MULTIPLE
VOICES
IN
FEMINIST
FILM
CRITICISM

MULTIPLE VOICES IN FEMINIST FILM CRITICISM

Diane Carson, Linda Dittmar, and Janice R. Welsch, editors

University of Minnesota Press

Minneapolis

London

Published by the University of Minnesota Press
2037 University Avenue Southeast, Minneapolis, MN 55455–3092
Printed in the United States of America on acid-free paper

Library of Congress Cataloging-in-Publication Data

Multiple voices in feminist film criticism / Diane Carson, Linda Dittmar, and
    Janice R. Welsch, editors.
        p. cm.
    Includes bibliographical references and index.
    ISBN 0-8166-2272-8. – ISBN 0-8166-2273-6 (pbk.)
    1. Women in motion pictures. 2. Feminist film criticism. I. Carson, Diane. II.
Dittmar, Linda, 1938– . III. Welsch, Janice R.
PN1995.9.W6M82   1994
791.43'015'082 – dc20   93-13743
                                                                          CIP

The University of Minnesota is an
equal-opportunity educator and employer.

Contents

Part III. Course Files

Preface

In the process of developing this anthology, we have become increasingly indebted to many scholars, activists, and artists committed to feminist principles and perspectives both within and beyond the academy. In particular, we want to acknowledge all the pioneers of feminist film studies who shaped its direction. Like the activists and artists who have influenced our thinking, these scholars have enriched us in innumerable ways. We are deeply conscious of our dependence on their insights and courage and on the support they have provided us. Each of us has also benefited personally and professionally from the strong, dynamic friendships and associations born out of feminism, and each of us owes much appreciation to a large circle of colleagues, students, and friends who have, knowingly and often unknowingly, informed our perspectives and moved us closer to a vision of feminism that is simultaneously idealistic and pragmatic. We thank all of you.

We owe special thanks to our contributors, our readers, our editor at the University of Minnesota Press, Janaki Bakhle, and her assistant, Robert Mosimann, and to Judi Hardin, whose word-processing skills kept us in touch and on line.

Introduction

Linda Dittmar, Janice R. Welsch, and Diane Carson

Sisterhood in Dialogue: Gender, Difference, and Film Study

What we most take for granted is always worth looking at afresh, as it is
precisely our neglect of the obvious that sets us up for surprises. Too often,
feeling sure that something goes without saying merely hides the fact that
thought lay fallow and that the time has come for reassessment. With
Multiple Voices in Feminist Film Criticism, the first assumption we must
examine is that gender constitutes a meaningful category in film studies
and that it therefore makes sense to organize a text around the subject of
women. The steady growth of feminist scholarship since the early 1970s
obviously stakes out women as a subject worthy of study in its own right,
but the basis for this claim may not be self-evident. Stepping back momentarily from the assumption that a focus on the category "women" is legitimate, let us raise the following questions: Is it useful to organize knowledge around women? That is, is the idea of gender a valid delineation of
subject matter? What does such an organization of knowledge accomplish
and what does it leave out?

Although they seem elementary, such questions are suggestive. On the
one hand, the recognition of women's studies as a field of inquiry and the
acceptance of feminist perspectives in a variety of disciplines affirm that
women do constitute an academic subject. In this respect, the parallel
emergence of "women" as an entrepreneurial and political entity is no acci-

dent. Both the lucrative marketing of "women" and feminism–through publications, media products, bookstore departments, and a variety of consumer items–and the political effects of women's organized opposition to patriarchy attest to a widely shared view of women as a meaningful category. While individuals may differ on the extent to which biological sex constructs identity, a broad consensus exists around the principle that gender inflects our material and conceptual realities in myriad tangible and intangible ways. On the other hand, debates among women, including feminists both inside and outside the academy, complicate this view. The early 1970s idea that women constitute a class and the euphoric discovery of unity that Robin Morgan articulated in *Sisterhood Is Powerful* (1970)[1] have given way to a sobering awareness of rifts, since women participate in multiple, and sometimes conflicting, modes of social organization. While we have discovered that we benefit from defining ourselves by gender, we also have had to face the full weight of differences in race and ethnicity, income and occupation, geography, religion, age, physical ability, marital and maternal status, and sexual orientation. Such differences have proven sufficiently divisive to challenge the notion of sisterhood and have led to reevaluation of reductionist notions of female essence as well as to greater understanding of ways women's interests may conflict. More important, this new awareness laid bare the operations of privilege, notably, that some women's gains occur at a cost to others.[2]

The more one studies women's recent history, the clearer this issue becomes. The notion that "sisterhood is powerful" captures the inspirational optimism the women's movement felt about women's shared identity and underscores the reality that we have fallen sadly short of that dream. In no time at all, it now seems, the feminist ideal of a gender-based movement for egalitarian social change came up against dissension within the ranks. Neither women's far-reaching hope that a feminist perspective would transform progressive politics in general nor even the more limited efforts to build feminist organizations based on equality proved simple. The last three decades witnessed not only the enthusiastic founding of many feminist coalitions and projects, but also considerable internal strife. Racism, homophobia, class conflict, and ethnic prejudice all surfaced, in addition to pragmatic problems such as wheelchair access, child care, and the need for second-language interpreters or sign readers. Despite its utopian invocation of caring, nurturing, communalism, and globalism, the familial concept of sisterhood has not, indeed could not, escape the burden of society's prevailing inequities.[3]

We review this history not to negate the substantive gains women have made in recent years but to introduce *Multiple Voices* with a caution against considering women exclusively in terms of gender. We do so fully aware that this position perches us between two abysses. On one side lie reductionism, essentialism, and the further oppression of women by women, since an undifferentiated focus on gender reduces all women's experience to a false common denominator, mistaking biology for destiny, despairing of efforts to effect social change, and ultimately blinding us to ways we benefit or suffer from differences that translate into inequities. On the other side loom the risks of disagreement, demoralization, and the appropriation of gender identity to serve antifeminist agendas, for a heightened attention to differences threatens potentially useful coalitions. In addition, because the complex interrelations of difference are ill defined, a focus on our diversity subjects us to competing loyalties and pressures us to suspend feminism in favor of other critical agendas such as national liberation movements, class struggle, antiracism, AIDS activism, and antimilitarism.[4]

While acknowledging these very real risks, we maintain that conflicting claims of diversity must be sustained dialectically. That is, the essays in *Multiple Voices* invite a reading of films and film scholarship responsive to multivalent feminist agendas. In addition to critiquing patriarchy's use of an undifferentiated concept of gender to promote an ideology of dominance, they also question ways films represent and define issues of difference and inequality among women. Acknowledging film's power as an instrument whose audiovisual and narrative capabilities profoundly affect public attitudes and beliefs, these essays participate in the broader reassessment of issues of multiculturalism and canon current in film studies and other fields. They stress that feminist filmmakers and critics must examine their representations and readings of gender, but they also treat the social construction of gender as inextricable from other constructions of hegemony, the common thread being the interaction of power relations.

This emphasis on the dialectics of power relations involves a certain instability about which mark of identity is primary or secondary. What Isaac Julien and Kobena Mercer describe as "the familiar 'race, class, gender' mantra" cannot obscure such sliding among hegemonies.[5] For example, while the economic disempowerment caused by racism clearly serves capitalist interests, gender relations sustain this configuration by encouraging men of color to feel empowered at the expense of their female counterparts. Each case involves a shifting panorama of winners and losers. Each rests on an ideology of separatism and division in which, as Trinh T. Minh-ha puts it, " 'difference' is no more than a tool for self-defence and conquest."[6]

Awareness of women's place within this changing topography is central to our present focus. Partly a review of the impressive body of feminist film criticism, theory, and curriculum development over the last twenty years, this volume surveys a range of perspectives and methodologies scholars have been using to document and explain ways patriarchy has appropriated cinematic representation and reception. In this respect it moves beyond the initial feminist concern with delineations of image and archetype and reconstruction of women's place in film history to include a variety of more recent approaches. Adapting and extending the contemporary practices and methodologies of semiotics, psychoanalysis, Marxism, deconstruction, and new historicism, as well as pivotal studies of genre and auteurism, it makes a compelling case for gender-focused scholarship as directly germane to women's social identity within patriarchy. In particular, it attests to gains women have made within the academy and signals a claiming of territory.

But what has not yet emerged as clearly is the next step, the relation between this feminist work and other ideological readings of film. While the attainments described above place white, middle-class feminist thought in the vanguard of film studies, scholarship linking gender to multiculturalism and the film canon has just begun. *Multiple Voices* chronicles some of this work, making it available for comparative readings. In doing so, it urges a constructive feminist engagement with issues of diversity through essays that treat women as social and political entities defined not only by gender within patriarchy but also by other power relations. Organized so as to highlight this latter point, *Multiple Voices* aims to promote awareness of ways diverse claims of difference intersect in filmic representations and receptions. Cautioning against an eclectic pluralism, it asserts that in practice difference translates into qualities that entail conflict but that also create opportunities for change. Issues of difference must be identified, analyzed, and theorized, in short, not only because they affect how films get made and seen, but also because they remain open to intervention. Filmic definitions of identity by category—by gender, sexual orientation, race, or class, for example—reflect and reinforce socially constructed notions of identity as essential. They thus describe a master narrative we must challenge. The practice of reading film against the grain that feminists have modeled so productively in matters of gender can and should be applied to a more complex notion of identity.

The Organization of *Multiple Voices*

Conceived as a text for readers sympathetic to feminist perspectives on film but not necessarily versed in feminist scholarship in this area, *Multiple Voices* illuminates the range of theoretical, critical, and educational directions feminist scholars have explored in recent years. Suggestive rather than exhaustive, the content and organization of each section encourage readers to reflect critically about the directions open to feminist film scholarship and to participate in sustaining, modifying, or changing the critical climate in which films are produced and received.

In practice, this sampling of possibilities translates into three different applications, with each of the book's three parts addressing a particular aspect of feminist scholarship. Part I includes theoretical approaches to film study and provides a framework for the critical analyses that constitute part II. Although the boundary between the two groups of essays is not sharply defined (in that theory and practice frequently overlap), enough divergence exists between them to argue for separation. The essays in part I survey various approaches available to feminist film study, while those in part II cover a variety of films and cinemas in order to illuminate diverse relations between film and social context.

Part III offers a separate but related focal point. It explores the rationale for and organization of selected feminist film courses. Shaped by the theory and criticism that necessarily inform what goes on in the classroom, the files uncover interrelations among films and highlight ways films and critical readings can be meaningfully organized. Moreover, shifting the emphasis from the private reflection each of us does to public and collaborative reflection by students and teachers, the course files affirm the interactive and dynamic nature of scholarship. They encourage a critical awareness of the selection and ordering process at work in all critical thought, including an assessment of the work in this anthology. Part III links the self-reflexivity of part II and the contextual emphasis of Practice to the classroom.

The representative feminist approaches of these essays question notions of ideology, audience, and canon. Taking as their starting point the work that has become the hallmark of feminist film studies, they pursue scholarship that underscores interlocking issues of social marginalities. Politically, the volume's inclusiveness could be misperceived as a mainstreaming and equalizing model that blurs conflict. In this respect, the course files prove particularly helpful because they demonstrate that questions of difference should be examined through specific courses, blueprints, and texts. Refocusing both the political and the scholarly aspects of what we might call mainstream, margin, and canon, each of them provides a larger framework from which to systematically question existing courses.

The three parts of *Multiple Voices* are unified, then, by the feminist perspective each brings to bear on its distinct tasks. In a collection of essays that foregrounds breadth as an organizing priority, such a common thread is necessary. This unifying perspective emerges from a set of questions the entire volume addresses, questions that concern the ways both films and the critical, theoretical, and pedagogical discourses surrounding them do or do not serve women's need for representations that promote their egalitarian, autonomous, and multiple places in society. Ultimately, these diverse materials demand critical readings attentive to differences and conflicts among them as well as to overlaps and consensus. In keeping with our intention of laying out a variety of feminist approaches to film study, a comparative reading of the essays should encourage both assessment of the different priorities and consequences each approach entails and critical reflection concerning our own positions and practices.

Part I: Perspectives

Over the past two decades, the emergence of feminist scholarship within film study has led to new thinking and new approaches concerning both substance and methods. While these constitute the theoretical bases of feminist film study, it is not altogether accurate to simply label this "theory." As is clearly evident in feminist applications of psychoanalysis to film scholarship, theory and method have complemented each other with striking coherence. In other instances the relation of theory to method has been harder to specify partly because certain issues, such as lesbian spectatorship and racial differences, have not yet generated a large enough body of scholarship to support a systematic formulation of positions and procedures. Yet, at given moments in history, certain theoretical perspectives have contributed to politically nuanced scholarship—for example, the influence of Althusser, Bakhtin, and semiotic theory on Marxist and other discussions of difference. Still, no essential match can exist between film theory and politics. Titling part I "Perspectives" signals the difficulty of labeling some of the scholarship in this section as theoretical, for while our title assumes the theoretical orientation of the essays, it acknowledges that such an orientation is not exhaustive.

Taken together, these essays survey a theoretical landscape of both striking breakthroughs and frustrating blockages. They highlight feminist contributions to film study as well as the uncertainties this scholarship and practice face. Registering the liminal and therefore precarious state of this work, they address key issues such as the need for a language appropriate to a feminist practice of film production and scholarship; assessments of the part film discourses play in social formation, including ways they may sustain or disrupt patriarchal ideology; the emergent debates within feminist film theory, criticism, and production concerning the tensions between classical Hollywood and independent cinemas, feminism and psychoanalysis, history and identity, or theory and culture; counterreadings of mainstream cinema's erasures of women's specificity in terms of their social class, race, ethnicity, age, or sexual orientation; and the political effects of film canons as these are formed within the academy.

Overall, this section's focus on thresholds, debates, omissions, and unanswered questions stresses the need for ongoing work, notably concerning the unresolved question of how one names oneself in a society that strategically describes women as other. The debates over essentialist and socially constructed views of gender, race, or social class illustrate the problems that attend self-naming. Ideology is at the heart of these questions precisely because it embeds personal desires in social contexts. What finally emerges from "Perspectives" is recognition of feminists' pioneering but unfinished agendas. B. Ruby Rich makes this point forcefully in her "Postscript," in which her regret for the lost innocence of earlier feminist film criticism and practice mingles with her optimism concerning filmmaking by feminists of color and the recent invigoration of lesbian and gay studies.

The first three essays in part I provide overviews of the development of feminist film studies from different points of view. Rich addresses the search for a language capable of sustaining feminist film production and criticism during the transition from the 1970s to the 1980s; Judith Mayne surveys the formative debates that engaged feminist film scholars during that same period; and Patrice Petro ties the evolution of film studies to ways it has mapped the female subject in history. Published between 1980 and 1990, these essays capture the rapidly evolving preoccupations of this period and scan a substantial and diverse body of work whose aggregate accomplishment has been to establish feminist perspectives as a necessary aspect of film study.

Next, psychoanalysis pinpoints considerations feminists have been applying to film study. Writing some ten years apart, Janet Walker and Jackie Byars review this field from different vantage points but with a shared awareness of its important contribution to helping us theorize the relation between spectatorship and representation, desire and gender. Central to this work have been the visual attraction the medium holds for its audiences, the appropriation of that attraction to patriarchal ends, and the question of feminist intervention through oppositional readings and alternative film production. The usefulness of psychoanalysis for feminists reflects a passionate investment in retrieving and affirming women as subjects in the realm of representation, spectatorship, scholarship, and production.

Not surprisingly, this emphasis on women as producers of meanings coincided with the development of poststructuralist thought and the strengthening of women's position within the academy. In this context, feminist psychoanalytical approaches at once empower women as scholars, spectators, and professionals and create new problems. One difficulty is the tendency of psychoanalysis to draw film discourse into a phallocentric orbit and ascribe to identities an aura of universality and inevitability that can lapse into an essentialist view of gender. In addition, psychoanalysis inappropriately imposes the demographically unrepresentative model of the white middle-class, nuclear family on an array of social and familial arrangements to which it does not apply. Although by no means the only contested issues affecting feminism and psychoanalysis, these bear most directly on the intersections of difference *Multiple Voices* seeks to uncover.

Interestingly, Laura Mulvey, whose essay "Visual Pleasure and Narrative Cinema" (1975) was the cornerstone of psychoanalytical feminist film study, notes in her introduction to *Visual and Other Pleasures* (1989) the need to reclaim Marxism as an equal partner in the feminist psychoanalytic project.[7] This complementarity reflects the fact that both approaches recognize the role of human agency in the production of meanings. Marxism differs from psychoanalysis, however, in its emphasis on agency as embedded in material and historical conditions. As Christine Gledhill emphasizes in the next essay, film and its reception are determined by socioeconomic forces, and the representations films construct through their plots, characters, mise-en-scènes, and other filmic and narrative devices reveal their social function. Meanings are not waiting to be uncovered in the text but are constructed and reconstructed in response to forces at work at the time of a given text's production and reception. Awareness of films as constructs foregrounds the role of choice–of human agency!–in assigning meanings.

Agency and our ability to bring about change are also the point on which psychoanalytic and Marxist feminism part ways when considered from a political perspective. Locating change in individuals, psychoanalytic film theory has generally grounded personal and even intensely private aspects of film reception in close textual readings with gender negotiated within intimate, often familial, social nuclei. This approach does not preclude more inclusive theories of social construction, but its orientation promotes a view that locates agency in individuals. In contrast, Marxism favors collective agendas. While these differences are hard to resolve, the combined effect of Marxist and psychoanalytical film criticism has been to uncover discourses that reposition us and implicitly all marginalized others as agents capable of working in our own best interest.

This concern with ways discourse resituates women in relation to their agency informs the rest of this section. Accordingly, the next two essays focus on feminist cinemas of resistance and intervention and raise questions of strategy in relation to both prevailing and radically oppositional narrative practices. Lisa Cartwright and Nina Fonoroff analyze ways narrative reproduces the patriarchal order and argue for an avant-garde that avoids referentiality altogether. Their exacting analysis of the aesthetics of subversion challenges even oppositional feminist narration, let alone orthodox cinema's dependence on visual pleasure, narrative, and identification. In contrast, Teresa de Lauretis's explanation of filmic address, female spectators, and especially representations of difference allows for feminist appropriations of narrative and encourages a more inclusive treatment of feminist interventions. At issue for her are immediate political struggles around the traditionally invisible issues of racial and lesbian difference and ways multiple narrative viewpoints destabilize the positions of identification available to spectators. Welsch's application of Bakhtin's concept of dialogism to feminist documentaries continues this discussion of feminist adaptations and disruptions of patriarchal discourse.

Addressing questions of language already introduced by Rich, the three essays foreground multiple utterances and positions of identification and reception as they reflect ways languages register cultural diversity and political debate. Interestingly, these considerations apply to both fiction and avant-garde films on the one hand and to documentaries on the other, pointing to a shared preoccupation with the relation between textual practice and social ideals. If anything, the interactive, dialogic texts speak of communities where wisdom is conveyed through diverse voices and emerges through a confluence of ideas, experiences, and insights. In actuality, such a sisterhood has not yet come into being. As the following essay by Jane Gaines shows, considerable work remains in understanding and appreciating relations that involve difference, social marginality, and injustice. Focusing on racially defined spectator positions as sites of ideological struggle, Gaines cautions against facile applications of feminist readings to women of color. Theorizing the racial other tends to elude feminist scholarship, she notes, precisely because of its treatment of women as a seemingly universal category.[8]

As the above suggests, film studies participate in the construction of ideology and social practice. The films a scholar selects for her focus and the theoretical perspective she adopts forge a compatibility, a fit, that makes her critical position assume a compelling and seemingly natural authority we need to consider cautiously and even skeptically. While valuing the insights a given position yields, we need to be mindful of the assumptions that limit it. Taken as a whole part I suggest that, once we compare and contrast the thinking that informs individual essays, we uncover dissonance as well as complementarity.

Accordingly, coming at the end of part I, Janet Staiger's survey of the evolution of film canons within the academy reminds us that our own choices of subject matter and methodology are never politically neutral. Although this concluding essay focuses mostly on the evolution of male-defined film canons, it suggests that feminist designations of pivotal films, genres, theories, and methods can function similarly. Canons may project an aura of inevitability that propels certain texts into an unquestioned and enduring prominence, but the choice of subjects and perspectives has more to do with historical contingencies than with the intrinsic value of particular films or critical perspectives. Considered in tandem with the preceding essays, this discussion of canon formation reminds us of the responsibilities we bear by virtue of our own agency.

Part II: Practice

In contrast with the theoretical emphasis of part I, part II of *Multiple Voices* centers on close readings of specific films and film clusters. The essays in part II share with those in part I an awareness that individual analyses fit into larger conceptual frameworks, but their primary focus rests on particular film choices and their social functions. Emphasizing ways films convey their subject matter and ways we read them, the essays suggest that both film and film analysis embody choices made by filmmakers and audiences, critics included. They posit films as constructed systems of audiovisual representation and film reception and critical writings as systems of interpretation that are ultimately imaginative, sense-making activities. Rather than capture preexisting realities, a film's subject matter is interpreted, altered, reimagined, and reconstituted at the site of its reception. Applying this view to a range of issues and cinemas, the essays in this section show that such recasting is never politically and ideologically neutral. Accordingly, they highlight the usefulness of a cross-cultural perspective and the importance of addressing the specificity of women's experiences of race, ethnicity, work, social class, and familial and sexual relations as they are represented in a diverse body of films.

That many of the essays address ways gender intertwines with other social identities at once broadens the scope of feminist film study and makes it more precise. In particular, our selection and sequencing show that women's diversity resists an essentialist and ahistorical view of gender that treats women interchangeably. Instead of subsuming the notion of "difference" exclusively under gender, the essays foreground its interlocking effects by analyzing its multiple operations in filmic representations of women's lives and by raising questions of authorship and reception. Examples include the racial/ethnic, economic, and political subordination of Asian women under occupation; the effects of post-World War II recovery agendas on working-class families in the United States; lesbian spectatorship as a site of resistance; the use of the female voice to signal personal and political displacement and/or empowerment; and the relation between representation and self-representation in films about and by African-American women.

Taken together, then, the essays question current constructions of difference and propose that we reassess the dominant ideology's existing power relations. At this point in the history of film studies, the usefulness of this approach lies mainly in reminding us that feminist film scholarship participates in the ideology found in all considerations of difference. All of us, including you, our readers, are critical participants in this process.

Such awareness unifies the essays in part II, for they all read film and ideology skeptically. Resisting patriarchal pressure, they unmask ways patriarchy depends on women's acceptance of its values. But while it has become relatively easy for feminists to read patriarchal texts against the grain, extending such skepticism to one's own practice presents a more difficult task. Nonetheless, several of our authors question the priorities and procedures of feminist filmmaking and scholarship, offering a healthy alternative to a homogenizing ideal of sisterhood by uncovering differences among women. These conflicting interests within gender make reading against the grain a necessary point of entry into feminist scholarship.

Significantly, a skeptical stance applies to our choice of subject matter as well as to its treatment. The selection of essays in part II resists both the idea of canon formation and a feminist countercanon. Rather, the essays provide examples of the strategic questioning one can bring to a variety of films. This openness echoes our earlier discussion of the as yet undertheorized state of feminist film scholarship when it comes to interrelations of difference. Read singly, the essays raise important questions about specific kinds of difference within gender. Read collectively, they point out the need to develop analogous lines of inquiry across multiple differences.

The internal organization of part II establishes a thematic and rhetorical order that responds to this need and to our seeing individual essays as models of inquiry. Our overall outline recalls part I in that it starts with the founding questions and practices of feminist film criticism and gradually moves toward current margins. Anchored in counterreadings of mainstream cinema's containment of women within patriarchy, part II illuminates double standards and contradictions within this hegemonic stance, instances of resistance on the level of plot and spectatorship, and, finally, women's emergence and self-articulation. Read comparatively, the essays highlight formal differences among films that share a historical context (1950s representations of the family, for instance, or 1980s black women directors), a generic focus (on melodrama or screwball comedy), or a thematic focus (on lesbian spectatorship, the Asian other, or the postcolonial condition). They also reveal theoretical and methodological differences among contributors who bring to their writing diverse experiences as filmmakers, social activists, or scholars in film studies and other disciplines. Read in sequence, the organization of this section is also rhetorical. While not suggesting that women's political history can be charted as smooth progress toward empowerment, we find it encouraging to observe the emergence of films that, despite their unresolved relation to a less-than-perfect world, show women's capacity for articulation and self-determination.

The first four essays participate in the well-established feminist project of reading patriarchal films against the grain. Beginning with three essays that explore classic and recent Hollywood films, the sequence ends with a similar analysis of classic Mexican cinema, often considered a colonized extension of Hollywood. The shared focus on mainstream practices gives the essays a coherence suggested by their attention to the repetitive function of stereotypes and genres, and by the authors' attention to race, class, nationality, ethnicity, and historical context.

Within this cluster, Diane Carson's discussion of 1930s screwball comedies and Judith Smith's discussion of 1950s working-class dramas concern films that downplay differences among women and assume a unified social subject as part of a larger strategy to promote reconciliation to the *status quo*. In this formula all women are white and heterosexual, and all upper- and middle-class women enjoy an unspecified ethnicity and an aura of classlessness that is projected by the films' obliviousness to class issues. Their privilege taken for granted, it becomes invisible and impervious to considerations of difference. Although Gina Marchetti's discussion of the effects of romance in *Sayonara* (1957) and Ana López's discussion of melodrama in Mexican cinema both examine complexities of otherness through prisms of class, race, and nation, they also reveal ways in which Hollywood and Mexican cinemas respectively reconcile or suppress the ideological contradictions inherent in their subject matter, presenting complex differences and inequalities as natural and inevitable, and offering us romance and melodrama as cathartic panaceas.

Such erasures occur across many of the films discussed in *Multiple Voices* and continue to frame our discussion as we shift to films that challenge patriarchy's hold over gender definitions. Beverle Houston's essay on Dorothy Arzner is an apt point of departure because Arzner's work exists within the tradition of classical Hollywood cinema. As in the essays by Esther Yau and Poonam Arora, the possibility for feminist intervention in dominant ideology and prevailing film practices is at stake. Thus, despite the gulf between recent mainland Chinese and Indian cinemas and Arzner's Hollywood of half a century ago, considering them side by side allows for an interesting inquiry into the ways women directors negotiate compromises that allow them to sidestep total co-optation. Houston emphasizes ways Arzner disrupts, however obliquely, the very codes that Mulvey and others see as central to film's containment of female agency.[9]

Although the films discussed in the next two essays address women's position within patriarchy more directly, they also sustain a tension between exposing and suppressing the very feminist questions they address. Julianne Burton-Carvajal's essay concerns Cuba in the 1970s and Mimi

White's the United States during World War II, two very different historical moments. Both center on films about women's struggle with the ideals
of domesticity within the familial-patriarchal order and the autonomy
made feasible when women take on wage labor. A colonizing spectatorship
compromising women's capacity to disrupt patriarchy (as analyzed by
Houston, Yau, and Arora) is less the problem than that these films do not,
finally, clarify for their audiences the very issues they single out for feminist consideration. Their focus on questions of labor and social class, which
embeds them in material-historical considerations such as the working-
class films Judith Smith discusses, escapes the complications of racial and
ethnic exoticism that concern Marchetti, López, Yau, and Arora. Yet the
intersection of urgent national and economic imperatives with an emerging feminist sense of women's need for self-determination enmeshes this
latter body of films in contradictions they fail to resolve. Unlike the forms
in part I, on cinematic and narrative devices that camouflage underlying
contradictions, here we have films that are more frank but also more ambivalent and irresolute about the struggles they portray.

The essays' wide-ranging contexts, political agendas, and subject matter all concern contradictory representations of female emergence. Read
singly, they apply ideological points of view to specific films. Taken together, they encourage a cross-cultural awareness of films' participation
in processes of social and cultural change. This said, part II of *Multiple
Voices* turns increasingly to films that affirm women as subjects. Not accidentally, this underscoring of women's agency is closely allied with access to voice. Disrupting mainstream cinema's investment in sutured
representation as a mode of knowing and in the gaze as a vehicle for reinforcing gendered power relations, the next cluster of essays explores the
issues of access and agency as they are filtered through oppositional audiovisual strategies and representations. Most of the essays focus on films
made by women; many of them concentrate on feminist questions of address and reception; and all involve representations of women and
women's agency.

Andrea Weiss and Chris Straayer investigate lesbian desire and empowerment in mainstream films coded as heterosexual but that create a
sexually indeterminate space drawing in lesbian spectators and allowing,
even encouraging, lesbian identification. Interestingly, the two kinds of
films under discussion and the different spectatorship each presupposes in
relation to its particular historical context lead Weiss and Straayer in
different directions. Weiss's work complements Houston's in its focus on
lesbian agency made possible through its flexible and ambiguous representations in 1930s Hollywood films. In contrast, Straayer's focus on recent
French art films directed by women is less sanguine precisely because
these films at once invoke and frustrate lesbianism within a cultural cli-

mate that balks at such ambivalence. It seems that classical cinema makes us thankful for any glimmer of empowerment, while contemporary films that stake out feminist reception evoke higher expectations. Still, the salient issue in both essays is the availability of alternative spectatorial perspectives and the possibility for individual desires, subjectivities, sexualities, and gender constructions to assert themselves in the gaps and fissures of normative heterosexuality.

This notion of fissures is critical when one counterreads mainstream cinemas. In such readings marginalized spectators may insert themselves into modes of reception and production that sustain their self-definitions individually and collectively within cinemas generally intended to erase them. In contrast, the last seven essays in part II foreground practices that retrieve the repressed voices and erased identities of diversely marginalized women. These films claim the territory of cinematic enunciation as the rightful domain of all women. Women's acquisition of their own voices – literally and metaphorically – is central to their affirmative stance. These essays focus on filmic challenges to racism by African-American and Caribbean women directors, discuss the silencing, mediation, and assertion of women's voices within colonialism and its aftermath, probe the voice's ability to disrupt mainstream cinema's specular regime, and explore an oppositional wild zone of articulation outside male discourse. Most of them concern recent work by women directors, reminding us of the progress possible when we, women, act on our own behalf and recognize men's potential participation in the process of our empowerment. Perhaps most striking is the undercurrent of shared experience and hope that emerges and draws us toward new visions and new ways of acting.

The essays' specific emphasis on women's self-articulation contrasts with the earlier essays' stress on women's representation. This difference distinguishes the passively specular object positions allotted women by traditional cinemas from their actively enunciating subject positions in feminist films. While they vary widely in subject matter, time and place of production, and audiences, the films discussed toward the end of part II redefine women and reconceptualize the ideology of difference. This agenda does not deny inequities and social antagonisms; on the contrary, the authors show that viewers' varying social identities interact significantly with the content, formal procedures, and reception of individual films. At the same time, an underlying commitment to equality and justice avoids the impasse created by binary conceptions of difference and equality. Emphasizing the role of self-articulation within social processes, the essays' attention to differences assumes that as spectators and readers we are capable of fluid, roving identifications that broaden our ability to feel solidarity with others.

These issues are central to bell hooks's essay, which considers representation, reception, and political solidarity in Euzhan Palcy's *A Dry White Season* (1989). The film's treatment of apartheid in South Africa revolves around a liberal white male protagonist, offering white spectators opportunities to adopt a self-critical perspective that recognizes how both racism and liberalism implicate us in injustice. Beyond this identification from positions of privilege is empowerment through resistance to oppression and the film's location of militant resistance in various black characters. The essay's focus on black resistance and white support foregrounds the relation between culture and social action.

Questions of identification and solidarity and their social application for racially mixed audiences come up again in the next two essays, this time through independent films made by black women in the United States during the 1980s, notably, Kathleen Collins, Ayoka Chenzira, Julie Dash, and Camille Billops. Produced within the economic constraints that routinely affect independent filmmakers, especially when their work is politically oppositional, these films are less technically polished but more formally innovative than Palcy's 35mm feature-length color film made for commercial distribution. In contrast, these films target film festivals, community-based screenings, and educational forums. They posit racially mixed and politically informed audiences. Gloria Gibson-Hudson treats their directors as cultural storytellers whose work catalyzes introspection, self-affirmation, and social change for African-American women, while in a similar vein Valerie Smith focuses on how documentary filmmaking can dislodge received notions of family, work, and personal beauty. Both authors examine film practices that dismantle familiar modes of reception and create fissures that allow spectators to critique traditional social constructions of race and gender. Disruption is offered as a strategy for attaining new insights of special urgency to the African-American community in general and to feminists of color in particular.

Locating women's oppression and agency within the ongoing effects of conquest and national displacement, the next two essays continue political reading of female articulation. Linda Dittmar examines films in which women's silencing registers the combined influence of traditional patriarchy and colonialism, where relations of hierarchy feed on myths of the racial, ethnic, or national superiority of the invader. Her reading of *Salt of the Earth* (1953) stresses women's assertion of their right to and capacity for self-articulation as they participate in their community's growing empowerment. Amy Lawrence continues this exploration in her explanation of ways linguistic hierarchies in *Surname Viet, Given Name Nam* (1989) reflect and support political hegemonies. She emphasizes the film's dissociation of exiled Vietnamese women's images from their voices and how this effects a subjectivity that is multiple, shifting, and communal. Both essays' attention to language as a denaturalized artifact—spoken, transcribed, and translated – clarifies how language works for female spectators as well as for the women on screen.

This focus on language as a site of resistance is of special urgency in feminist analyses of films set within patriarchal contexts. In *Salt of the Earth*, for instance, the repression and emergence of the Chicana voice captures a radical shift in gender-based power relations. In *Hair Piece: A Film for Nappy-Headed People* (1984) and *Illusions* (1983), discussed by Gibson-Hudson, the black female voice treats identity politics as an opportunity for black women to define themselves. We have come a long way from the erasures discussed earlier in part II. Still, that the final two essays take us back to films made by Caucasian women reminds us that even these relatively privileged women engage in struggles against erasure. Reviewing the pioneering work of directors Alice Guy, Germaine Dulac, Lis Rhodes, and Joanna Davis, authors Lis Rhodes and Felicity Sparrow continue the focus on women as self-articulating subjects resisting mainstream cinema's tradition of containing women within patriarchal specularity. That their films link women's cinematic containment to their historic containment echoes the discussion of female agency in the immediately preceding essays as well as in Linda Williams's reading of *A Question of Silence* (1982). While the function of the voice as a means of self-definition is central to this group of essays, Williams brings out its potential for affirmative anarchy and generative deviance and disruption.

Straining against boundaries becomes increasingly evident in both the representational content (i.e., characters, plots) and the formal operations under discussion in *Multiple Voices*. We see women repudiate the restraints of patriarchy and step outside the hegemonic hold of conventional codes of behavior and representation. Within the terrain bounded by the disintegrating female power of screwball comedies and the erupting defiance of *A Question of Silence*, increasingly overt challenges and nonconformist film practices are at work. Significantly, this movement does not register actual historical developments. To some extent, the apparent movement toward more assured and explicit depictions of feminist agendas registers a shift in views of women's place within patriarchy. But this growing confidence is also very much a product of our selection and arrangement of essays within part II and is not without exceptions. Ours is a rhetorical construct, similar to the organization of part I. Thus, instead of organizing part II thematically or focusing it on mainstream cinemas, we chose to build up a comparative and cumulative sense of ways disempowerment, ambivalence, and resistance are articulated in an array of films open to feminist readings. In short, the essays included in this section increasingly foreground thematic and formal practices that offer women dynamic and viable options.

From the perspective of patriarchy, such strategies necessarily edge toward revolution. Williams's reference to Showalter's metaphor of "the wild zone" and her use of the concept of deviance highlight the violence and defiance entailed in such ventures. Accordingly, the violence of emergence is a recurrent concern for our authors, regardless of the extent to which individuals focus on women's repression or resistance. For those long trained in accommodation as a means of survival, resistance of any sort, even the most minimal and barely noticeable, is transgressive. The protagonists of *A Portrait of Teresa* (1979) or *Salt of the Earth*, for example, share with Billops's interviewees in *Suzanne, Suzanne* (1982) a struggle with barriers embedded in their socially structured diversity; the lesbian audiences discussed by Weiss and Straayer share with the audiences constructed by *Hair Piece* modes of reception that require one to acknowledge difference; and *Surname Viet, Given Name Nam* shares with the films of Dulac, Arzner, and Rhodes ruptures that clearly resist mainstream cinema's air of naturalness. In different ways, large and small, all of these transgress patriarchal norms. Williams's essay reveals the sense of illegitimacy bordering on insanity that haunts all emergence. At the same time, her essay, together with others that precede it, captures the exhilaration accompanying such empowerment.

Part III: Course Files

The third section of *Multiple Voices* may seem to take a direction different from the two preceding ones. Focused on course design, resources, and related curricular matters, part III is distinct in scope and format, though not in goals. Readily seen as helpful to instructors, the course files are also relevant to students, inviting them, too, to examine the principles and perspectives that define a course, including ties across parts I and II. Designating the files as equal partners in this volume also reemphasizes our suggestion that *Multiple Voices* is thinking-in-progress, part of the continuing evolution of feminist scholarship.

The course files direct attention to connections between research and pedagogy. In delineating subject matter for specific courses, articulating perspectives from which this subject matter can be approached, selecting films and readings through which such thinking can be pursued, and sequencing this work purposefully, they suggest but do not exhaust the curricular potential of feminist film criticism. Given *Multiple Voices*'s underlying assumption that we, students as well as instructors, all participate in this reshaping of the field, the inclusion of analytic and self-reflexive course files affirms joint inquiry as an ongoing process. This section is, then, an invitation to all readers to think critically about diverse configurations of feminist film study and of the reciprocity of research, teaching, and learning.

These courses integrate this dynamic into feminist film study through questions of social context and political use. Although clearly only a sampling of possible approaches, they help us envision additional possibilities and rethink existing courses. For this reason, the "Feminist Film Theory/Criticism" and "Women Filmmakers" files champion some established but infrequently taught materials, while the files outlining courses on women of color and sexual representations reclaim areas in feminist film study generally ignored or given minimal attention. Recognizing that this erasure is at once institutional and political, we introduce alternative models to affirm the necessity of a feminist film study encompassing diverse communities, all of them active in the formation of culture and ideology. Especially when considered as a group, the files encourage attention to the interrelations of difference within gender. At the same time, because the files emphasize issues often treated as marginal to feminist film study, they invite debate about what needs to be taught and to what ends.

Ultimately, at issue throughout this volume is canon formation, in the classroom as well as in scholarship. In both instances the definition of the discipline, what we study and what we bypass, is critical. The course files promote a self-reflexive awareness of our positions as film viewers, students, and scholars in relation to the priorities and agendas inevitably influencing our discussions and work. They do this by shifting certain cinemas, films, and debates from the margins of film study to the center of this anthology; including discussion of the rationale for the choices made; noting ways models function provisionally and allow for restructuring; and providing bibliographies and filmographies to help modify or rework the material to meet individual class needs.

Uncovering the relations among scholarship, learning, and social practice, the course files thus question implicitly the idea that academic work is a neutral pursuit and insist that all inquiry is socially as well as intellectually motivated. Noting the interdependence of individual and collective thought, they stress the political nature of film study. Most important, the very presence of course files elicits an assessing metacriticism of our own practice. Raising questions about the courses taught in academia and the values they reproduce through their design, this section highlights the fact that individuals choose and organize their knowledge in politically significant ways.

Following the pattern of the volume as a whole, Janice Welsch's "Feminist Film Theory/Criticism in the United States" establishes a theoretical framework for the more specialized courses that follow. Its review of three decades of intense feminist engagement in film production and criticism uncovers debates about the agendas, theoretical frameworks, and methodologies associated with feminist film study. While devoting space to the most influential and highly visible work of feminists to date, the file anchors the discussion of feminist applications of poststructuralist discourse in the women's movement, doing so from a multicultural perspective that encompasses important work outside mainstream film study. After a review of the rapid evolution of contemporary feminist thought, Welsch emphasizes discourses of difference as an appropriate response to social realities and as a counterbalance to divisions within feminism.

Diane Carson's "Women Filmmakers" complements this focus on scholarship and reception by providing an overview of women's role in film production. Covering nine decades of work too often marginalized or totally absent in film studies, this course emphasizes women's historic roles in film production. Clearly comprehensive in its intent, the course covers several areas of production women helped shape, including live action and animation, fiction and nonfiction, classical narrative and experimental work, all across national borders. The course's priority is to note representative work by women from diverse cultures and to provide readers with strategies for feminist interpretation of such films. Celebrating the imagination and invention that characterized women's technical and artistic accomplishments, the course helps correct a view of the industry as exclusively male and U.S.-dominated.

The other courses in part III are more narrowly conceived, but each aims for an overview of its subject matter. Accordingly, Julia Lesage, in "Latin American and Caribbean Women in Film and Video," defines her subject matter historically and geographically. Reiterating other contributors' interest in interrelations among gender, class, and ethnicity, she centers her discussion on oppressed people's struggles to build just societies and create empowering representations of themselves. The course challenges institutional powers in ways likely to speak to students' comparable needs. These concerns are addressed through discussion of semiotics, aesthetics, the relation between documentary film and anthropology, national and regional specificity, and global economics. Interweaving critical and political considerations, the file uncovers possibilities for resistance as well as insight and underscores media as a participant in social transformation.

Elizabeth Hadley Freydberg's course "Women of Color: No Joy in the Seduction of Images" charts the intersection of racism and sexism, which present dual obstacles for women of color. Noting the effects of this combined barrier to emergence, the course centers on struggle and empowerment. There is no joy in demeaning, stereotypical images, Hadley Freydberg indicates, but there is clearly considerable power in critiquing, undermining, and displacing them. To this end, the course affirms community as basic to survival without negating significant differences that distinguish women of color. The films, primarily independent political documentaries, emphasize honest images, independent production, and viewer access as Aboriginal, African, Asian, Latina, lesbian (of color), Native-American, and Caribbean women are considered separately before interracial alliances are explored and issues are analyzed thematically. Stressing that color is too inclusive a concept to register women's cultural and political specificity, this organization highlights the distinctions that can be drawn within and across communities while also noting points of contact and mutual interest.

In contrast with the preceding course's organization around the heterogeneity of women's communities, Frances Stubbs and Elizabeth Hadley Freydberg's "Black Women in American Films: A Thematic Approach" explores one community thematically. While the authors note the potential for flexibility in their themes and organization, their approach encourages a closer examination of ways representations can sustain or resist women's current social, economic, familial, and sexual status. They begin with a survey of the stereotyping of black women in mainstream cinema in the United States and counter this production of images with discussions of African-American filmmaking from the 1920s and 1930s to the present. Using the tools of black feminism, feminist film theory, and black film history, this course examines the intricate interplay of race, gender, class, and caste as it challenges the more common but reductive paradigm of gender oppression that subsumes black women's diverse experiences and identities under white middle-class values. Its thematic approach suggests alternative perspectives and sensitizes us to film's ideological functions and implications. Most important, its emphasis on the colonizing effects of representation affirms the authors' view that African Americans have a responsibility to become agents in the production of film discourse and to rescue their own images and put them to new uses.

While the three preceding course files suggest ways of studying how filmic representations inflect women's national, racial, and ethnic identities, Chris Straayer's "Sexual Representation in Film and Video" takes up issues conventionally linked to the private sphere. Straayer challenges this linkage by defining sexuality as a political (that is, public and collective) matter, despite ongoing attempts to ignore and suppress the behaviors through which sexual politics are socially enacted. Specifically, the course file centers on the politics of sexualities and ideologies of gender as mediated through voyeurism, exhibitionism, aggression, transgression, knowledge, and displacement. The course's exploration of sexually explicit imagery requires careful introduction and adequate cautioning of students who need to be fully advised of its content before enrolling in it. Straayer provides assistance through her suggestions for readings and strategies that promote a scholarly and critical orientation to the material. Addressing potentially volatile issues from a variety of perspectives, the course underscores the need for analysis and theory as a complement to reception. Beginning with a generic study of how sexuality intersects with fantasy, the course reveals the nuanced and sometimes covert effects of sexual ideology, including its political underpinnings. In so doing it shifts its focus from considerations of patriarchal dominance to representations that counter or circumvent it altogether by establishing female sexualities as autonomous and self-motivated, whether heterosexual or lesbian.

This and preceding course files question power and self-determination. Representations of sexuality, nationality, race, ethnicity, and social class are all entwined in hegemonic practices subject to counter readings and counter representations. However, as all the files included in *Multiple Voices* suggest, the resisting practices available to feminists as filmmakers and viewers are not always clear-cut or satisfying. They involve complex, nuanced, and sometimes contradictory understandings of power and definitions of self-interest. But they all recognize the importance of articulating feminist orientations toward film study where differences intersect with gender in productive ways. Most usefully, they focus on agency and positionality as liberating and necessary topics for feminist inquiry and, not incidentally, for all considerations of social justice.

Debates and Options

As the preceding discussion stresses, the three sections that compose *Multiple Voices* are joined by a common goal and complementary concerns. In particular, all three sections aim to refocus feminist film study so as to draw in marginalized films, representations, and perspectives. Ultimately, the thrust of this work is to question received notions of canon, margins, and center. Emphasizing the dialectics of difference, it proposes a dialogic dissonance that allows for exchange without the erasures so readily brought about in the name of universality. Together, the theoretical, critical, and pedagogic essays making up this volume underscore the ideological and the political functions of a film's subject matter as well as its production and reception.

Obviously, our focus on certain materials involved a process of selection and sequencing that is itself ideological. We note this to reiterate that this volume presents thinking in progress and to call attention to the debates and possibilities available to us. We are not proposing a feminist counter-canon but urging critical self-reflexivity about all our work as it relates to the differentials of power and privilege affecting women's position within gender. In practice, canon formation is not entirely avoidable: certain films get screened in class, in festivals, and in movie houses more often than others, and certain authors are anthologized or cited with greater frequency than others. Canons are formed because they speak to the needs of the hour. Still, our overall intention has been to include a broad sampling of possibilities for feminist film reception and scholarship, to encourage critical thinking about the role of films and film studies in social formation, and to contribute to the ongoing discussion feminist film criticism has initiated.

Notes

1. Robin Morgan, *Sisterhood Is Powerful: An Anthology of Writings from the Women's Movement* (New York: Vintage Books, 1970).

2. Peggy McIntosh, "White Privilege and Male Privilege: A Personal Account of Coming to See Correspondences through Work in Women's Studies," in *Race, Class, and Gender*, ed. Margaret L. Andersen and Patricia Hill Collins (Belmont, Calif.: Wadsworth, 1992).

3. For useful analyses of the history and issues at stake, see Zillah Eisenstein, "Specifying US Feminism in the 1990s: The Problem of Naming," *Socialist Review* 2 (1990): 45–56. See also Linda Gordon, "On Difference," *Genders*, no. 10 (Spring 1991): 91–111. Paula Rothenberg relates these issues to teaching in "Integrating the Study of Race, Gender, and Class: Some Preliminary Observations," *Feminist Teacher* 3 (Fall-Winter 1988): 37–42.

4. Debates surrounding *The Color Purple*, especially regarding its commercially screened film adaptation, illustrate the point. Alice Walker's "womanist" protest against African-American women's subjection to incest and physical abuse was widely criticized by African-American men for its undermining of racial solidarity. See Jacqueline Bobo, "*The Color Purple*: Black Women as Cultural Readers," in *Female Spectators: Looking at Film and Television*, ed. E. Deidre Pribram (London: Verso, 1988). See also Trudier Harris, "On *The Color Purple*, Stereotypes, and Silence," *Black American Literature Forum* 18 (1984): 155–61, and Mel Watkins, "Sexism, Racism and Black Women Writers," *New York Times Book Review*, June 12, 1986, 1 and 35–37.

5. Isaac Julien and Kobena Mercer, "Introduction–De Margin and De Centre," *Screen: The Last "Special Issue" on Race?* 29 (Autumn, 1988): 8.

6. Trinh T. Minh-ha, "Difference: A Special Third World Women Issue," in *Woman, Native, Other: Writing Postcoloniality and Feminism* (Bloomington: Indiana University Press, 1989), 79–116. See also Sara Suleri, "Woman Skin Deep: Feminism and the Postcolonial Condition," *Critical Inquiry* 18, no. 4 (1992): 756–69.

7. Laura Mulvey, *Visual and Other Pleasures* (Bloomington: Indiana University Press, 1989).

8. Along parallel lines, Richard Dyer's essay "White" strips the aura of universality away from Western cinema's normative rendition of whiteness as universal: *Screen: The Last "Special Issue" on Race?* 29, no. 4 (1988): 44–64. See also the discussion of "identity politics" in *The Combahee River Collective Statement: Black Feminist Organizing in the Seventies and Eighties* (Albany, N.Y.: Kitchen Table: Women of Color Press, 1986) and Linda Alcoff's discussion of "positionality" in "Cultural Feminism versus Poststructuralism: The Identity Crisis in Feminist Theory," *Signs: Journal of Women in Culture and Society* 13, no. 3 (1988): 405–36.

9. Forging beyond what Houston describes as her "modest claims" on Arzner's behalf, Judith Mayne has since gone on to foreground Arzner's lesbian authorship as resistance to the heterosexual master narrative. See Judith Mayne, "Female Authorship Reconsidered," in *The Woman at the Keyhole: Feminism and Women's Cinema* (Bloomington: Indiana University Press, 1990), 89–123.

Part I

Perspectives

In the Name of Feminist Film Criticism[1]

B. Ruby Rich

> Whatever is unnamed, undepicted in images, whatever is omitted
> from biography, censored in collections of letters, whatever is mis-
> named as something else, made difficult-to-come-by, whatever is bu-
> ried in the memory by the collapse of meaning under an inadequate
> or lying language–this will become, not merely unspoken, but un-
> speakable.
>
> *–Adrienne Rich[2]*

The situation for women working in filmmaking and film criticism today
is precarious. While our work is no longer invisible, and not yet unspeakable, it still goes dangerously unnamed. There is even uncertainty over
what name might characterize that intersection of cinema and the
women's movement within which we labor, variously called "films by
women," "feminist film," "images of women in film," and "women's films."
All are vague and problematic. I see the lack of proper name here as symptomatic of a crisis in the ability of feminist film criticism thus far to come
to terms with the work at hand, to apply a truly feminist criticism to the
body of work already produced by women filmmakers. "Feminist" is a
name that may have only a marginal relation to the film text, describing
more persuasively the context of social and political activity from which
the work sprang.

The History

The great contribution of feminism, as a body of thought, to culture in our
time has been that it has something fairly direct to say, a quality all too
rare today. And its equally crucial contribution, as a process and style, has
been women's insistence on conducting the analysis, making the statements, in unsullied terms, in forms not already associated with the media's
oppressiveness toward women. It is this freshness of discourse and dis-

27

trust of traditional modes of articulation that placed feminist cinema in a singular position vis-à-vis both the dominant cinema and the avant-garde in the early 1970s. By the "dominant," I mean Hollywood and all its corresponding manifestations in other cultures; but this could also be termed the Cinema of the Fathers. By the "avant-garde," I mean the experimental/personal cinema, which is positioned, by self-inclusion, within the art world; but this could also be termed the Cinema of the Sons. Being a business, the Cinema of the Fathers seeks to do only that which has been done before and proved successful. Being an art, the Cinema of the Sons seeks to do only that which has not been done before and so prove itself successful.

Into such a situation, at the start of the 1970s, entered a feminist cinema. In place of the Fathers' bankruptcy of both form and content, there was a new and different energy: a cinema of immediacy and positive force now opposed the retreat into violence and the revival of a dead past that had become the dominant cinema's mainstays. In place of the Sons' increasing alienation and isolation, there was an entirely new sense of identification—with other women—and a corresponding commitment to communicate with this now-identifiable audience, a commitment that replaced, for feminist filmmakers, the elusive public ignored and frequently scorned by the male formalist filmmakers. Thus, from the start, its link to an evolving political movement gave feminist cinema a power and direction entirely unprecedented in independent filmmaking, bringing such traditional issues as theory/practice, aesthetics/meaning, process/representation into focus.

The unity, discovery, energy, and brave we're-here-to-stay spirit of the early 1970s underwent a definite shift in 1975, mid-decade. Since then, the field of vision has altered. There is now increased specialization, both in the direction of genre studies (such as film noir) and film theory (particularly semiotic and psychoanalytic); the start of sectarianism, women partitioned off into enclaves defined by which conferences they attend or which journals they subscribe to; increased institutionalization, both of women's studies and cinema studies departments—twin creations of the 1970s; a backlash emphasis on "human" liberation, which by making communication with men a priority can leave woman-to-woman feminism looking déclassé. Overall, there is a growing acceptance of feminist film as an area of study rather than as a sphere of action. And this may pull feminist film work away from its early political commitment, to encompass a wide social setting; away from the issues of life that go beyond form; away from the combative (as an analysis of and weapon against patriarchal capitalism) into the merely representational. Cross-fertilization between the women's movement and cinema took place initially in the area of practice rather than in written criticism. The films came first. In fact, we find two different currents feeding into film work: one made up of women who were feminists and thereby led to film, the other made up of women already working in film and thereby led to feminism. It was largely the first group of women who began making the films that were naturally named "feminist,"[3] and largely the second group of women, often in university film studies departments, who began holding the film festivals, just as naturally named "women and/in film." Spadework has continued in both directions, creating a new women's cinema and rediscovering the antecedents, with the two currents feeding our film criticism.

Returning to Rich's original warning, however, we reach the end of history's comforts and arrive at our present danger: "Whatever is unnamed, . . . buried in the memory by the collapse of meaning under an inadequate or lying language – this will become, not merely unspoken, but unspeakable." Herein lies the crisis facing feminist film criticism today, for after a decade of film practice and theory, we still lack our proper names. The impact of this lack on the films themselves is of immediate concern.

The Films

One classic film rediscovered through women's film festivals indicates the sort of misnaming prevalent in film history. Leontine Sagan's *Maedchen in Uniform*, a 1931 German film, details the relationship between a student and her teacher in a repressive girls' boarding school.[4] The act of naming is itself a pivotal moment in the narrative. Toward the end of the film, the schoolgirls gather at a drunken party after the annual school play. Manuela has just starred as a passionate youth and, drunk with punch, still in boy's clothing, she stands to proclaim her happiness and love – naming her teacher Fräulein von Bernburg as the woman she loves. Before this episode, the lesbian substructure of the school and the clearly shared knowledge of that substructure have been emphasized; the school laundress even points to the prevalence of the Fräulein's initials embroidered on the girls' regulation chemises as evidence of the adulation of her adolescent admirers. This eroticism was *not* in the closet. But only when Manuela stands and names that passion is she punished, locked up in solitary – for her speech, not for her actions.

Such is the power of a name and the valor of naming. It is ironic that the inscription of the power of naming within the film has not forestalled its own continuous misnaming within film history, which has championed its antifascism while masking the lesbian origins of that resistance. The problem is even more acute in dealing with contemporary films, where the lack of an adequate language has contributed to the invisibility of key aspects of our film culture – an invisibility advantageous to the prevailing film traditions.

The act of misnaming functions not as mere error but as a strategy of the patriarchy. The lack of proper names facilitates derogatory name-calling; the failure to assign meaningful names to contemporary feminist films eases the acquisition of misnomers. Two key films of the 1970s reveal this process and the disenfranchisement we suffer as a result.

Chantal Akerman's *Jeanne Dielman, 23 Quai du Commerce, 1080 Bruxelles* (1975) is a chronicle of three days in the life of a Brussels house-wife, a widow and mother who is also a prostitute. It is the first film to scru-tinize housework in a language appropriate to the activity itself, showing a woman's activities in the home in real time to communicate the alienation of woman in the nuclear family under European postwar economic condi-tions. More than three hours in length and nearly devoid of dialog, the film charts Jeanne Dielman's breakdown via a minute observation of her per-formance of household routines, at first methodical and unvarying, later increasingly disarranged, until by film's end she permanently disrupts the patriarchal order by murdering her third client. The film was scripted, directed, photographed, and edited by women with a consciously feminist sensibility.

The aesthetic repercussions of such a sensibility are evident throughout the film. For example, the choice of camera angle is unusually low. In inter-views, Akerman explained that the camera was positioned at her own height; since she is quite short, the entire perspective of the film is differ-ent from what we are used to seeing, as shot by male cinematographers. The perspective of every frame thus reveals a female ordering of that space, prompting a reconsideration of point of view that I had felt before only in a few works shot by children (which expose the power of tall adults in every shot) and in the films by the Japanese director Yasujiro Ozu (where the low angle has been much discussed by Western critics as an en-try into the "oriental" detachment of someone seated on a tatami mat, ob-serving). Akerman's decision to employ only medium and long shots also stems from a feminist critique: the decision to free her character from the exploitation of a zoom lens and to grant her an integrity of private space usually denied in close-ups, thereby also freeing the audience from the in-sensitivity of a camera barreling in to magnify a woman's emotional crisis. Similarly, the activities of shopping, cooking, and cleaning the house are presented without ellipses, making visible the extent of time previously omitted from cinematic depictions. Thus, the film is a profoundly feminist work in theme, style, and representation; yet it has been critically received in language devoted to sanctifying aesthetics stripped of political consequence.

Shortly after *Jeanne Dielman*'s premiere at the Cannes film festival, European critics extolled the film as "hyperrealist" in homage both to the realist film (and literary) tradition and to the superrealist movement in painting. Two problems arise with such a name: first, the tradition of cinematic realism has never included women in its alleged veracity; second, the comparison with superrealist painters obscures the contradiction between their illusionism and Akerman's anti-illusionism. Another name applied to *Jeanne Dielman* was "ethnographic," in keeping with the film's insistence on real-time presentation and nonelliptical editing. Again, the name negates a basic aspect by referring to a cinema of clinical observation, aimed at "objectivity" and noninvolvement, detached rather than engaged. The film's warm texture and Akerman's committed sympathies (the woman's gestures were borrowed from her own mother and aunt) make the name inappropriate.

The critical reception of the film in the *Soho Weekly News* by three different reviewers points up the confusion engendered by linguistic inadequacy.[5] Jonas Mekas questioned, "Why did she have to ruin the film by making the woman a prostitute and introduce a murder at the end, why did she commercialize it?" Later, praising most of the film as a successor to *Greed*, he contended that the heroine's silence was more "revolutionary" than the murder, making a case for the film's artistic merit as separate from its social context and moving the work into the area of existentialism at the expense of its feminism. Amy Taubin considered the film "theatrical" and, while commending the subjectivity of the camera work and editing, she attacked the character of Jeanne: "Are we to generalize from Jeanne to the oppression of many women through their subjugation to activity which offers them no range of creative choice? If so, Jeanne Dielman's pathology mitigates against our willingness to generalize." By holding a reformist position (i.e., that she should vary her menu, change her wardrobe) in relation to a revolutionary character (i.e., a murderer), Taubin was forced into a reading of the film limited by notions of realism that she, as an avant-garde film critic, would have ordinarily tried to avoid: her review split the film along the lines of form/content, annexing the aesthetics as "the real importance" and rejecting the character of Jeanne as a pathological woman. Again we find a notion of pure art set up in opposition to a feminism seemingly restricted to positive role models. Finally, Annette Michelson wrote a protest to Mekas that defended the film for "the sense of renewal it has brought both to a narrative mode and the inscription *within it* of feminist energies" (my italics). Yes, but at what cost? Here the effect of inadequate naming is precisely spelled out: the feminist energies are being spent to create work quickly absorbed into mainstream modes of art that renew themselves at our expense. Already, the renaissance of the "new narrative" is under way in film circles with nary a glance back at filmmakers such as Akerman or Yvonne Rainer, who first incurred the wrath of the academy by reintroducing characters, emotions, and narratives into their films.

The critical response to Rainer's recent films, especially *Film about a Woman Who* . . . , adds instances of naming malpractice.[6] Much of the criticism has been in the area of formal textual analysis, concentrating on the "postmodernist" structures, "Brechtian" distancing, or cinematic deconstruction of the works. Continuing the tactic of detoxifying films via a divide-and-conquer criticism, critic Brian Henderson analyzed the central section in *Film about a Woman Who* . . . according to a semiological model, detailing the five channels of communication used to present textual information.[7] The analysis was exhaustive on the level of technique but completely ignored the actual meaning of the information (Rainer's "emotional accretions")–the words themselves and the visualization (a man and woman on a stark bed/table). At the opposite extreme, a *Feminist Art Journal* editorial condemned Rainer as a modernist, "the epitome of the alienated artist," and discounted her film work as regressive for feminists, evidently because of its formal strategies.[8]

Rainer's films deal with the relations between the sexes and the interaction of life and art within a framework combining autobiography and fiction. Whatever the intent of Rainer's filmmaking in political terms, the work stands as a clear product of a feminist cultural milieu. The films deal explicitly with woman as victim and the burden of patriarchal mythology; they offer a critique of emotion, reworking melodrama for women today, and even provide an elegy to the lost innocence of defined male/female roles (*Kristina Talking Pictures*). Yet little of the criticism has managed to reconcile an appreciation for the formal elements with an understanding of the feminist effect. Carol Wikarska, in a short review for *Women & Film*, could only paraphrase Rainer's own descriptions in a stab at *Film about a Woman Who* . . . seen in purely art-world terms.[9] More critically, the feminist-defined film journal *Camera Obscura* concentrated its first issue on Rainer but fell into a similar quandary. While an interview with Rainer was included, the editors felt obliged to critique the films in the existing semiological vocabulary, taking the feminist value for granted without confronting the points of contradiction within that methodology. The lack of vocabulary once again frustrates a complete consideration of the work.

Lest the similarity of these misnamings merely suggest critical blindness rather than a more deliberate tactic, an ironic reversal is posed by the response to Anne Severson's *Near the Big Chakra*. Silent and in color, the film shows a series of thirty-six women's cunts photographed in unblinking close-up, some still and some moving, with no explanations or gratuitous presentation. Formally the film fits into the category of "structuralist" cinema: a straightforward listing of parts, no narrative, requisite attention to a predetermined and simplified, structured, and fixed camera position (as defined by the namer–P. Adams Sitney). Yet Severson's image is so powerfully unco-optable that her film has never been called "structuralist" to my knowledge, nor–with retrospective revisionism–have her earlier films been so named. Evidently, any subject matter that could make a man vomit (as happened at a London screening in 1973) is too much for the critical category, even though it was founded on the "irrelevance" of the visual images. Thus a name can be withheld by the critical establishment if its application alone won't make the film fit the category.

"Whatever they have not laid hands on . . . does not appear in the language you speak," wrote Monique Wittig.[10] Here is the problem: not so much that certain names are used, but that other names are not–and therefore the qualities they describe are lost. Where patriarchal language holds sway, the silences, the characteristics that are unnamed, frequently hold the greatest potential strength. In Chantal Akerman's work, what is most valuable for us is her decoding of oppressive cinematic conventions and her invention of new codes of nonvoyeuristic vision; yet these contributions go unnamed. In Yvonne Rainer's work, the issue is not one of this or that role model for feminists, not whether her women characters are too weak or too victimized or too individualistic. Rather, we can value precisely her refusal to pander (visually and emotionally), her frustration of audience expectation of spectacle (physical or psychic), and her reworking of traditional forms of melodrama and elegy to include modern feminist culture. Yet these elements, of greatest value to us, are not accorded critical priority.

The effect of not naming is censorship, whether caused by the imperialism of the patriarchal language or the underdevelopment of a feminist language. We need to begin analyzing our own films, but first it is necessary to learn to speak in our own name. The recent history of feminist film criticism indicates the urgency of that need.

"Feminist Film Criticism: In Two Voices"

There have been two types of feminist film criticism,[11] motivated by different geographical and ideological contexts, each speaking in a very different voice:

> History of philosophy has an obvious, repressive function in philosophy; it is philosophy's very own Oedipus. "All the same, you won't dare speak your own name as long as you have not read this and that, and that on this, and this on that. . . . To say something in one's own name is very strange." (Gilles Deleuze)[12]

Speaking in one's own name versus speaking in the name of history is a familiar problem to anyone who has ever pursued a course of study, become involved in an established discipline, and then tried to speak out of personal experience or nonprofessional/nonacademic knowledge without suddenly feeling quite schizophrenic. Obviously it is a schizophrenia especially familiar to feminists. The distinction between one's own voice and the voice of history is a handy one by which to distinguish the two types of feminist film criticism. At least initially, these two types could be characterized as either American or British: the one, American, seen as sociological or subjective, often a speaking out in one's own voice; the other, British, seen as methodological or more objective, often speaking in the voice of history. (The work of the past few years has blurred the original nationalist base of the categories: for example, the Parisian perspective of the California-based *Camera Obscura.*)

The originally American, so-called sociological, approach is exemplified by early *Women & Film* articles and much of the catalogue writing from festivals of that same period. The emphasis on legitimizing women's own reactions and making women's contributions visible resulted in a tendency toward reviews, getting information out, a tendency to offer testimony as theory. Fruitful in this terrain, the weakness of the approach became the limits of its introspection, the boundaries established by the lack of a coherent methodology for moving out beyond the self. An example of this approach would be Barbara Halpern Martineau's very eccentric, subjective, and illuminating analyses of Nelly Kaplan and Agnés Varda films.[13] A dismaying example of the decadent strain of this approach was Joan Mellen's mid-1970s book *Big Bad Wolves*, which offered personal interpretations of male characters and actors in a move to shift attention to the reformist arena of "human liberation."

The originally British, so-called theoretical, approach is exemplified by the British Film Institute monograph on women and film, by articles in *Screen*, and by the initial issues of *Camera Obscura* (which, like the British writing, defers to the French authorities). Committed to using some of the most advanced tools of critical analysis, such as semiology and psychoanalysis, this approach has tried to come to terms with *how* films mean – to move beyond regarding the image to analyzing the structure, codes, the general subtext of the works. Fruitful for its findings regarding signification, the weakness of the approach has been its suppression of the personal and a seeming belief in the neutrality of the analytic tools, so that the critic's feminist voice has often been muted by this methodocracy. Two of the most important products of this approach are pieces by Laura Mulvey and Claire Johnston.[14] Johnston has critiqued the image of woman in male cinema and finds her to be a signifier, not of woman, but of the absent phallus, a signifier of an absence rather than any presence. Similarly, Mulvey has analyzed the nature of the cinematic spectator and finds evidence – in cinematic voyeurism and in the nature of the camera look – of the exclusively male spectator as a production assumption.

Another way of characterizing these two approaches would be to identify the American (sociological, or in one's own voice) as fundamentally
phenomenological, and the British (theoretical, or the voice of history) as
fundamentally analytical. Johnston and Mulvey's texts taken together, for
example, pose a monumental absence that is unduly pessimistic. The misplaced pessimism stems from their overvaluation of the production aspect
of cinema, a misassumption that cinematic values are irrevocably embedded at the level of production and, once there, remain pernicious and invio-
lable. Woman is absent on the screen and she is absent in the audience,
their analysis argues. And yet here a bit of phenomenology would be helpful, a moment of speaking in one's own voice and wondering at the source
in such a landscape of absence. As a woman sitting in the dark, watching
that film made by and for men with drag queens on the screen, what is my
experience? Don't I in fact interact with that text and that context, with
a conspicuous absence of passivity? For a woman's experiencing of culture
under patriarchy is dialectical in a way that a man's can never be: our experience is like that of the exile, whom Brecht once singled out as the ultimate dialectician for that daily working out of cultural oppositions within
a single body. It is crucial to emphasize here the possibility for texts to be
transformed at the level of reception and not to fall into a trap of condescension toward our own developed powers as active producers of meaning.

The differences implicit in these two attitudes lead to quite different positions and strategies, as the following selection of quotations helps to
point up.[15] When interviewed regarding the reason for choosing her
specific critical tools (auteurist, structuralist, psychoanalytic), Claire Johnston replied, "As far as I'm concerned, it's a question of what is theoretically correct; these new theoretical developments cannot be ignored, just
as feminists cannot ignore Marx or Freud, because they represent crucial
scientific developments." In contrast to this vision of science as ideologically neutral would be the reiteration by such theoreticians as Adrienne
Rich and Audre Lorde that "you have to be constantly critiquing even the
tools you use to explore and define what it is to be female." In the same
interview as Johnston, Pam Cook elaborated on their aim: "Women are
fixed in ideology in a particular way, which is definable in terms of the patriarchal system. I think we see our first need as primarily to define that
place – the place that women are fixed in." In marked contrast to such a
sphere of activity, the Womanifesto of the 1975 New York Conference of
Feminists in the Media stated, "We do not accept the existing power structure and we are committed to changing it by the content and structure of
our images and by the ways we relate to each other in our work and with
our audience." In her own article, Laura Mulvey identified the advantage
of psychoanalytical critiques as their ability to "advance our understand-

ing of the status quo," a limited and modest claim; yet she herself went beyond such a goal in making (with Peter Wollen) *The Riddles of the Sphinx*, a film that was meant to represent a part two of her original theory.

I have termed the British approach pessimistic, a quality that may be perceived by supporters as realistic or by detractors as colonized. I have termed the American approach optimistic, a quality that may be viewed by supporters as radical or by detractors as unrealistic, utopian. It is not surprising, however, that such a dualism of critical approach has evolved. In *Woman's Consciousness, Man's World*, Sheila Rowbotham points out that "there is a long inchoate period during which the struggle between the language of experience and the language of theory becomes a kind of agony."[16] It is a problem common to an oppressed people at the point of formulating a new language with which to name that oppression, for the history of oppression has prevented the development of any unified language among its subjects. It is crucial for those of us working in the area of feminist film criticism to mend this rift, confront the agony, and begin developing a synthesis of maximally effective critical practice. Without names, our work remains anonymous, insecure, our continued visibility questionable.

Anticlimax: The Names

Without new names, we run the danger of losing title to films that we sorely need. By stretching the name "feminist" beyond all reasonable elasticity, we contribute to its ultimate impoverishment. At the same time, so many films have been partitioned off to established traditions, with the implication that these other names contradict or negate any application of the name "feminist" to the works so annexed, that the domain of "feminist" cinema is fast becoming limited to that work concerned only with feminism as explicit subject matter. "Feminist," if it is to make a comeback from the loss of meaning caused by its all-encompassing overuse, requires new legions of names to preserve for us the inner strengths, the not-yet-visible qualities of these films still lacking in definition.

Because this need is so very urgent, I here offer an experimental glossary of names as an aid to initiating a new stage of feminist criticism. These names are not likely to be an immediate hit. First of all, it's well and good to call for new names to appear in the night sky like so many constellations, but it's quite another thing to invent them and commit them to paper. Second, there's the inevitable contradiction of complaining about names and then committing more naming acts. Third, there's the danger that, however unwieldy, these new names might be taken as formulas to be applied to every hapless film that comes our way. The point, after all, is not to set up new power institutions (feminist banks, feminist popes, feminist names) but rather to open the mind to new descriptive possibilities. Not to require alternate glossaries of Talmudic herstory, but to suggest the revolutionary possibilities of nonpatriarchal, noncapitalist imaginings.

Validative

One of feminist filmmaking's greatest contributions is the body of films about women's lives, political struggles, organizing, and so on. These films have been vaguely classified under the *cinéma vérité* banner, where they reside in decidedly mixed company. Since they function as a validation and legitimation of women's culture and individual lives, the name "validative" would be a better choice. It has the added advantage of aligning the work with products of oppressed peoples (with the filmmaker as insider), whereas the *cinéma vérité* label represents the oppressors, who make films as superior outsiders documenting alien, implicitly inferior cultures, often from a position of condescension. The feminist films of the early 1970s were validative, and validative films continue to be an important component of feminist filmmaking. They may be ethnographic, documenting the evolution of women's lives and issues (as in *We're Alive*, a portrait and analysis of women in prison) or archaeological, uncovering women's hidden past (as in *Union Maids*, with its recovery of women's role in the labor movement, or Sylvia Morales's *Chicana*, the first film history of the Mexican-American woman's struggle). The form is well established, yet the constantly evolving issues require new films, such as *We Will Not Be Beaten*, a film on domestic violence culled from videotaped interviews with women. By employing the name "validative" in place of *cinéma vérité*, we can combat the patriarchal annexation of the woman filmmaker as one of the boys, that is, as a professional who is not of the culture being filmed. It is a unifying name aimed at conserving strength.

Correspondence

A different name is necessary for more avant-garde films, such as those of Yvonne Rainer, Chantal Akerman, Helke Sander, or Laura Mulvey and Peter Wollen. Looking to literary history, we find a concern with the role played by letters ("personal" discourse) as a sustaining mode for women's writing during times of literary repression. The publication of historical letters by famous and ordinary women has been a major component of the feminist publishing renaissance, just as the long-standing denigration of the genre as not "real" writing (i.e., not certified by either a publishing house or monetary exchange) has been an additional goad for the creation of feminist alternatives to the literary establishment. A cinema of "correspondence" is a fitting homage to this tradition of introspective missives sent out into the world. Equally relevant is the other definition of "correspondence" as "mutual response, the answering of things to each other," or, to take Swedenborg's literal doctrine of correspondence as an example, the tenet that "every natural object symbolizes or corresponds to some spiritual fact or principle which is, as it were, its archetype."[17] Films of correspondence, then, would be those investigating correspondences, for example, between emotion and objectivity, narrative and deconstruction, art and ideology. Thus *Jeanne Dielman* is a film of correspondence in its exploration of the bonds between housework and madness, prostitution and heterosexuality, epic and dramatic temporality.

What distinguishes such films of correspondence from formally similar films by male avant-garde filmmakers is their inclusion of the author within the text. *Film about a Woman Who* . . . corresponds to very clear experiences and emotional concerns in Rainer's life, and *Jeanne Dielman* draws on the gestures of the women in Akerman's family. (Of course, there is a tradition of "diary" movies by men as well as women, but, significantly, the presence of Jonas Mekas in most of his diary films – like that of Godard in *Numero Deux* – is of the filmmaker rather than the "man" outside that professional role.) Similarly, Helke Sander in *The All-Round Reduced Personality/Redupers* revises the ironic, distanced narration of modernist German cinema to include the filmmaker in a same first-person-plural with her characters. It is this resolute correspondence between form and content, to put it bluntly, that distinguishes the films of correspondence. Such films are essential to the development of new structures and forms for the creation and communication of feminist works and values; more experimental than validative, they lay the groundwork of a feminist cinematic vocabulary.

Reconstructive

Several recent films suggest another name, located midway between the two described above and dealing directly with issues of form posed by the political and emotional concerns of the work. One such film is Sally Potter's *Thriller*, a feminist murder mystery related as a first-person inquiry by the victim: Mimi, the seamstress of Puccini's *La Bohème*, investigates the cause of her death and the manner of her life, uncovering in the process the contradictions hidden by the bourgeois male artist. Michelle Citron's *Daughter Rite* probes relations between women in the family, using dramatic sequences to critique *cinéma vérité* and optical printing to reexamine home movies, that U.S. index to domestic history. Both *Thriller* and *Daughter Rite* are reconstructive in their rebuilding of other forms, whether grand opera or soap opera, according to feminist specifications. At the same time both Potter and Citron reconstruct some basic cinematic styles (psychodrama, documentary) to create new feminist forms, in harmony with the desires of the audience as well as the theoretical concerns of the filmmakers. By reconstructing forms in a constructive manner, these films build bridges between the needs of women and the goals of art.

Medusan

Humor should not be overlooked as a weapon of great power. Comedy requires further cultivation for its revolutionary potential as a deflator of the patriarchal order and an extraordinary leveler and reinventer of dramatic structure. An acknowledgment of the subversive power of humor, the name "Medusan" is taken from Hélène Cixous's "The Laugh of the Medusa," in which she celebrates the potential of feminist texts "to blow up the law, to break up the 'truth' with laughter."[18] Cixous's contention that when women confront the figure of Medusa she will be laughing is a rejoinder to Freud's posing the "Medusa's head" as an incarnation of male castration fears. For Cixous, women are having the last laugh. And, to be sure, all the films in this camp deal with combinations of humor and sexuality. Vera Chytilova's *Daisies* was one of the first films by a woman to move in the direction of anarchic sexuality, though its disruptive humor was received largely as slapstick at the time. Nelly Kaplan's two films, *A Very Curious Girl* and *Nea*, also offered an explosive humor coupled with sexuality to discomfort patriarchal society (even though her fondness for "happy" endings that restore order has discomfited many feminist critics). Jan Oxenberg's *A Comedy in Six Unnatural Acts* is an excellent example of a Medusan film, attacking not just men or sexism but the heterosexually defined stereotypes of lesbianism; its success has been demonstrated by its raucous cult reception and, more pointedly, by its tendency to polarize a mixed audience along the lines not of class but of sexual preference. It is disruptive of homophobic complacency with a force never approached by analytical films defending lesbianism.

Another highly Medusan film is Jacques Rivette's *Celine and Julie Go Boating* (which may be curious, as it is directed by a man, but production credits claim a total collaboration with the four actresses and coscenarists). Celine and Julie enter each other's lives by magic and books, joined in a unity of farce; once they are together, each proceeds to demolish the other's ties to men (an employer, a childhood lover) by using humor, laughing in the face of male fantasies and expectations and thus "spoiling" the relationships with a fungus of parody. The film has been criticized as silly, for Juliet Berto and Dominique Labourier do laugh constantly—at the other characters, themselves, the audience, acting itself—yet their laughter ultimately proves their finest arsenal, enabling them to rescue the plot's girlchild from a darkly imminent Henry Jamesian destruction simply through a laughing refusal to obey the rules. Again, *Celine and Julie* has consistently divided its audience according to whom it threatens: it has become a cult feminist movie even as the male critical establishment (except for Rivette fan Jonathan Rosenbaum) has denounced the film as silly, belabored, obvious, and the like.

Corrective Realism

As mentioned earlier, the tradition of realism in the cinema has never done well by women. Indeed, extolling realism to women is rather like praising the criminal to the victim, so thoroughly have women been falsified under its banner. A feminist feature cinema, generally representational, is now developing with a regular cast of actresses and a story line aimed at a wide audience and generally accepting of many cinematic conventions. The women making these films, however, are so thoroughly transforming the characterizations and the narrative workings of traditional realism that they have created a new feminist cinema of "corrective realism." Thus in Margarethe von Trotta's *The Second Awakening of Christa Klages*, it is the women's actions that advance the narrative; bonding between women functions to save, not to paralyze or trap, the characters; running away brings Christa freedom, while holding his ground brings her male lover only death. Marta Meszaros's *Women* presents a profound reworking of socialist realism in its depiction of the friendship between two women in a Hungarian work hostel. The alternating close-ups and medium shots become a means of social critique, while the more traditional portrayal of the growing intimacy between the two women insistently places emotional concerns at the center of the film. Both films successfully adapt an existing cinematic tradition to feminist purposes, going beyond the "positive role model" in their establishment of a feminist cinematic environment within which to envision female protagonists and their activities.

These, then, are a few of the naming possibilities. However, it is not only the feminist films that demand new names, but also (for clarity) the films being made by men about women.

Projectile

One name resurrected from the 1950s by 1970s criticism, via Molly Haskell's recoining, was the "woman's film," that matinee melodrama that, cleared of pejorative connotations, was refitted for relevance to women's cinematic concerns today. Wishful thinking. The name was Hollywood's and there it stays, demonstrated by the new "woman's films" that are pushing actual women's films off the screen, out into the dark. These are male fantasies of women—men's projections of themselves and their fears onto female characters. The name "projectile" identifies these films' true nature and creates an added awareness of the destructive impact of male illusions on the female audience. It is time the bluff was called on the touted authenticity of these works, which pose as objective while remaining entirely subjective in their conception and execution. The clearest justification for this name can be found in director Paul Mazursky's description of his *An Unmarried Woman*:

> I don't know if this is a woman's movie or not. I don't know what that means anymore. . . . I wanted to get inside a woman's head. I've felt that all the pictures I've done, I've done with men. I put myself inside a man's head, using myself a lot. I wanted this time to think like a woman. That's one of the reasons there was so much rewriting. . . . There were many things the women I cast in the film . . . wouldn't say. They'd tell me why, and I'd say, 'Well, what would you say?' and I'd let them say that. I used a real therapist; I wanted a woman, and I had to change what she said based on what she is. In other words, the only thing I could have done was to get a woman to help me write it. I thought about that for a while, but in the end I think it worked out.[19]

Films such as this one (and *The Turning Point, Pretty Baby, Luna,* and so on ad infinitum) are aimed fatally at us; they deserve to be named "projectile."

Certainly the names offered here do not cover all possibilities, nor can every film be fitted neatly into one category. But I hope their relative usefulness or failings will prompt a continuation of the process by others. The urgency of the naming task cannot be overstated.

Warning Signs: A Postscript

We are now in a period of normalization, a time that can offer feminists complacency as a mask for co-optation. Scanning the horizon for signs of backlash and propaganda, we see that the storm clouds within feminist film criticism are gathering most clearly over issues of form.

It has become a truism to call for new forms. Over and over, we have heard the sacred vows: you can't put new revolutionary subjects/messages into reactionary forms; new forms, a new antipatriarchal film language for feminist cinema, must be developed. While certainly true to an extent, form remains only one element of the work. And the valorization of form above and independent of other criteria has begun to create its own problems.

There is the misconception that form, unlike subject matter, is inviolate and can somehow encase meaning in protective armor. But form is as co-optable as other elements. A recent analysis by critic Julianne Burton of the *cinema novo* movement in Brazil raised this point by demonstrating how the Brazilian state film apparatus took over the forms and styles of *cinema novo* and stripped them of their ideological significance as one means of disarming the movement.[20] If we fetishize the long take, the unmediated shot, and such, as feminist per se, then we will shortly be at a loss over how to evaluate the facsimiles proliferating in the wake of such a definition. Furthermore, the reliance on form as the ultimate gauge of a film's worth sets up an inevitable hierarchy that places reconstructive films or films of correspondence at the top of a pyramid, leaving corrective realist or validative approaches among the baser elements. This itself is a complex problem. First, such a view reproduces the notion of history as "progress" and supposes that forms, like technology, grow cumulatively better and better. Some believe in that sort of linear quality, but I don't. Second, recent criticism by Christine Gledhill (of film) and Myra Love (of literature) has questioned the naturalness of the Brechtian, postmodernist, deconstructive model as a feminist strategy, pointing out the real drawbacks of its endemic authoritarianism and ambiguity.[21] Third, our very reasons for supporting such work must at least be examined honestly. Carolyn Heilbrun's point should be well taken: "Critics, and particularly academics, are understandably prone to admire and overvalue the carefully constructed, almost puzzlelike novel [read: film], not only for its profundities, but because it provides them, in explication, with their livelihood."[22] Just as a generosity of criticism can provide the strongest support for feminist filmmakers, so acceptance of a variety of filmic strategies can provide the vigor needed by the feminist audience.

For we must look to the filmmaker and viewer for a way out of this aesthetic cul-de-sac. Aesthetics are not eternally embedded in a work as a penny in a cube of Lucite. They are dependent on and subject to the work's reception. The formal values of a film cannot be considered in isolation, cut off from the thematic correspondents within the text and from the social determinants without. Reception by viewers as well as by critics is key to any film's meaning. As a look at history shows, feminist cinema arose out of a need not only on the part of the filmmakers and writers, but on the part of the women they knew to be their audience. Today we must constantly check feminist film work to gauge how alive this thread of connection still is, how communicable its feminist values are. We are in a time of transition now, when we still have the luxury of enjoying feminist work on its makers' own terms, without having to sift the sands paranoically for imposters. But this transitional period is running out: as the cultural lag catches up, the dominant and avant-garde cinema may begin to incorporate feminist success before we recognize what we've lost. The emphasis on form makes that incorporation easier. Burton ended her article with a call for the inscription of modes of production within the body of Third

World film criticism. Therein lies a clue. Feminism has always emphasized process; now it's time that this process of production and reception be inscribed within the critical text. How was the film made? With what intention? With what kind of crew? With what relationship to the subject? How was it produced? Who is distributing it? Where is it being shown? For what audience is it constructed? How is it available? How is it being received? There is no need to establish a tyranny of the productive sphere over a film's definition, nor to authorize only immediately popular films, but it will prove helpful in the difficult times ahead of us to keep this bottom line of method and context in mind, to avoid painting ourselves into a corner.

Formal devices are progressive only if they are employed with a goal beyond aesthetics alone. Here, finally, is the end of the line. Feminist film criticism cannot solve problems still undefined in the sphere of feminist thought and activity at large. We are all continually borrowing from and adding to one another's ideas, energies, insights, across disciplines. We also need to develop lines of communication across the boundaries of race, class, and sexuality. Last year (1978) in Cuba, I heard a presentation by Alfredo Guevara, founder and director of the Cuban Film Institute. He explained its efforts to educate the Cuban audience to the tricks of cinema, to demystify the technology, to give the viewers the means with which to defend themselves against cinematic hypnosis, to challenge the dominant ideology of world cinema, to create a new liberated generation of film viewers. I will never forget his next words: "We do not claim to have created this audience already, nor do we think it is a task only of cinema." The crisis of naming requires more than an etymologist to solve it.

Yet Another Postscript (1991)

Writing in the 1970s, with no crystal ball at hand, I could not have foreseen how changed a landscape would welcome this essay back into print. Now, in the first decade of the post-cold war, of the total militarization of American life, of worldwide recession, the end of communism and socialism as viable alternatives, the rollback of civil rights and reproductive rights, the evolution of a quasi-fascist form of capitalism, and the emergence of a repressive apparatus directed explicitly at representation (photography and film, in particular, although the art world as a whole is under siege), this essay shines for me today brightly but innocently, a clarion cry from another era.

This is not to say that its lessons have gone out of date, that its insights are not still relevant, its terminologies obsolete. Not at all. But they are insufficient. Within the world of feminist film, three shifts of direction since this essay's first appearance are particularly striking.

First, narrative has assumed precedence over documentary as the favored medium for women filmmakers and video artists. In part, this turn to fiction has been necessitated by changes in economics and funding patterns (the politically motivated withdrawal of the National Endowment for the Humanities monies that funded the early ambitious documentaries, the increased costs of shooting in film at the ratio demanded by the 1970s working methods, and the development of investment models for film production by independent director/producers). In equal part, however, it was probably a response to the very real pressures brought to bear on filmmakers who took on the burden of uplifting the gender: fiction allows more leeway, sits more easily with the auteurist style demanded by the age, and offers more freedom from collective expectations. Secondarily, the short film has lost ground to the feature in terms of prestige, with many filmmakers trying hard to make the transition. Although numerous films are still made in the short format (particularly by women of color), the market that once sustained that arena is diminished.

Second, the whiteness that is so pronounced a characteristic of this text has been thankfully eradicated by the important works produced in the United States throughout the 1980s and 1990s by women of color. A filmography and videography of considerable length would be required to do justice to the subject; any such list would certainly have to include the independent works of Martina Attille, Camille Billops, Shu-Lea Cheang, Ayoka Chenzira, Christine Choy, Julie Dash, Zeinabu Davis, Leslie Harris, Indu Krishnan, Daresha Kyi, Alile Sharon Larkin, Tracey Moffatt, Sylvia Morales, Emiko Omori, Midi Onodera, Ngozi A. Onwurah, Michelle Parkerson, Pratibha Parmar, Lourdes Portillo, Demetria Royals, Kathe Sandler, Jacqueline Shearer, Valerie Soe, Renee Tajima, Rea Tajiri, Pam Tom, Janice Tanaka, Trinh T. Minh-ha, and dozens more.

The genre choices and narrative strategies are wildly divergent, as would be expected from such a broad movement of what is increasingly (and inadequately) seen as "multiculturalism" in a female chord. But already—to take just one example—in the lyrical revivalism of Dash's first feature, *Daughters of the Dust*, there are dream glimpses of a future of a different color, in which aesthetic decisions follow a different history. Further, the arrival of a critical film theory advanced by women of color has begun to parallel the evolution of the films and videotapes: writers such as Jacqueline Bobo, Rosa Linda Fregoso, Coco Fusco, bell hooks, Lisa Jones, and Michele Wallace are redefining the field, moving easily outside the parameters of official haute theory within which so many texts are restricted and from which so many actual films and videotapes are excluded. They are looking, sometimes for the first time, at the aesthetic foundations of these new works and, just as important, critiquing productions from the brothers (Spike Lee, Luis Valdez) whose films are filling the commercial screens still empty of women.

Third, and perhaps most obvious, is the degree to which the shape and structure of feminist film criticism has moved decisively into the academy since the original writing of this piece – and as a result, how much further it has moved away from the women making films and videotapes today. No longer are festivals and nonuniversity-based conferences likely to be cited in an imaginary timeline of significances. No longer do diverse sectors of the women's "community" meet in fractious dialogue in a common space occasioned by a film screening. The very word has changed: the operative noun is theory – not criticism, not history, not women's studies.

One positive development within academia is the sudden explosion of "queer studies," with the annual gay and lesbian studies conference besieged by papers on films and videotapes and popular culture (the most recent event even included a reconsideration of Dusty Springfield). Most exciting here is the common cause made by critics, activists, academics, filmmakers, and video artists, not yet separated by the conflicting allegiances and career paths that will undoubtedly set in later. Even in the established bedrock of film studies, established scholars such as Judith Mayne and Terese de Lauretis have moved increasingly into the development of a lesbian theory for film analysis and viewing, while other scholars such as Sue-Ellen Case and Martha Gever challenge the heterosexual biases of mainstream feminist theory. In film and video, artists including Sheila McLaughlin, Cecilia Doughterty, Sadie Benning, Jane Cottis and Kaucyila Brooke, Julie Zando (and Onodera, Parkerson, and Parmar, mentioned above) are inventing new vernaculars for the future. Others are continuing the example they've already set (Ulrike Ottinger, for instance) or preparing to have their work reflect a changed status (the newly out Yvonne Rainer).

The field has changed a great deal, and, with any luck, it will change even more. For these are urgent times that we face. It's already clear that the old categories and ways of thinking will not work well enough for us. Hopefully, the decade of the 1990s will bring exciting breakthroughs from new generations, forged in struggles against increasing oppression, but speaking also from the power and authority and sense of self that the work of the 1970s and 1980s has made possible. Now, for the first time, we have communities constituted that can speak in (their own) tongues. We don't all speak the same language, but translation is still possible.

Of course, the diversity of the field depends upon the ability to move forward against today's strong current of racism. Relations between the races are the worst I've seen in my lifetime, with segregation, both exclusionary and chosen, increasingly the major form of social organization. Like the rest of society, this field must come to terms with racism, up to and well beyond the element of curriculum inclusion, so that full participation can ensure the field's renewal, heterogeneity, and value. Like patients on the couch, we need the "talking cure." Like patients rising up to leave the session, we need action, too. If the field of feminist film studies, encompassing video and including theory alongside practice, can transcend the status quo, build on its foundation, and move forward, then the worst of times could be the best of times – soon.

Notes

1. This is an abbreviated version of an article that first took shape as a paper presented at the 1978 Purdue Film Conference and was subsequently published, in differing forms, in *Jump Cut*, no. 19, and *Heresies*, no. 9.

2. Adrienne Rich, "It Is the Lesbian in Us," *Sinister Wisdom* 3 (1977).

3. Women artists working in film continued, as before, to make avant-garde films, but those without feminist material lie outside my present concerns.

4. For a fuller discussion of the film, see my "*Maedchen in Uniform*: From Repressive Tolerance to Erotic Liberation," *Jump Cut*, nos. 24–25 (1981), and *Revision: Essays in Feminist Film Criticism*, ed. Mary Ann Doane, Patricia Mellencamp, and Linda Williams (Frederick, Md.: University Publications of America, 1984).

5. See *Soho Weekly News*, November 18 (36), November 25 (31), and December 9 (35), all 1976.

6. See also my "Yvonne Rainer: An Introduction," in Rainer, *The Films of Yvonne Rainer* (Bloomington: Indiana University Press, 1990).

7. Presented at the International Symposium of Film Theory and Practical Criticism, Center for Twentieth-Century Studies, University of Wisconsin-Milwaukee, in 1975.

8. Cindy Nemser, "Editorial: Rainer and Rothschild, an Overview," *Feminist Art Journal* 4 (1975): 4. The same issue contained Lucy Lippard's "Yvonne Rainer on Feminism and Her Film." Lippard, however, is the exception in her ability to handle both the formal value and feminist strengths of Rainer's work.

9. *Women & Film* 8: 86; also *Camera Obscura* 1 (1977).

10. Monique Wittig, *Les Guerilleres* (New York: Avon, 1973), 112–14.

11. Here I am considering only English-language feminist film criticism; there are other complex issues in French and German criticism, for example.

12. Gilles Deleuze, "I Have Nothing to Admit," *Semiotexte* 6 (1977): 112.

13. See Barbara Halpern Martineau, "Nelly Kaplan" and "Subjecting Her Objectification; or, Communism Is Not Enough," in *Notes on Women's Cinema*, ed. Claire Johnston (London: Society for Education in Film and Television, 1973).

14. See Claire Johnston, "Women's Cinema as Counter-Cinema," in *Notes on Women's Cinema*, and Laura Mulvey, "Visual Pleasure and Narrative Cinema," *Screen* 16 (Autumn 1975): 6–18.

15. Quotations are taken from E. Ann Kaplan, "Interview with British Cine-Feminists," in *Women and the Cinema*, ed. Karyn Kay and Gerald Peary (New

York: Dutton, 1977), 400–401; Barbara Charlesworth Gelpi and Albert Gelpi, *drienne Rich's Poetry* (New York: Norton, 1975), 115; Barbara Halpern Martineau, "Paris/Chicago," *Women & Film* 7:11; Laura Mulvey, "Visual Pleasure and Narrative Cinema," 414, as well as personal communications. See also E. Ann Kaplan, "Aspects of British Feminist Film Theory," *Jump Cut*, nos. 12–13, for an in-depth examination of the British theories and their implications.

16. Sheila Rowbotham, *Woman's Consciousness, Man's World* (London: Penguin, 1973), 33. See also her statement (32) that language always is "carefully guarded by the superior people because it is one of the means through which they conserve their supremacy."

17. *The Compact Edition of the Oxford English Dictionary.*

18. Hélène Cixous, "The Laugh of the Medusa," *Signs: Journal of Women in Culture and Society* 1, no. 4 (1976): 888.

19. "Paul Mazursky Interviewed by Terry Curtis Fox," *Film Comment* 14, no. 2 (1978): 30–31.

20. These remarks by Burton are taken from memory of her talk at the 1979 Purdue Conference on Film.

21. Christine Gledhill, "Recent Developments in Feminist Criticism," *Quarterly Review of Film Studies* 3, no. 4 (1979), and Myra Love, "Christa Wolf and Feminism: Breaking the Patriarchal Connection," *New German Critique* 17 (1979).

22. Carolyn G. Heilbrun, "Introduction to May Sarton," in *Mrs. Stevens Hears the Mermaids Singing* (New York: Norton, 1974), xii.

Feminist Film Theory and Criticism

Judith Mayne

It is only a slight exaggeration to say that most feminist film theory and criticism of what might be called the "first" decade, from the mid-1970s to the mid-1980s, has been a response, implicit or explicit, to the issues raised in Laura Mulvey's ground-breaking article "Visual Pleasure and Narrative Cinema": the centrality of the look, cinema as spectacle and narrative, psychoanalysis as a critical tool.[1] Most important, Mulvey attributed the polarity of gender, of masculinity versus femininity, to the very structures of pleasure and identification in the classical cinema. "In a world ordered by sexual imbalance, pleasure in looking has been split between active/male and passive/female," writes Mulvey. "The determining male gaze projects its phantasy onto the female figure which is styled accordingly. In their traditional exhibitionist role women are simultaneously looked at and displayed, with their appearance coded for strong visual and erotic impact so that they can be said to connote *to-be-looked-at-ness*."[2]

My aim in this essay, a survey of feminist film theory and criticism up to 1984, is to examine what I call the ambivalent terrain of feminism and the cinema. I will argue that the most interesting and challenging work on women and film—interesting in the ways it asks us to think about the cinema and about images within and through culture, and challenging in the distinct perspectives it brings to feminist work as a whole—addresses the central problem of contradiction. In film terms, this means, for example, a simultaneous fascination with and contempt for the Hollywood cinema. In broader terms, it means an understanding of patriarchy as oppressive and as vulnerable, and the attendant sense that the work of feminism is to exploit the vulnerability, while knowing full well the dangers of a vigorous backlash.

The development of feminist film theory and criticism in the United States has been shaped by three major forces, all of which are, like feminist film theory itself, phenomena of the late 1960s and early 1970s: the women's movement, independent filmmaking, and academic film studies. Although the first two movements emphasized a political agenda for feminist film critics, university film studies stressed a theoretical one—not necessarily apolitical, but certainly not political in the same way.

From the outset, the contemporary U.S. women's movement had a distinct cultural focus. Feminist attention to stereotyped images of women dominant in patriarchal culture made cinema—and, first and foremost, Hollywood cinema—a likely target for critique. Much of what might be called the first stage of feminist film criticism focused on film images of women and their disparity with women's actual lives.[3] Since many women attracted to film study were part of the first generation of North Americans reared on visual culture, their simultaneous recognition of the power of the image and the power of the versions of femininity presented therein came as a major revelation. The question that Marjorie Rosen poses in her preface to *Popcorn Venus* conveys the enormity of that discovery: "How profoundly Hollywood's values have influenced a gullible Public—like myself. But why did the public—and especially its females—so passively embrace the industry's interpretations of life?"[4]

The new feminist documentaries inspired by independent filmmaking and the women's movement were also aimed at rejecting stereotyped images of women. Films such as Julia Reichert and James Klein's *Growing up Female* (1971) and Geri Ashur's *Janie's Janie* (1971) presented feminist issues in a direct, accessible way as a form of political consciousness-raising.[5] Although women's independent filmmaking was not limited to documentaries, their explicit concern with women's issues marked them as independent films' most decisive influence on feminist film theory and criticism.

The women's movement and independent filmmaking seemed to suggest a clear-cut agenda for feminist film criticism: demystify the "negative" images of Hollywood and praise the "positive" images offered by feminist filmmakers. But equally influenced by new development in film studies, feminists began to question the very notion of woman as "image."[6]

Interest in academic film study was revived at the same time that literary semioticians were testing the linguistic paradigm against other nonlinguistic forms, such as film; "interdisciplinary" studies were simultaneously becoming more important within the university. The theoretical scope of film studies was rigorous and complex, as evidenced in particular by the British journal *Screen*, in which Laura Mulvey's essay first appeared. Throughout the 1970s, *Screen* was the most important testing ground for the methodologies that have shaped contemporary film theory: semiotics, Marxism, and psychoanalysis. Central to each is an issue of representation. According to the semioticians, film was to be understood as a systematic network of binary oppositions, organized metaphorically, if not literally, like language. Marxists, especially those influenced by the work of Louis Althusser, stressed that ideology was a function of representation, and the function of film as an ideological medium would be evaluated in terms of its forms of address to the spectator. And psychoanalytic critics, particularly those following Jacques Lacan, insisted that the cinema be understood through structures of the look that are central to cinematic identification, here understood as an imaginary coherence of the subject. If feminist film theory emerged under the influence of these methodologies, it seemed to offer nonetheless a new perspective on their potential. To paraphrase an old Marxist catchphrase, feminism seemed to offer a way not only to understand the cinema but to change it.

Writing from the vantage point of both a theorist and a filmmaker, Laura Mulvey examines classical narrative cinema, that is, realist films using the basic storytelling devices of the nineteenth-century novel: plots of crisis and resolution, strong identification between readers/viewers and characters, and an overall point of view, or narrative intelligence. That "classical narrative cinema" and "Hollywood cinema" are used almost interchangeably is a function, of course, of Hollywood's centrality in defining the cinema in both an aesthetic and a cultural sense. Mulvey proposes, then, a demystification of the classical narrative cinema from which the possibilities of a new, alternative film practice would emerge. While Mulvey concludes that the goal of feminist cinema is to destroy the forms of pleasure associated with the classical cinema, the appeal of Hollywood has been decidedly stronger in the development of feminist film theory than she anticipated, and Mulvey herself has since reevaluated this position.[7] Claire Johnston has argued that the classical cinema should not be so quickly declared an enemy to feminist ends: "At this point in time, a strategy should be developed which embraces both the notion of film as a political tool and film as entertainment. For too long these have been regarded as two opposing poles with little common ground."[8]

Whatever connections feminists have made between a theory of the classical cinema and the evaluation of an alternative women's cinema, I would argue that the tension between the two is a persistent feature of feminist work on film. A major task for all feminist critics is to rethink dualism itself, a process that E. Ann Kaplan describes as the need to move beyond those "long-held cultural and linguistic patterns of oppositions."[9]

And yet central to the most exciting work on women and film is a contradiction: however compelling the desire to "move beyond," the dualistic patterns have a hypnotic power to fascinate, especially when projected on a movie screen.

Looking at the Classical Cinema

Given classical cinema's obsession with sexual hierarchy, feminist film critics could choose the somewhat obvious task of amassing more and more evidence of woman's exclusion and victimization, or they could undertake the more complex and challenging project of examining the contradictions in classical films, that is, what is repressed or unresolved, and potentially threatening to the patriarchal status quo. Thus Claire Johnston writes of those films in which "there exists an 'internal tension' so that the ideology no longer has an independent existence but is 'presented' by the film. The pressure of this tension cracks open the surface of the film; instead of its ideology being simply assumed and therefore virtually invisible, it is revealed and made explicit."[10]

In practice, the notion of contradiction has been used in different ways. Some films have attracted interest because they offer exaggerated representations of woman as the object of the look; analysis thus lays bare the very mechanisms that in other films would be concealed. Hence musicals, in which the display of the body (and the female body in particular) is central, have been examined as strategic examples of just what the definition of woman as spectacle, or woman as image, entails.[11] The genre of *film noir* is taken up with evil and corruption, and its use of two women—one sexual and treacherous, the other chaste and good—to symbolize a male hero's conflict has been identified by feminist critics as a virgin/whore dichotomy characteristic of women's general representation in classical cinema.[12]

Contradiction has also been understood as inconsistency, a blind spot that reveals weakness in the sexual hierarchy. Gertrud Koch has revealed a contradiction between "woman" and "female" in Howard Hawks's film *Rio Bravo*. The central woman character, portrayed by Angie Dickinson, is a stereotypical sex object. But there is also a character who performs the female nurturing roles of housewife and mother, and this individual happens to be portrayed by Walter Brennan. By splitting the functions of "female" and "woman," the film assures that the image of a woman will denote only sexuality. But when read against the grain, this split reveals a fear of dependence on female labor.[13]

More along the specific lines that Claire Johnston proposes, contradiction has come to stand for something akin to deconstruction, that is, as a critique of dominant ideology from within. Hence a given film may "seem" to function as a simple vehicle for sexist ideology, but when read in a critical way is shown to undermine the very values it presumably conveys. For example, Sylvia Harvey has argued that *film noir* contains a critique of the nuclear family so devastating that no narrative can resolve it.[14]

Feminist readings of the different kinds of contradiction in the classical cinema are provocative for what they suggest about the complexity of film, but they are also problematic. The very term *contradiction* has come to refer to an irresolvable conflict within patriarchy, but it is not always clear what differentiates contradiction from the conflicts or tensions essential to any narrative. Catherine Johnson's analysis of the apparently contradictory views of marriage – marriage for love or marriage for money – in the comedy *How to Marry a Millionaire* is instructive in this regard. Johnson argues that the film transforms this potential contradiction into an opposition, between men (who marry for money) and women (who marry for love). Through this separation of the conflicting terms, the potential contradiction is superseded by an opposition, and "the debate between marriage-for-love and marriage-for-money maintains the women's fates entirely within the realm of marriage."[15]

A contradiction can, in other words, be deceptive. Along similar lines, it could be argued that there is nothing particularly unusual about the obvious contradictions, deceptive or otherwise, in a given film. Any weak links or blind spots are perhaps more than adequately compensated for by the film's overall movement toward resolution and containment. Indeed, Janet Bergstrom has argued that the classical cinema has an "unlimited capacity . . . to create gaps, fissures, ruptures . . . only to recover them ultimately and to efface the memory, or at least the paths, of this heterogeneity."[16] Put another way, it is not always clear to what extent the contradictions revealed by feminist analysis are the exceptions to, rather than the rules of, the classical cinema.

The preferred mode of analyzing the classical cinema has been through close reading of individual films. Textual analysis has been a crucial tool in feminist film criticism, for it emphasizes the importance of understanding cinematic representation in any evaluation of women in film. Yet detailed readings of individual films beg the question of how influential the encounter with contradiction is for a viewer seeing a film in a movie theater rather than with an analyst projector. Do the contradictions in a given film truly make it subversive, and if so, what are the implications of those contradictions?

The contradictions of the classical cinema are often evoked in the name of an alternative film practice, a subject to which I will return. Their reading thus suggests two possible directions for feminist film criticism: encouraging filmmakers to formulate another kind of cinema with a feminist perspective, or encouraging film viewers to understand cinema as sympto-matic of women's contradictory investments in patriarchal society.

Whatever the contradictory status of a film might be, most feminist critics have assumed that the classical cinema is identified with a male van-tage point and is addressed to a male spectator. While Hollywood films of the 1930s and 1940s are usually understood as representative examples of the institution of the cinema, one must examine film history carefully to determine how such an alignment with the male perspective occurred and if it has always been a feature of the cinema. Analysis of the emerging nar-rative and visual conventions of the early cinema is particularly important in this context. Lucy Fischer and Linda Williams have examined the films of early French director Georges Méliès, who is credited with perfecting the trick film and who introduced, in the 1890s, many of the fantastic effects that established cinema's reputation as a magical medium.

That the magical appeal of the cinema had something to do with men, women, and the power of the look is suggested by *The Vanishing Lady* (1896), a film in which a male magician drapes a woman's body and then removes the cloth to reveal a skeleton in her place. Using this film as a point of departure, Fischer argues that the cinema, like magic, is informed by a "submerged discourse on sexual politics," and she concludes that the male subject of this and other early magic films is a contradictory entity: "The male enacts a series of symbolic rituals in which he expresses numer-ous often-contradictory attitudes towards woman."[17] As a cultural institu-tion that tapped other nineteenth-century forms of entertainment such as magic, then, the cinema offered a fantasy land for the acting out of male envy of female power (and particularly, Fischer argues, female procrea-tive powers).

Linda Williams also examines the male subject of early films and fo-cuses on the appeal of cinema's representation of the body. Unlike Fischer, Williams suggests that the male subjectivity at work in the films of Méliès obsessively repeats the same structure. Williams argues that the cinema addresses the male fear of castration that the female represents; hence the woman's body, as represented on screen, becomes a fetish as the denial of sexual difference: "[The female body] poses a problem of sexual difference which it then becomes the work of the incipient forms of narrative and mise-en-scène to overcome."[18] Whether or not male subjectivity is riddled with contradictions is, from this perspective, beside the point. If, in Fischer's reading, cinema's function is to express those contradictions, ac-cording to Williams, its function is to repress them.

If Méliès can be taken as a privileged example of emerging cinematic structures, then Fischer's and Williams's studies suggest the centrality of the male subject. Where they differ is in their assessment of the kind of identity that subject assumes. But their agreement about the male subject's central role raises other perplexing questions: Do all examinations of contradiction in the classical cinema lead inevitably to the male psyche? Is woman therefore–whether feminist film critic or image on the screen–always designated as the outsider?

Feminist work on Alfred Hitchcock's films is particularly interesting in this context, for his work relentlessly insists that if cinema is a voyeuristic medium, then women must be objectified. One perspective on Hitchcock has been most influenced by the work of French critic Raymond Bellour, who argues for the centrality of male subjectivity in the films: "The woman occupies a central place only to the extent that it's a place assigned to her by the logic of masculine desire."[19] In contrast, Jacqueline Rose, writing on *The Birds*, stresses the fragmented nature of whatever "cohesion" the film achieves. Whereas in Bellour's terms, Hitchcock's films assume a male point of view and appeal to a male spectator, Rose assigns the viewing subject a more complex status and a more fluid sexual identity; indeed, she questions the very possibility of ascribing a gender to the subject of cinema.[20] Tania Modleski challenges the view of Hitchcock's cinema as a monument to male desire by reading Hitchcock's *Rebecca* as a female oedipal drama. She literally turns the recurrent male-centered story on its head by suggesting that, while *Rebecca* shows a woman trying to "make her desire the mirror of the man's desire," it "makes us experience the difficulties involved *for the woman* in this enterprise. . . . From the woman's point of view, then, man becomes an enigma, his desire difficult to know."[21]

While the kind of analysis Bellour and others have done illustrates how thoroughly the classical cinema is defined by and obsessed with sexual difference, Modleski's comment is well taken: "Feminine sexuality must undergo a complete suppression, feminine desire, an utter silencing, so there is nothing left for the feminist critic to do but outline the process by which this silencing is inscribed in the text."[22] Modleski's reading, by focusing on the exception to the rule, questions the hegemony of the male oedipal crisis, if not its foundations. And Jacqueline Rose's reading does not so much oppose "female" to "male" as it poses a split subject for which the safe and secure boundaries of gender do not exist. Hence the issue is recast: not male or female, but the very question of sexual identity itself.

But there are films that address themselves, however problematically, to women viewers. Specifically, the "woman's film"–or, more pejoratively, the "weepie"–popular during the 1940s and 1950s had a female-centered plot and was presumably addressed to a largely female audience. Lea Jacobs offers a provocative reading of one such "woman's film," *Now, Voyager*, in which Bette Davis as Charlotte Vale is transformed, thanks to a sympathetic doctor, from ugly duckling to attractive woman. Jacobs analyzes the implications of the film's tension between the doctor as narrating authority and Charlotte Vale as subject of the film. However central the doctor's authority, Jacobs writes that "another kind of identification is possible, an identification which posits Charlotte's pleasure as a source and endpoint of the narrative processes and which is based on her desire, like our own, to *experience* narrative."[23] The contradiction in this film between male discourse and female investment in narrative is significant for the other space it opens up – a space for women's film viewing.

Jacobs's analysis of *Now, Voyager* illustrates feminist critics' increasing preoccupation with the female spectator and with the implications of classical film narrative for what might then be called "female spectatorship." If the cinema is indeed a function of male desire, then woman's position is rather predictable; as Mary Ann Doane writes: "Above and beyond a simple adoption of the masculine position in relation to the cinematic sign, the female spectator is given two options: the masochism of overidentification or the narcissism entailed in becoming one's own object of desire, in assuming the image in the most radical way."[24] Some feminist critics have argued that women's presumed alienation from the cinematic apparatus might be advantageous rather than purely negative. In B. Ruby Rich's wonderful phrase, the woman viewer is the "ultimate dialectician."[25] Some of the most interesting work in feminist criticism has explored the complexity of female spectatorship; for instance, the female viewer has been analyzed in terms of transvestism and masquerade, as well as used as a model for alternative theories of filmic identification.[26]

If the woman viewer is a contradiction in terms, she embodies contradiction in a potentially productive way. And in addressing the issue of female spectatorship, feminist critics are posing that fundamentally perplexing question concerning feminist work on the classical film: Just why are feminists attracted to this kind of study? Are they really dutiful daughters, trying to rescue the cinema, or are they motivated by a utopian wish to establish entirely new relations of looking and telling, of spectacle and narrative? The danger in theories of female spectatorship is the potential romanticization of the female viewer; feminist critics may well be projecting their own desires to define their prefeminist investment in the movies as something "positive," or at least as not completely under the sway of dominant ideology.

A distinctive feature of what I am calling the "ambivalent terrain" of feminist film theory is the recognition that "female" and "feminist" are connected, yet different. Some feminist critics thus write in a divided voice that calls on that difference. For example, in analyzing D. W. Griffith's *Broken Blossoms*, Julia Lesage speaks in the voice of feminism when she writes, "I do know that, as a feminist, it is my being drawn into cinematic depictions of this kind of sexual perversion that disturbs me most. It seems a gauge of my own colonized mind." She also speaks as a woman viewer, certainly not in opposition to the feminist, but with a different frame of reference: "*Broken Blossoms*' patriarchal, extreme depiction of father-daughter relations also reflects my own internalized and eroticized fears of male authority, dominance, and control."[27] This reading not only pulls out the contradictions of the film but sets those contradictions of the text alongside the conflicting responses that women viewers bring to the cinema.

Psychoanalysis and Feminist Film Theory

I have suggested that contradiction is the central issue in feminist film theory and criticism, and to many observers the centrality of psychoanalysis in so much recent feminist work on film is itself a contradiction in terms. In contemporary film theory, it has become a commonplace that the simultaneous development of cinema and psychoanalysis at the end of the nineteenth century was not accidental. The affinity between the two has been described in a variety of ways, from cinema's obsessive reenactment of those oedipal crises theorized by psychoanalysis to the cinema as a manifestation of Freud's description of the psychic apparatus. Even the most basic features of the cinema suggest the affinity – from projection and identification to the similarity between dreaming and watching a film.

What has made psychoanalysis a controversial subject in feminist film theory is not so much the historical and ideological dimension of this affinity but, rather, the fact that contemporary theories of the viewing subject have taken Jacques Lacan's work as their point of departure. There is an almost irresistible fit between the "mirror stage" and the movie screen, and the relationship between the imaginary and the symbolic has become a grand metaphor for film viewing as, simultaneously, regressive and authoritarian. And for cinema, as for Lacanian psychoanalysis, sexual difference is the central, determining force.

It is clear that a Lacanian perspective on sexual difference and a feminist one do not necessarily intersect, and Lacan's characteristically sexist wit has made it difficult for many observers to understand what possible interest his work holds for feminists. While a critical appropriation of psychoanalysis is certainly important, the danger, of course, is the fine line that separates "appropriation" from "co-optation." As Lesley Stern writes, "Whilst, from a feminist perspective, one would not deny that the patriarchal unconscious is inscribed within cinematic discourse, there is a danger that such an assertion stops at the point of demonstrating the dualities of oppression and seduction and blocks the question of woman's desire: who speaks it, how is it spoken?"[28] Too often, the "question of woman's desire" is posed only within the psychoanalytic parameters of woman's exclusion from the symbolic, and as Stephen Heath says, "the difference inverted is also the difference maintained."[29] The problem has been taken up by a variety of theorists who read psychoanalysis in a feminist framework, from Constance Penley's analysis of the avant-garde to Kaja Silverman's account of theories of the subject in semiotics and psychoanalysis.[30]

The intersection of psychoanalysis and feminism, in film as elsewhere, has been debated too facilely in terms of whether one is "for" or "against" psychoanalysis. The more crucial question, it seems to me, is, Does psychoanalysis constitute a theory to which feminists bring a new perspective? Or is there a feminist theory of the cinema that might borrow, as it were, from other discourses, but that would nonetheless constitute a theory in its own right? Such questions about the very status of feminism as a theory of the cinema are just beginning to be raised.

If dualism and sexual difference are obsessive concerns in psychoanalysis as they are in the cinema, the task for feminists is to engage with the dualisms, while insisting on the possibilities of other approaches, other modes of thought. This formidable task has been brilliantly undertaken by Teresa de Lauretis in *Alice Doesn't: Feminism, Semiotics, Cinema*. Using psychoanalysis as well as other theories of subject formation such as semiotics and anthropology, de Lauretis insists that the distinctive and irreducible gap between woman as image – as object for the male subject – and women as historically defined subjects is most often ignored or suppressed in analyses of difference and representation. The goal of feminist theory, in de Lauretis's view, is not some utopian mediation of that gap but, rather, the articulation of its attendant contradictions in the name of women as historical subjects.[31]

Women's Cinema and Feminist Criticism

Feminist film critics, influenced by psychoanalytic theory, have become accustomed to asking not just how to define women's cinema but whether it can be defined. At best, this has meant that the definition of women's cinema is a theoretically complex endeavor in which the very notion of a cinema by and/or for women is problematized; at worst, it has meant a certain hesitation to affirm women's contributions to the cinema at all. The definition of women's alternatives to the classical cinema is not always clear: should women filmmakers somehow "resolve" the contradictions of Hollywood cinema? Or rather, should their analysis of its contradictions lead to a new film practice, as well as theory, that examines the structure of film language in a critical and self-reflexive way? If the former goal naively assumes that aesthetic intervention can occur in a noncontradictory realm, the latter risks restricting women's cinema to a mirror reflection of film critics' theoretical preoccupations.

The definition of women's cinema has entailed both exploring women's involvement with film production in the past and examining recent examples of women's filmmaking. The first potentially involves rereading film history to seek out little-known women directors or to evaluate the "hidden" ways in which women have worked in the film industry: as cutters and editors, as screenwriters, as actresses who may have exercised artistic control in their films. By and large, however, feminist explorations of film history have focused on the film director.

Dorothy Arzner, one of the few women to have had a successful career as a director (she began her career in motion pictures, as chance would have it, as a script typist, then a cutter, then a screenwriter) in Hollywood from the late 1920s to the early 1940s, was a major rediscovery for feminist film critics. Arzner's films have been seen as films that critique Hollywood's cinematic conventions from within, thus providing examples of the very contradictions central to feminist writing about the cinema. Claire Johnston writes, "In general, the woman in Arzner's films determines her own identity through transgression and desire in a search for an independent existence beyond and outside the discourse of the male." Johnston's claims for Arzner's work are based on the limited nature of the critique, and the crucial question thus posed is whether it is "possible to sweep aside the existing forms of discourse in order to found a new form of language."[32]

While Johnston has always argued for the necessity of critical engagement with Hollywood cinema, other feminists have assumed that women's cinema will be a more likely possibility outside the industrial and cultural constraints of Hollywood. Hence the work of Germaine Dulac, an independent French filmmaker of the 1920s, has generated much interest, particularly her film *The Smiling Madame Beudet*, about a creative yet frustrated woman in the French provinces married to a boorish man. Sandy Flitterman-Lewis's analysis of the film proposes that its interest in feminist terms has less to do with the story or the characterizations than with its textual system.[33] Wendy Dozoretz argues that the importance of *The Smiling Madame Beudet* lies in the way Dulac inscribed her own presence into the film and, specifically, in her own identification with Madame Beudet.[34]

These approaches to Arzner and Dulac suggest three different methods of defining film authorship in female terms. For Johnston, Arzner's role as a woman director highlights her status within and without the system of classical cinema. If one reads Arzner's work as a critique of dominant ideology, it is in part because of her ambivalent status as director. Ambivalence is also characteristic of Dulac's work, according to Flitterman-Lewis, but this ambivalence stems from the director's distance from the Hollywood model and her continuing investment in narrative cinema. Dozoretz suggests another view—that it is in defining authorship as the director's immediate, at times autobiographical, investment in the film that the possibilities of female inscription on film are raised.

While all these analyses constitute important interventions and while the work of many other women directors remains to be explored, it is unfortunate that a historical view of women's cinema has been by and large limited to films by women directors. At the same time that feminist critics ask what kinds of films women have made, they must ask just how women have been involved in the cinema if not primarily as directors. Part of the problem here, as in discussions of the female spectator, is the risk of romanticizing women's exclusion from the actual production of films. The assumption that women were either directors or nothing at all betrays a certain failure of the imagination. Women have often written about the cinema, for instance, and in a variety of roles.[35] Assumptions about the male vantage point of the cinema aside, we know that women have always gone to the movies, and examination of female audiences, particularly at crucial moments of cinematic history, is another fruitful area of research.[36]

In her work on the poet H. D., Anne Friedberg has done the most productive rethinking of women in film history. Although H. D. did not make films, she was attracted to and seduced by the cinema in a variety of ways, incorporating its images in her work and writing about it while associated with the journal *Close-Up*. Describing her fascination with films, H. D. said: "Just at the moment I am involved with pictures. . . . The work has been enchanting, never anything such fun and I myself have learned to use the small projector and spend literally hours alone in my apartment making the mountains and village streets and my own acquaintances reel past me in the light and light and light."[37] As Friedberg writes, the acquisition of this skill was "not an insignificant act, but a skill imbued with a euphoria of control which suggests not a full challenge to patriarchy, but a sidling up to, a siblinghood of shared power."[38] The gesture of "sidling up to patriarchy" strikingly conveys women's simultaneous exclusion from and investment in the cinema. Furthermore, Friedberg's engagement with H. D. and the cinema suggests some new perspectives on questions of modernism, psychoanalysis, and bisexuality that have been central to feminist evaluations of H. D.'s career. What Friedberg suggests, in short, is that "opening up" the contradictions of women and film history might give feminist critics some metaphorical distance from the cinema, distance that would allow other connections to be made.

The attempt to define women's cinema today has raised some of the same issues that emerge when feminists evaluate the classical cinema. Because the first and most visible way women broke into independent filmmaking in the early 1970s was through documentary cinema in the name of feminism, debates immediately arose concerning issues of realism, politics, and representation.[39] However, the films and filmmakers that command the most interest among feminist film critics are concerned with the problematic fit between cinematic form and female expression. Hence feminist documentary is an area of interest in those films that challenge the very notion of documentary as truth, such as Michelle Citron's *Daughter Rite* (1979), in which "fake" *cinéma vérité* interviews with two women alternate with home movie footage.[40]

The preferred films in discussions of contemporary women's cinema are those that engage with the contradictions central to feminist work on the classical cinema: between spectacle and narrative, between the male look and the female image, between feminism and femininity. For instance, feminists have been attracted to Laura Mulvey and Peter Wollen's *Riddles of the Sphinx* (1977) for its retelling of the oedipal myth through the questioning voice of the sphinx–the voice located outside established discourse–and to the films of Yvonne Rainer for their suggestion of the problematic affiliation between an avant-garde aesthetic and the female voice.[41]

A recurrent motif in discussions of these and other films is the fine line between critique and celebration. It has been suggested, for instance, that *The Riddles of the Sphinx* comes dangerously close to celebrating women's exclusion from patriarchy, and the fascination with woman as victim in Rainer's films might well be taken as the perpetuation of the very stereotype under investigation.[42] I am not suggesting that the issue of this fine line should somehow be resolved either in the films or in criticism and theory; however, it needs greater theoretical definition and creative exploration.

Sally Potter's *Thriller* (1979) illustrates the dilemma perfectly. The film, a rereading of Puccini's *La Bohème* from Mimi's point of view, makes frequent reference to issues of contemporary feminist film theory. At one point, for instance, Mimi reads from a collection of writings by Parisian structuralists and bursts into laughter. At the film's conclusion, Mimi and Musetta embrace while the men exit through the window. The final words of the film, spoken by Mimi, suggest that female bonding is what is repressed in a work like *La Bohème*.[43] Many claims have been made for *Thriller*, and its praise by feminist critics of quite different persuasions has lent it unique status. Yet a fundamental contradiction of the film has remained unaddressed. After the film has challenged the definition of woman's desire and called the very notion of identity into question, the embrace between the two women with which it concludes easily reads as a radical feminist gesture tacked on to a deconstructive film. The ambivalence of *Thriller* is its simultaneous affirmation of a feminist critique and its exploration of the difficulties involved in such a project. The task of feminist criticism is not to resolve the ambivalence – to label *Thriller* as either radical feminist or deconstructive – but rather to analyze the complex issues such ambivalence evokes.

Such attention to ambivalence and contradiction is central to the complex theoretical examination contemporary women's films deserve. Lizzie Borden's *Born in Flames* (1983), for instance, poses a series of speculations concerning feminism and socialism, race and sexuality; and Bette Gordon's *Variety* (1983) takes on an equally complex set of questions about female fantasies and the pornography industry. Such films present genuine challenges to feminist film critics, challenges to rethink and advance the ideas about contradiction that have shaped our critical project. While the close relationship between theory and practice is an appealing feature of feminist work on film, it has been problematic in its own way, tending to create a somewhat closed field of inquiry. Ironically, film theory and criticism are perhaps the areas of feminist thought where the question of contradiction is posed most thoroughly and obsessively, yet the same contradictions tend to emerge again and again.

The term *difference*, for instance, tends to be understood rather narrowly. That the cinema is obsessed with the polarities of masculine and feminine is a basic assumption of feminist film theory. But cinema's role in orchestrating other forms of difference – sexuality outside the heterosexual paradigm, or class and race difference – has not been a central area of inquiry. Not all national cinemas, for instance, fit into the easy opposition of "dominant" versus "alternative" film that has structured contemporary film studies. The women filmmakers whose works have received the most sustained critical attention tend to be white, European, and heterosexual; hence examination of films by women filmmakers marginalized in multiple ways could suggest new definitions of alternative film practice. And a recent collection of essays on lesbians and film in *Jump Cut* takes the theoretical preoccupations of feminist film theory – women in film history, textual analysis, female spectatorship, women's desire – into what has been up until now virtually unexplored territory in feminist work on film.[44]

The need to expand the field of inquiry, to get beyond dualistic categories while understanding their power to attract, is suggested by a word that appears more and more frequently in feminist film theory and criticism: *risk*.[45] While feminist critics are cognizant of the fine line between critique and celebration, that very opposition can become so reified that a given film or a set of theoretical terms must be defined as one or the other. And more and more, feminist film theorists and critics are emphasizing, implicitly or explicitly, that we must take the risk of rethinking the oppositions on which our most profound assumptions are based.

Notes

1. Laura Mulvey, "Visual Pleasure and Narrative Cinema," *Screen* 16 (Autumn 1975): 6–18.

2. Ibid., 12.

3. The first and most influential studies of images of women in film are Molly Haskell, *From Reverence to Rape: The Treatment of Women in the Movies* (New York: Holt, Rinehart and Winston, 1974), and Marjorie Rosen, *Popcorn Venus: Women, Movies & the American Dream* (New York: Coward, McCann and Geoghegan, 1973).

4. Rosen, *Popcorn Venus*, 9.

5. For a history of the feminist documentary cinema, see Jan Rosenberg, *Women's Reflections: The Feminist Film Movement*, Studies in Cinema no. 22 (Ann Arbor: University of Michigan Research Press, 1983).

6. See Elizabeth Cowie, "Woman as Sign," *m/f*, no. 1 (1978): 49–63, and Griselda Pollock, "What's Wrong with Images of Women?" *Screen Education*, no. 24 (Autumn 1977): 25–34.

7. Mulvey, "Visual Pleasure," 18, and Laura Mulvey, "Afterthoughts on 'Visual Pleasure and Narrative Cinema' Inspired by *Duel in the Sun* (King Vidor, 1946)," *Framework*, nos. 15–17 (1981): 12–15.

8. Claire Johnston, "Women's Cinema as Counter-Cinema," in *Notes on Women's Cinema* (London: Society for Education in Film and Television, 1973), 24–31, esp. 31.

9. E. Ann Kaplan, *Women and Film: Both Sides of the Camera* (New York: Methuen, 1983), 206.

10. Claire Johnston, "Dorothy Arzner: Critical Strategies," in *The Work of Dorothy Arzner: Towards a Feminist Cinema* (London: British Film Institute, 1975), 1–8, esp. 3.

11. See Lucy Fischer, "The Image of Woman as Image: The Optical Politics of *Dames*," *Film Quarterly* 30 (Fall 1976): 2–11; Patricia Mellencamp, "Spectacle and Spectator: Looking through the American Musical Comedy," *Ciné-tracts* 1 (Summer 1977): 27–35; Paula Rabinowitz, "Commodity Fetishism: Women in *Gold Diggers of 1933*," *Film Reader*, no. 5 (1982): 141–49; and Maureen Turim, "Gentlemen Consume Blondes," *Wide Angle* 1, no. 1 (1976): 68–76.

12. See E. Ann Kaplan, ed., *Women in Film Noir* (London: British Film Institute, 1978).

13. Gertrud Koch, "Was ist und wozu brauchen wir eine feministische Filmkritik [What feminist film criticism is and why we need it]," *frauen und film*, no. 11 (1977): 7.

14. Sylvia Harvey, "Woman's Place: The Absent Family in Film Noir," in *Women in Film Noir*, 22–34.

15. Catherine Johnson, "Marriage and Money: *How to Marry a Millionaire*," *Film Reader*, no. 5 (1982): 67–75, esp. 74.

16. Janet Bergstrom, "Rereading the Work of Claire Johnston," *Camera Obscura*, nos. 3–4 (Summer 1979): 21–31, esp. 27.

17. Lucy Fischer, "The Lady Vanishes: Women, Magic, and the Movies," *Film Quarterly* 33 (Fall 1979): 30–40, esp. 31.

18. Linda Williams, "Film Body: An Implantation of Perversions," *Ciné-tracts* 3 (Winter 1981): 19–35, esp. 31. See also Susan Lurie, "The Construction of the 'Castrated Woman' in Psychoanalysis and Cinema," *Discourse*, no. 4 (Winter 1981–82): 52–74.

19. Janet Bergstrom, "Alternation, Segmentation, Hypnosis: Interview with Raymond Bellour," *Camera Obscura*, nos. 3–4 (Summer 1979): 71–103, esp. 93. See also Raymond Bellour, "Hitchcock the Enunciator," *Camera Obscura*, no. 2 (Fall 1977): 66–91, and "Psychosis, Neurosis, Perversion," *Camera Obscura*, nos. 3–4 (Summer 1979): 105–32; Janet Bergstrom, "Enunciation and Sexual Difference," *Camera Obscura*, nos. 3–4 (Summer 1979): 33–69; Sandy Flitterman, "Woman, Desire and the Look: Feminism and the Enunciative Apparatus in Cinema," in *Theories of Authorship*, ed. John Caughie (London and Boston: Routledge and Kegan Paul, 1981), 242–50; Barbara Klinger, "*Psycho*: The Institutionalization of Female Sexuality," *Wide Angle* 5, no. 1 (1982): 49–55; Deborah Linderman, "The Screen in Hitchcock's *Blackmail*," *Wide Angle* 4, no. 1 (1980): 20–28; and Michael Renov, "From Identification to Ideology: The Male System of Hitchcock's *Notorious*," *Wide Angle* 4, no. 1 (1980): 30–37.

20. Jacqueline Rose, "Paranoia and the Film System," *Screen* 17 (Winter 1976–77): 85–104.

21. Tania Modleski, "Never to Be Thirty-Six Years Old . . . *Rebecca* as Female Oedipal Drama," *Wide Angle* 5, no. 1 (1982): 34–41, esp. 38.

22. Ibid., 34.

23. Lea Jacobs, "*Now, Voyager*: Some Problems of Enunciation and Sexual Difference," *Camera Obscura*, no. 7 (1981): 89–109, esp. 95.

24. Mary Ann Doane, "Film and the Masquerade: Theorising the Female Spectator," *Screen* 23 (September–October 1982): 74–88, esp. 87.

25. B. Ruby Rich, in Michelle Citron et al., "Women and Film: A Discussion of Feminist Aesthetics," *New German Critique*, no. 13 (Winter 1978): 83–107, esp. 87.

26. On transvestism, see Mulvey, "Afterthoughts" (note 7 above); on masquerade, see Doane, "Film and the Masquerade" (note 24 above); and on identification, see Teresa de Lauretis, *Alice Doesn't: Feminism, Semiotics, Cinema* (Bloomington: Indiana University Press, 1984).

27. Julia Lesage, "*Broken Blossoms*: Artful Racism, Artful Rape," *Jump Cut*, no. 26 (1981): 51–55, esp. 54 and 55.

28. Lesley Stern, "Point of View: The Blind Spot," *Film Reader*, no. 4 (1979): 214–36, esp. 222.

29. Stephen Heath, "Difference," *Screen* 19, no. 3 (1978): 51–112, esp. 98.

30. Constance Penley, "The Avant-Garde and Its Imaginary," *Camera Obscura*, no. 2 (Fall 1977): 3–33; Kaja Silverman, *The Subject of Semiotics* (New York: Oxford University Press, 1983).

31. De Lauretis (note 26 above).

32. Johnston, "Dorothy Arzner" (note 10 above).

33. Sandy Flitterman, "Montage/Discourse: Germaine Dulac's *The Smiling Madame Beudet*," *Wide Angle* 4, no. 3 (1980): 54–59. See also Sandy Flitterman-Lewis, *To Desire Differently: Feminism and the French Cinema* (Urbana: University of Illinois Press, 1990).

34. Wendy Dozoretz, "Madame Beudet's Smile: Feminine or Feminist?" *Film Reader*, no. 5 (1982): 41–46.

35. See Marsha McCreadie, *Women on Film: The Critical Eye* (New York: Praeger Publishers, 1983), for a discussion of the relative invisibility women have had as film critics.

36. See, for instance, Elizabeth Ewen, "City Lights: Immigrant Women and the Rise of the Movies," *Signs: Journal of Women in Culture and Society* 5 (Spring 1980): 545–66, and Judith Mayne, "Immigrants and Spectators," *Wide Angle* 5, no. 2 (1982): 32–41.

37. Cited in Anne Friedberg, "On H. D., Woman, History, Recognition," *Wide Angle* 5, no. 2 (1982): 26–31, esp. 28.

38. Ibid., 31.

39. See Julia Lesage, "The Political Aesthetics of the Feminist Documentary Film," *Quarterly Review of Film Studies* 3 (Fall 1978): 507–23, and Eileen McGarry, "Documentary Realism and Women's Cinema," *Women & Film* 2, no. 7 (1975): 50–59.

40. See Jane Feuer, "*Daughter Rite*: Living with Our Pain and Our Love," *Jump Cut*, no. 23 (1980): 12–13; Kaplan (note 9 above), 181–88; Annette Kuhn, *Women's Pictures: Feminism and Cinema* (Boston and London: Routledge and Kegan Paul, 1982), 171–73; and B. Ruby Rich and Linda Williams, "The Right of Re-Vision: Michelle Citron's *Daughter Rite*," *Film Quarterly* 35, no. 1 (1981): 17–21.

41. On *The Riddles of the Sphinx*, see Sandy Flitterman and Jacquelyn Suter, "Textual Riddles: Woman as Enigma or Site of Social Meanings? An Interview with Laura Mulvey," *Discourse*, no. 1 (1979): 86–127, and Kaplan (note 9 above), 171–81. On the films of Yvonne Rainer, see "Yvonne Rainer: An Introduction" and "Yvonne Rainer: An Interview," *Camera Obscura*, no. 1 (Fall 1976): 53–96; Kaplan (note 9 above), 113–24; Yvonne Rainer, "Looking Myself in the Mouth," *October*, no. 17 (Summer 1981): 65–76; and B. Ruby Rich, *Yvonne Rainer* (Minneapolis, Minn.: Walker Art Center, 1981).

42. Heath (note 29 above), 73; Mary Ann Doane, "The Woman's Stake: Filming the Female Body," *October*, no. 17 (Summer 1981): 23–36.

43. See Kaplan (note 9 above), 154–61, and Jane Weinstock, "She Who Laughs First Laughs Last," *Camera Obscura*, no. 5 (Spring 1980): 100–110.

44. *Jump Cut*, nos. 24–25 (1981): 17–52.

45. See in particular Doane and Heath's discussion of the risk of essentialism in *The Riddles of the Sphinx* (note 42 above).

Feminism and Film History

Patrice Petro

> It's now too easy to assume that if a text is labeled "feminist" theory, then it can't properly "count" or "figure" as anything else ("woman's sphere," again).
>
> *Meaghan Morris*[1]

At a time of inflated rhetoric about the importance of history to textual analysis and criticism, it is perhaps not surprising that film studies has recently experienced a turn to history and historical inquiry. Well before the new historicism in literary studies,[2] however, film scholars had engaged in extended debates about the problems and inadequacies of traditionally conceived histories and attempted to bridge the critical separation of texts from contexts, and history from theory.[3]

For all of their self-consciousness and theoretical sophistication, these early debates about film history nevertheless remained curiously silent about feminist challenges to conventional ways of thinking about the past. And some of the most recent work in film history (or, at least, the work that most explicitly and unreservedly names itself as such) has only exacerbated this trend, either by excluding feminism from consideration altogether, or by relegating feminist work to the specialized realm of gender criticism and speculative theory.[4]

Needless to say, the repeated call for greater rigor in film studies, an argument typically cast in terms of a need for archival research and hard empirical study, has had the additional effect of implying that feminists working in film theory have had relatively little to say about questions of film history.[5] As a result, it would appear from the writings of some film scholars that a certain division of labor has come to characterize film studies as a discipline—a discipline in which "historians" pursue the realm of the empirical, the quantifiable, the concretely known (the realm of history proper), and "feminists" explore the more intangible realm of theoretical speculation (the realm of interpretation).

There are, of course, obvious and immediate problems with situating such an impassable (and impossible) divide between historians and feminists, history and theory, empirical research and theoretical analysis. Such a divide intensifies the current state of film historical debate. More important, by ignoring feminist film theory's long-standing desire to differentiate and particularize notions of subjectivity, it also functions to consign much feminist work on film history to oblivion.

To be sure, feminist film criticism and theory are often unrecognizable as "history" understood in a conventional way (history as the study of unique individuals; history as the development of aesthetic forms; history as the evolution of industrial and legal structures – what one feminist has called "history as usual").[6] Not surprisingly, the methods and approach of traditional histories have proven problematic for feminists, not least of all because so many documents preserved from the past offer only limited traces of women's presence, while presenting massive evidence of their marginality and repression. But what is fundamentally at issue here is not a lack of adequate documentation. Indeed, as many feminists have shown, the project of reconstituting film history from a feminist perspective is not merely a matter of making the invisible "visible." It also involves submitting regimes of visibility to a general critique of objectivity and subjectivity in the writing of film history, and rethinking critical methods and theoretical procedures in contemporary film theory (e.g., the status of textual analysis, the relationship between authorship and biography, the role of extratextual determinations on the cinema and its audiences).

A larger and more important distinction in film historiography is therefore obscured by debates over the relative merits of empiricism and theoretical speculation: namely, the difference between a history of film as institutionally and formally *produced* (the history of film as a privileged object) and a history of film as it is *received* in culture (the history of the spectator-subject). As Fredric Jameson has remarked, there are always two historicities, two paths of historical inquiry: "the path of the object, and the path of the subject, the historical origins of the things themselves and that more intangible historicity of the concepts and categories by which we attempt to understand those things."[7]

The difference between these two historicities in film studies is perhaps best described as the difference between a *formal* history of filmic conventions and institutions and a *cultural* history of film reception and spectatorship. Whereas formal film histories are characterized by an attempt to discern developments within institutional constraints and generic conventions, for example, cultural film histories aim to locate films within the history of larger cultural forces, such as consumerism, censorship, or re-form. Given these alternatives, it is no coincidence that feminists have cho-sen to pursue issues in cultural history, thereby following the path of the subject and the more intangible historicity of subjectivity. In contrast to formalist film historians, who seek to recover what is increasingly becom-ing a lost object, feminists have been primarily concerned about unearth-ing the history of the (found) female subject.

Having posed the issue in this way, I would not want to imply that the distinction between formal and cultural histories exhausts the kinds of historical writing in film studies today, or, indeed, that there is no overlap between formalist and culturalist approaches. Furthermore, as I will sug-gest later on, the very opposition between subject and object remains in-herently problematic and especially limiting for feminist film histories, failing as it does to account for the paradoxical status of woman in film his-tory as both subject and object of representation, as both consumer of im-ages and as the quintessential image of the consumer. Finally, as the his-tory of feminist film theory so clearly demonstrates, the very attempt to "find" a female subject has led to a paralyzing situation in some feminist film histories, which tend either to affirm a socially constructed feminine identity or to reject any attempt at self-naming at all.

This said, there is something to be gained, however, by recognizing the historical dimension of feminist film criticism and theory, and by discern-ing the more general feminist concern with mapping the path of the (fe-male) subject in history. Although feminist work in film studies has rarely been thought to "count" or "figure" as history, I would like to suggest how it reveals a consistent concern with questions of history and representa-tion, as well as a shift from grand, teleological narratives of the represen-tation of women in film to more limited histories of authorship, spectator-ship, and consumerism. In the analysis that follows—an analysis that admittedly remains suggestive rather than exhaustive—I hope to show how historical questions loom large in feminist writing on film, where the stakes of historical knowledge turn less on debating the merits of empiri-cism and interpretation, and more on rethinking the vexed relationships between identity and difference in culture.

Feminism and Reflection Theory

Women have served all these centuries as looking glasses possessing the magic and delicious power of reflecting the figure of man at twice its natural size.

Virginia Woolf, quoted by Molly Haskell
in the introduction to From Reverence to Rape[8]

The earliest accounts of film history written from a feminist perspective – Marjorie Rosen's *Popcorn Venus: Women, Movies & the American Dream* (1973) and Molly Haskell's *From Reverence to Rape: The Treatment of Women in the Movies* (1974) – are now dismissed as popularized and theoretically unsophisticated histories, noted for their sweeping and teleological historical claims.[9] Detailing the decade-by-decade repression of women in the Hollywood cinema, both books are also criticized for their historical reductionism, for their assumption of an identity between text and context, audience and screen: in short, for their reliance on a what is commonly referred to as "reflection theory."[10]

"Movies are one of the clearest and most accessible of looking glasses into the past, being both cultural artifacts and mirrors," writes Molly Haskell in the introduction to *From Reverence to Rape*.[11] Similarly, in the preface to *Popcorn Venus*, Marjorie Rosen asks whether "art reflects life," only to provide the following unequivocal answer: "In movies, yes. Because more than any other art form, films have been a mirror held up to society's porous face. They therefore reflect the changing societal image of women – which, until recently, has not been taken seriously enough."[12] The metaphor of the mirror that is invoked here, while serving to establish a relationship between film and culture, the textual and the social body, nevertheless fails to consider the far more difficult issue of the relationship between text and ideology. Thus, according to Jameson's formulation: "Is the text a free-floating object in its own right, or does it reflect some context or ground, and in that case does it simply replicate the latter ideologically, or does it possess some autonomous force in which it could also be seen as negating that context?"[13]

Rosen's account of women and film history remains unconcerned with the question of the relationship between text and ideology, invested as it is in the terms of traditional sociological analysis. Haskell's account, by contrast, often suggests a far more nuanced view of how films can function as historical evidence, addressing the ways in which the cinema both reflects social conditions and distorts women's experience of those conditions. In one of the most frequently cited passages from her book, Haskell writes:

> Women have grounds for protest, and film is a rich field for the mining of female stereotypes. At the same time, there is a danger in going too far the other way, of grafting a modern sensibility onto the past so that all film history becomes grist in the mills of outraged feminism. . . . We can, for example, deplore the fact that in every movie where a woman excelled as a professional she had to be brought to heel at the end, but only as long as we acknowledge the corollary: that at least women *worked* in the films of the thirties and forties, and, moreover, that early film heroines were not only proportionately more active than the women

who saw them, but more active than the heroines of today's films. Here we are today, with an unparalleled freedom of expression and a record number of women performing, achieving, choosing to fulfill themselves, and we are insulted with the worst–the most abused, neglected, and dehumanized–screen heroines in film history.[14]

In this passage, Haskell challenges the conventional view of "progress" and "development" in the Hollywood cinema and insists that critics respect the otherness of the past and account for its fundamental difference from the present. Questioning the basic tenets of reflection theory, she also maintains that the mirror held up to women in film does not simply "reflect" their social reality, but rather reveals how the cinema has functioned historically to obscure women's accomplishments and further invest the male point of view with what she calls the "big lie" of Western civilization–the idea of women's inferiority. Interestingly enough, Haskell avoids the pitfalls of reflection theory by setting up an atemporal and normative ideal of heterosexual romance against which the trajectory of film history is judged. Significantly, the metaphor of the mirror is often invoked pejoratively in Haskell's text, usually in reference to contemporary cinema and in relation to questions of sexual difference. In recent seventies films, for example, Haskell detects a breakdown in the representation of heterosexual romance, claiming that the male-female protagonists, "like so many modern couples, come together in their weaknesses rather than their strength; they are mirror reflections of each other's neuroses."[15] The male-buddy film, moreover, is analyzed in strikingly similar terms, although it comes in for additional criticism for its exclusion of women and its narcissistic indifference to heterosexuality:

Sexual desire is not the point, nor "homoeroticism" the term for these relationships or for men fighting together shoulder to shoulder at the front . . . ; rather the point is love–love in which men understand and support each other, speak the same language, and risk their lives to gain each other's respect. But this is also a delusion; the difficulties of the adventure disguise the fact that this is the easiest of loves: a love that is adolescent, presexual, tacit, the love of one's *semblable*, one's mirror reflection.[16]

Despite her remarks to the contrary, Haskell's critique of the buddy film is at least in part a critique of homoeroticism that she extends to contemporary cinema as well. "We have succumbed to a kind of emotional laziness and passivity," Haskell writes, "a state in which only violence can rouse us, and we are inclined to choose as our partners those who are reflections of, rather than challenges to, the soul. The homophile impulse, like most decadent tropisms, like incest, is, or can be, a surrender, a sinking back into one's own nature."[17]

Although critical of the institution of marriage and what she refers to as "a disease called middle-class family life," Haskell upholds the "male-female chemistry" as a standard by which to evaluate film history and indulges in an uncritical celebration of heterosexual romance (as represented by "films in which the two points of view are separate but equal," such as those starring Lauren Bacall and Humphrey Bogart or Katharine Hepburn and Spencer Tracy). While commonly criticized for its sweeping and teleological claims, *From Reverence to Rape* can also be criticized for imposing an identity on film history—for reducing the history of women and film to the (failed) history of heterosexual romance in contemporary American cinema and culture.

In any case, Haskell's narrative version of film history was quickly abandoned in favor of more theoretically sophisticated, and more historically limited, approaches to issues of women and film. Questions of authorship, in particular, allowed feminist theorists to challenge established ways of writing about film history, and to rethink, at the level of production, the complicated relationships between gender identity and sexual difference in film.

Feminism and Film Authorship

> Women and film can only become meaningful in terms of a theory, in an attempt to create a structure in which films such as Arzner's can be examined in retrospect.
>
> *Claire Johnston*[18]

It has often been remarked that the poststructuralist critique of authorship functioned to exclude the very questions of identity and subjectivity central to an emerging feminist literary criticism. As Nancy Miller explains, "The removal of the Author has not so much made room for a revision of the concept of authorship as it has, through a variety of rhetorical moves, repressed and inhibited discussion of any writing identity in favor of the (new) monolith of anonymous textuality. . . . "[19]

In the context of film studies, however, the advent of poststructuralism had the opposite effect on feminist criticism; at least initially, it enabled the discussion of women directors in the cinema and revitalized debates about authorship that had dominated film studies since the early 1960s. Appearing in 1975, only a year after the publication of *From Reverence to Rape*, Claire Johnston's and Pam Cook's essays on Dorothy Arzner effectively redefined the terms of traditional *auteur* criticism by submitting the concept of film authorship to poststructuralist revision and to a thoroughgoing feminist critique.[20]

Importantly, Johnston and Cook understood their project to be a *po-*

lemical intervention into contemporary debates about the function of feminist criticism and an emerging feminist film practice. Challenging established ways of writing film history for their excluding the contributions of women (e.g., the *auteurism* championed by Andrew Sarris and the sociological histories of Kevin Brownlow and Lewis Jacobs), they also challenged feminist "discoveries" of female directors in the Hollywood cinema and criticized attempts to reclaim films directed by women for an unbroken tradition of "feminist art." A feminist film history, Johnston argued, is not simply a matter of "reintroducing" women into an untransformed history, as yet another series of "facts" to be assimilated into a preexisting chronology:

> "History" is not some abstract "thing" which bestows significance on past events in retrospect. Only an attempt to situate Arzner's work in a theoretical way would allow us to comprehend her real contribution to film history. . . . This is not, however, to ignore the political importance of asserting the real role women have played in the history of the cinema. . . . [But] the role of women in film history . . . inevitably raises questions about the nature of film history as such, and it is for this reason that this pamphlet has approached Dorothy Arzner's work from the point of view of feminist politics and feminist theory, as prerequisite research before any attempt at insertion into film history can be undertaken.[21]

For Johnston, as for Cook, the place of the female director in the Hollywood cinema can be assessed only in relation to a *history* that made it impossible for feminist statements to emerge from the studio system, and in terms of a *theory* that understands film authorship to be a function of discourse rather than individual intent. In Arzner's case, this amounts to analyzing the ways in which her films displace identification with characters and generate a series of competing discourses that "denaturalize" patriarchal ideology and "disturb" the fixed position of the spectator. "In Arzner's work," Johnston explains "the discourse of the woman, or rather her attempt to locate it and make it heard, is what gives the system of the text its structural coherence. . . . These women do not sweep aside the existing order and found a new, female order of language. Rather, they assert their own discourse in the face of the male one by breaking it up, subverting it, and, in a sense, rewriting it."[22]

Dance, Girl, Dance provides both critics with a wealth of examples to support this idea of the "subversive text." The final scene in which Judy O'Brien (Maureen O'Hara) discovers Steve Adams's identity as director of a dance academy, and hence the real reason for his pursuit of her (i.e., her abilities as a dancer), is cited by Johnston as a compelling instance of denaturalization: "*Dance, Girl, Dance* shows Judy exchanging the humiliation of the spectacle for the defeat of the final embrace with Steve Adams, the patriarchial presence which has haunted her throughout the film. . . . As she turns to the camera, her face obscured by a large, floppy hat, Judy, half crying, half laughing, exclaims 'when I think how simple things could have been, I just have to laugh.' This irony marks her defeat and final engulfment, but at the same time it is the final mark of subversion of the discourse of the male."[23] Of this same scene, Cook writes:

> In this final ironic reversal Judy "gets what she wants" at the expense of any pretensions to "independence" she has. Again, by displacing our ex-pectations of identification with Judy's positive qualities into a recogni-tion of the weakness of her position within male-dominated culture, the film's ending opens up the contradictions inherent in that position (our position) thus encouraging us as spectators to recognize the all-important problematic of the difficulties of the working through of female desire un-der patriarchy.[24]

Four years after the appearance of their work on Dorothy Arzner, John-ston's and Cook's approach to the analysis of the subversive text was sub-jected to detailed criticism by Janet Bergstrom and Jacquelyn Suter in the pages of *Camera Obscura*.[25] Bergstrom, in particular, questioned John-ston's attempt to specify—on the basis of a largely thematic analysis—reactions or reflexive thoughts on the part of the spectator. For all of John-ston's interpretive claims, Bergstrom argued, she fails to provide a textual analysis that adequately demonstrates "the working through of the wo-man's desire" or the positioning of the woman's discourse in terms of a film system: "The irony which Johnston sees operating in these Arzner endings is stated as if it is part of a factual account of the narrative. It is assumed that these endings will be understood as ironic by everyone, and that this irony will work, for all spectators, in the woman's favor."[26] In addition to Johnston's problematic use of textual evidence, Bergstrom further con-tends that her analysis of the "rupturing activity" of the classical film relies on a rather dubious view of the workings of the Hollywood cinema:

> Although Johnston refers to Stephen Heath's analysis of *Touch of Evil* . . . his article serves to demonstrate what, at the very least, presents a major paradox for what she is arguing—that is, the seemingly unlimited capacity for classical narrative film to create gaps, fissures, ruptures, generated most of all by its difficulty in containing sexual difference, only to recover them ultimately and to efface the memory, or at least the paths, of this heterogeneity. It is just this rupturing activity that is said to be characteristic of the classical text, and which, more-over, is thought to be the condition of a large part of its pleasure.[27]

In underscoring the problems that follow from highly interpretive ana-lyses such as Johnston's, Bergstrom provides a compelling critique of attempts to generalize audience response on the basis of single analysis, and, in the process, raises important reservations about assigning subversive or feminist readings to classical texts. Bergstrom's description of the Hollywood cinema, which draws largely upon the work of Raymond Bellour, Stephen Heath, and Thierry Kuntzel, nevertheless presents its own problems for the study of female authorship in the classical film – problems that become strikingly apparent in Jacquelyn Suter's analysis of Arzner's *Christopher Strong*. Simply put, if the classical film functions, consistently and inevitably, to contain the excesses and contradictions it so clearly generates, is the study of female authorship in the Hollywood cinema a questionable endeavor, merely another version of what Constance Penley calls "the easily accepted (because narcissistically desired)"?[28]

Suter's discussion of Arzner's film attempts to provide a provisional answer. In her view, a film such as *Christopher Strong* generates certain formal transgressions that might be associated with a feminine discourse, and yet these "isolated interruptions do not necessarily deconstruct the narrative discourse in any significant way."[29] According to Suter, the classic text is bound up with a narrative logic that necessarily precludes the forceful articulation of authorship that one finds, for example, in Chantal Akerman's films. In *Jeanne Dielman*, she contends, "instead of isolated interventions into a classic text, we have a systematic reordering of certain crucial elements upon which the classic text depends, and a recognition of other elements which the classic text chooses invariably to ignore."[30] For Suter, the Hollywood film thus remains a self-contained and, by implication, closed system – at least insofar as female authorship in concerned.

While Johnston and Cook, and Bergstrom and Suter, generally agree about what constitutes authorship in the cinema – that is, they all define it as a discursive practice – they nevertheless disagree about what constitutes a subversive reading and hence about critical methodology. Importantly, however, none of these theorists (with the exception of Johnston) addresses the difficulty or the necessity of thinking about authorship in extratextual terms, and they therefore fail to consider the problem of authorship as it intersects with issues of history, biography, and textuality.

Paradoxically, then, what began as an attempt to *revise* the concept of film authorship by rethinking the place of the female director in the history of the Hollywood cinema ended up in debates about the concept of the subversive text – and in arguments (to borrow from Nancy Miller) for a "(new) monolith of anonymous textuality" that inhibited further discussion of female authorship in the development of the classical film. To be sure, feminists continued to consider the possibility of locating female enunciation in the Hollywood cinema, and studies of female authorship in the independent and avant-garde cinema proceeded as if the relationship between biography and textual analysis were simpler, or at least less problematic, than in Arzner's case. In any event, both the role of the woman director in Hollywood and the troubling theoretical question of biography were virtually set aside as theorists turned from the production context to explore questions of film history through a consideration of spectatorship and discourses on consumption.

Feminism, Spectatorship, and Consumerism

> If the apparatus stages an eternal, universal and primordial wish to create a simulacrum of the psyche, then Baudry's argument is blind to the economic, social or political determinations of cinema as well as its basic difference from other art forms.
>
> *Constance Penley*[31]

> What is elided in the conceptualization of the spectator is not only historical but sexual specificity.
>
> *Mary Ann Doane*[32]

Studies of consumerism and female spectatorship emerged in response to the most significant film theories of the 1970s: Jean-Louis Baudry's and Christian Metz's theories of the cinematic apparatus and Laura Mulvey's theory of narrative cinema and masculine visual pleasure.[33] Both apparatus theory and the theory of the spectator developed by Mulvey signaled an important conceptual shift in film studies: the shift from a formal analysis of the film text (the structural organization of the fiction) to a consideration of the metapsychology of film viewing (the place of the spectator with respect to the fiction).

Although setting the terms for a sophisticated analysis of perception and identification in film, apparatus theory and the conceptualization of the spectator that underpinned it quickly became the focus of extensive criticism and debate. Feminist theorists, in particular, challenged claims for the eternal, universal effects of the cinematic apparatus, as opposed to its historically specific and sexually differentiated constructions.

As Jacqueline Rose has pointed out, Metz's psychoanalytic reading of visual perception and, specifically, his use of the concept of disavowal to describe the ways in which cinema achieves its impression of reality failed to address the problem or the difficulty of sexual difference.[34] In a similar way, Baudry's assumption of a transhistorical, indeed primordial, desire for cinematic pleasure neglected to consider pleasures and subjectivities that were historically produced as well as sexually inflected. Baudry's model, as Constance Penley has explained, is "not only ahistorical but also strongly teleological."

The shackled prisoners fascinated by the shadows on the wall of Plato's cave are the first "cinema" spectators; the only historical changes in the apparatus since then have been little more than technological modifications. . . . Baudry's teleological argument [further] asserts that the cinema aims at pleasure alone, and that it unfailingly achieves it, an assertion, moreover, that is merely stated and not supported. . . . The question of pleasure has been a crucially troubling one for feminist theory and filmmaking and the theory of the apparatus appears to answer the question before it is even raised.[35]

The question of sexually inflected pleasures was, of course, central to Mulvey's now classic theorization of the Hollywood film. However, in assuming masculine subjectivity as a sole point of reference, Mulvey's analysis of structures of looking in the cinema tended to reproduce the problems and blind spots of apparatus theory. In an effort to reintroduce both historical and sexual specificity into theories of cinematic perception, feminists therefore increasingly turned to questions of consumerism and female spectatorship, exploring the ways in which a particular history (the history of consumer capitalism) transformed not just the organization of narrative and visual pleasure, but also the forms of subjectivity associated with a female spectator-subject.

Mary Ann Doane's book *The Desire to Desire: The Woman's Film of the 1940s* (1987) stands as the most important contribution to the reconsideration of spectatorship and apparatus theory from a feminist perspective.[36] Challenging the assumption that the cinematic apparatus is sexually indifferent—that it stages a "universal and hence ahistorical condition of the human psyche"—Doane sets out to trace the contours of female subjectivity in the woman's film, charting the difficulties and failures of Hollywood's attempt to construct a position for the female spectator. The woman's film, Doane explains,

> does not provide us with an access to a pure and authentic female subjectivity, much as we might like it to do so. It provides us instead with an image repertoire of poses—classical feminine poses and assumptions about the female appropriation of the gaze. Hollywood women's films of the 1940s document a crisis in subjectivity around the figure of woman— although it is not always clear whose subjectivity is at stake."[37]

As this quote implies, Doane's challenge to apparatus theory remains within the terms of its own analysis. Her study of the woman's film, for example, does not address the habits and responses of actual moviegoers, but rather provides an investigation of "classical feminine poses" or discourses of feminine subjectivity during the period. This is not to say, however, that Doane is unconcerned with questions of history or the context of reception. Indeed, although she is careful to distinguish between social and psychical descriptions of the subject, she nevertheless attempts to examine the historical process whereby the address to women as consumers became indistinguishable from the objectification of woman as image.

Drawing on the work of Charles Eckert and Jeanne Allen,[38] Doane sketches the relationship between the cinema and commodity fetishism and shows how the commodity form inflected filmic representation and spectatorship. With reference to Walter Benjamin's argument about large-scale historical changes in human perception,[39] Doane further suggests how the commodity form collapses traditional distinctions between subject and object and restructures spatial and temporal registers of looking and perception. "It is not accidental," she writes, "that the logic of consumerism and mechanical reproduction corresponds to a logic of perception attributed to the female spectator whose nonfetishistic gaze maintains a dangerous intimacy with the image."[40] Proximity rather than distance, a disabling closeness to the image – these are the tropes that link femininity and consumerism and the female spectator. As Doane explains,

> In her desire to bring the things of the screen closer, to approximate the bodily image of the star, and to possess the space in which she dwells, the female spectator experiences the intensity of the image as lure and exemplifies the perception proper to the consumer. The cinematic image for the woman is both shop window and mirror, the one simply a means of access to the other. The mirror/window takes on then the aspect of a trap whereby her subjectivity becomes synonymous with her objectification.[41]

Doane's efforts to historicize apparatus theory represent a remarkable achievement, and yet her assessment of female spectatorship during the 1940s raises important questions about historical periodization and critical method. One could argue, for example, that Doane describes a form of spectatorship that embraces the history of the cinema in its entirety, rather than a particular subjectivity at a precise historical moment. To be sure, the history of consumer capitalism provides a more limited temporal frame for an analysis of cinema and subjectivity than Baudry's appeal to Plato's allegory of the cave. Nevertheless, in situating her discussion of the female spectator within such an expanded historical perspective, Doane might be faulted by historians for subordinating historical analysis to theoretical interpretation – for producing a theory of the woman's film instead of a history.

Importantly, however, Doane's attempt to *theorize* the context of film reception in the 1940s allows her to explore questions of historical spectatorship through textual analysis. In contrast to other recent studies of cinema and consumerism,[42] *The Desire to Desire* seeks to integrate film analysis with a larger, and more extensive, discussion of film culture during a historical period – hence, the appeal to consumerism as a critical concept, and the close analysis of films such as *Caught*, which inscribe female desire according to the logic of the commodity. This is not to say, however, that Doane aims simply to respond to the formalist question, Can film history survive without the analysis of individual films? Indeed, by considering consumerism as it inflects modes of looking and representation, she also confronts a far more crucial issue, namely, can a feminist film history be confined to a history of film? From this perspective, studies of consumerism and the female spectator, rather than necessarily implying the triumph of theory over history or the disappearance of film as a privileged object, might more usefully be understood as redefining the object of a specifically feminist film history. As Doane herself has written, "Feminism cannot be a formalism. The object is cinema only insofar as cinema is understood not as formal object or as a repository of meanings but as a particular – and quite specific – mode of representing and inscribing subjectivities which are sexually inflected."[43]

All of this is not to suggest some sort of teleology in the development of feminist film theory, in which consumerism replaces authorship, which replaced social history, as the most viable concept for organizing film history. Studies of the female spectator-consumer, moreover, pose a number of difficulties and problems, most obviously with respect to the history of American consumer culture itself. One might ask, for example, What distinguishes discourses on consumption in the 1940s (a privileged area for feminist research) from discourses on consumerism in the early part of the century? Does the history of consumer capitalism form an unbroken continuum, or does it rather reveal a series of radical shifts and dislocations? And what of the relationships among cinema, sexual difference, and consumerism in Second and Third World nations? Given the inordinate amount of attention to the Hollywood cinema in feminist film theory, it is now important to begin to account for the history of other national cinemas from a feminist perspective.[44] But can the model of the spectator-consumer developed by feminist theory be easily exported to explain developments in other cinemas or national traditions?

While studies of consumerism raise important questions and suggest areas for further research, I also believe it is crucial for feminists to return to earlier debates on film history to address issues that were too hastily dismissed or prematurely foreclosed. The relationship between biography and textuality, for instance, remains a crucial issue for feminist film history, although more attention has been paid to the biographical dimension of filmic textuality than to the textual dimension of biography. Certainly, a study like Haskell's highlights the place of the female star in the Hollywood cinema, and biographical information remains central to her attempt to detail the contradictions between cinematic representation and the everyday lives of female stars. In view of recent theoretical work on cinema and the star system, however, Haskell's social history could be usefully extended and updated. How, for example, might the concepts of biography and textuality be theorized to enable the study of differences outside of a heterosexual problematic? As Judith Mayne points out in *The Woman at the Keyhole*, while it was well known in Hollywood amongst feminist critics that Arzner was a lesbian, this "striking aspect of her persona—and her films—has been largely ignored."[45] How, then, might studies of female authorship open up discussion about the tensions and negotiations of the production context, and hence generate accounts of sexual *differences* in the history of the Hollywood film?

Finally, as the history of feminist film theory so clearly demonstrates, the analysis of individual films goes only so far in explaining the complexities of audience expectation and spectator response. But if film theory cannot exist without film analysis, and if feminism cannot be a formalism, then what precisely is the role of textual analysis in feminist film history? The issue here, as I suggested earlier, is not one of retrieving film analysis from the perceived excesses of theory, or of reducing feminist film history to a formalist study of film. It is instead a matter of rethinking what claims can be made on the basis of film analysis, and of reconceptualizing what constitutes textual evidence in relation to questions of sexual difference. For what is finally at stake for feminism is not so much the problem of claiming too much for textual analysis, but that of claiming too little, thereby leaving the writing of film history to those who would exclude sexual difference from the study of the cinema entirely.

Notes

1. Meaghan Morris, *The Pirate's Fiancée: Feminism, Reading, Postmodernism* (New York: Verso, 1988), 4–15.

2. On the new historicism, see Brook Thomas, "The New Historicism and the Privileging of Literature," *Annals of Scholarship: Metastudies of the Humanities and Social Sciences* 4, no. 4 (1987): 23–48; David Simpson, "Literary Criticism and the Return to History," *Critical Inquiry* 14 (1988): 721–47; and Gregory Jay, *America the Scivener: Deconstruction and the Subject of Literary History* (Ithaca, N.Y.: Cornell University Press, 1990).

3. On early debates over the relationship between film theory and film history, see Robert C. Allen, "Film History: The Narrow Discourse," in *The 1977 Film Studies Annual: Part Two* (New York: Redgrave, 1977): 9–16; Charles F. Altman, "Towards a Historiography of American Film," *Cinema Journal* 16, no. 2 (1977): 1–25; Edward Branigan, "Color and Cinema: Problems in the Writing of Film History," *Film Reader* 4 (1979): 16–34; John Ellis, "The Institution of Cinema," *Edinburgh '77 Magazine* 2 (London: British Film Institute, 1977): 56–66; Gerald Mast, "Film History and Film Histories," *Quarterly Review of Film Studies* 1 (1976):

297–314; Mark Nash and Steve Neale, "Film History/Production/Memory," *Screen* 18, no. 4 (1977–78): 71–91; Geoffrey Nowell-Smith, "Facts about Films and Facts of Film," *Quarterly Review of Film Studies* 1 (1976): 272–75.

4. See, for example, Robert C. Allen and Douglas Gomery, *Film History: Theory and Practice* (New York: Knopf, 1985); David Bordwell, Janet Staiger, and Kristin Thompson, *The Classical Hollywood Cinema: Film Style and Mode of Production to 1960* (New York: Columbia University Press, 1985).

5. See, for example, David Bordwell, *Making Meaning: Inference and Rhetoric in the Interpretation of Cinema* (Cambridge, Mass.: Harvard University Press, 1989). To be sure, in his final chapter, Bordwell does mention at least one feminist's work on film history. Typically, however, his praise for this work turns entirely on its attention to archival sources and "concrete institutional negotiations among filmmakers, studio executives, and censors"; in other words, on its rigorous empirical foundation. While empirical research is, of course, crucial to rethinking film history from a feminist perspective, Bordwell fails to consider the central role played by feminist theory in generating the questions that feminist historians attempt to answer through archival study.

6. Judith Newton, "History as Usual? Feminism and the 'New Historicism,'" *Cultural Critique* 9 (1988): 87–121.

7. Fredric Jameson, *The Political Unconscious: Narrative as a Socially Symbolic Act* (Ithaca, N.Y.: Cornell University Press, 1981), 9.

8. Molly Haskell, *From Reverence to Rape: The Treatment of Women in the Movies* (New York: Holt, Rinehart and Winston, 1974), 1.

9. Marjorie Rosen, *Popcorn Venus: Women, Movies & the American Dream* (New York: Coward, McCann and Geoghegan, 1973); Haskell, *Reverence*.

10. For a compelling analysis of *From Reverence to Rape* and *Popcorn Venus* as feminist film histories, see Claire Johnston, "Feminist Politics and Film History," *Screen* 16, no. 3 (1975): 115–24.

11. Haskell, *Reverence*, xiv.

12. Rosen, *Popcorn Venus*, 9.

13. Jameson, *The Political Unconscious*, 38.

14. Haskell, *Reverence*, 30.

15. Haskell, *Reverence*, 27.

16. Haskell, *Reverence*, 24.

17. Haskell, *Reverence*, 28.

18. Claire Johnston, "Dorothy Arzner: Critical Strategies," in *The Work of Dorothy Arzner: Towards a Feminist Cinema*, ed. Claire Johnston (London: British Film Institute, 1975), 2.

19. Nancy Miller, "Changing the Subject: Authorship, Writing, and the Reader" in *Feminist Studies/Critical Studies*, ed. Teresa de Lauretis (Bloomington: Indiana University Press, 1986), 104.

20. Johnston, "Dorothy Arzner," 1–8; Pam Cook, "Approaching the Work of Dorothy Arzner," *Dorothy Arzner*, 9–18. Both of these essays have been reprinted in *Feminism and Film Theory*, ed. Constance Penley (New York: Routledge, 1988).

21. Johnston, "Dorothy Arzner," 2.

22. Johnston, "Dorothy Arzner," 4.

23. Johnston, "Dorothy Arzner," 7.

24. Cook, "Approaching the Work of Dorothy Arzner," 11.

25. Janet Bergstrom, "Rereading the Work of Claire Johnston," *Camera Obscura* 3, no. 4 (1979): 21–31 (reprinted in *Feminism and Film Theory*, 80–88); Jacquelyn Suter "Feminine Discourse in *Christopher Strong*," *Camera Obscura* 3, no. 4 (1979): 135–50 (reprinted in *Feminism and Film Theory*, 89–103. Citations are taken from the later edition).

26. Bergstrom, "Rereading," 84.

27. Bergstrom, "Rereading," 85.

28. Penley, "The Lady Doesn't Vanish: Feminism and Film Theory," *Feminism and Film Theory*, 2.

29. Suter, "Feminine Discourse," 101.

30. Suter, "Feminine Discourse," 102.

31. Penley, "Feminism, Film Theory, and the Bachelor Machines," *m/f* 10 (1985): 42.

32. Mary Ann Doane, "The 'Woman's Film': Possession and Address," in *Revision: Essays in Feminist Film Criticism*, ed. Mary Ann Doane, Patricia Mellencamp, and Linda Williams (Frederick, Md.: University Publications of America, 1984), 68.

33. Jean-Louis Baudry, "Ideological Effects of the Basic Cinematographic Apparatus," trans. Alan Williams, *Film Quarterly* 27, no. 2 (1974): 39–47; Baudry, "The Apparatus," trans. Jean Andrews and Bertrand Augst, *Camera Obscura* 1 (1979): 104–26; Christian Metz, *The Imaginary Signifier: Psychoanalysis and the Cinema*, trans. Celia Britton, Annwyl Williams, Ben Brewster, and Alfred Guzzetti (Bloomington: Indiana University Press, 1982); Laura Mulvey, "Visual Pleasure and Narrative Cinema," *Screen* 16, no. 3 (1975): 6–18.

34. Jacqueline Rose, "The Cinematic Apparatus: Problems in Current Theory," *The Cinematic Apparatus*, ed. Teresa de Lauretis and Stephen Heath (New York: St. Martin's, 1980), 172–86.

35. Penley, "Bachelor Machines," 42.

36. Doane, *The Desire to Desire: The Woman's Film of the 1940s* (Bloomington: Indiana University Press, 1987).

37. Doane, *Desire*, 4.

38. Charles Eckert, "The Carole Lombard in Macy's Window," *Quarterly Review of Film Studies* 3, no. 1 (1978): 1–22; Jeanne Allen, "The Film Viewer as Consumer," *Quarterly Review of Film Studies* 5, no. 4 (1980): 481–99.

39. Doane refers especially to Benjamin's most famous essay in English translation, "The Work of Art in the Age of Mechanical Reproduction," reprinted in *Illuminations*, trans. Harry Zohn, ed. Hannah Arendt (New York: Schocken, 1969).

40. Doane, *Desire*, 32.

41. Doane, *Desire*, 32–33.

42. For a sampling of recent essays on cinema and consumerism, see *Quarterly Review of Film and Video* 11, no. 1 (1989), special issue "Female Representation and Consumer Culture" ed. Michael Renov and Jane Gaines.

43. Doane, "Feminist Film Theory and the Enterprise of Criticism," unpublished paper.

44. A number of recent feminist studies have addressed precisely this issue. See, for example, Rey Chow, "Silent Is the Ancient Plain: Music, Filmmaking, and the Conception of Reform in China's New Cinema," *Discourse* 12, no. 2 (1990); Sandy Flitterman-Lewis, *To Desire Differently: Feminism and the French Cinema* (Urbana: University of Illinois Press, 1990); Judith Mayne, *Kino and the Woman Question: Feminism and Soviet Silent Film* (Columbus: Ohio University Press, 1989); and Patrice Petro, *Joyless Streets: Women and Melodramatic Representation in Weimar Germany* (Princeton, N.J.: Princeton University Press, 1989).

45. Judith Mayne, *The Woman at the Keyhole: Feminism and Women's Cinema* (Bloomington: Indiana University Press, 1990), 104.

Psychoanalysis and Feminist Film Theory:
The Problem of Sexual Difference and Identity

Janet Walker

Author's note: This article was written in Paris in 1981. As such it reflects
contemporary feminist film theory's concentration on European feminist
perspectives, a concentration that has intensified in the intervening years
as French feminist work, in particular, has become more plentiful and accessible through English translation.[1] Happily, the early impulse (examined in part III of this article) to study problems of female spectatorship
and sexual and cultural identity as problems pertinent to cultural
representation seen historically has developed significantly and might be
pursued in the writings of feminist media scholars Patrice Petro, Tania
Modleski, Maureen Turim, Constance Penley, and Diane Waldman, among
many others.[2] For an excellent overview of contemporary feminist work
on film and television see "The Spectatrix," *Camera Obscura*, nos. 20–21
(May-September 1989).

This article provides an overview of how psychoanalytic thought has been
applied to feminist film theory in order to pursue questions of women's material and imagistic oppression and to imagine possibilities for women's
liberation. I have divided my discussion into three areas to chart the development and variations in psychoanalytic applications. The first area to
be discussed concerns the use of psychoanalysis to explain the irrevocably
patriarchal nature of the constitution of sexual difference and identity and

its reinforcement in filmic representation. The second application envisions a psychoanalysis in which femininity is problematized and in which the gaps and lacunae within (primarily Freudian) psychoanalytic theory become the site of the (missing) formulation of feminine psychic structures. Hollywood films, under this view, may be interrogated for subversive moments when a given film's "unconscious" surfaces in the form of heretofore repressed femininity, or moments when the film presents contradictory notions of the feminine. A third application of psychoanalysis to film studies emphasizes the potential of psychoanalysis to address the cultural as well as the psychological register. This application has as its goal the understanding of the place of women in cultural representation as neither absent nor totally repressed or punished, but rather underappreciated by theoreticians whose thinking has been constructed precisely through psychoanalytic processes.

To Illuminate Patriarchal Oppression

Laura Mulvey's "Visual Pleasure and Narrative Cinema" is the touchstone article in the field of feminism, psychoanalysis, and film.[3] Not only does "Visual Pleasure" mount an uncompromising feminist critique of cinematic representation, but it links psychoanalytic processes and cinema spectating by more than the previously explored "film as dream" metaphor. Using concepts of scopophilic voyeurism and scopophilic narcissism, Mulvey explores how the psychological processes that constitute and govern psychosexual identity also enable the pleasure of cinema spectating.

The fascinating world of the cinema screen is exhibited and, for the spectator alone in the dark, it is also private. Thus, cinema engages what Freud, in *Three Essays on the Theory of Sexuality* (1905), described as scopophilia: the pleasure in subjecting others to a curious, controlling gaze. But, argues Mulvey, cinema also engages narcissistic scopophilia, described by Freud in *Instincts and Their Vicissitudes* (1915). In this incarnation, "the wish to look intermingle[s] with a fascination with likeness and recognition: the human face, the human body, the relationship between the human form and its surroundings."[4] Thus, scopophilic pleasure in taking another person as a sexual object is identified as one essential psychic process involved in cinematic spectating. Processes of identification and the constitution of the ego make up the second half of the pair.

However, these processes of psychosexuality and identity construction are imbalanced across the sexes. The male is the active "bearer of the look," where the female is the passive object of the look. "In a world ordered by sexual imbalance," writes Mulvey, "pleasure in looking has been split between active/male and passive/female." Applied to cinema spectating, then, and in particular the films of Alfred Hitchcock, it is only the male spectator in his identification with the camera and the male actors, his surrogates, who gains pleasure in looking, while the female *performer* "connotes *to-be-looked-at-ness*."[5]

And yet this process is not so straightforward. First, identification with a male protagonist is inherently problematic because such identification reanimates what Jacques Lacan has described as the "misrecognition" that takes place in infancy during the mirror stage when the infant sees in his own reflection a more discrete and capable physical being than is actually the case. Second, both voyeuristic scopophilia and narcissistic scopophilia are defenses against the male's recognition of his own limitations, which recognition threatens all the more acutely when a "castrated" being, the woman according to the man's view, comes into focus:

> The woman as icon, displayed for the gaze and enjoyment of men, the active controllers of the look, always threatens to evoke the anxiety it originally signified. The male unconscious has two avenues of escape from this castration anxiety: preoccupation with the re-enactment of the original trauma (investigating the woman, demystifying her mystery), counterbalanced by the devaluation, punishment, or saving of the guilty object (an avenue typified by the concerns of the *film noir*); or else complete disavowal of castration by the substitution of a fetish object or turning the represented figure itself into a fetish so that it becomes reassuring rather than dangerous (hence over-valuation, the cult of the female star).[6]

Filmic representation in classical Hollywood cinema, then, is predicated on the patriarchally required denial of sexual difference. Films that seem to offer alternatives by allowing a certain openness suggested by the *femme fatale* or the spectacular image of, say, Marlene Dietrich in the films of Josef von Sternberg, in fact only allow this openness to the extent that it is predicated on closure. The feminine position is, by definition, inaccessible.

Mulvey carefully foregrounds her own use of psychoanalytic theory as "a political weapon." In response to feminists who suggest that Mulvey's formulation reiterates the oppression she is set to struggle against, Mulvey may reply that psychoanalysis is used in her piece as a *description* of society and not as a naturalized *prescription*. And yet, Mulvey's recruitment of psychoanalytic theory into the service of its own critique seems to me only partly realized. The view of psychoanalysis and that of Hollywood cinema seem overly monolithic and unable to account for the spaces of female resistance that give rise, for example, to classical film texts that depart in places from the model, to radically other sorts of pleasurable filmic representation, and even to critical writing such as Mulvey's own.

What Does a Woman Want?

> The great question that has never been answered and which I have
> not yet been able to answer despite my thirty years of research into
> the feminine soul, is "What does a woman want?"
>
> *Freud, to Marie Bonaparte*[7]

If Mulvey's piece is representative of a feminist critique of patriarchy that
turns on the recognition and analysis of the impossibility of the female position, another body of critical writings takes as its point of departure
Freud's question, "What does a woman want?" But, there can be little
smoothness or closure in an argument resting on such a volatile notion as
female pleasure. Thus, theoretical work in this realm, in contradistinction
to the solid critique of patriarchal representation described above, establishes itself as being *of necessity* tentative, unfinished, and inherently
problematic. Freud's question is asked, but remains partially unanswered.

Juliet Mitchell and Jacqueline Rose both excavate Freud's work for
evidence of his dissatisfaction with his own formulations of femininity.[8]
Rose points out that from 1923, with "The Infantile Genital Organization:
An Interpolation into the Theory of Sexuality," to 1933, with "Femininity," Freud talks about nothing as much as he talks about sexual difference.[9] Unsatisfied, he returns to his early ideas in *Studies on Hysteria*
(1893–1895) and *Three Essays on the Theory of Sexuality* (1905).[10] In
"Femininity" (1933) Freud makes the following inconclusive remark: "That
is all I had to say to you about femininity. It is certainly incomplete and
fragmentary and does not always sound friendly."[11]

In order to avoid naturalizing the male as "having" the phallus and the
female as "lacking" the phallus (the trap that threatens to snare Mulvey),
Rose emphasizes that the boy has often *seen* that his mother does not have
a penis, without really *noticing*. The observation becomes significant only
when social taboos begin to function, enacting the threat of castration if
the boy continues to desire his mother. The sight, then, is meaningless outside of *social difference*, and gender identity is conceived as a process of
questioning carried on during the child's attempt to discover his or her
own origin. Here the problem of sexual difference is assigned outside of
biology and it relates to the ways in which the child learns to understand
and represent himself or herself.

It is in this sociologically insinuated context that Freud's definition of
the three paths open to women must be seen. A woman has the alternatives of repressing all sexuality, of functioning with a masculinity complex,
or of taking the "very circuitous path" to "normal feminine attitude."[12] The
third option implies that the process of becoming a woman is undertaken
through a series of violences, destructions, or repressions that occur as the

girl changes the sex of her object choice and as her actions change from activity to passivity. But the very need for the repressive apparatus reveals active female sexuality and calls into question maternity as the ultimate expression of adult female sexuality.

The reader might be wondering what ever happened to feminist *film* theory. In 1981, Laura Mulvey published an article entitled, "Afterthoughts on 'Visual Pleasure and Narrative Cinema' Inspired by *Duel in the Sun* (King Vidor, 1946)."[13] Mulvey begins this article by asking, "What about the women in the audience?" and "What happens when there is a female character occupying the center of the narrative arena?" Those queries inaugurate her participation in the search for the theoretical location of female pleasure.

From the start, the problems encountered are different from those at hand when the spectator being theorized is a male. The fact that the psychoanalytic description of feminine sexual identity includes the possibility of "masculinization" when applied to film spectatorship suggests that the female spectator would identify with both male and female protagonists.[14] A change in the gender of the spectator shifts the focus from castration and the oedipal scenario to the areas outlined above relating to problematized femininity. It also shifts critical attention to a different group of films: melodramas with a woman at the story's center are studied instead of films with a male hero, thus providing evidence that the selection of films influences film theory.

In "Afterthoughts on 'Visual Pleasure'" Mulvey concentrates on films in which "a woman central protagonist is shown to be unable to achieve a stable sexual identity, torn between the deep blue sea of passive femininity and the devil of regressive masculinity."[15] The heroine's dilemma echoes the predicament of the female spectator who must accept "masculinization" to identify with a male hero. All women in question, "real" or fictional, are constructed in relation to instability and oscillation.

This time around, Mulvey describes female psychical life as it exists *over time*, rather than dwelling on any formative moment or even stage of identity construction. Residual ambiguities in sexual identity continue to erupt throughout a woman's life. They are never "taken care of" for good. Mulvey quotes Freud in "Femininity":

> I will only emphasize here that the development of femininity remains exposed to disturbances by the residual phenomenon of the early masculine period. Regressions to the pre-Oedipus phase very frequently occur; in the course of some women's lives there is a *repeated alternation* between periods in which femininity or masculinity gain the upper hand.[16]

Duel in the Sun, Mulvey's inspiration, takes as its heroine a girl named Pearl. The plot describes her attempt to find and live a mature femininity that is not repressive. Two brothers offer her alternative paths of development. One brother is socially sanctioned, upright, cultured; the other wild, sexual, macho. They personify the qualities with which Pearl's femininity could find symbiosis. In the end, Pearl is unable to settle on "a 'femininity' in which she and the male world can meet."[17] In the desert heat, Pearl and Lewt (the wild, sexual brother) hunt each other down, shoot each other, and die in a sweaty embrace. Through this film, one can see that femininity need not signify sexuality in a simple sense, nor need femininity be merely an object of patriarchal domination. The very exploration in and of itself of the conflicted feminine position can provide the premise of a Hollywood narrative.

Psyche and Culture

The first area analyzed above included work characterizing the textual representation of the position of woman as absent. The second area saw femininity as present but "problematized" by definition. Both approaches articulate the *relationship* between psychoanalytic formulations of sexual difference and identity. Both assume that these two psychic processes must be taken together, the first seeing the pairing as resulting in an impossible feminine position while the second sees this pairing as resulting in a fundamentally unstable and contradictory feminine position. Monique Plaza, whose work I accept as laying out the theoretical base for the third area to be identified, steps back to question the results of the sexual difference/identity couple. Her work is not a refusal of "sexual difference" in the sense in which the term has been central for feminist film theory, where the recognition of sexual difference is the recognition that woman is *other than* not-male. It is, rather, a look at the problems of "difference" where woman is posited as other *and* not-male.

In " 'Phallomorphic Power' and the Psychology of 'Woman': A Patriarchal Chain," Plaza critiques the contention that "woman" does not exist.[18] She points out that the argument for the absence of "woman" must be based on an analysis of patriarchal discourses such as philosophy and literature (one could go on here to cite art, architecture, government, and so on) that do not often include contributions by women as preserved artifacts. This latter point is also granted by those adherents to the first category outlined. They do not mean to argue that individual women or women in general do not exist. Their own publications and existence immediately negate that point of view. They too are arguing that it is patriarchal discourse that excludes women. However, there *is* a basic difference in the two points of view. While the work described in the first section of this article theorizes a patriarchal structure *virtually effective* in its repressive strategies, Plaza envisages a nonmonolithic patriarchy that is *not* exhaus-

tive in its control and descriptions of the material world. To posit alternative women's or radical discourses is not to invent an "elsewhere" outside
of ideology, but rather to recognize the limitations of patriarchal ideology.
Patriarchy is simply *not* all-inclusive. Discourse, even discourse produced
by men, is *phallocentric*, but not *phallomorphic*.

The theory of sexual difference is used by feminists who want a way to
talk about women that does not fall into the male/not-male binarism of the
first group. But Plaza is not at all convinced that the attempt has been successful, since sexual difference is still understood to be ordered around
"having" or "lacking" the phallus. In theoretical practice, the phallus is a
metaphor, a sign imposed by patriarchal symbolic order and not a "real"
lack in women. Nonetheless, it must still be viewed as a metaphor that is
"propped" on or exists in inextricable relation to the anatomical realm.[19]
Plaza argues that this way of thinking poses a division of labor that implies
not only *differentiation*, but also *hierarchization*, since to have the phallus
is valorized by the social system that formulates the metaphor. For Plaza,
posing sexual difference in this light is only the flip side of the denial of
difference that the first and second groups note as a characteristic of classical representation.

A significant difficulty arises from the fact that psychoanalysis does not
sufficiently differentiate the processes through which identity is constituted (the separation of self and other) from the processes of sexual
differentiation. But, since processes of sexual differentiation carry an inherently hierarchical structure that is socially prescribed, it is a mistake
to collapse the two. Plaza argues:

> If the category of sex has such an important position in patriarchal logic,
> this is not because sex gives its shape to the social; it is because the so-
> cial is able to make sexual forms seem obvious and thereby hide oppres-
> sive systems.[20]

Thus, Plaza demonstrates the necessity of understanding the psychic process of sexual differentiation as propped on the biological *and* as further ordered by the sociological.

In the social realm, the concept of a man does not rest only on his sexual
identity. It expands to embody other "human" qualities possessed by
"mankind" that are collectively understood as good qualities. Therefore, to
base the singularity of individuals on their gender identity means something different for the man and the woman since a woman has a lower place
in the symbolic hierarchy. Feminist theory, if it is to be feminist, must resist the total fusion of singularity and gender identity. Woman is *not only*
woman. For Plaza,

To reveal its existence and lay bare its mechanisms, it is necessary to bring down the idea of "woman," that is, to denounce the fact that the category of sex has invaded gigantic territories for oppressive ends. . . . At the psychological level, it is the signifier "woman" which must summarize for the woman the whole of her existence. The weight of this signifier in her psychic system is made possible by her subjection to the patriarchal symbolic arrangements. . . . Woman exists too much as signifier. Woman exists too much as subjected, exploited individual.[21]

The concept of woman must be extended to a general, human category, without the loss of either the sexual or cultural specificity of femaleness.

It would be difficult to go on from here without reference to the work of Mary Ann Doane wherein is proposed an approach to the sexual difference/self-identity quandry different from Plaza's call for sociological correction. In "Woman's Stake: Filming the Female Body," Doane presents the terms of the feminist critique of essentialism and the problems encountered by that position. Antiessentialist feminist theory tiptoes around notions of the female body, thus collapsing its focus onto male psychic development at the expense of an account of female psychic development.[22] Doane argues for the reformulation of the relation between body and psyche as a way out of the essentialist/antiessentialist impasse. The concept of "propping" or "anaclisis" used by Jean Laplanche provides a way to explain this relation between body and psyche, as does Lacanian work. Here the phallus is a necessary signifying presence, and gender-differentiated relationships to discourse are based on differing relationships to that representational stake. Since we know that women do "speak," the project Doane identifies is to interrogate the complex body-psyche relation, where body is not an essence but a condition of discursive practice, to define a construction of feminine specificity.[23]

This is not so simple. Critical discourse about the cinema in general is easily elided into an extension of that institution. As Christian Metz puts it, "Knowledge of the cinema is obtained via a 'reprise' of the native discourse in two senses of the word: taking it into consideration and reestablishing it."[24] In feminist film theory, the danger is twice as common and twice as potent, to the extent that feminist theoretical work that provides a reprise of the repressive textual function in relation to the position of the woman seems intuitively to account wisely for textual operations. But by concentrating on the classical text, isn't the feminist theorist undercutting both possibilities for experimentation with the film medium and alternatives in critical discourse? This trap is one that Monique Plaza terms "patriarchal *bouclage*," meaning that feminist work can easily loop or buckle over on itself in such a way as to become an arm of the patriarchal critical institution it aims to react against.[25]

Those who recognize this pitfall have pioneered several routes of resistance. First of all, not all Hollywood classical films need be read as totally recuperative of feminine desire. For example, Mary Ann Doane's analysis of *Caught* and *Rebecca* points to cinematic passages that operate to resist the objectification of the woman as spectacle for the male gaze.[26] These films are obsessed with female fantasy, rehearsing the relationship between female subjectivity and desire. Another option is the work currently being done by the British Film Institute on the production and marketing of "stars." For example, even if Joan Crawford as Mildred Pierce (in the film of that title) is remanded to the family at the end of the film, Joan Crawford as "star" lives on through subsidiary images of publicity and press coverage. Finally, women filmmakers are experimenting with the medium to discover its capacity to express our desire. This work must be supported by feminist critical readings of their films.

One certainly hesitates to authorize feminist speech by quoting from Freud, but at the same time it is satisfying to realize that his challenge to learn about femininity by "inquir[ing] from your own experiences of life, or turn[ing] to the poets, or wait[ing] until science can give you deeper and more coherent information" is being met and even gone beyond.[27] The enigma not just of femininity but of the relationship between psychosexuality and culture is an enigma currently subject to critical interrogation by numerous feminist thinkers, the work of some of whom it has been the purpose of this article to explore.

Notes

1. See, for example, Luce Irigaray, *Speculum de l'autre femme* (Paris: Editions de Minuit, 1974) and *Ce sexe qui n'en est pas un* (Paris: Editions de Minuit, 1977), translated by R. Albury and P. Foss as "That Sex Which Is Not One," in *Language, Sexuality, Subversion*, ed. Paul Foss and Meaghan Morris (Darlington, Australia: Feral Publications, 1978); Sarah Kofman, *L'Enigme de la femme: La femme dans les textes de Freud* (Paris: Editions Galilée, 1980), and "The Narcissistic Woman: Freud and Girard," *Diacritics* 10 (Fall 1980): 36–45; Julia Kristeva, "Le Sujet en proces: Le langage poetique," in *L'identité* (Paris: Editions Grasset et Fasquelle, 1977). English translations of works by French feminists that have appeared since the original publication of this article include Luce Irigaray, *Speculum of the Other Woman* (Ithaca, N.Y.: Cornell University Press, 1985), and *This Sex Which Is Not One* (Ithaca, N.Y.: Cornell University Press, 1985); Kofman, *The Enigma of Woman: Woman in Freud's Writings* (Ithaca, N.Y.: Cornell University Press, 1985); and Kristeva, *Powers of Horror* (New York: Columbia University Press, 1982). For a contribution by British feminists, see *Feminine Sexuality: Jacques Lacan and the école freudienne*, trans. Jacqueline Rose, ed. and intro. Juliet Mitchell and Jacqueline Rose (New York: Norton, 1983).

2. Patrice Petro, *Joyless Streets: Women and Melodramatic Representation in Weimar Germany* (Princeton, N.J.: Princeton University Press, 1989); Tania

Modleski, *Feminism without Women: Culture and Criticism in a "Postfeminist Age"* (New York and London: Routledge, 1991); Diane Waldman, "Film Theory and the Gendered Spectator: The Female or the Feminist Reader?" *Camera Obscura* 18 (1989): 80–94; Constance Penley, *The Future of an Illusion: Film, Feminism, and Psychoanalysis* (Minneapolis: University of Minnesota Press, 1989); Maureen Turim, *Flashbacks in Film: Memory and History* (New York and London: Routledge, 1989).

3. Laura Mulvey, "Visual Pleasure and Narrative Cinema," *Screen* 16 (Autumn 1975): 6–18.

4. Ibid., 9.

5. Ibid., 11.

6. Ibid., 13–14.

7. Quoted in Ernest Jones, M.D., *The Life and Work of Sigmund Freud*, vol. 2, 1901–1919 (New York: Basic Books, 1955), 421.

8. Juliet Mitchell, *Psychoanalysis and Feminism* (Harmondsworth, England: Penguin, 1975); Jacqueline Rose, "Psychoanalysis and Feminism," minicourse for the Centre Universitaire Americain du Cinéma à Paris, December 1981. The publication of *Feminine Sexuality: Jacques Lacan and the école freudienne* has occurred since this article was originally published. It is in their lengthy introductions to the selected essays that Juliet Mitchell and Jacqueline Rose elaborate on the ideas referred to here.

9. Sigmund Freud, "The Infantile Genital Organization: An Interpolation into the Theory of Sexuality" (1923), in *The Ego and the Id*, vol. 19 of *The Standard Edition of the Complete Psychological Works of Sigmund Freud*, ed. and trans. James Strachey (London: The Hogarth Press and the Institute of Psychoanalysis, 1953–1974); "Femininity" (1933), in *New Introductory Lectures on Psychoanalysis*, vol. 22 of *The Standard Edition*.

10. Joseph Breuer and Sigmund Freud, *Studies on Hysteria* (1893–1895), vol. 2, *The Standard Edition*; Sigmund Freud, *Three Essays on the Theory of Sexuality* (1905), vol. 7, *The Standard Edition*.

11. Freud, "Femininity" (1933), vol. 21, *The Standard Edition*, 135.

12. Freud, "Feminine Sexuality" (1931), vol. 21, *The Standard Edition*.

13. Laura Mulvey, "Afterthoughts on 'Visual Pleasure and Narrative Cinema' inspired by *Duel in the Sun* (King Vidor, 1946)," *Framework* 15–17 (1981): 12–15.

14. Since this article was originally published the possibility that male spectators might identify with a female protagonist has been explored by Richard Dyer (*Gays and Film* [New York: Zoetrope, 1984]), among others.

15. Mulvey, "Afterthoughts," 12.

16. Mulvey, "Afterthoughts," 13.

17. Mulvey, "Afterthoughts," 15.

18. Monique Plaza, " 'Phallomorphic Power' and the Psychology of 'Woman': A Patriarchal Chain," trans. Miriam David and Jill Hodges, in *Human Sexual Relations: Towards a Redefinition of Sexual Politics*, ed. Mike Brake (New York: Pantheon, 1982). Originally, "Pouvoir 'Phallomorphique' et la psychologie de 'la Femme,'" *Questions Feminist* 1 (November 1977).

19. Jean Laplanche, *Life and Death in Psychoanalysis*, trans. Jeffrey Mehlman

(1970; Baltimore: The Johns Hopkins University Press, 1976). The discussion of "propping" is central to this book.

20. Plaza, " 'Phallomorphic Power,' " 328.

21. Plaza, " 'Phallomorphic Power,' " 347–48.

22. Mary Ann Doane, "Woman's Stake: Filming the Female Body," *October* 17 (Summer 1981): 23–36. Doane cites Michele Montrelay, "Inquiry into Femininity," *m/f* 1 (1978): 83–101. "Woman's Stake" has recently been collected as chap. 1 in Mary Ann Doane, *Femmes Fatales: Feminism, Film Theory, Psychoanalysis* (New York and London: Routledge, 1991).

23. Doane cites the work of Julia Kristeva in this context.

24. Christian Metz, "The Imaginary Signifier," *Screen* 16 (Summer 1975): 14–76. Translated from the original French version, which appeared in *Communications* 23 (1975): 3–55.

25. Miriam David and Jill Hodges, the translators of Plaza's " 'Phallomorphic Power,' " have translated *bouclage* as "chain."

26. Mary Ann Doane, "*Caught* and *Rebecca*: The Inscription of Femininity as Absence," *Enclitic* 5, no. 2 (Fall 1981), and 6, no. 1 (Spring 1982): 75–89. This article has been revised as "Female Spectatorship and Machines of Projection: *Caught* and *Rebecca*," chap. 6 in Mary Ann Doane, *The Desire to Desire: The Woman's Film of the 1940s* (Bloomington: Indiana University Press, 1987).

27. Freud, "Feminine Sexuality," 135.

Feminism, Psychoanalysis, and Female-Oriented Melodramas of the 1950s

Jackie Byars

In the aftermath of World War II, upwardly and physically mobile families were uprooted and American commitment to the extended family (always more of a utopian fantasy than an actuality) waned.[1] Even as Americans seemed to embrace a model of the nuclear family centered on a heterosexual couple with the male as the sole breadwinner, the nuclear family seemed threatened as increasing numbers of women left their homes to enter the work force. Sociohistorical and economic conditions began to allow the questioning of the family, the foundation of American society: was it a "natural" or a social collective? Hollywood, too, moved in this direction of inquiry as filmmakers working in a variety of genres—from Westerns to thrillers—turned to the family.[2] The genre that most effectively and directly addressed this institution and the tensions of heterosexual desire was the melodrama. The various film melodramas of the 1950s—maternal melodramas, patriarchal melodramas, lover-centered melodramas—laid bare the family's internal contradictions more explicitly than any other film genre, as Geoffrey Nowell-Smith explains:

> Melodrama can . . . be seen as a contradictory nexus, in which certain
> determinations (social, physical, artistic) are brought together but in
> which the problem of the articulation of these determinations is not suc-
> cessfully resolved. The importance of melodrama . . . lies precisely in its
> ideological failure. Because it cannot accommodate its problem, either in

a real present or in an ideal future, but lays them open in their shame-
less contradictoriness, it opens a space which most Hollywood forms have
studiously closed off.[3]

During the 1950s, a distinctly family-oriented melodramatic form developed, a form focused on conflict indigenous to the family. This rich and ambiguous group of film melodramas simultaneously championed and criticized the institution of the family and the gender roles it entails. And
although a majority of these family melodramas were male oriented, a substantial minority were organized around a woman's point of view, her
problems, and her desires.[4] These films called attention to gendered identity construction during a period when precisely what it means to be a
woman and, as a result, what it means to be a man were becoming controversial, and the space they opened was a space for women's voices.

Because psychoanalysis attempts to theorize the construction of the individual identity within the patriarchal family and, at the same time, to account for patriarchy itself, feminists have argued that it offers some potential for demystification of the status quo and, therefore, for analysis of
gender representation. Psychoanalysis would seem, then, a useful tool for
understanding melodrama, but because they do not encourage us to analyze (or recognize) women's voices in our cultural texts, the psychoanalytic
theories of Freud and Lacan that have recently dominated feminist film
theory and criticism have proved to be of only limited value in understanding these films, particularly as they relate to the material conditions of
their production and reception.

Although their work has received little attention from feminist film theorists and critics, the newer psychoanalytic models presented by Nancy
Chodorow and Carol Gilligan offer a more productive framework for
analyzing melodrama. Chodorow and Gilligan have described socially constructed gender-linked differences in modes of thinking and communicating that do not present the male as normative, and their descriptions of
these identity differences—and modes of interpersonal interactions that
result from them—correspond remarkably closely to the representations
of gender in the female-oriented melodramas of the fifties. In this essay,
I will examine the limitations of Freudian and Lacanian theories, showing
how they are insufficient for the project of feminist film theory and criticism, particularly for explaining female-oriented films. Then I will address
the advantages and limitations of Chodorow's and Gilligan's theorizing, explaining how they have helped me to more adequately understand the contradictions inherent in female-oriented melodramas of the 1950s.

In her pioneering 1975 *Screen* article, "Visual Pleasure and Narrative
Cinema," Laura Mulvey laid the groundwork for a political use of psychoanalysis in feminist film studies, charging that previous work in the

area had not sufficiently addressed representation of "the female form in a symbolic order in which in the last resort, it speaks castration and nothing else." Claiming that psychoanalysis gives an "exact rendering of the women's frustration experienced under the phallocentric order" (a claim I dispute), she launched her examination of filmic representation of women on the basis that "psychoanalytic theory as it stands can at least advance our understanding of the status quo, of the patriarchal order in which we are caught" (a claim I do not dispute).[5] Many on the left have considered progressive political analysis (generally Marxist) incommensurable with psychoanalysis,[6] but many feminists, even Marxist feminists (with the inherent feminist focus on the private sphere) have, since the mid-1970s, turned to psychoanalysis for an explanatory theory. American literary theorist Jane Gallop, for example, has supported the political use of psychoanalysis. In *The Daughter's Seduction*, she argued that

> one of psychoanalysis' consistent errors is to reduce everything to a family paradigm. Sociopolitical questions are always brought back to the model father-mother-child. Class conflict and revolution are understood as a repetition of parent-child relations. This has always been the pernicious apoliticism of psychoanalysis. . . . [And] what is necessary to get beyond this dilemma is a recognition that the enclosed, cellular model of the family used in such psychoanalytic thinking is an idealization, a secondary revision of the family. The family never was, in any of Freud's texts, completely closed off from questions of economic class.[7]

Freudian and Lacanian psychoanalysis became a primary tool for feminist film analysis, initially among the members of the editorial board of the British film journal *Screen*, among French film theorists, and later among their students and readers, many of them American. However, although these theorists and critics were generally critical of the power imbalance inherent in society and in the modern nuclear family, they based their work on Freudian and Lacanian theories of psychoanalysis, which describe the masculine as normative and the feminine as aberrant. These theories, unless modified significantly, cannot account for resistance and ideological struggle; they represent, instead, the psychic mechanisms for reinforcing dominant ideologies. The resulting film theory does explain a remarkable number of Hollywood films, but it fails to explain and, in fact, misrepresents a significant minority of these texts. This theoretical approach–which incorporated the totalizing notion of "classic realist cinema" with the universalizing of a male-oriented theory of psychoanalysis–underestimates both the complexity and variety of mainstream narratives and the potential for consuming them in ways that challenge patriarchy.

The earliest influence of psychoanalysis on film theory and criticism produced an approach focused on the oedipal "family romance," which, it was claimed, generates plot patterns. Popular in the late 1960s and early 1970s, this Freudian mode of interpretation, which concentrated on narrative content, began to lose favor in the mid- to late seventies, when film theorists turned to a second strain that had a more linguistic orientation, focusing on filmic texts as signifying processes and analyzing their enunciative patterns.[8] But even in the late 1970s, Stephen Heath and Geoffrey Nowell-Smith, writing for *Screen*, argued that "to understand melodrama in the cinema is necessarily to attempt to focus the investment in a constant repetition of family romance fantasizing both in its themes and its process of relations and positions of the subject-spectator."[9] While many film theorists were moving away from this (chronologically) first strain, these *Screen* theorist-critics believed, correctly, that the first is as important as the second strain, especially in relation to the family melodrama, but interpretation in terms of Freud's description of the oedipal scenario is, alone, insufficient.

Freud's description of the "family romance" depends on a notion of psychic development beginning with a masculine origin that he dissimulated as unisex. He described male development as normal, juxtaposing female development in terms of its deviance from this norm. According to Freud, the relationship of the male child with his mother eventually takes on sexual overtones, and the child begins to see his father as a rival for his mother's affections. He fantasizes murdering or castrating his father but then fears retaliation (his own castration) and so denies himself the love for his mother, instead identifying with his father, and is reassured of his sexual superiority to all that is feminine. For the male, the entry into the adult social order is the road to normalcy, and he "naturally" transfers his early, primary narcissistic self-love to "normal" object love, first to his mother and later to some other woman.

For the female, Freud believed, this was impossible. Focusing on anatomical difference, with the male as norm, Freud posited a "genital trauma" in the female child as she realizes that she is anatomically "inferior" – she does not possess a penis. She comes to despise herself and all those like her, especially her mother, and the feelings of castration and inadequacy manifest themselves in "penis envy." She turns angrily from her mother, who is not only penisless but also a rival for the affections of her father, now the object of her love. Eventually, she regains self-esteem through a narcissistic vanity. But, according to Freud, women never develop "normal" object-love, which he privileged as ethically superior; they experience, he argued, an artificial object-love through their children. Women may appear to "win," but there is no normalcy for women. Woman is the unknown, the unknowable, the Other – not male. Fundamentally narcissistic and penisless (castrated), woman only artificially displaces her narcissism with object-love.

Laura Mulvey has used Freudian theory in attempting to explain how the female viewer derives pleasure from a Hollywood genre film that is "structured around masculine pleasure, offering an identification with the *active* point of view."[10] She argued that this identification allows a woman spectator "to rediscover that lost [masculine] aspect of her sexual identity," the never fully repressed bedrock of feminine repression. Mulvey insisted that such an accomplishment is derived through a transsex identification in which the female spectator temporarily remembers her masculine, active stage. Within a theory based on Freudian psychoanalysis, as Mulvey's is, the male or masculine is inherently, essentially both active and normative, and the female or feminine is explicable only through reference to this norm.[11] Within this realm of film theory, then, there is no way to explain resisting, different "voices" that function at both the narrative and the enunciative levels, and there is no way to explain the pleasure of the female spectator without reference to a masculine "norm."

Indeed, a primary obstacle for feminist film studies is this dependence on Freudian and Lacanian psychoanalytic theories, which tie gender to biology rather than to social structures. Both Freudian and Lacanian theories of psychoanalysis operate conservatively to extend and naturalize the repression of women, defining "woman" in terms of aberrance and deviance and effectively obscuring any variant "voice." According to Lacanian psychoanalysis, in fact, sexuality is produced only in and through language, and language constructs woman as *not* man. The male—or masculine—voice that dominates our society and structures sexuality and gender also structures the very theories we use to explain them. Male-dominant theorizing consigns women to an inevitable secondary status and obscures nondominant voices.[12] Recent developments in psychoanalytic theory and in the social sciences challenge Freud's attitude toward narcissism and his interpretation of psychosexual development; however, most psychoanalytic film theory and analysis remains based on either an orthodox Freudianism or on Lacan's rereading of Freud, which is also skewed in favor of the masculine.[13]

Lacan argued powerfully that the individual *is* constructed socially; he saw the individual as constituted through language, through a process of initiation into "the" Symbolic order that establishes for the individual a sense of separateness from the rest of the world and awareness of the nature of signification. Sexuality, he argued, is only ever in language, and language defines woman as *not* man. This symbol system privileges, not surprisingly, the masculine authority it supports and is supported by; it expresses prohibition and the law in terms of the phallus, which Lacan claimed is an abstraction with no necessary reference to anatomy. Even within the Lacanian tradition, challenges have been made to this theory. Some of his followers assign femininity a prelinguistic, presymbolic point of origin. For Lacan, however, there is no prediscursive reality, and these challenges attack the very crux of his theory, the determinant nature of the Symbolic.[14] But his arguments are persuasive, and even if the terms he uses and his privileging of the masculine are offensive, his emphasis on the social construction of individuals is useful. And his argument that authority is vested in the masculine is, at least in our society, difficult to dispute; a Lacanian approach does account for the bulk of Hollywood films, which are, in fact, male-oriented. As Jacqueline Rose argues:

> Lacan gives an account of how the status of the phallus in human sexuality enjoins on the woman a definition in which she is simultaneously symptom and myth. As long as we continue to feel the effects of that definition, we cannot afford to ignore this description of the fundamental imposture which sustains it.[15]

But significant problems within Lacanian theory limit its usefulness for cultural studies. Lacan's emphasis on the linguistic obscures, even ignores, the very real nonlinguistic determinants in the constitution of an individual. And there is a distinct tendency on the part of Lacan and his followers to universalize his theory, to assume that all individuals ("subjects") in all societies at all times are constituted in the same way. This transcendentalism is basically incompatible with any notion of historical materialism. In a critique of what he and his compatriots at the Center for Contemporary Cultural Studies at the University of Birmingham called "screen theory," Stuart Hall addressed this problem in Lacan's theory, arguing that subject formation is neither transhistorical nor transsocial. He noted that it is "difficult, if not impossible to square this universal form of argument with the premises of historical materialism . . . which historicizes the different forms of subjectivity and which needs a reference to specific modes of production, to definite societies at historically specific moments and conjunctures. The two kinds of theory are conceptually incompatible in the form of their argument."[16]

Because of the tendency to universalize, the Lacanian approach fails to account for differences among various patriarchal ideologies, for any nondominant ideologies, and for any concept of struggle and change in ideology. In addition, Lacan's highly phallocentric theory appears to consign women necessarily and irreversibly to patriarchy, and although it is the case that our society is patriarchal, this approach fails to account for the challenges to and changes in our social structure, challenges and changes that mitigate against patriarchy. Although the Lacanian description of identity development has value as a description of the status quo, it is incomplete and cannot be used to explain ideological change. Neither can it explain all cultural texts, even mass-produced texts, even in a patriarchal society.

Mainstream film texts cannot be removed from the material conditions in which they are produced and consumed, nor can they be separated from the ideological struggles of which they are a part. They are not simple texts; they not only are not necessarily ideologically coherent but also are not monolithically repressive.[17] They are participants in an ongoing ideological process; real ideological struggle goes on in and with mainstream entertainment texts, and ideological struggle goes on in theory as well. To understand and explain this struggle and the existence and role of "different voices" in Hollywood's films, we must read Freudian and Lacanian theories of psychoanalysis through the eyes of contemporary feminism–if we keep these theories at all, which some theorists feel we shouldn't. I find them helpful but feel that we must rework these powerful theoretical constructs in ways that both acknowledge the validity of female experience and help to explain the active role of women in ideological change. The work of Nancy Chodorow and of Carol Gilligan–and that of their critics–offers fertile ground for feminist film theory.

Chodorow's pioneering *The Reproduction of Mothering* has been hailed as "the most comprehensive and articulate explanation of gender difference as a social fact to date."[18] Because of social, economic, political, and cultural inequities, women's experiences of the world are different from those of men, and they develop in qualitatively different (not inferior or superior) ways. Chodorow presented a basic rereading of Freudian theory, a theoretical account for the asymmetrical organization of gender that she contended is generated by and reproduces women's mothering. Chodorow works in the tradition of "object relations" theory, which posits, like Lacan, that the individual is a social construction but which claims, against Lacan, that the child's social relations determine psychological growth and identity formation. Object-relations psychoanalysts focus their attention on the infant-mother relationship, seeing the mother as the infant's most important object, and Chodorow described the process by which women reproduce themselves by producing female children who want to mother.

Chodorow drew on clinical evidence and a consideration of the social setting in which it was obtained, and she presented a positive reassessment of female development. Rejecting Freud's emphasis on the child's discovery of anatomical difference, she focused much more extensively on the pre-oedipal phase. Her evidence showed that the first identification for both male and female infants is with the primary parent, the mother, contradicting Freud by asserting that the boy's development involves a negation of the primary identity but that the girl's does not. Chodorow also countered Freud in her insistence that the girl child does not give up her attachment to her mother during the oedipal stage but develops instead a triadic model for relationships. The male, on the other hand, represses his identification with the mother and develops a sense of difference and separateness. Because girls are parented by a person of the same gender, they experience themselves as more continuous with the external world than do boys. Girls develop more flexible ego boundaries and more fluid senses of identity; they define themselves in terms of relationships rather than in terms of separateness and individuality. Also, because they don't develop the masculine sense of justice and morality that is based on a denial of relationship and connection and that is dependent on an uncompromising superego, females are more capable of empathy.

In this society, which assigns primary responsibility for parenting to women, men and women develop into incompatible people. Both males and females desire a return to the original emotional nurturance they experienced as infants, but the male sense of separateness brought about by being parented by a person of a different gender causes most men to be incapable of providing this sort of nurturance. Women, on the other hand, are conditioned to give it as well as to desire it, but they rarely receive it from men. And whereas men form dyadic relationships, the triadic model—formed in females during the oedipal period—is followed by women as they extend their affection also to their children and maintain close ties to their mothers and other women friends.

Although Chodorow noted that all known sex-gender systems have been male dominated, her feminist position and her attention to historical and material conditions have led to a theory that, with modification, may have the potential to account for change. Women's roles are historical and social products and the nature of women's mothering is not transcultural or universal, Chodorow argued, pointing to contradictions within the process that reproduces mothering. The forms of the tensions and strains created by these contradictions are, she argued, dependent partially on internal developments within the sex-gender system and partially on external historical conditions, particularly on changes in the organization of production. A fusion of these forces can lead, as it has in our time, to widespread and even explicitly political resistance to dominant patterns. Chodorow noted particularly the recent attention to males involved in primary parenting, speculating that

> equal parenting [by males and females] would leave people of both
> genders with the positive capacities each has, but without the destruc-
> tive extremes these currently tend toward. . . . Men would be able to
> retain the autonomy which comes from differentiation without that
> differentiation being rigid and reactive, and women would have more op-
> portunity to gain it. People's sexual choices might become more flexible,
> less desperate.[19]

The notion of equal parenting constitutes a basic challenge to our social, economic, and ideological organization, but the "more positive" development of gender proposed by Chodorow would depend on significant social, economic, and ideological changes – changes that might be welcomed by even those who feel that Chodorow's theorizing stops short.

Chodorow's documentation of the emotional primacy of women for other women has tantalized some feminist theorists who want to push her theorizing further, to account for a range of female friendships. They feel she fails to acknowledge and theorize the range of important female relationships, as well as the practical impediments to these relationships imposed by a society in which heterosexuality is dominant (witch burning, male control of law, production of narrative texts – like Hollywood films – driven by a celebration of heterosexual romance, for example).[20] Noting that Chodorow comes "close to the edge of an acknowledgement of lesbian existence," Adrienne Rich has critiqued Chodorow's assumption that heterosexuality is the norm, describing Chodorow as "stuck with trying to reform a man-made institution – compulsory heterosexuality – as if, despite profound emotional impulses drawing women toward women, there is some mystical/biological heterosexual inclination, a 'preference' or 'choice' which draws women to men."[21] Janice Raymond pushed the critique further, arguing that Chodorow's theories actually – though not consciously – boost "hetero-reality" by failing to emphasize the importance of women's relationships with women and subtly encouraging women to "live for men."[22] Raymond argued that male parenting will actually enhance male supremacy by giving men more power than they already have rather than encouraging acknowledgement of female friendships; power is at stake here, political considerations are primary. And Rich pointed in a profitable direction for adapting Chodorow's work by suggesting that "heterosexuality, like motherhood, needs to be recognized as a *political institution*."[23]

Like all dominant political institutions, heterosexuality receives constant ideological (and sometimes compulsory) reinforcement. In the bulk of Hollywood films, heterosexual relationships and male relationships with other men dominate, with women represented only in terms of their relationships with men or in terms of their conflict or competition with other women. But in a significant minority of films – even very successful films – women's emotional attachments to other women are prominent, and teasing out this tendency in Chodorow's theorizing produces a potentially emancipatory approach to interpreting these female-oriented films. Understanding the possibilities for resistance empowers more than a simple understanding of victimization; we must, in fact, understand the conditions of victimization and the possibilities for agency under oppression.[24]

Carol Gilligan's research and theorizing productively complement Chodorow's, as do the critiques of the work; her emphasis on discourse is of particular value for film theory and criticism. Analyzing interviews with people on the topic of morality, Gilligan found distinct differences between the way males and females talk, differences strikingly similar to those found by Chodorow. Gilligan described two distinct perspectives, two modes of thinking, two different experiences of self. One, the male, is rooted in objectivity and impartiality, is premised "on a fundamental separation between other and self," and is characterized by reciprocity, the need to receive in response to one's giving. The other, the female perspective, is based in a blurring of boundaries between self and other, allows feelings to influence thought, and is characterized by response and connectedness. Addressing psychoanalytic theorizing, Gilligan argued that Freud's desire to eliminate contradictions within his theory "blinded him to the reality of women's experience" and to the asymmetrical personality development of males and females. He lived in a society "where women's lives were not considered to inform human possibility," and he worked with a notion of theory construction limited by a "conception of objectivity in science that led to a series of enforced separations" (the analytic situation) characteristic of the masculine perspective.[25]

Some of Gilligan's critics contend that other significant factors – such as occupation – can account for the distinctions she attributed to gender, and some are uneasy with linking these characteristics to sex differences. Joan Tronto, for instance, argued that Gilligan's equation of "care" with "female" has not been adequately supported and is fraught with philosophical peril.[26] Claudia Card, focusing on Gilligan's contrast between a female ethics of responsibility and a male ethics of rights, argued that Gilligan may have mistaken a misplaced female gratitude to men for their "benefactions" – which females could, in fact, not refuse – for a discourse of caring. Like Rich and Raymond, who objected to Chodorow's primary emphasis on psychological reasons for the reproduction of heterosexual dominance, Card wants Gilligan's analysis of discourse expanded to include attention to the material – and often violent – realities women live, realities in which they may seek male approval not for its own sake and not because they "care" about maintaining relationships but because they feel the approval is necessary for their security (for example, protection against violent assault or for job security).[27] Card suggested that such action and the discourse that naturalizes it actually entrench that need. In addition, she fears that Gilligan's focus on improving the quality of connectedness (a concern attributed to the female) may, politically, be self-defeating; separation can be more empowering than destructive relationships with men, and the discourse of connectedness works against that separation by naturalizing female concern with relationships.

In addition, some critics consider Gilligan and Chodorow essentialists, but in fact neither Gilligan nor Chodorow actually argued that the differences described are essentially gendered; the differences and the discourses that reinforce them are, however, very real and most often gender-connected in our society. Gilligan, for instance, reported that males and females describe themselves differently—females in terms of relationships, males in terms of separation—but she did not argue that these distinctions are absolute. Rather, she contended that once we see them, we may begin to see the existence of feminine traits in men and vice versa. Whatever the perils of these gendered differences, they are differences that are socially constructed and discursively reinforced. Theorizing such as that done by Chodorow, Gilligan, Rich, Raymond, and Card allows both the expansion of psychoanalytic theory to explain gender differences in social rather than biological terms and the theorizing of gender construction and representation in terms of hierarchies of power.[28] It may help us move toward a materialist psychoanalysis, toward a theory that can help us to understand the interaction of the economic, the psychosexual, and the discursive. They definitely aid an analysis of the female-oriented family melodramas of the 1950s.

Although neither Freudian nor Lacanian theories can provide a framework for understanding these plots, the models presented by Chodorow and Gilligan can. A model based on their theories explains certain things about the plots and about the enunciative processes of these films. Women, their lives, and their relationships with other women are important in these films, whereas they are marginalized (if not ignored) in other films. The optical point of view most frequently privileges female characters, the narratives are set in communities of women and children, and women's relationships with other women receive as much attention as their relationships with men. Chodorow argued that one way women fulfill the needs not met by a dyadic relationship is "through the creation and maintenance of important personal relations with other women," relationships generally ignored in male-oriented narratives and, indeed, in male-oriented theories. Chodorow observed that women "tend to have closer personal ties with other women" than men do with other men and that women "spend more time in the company of women than they do with men." She argued that these relationships "are one way of resolving and re-creating the mother-daughter bond and are an expression of women's general relational capacities and definition of self in relationship."[29]

Set in a community of women and children, the plot of the female-oriented melodrama is motivated by the absence of a patriarchal figure. It begins as the community is invaded by a young and virile "intruder-redeemer" who identifies the problem—the female protagonist's lack of connectedness to a male—and enables its solution: their coupling and integration into the larger community as the heterosexual core of a nuclear family unit. This narrative feature lends credence to readings arguing that family melodramas operate simply and straightforwardly to reinforce a repressive patriarchy, but a reading that focuses on the needs of the female protagonist—needs, Chodorow argued, that include the completion of a triadic relational model—requires an expansion of theory, an expansion that includes women's and men's experiences as equally valid and an expansion that recognizes the possibility of change. Such an expansion enables us to hear and see alternatives to currently dominant ideologies and struggles among ideologies, struggles made evident in the female-oriented melodramas precisely through the shamelessness of the contradictions they unveil.

The female-oriented melodramatic narratives are clearly organized around the female protagonist, and they even privilege her optical point of view, but the male is indeed central. He is crucial for the film's conclusion and for the female's entry into the larger social order; to achieve integration into the (heterosexual) social order, the female protagonist, who has lost the adult male in a triadic relationship, must acquire a mate and participate in a heterosexual dyad. For social reasons, she must create the dyad; for personal reasons, she strives to create or re-create a triad. Steve Neale noted that men are crucial to genres such as the war film and the Western, even as the genres go out of their way to incorporate "the direct representation of woman, no matter how 'contrived' or 'clumsy' this may seem in terms of the logic of a given narrative." But although melodramas and musicals tend to feature female characters, they almost always also include men as central figures. "Indeed, men are crucial to these genres, more so, perhaps than women to war films and westerns."[30]

The male *is* crucial to the narrative; he enables the female protagonist to complete a family unit, complete with often overlapping relational triads. But it is not the male's action that precipitates closure, and this marks the form as distinctly different from male-oriented melodramas. A contradictory combination of female independence (the willingness to confront social norms) and dependence (the need for male companionship) provides a common thread throughout the female-oriented melodramas of the 1950s. The solution may be obtained only through the action of the female protagonist or less frequently through her surrogate. She is enabled to act on her desires for the intruder-redeemer, even if she must challenge prevailing social standards, only because of a fantastic narrative rupture, which heightens the solution's artificiality and exposes the contradictions it so transparently attempts to overcome. The often improbable "happy endings" in female-oriented family melodramas have caused critics to ridicule the genre and its audience, leading to the notion that the films do function simply and solely to reinforce dominant ideology, to champion the heterosexual dyad.

The solution—the creation of the triadic model through the completion of a heterosexual dyad–does participate in the reproduction of a patriarchal sex-gender system. Of course these mainstream narratives reinforce dominant ideologies. That is a major function of mainstream cultural texts, and it would be surprising if they presented an overt and radical challenge to systems dominant at the time of their production. And contemporary American patriarchy–a patriarchy slightly altered by the struggles over gender construction that became increasingly obvious in the wake of World War II–is precisely the status quo described by both Chodorow and Gilligan. After World War II, at the same time increasing classes of women who–until the war–had never worked outside the home were entering the labor force and exerting unprecedented influence over financial decisions within the family, most Americans appeared to wholeheartedly embrace the model of the hierarchical nuclear family based on a heterosexual couple, with the man as the breadwinner (and therefore in charge of money matters) and the woman working in the home. The contradictions embodied in such a reality are the contradictions at the core of the female-oriented melodramas of the 1950s, which privilege women's experiences but insist that–in the end–she be firmly and happily partnered with a man, no matter how improbable the match. Chodorow and Gilligan have described an asymmetrically organized sex-gender system that privileges the male and the masculine but that also includes rewards for females, rewards that encourage, even necessitate, female participation in a system that represses women, and this group of films depicts a world in which women's needs (however contradictory, however complicitous with patriarchy) are significant. Unlike Freud and Lacan, Chodorow and Gilligan did not describe the masculine (or the feminine) as normative; neither did they describe patriarchy as inherent, inevitable, or unchangeable.

Chodorow and Gilligan describe contradiction, and they have enabled this critic to read the narrative contortions (ruptures?) that were necessary in order to produce the deus-ex-machina endings common to the female-oriented melodramas of the 1950s as contortions that expose contradictions rather than resolve them. A primary task of feminist criticism has been to expose the ideological grain of a text as we read against it, so that we may challenge it. Although their work is not without its flaws and they have not provided definitive guidance, Chodorow and Gilligan have allowed me to reread a group of films in a way that values women and their patterns of relating and communicating. Chodorow and Gilligan have led me to reflect on these films and the context in which they were produced and consumed in a way that calls attention to an ongoing struggle against oppression and silence in a period when gender construction and its relation to family structure were becoming controversial, but the vocabulary for the debate had not yet been developed–especially in the mainstream media.

Notes

1. The bulk of this essay was originally published as a portion of a chapter in my book, *All That Hollywood Allows: Re-reading Gender in 1950s Melodrama* (Chapel Hill: University of North Carolina Press; London: Routledge, 1991); see 136–48. Other parts of the chapter draw on Chodorow's and Gilligan's theorizing in reading the "family romance" plots and the enunciative patterns of female-oriented melodramas of the 1950s.

2. The plot of *The Searchers* (John Ford, 1956) is organized around the unification of the family, and *The Wrong Man* (Alfred Hitchcock, 1957) and *The Man Who Knew Too Much* (Hitchcock, 1956) both depict external forces pressuring a family unit and chronicle the resulting interpersonal conflicts.

3. Geoffrey Nowell-Smith, "Minnelli and Melodrama," *Screen* 18 (Summer 1977): 118.

4. During the 1950s, Ross Hunter recognized the potential profits from the audience that had previously supported the "women's films" so popular in the thirties and forties and polished Universal Studio's young contract players and refurbished old ones to provide an update of this previously popular genre. His exploitation of the female matinee audience brought Universal a growing share of the fragmenting American audience, and other studios followed suit. (See Andrew Dowdy, *The Films of the Fifties* [New York: William Morrow, 1973], 183.) Some of the films, in fact, must have appealed to more than just matinee audiences, since they reached *Variety*'s annual list of Top Twenty Moneymakers. *Magnificent Obsession* (1954)–directed by Douglas Sirk, produced by Ross Hunter for Universal Studios, and based on a 1935 film adapted from a Lloyd C. Douglas novel and directed by John Stahl–tied for number 7 on the *Variety* list in the year it was released. Prompted by its phenomenal success, Universal once again combined Ross Hunter with Douglas Sirk and an almost identical cast to make *All That Heaven Allows*; this film did not make the *Variety* list, but other studios followed suit anyway. *Picnic* (1955)–adapted for Columbia Pictures from William Inge's stage play and directed by Joshua Logan (also a Broadway director)–reached number 6 in 1956, and *Peyton Place* (1957)–adapted from Grace Metalious's controversial novel and directed by Mark Robson for Twentieth Century-Fox–was number 2 in 1958. Universal repeated its earlier success when *Imitation of Life* (1959)–directed by Douglas Sirk, a remake of the 1934 film of the same name that was directed by John Stahl and adapted from a Fannie Hurst best-seller–was number 4 in 1959.

5. Laura Mulvey, "Visual Pleasure and Narrative Cinema," *Screen* 16 (Autumn 1975): 7. For a description of *Screen*'s participation in this endeavor, 1971 to 1977, see Philip Rosen, "*Screen* and the Marxist Project in Film Criticism," *Quarterly Review of Film Studies* 2 (August 1977).

6. In conversations, sociologist Stanley Aronowitz has claimed the incommensurability of Marxism and psychoanalysis, and philosopher Nancy Fraser has also expressed serious doubts concerning the adequacy of (any theory of) psychoanalysis as an explanatory social theory.

7. Jane Gallop, *The Daughter's Seduction* (Ithaca, N.Y.: Cornell University Press, 1982), 144.

8. Charles F. Altman, in "Psychoanalysis and Cinema: The Imaginary Dis-

course," *Quarterly Review of Film Studies* 11 (August 1977), traces these two strains of psychoanalytic film analysis, as they were pursued by the French theoretical avant-garde, in his review of volume 23 of the French journal *Communications*, a special issue on psychoanalysis and the cinema edited by Christian Metz, Thierry Kuntzel, and Raymond Bellour.

9. Stephen Heath and Geoffrey Nowell-Smith, "A Note on 'Family Romance,' " *Screen* 18 (Summer 1977): 119.

10. Laura Mulvey, "Visual Pleasure and Narrative Cinema" and "Afterthoughts on 'Visual Pleasure and Narrative Cinema' Inspired by *Duel in the Sun* (King Vidor, 1946)" *Framework* 15-17 (1981): 12-15.

11. Mulvey, "Afterthoughts."

12. Researchers in numerous areas have found that the theories on which they based their analysis were themselves the problem. In *In a Different Voice* Carol Gilligan notes the difficulties she encountered in trying to explain female experiences with theories based on research on males. Researchers in interpersonal communication have met with a similar problem. Puzzled by their difficulty in interpreting data collected in their research on storytelling – data collected from women – Kristin Langellier and Deanna Hall realized that "research on storytelling has focused on stories gathered primarily from male subjects, and this research has analyzed stories from a 'male-as-norm' perspective." Women's communication experience had not previously been considered worthy of study, and women's storytelling had been described as deviant or deficient by comparison to male models. Such research implies that women cannot tell stories "right" and that what women tell are not "real" stories. In fact, their problem was that data had repeatedly been collected on men's storytelling, usually in public places, and generalized to the entire speech community. As a result, the structures, purposes, styles, strategies, and functions of women's storytelling have – until recently – been inadequately understood. (Quotes are from "Storytelling Strategies in Mother-Daughter Communication," a paper delivered at the International Communication Association annual conference, Chicago, May 1986.)

13. In "On Narcissism," *Telos* 44 (Summer 1980), sociologist Stanley Aronowitz argues that the sense of autonomy gained from a self-affirmative narcissism is necessary for sexual and political liberation. This radical departure from the negative attitude toward narcissism evidenced by Freud is also found in French psychoanalyst Sarah Kofman's article "The Narcissistic Woman: Freud and Girard," *Diacritics* 10 (Fall 1980). In this article, Kofman presents a thorough reading of Freud's essay "On Narcissism," one of the few points in the body of his work where he opens up in a less negative direction for studying the female.

14. For a description and analysis of this debate in the Lacanian camp, see Monique David-Menard, "Lacanians against Lacan," *Social Text* 6 (Fall 1982): 86-111.

15. Jacqueline Rose, "Introduction – II," in Jacques Lacan, *Feminine Sexuality*, trans. Jacqueline Rose, ed. Juliet Mitchell and Jacqueline Rose (New York: Norton, 1982), 57.

16. Stuart Hall, "Recent developments in theories of language and ideology: a critical note," in *Culture, Media, Language*, ed. Stuart Hall et al. (London: Hutchinson, 1980), 160.

17. I make this argument as it pertains to television in "Reading Feminine Discourse: Prime-Time Television in the U.S.," *Communication* 9, nos. 3–4 (1987), and in terms of both film and television in "Gazes/Voices/Power," in *Female Spectators: Looking at Film and Television*, ed. E. Deidre Pribram (New York: Verso, 1988). In the second article, I include summaries of the analyses of *All That Heaven Allows* and *Picnic* presented in chapter 4 of *All That Hollywood Allows*, as well as an analysis of a male-oriented melodrama, *Not as a Stranger*, showing how a Lacanian approach does help to explain male-oriented films.

18. This compliment to Chodorow comes from a review of her book by Jessica Benjamin, published with reviews by Mary Brown Parlee and Carol Nadelson in Leila Lerner, ed., "Special Book Review," *Psychoanalytic Review* 69 (Spring 1982). For a review of the influence of feminist theories of psychoanalysis on literary criticism that includes attention to the influence of Chodorow, see Judith Kegan Gardiner, "Mind Mother: Psychoanalysis and Feminism," in *Making a Difference: Feminist Literary Criticism*, ed. Gayle Greene and Coppelia Kahn (New York: Methuen, 1985).

19. Nancy Chodorow, *The Reproduction of Mothering: Psychoanalysis and the Sociology of Gender* (Berkeley: University of California Press, 1978), 218.

20. Adrienne Rich, "Compulsory Heterosexuality and Lesbian Existence," *Signs: Journal of Women in Culture and Society* 5 (Summer 1980): 635–37; Janice G. Raymond, *A Passion for Friends* (Boston: Beacon Press, 1986), 49–55.

21. Rich, "Compulsory Heterosexuality," 635 and 637.

22. Raymond, *A Passion for Friends*, 55.

23. Rich, "Compulsory Heterosexuality," 637.

24. See Sarah Lucia Hoagland, *Lesbian Ethics: Toward New Value* (Palo Alto, Calif.: Institute of Lesbian Studies, 1988). Hoagland's thesis is built around understanding precisely the possibilities of agency under oppression.

25. Carol Gilligan, "The Conquistador and the Dark Continent: Reflections on the Psychology of Love," *Daedalus* 113 (Summer 1984): 88. See also Gilligan's *In a Different Voice: Psychological Theory and Women's Development* (Cambridge, Mass.: Harvard University Press, 1982).

26. Joan C. Tronto, "Beyond Gender Difference to a Theory of Care," *Signs: Journal of Women in Culture and Society* 12 (Summer 1987): 646. Tronto feels that although an ethic of care is an important intellectual concern for feminists, it should be phrased in terms not of gender difference but of the ethic's adequacy as a moral theory.

27. Claudia Card, "Women's Voices and Ethical Ideals: Must We Mean What We Say?" *Ethics* 99 (October 1988).

28. This expansion allows us to consider intervention in both the social and the biological arenas.

29. Chodorow, *The Reproduction of Mothering*, 200.

30. Stephen Neale, *Genre* (London: British Film Institute, 1980), 59.

Image and Voice: Approaches to Marxist-Feminist Film Criticism

Christine Gledhill

A major concern of any oppressed group engaged in political struggle is to contest media representation. Marxist-feminist film and media theory has developed along two sometimes overlapping, sometimes diverging strands that emphasize, respectively, image and voice. This essay examines these two strands, concluding with speculations on future development.

Image and Reality

In the 1960s, left politics grew increasingly concerned with culture as a site of ideological struggle, developing the concept of ideology to explain the apparent failure of the working-class revolution predicted by Marxism. A basic definition of ideology refers to any particular belief system used to explain society. But Marx had pointed out that the class that rules because it owns the means of production controls not only that society's wealth but also the production of its ideas.[1] The established ideas of bourgeois society misrepresent class relations, making the dominance of the ruling class appear natural: hence the concept of dominant ideology and its corollary, false consciousness, whereby the working class accepts inequality as part of the natural order.

Early feminist cultural politics focused on *images of women* circulating in the media. Feminists attacked misrepresentation, arguing that gender stereotyping both expresses and normalizes patriarchal sexual inequality. In these polemics the deadly combination of patriarchal fantasy and consumer capitalism turn woman as sex object into a marketing device. This process was analyzed not only in advertising but in Hollywood fictions, which, drawing on deeply ingrained gender stereotypes and showcasing the cornucopia of capitalism, simultaneously produce woman as object of male desire and invite the female audience to consume. Against image, stereotype, sex object, and fantasy, early feminist criticism demanded representation of "real women" – women as they really are or could be. The ideological problem was located in Hollywood's commercial production of mass entertainment. European art cinema, organized around the creative artist and middle-class audiences, appeared free to treat film as an art form capable of exploring real human relationships. Out of this opposition emerged the search for positive images of women – realistic but also liberated – to contest the negative stereotypes of the mass media.[2] This paired opposition, positive/realist versus negative/stereotyped, was to prove problematic.

In the first place, Marxism contests idealist, essentialist conceptions of reality. Marxist materialism analyzes reality not as individual experience, empirical phenomena, or spiritual perceptions but as the historical production of contradictory socioeconomic forces. An early Marxist model of society comprised an economic "base" underpinning a cultural/ideological "superstructure."[3] Where liberal humanism holds that the progress of civilization lies in the development of ideas by inspired individuals, Marx argued the reverse. Social and cultural forms are determined by a particular society's means of producing material life. The developing contradictions between the forces and social relations of production provide the dynamic of historical change and development. For example, the exploitation of the materials and processes of industrial production depends on amassing a work force whose collective interests contradict private ownership and profit. The effects of such contradictions may be felt in everyday life – for instance, in strikes and lockouts – but understanding of their operation and interrelationships within a social totality can be grasped only in theory. Similarly, if personal experience of oppression leads women to interrogate and resist aspects of our world, only the developing theoretical framework of feminism will enable us to analyze the historical forces of patriarchy and so formulate the means of change. In this sense the meaning of woman is not immanent in the world waiting to be revealed. "Woman" is a social-sexual dynamic being produced by history.

A change in the conception of reality demands a corresponding change in the aesthetic practices that seek to represent it. However, the early Marxist model of a cultural superstructure determined by an economic base perpetuated rather than challenged the liberal humanist "reflec-

tionist" model of the relations between culture and society. But where idealist approaches assume that culture reflects truth, early Marxism argued
that bourgeois culture, by inverting the relation between ideas and society, offers distorted reflections. Accordingly, the early focus on "images"
of women contested bourgeois culture for what it reflected rather than for
the premise of reflection itself. For example, it is often argued that the
glamour of the female movie star reflects a distortion of femininity
demanded by consumerism and patriarchy; or that the threateningly independent femme fatale of *film noir*, who is ritually exorcised by the plot,
reflects the need of postwar capitalism to oust women from industrial
production. In general, it was argued, such sexist stereotypes reflect male
dominance of the media. A corollary of this view demanded women's control of the media as a means of changing images of women.

This approach was questioned by neo-Marxist aesthetics of the seventies. In the first place it fosters the notion of media producers consciously
conspiring to indoctrinate a largely passive mass audience. Yet accounts
of actual social relations offered by Marxists or feminists rarely dispelled
the false consciousness inculcated by the media. Feminists found this particularly true of patriarchal ideology, where romantic love, family, and
maternity bind the sexes together in an unequal relationship at an emotional as well as economic level. Three problematic assumptions underpin
the opposition implied here between ideology and reality, stereotypes and
real women, truth and fantasy: first, that feminist understanding of the
real world can be promoted by appeal to experiences that it is assumed all
women share; second, that language and form are transparent, acting as
vehicles for the accurate reflection of reality; and third, that representation of reality should be the major goal of art and entertainment. The last
two decades of Marxist-feminist aesthetics have seen each of these assumptions challenged, the last proving the most tenacious.

The Real World, Fictional Production, and Ideology

The challenge emerged initially from the changing focus of film theory
itself, which in the late sixties and seventies gradually shifted from authorship toward genre. In seeking to address Hollywood as mass entertainment, genre theory qualified the humanist realist aesthetics that underpinned auteurism's focus on the personal vision of the creative artist.[4]
While realism demands real life, truth, authenticity, and credibility, genre
production had been largely dismissed as the source of conventions,
stereotypes, formulaic plots, cliches, and ideologies.[5] For feminists, the
Hollywood genres produced macho heroes and a subordinate, objectified
place for women.[6] The new genre criticism, however, stressed the formal
and coded dimension of film fiction, where genre conventions evolve ac-

cording to their own internal logic and histories and provide a different kind of aesthetic resource to the filmmaker. In this respect, to judge generic plot conventions and character types against the real world is inappropriate. If genres relate only indirectly to reality, the question now posed for Marxists and feminists was at what level their meanings and ideological effects could be located.

This question demanded a break with the humanist literary tradition, which assumes that artistic devices and narrative structures are the vehicles of meanings that reflect the human condition. In this tradition form expresses metaphorically the artist's vision of life. Humanist literary interpretation depends on psychological realism manifested in the rounded, complex, and individualized character as opposed to the stereotype or social type. Characters are analyzed in terms of how we think people react and behave in real life. Students and critics become amateur psychologists. The rehabilitation of convention in genre criticism that foregrounded the presence and role of fictional rules and codes challenged the notion of cinema as a direct reflection of the world or artist's vision.

This challenge was consolidated by film theory's rediscovery of Russian formalist criticism and by the growth of structuralism and semiotics. The formalist Victor Shklovsky, for example, argued that the function of aesthetic form is not to reflect, but to distort or *make strange* everyday, normal appearances. Artistic device blocks automated recognition and enables us to see anew.[7] Semiotics goes further, arguing that words and images are signs that have meaning not because they reflect a preexisting reality but because of their structural place and function in a linguistic or semiotic system.[8] The world does not provide words and images with their meaning; rather, by articulating and naming, verbal and visual languages give meaning to the world. Thus meaning is not reflected but *produced*.

In the first instance the aim of this new critical project was greater rigor, demanding that before a film's content is assessed closer attention be paid to the specificities of cinematic production and particularly to how character is produced by textual operations such as narration, plot, and mise-en-scène. But it also implied investigation of a different order of meaning. The displacement of "reflection" by the term *production* made a conceptual link between Marxist analysis of the social structure and the formal analysis of semiotic, narrative, and generic structures. In place of the artistic reflection of life emerged the concept of fictional production and with it the suggestion that bourgeois and patriarchal ideology is embedded in the forms of representation itself.

This shift in the understanding of representation drew on the ideas of the French Marxist philosopher Louis Althusser, who challenged the hierarchical base/superstructure model that subordinated culture to the economy. Althusser conceived the social formation as comprising different, semiautonomous but interacting spheres or levels of social practice, each governed by its own history and process of development: the economic, the political, and the ideological. The latter itself comprised a range of practices, including education, family, religion, media. These different spheres of social practice do not necessarily develop in tandem, but at any particular moment one may be more important to the development of the total social formation than another. More radically, Althusser argued that the economic determines the relationship between spheres only indirectly and "in the last instance."[9] The effect of this new model of the social formation was to invalidate the notion of culture reflecting an economic base. It gave a much larger role to ideological determination through cultural practice and extended the concept of contradiction to art. Significantly, Althusser reworked the concept of ideology to include not only fully formulated ideas, but also commonsense wisdoms, images, myths, representations. The power of ideology lies in the fact that it operates not just as ideas in the head, but in the cultural assumptions that shape the way we do things. In this sense ideology is "materialized" in the habitual activities of everyday life. Ideologies are systematized in the institutional practices of home, school, church, and media, and in the professional and representational practices of journalism, fiction, film, television, advertising. For example, news broadcasting operates under the institutional rule of "balance," which effectively constructs the middle ground as the political norm and marginalizes groups who threaten the stability of the status quo.

This conception of ideology was consonant with structuralist and semiotic accounts of the constructive power of language and sign systems. Rather than a transparent means of expression, cinematic language and film forms constitute cultural systems with their own specific histories, structures, and therefore formative capacity to produce meanings and ideological effects. Realism, as a particular mode, depends on adherence to historically specific conventions that "signify" (rather than "reflect") reality. We may be more convinced by *Platoon* than *The Green Berets*, for example, not by comparing image and reality, but because we recognize conventions of filming in a war zone—for example, a shaky camera, grainy 16mm image, wild soundtrack—derived from newsreel. These conventions in turn change according to changing technology, social attitudes toward war, competition for audiences, and such. Thus the convincing character, the revealing episode, or the realistic image of the world is not a simple reflection of real life but a highly mediated production of cinematic practice.

From this perspective, meaning is produced out of the dynamic interplay of the various aesthetic, semiotic, and ideological processes that constitute the "work" of a film. Thus neo-Marxism changes the project of criticism from the *discovery of meaning* to that of *uncovering the means of its production.* For feminists seeking to deconstruct patriarchal culture, the pertinent question is less "What does this film mean?" than "How is its meaning produced?" The assumption that meaning is already constituted in the world or lies hidden in the work of art, waiting to be prized open, validates the ideology that constructs woman as unknowable other, outside history, in the realm of nature and eternal truth. The second question attempts to locate behind the manifest themes of a film another level of meaning that lies in the structural relationships of the text. Devices such as the close-up or voice-over construct meaning less by what they show or say than by the way they organize the female image into a patriarchal position, or, conversely, offer textual opportunities for resistance. What this reveals is not the expression of immanent truths about women, but rather an aspect of how patriarchy works. It explains, for example, the recognizable "reality" of stereotypes that turn the effects of the specific conditions of women's lives – for example, choplogic as an adaptation to the conflicting demands of domestic life – into an explanation of female nature – for instance, dumbness.[10]

Realism and Antirealism

Central to the Marxist conception of the social formation is the role of contradiction. The driving force of history lies in the conflict between the material forces and social relations of production and the consequent division of the social formation into opposing class interests. The task of bourgeois ideology is to *mask* these class contradictions through their illusory *unification*, using notions such as "human nature," the "common interest," or the "nation"; or by displacing them onto idealist oppositions that are amenable to *resolution* – such as the conflict between individual and society. Thus striking workers are often represented not as our compatriots but as extremists holding the nation to ransom. Nonstriking workers are defined not as failing in class solidarity but as decent family men, protecting their rights as individuals. Such concepts serve to "naturalize" conflicting historical forces, putting them outside human control and so beyond change.[11]

Seventies film theory developed a model of the "classic realist text" to analyze this process across the media, from Hollywood genre films to European art cinema, TV drama, news, and documentary.[12] Realist narrative is invested in the individual hero and a narrative pattern of disruption, conflict, and resolution, authenticated by recognizable settings connoting real life. This structure, it was argued, masks not only the social processes that produce reality, but also the semiotic processes of representation. Thus the classic realist text simultaneously renders natural the social and ideological constructions of capitalism and patriarchy and denies the cultural production of meaning. Realism, as Roland Barthes paradoxically claimed, produces myth.[13] This argument opposed earlier Marxist and feminist demands for realism as the responsible goal of art and entertainment seeking to counteract the false stereotypes of capitalist and patriarchal culture. Alternative practice espoused a combative antirealism. In Jean-Luc Godard's words, the task of radical filmmaking was not to reflect reality but to expose the reality of the reflection.[14]

Realism and Genre

While this model described the *ambition* of dominant ideology, it failed to take account of contradictory or resisting ideologies and aesthetic practices that might impede its realization. Genre criticism, however, had highlighted filmic procedures that, due to the economic needs of the studio system, necessarily foreground rather than conceal their systematic conventionality. Film genres provide material for the mass production of entertainment. On the one hand, the recognizable plots, stereotypes, and conventions of the different genres enable the industry to standardize studio practices, to predict market demand, and so stabilize production. On the other hand, the demand for novelty is met by innovative play with the conventions. Audiences return to watch yet another Western not to find out "what is going to happen next"–which they already know–but "how." Thus there is an underlying tension between the genre film's need to foreground its formulae and conventions and the needs of classic narrative for illusory realism, which depends on winning the audience's suspension of disbelief.

Feminist criticism became interested in this potential antagonism. The generic conventions and stereotypes of classic Hollywood represent highly visible codes that might be set into play one against another, or against the grain of a film's ideological themes. In this process the contradictions that it is a film's ideological project to unify may be exposed, even subverted. Thus feminist criticism that operates according to a perspective at odds with the ideology privileged as the film's "message" or "worldview" may be able to animate these effects to produce a subversive reading of an apparently reactionary film, or an ideological reading of an apparently progressive film.

Marxism Meets Psychoanalysis

It was the exposure of patriarchal ideology that came to predominate in the ensuing encounter of neo-Marxist/feminist film criticism with psychoanalysis. In extending the concept of ideology from political beliefs to include commonsense wisdoms and everyday life, Louis Althusser had argued the determining role of unconscious assumptions in the way we do things. Drawing on the theories of French psychoanalyst Jacques Lacan, Althusser suggested not only the profoundly unconscious way dominant ideology infiltrates everyday life, but also the way it controls our identities as "subjects"—our everyday sense of self at the center of our world. This argument pointed away from Marx, via Lacan to Freud and the much-debated relationship between Marxism and psychoanalysis.

The link between them, it was argued, lay in language. Marxism analyzes social history as the dialectical interaction between contradictory social and economic forces: thesis > antithesis > synthesis, which becomes the next thesis, and so on. The linguist Ferdinand de Saussure had similarly argued that meaning is produced in the structural interactions among a series of sociolinguistic differences.[15] Just as the difference between *t* and *d* enables us to distinguish *tin* from *din*, the meaning of, say, *lamb* shifts depending on whether it is defined against sheep or against mutton. The meaning of *lamb* resides not in the word, *l-a-m-b*, or in a verbal concept positively attached to the word, but in its difference from an adjacent concept. In their early formations both Marxism and structural linguistics had assumed as given the psychological identity of the agents of historical process and of language in the form either of the class subjects of history or the individual language user—the linguistic "I." However, Lacan made the conceptual link between the processes of language and the psyche, drawing on the analogous role of difference between self and other in the production of identity to argue that "self" and "other" are the unconscious products of linguistic positions—"I," "you," "they"—created in language. Subjectivity is a product of meanings that are produced through the play of linguistic structures. In other words, language, meaning, and subjectivity are all in different ways dependent on "difference." The founding moment that for Lacanian psychoanalysis knots these instances together in mutual determination is derived from Freud's theory of the Oedipus complex, which is triggered by the oedipal (male) child's traumatic perception of sexual difference in the maternal body as castration. According to Lacan, this perception is both essential to the child's becoming a subject in language and at the same time impossible to acknowledge if coherent subjecthood and language use are to be attained. Knowledge of difference is repressed for the sake of unified identity expressed in the apparent mastery of the linguistic subject position, "I." This mastery is, however, illusory; difference continues to exercise control from the unconscious.[16]

The insight of Lacanian psychoanalysis that identity, like meaning, is both production and process, based on the dynamic of difference, resonated with the Marxist concept of the dialectical process of history based on contradiction. Thus, it was argued, not only does bourgeois ideology mask social contradictions and deny meaning as construct, it also represses the role of difference and other in the production of identity. Neo-Marxism uses Lacanian psychoanalysis to challenge the centrality of the subject – whether individual or class subject – conceived as autonomous source of meaning.

For feminism this argument led away from Marxism toward Freudian psychoanalysis and a theory of patriarchal representation. Feminists focused on the fact that the key difference, essential to the formation of the patriarchal subject and the operation of language, is sexual difference. What the oedipal moment represses for the patriarchal subject is femininity. Woman, it was argued, functions as other not only in the content of male fantasy, but also in the very structuring of language and representation. In cinema, photography and narrative organize the image of woman for a male gaze that replays the founding moments of patriarchal identity. The image of woman cannot represent real women either visually or narratively, for in evoking male desire she also speaks of castration. The female image is therefore constructed as glamorized fetish or is voyeuristically investigated and punished. Both strategies repress the difference represented by femininity that threatens the coherence and mastery of patriarchal identity.[17]

These arguments focused attention on spectatorship. A film includes in its structure the positions from which it must be viewed and understood. The male hero is the principal agent of the narrative. Camera position, framing, and editing offer spectatorial positions of identification with his look and, through his look, access to the woman. Centered within the frame and narrative, the woman is photographed to be looked at. The spectator created by the text is masculine.[18] Thus identification, the notion of identity itself, was accounted a mechanism of patriarchy.[19] Consequently, spectatorship for the female viewer of the image of woman produces either masochistic or narcissistic identifications. Women as women could not be represented. At the same time, the conceptualization of subjectivity in terms of difference, negativity, instability led to an equation of femininity with difference itself. Progressive critical and filmmaking practice, it was argued, should seek to destroy the illusions and pleasures of realist recognition, of identification with characters in a coherent fictional world, by dissolving the subject in an endless play of radical difference. For feminist filmmaking, this implied antirealist, deconstructionist, avant-garde strategies.[20]

Ultimately, however, this proved an intellectually and politically untenable outcome for feminists who look for understanding of social and psychic structures in order to change them. The first stage in any political movement involves recognition of and identification with new politicized identities. The new filmmaking practices were accessible only to an educated minority, while the pleasures the majority of women take in mainstream media (which even feminists rarely forgo completely) remained outside cultural struggle. Feminist psychoanalytic work of the last decade has turned to the urgent problem of the female spectator, the formation of female identity in the oedipal triangle, and the relationship of femininity to language as a means of understanding female identification and pleasure. However, alongside the psychoanalytic theorization of image and representation, a different line of inquiry has developed, focusing less on woman's image than on her voice and discourse, and it is to this strand in Marxist-feminist analysis to which I now want to turn.

Women's Voices: Theories of Discourse

While the essentialism of the bourgeois masculine or feminine subject may readily be challenged, feminists have difficulty in abandoning the category "women" altogether. The specificity of women arises from the fact that we are positioned differently from men in the social formation. Women experience work, parenthood, and personal heterosexual and family relations in gender-specific ways. These differences arise not from essential femininity but from the different sociocultural and psychic conditions of women's lives, which frequently contradict patriarchal constructions. For example, the fifties cult of motherhood was one thing; living it, as the emerging women's movement showed, was another. This suggests a gap between textual spectator theorized by cine-psychoanalysis and social audience. Increasingly, feminist theory has sought to bridge this gap.[21]

The concept of *women's discourse* focuses not on the image of woman centered in character or psychic fetish, but on the "woman's voice" heard intermittently among the social discourses drawn into the text of a film. A discourse defines and is used by a socially constituted group of speakers. It comprises all those terms—aesthetic, semantic, ideological, social—that speak for or refer to those whose discourse it is, controlling what can or cannot be said. In textual analysis, discourse is distinguished from point of view in that the latter is attached to a particular character or authorial position, while a discourse stretches across the text through a variety of articulations of which character is only one; it need not be continuous but can be broken by gaps or silences during which contesting discourses may interrupt or take over.

The value of this concept is that it avoids the humanist reduction of textual productivity to character or image and cuts across the division between text and society, thus permitting reference to social life outside the text without falling into the trap of reflectionism. A film, in constructing a recognizable fictional world, draws discourses circulating in society and in other cultural forms into the fabric of the film. Fashion is an obvious example. Others include discourses of motherhood (*Mildred Pierce*), of class

(*Stella Dallas*), domesticity (*Craig's Wife*); but also, more recently, of women's liberation (*Coma*) or black feminism (*The Color Purple*). Thus a filmic text is composed of a variety of different discourses that may be organized along class, ethnic, gender, and sexual lines. The coherence of the classic realist text derives from the hierarchical organization of its discourses through which ideological dominance is gained by that discourse with the power to place and define the "truth" of the others—in mainstream fiction film, "patriarchal discourse." This suggests potential struggle among discourses, and feminists have looked for those moments when in the tension between the genre conventions and realism's need to seek the recognition of a female audience, patriarchal discourse loses control; the woman's voice disrupts it, making its assumptions seem "strange." Claire Johnston and Pam Cook explored this approach in relation to the work of Dorothy Arzner.[22] From this perspective the questions the feminist critic asks are, What is being said about women here? Who is speaking? And for whom?

Ideology and Negotiation

Any area of social activity can be analyzed as discursive practice. Cultural studies took up "discourse analysis" to examine lived subcultures, at the same time exploring the life of the text in society. Charlotte Herzog and Jane Gaines, for example, analyze the way the costumes worn by stars provide raw material for the discursive practice of dressmaking.[23] Such considerations raise the important issue of audiences, of reading, and of the conditions of reception. For feminists, concerned with the productivity of theory for the lives of women, work with audiences has been crucial.

Analysis of reception draws on a revised concept of ideology made possible by a return to the work of the Italian Marxist Antonio Gramsci.[24] Although the Althusserian model of the social formation acknowledges contradictions between its different levels and practices, the conception of dominant ideology that works unconsciously to interpolate the subject into its structures severely restricts the productive possibilities of contradiction. In place of dominant ideology and interpolation, Marxist cultural studies deploys concepts of hegemony and negotiation. According to Gramsci, since ideological power in a social democracy is as much a matter of persuasion as force, it is never secured once and for all. Consent to the rule of the dominant class has continually to be rewon in a struggle between contesting groups. Hegemony describes the negotiations between socioeconomic, ideological, and political forces through which power is maintained and contested. The culture industries play a part in this negotiation.

Bourgeois democratic culture, in its attempt to make society cohere, must constantly address subordinate groups by invoking and manipulating the discourses through which they recognize themselves. This opens up the processes of meaning production to negotiation within and between the intersecting levels of production and reception. Whereas the culture industries must look for exchange-value as a source of profit, audiences look for use-value.[25] If the use-value of a washing machine or car can more or less be defined by industrial planners and designers, the use-values of cultural products (which lie in a complex of pleasures and meanings) are more difficult to predict and control. There is a dislocation between the economic and ideological goals of industry and audience. Moreover, "creative" personnel intervene between producer and product with their own professional and personal goals. The popular TV series "Cagney & Lacey" exemplifies such struggles. While its writers, inspired by feminist critiques of the male buddy movie, made a female duo the center of their crime series, the production company, anxious about conservative advertisers, sought to dispel any suggestion of lesbianism. A change of actress failed to resolve the contradictions around female sexuality, since the more conventionally glamorous Sharon Gless already had a cult lesbian following. Moreover, a strong female partnership at the center of the male crime genre must, if it is to command audience recognition in a period of public struggles around women's liberation, encounter sexism in the course of the plot. The series spoke to an articulate middle-class female audience whose vigorous campaigning kept it alive some time after the producers sought to cancel it.[26] Thus meaning is neither imposed by a ruling-class or media conspiracy nor passively imbibed by unconsciously interpolated audiences, but arises out of a struggle or negotiation between competing motivations and frames of reference at all three levels of production, text, and audience.

In this respect the concept of negotiation brings cultural studies close to the insights of semiotic and psychoanalytic textual analysis, which stresses meaning and identity as always in process, never finally achieved or fixed. Psychoanalytic textual analysis, like the model of the classic realist text, has tended to close down the productivity of these insights in its emphasis on narrative closure. According to this perspective, mainstream fiction engages class, gender, or ethnic difference as a means of narrative disruption only to disavow it in recuperative endings that replay oedipal repression, repositioning the resistant heroine under patriarchal control. However, the notion of recuperation treats the film as a fixed object, assuming that narrative closure also "fixes" the audience's experience and memory of the film.

The value of negotiation is that it recognizes the different and competing determinations, professional practices and cultural traditions operating in any media exchanges that potentially "unfix" the text. These traditions, moreover, include realism, which negotiation both admits as a demand of the culture and relativizes as a site of cultural struggle. While criticizing the realist project as bourgeois ideology, film theory has never escaped realist epistemology: the real has simply shifted from phenomenal appearances to the underlying realities revealed by Althusserian-Lacanian Marxism: the real relations of production, real structures of language, real conditions of subjectivity. The concepts of hegemony and negotiation make possible a different theorization of the social production of reality and meaning and thus a different approach to issues of realism and identity. The Gramscian formulation conceives the social formation as a struggle for hegemony between different socially located and historically determined positions and identities.

If the real is in constant production, realism should be seen as itself a part of this process. Struggles over representation contribute to the construction, deconstruction, and reforming of the real. In a similar vein, recent feminist and ethnic work on identity questions the conception of identity and other as mutually exclusive positions. Feminist analysis of the female child's position in the oedipal triangle argues that she add the father to the original maternal dyad. This suggests an extension of identities rather than their repression under a singular identity.[27] Thus subjects move in and out of different identities constructed by ethnicity, class, gender, sexual orientation, and so on. Similarly, cultural products offer a range of often conflicting positions for identification. This is not to suggest that identities are freely available for the choosing at a sort of cultural supermarket. Identity, like the real, is a site of social and cultural negotiation and contest. Recent ethnographic studies analyze such negotiations and the social and discursive conditions that permit them.[28] Such a conception of realism and identification does not assume free self-determining subjects; at the same time it does not rule out human agency. Subjects are socially, culturally situated, but they may, in reaction to the contradictions of their daily lives, contest dominant determinations. Thus realism and identity are not ideologically predetermined, static, invested in the status quo, but involved in the process of historical change, in which we as subjects, working from specific social and political positions, can intervene.

Conclusion: The Project of Feminist Criticism

If we accept the heterogeneous and inexhaustible nature of the cultural product as a site in which different voices, aesthetic traditions, and ideologies struggle to impose or challenge, negotiate or displace definitions and identities, then feminist criticism opens up the negotiations of the text in order to *animate its contradictions*, to enter the polemics of cultural negotiation by drawing the text into a female or feminist orbit. Such cultural criticism is not concerned with the progressiveness or reactionariness of the text, but with tapping its cultural energy, making it productive for feminist debate and practice.

Notes

1. Karl Marx and Friedrich Engels, *The German Ideology* (London: Lawrence and Wishart, 1974).

2. See the early feminist film journal *Women & Film*; e.g., Christine Mohanna, "A One-Sided Story: Women in the Movies," *Women & Film*, no. 1 (1972).

3. See Sylvia Harvey, "Ideology: The 'Base and Superstructure' Debate," in *Photography/Politics: One*, ed. Terry Dennett and Jo Spence (London: Photography Workshop, 1979).

4. See especially Lawrence Alloway, *Violent America* (New York: Museum of Modern Art, 1971), and "Iconography of the Movies," in *Movie Reader*, ed. Ian Cameron (London: November Books, 1972).

5. Judith Hess, "Genre Film and the Status Quo," in *Film Genre: Theory and Criticism*, ed. Barry Grant (Metuchen, N.J.: Scarecrow Press, 1977).

6. Jacqueline Levitin, "The Western: Any Good Roles for Women?" *Film Reader*, no. 5 (1982).

7. Victor Shklovsky, "Art as Technique," in *Russian Formalist Criticism*, ed. Less T. Lemon and Marion J. Reis (Lincoln: University of Nebraska Press, 1965).

8. Terence Hawkes, *Structuralism and Semiotics* (reprint, London: Routledge, 1991).

9. Louis Althusser, "Marxism and Humanism," in *For Marx* (Harmondsworth, England: Penguin, 1969), and "Ideology and Ideological State Apparatuses," in *Lenin and Philosophy and Other Essays* (London: New Left Books, 1971).

10. See Tessa Perkins, "Rethinking Stereotypes," in *Ideology and Cultural Production*, ed. Michele Barrett et al. (London: Croom Helm, 1979).

11. See Stuart Hall, "Culture, the Media and the 'Ideological Effect,' " in *Mass Communication and Society*, ed. James Curran et al. (London: Edward Arnold, 1977).

12. See Colin MacCabe, "Realism and the Cinema: Notes on Some Brechtian Theses," *Screen* 15 (Summer 1974).

13. Roland Barthes, "Myth Today," in *Mythologies*, trans. Annette Lavers (New York: Hill and Wang, 1972).

14. Jean-Luc Godard, *Vent D'Est*, 1970.

15. Ferdinand de Saussure, *A Course in General Linguistics* (London: Fontana, 1974).

16. See Steve Burniston and Christine Weedon, "Ideology, Subjectivity and the Artistic Text," in *Working Papers in Cultural Studies* no. 10 (Birmingham: Centre for Contemporary Cultural Studies, 1977), and Steve Burniston et al., "Psychoanalysis and the Cultural Acquisition of Sexuality and Subjectivity," in *Women Take Issue: Aspects of Women's Subordination*, ed. Women's Studies Group, Birmingham University Centre for Contemporary Cultural Studies (London: Hutchinson, 1978).

17. See Claire Johnston, "Woman's Cinema as Counter Cinema," in *Notes on Women's Cinema* (London: Society for Education in Film and Television, 1973), reprinted in *Movies and Methods*, ed. Bill Nichols (Berkeley: University of California Press, 1976), and Elisabeth Cowie, "Women, Representation and the Image," *Screen Education*, no. 23 (Summer 1977).

18. Laura Mulvey, "Visual Pleasure and Narrative Cinema," *Screen* 16 (Autumn 1975): 6-18.

19. Anne Friedberg, "Identification and the Star: A Refusal of Difference," in *Star Signs*, ed. Christine Gledhill (London: British Film Institute Education Department, 1982).

20. See Claire Johnston, "Femininity and the Masquerade," in *Jacques Tourneur*, ed. Claire Johnston and Paul Willemen (Edinburgh, Scotland: Edinburgh Film Festival, 1975), and "Towards a Feminist Film Practice: Some Theses," *Edinburgh '76 Magazine*, no. 1.

21. Annette Kuhn, "Women's Genres: Melodrama, Soap Opera and Theory," in *Home Is Where the Heart Is: Studies on Melodrama and the Woman's Film*, ed. Christine Gledhill (London: British Film Institute, 1987).

22. See Claire Johnston's and Pam Cook's essays in *The Work of Dorothy Arzner: Towards a Feminist Cinema*, ed. Claire Johnston (London: British Film Institute, 1975). Also Pam Cook, " 'Exploitation' Films and Feminism," *Screen* 17 (Summer 1976).

23. Charlotte Cornelia Herzog and Jane Marie Gaines, " 'Puffed Sleeves before Tea-time': Joan Crawford, Adrian and Women Audiences," in *Stardom: Industry of Desire*, ed. Christine Gledhill (London: Routledge, 1991).

24. Antonio Gramsci, *Selections from the Prison Notebooks* (London: Lawrence and Wishart, 1971).

25. Terry Lovell, "Ideology and *Coronation Street*," in *Television Monograph 13*, ed. Richard Dyer et al. (London: British Film Institute, 1981).

26. Julie D'Acci, "The Case of Cagney and Lacey," in *Boxed In: Women and Television*, ed. Helen Baehr and Gillian Dyer (London: Pandora, 1987).

27. See Janet Walker, "Feminist Critical Practice: Female Discourse in *Mildred Pierce*," *Film Reader*, no. 5 (1982), and Jackie Byars, "Gazes, Voices, Power," in *Female Spectators: Looking at Film and Television*, ed. E. Deidre Pribram (London: Verso, 1988), and *All That Hollywood Allows* (Chapel Hill: University of North Carolina Press, 1991). Both writers make use of Nancy Chodorow, *The Reproduction of Mothering: Psychoanalysis and the Sociology of Gender* (Berkeley: University of California Press, 1978), and Carol Gilligan, *In a Different Voice* (Cambridge, Mass.: Harvard University Press, 1982).

28. See for example, Dorothy Hobson, *Crossroads: The Drama of a Soap Opera* (London: Methuen, 1982); Charlotte Brunsdon, "*Crossroads*: Notes on a Soap Opera," in *Regarding Television: Critical Views – an Anthology*, ed. E. Ann Kaplan (Los Angeles: American Film Institute, 1982); Ien Ang, *Watching Dallas* (London: Methuen, 1985); and Ellen Seiter et al., *Remote Control* (New York and London: Routledge, 1991).

Narrative Is *Narrative*: So What Is New?

Lisa Cartwright and Nina Fonoroff

1992 Introduction

We wrote the essay "Narrative Is *Narrative*; So What Is New?" in 1983 for a special Film/Video issue of *Heresies*, a feminist publication on art and politics. At the time, Nina was at the beginning of her career as an independent filmmaker and Lisa was a recent graduate of film school. As art students in the late 1970s and early 1980s, we were introduced to two spheres of thinking that would come to define our work: feminist politics (both inside and outside film studies) and the ideas of the North American and British experimental film avant-garde (from Maya Deren and Alexander Hammid to Shirley Clarke, Marie Menken, Stan Brakhage, Michael Snow, and Peter Gidal).

We had studied filmmaking initially in an art school context, where the conventions of mainstream narrative cinema had very little currency. Experimental film was presented to us as a semiautonomous art form engaging a set of techniques, aesthetics, and politics independent from those of mainstream or documentary cinema. We were given to understand that this sector of filmmaking was done on a small scale in something like an artisanal fashion. The filmmaker would be responsible for all aspects of a production, most likely distribute it her- or himself or through a film cooperative, and show the work at museums, universities, archives, or workshops.[1] This model came out of the traditions of North American structural, visionary, and personal film. The antecedent of these traditions was the historical avant-garde of the teens and twenties (for example, the work of Viking Eggeling in Germany, Germaine Dulac in France, and James Watson, Jr., in the United States).[2] These traditions had in common their strong affinities with the aesthetic concerns and conventions of the plastic arts and poetry, and a distance from (and, in some cases, a critique of) the conventions of theater, the novel, and commercial cinema.

Among many North American experimental filmmakers, there was a tacit belief that an experimental tradition could exist in isolation from the social and economic conditions of industry production and larger political and social issues. However, as we became more familiar with the Althusserian Marxist and feminist critique of representation forwarded in journals such as *Screen* in Britain and *Camera Obscura* in the United States, we began to question the supposed insularity of the U.S. experimental film community and the politics of its small-scale auteur system, where traditional notions of mastery and discipleship still held sway. We felt that the avowedly apolitical nature of the work of many experimental filmmakers such as Stan Brakhage and Michael Snow constituted, in fact, a tacit involvement in the idealist values of a conservative artworld milieu.

The film and writing coming out of the Co-op movement of seventies Britain seemed to us a useful model for politicizing the course of experimental film on this side of the Atlantic.[3] Even more central to our thinking were the actively feminist films and writings produced by experimental filmmakers such as Lis Rhodes (a cofounder of the Circles film collective) in London and Su Friedrich in the United States. This work challenged not only the conventions of mainstream cinema, but those of the fratriarchy that long had been dominant in experimental film.

While male avant-garde filmmakers such as Brakhage and Snow were the subject of critical and historical writing, we found only a very few feminist analyses of women filmmakers' interventions in experimental form. Two important published essays are Lis Rhodes's 1976 "Whose History?"[4] and Constance Penley and Janet Bergstrom's 1978 "The Avant-Garde: Histories and Theories."[5] But some important new approaches were never published (such as Nancy Woods's analysis of the aesthetic politics of Rhodes's *Light Reading,* 1979) or appeared in print only recently (Sandy Flitterman's book on Germaine Dulac and Marie Epstein was published in 1990,[6] and Lauren Rabinovitz's study of the work of Joyce Wieland, Shirley Clarke, and Maya Deren appeared in print in 1991).[7] Marie Menken, a central figure in postwar experimental cinema who began making films in 1945, has yet to receive consideration.[8]

At the time that we wrote our critique of narrative in avant-garde cinema, there were two important sources for writing on feminism and film in the United States. *Women & Film,* the early seventies journal published in Los Angeles by Siew-Hwa Beh and Saunie Salyer, addressed a range of concerns but did not take up experimental cinema to a great extent, although the journal did consider overlooked Hollywood women directors such as Ida Lupino and Dorothy Arzner as well as political documentary. *Camera Obscura*, the journal of feminism and film theory formed by some of the members of the *Women & Film* collective, offered an alternative to the sociological and empirical approach represented in *Women & Film*.[9] Maintaining a more subtle and less totalizing critique of mainstream cinematic conventions, the journal brought to light avant-garde films by women who were working against industry standards by engaging directly with many of the conventions of Hollywood's dramatic narratives–the work of Yvonne Rainer, Jackie Raynal, Chantal Akerman, Marguerite Duras, Sally Potter, and Laura Mulvey and Peter Wollen. While these were clearly important experimental and avant-garde films, they engaged a different set of questions than those films that drew on the conventions of music, poetry, or painting and sculpture, rather than those of narrative cinema, theater, or the novel.

In the discourse that surrounded independent film in the late seventies and early eighties, nonnarrative filmmaking in the visionary, structural, or personal mode was, more often than not, criticized. Peter Wollen's polemical survey of avant-garde film movements, "The Two Avant-Gardes," reduced the avant-garde tradition to two politically opposed spheres.[10] Wollen relegated nonnarrative work–even that which claimed to uphold Marxist and feminist agendas–to an idealist art-world history and context (and, in another essay, to a discourse in ontology).[11] Industry-influenced avant-garde narrative strategies–the methods and theories of Jean-Luc Godard and the French New Wave that had influenced Wollen's own filmmaking practice–were identified as *the* effective strategies in leftist and feminist political cinema. We agreed with Teresa de Lauretis's statement that "the present task of theoretical feminism and of feminist film practice is to articulate the relations of the female subject to representation, meaning, and vision, and in so doing to construct the terms of another frame of reference, another measure of desire." However, we disagreed with her claim, directly following, that "this cannot be done by destroying all representational coherence, by denying the 'hold' of the image in order to prevent identification and subject reflection."[12] The feminist strategy of "narrative with a vengeance" that de Lauretis advocated did not seem to us a useful one for women working in areas of filmmaking where narrative had never been a central mode, and where equally critical questions of representation were being engaged through nonnarrative work.[13]

The question that confronted us was this: *Must* filmmakers engage in the conventions of narrative in order to maintain feminist concerns? To us, such a switch would have been tantamount to switching fields altogether.

We felt there was a tacit advocacy of commercial industry standards in the criticism we read. Finally, we felt that certain very basic problems of representation fundamental to feminist concerns could be raised *only* through works outside industry conventions. Popular industry conventions could not constitute *all* of the cinematic strategies in question, after all. Our 1983 article was intended as a means of claiming the existence of a feminist methodology within the sphere of nonnarrative experimental film. However, our essay addressed very few of our ideas on actual film practices that we supported. It functioned, finally, as a polemic against narrative strategies.

In the ten years since we wrote "Narrative Is *Narrative*," the ideological function of narrative, the politics of the film avant-garde, and the positions taken by each of us respectively, have changed considerably. The issues and questions important to independent film have shifted dramatically over the past decade. Coco Fusco's 1988 critique of the very concept of an "independent" sector (and her exposure of the white middle/upper-class conditions that tacitly underlie the self-designated film avant-garde) poses some of the issues that we believe to be most important currently.[14] Independent films and critical writings on the avant-garde by members of Sankofa Audio/Film Production and the Black Audio Film Collective of London have foregrounded the presence of a black modernity that constitutes an important, but historically repressed, area of avant-garde visual production. The AIDS and health-care systems crisis, the collapsing U.S. economy, increasing police brutality, and the decline in public arts funding are just a few conditions of the eighties that have influenced many independent filmmakers to foreground social issues. But this has not precipitated a return to conventional documentary or narrative strategies; for example, experimental films such as Martina Attille's *Dreaming Rivers* (1988), Su Friedrich's *The Ties That Bind* (1984) and *Sink or Swim* (1990), Nina Fonoroff's *A Knowledge They Cannot Lose* (1989), and Julie Dash's *Daughters of the Dust* (1991) all draw in very different ways from nonnarrative, narrative, and documentary modes to consider issues of sexuality, race, nationality, and familial relations from deeply personal, historical, and political perspectives. Meanwhile, the adoption of "experimental" techniques in popular cultural productions (in TV commercials and MTV, for example) has raised questions about the value of an avant-gardist approach, and the potential for political work in popular culture. As the categories of independent film and industry practice shift and disintegrate, distinctions between narrative and nonnarrative are no longer highly charged with political importance. However, consideration of the history and terms of the debates around narrative and nonnarrative during the seventies and early eighties remains critical if we are to consider the long-term implications for contemporary political cinema.

Narrative Is Narrative: So What Is New?

Over the past several years there has been a growing trend toward "new" uses of narrative by avant-garde independent filmmakers. Work toward the development of feminist experimental film that breaks from a use of narrative altogether is being foreclosed by the currently popular use of narrative in film.

Much feminist study has been devoted to the development of a discourse that addresses the ways in which narrative functions to reproduce the patriarchal order.[15] Processes of identification (with camera point of view, with characters depicted within the film), temporal continuity, the "kind" of viewing required for narrative films – these are just a few aspects of narrative cinema that are called into question. With only a few exceptions,[16] however, little attention has been given to the possibility of a radical feminist experimental film – one that breaks from the use of narrative altogether.

Writings on narrative films maintain that dominant cinema must be criticized *from within* (through further narrative work) in order to undermine its politically repressive impact. In light of recent work on narrative it is evident that this results in a deeper investment in the very principles that are ostensibly being subverted. The "new," "disjunctive," "deconstructive," and "oblique" narrative films employ the *same old* values of mainstream cinema. The belief that there is a direct or natural connection between an image and what that image represents, between what is seen and what is known, is necessarily reinforced in narrative film. New narrative filmmakers do acknowledge this "obvious" relation as an ideological construct. Nevertheless, they fall back on a provisional acceptance of this "reality" in their own films. The confessed *need* for the particular pleasure provided by narrative has been overemphasized to the point of forcing an equation between narrative and pleasure, and, by implication, nonnarrative and nonpleasure. This equation fails to acknowledge other less obvious possibilities for pleasure in film viewing and making, and reinforces another "natural" connection – that which is understood to exist between film and narrative. As this work on narrative gains political credence and authority, narrative takes on the appearance of inevitability.

The development of feminist experimental work that attempts to break from a use of narrative altogether has been suppressed by the principles upheld in mainstream cinema, but now the same principles are also being employed within an avant-garde that originally set out to oppose the mainstream. Due to the growing indifference to nonnarrative, experimental film, younger filmmakers barely stand a chance of hearing more than the most reduced version of its history, and only the most determined will succeed in producing experimental films in an emerging cultural/political climate that increasingly inhibits the development of such work.

Audience: The Prophet Motive

Proponents of the new narrative argue that if a film departs too radically from familiar narrative elements, the audience will decrease and the film will be consigned to obscurity, limiting its potential for large-scale political effectiveness. It is assumed that the most effective means of undermining mainstream cinema is to preserve selected narrative elements, within which departures can be made. The idea is that one elicits a set of accustomed formal viewing expectations, all the better to shatter them.

Here makers of new narratives find themselves in the perfect double bind. A need for a break from narrative is nobly acknowledged by filmmakers, but deployment of narrative "form" is justified by a saving grace: political content. That their films depend on the very principles being questioned is leniently excused – *silenced* – by a liberal audience, sympathetic to the filmmakers' avowed radical intentions and willing to overlook the discrepancy between these intentions and the actual films.

The work of British filmmakers Laura Mulvey and Peter Wollen is indicative of this trend toward greater accessibility – *and* toward a classical use of film. Mulvey has stated, "We see each film we make as potentially reaching a wider audience than the one before. . . . I don't feel that *AMY!* breaks new ground in the way that *Riddles [of the Sphinx]* did. But at the same time it's more accessible and consumable, and in that sense it could appeal to a wider group of people."[17]

The first Mulvey-Wollen feature, *Penthesilea* (1975), attempts to replace the structuring device of narrative with theoretical and historical text. The film is divided into four formally different sequences, addressing the Amazon legend and women's place in patriarchal language. Their second feature, *The Riddles of the Sphinx* (1977), again reflects feminist concerns, highlighting the issue of women's place in language from the position of the mother. This film, too, is structured by formally distinct sequences. Each sequence, however, is a narrative within itself, providing the basic framework of a diegesis, character development (however limited), temporal continuity, and so on. *AMY!* (1980) provides an even less altered version of narrative, offering a feminist rendering of the story of aviator Amy Johnson. The film's linearity is broken only intermittently by short interludes such as a poetic stop-action bird-in-flight sequence or a mapping sequence. *Crystal Gazing* (1982), their fourth feature, is a narrative film in the strict sense. Its avant-garde function can be read only in the content "side" of the film: it is about "surviving in London in the eighties"[18] and deals with the issues of Thatcherism and rock and roll. Interestingly, this classical narrative is also the first of their films that does not focus on the central issue of patriarchy, but instead pictures the present relations of capital in London. With a generous British Film Institute grant, its rendering of a desperate political climate brings into question their own position within that climate.

The issue of economic survival is of paramount importance, and the move to narrative reflects this concern. As funds for filmmaking become scarce, it becomes increasingly difficult and risky to depend on granting systems for support. Much current work is done with a view toward marketing potential: larger budgets, "better" production values, and more topical themes all signal the move toward making films that are commercially viable products – lifted from obscurity to greater "public acceptance," from small film-screening spaces to art-movie houses – and, by design or default, a shift from a concern for the possibilities of new uses of film to a concern for marketability and accessibility. These "formally accessible" films require the sophisticated tools of mainstream cinema to effect the degree of illusion necessary to be read *familiarly*. This shift toward the use of an expensive, accessible form for political content is apparent in the Mulvey-Wollen films. One sees it also in Sally Potter's move from the relatively low-budget *Thriller* (1979) to her epic drama *Gold Diggers* (1984), budgeted at $230,000, and in Bette Gordon's move from *Empty Suitcases* (1980), a film (falsely) heralded as both experimental and feminist, to her highly funded production *Variety* (1983), a disjunctive narrative about pornography.

True, one might conclude from this upward mobility of the "avant-garde" that, *finally*, new avant-garde film work is being acknowledged with funds. But a more accurate reading might be that the avant-garde is formulating its own "new" Hollywood through private and government money. This situation is neither new nor advanced.

We are not suggesting that the audience should never be considered in making films. But it is hazardous to endow the audience with a limited understanding or tolerance and to thereby assume a limit of intelligibility within a film, beyond which it will be too obscure to sustain people's interest. And this fallacy often goes unchallenged – is excused and even justified – by an avant-garde audience sympathetic to the filmmakers' political intentions. With such unequivocal trust, the filmmakers assume a position of omnipotence; they are allowed a condescending attitude toward their potential audience. The questions most often raised concern "what *they* want" and "what *they* need to know," in a style resembling market research. The fact that filmmakers are playing into a romantic myth of the artist as prophet/mentor is never stated. And the vague conjectures about the limit of tolerance within film remain the dividing line in this hierarchy, implicit in the films and in discussions about them.

"But the discourse must go on. So one invents obscurities."[19]

One strategy in the new films that is supposed to subvert traditional narrative is quotation, often taking the form of written or spoken text within the film. In an effort to undercut the seductive power of the image, voiceover narration literally speaks ideas developed out of Marxism, psychoanalysis, and semiotics. Constance Penley has stated: "Images have very little power in themselves; their power of fascination and identification is too strong. That is why there must always be a commentary *on* the image simultaneously *of* and *with* them."[20]

The work of Jean-Luc Godard has been a source of inspiration for many filmmakers who employ this strategy. A case in point is his film *Le Gai Savoir* (1968), in which media images, acted sequences, documentary-style sequences, and political theorizing/poeticizing are intercut and overlapped in a dense intertextual montage. Spoken/written language is intended as commentary on and analysis of the ideology manifested in the images. The inclusion of a multiplicity of elements purportedly provides a prime situation for a more dialectical viewing: the greater the amount of elements placed before us, the greater the number of juxtapositions of meanings that can occur. Knowledge of Godard's intention for a more dialectical viewing situation, however, fails to effect that experience. In watching the film we are provided with a complicated picture or model of dialectics— with a confusion of relations between image and image, image and sound, sound and sound. But this presentation never addresses the complex dialectical relation between image and meaning—the actual workings of representation within and through images.

Yvonne Rainer's *Journeys from Berlin* (1979) also provides a dense intertextual construction, and *Sigmund Freud's Dora* (1979),[21] although its combination of texts is less dense and more clearly *readable*, works in much the same way. Such films, which speak a critical, historical, or theoretical tract, compound rather than subvert the power of fascination and identification exerted by film images. The use of texts drawn from other areas obfuscates the still untouched relation between the image and what that image is intended to represent. A text can go no further than to instruct us within its own terms, providing, literally, a *reading* of the function of images. Further, to assume that discursive language breaks the hold of images is to assume that the spoken text is without its own powers of seduction. The authority-of-voice/voice-of-authority compounds the authority of image.

"Quotation" is also used in films in the form of references: to the films of a particular director; to the filmmakers' own past work; and to popular genres of both Hollywood and nonmainstream narrative film. The work of Amos Poe (*Subway Riders, The Foreigner, Unmade Beds*), Beth and Scott

B (*Vortex*), and Manuel de Landa (*Raw Nerves*) reflects the current interest in *film noir*. Particularly in the case of *Raw Nerves* and *Subway Riders*, Christine Noll-Brinckmann and Grahame Weinbren see a radical departure from the genre that inspired them, and indeed from narrative form itself, through these films' inclusion (and exclusion) of elements that render them *opaque*. Opacity is distinguished from the principle of transparency that is at work in mainstream films:

> Traditional narrative is based on the rule that all elements should combine to form a unity, that each element should have its proper, intelligible place in the text and that an ending before the text has succeeded in integrating and explaining them all would be an untimely one indeed. The new narrative ignores this rule. Opacity, quotations from all sorts of sources without stating what their relevance might be, and the fluctuating status of sequences as fiction or non-fiction are evidences of this.[22]

Opacity indicates self-consciousness on the part of the filmmaker, thus foregrounding his/her presence within the work. It also indicates the presence of critical/theoretical work:

> Opacity often leads the viewer to assume the presence of theoretical groundwork and therefore to look for it, and it also signals an inexhaustibility to the work, an idea that it needs repeated screenings to be understood to any degree. But the sense of opacity often remains even after the theory has been understood. This grows out of a general toleration these films have for loose ends; and the general opposition to the notion that every element of a text should be accounted for by the text. The opacity is, in many cases, no more than the impossibility of accounting for some of its elements.[23]

The writers go on to imply that the theoretical underpinnings of a film are often difficult to grasp. And although opacity is not discussed here in relation to transparency, one assumes that it is intended to set up an experience whereby there is limited possibility for identification because the relationship between reality and what is being represented is called into question. Instead, the authors link "opacity" with "unaccountability," as though certain elements of the story were omitted, disrupting the customary cause-and-effect relation between events, but only to the extent that it leads the viewer to wonder about—and search for—the missing parts. One wonders whether "opacity" here isn't being used synonymously with "obscurity" and "inscrutability"—which would, in the end, leave the viewer in the same relation to the film as would a Hollywood *noir* film wherein some key moments in the drama were arbitrarily omitted. The authors go on to say,

Opacity can become a reassuring quality for the viewer, convincing her or him that everything is, after all, in its proper place, that the artist remains in control by making use of mechanisms that are not fully apparent to the audience. Opacity gives one the idea that theory is behind the film, clear to the filmmakers, and that therefore everything in the work is motivated, and that it is worthy of trust. And this, in turn, justifies the opacity. A neat circle of opacity, motivation, trustworthiness, justification, acceptance, and again opacity.[24]

It seems ironic that a theory intended originally to prescribe an *active* viewing possibility, directed toward criticism and questioning of motivation and the process of viewing itself, should not be called upon to produce a very different effect: trust, unequivocal acceptance of what is presented because the filmmaker "knows what he/she is doing," and, ultimately, yet another case of investment in the myth of the artist as mentor/prophet. The foregrounding of the filmmaker: the cult of personality.

The inscription of theory in many of the new narratives makes a certain *kind* of analysis not only possible but necessary. The confusion between the problems specific to film theory/analysis and film practice has led to a use of literary analysis as a primary mode of film viewing. The success of the film is measured by how well it illustrates a particular issue, which can then be subjected to analysis. In turn a particular theoretical take is required to understand the film, and a particular theoretical background is presupposed. *Reading* a film as an illustration of literary ideas has come to be regarded not only as a possible means for knowledge of a certain kind in *certain* films, but as *the* means, *par excellence*, for certain knowledge in/of all film work.

In this scheme, the filmmaker and the critic/theorist have entered into a curious symbiotic relationship, in which the filmmaker buries a bone that the critic, at some later point, can unearth. Many recent narrative films function as setups for critical analysis: theoretical discourse becomes the subtext of the film, which becomes a sitting duck for the critic, whose reading was prepared beforehand. Films that play on such a symbiotic relationship seem to suggest that nothing new can be done in film—that the best a contemporary filmmaker can do is to repeat endless variations of old forms.[25]

In the absence of characters with whom to identify, the sophisticated avant-garde film spectator now identifies with a body of knowledge, with theory. The dramaturgy of traditional narrative has simply been supplanted by a grammaturgy of theoretical principles. The traditional story has been replaced by a larger story—theory. The "story" becomes even grander when the psyche of the filmmaker is brought into the picture as a subject to be analyzed conjointly with the film. The theory of psychoanalysis is used as a cover, merging the respective narratives of the filmmakers' psyche and the film itself into an aggregate "case history."

Shifting Signifier

Another strategy that is supposed to challenge traditional narrative codes is that of thwarting character development. The depiction of human beings with elusive identities allegedly serves to subvert empathy and identification between the viewer and the protagonist.

The device of the "shifting signifier" is commonly employed in new narrative films. Yvonne Rainer's *Film about a Woman Who . . .* (1974) and *Kristina Talking Pictures* (1976) are two early films that experiment with this device as a strategy for breaking the power of character identification. Gordon's *Empty Suitcases* is a later use of this device in which the pronoun "she" is used, in voice-over narration and intertitles, to refer to a number of different female protagonists, all of whom appear on the screen at different times and in different settings. Since no cohesive story is built around a central protagonist, an ambiguity develops in regard to the identity of "she" at any given point in the film. The female characters thus become interchangeable with one another.

Instead of the highly developed characters presented by mainstream cinema, we now have an assortment of appearances, semblances, and archetypes. What takes place is a "shattering" of character in which each fragment carries the earmarks of the whole that engendered it.

The use of the archetype claims to bring about an awareness of the archetypal nature not only of the characters within the particular film, but also, by implication, of all filmic depiction of human behavior. As a reduced model, the archetype supposedly facilitates the process of analysis and dissection for the viewer. Identification is no longer elicited through empathy with a character undergoing conflict, but through the vicarious experience of style. Instead of a real break with unity of character, we are left with a multiplicity of reduced archetypes, with "whom" we can still identify, albeit in a more ambiguous way. But *ambiguous processes of identification still remain processes of identification.*

Whence the Supposition That Analysis Precludes Seduction?

Laura Mulvey's article "Visual Pleasure and Narrative Cinema"[26] advanced feminist film study by proposing a political use of psychoanalysis in the study of mainstream narrative cinema. It was not a prescriptive theory for film practice. Her emphasis is on the use of psychoanalysis to reveal and dismantle the workings of patriarchy *within narrative cinema,* especially in regard to representations of women in subservience to the *male gaze.*

Gordon's *Empty Suitcases* and Jackie Raynal's *Deux Fois* (1970) have been cited as films that address this problem. In the case of Raynal, the filmmaker turns the camera on herself, at times defiantly staring into it – at once the object and the subject of her own gaze, at once "male" and "female." This simultaneous engagement with and critical/analytical relation to her own image is intended to promote the viewer's awareness of – and therefore rupture with – the problematic seductive nature of the image. Yet a picture of a seductive woman "tells" us nothing about the nature of pictures, seduction, or women. Without prior knowledge of the theory behind this sequence, it is doubtful whether one will read it as *against* seduction. If anything, the "male" nature of the gaze is reinforced by such a strategy. Analysis, bearing no relation to the film itself, is what prevents this scene from functioning as it would in any mainstream film.

The interruption or disjunction of the narrative line is yet another strategy employed to undermine the viewer's engagement. This tactic is evident in the fractured narratives of such films as *Empty Suitcases*, which, rather than breaking with narrative, provide multiple, limited narrative developments in an endless deferral of completion. This process is intended to unfix meaning, opening up multiple readings and disengaging the viewer from the drive for completion, yet providing enough narrative satisfaction. But how long can a story continue before something takes place, before some specific meaning is produced? This strategy assumes a calibrated model of narrative, in which the viewer's engagement (and subsequent fixing of meaning) occurs only at certain intervals. The filmmaker functions as manipulator, intermittently leading on and closing off the viewer. This kind of withdrawal tactic assumes that the only moment when "something" takes place is at the instance of climax – a dangerously mistaken assumption. The comparatively straightforward appeal of mainstream narrative has taken on a coy seductiveness in these altered versions, *veiling* the operations of narrative in a game of hard-to-get. Complication is simply posing as dialectics.

Diegesis

The term *diegesis* has considerable currency in discussions about narrative film. Diegetic elements within film are defined as those elements that take place "naturally," within the world constructed by the story of the film – that is, any situation, thought, or dream that is plausible within the context of the constructed fiction. Nondiegetic elements, on the other hand, are those that constitute other "information" that falls outside the realm of the film's fictional world (e.g., background music). The dividing line between diegesis and nondiegesis is growing increasingly blurred, it is said, in new narrative films.

The very concept of diegesis presupposes that a separation can be made between a kind of parareality and what are obviously nonrealistic materials, all within the *same* experience of watching the *same* film. This model fails to account for the fact that a film establishes its own terms, its own context. What is constructed, therefore, sets the terms of its own reality as film. Everything that takes place within a particular film is by definition "diegetic" – it belongs to a particular framework that may be modeled in the image of the everyday world but which nonetheless becomes something different, on the level of experience, once it is placed within the film-viewing context. There is a fundamental misunderstanding about the nature of film in the very designation of diegetic and nondiegetic elements. "Blurring" a nondistinction seems absurd. As far as nonnarrative filmmakers are concerned, the only nondiegetic moment occurs when the film stops, and the film-viewing experience is over.

The idea of "blurring distinctions" forms the cornerstone of the discussion of recent developments in narrative film. Diegesis/nondiegesis, fiction/nonfiction, form/content, personal/political, objective/subjective – how did these elements gain the stability as fixed categories to be expressed as pairs of opposites, and then to be posited as "blurred distinctions"? To accept such distinctions as more than what they are (*terms of convenience*), one must first accept narrative convention as the very foundation of all film practice. We do not accept this precondition; we believe it is necessary to shatter this conceptual framework in order to proceed with film.

History

The case for narrative film is based on the belief that a film practice cannot develop "out of the blue"; that one has to start *somewhere*, within the history of film. Yet a history, theory, and practice of nonnarrative feminist experimental film is not only possible, but already exists. From the experimental work of Germaine Dulac, rarely shown and often overlooked in favor of her more commercial, narrative films, to current work such as that of Su Friedrich and Leslie Thornton in the United States and that of Lis Rhodes in England, it is evident that feminist nonnarrative experimental film can be made.

As with any other area, experimental film is not without its own specific problems, which need to be addressed within the terms of feminism. A fratriarchy of experimental film has developed with its own standards of "quality" to protect, with an absolute faith in certain principles and ideals, which themselves mirror patriarchal ideology. The North American structural film movement, for example, took the ideal of a positivist science as its starting point, and the work of Michael Snow, Hollis Frampton, George Landow, and others relies heavily on the aims and methods of that discipline.

In these films it is evident that the answer being sought, the object of the experiment, is inscribed in the very questions asked: the "knowledge" to be gained is determined in advance. The very terms of this film practice, the set of rules that govern it, delineate and restrict the area of inquiry and thereby foreclose the possibility of any result that was not already known from the outset of the process. The ideal of pure Science, applied to film, provides no guarantee of freedom from the ideology inscribed within the very materials of film. On the contrary, it reflects the patriarchal ideology from which it originated, and which it continues to serve.

Another development, the "lyrical" or "visionary" film (e.g., Stan Brakhage), posits a world in which an entirely new set of physical and social principles is in operation. In a pseudonaïf search for a more "pure" vision, a return to an unadulterated mode of seeing, visionary filmmakers exempt themselves from the responsibility of examining and challenging the very myths and ideals of an ideology that they buy into in their use of the tools of cinema.

Men who have sought a break with the cinema of the past have launched unified theories, positing fixed methods and procedures. We are loath to posit an argument that would assert, definitively, the last word – the ultimate strategy – in a long history of attempts at anti-illusionist filmmaking. We mistrust the sense of conclusiveness implicit in the very act of assertion. The nature of *experimental* film belies any attempt at a fixed method or procedure: the work needs to proceed in a manner that assumes no ultimate end, no goal for film outside of the real materials and conditions of film itself. *By proposing a feminist film practice, we are necessarily proposing an experimental method* – a method that questions the very grounds of film, assuming nothing as given but the materials of film themselves – not simply film stock, camera, and so on, but especially the processes and relations of filmmaking and film viewing. This reflects the desire not to reproduce already-existing representations, which have been immeasurably limiting and damaging to us. The present impossibility for women to represent themselves properly, accurately, has led to an awareness not only of the inadequacy of the aims and intentions of dominant cinema but also of the impossibility of its main task: to represent. We wish to finally acknowledge this impossibility and to move on to a use of film that attempts no mastery of meaning, assumes no ultimate knowledge of reality through film. For film will fail to advance any understanding of these problems unless it first deals with the complex problems *within the terms of film*:

Film first of all has to function in cinematographic terms as any art or science must operate in reference to the development of its particular mode of expression. This does not evacuate "content" as it assumes it to be a preliminary question what film content could be, and to study, contrive, invent the precise ways it could be inscribed in film.[27]

In order to do this it is necessary to open up the possibility for the making and viewing of films that provide a "kind" of pleasure that does not depend on the patriarchal narrative mode (nor on its inverse in the form of a "neofeminist" use of film for "different" representations of women). A use of film that breaks with the patriarchal foundation of sexual division is necessary for feminist film work to proceed.

The ultimate impossibility of film in its use for patriarchy – the problematic lack of correspondence between image and meaning, between the real of film and that of other areas of life – is no longer a cause for lament, but a source of relief and inspiration for women working in film.

Notes

1. Some important institutions include the Film-makers' Co-op and Circles Film Distribution in London, the Pacific Film Archive and Canyon Cinema in the San Francisco Bay Area, and the Anthology Film Archive, the Millennium Film Workshop, the Filmmakers' Co-op, and the now-defunct Collective for Living Cinema in New York City.

2. See P. Adams Sitney, *Visionary Film: The American Avant-Garde 1943–1978* (New York: Oxford University Press, 1974); see also his collection of essays on the historical film avant-garde, *The Avant-Garde Film: A Reader of Theory and Criticism* (New York: Anthology Film Archives, 1978).

3. See Lis Rhodes and Felicity Sparrow, "Her Image Fades as Her Voice Rises," in this anthology (originally published in *Heresies* 16 [1983]: 63–66). See also Peter Gidal, *Materialist Film* (London and New York: Routledge, 1989).

4. This essay appeared in a British Film Institute exhibition catalog for a show of British avant-garde cinema called *Film as Film* (London: British Film Institute, 1976).

5. *Screen* 19, no. 3 (1978): 113–27.

6. Sandy Flitterman-Lewis, *To Desire Differently: Feminism and the French Cinema* (Urbana: University of Illinois Press, 1990).

7. Lauren Rabinovitz, *Points of Resistance: Women, Power and Politics in the New York Avant-Garde Cinema, 1943–71* (Urbana: University of Illinois Press, 1991).

8. Menken's films include *Geography of the Body* (produced in 1943 with Norman McLaren and the Gryphon Group); *Visual Variations on Noguchi* (1945); *Glimpse of the Garden* (1957); and *Hurry, Hurry!* (1957).

9. For an account of the development of the *Camera Obscura* collective, see the collectively written "Chronology," *Camera Obscura* 3–4 (1979): 6–13.

10. Peter Wollen, "The Two Avant-Gardes," *Studio International* (December 1975). Reprinted in Peter Wollen, *Readings and Writings* (London: Verso, 1982): 92–104.

11. Peter Wollen, " 'Ontology' and 'Materialism' in Film," *Screen* 17, no. 1 (1976): 7–23.

12. Teresa de Lauretis, *Alice Doesn't: Feminism, Semiotics, Cinema* (Bloomington: Indiana University Press, 1984), 68.

13. A special issue of *October* devoted to "the New Talkies" is a good example of the trend we were critiquing in our essay (*October* 14 [1983]).

14. Coco Fusco, "Fantasies of Oppositionality – Reflections on Recent Conferences in New York," *Screen* 29 (Autumn 1988): 80–93.

15. The writings of the *Camera Obscura* collective, Claire Johnston, E. Ann Kaplan, and Mary Ann Doane are just a few instances in a long line of different approaches to deconstructing/analyzing narrative within an avant-garde context.

16. Constance Penley, Felicity Sparrow, Lis Rhodes, Nancy Woods, and Su Friedrich are a few women who have begun a written feminist discourse addressing the problems and possibilities of experimental film work for women.

17. Interview with Laura Mulvey by Nina Danino and Lucy Moy-Thomas, *Undercut* 6 (Winter 1982–83): 11.

18. Ad copy from film journals.

19. Samuel Beckett, *Ill Seen Ill Said* (New York: Grove Press, 1974).

20. Constance Penley, "The Avant-Garde and Its Imaginary," *Camera Obscura* 2 (Fall 1977): 25.

21. A film by Claire Pajaczkowska, Jane Weinstock, Andrew Tyndall, and Anthony McCall.

22. Christine Noll-Brinckmann and Grahame Weinbren, "Mutations of Film Narrative," *Idiolects* 12 (Fall 1982): 28.

23. Ibid.

24. Ibid.

25. "Theory films" that function as studies in Marxist, psychoanalytic, and semiotic analyses make redundant what already exists in dominant cinema. This redundancy becomes evident when we note that these theories have been applied with equal success to new avant-garde narrative and to old Hollywood narratives – particularly those of the forties and fifties, in which the operations of seduction are so visible as to have provided perfect case studies for such analysis.

26. Laura Mulvey, "Visual Pleasure and Narrative Cinema," *Screen* 16 (Autumn 1975): 6–18.

27. Rose Lowder, "Reflections on Experimental Film," *Feminism/Film* 1 (1984): 30–31.

Rethinking Women's Cinema:
Aesthetics and Feminist Theory

Teresa de Lauretis

When Silvia Bovenschen in 1976 posed the question "Is there a feminine aesthetic?" the only answer she could give was, yes and no: "Certainly there is, if one is talking about aesthetic awareness and modes of sensory perception. Certainly not, if one is talking about an unusual variant of artistic production or about a painstakingly constructed theory of art."[1] If this contradiction seems familiar to anyone even vaguely acquainted with the development of feminist thought over the past fifteen years, it is because it echoes a contradiction specific to, and perhaps even constitutive of, the women's movement itself: a twofold pressure, a simultaneous pull in opposite directions, a tension toward the positivity of politics, or affirmative action in behalf of women as social subjects, on one front, and the negativity inherent in the radical critique of patriarchal, bourgeois culture, on the other. It is also the contradiction of women in language, as we attempt to speak as subjects of discourses that negate or objectify us through their representations. As Bovenschen put it, "We are in a terrible bind. How do we speak? In what categories do we think? Is even logic a bit of virile trickery? . . . Are our desires and notions of happiness so far removed from cultural traditions and models?" (119).

Not surprisingly, therefore, a similar contradiction was also central to the debate on women's cinema, its politics and its language, as it was articulated within Anglo-American film theory in the early 1970s in relation to feminist politics and the women's movement, on the one hand, and to artistic avant-garde practices and women's filmmaking, on the other. There, too, the accounts of feminist film culture produced in the mid- to late seventies tended to emphasize a dichotomy between two concerns of the women's movement and two types of film work that seemed to be at odds with each other: one called for immediate documentation for purposes of political activism, consciousness-raising, self-expression, or the search for "positive images" of woman; the other insisted on rigorous, formal work on the medium – or, better, the cinematic apparatus, understood as a social technology – in order to analyze and disengage the ideological codes embedded in representation.

Thus, as Bovenschen deplores the "opposition between feminist demands and artistic production" (131), the tug of war in which women artists were caught between the movement's demands that women's art portray women's activities, document demonstrations, and such, and the formal demands of "artistic activity and its concrete work with material and media," so does Laura Mulvey set out two successive moments of feminist film culture. First, she states, there was a period marked by the effort to change the *content* of cinematic representation (to present realistic images of women, to record women talking about their real-life experiences), a period "characterized by a mixture of consciousness-raising and propaganda."[2] It was followed by a second moment, in which the concern with the language of representation as such became predominant, and the "fascination with the cinematic process" led filmmakers and critics to the "use of and interest in the aesthetic principles and terms of reference provided by the avant-garde tradition" (7).

In this latter period, the common interest of both avant-garde cinema and feminism in the politics of images, or the political dimension of aesthetic expression, made them turn to the theoretical debates on language and imaging that were going on outside of cinema, in semiotics, psychoanalysis, critical theory, and the theory of ideology. Thus it was argued that in order to counter the aesthetic of realism, which was hopelessly compromised with bourgeois ideology, as well as Hollywood cinema, avant-garde and feminist filmmakers must take an oppositional stance against narrative "illusionism" and in favor of formalism. The assumption was that "foregrounding the process itself, privileging the signifier, necessarily disrupts aesthetic unity and forces the spectator's attention on the means of production of meaning" (7).

While Bovenschen and Mulvey would not relinquish the political commitment of the movement and the need to construct other representations of woman, the way in which they posed the question of expression (a "feminine aesthetic," a "new language of desire") was couched in the terms of a traditional notion of art, specifically the one propounded by modernist aesthetics. Bovenschen's insight that what is being expressed in the decoration of the household and the body, or in letters and other private forms of writing, is in fact women's aesthetic needs and impulses, is a crucial one. But the importance of that insight is undercut by the very terms that define it: the *"pre-*aesthetic realms." After quoting a passage from Sylvia Plath's *The Bell Jar*, Bovenschen comments:

> Here the ambivalence once again: on the one hand we see aesthetic ac-
> tivity deformed, atrophied, but on the other we find, even within this
> restricted scope, socially creative impulses which, however, have no out-
> let for aesthetic development, no opportunities for growth. . . . [These
> activities] remained bound to everyday life, feeble attempts to make this
> sphere more aesthetically pleasing. But the price for this was narrow-
> mindedness. The object could never leave the realm in which it came into
> being, it remained tied to the household, it could never break loose and
> initiate communication. (132–33)

Just as Plath laments that Mrs. Willard's beautiful home-braided rug is not hung on the wall but put to the use for which it was made, and thus quickly spoiled of its beauty, so would Bovenschen have "the object" of artistic creation leave its context of production and use-value in order to enter the "artistic realm" and so to "initiate communication"; that is to say, to enter the museum, the art gallery, the market. In other words, art is what is enjoyed publicly rather than privately, has an exchange-value rather than a use-value, and that value is conferred by socially established aesthetic canons.

Mulvey, too, in proposing the destruction of narrative and visual pleasure as the foremost objective of women's cinema, hails an established tradition, albeit a radical one: the historic left avant-garde tradition that goes back to Eisenstein and Vertov (if not Méliès) and through Brecht reaches its peak of influence in Godard, and on the other side of the Atlantic, the tradition of American avant-garde cinema. "The first blow against the monolithic accumulation of traditional film conventions (already undertaken by radical film-makers) is to free the look of the camera into its materiality in time and space and the look of the audience into dialectics, passionate detachment."[3] But much as Mulvey and other avant-garde filmmakers insisted that women's cinema ought to avoid a politics of emotions and seek to problematize the female spectator's identification with the on-screen image of woman, the response to her theoretical writings, like the reception of her films (codirected with Peter Wollen), showed no consensus. Feminist critics, spectators, and filmmakers remained doubtful. For example, Ruby Rich:

> According to Mulvey, the woman is not visible in the audience which is
> perceived as male; according to Johnston, the woman is not visible on the
> screen. . . . How does one formulate an understanding of a structure
> that insists on our absence even in the face of our presence? What is

there in a film with which a woman viewer identifies? How can the contradictions be used as a critique? And how do all these factors influence what one makes as a woman filmmaker, or specifically as a feminist filmmaker?[4]

The questions of identification, self-definition, the modes or the very possibility of envisaging oneself as subject – which the male avant-garde artists and theorists have also been asking, on their part, for almost one hundred years, even as they work to subvert the dominant representations or to challenge their hegemony – are fundamental questions for feminism. If identification is "not simply one psychical mechanism among others, but the operation itself whereby the human subject is constituted," as Laplanche and Pontalis describe it, then it must be all the more important, theoretically and politically, for women who have never before represented ourselves as subjects, and whose images and subjectivities – until very recently, if at all – have not been ours to shape, to portray, or to create.[5]

There is indeed reason to question the theoretical paradigm of a subject-object dialectic, whether Hegelian or Lacanian, that subtends both the aesthetic and the scientific discourses of Western culture; for what that paradigm contains, what those discourses rest on, is the unacknowledged assumption of sexual difference: that the human subject, Man, is the male. As in the originary distinction of classical myth reaching us through the Platonic tradition, human creation and all that is human – mind, spirit, history, language, art, or symbolic capacity – is defined in contradistinction to formless chaos, *phusis* or nature, to something that is female, matrix and matter; and on this primary binary opposition, all the others are modeled. As Lea Melandri states,

> Idealism, the oppositions of mind to body, of rationality to matter, originate in a twofold concealment: of the woman's body and of labor power. Chronologically, however, even prior to the commodity and the labor power that has produced it, the matter which was negated in its concreteness and particularity, in its "relative plural form," is the woman's body. Woman enters history having already lost concreteness and singularity: she is the economic machine that reproduces the human species, and she is the Mother, an equivalent more universal than money, the most abstract measure ever invented by patriarchal ideology.[6]

That this proposition remains true when tested on the aesthetic of modernism or the major trends in avant-garde cinema from visionary to structural-materialist film, on the films of Stan Brakhage, Michael Snow, or Jean-Luc Godard, but is not true of the films of Yvonne Rainer, Valie Export, Chantal Akerman, or Marguerite Duras, for example; that it remains valid for the films of Fassbinder but not those of Ottinger, the films of Pasolini and Bertolucci but not Cavani's, and so on, suggests to me that it is perhaps time to shift the terms of the question altogether.

To ask of these women's films, What formal, stylistic, or thematic markers point to a female presence behind the camera? and hence to generalize and universalize, to say, This is the look and sound of women's cinema, this is its language—finally only means complying, accepting a certain definition of art, cinema, and culture, and obligingly showing how women can and do "contribute," pay their tribute, to "society." Put another way, to ask whether there is a feminine or female aesthetic, or a specific language of women's cinema, is to remain caught in the master's house and there, as Audre Lorde's suggestive metaphor warns us, to legitimate the hidden agendas of a culture we badly need to change. Cosmetic changes, she is telling us, won't be enough for the majority of women—women of color, black women, and white women as well; or, in her own words, "assimilation within a solely western-european herstory is not acceptable."[7]

It is time we listened. Which is not to say that we should dispense with rigorous analysis and experimentation on the formal processes of meaning production, including the production of narrative, visual pleasure, and subject positions, but rather that feminist theory should now engage precisely in the redefinition of aesthetic and formal knowledges, much as women's cinema has been engaged in the transformation of vision.

Take Akerman's *Jeanne Dielman, Quai du Commerce, 1080 Bruxelles* (1975), a film about the routine daily activities of a Belgian middle-class and middle-aged housewife, and a film in which the pre-aesthetic is already fully aesthetic. That is not so, however, because of the beauty of its images, the balanced composition of its frames, the absence of the reverse shot, or the perfectly calculated editing of its still-camera shots into a continuous, logical, and obsessive narrative space; it is so because it is a woman's actions, gestures, body, and look that define the space of our vision, the temporality and rhythms of perception, the horizon of meaning available to the spectator. So that narrative suspense is not built on the expectation of a "significant event," a socially momentous act (which actually occurs, though unexpectedly and almost incidentally, one feels, toward the end of the film), but is produced by the tiny slips in Jeanne's routine, the small forgettings, the hesitations between real-time gestures as common and "insignificant" as peeling potatoes, washing dishes, or making coffee—and then not drinking it. What the film constructs—formally and artfully, to be sure—is a picture of female experience, of duration, perception, events, relationships, and silences that feels immediately and unquestionably true. And in this sense the "pre-aesthetic" is *aesthetic* rather than *aestheticized*, as it is in films such as Godard's *Two or Three Things I Know about Her*, Polanski's *Repulsion*, or Antonioni's *Eclipse*. To say the same thing in another way, Akerman's film addresses the spectator as female.

The effort, on the part of the filmmaker, to render a presence in the feeling of a gesture, to convey the sense of an experience that is subjective yet socially coded (and therefore recognizable), and to do so formally, working through her conceptual (one could say, theoretical) knowledge of film form, is averred by Chantal Akerman in an interview on the making of *Jeanne Dielman*:

> I *do* think it's a feminist film because I give space to things which were never, almost never, shown in that way, like the daily gestures of a woman. They are the lowest in the hierarchy of film images. . . . But more than the content, it's because of the style. If you choose to show a woman's gestures so precisely, it's because you love them. In some way you recognize those gestures that have always been denied and ignored. I think that the real problem with women's films usually has nothing to do with the content. It's that hardly any women really have confidence enough to carry through on their feelings. Instead the content is the most simple and obvious thing. They deal with that and forget to look for formal ways to express what they are and what they want, their own rhythms, their own way of looking at things. A lot of women have unconscious contempt for their feelings. But I don't think I do. I have enough confidence in myself. So that's the other reason why I think it's a feminist film—not just what it says but *what* is shown and *how* it's shown.[8]

This lucid statement of poetics resonates with my own response as a viewer and gives me something of an explanation as to why I recognize in those unusual film images, in those movements, those silences, and those looks, the ways of an experience all but unrepresented, previously unseen in film, though lucidly and unmistakably apprehended here. And so the statement cannot be dismissed with commonplaces such as authorial intention or intentional fallacy. As another critic and spectator points out, there are "two logics" at work in this film, "two modes of the feminine": character and director, image and camera, remain distinct yet interacting and mutually interdependent positions. Call them femininity and feminism; the one is made representable by the critical work of the other; the one is kept at a distance, constructed, "framed," to be sure, and yet "respected," "loved," "given space" by the other.[9] The two "logics" remain separate:

> The camera look can't be construed as the view of any character. Its interest extends beyond the fiction. The camera presents itself, in its evenness and predictability, as equal to Jeanne's precision. Yet the camera continues its logic throughout; Jeanne's order is disrupted, and with the murder the text comes to its logical end since Jeanne then stops altogether. If Jeanne has, symbolically, destroyed the phallus, its order still remains visible all around her.[10]

Finally, then, the space constructed by the film is not only a textual or filmic space of vision, in frame and off—for an off-screen space is still inscribed in the images, although not sutured narratively by the reverse shot but effectively reaching toward the historical and social determinants that define Jeanne's life and place her in her frame. But beyond that, the film's space is also a critical space of analysis, a horizon of possible meanings that includes or extends to the spectator ("extends beyond the fiction") insofar as the spectator is led to occupy at once the two positions, to follow the two "logics," and to perceive them as equally and concurrently true.

In saying that a film whose visual and symbolic space is organized in this manner *addresses its spectator as a woman*, regardless of the gender of the viewers, I mean that the film defines all points of identification (with character, image, camera) as female, feminine, or feminist. However, this is not as simple or self-evident a notion as the established film-theoretical view of cinematic identification, namely, that identification with the look is masculine, and identification with the image is feminine. It is not self-evident precisely because such a view—which indeed correctly explains the working of dominant cinema—is now accepted: that the camera (technology), the look (voyeurism), and the scopic drive itself partake of the phallic and thus somehow are entities or figures of a masculine nature.

How difficult it is to "prove" that a film addresses its spectator as female is brought home time and again in conversations or discussions between audiences and filmmakers. After a screening of *Redupers* in Milwaukee (in January 1985), Helke Sander answered a question about the function of the Berlin wall in her film and concluded by saying, if I may paraphrase: "But of course the wall also represents another division that is specific to women." She did not elaborate, but again, I felt that what she meant was clear and unmistakable. And so does at least one other critic and spectator, Kaja Silverman, who sees the wall as a division other in kind from what the wall would divide—and can't, for things do "flow through the Berlin wall (TV and radio waves, germs, the writings of Christa Wolf)," and Edda's photographs show the two Berlins in "their quotidian similarities rather than their ideological divergences."

> All three projects are motivated by the desire to tear down the wall, or at least to prevent it from functioning as the dividing line between two irreducible opposites. . . . *Redupers* makes the wall a signifier for psychic as well as ideological, political, and geographical boundaries. It functions there as a metaphor for sexual difference, for the subjective limits articulated by the existing symbolic order both in East and West. The wall thus designates the discursive boundaries which separate residents not only of the same country and language, but of the same partitioned space.[11]

Those of us who share Silverman's perception must wonder whether in fact the sense of that other, specific division represented by the wall in *Redupers* (sexual difference, a discursive boundary, a subjective limit) is in the film or in our viewers' eyes. Is it actually there on screen, in the film, inscribed in its slow montage of long takes and in the stillness of the images in their silent frames; or is it, rather, in our perception, our insight, as—precisely—a subjective limit and discursive boundary (gender), a horizon of meaning (feminism) that is projected into the images, onto the screen, around the text?

I think it is this other kind of division that is acknowledged in Christa Wolf's figure of "the divided heaven," for example, or in Virginia Woolf's "room of one's own": the feeling of an internal distance, a contradiction, a space of silence that is there alongside the imaginary pull of cultural and ideological representations without denying or obliterating them. Women artists, filmmakers, and writers acknowledge this division or difference by attempting to express it in their works. Spectators and readers think we find it in those texts. Nevertheless, even today, most of us would still agree with Silvia Bovenschen.

"For the time being," writes Gertrud Koch, "the issue remains whether films by women actually succeed in subverting this basic model of the camera's construction of the gaze, whether the female look through the camera at the world, at men, women and objects will be an essentially different one."[12] Posed in these terms, however, the issue will remain fundamentally a rhetorical question. I have suggested that the emphasis must be shifted away from the artist behind the camera, the gaze, or the text as origin and determination of meaning, toward the wider public sphere of cinema as a social technology: we must develop our understanding of cinema's implication in other modes of cultural representation, and its possibilities of both production and counterproduction of social vision. I further suggest that, even as filmmakers are confronting the problems of transforming vision by engaging all of the codes of cinema, specific and nonspecific, against the dominance of that "basic model," our task as theorists is to articulate the conditions and forms of vision for another social subject, and so to venture into the highly risky business of redefining aesthetic and formal knowledge.

Such a project evidently entails reconsidering and reassessing the early feminist formulations or, as Sheila Rowbotham summed it up, "look[ing] back at ourselves through our own cultural creations, our actions, our ideas, our pamphlets, our organization, our history, our theory."[13] And if we now can add "our films," perhaps the time has come to rethink women's cinema as the production of a feminist social vision. As a form of political critique or critical politics, and through the specific consciousness that women have developed to analyze the subject's relation to sociohistorical reality, feminism not only has invented new strategies or created new texts, but, more important, it has conceived a new social subject, women: as speakers, writers, readers, spectators, users, and makers of cultural forms, shapers of cultural processes. The project of women's cinema, therefore, is no longer that of destroying or disrupting man-centered vision by representing its blind spots, its gaps, or its repressed. The effort and challenge now are how to effect another vision: to construct other objects and subjects of vision, and to formulate the conditions of representability of another social subject. For the time being, then, feminist work in film seems necessarily focused on those subjective limits and discursive boundaries that mark women's division as gender-specific, a division more elusive, complex, and contradictory than can be conveyed in the notion of sexual difference as it is currently used.

The idea that *a film may address the spectator as female*, rather than portray women positively or negatively, seems very important to me in the critical endeavor to characterize women's cinema as a cinema for, not only by, women. It is an idea not found in the critical writings I mentioned earlier, which are focused on the film, the object, the text. But rereading those essays today, one can see, and it is important to stress it, that the question of a filmic language or a feminine aesthetic has been articulated from the beginning in relation to the women's movement: "the new grows only out of the work of confrontation" (Mulvey 4); women's "imagination constitutes the movement itself" (Bovenschen 136); and in Claire Johnston's nonformalist view of women's cinema as countercinema, a feminist political strategy should reclaim, rather than shun, the use of film as a form of mass culture: "In order to counter our objectification in the cinema, our collective fantasies must be released: women's cinema must embody the working through of desire: such an objective demands the use of the entertainment film."[14]

Since the first women's film festivals in 1972 (New York, Edinburgh) and the first journal of feminist film criticism (*Women & Film*, published in Berkeley from 1972 to 1975), the question of women's expression has been one of both self-expression and communication with other women, a question at once of the creation/invention of new images and of the creation/imaging of new forms of community. If we rethink the problem of a specificity of women's cinema and aesthetic forms in this manner, in terms of address—who is making films for whom, who is looking and speaking, how, where, and to whom—then what has been seen as a rift, a division, an ideological split within feminist film culture between theory and practice, or between formalism and activism, may appear to be the very strength, the drive and productive heterogeneity of feminism. In their introduction to the recent collection *Re-vision: Essays in Feminist Film*

Criticism, Mary Ann Doane, Patricia Mellencamp, and Linda Williams point out:

> If feminist work on film has grown increasingly theoretical, less oriented towards political action, this does not necessarily mean that theory itself is counter-productive to the cause of feminism, nor that the institutional form of the debates within feminism have simply reproduced a male model of academic competition. . . . Feminists sharing similar concerns collaborate in joint authorship and editorships, cooperative filmmaking and distribution arrangements. Thus, many of the political aspirations of the women's movement form an integral part of the very structure of feminist work in and on film.[15]

The "re-vision" of their title, borrowed from Adrienne Rich ("Re-vision — the act of looking back, of seeing with fresh eyes," writes Rich, is for women "an act of survival"), refers to the project of reclaiming vision, of "seeing difference differently," of displacing the critical emphasis from "images of" women to "the axis of vision itself — to the modes of organizing vision and hearing which result in the production of that 'image.' "[16]

I agree with the *Re-vision* editors when they say that over the past decade, feminist theory has moved "from an analysis of difference as oppressive to a delineation and specification of difference as liberating, as offering the only possibility of radical change" (12). But I believe that radical change requires that such specification not be limited to "sexual difference," that is to say, a difference of women from men, female from male, or Woman from Man. Radical change requires a delineation and a better understanding of the difference of women from Woman, and that is to say as well, *the differences among women.* For there are, after all, different histories of women. There are women who masquerade and women who wear the veil; women invisible to men, in their society, but also women who are invisible to other women, in our society.[17]

The invisibility of black women in white women's films, for instance, or of lesbianism in mainstream feminist criticism, is what Lizzie Borden's *Born in Flames* (1983) most forcefully represents, while at the same time constructing the terms of their visibility as subjects and objects of vision. Set in a hypothetical near-future time and in a place very much like lower Manhattan, with the look of a documentary (after Chris Marker) and the feel of contemporary science-fiction writing (the post-new-wave sci-fi of Samuel Delany, Joanna Russ, Alice Sheldon, or Thomas Disch), *Born in Flames* shows how a "successful" social democratic cultural revolution, now into its tenth year, slowly but surely reverts to the old patterns of male dominance, politics as usual, and the traditional Left disregard for "women's issues." It is around this specific gender oppression, in its various forms, that several groups of women (black women, Latinas, lesbians, single mothers, intellectuals, political activists, spiritual and punk performers, and a Women's Army) succeed in mobilizing and joining together not by ignoring but, paradoxically, by acknowledging their differences.

Like *Redupers* and *Jeanne Dielman*, Borden's film addresses the spectator as female, but it does not do so by portraying an experience that feels immediately one's own. On the contrary, its barely coherent narrative, its quick-paced shots and sound montage, the counterpoint of image and word, the diversity of voices and languages, and the self-conscious science-fictional frame of the story hold the spectator across a distance, projecting toward her its fiction like a bridge of difference. In short, what *Born in Flames* does for me, woman spectator, is exactly to allow me "to see difference differently," to look at women with eyes I've never had before and yet my own, for, as it remarks the emphasis (the words are Audre Lorde's) on the "interdependency of different strengths" in feminism, the film also inscribes the differences among women as *differences within women*.

Born in Flames addresses me as a woman and a feminist living in a particular moment of women's history, the United States today. The film's events and images take place in what science fiction calls a parallel universe, a time and a place elsewhere that look and feel like here and now, yet are not, just as I (and all women) live in a culture that is and is not our own. In that unlikely, but not impossible, universe of the film's fiction, the women come together in the very struggle that divides and differentiates them. Thus, what it portrays for me, what elicits my identification with the film and gives me, spectator, a place in it, is the contradiction of my own history and the personal/political difference that is also within myself.

"The relationship between history and so-called subjective processes," says Helen Fehervary in a recent discussion of women's film in Germany, "is not a matter of grasping the truth in history as some objective entity, but in finding the truth of experience. Evidently, this kind of experiential immediacy has to do with women's own history and self-consciousness."[18] That, how, and why our histories and our consciousness are different, divided, even conflicting, is what women's cinema can analyze, articulate, reformulate. And, in so doing, it can help us create something else to be, as Toni Morrison says of her two heroines:

> Because each had discovered years before that they were neither white nor male, and that all freedom and triumph was forbidden to them, they had set about creating something else to be.[19]

In the following pages I will refer often to *Born in Flames*, discussing some of the issues it has raised, but it will not be with the aim of a textual analysis. Rather, I will take it as the starting point, as indeed it was for me, of a series of reflections on the topic of this essay.

Again, it is a film, and a filmmaker's project, that bring home to me with greater clarity the question of difference, this time in relation to factors other than gender, notably race and class – a question endlessly debated within Marxist feminism and recently rearticulated by women of color in feminist presses and publications. That this question should reemerge urgently and irrevocably now is not surprising, at a time when severe social regression and economic pressures (the so-called feminization of poverty) belie the self-complacency of a liberal feminism enjoying its modest allotment of institutional legitimation. A sign of the times, the recent crop of commercial, man-made "woman's films" (*Lianna, Personal Best, Silkwood, Frances, Places of the Heart*, and so on) is undoubtedly "authorized," and made financially viable, by that legitimation. But the success, however modest, of this liberal feminism has been bought at the price of reducing the contradictory complexity – and the theoretical productivity – of concepts such as sexual difference, the personal is political, and feminism itself to simpler and more acceptable ideas already existing in the dominant culture. Thus, to many today, "sexual difference" is hardly more than sex (biology) or gender (in the simplest sense of female socialization) or the basis for certain private "life-styles" (homosexual and other nonorthodox relationships); "the personal is political" all too often translates into "the personal instead of the political"; and "feminism" is unhesitantly appropriated, by the academy as well as the media, as a discourse – a variety of social criticism, a method of aesthetic or literary analysis among others, and more or less worth attention according to the degree of its market appeal to students, readers, or viewers. And, yes, a discourse perfectly accessible to all men of good will. In this context, issues of race or class must continue to be thought of as mainly sociological or economic, and hence parallel to but not dependent on gender, implicated with but not determining of subjectivity, and of little relevance to this "feminist discourse" that, as such, would have no competence in the matter but only, and at best, a humane or "progressive" concern with the disadvantaged.

The relevance of feminism (without quotations marks) to race and class, however, is very explicitly stated by those women of color, black and white, who are not the recipients but rather the "targets" of equal opportunity, who are outside or not fooled by liberal "feminism," or who understand that feminism is nothing if it is not at once political and personal, with all the contradictions and difficulties that entails. To such feminists it is clear that the social construction of gender, subjectivity, and the relations of representation to experience do occur within race and class as much as they occur in language and culture, often indeed across languages, cultures, and sociocultural apparati. Thus, not only is it the case that the notion of gender, or "sexual difference," cannot be simply accommodated into the preexisting, ungendered (or male-gendered) categories by which the official discourses on race and class have been elaborated; but it is

equally the case that the issues of race and class cannot be simply subsumed under some larger category labeled femaleness, femininity, womanhood, or, in the final instance, Woman. What is becoming more and
more clear, instead, is that all the categories of our social science stand to
be reformulated *starting from* the notion of gendered social subjects. And
something of this process of reformulation – re-vision, rewriting, rereading, rethinking, "looking back at *ourselves*" – is what I see inscribed in the
texts of women's cinema but not yet sufficiently focused on in feminist film
theory or feminist critical practice in general. This point, like the relation
of feminist writing to the women's movement, demands a much lengthier
discussion than can be undertaken here. I can do no more than sketch the
problem as it strikes me with unusual intensity in the reception of Lizzie
Borden's film and my own response to it.

What *Born in Flames* succeeds in representing is this feminist understanding: that the female subject is en-gendered, constructed, and defined
in gender across multiple representations of class, race, language, and social relations; and that, therefore, differences among women are differences *within* women, which is why feminism can exist despite those differences and, as we are just beginning to understand, cannot continue to exist
without them. The originality of this film's project is its representation of
woman as a social subject and a site of differences; differences that are not
purely sexual or merely racial, economic, or (sub)cultural, but all of these
together and often enough in conflict with one another. What one takes
away after seeing this film is the image of a heterogeneity in the female
social subject, the sense of a distance from dominant cultural models and
of an internal division within women that remain, not in spite of but concurrently with the provisional unity of any concerted political action. Just
as the film's narrative remains unresolved, fragmented, and difficult to follow, heterogeneity and difference within women remain in our memory as
the film's narrative image, its work of representing, which cannot be col-
lapsed into a fixed identity, a sameness of all women as Woman, or a
representation of Feminism as a coherent and available image.

Other films, in addition to the ones already mentioned, have effectively
represented that internal division or distance from language, culture, and
self that I see recur, figuratively and thematically, in recent women's
cinema (it is also represented, for example, in Gabriella Rosaleva's *Pro-
cesso a Caterina Ross* and in Lynne Tillman and Sheila McLaughlin's
Committed). But *Born in Flames* projects that division on a larger social
and cultural scale, taking up nearly all of the issues and putting them all
at stake. As we read on the side of the (stolen) U-Haul trucks that carry
the free women's new mobile radio transmitter, reborn as Phoenix-
Regazza (girl phoenix) from the flames that destroyed the two separate
stations, the film is "an adventure in moving." As one reviewer saw it,

> An action pic, a sci-fi fantasy, a political thriller, a collage film, a snatch of the underground: *Born in Flames* is all and none of these. . . . Edited in 15-second bursts and spiked with yards of flickering video transfers . . . *Born in Flames* stands head and shoulders above such Hollywood reflections on the media as *Absence of Malice, Network*, or *Under Fire*. This is less a matter of its substance (the plot centers on the suspicious prison "suicide," à la Ulrike Meinhoff, of Women's Army leader Adelaide Norris) than of its form, seizing on a dozen facets of our daily media surroundings.[20]

The words of the last sentence, echoing Akerman's emphasis on form rather than content, are in turn echoed by Borden in several printed statements. She, too, is keenly concerned with her own relation as filmmaker to filmic representation ("Two things I was committed to with the film were questioning the nature of narrative . . . and creating a process whereby I could release myself from my own bondage in terms of class and race").[21] And she, too, like Akerman, is confident that vision can be transformed because hers has been: "Whatever discomfort I might have felt as a white filmmaker working with black women has been over for so long. It was exorcized by the process of making the film." Thus, in response to the interviewer's (Anne Friedberg) suggestion that the film is "progressive" precisely because it "demands a certain discomfort for the audience, and forces the viewer to confront his or her own political position(s) (or lack of political position)," Borden flatly rejects the interviewer's implicit assumption.

> I don't think the audience is solely a white middle-class audience. What was important for me was creating a film in which that was *not* the only audience. The problem with much of the critical material on the film is that it assumes a white middle-class reading public for articles written about a film that they assume has only a white middle-class audience. I'm very confused about the discomfort that reviewers feel. What I was trying to do (and using humor as a way to try to do it) was to have various positions in which everyone had a place on some level. Every woman— with men it is a whole different question—would have some level of identification with a position within the film. Some reviewers over-identified with something as a privileged position. Basically, none of the positioning of black characters was *against* any of the white viewers but more of an invitation: come and work with us. Instead of telling the viewer that he or she could *not* belong, the viewer was supposed to be a repository for all these different points of view and all these different styles of rhetoric. Hopefully, one would be able to identify with one position but be able to evaluate all of the various positions presented in the film. Basically, I feel this discomfort only from people who are deeply resistant to it.[22]

This response is one that, to my mind, sharply outlines a shift in women's cinema from a modernist or avant-garde aesthetic of subversion to an emerging set of questions about filmic representation to which the term *aesthetic* may or may not apply, depending on one's definition of art, one's definition of cinema, and the relationship between the two. Similarly, whether or not the terms *postmodern* or *postmodernist aesthetic* would be preferable or more applicable in this context, as Craig Owens has suggested of the work of other women artists, is too large a topic to be discussed here.[23]

At any rate, as I see it, there has been a shift in women's cinema from an aesthetic centered on the text and *its* effects on the viewing or reading subject – whose certain, if imaginary, self-coherence is to be fractured by the text's own disruption of linguistic, visual, and/or narrative coherence – to what may be called an aesthetic of reception, where the spectator is the film's primary concern – primary in the sense that it is there from the beginning, inscribed in the filmmaker's project and even in the very making of the film.[24] An explicit concern with the audience is of course not new either in art or in cinema, since Pirandello and Brecht in the former, and it is always conspicuously present in Hollywood and TV. What is new here, however, is the particular conception of the audience, which now is envisaged in its heterogeneity and otherness from the text.

That the audience is conceived as a heterogeneous community is made apparent, in Borden's film, by its unusual handling of the function of address. The use of music and beat in conjunction with spoken language, from rap singing to a variety of subcultural lingos and nonstandard speech, serves less the purposes of documentation or cinema vérité than those of what in another context might be called characterization: they are there to provide a means of identification of and with the characters, though not the kind of psychological identification usually accorded to main characters or privileged "protagonists." "I wanted to make a film that different audiences could relate to on different levels – if they wanted to ignore the language they could," Borden told another interviewer, "but not to make a film that was anti-language."[25] The importance of "language" and its constitutive presence in both the public and the private spheres is underscored by the multiplicity of discourses and communication technologies – visual, verbal, and aural – foregrounded in the form as well as the content of the film. If the wall of official speech, the omnipresent systems of public address, and the very strategy of the women's takeover of a television station assert the fundamental link of communication and power, the film also insists on representing the other, unofficial social discourses, their heterogeneity, and *their* constitutive effects vis-à-vis the social subject.

In this respect, I would argue, both the characters and the spectators of Borden's film are positioned in relation to social discourses and representations (of class, race, and gender) within particular "subjective limits and discursive boundaries" that are analogous, in their own historical specificity, to those which Silverman saw symbolized by the Berlin Wall in *Redupers*. For the spectators, too, are limited in their vision and understanding, bound by their own social and sexual positioning, as their "discomfort" or diverse responses suggest. Borden's avowed intent to make the spectator a locus ("a repository") of different points of view and discursive configurations ("these different styles of rhetoric") suggests to me that the concept of a heterogeneity of the audience also entails a heterogeneity of, or in, the individual spectator.

If, as is claimed by recent theories of textuality, the Reader or the Spectator is implied in the text as an effect of its strategy – either as the figure of a unity or coherence of meaning that is constructed by the text (the "text of pleasure"), or as the figure of the division, dissemination, incoherence inscribed in the "text of jouissance" – then the spectator of *Born in Flames* is somewhere else, resistant to the text and other from it. This film's spectator is not only *not* sutured into the "classic" text by narrative and psychological identification; nor is it bound in the time of repetition, "at the limit of any fixed subjectivity, materially inconstant, dispersed in process," as Stephen Heath aptly describes the spectator intended by avant-garde (structural-materialist) film.[26] What happens is that this film's spectator is finally not liable to capture by the text.

And yet one is engaged by the powerful erotic charge of the film; one responds to the erotic investment that its female characters have in each other, and the filmmaker in them, with something that is neither pleasure nor *jouissance*, oedipal nor preoedipal, as they have been defined for us; but with something that is again (as in *Jeanne Dielman*) a recognition, unmistakable and unprecedented. Again the textual space extends to the spectator, in its erotic and critical dimensions, addressing, speaking-to, making room, but not (how very unusual and remarkable) cajoling, soliciting, seducing. These films do not put me in the place of the female spectator, do not assign me a role, a self-image, a positionality in language or desire. Instead, they make a place for what I will call me, knowing that I don't know it, and give "me" space to try to know, to see, to understand. Put another way, by addressing me as a woman, they do not bind me or appoint me as Woman.

The "discomfort" of Borden's reviewers might be located exactly in this disappointment of spectator and text: the disappointment of not finding oneself, not finding oneself "interpellated" or solicited by the film, whose images and discourses project back to the viewer a space of heterogeneity, differences, and fragmented coherences that just do not add up to one individual viewer or one spectator-subject, bourgeois or otherwise. There is no one-to-one match between the film's discursive heterogeneity and the discursive boundaries of any one spectator. We are both invited in and held at a distance, addressed intermittently and only insofar as we are able to occupy the position of addressee; for example, when Honey, the Phoenix Radio disc jockey, addresses to the audience the words "Black women, be ready. White women, get ready. Red women, stay ready, for this is our time and all must realize it."[27] Which individual member of the audience, male or female, can feel singly interpellated as spectator-subject or, in other words, unequivocally addressed?

There is a famous moment in film history, something of a parallel to this one, which not coincidentally has been "discovered" by feminist film critics in a woman-made film about women, Dorothy Arzner's *Dance, Girl, Dance*: it is the moment when Judy interrupts her stage performance and, facing the vaudeville audience, steps out of her role and speaks to them as a woman to a group of people. The novelty of this direct address, feminist critics have noted, is not only that it breaks the codes of theatrical illusion and voyeuristic pleasure, but also that it demonstrates that no complicity, no shared discourse, can be established between the woman performer (positioned as image, representation, object) and the male audience (positioned as the controlling gaze); no complicity, that is, outside the codes and rules of the performance. By breaking the codes, Arzner revealed the rules and the relations of power that constitute them and are in turn sustained by them. And sure enough, the vaudeville audience in her film showed great discomfort with Judy's speech.

I am suggesting that the discomfort with Honey's speech has also to do with codes of representation (of race and class as well as gender) and the rules and power relations that sustain them—rules that also prevent the establishing of a shared discourse, and hence the "dream" of a common language. How else could viewers see in this playful, exuberant, science-fictional film a blueprint for political action that, they claim, wouldn't work anyway? ("We've all been through this before. As a man I'm not threatened by this because we know that this doesn't work. This is infantile politics, these women are being macho like men used to be macho. . . . ")[28] Why else would they see the film, in Friedberg's phrase, "as a *prescription* through fantasy"? Borden's opinion is that "people have not really been upset about class and race. . . . People are really upset that the women are gay. They feel it is separatist."[29] My own opinion is that people are upset with all three, class, race, and gender—lesbianism being precisely the demonstration that the concept of gender is founded across race and class on the structure that Adrienne Rich and Monique Wittig have called, respectively, "compulsory heterosexuality" and "the heterosexual contract."[30]

The film-theoretical notion of spectatorship has been developed largely in the attempt to answer the question posed insistently by feminist theorists and well summed up in the words of Ruby Rich already cited above: "How does one formulate an understanding of a structure that insists on our absence even in the face of our presence?" In keeping with the early divergence of feminists over the politics of images, the notion of spectatorship was developed along two axes: one starting from the psychoanalytic theory of the subject and employing concepts such as primary and secondary, conscious and unconscious, imaginary and symbolic processes; the other starting from sexual difference and asking questions such as, How does the female spectator see? With what does she identify? Where/How/In what film genres is female desire represented? and so on. Arzner's infraction of the code in *Dance, Girl, Dance* was one of the first answers in this second line of questioning, which now appears to have been the most fruitful by far for women's cinema. *Born in Flames* seems to me to work out the most interesting answer to date.

For one thing, the film assumes that the female spectator may be black, white, "red," middle class or not middle class, and wants her to have a place within the film, some measure of identification—"identification with a position," Borden specifies. "With men [spectators] it is a whole different question," she adds, obviously without much interest in exploring it (though later suggesting that black male spectators responded to the film "because they don't see it as just about women. They see it as empowerment").[31] In sum, the spectator is addressed as female in gender and multiple or heterogeneous in race and class; which is to say, here too all points of identification are female or feminist, but rather than the "two logics" of character and filmmaker, like *Jeanne Dielman, Born in Flames* foregrounds their different discourses.

Second, as Friedberg puts it in one of her questions, the images of women in *Born in Flames* are "unaestheticized": "You never fetishize the body through masquerade. In fact the film seems consciously de-aestheticized, which is what gives it its documentary quality."[32] Nevertheless, to some, those images of women appear to be extraordinarily beautiful. If such were to be the case for most of the film's female spectators, however socially positioned, we would be facing what amounts to a film-theoretical paradox, for in film theory the female body is construed precisely as fetish or masquerade.[33] Perhaps not unexpectedly, the filmmaker's response is amazingly consonant with Chantal Akerman's, though their films were visually quite different, and the latter's is in fact received as an "aesthetic" work.

> BORDEN: "The important thing is to shoot female bodies in a way that they have never been shot before. . . . I chose women for the stance I liked. The stance is almost like the gestalt of a person."[34]

> And AKERMAN (cited above): "I give space to things which were never, almost never, shown in that way. . . . If you choose to show a woman's gestures so precisely, it's because you love them."

The point of this cross-referencing of two films that have little else in common beside the feminism of their makers is to remark the persistence of certain themes and formal questions about representation and difference that I *would* call aesthetic, and that are the historical product of feminism and the expression of feminist critical-theoretical thought.

Like the works of the feminist filmmakers I have referred to, and many others too numerous to mention here, *Jeanne Dielman* and *Born in Flames* are engaged in the project of transforming vision by inventing the forms and processes of representation of a social subject – women – that until now has been all but unrepresentable; a project already set out (looking back, one is tempted to say, programmatically) in the title of Yvonne Rainer's *Film about a Woman Who* . . . (1974), which in a sense all of these films continue to reelaborate. The gender-specific division of women in language, the distance from official culture, the urge to imagine new forms of community as well as to create new images ("creating something else to be"), and the consciousness of a "subjective factor" at the core of all kinds of work – domestic, industrial, artistic, critical, or political work – are some of the themes articulating the particular relation of subjectivity, meaning, and experience that en-genders the social subject as female. These themes, encapsulated in the phrase "the personal is political," have been formally explored in women's cinema in several ways: through the disjunction of image and voice, the reworking of narrative space, the elaboration of strategies of address that alter the forms and balances of traditional representation. From the inscription of subjective space and duration inside the frame (a space of repetitions, silences, and discontinuities in *Jeanne Dielman*) to the construction of other discursive social spaces (the discontinuous but intersecting spaces of the women's "networks" in *Born in Flames*), women's cinema has undertaken a redefinition of both private and public space that may well answer the call for "a new language of desire" and actually have met the demand for the "destruction of visual pleasure," if by that one alludes to the traditional, classical and modernist, canons of aesthetic representation.

So, once again, the contradiction of women in language and culture is manifested in a paradox: most of the terms by which we speak of the construction of the female social subject in cinematic representation bear in their visual form the prefix *de-* to signal the deconstruction or the destructuring, if not destruction, of the very thing to be represented. We speak of the de-aestheticization of the female body, the desexualization of violence, the de-oedipalization of narrative, and so forth. Rethinking women's cinema in this way, we may provisionally answer Bovenschen's question thus: There is a certain configuration of issues and formal problems that have been consistently articulated in what we call women's cinema. The way in which they have been expressed and developed, both artistically and critically, seems to point less to a "feminine aesthetic" than to a feminist *de-aesthetic*. And if the word sounds awkward or inelegant . . .

Notes

This essay was written initially as a contribution to the catalogue of *Kunst mit Eigen-Sinn* (edited by Silvia Eiblmayr, Valie Export, and Monika Prischl-Meier [Vienna and Munich: Locker. 1985]), an international exhibition of contemporary women's art held at the Museum des 20. Jahrhunderts in Vienna, 1985. It was first published in the present expanded version, and with the title "Aesthetics and Feminist Theory: Rethinking Women's Cinema," in *New German Critique*, no. 34 (Winter 1985). Reprinted here with minor changes in editorial style and format.

I am very grateful to Cheryl Kader for generously sharing with me her knowledge and insight from the conception through the writing of this essay, and to Mary Russo for her thoughtful critical suggestions.

1. Silvia Bovenschen, "Is There a Feminine Aesthetic?" trans. Beth Weckmueller, *New German Critique*, no. 10 (Winter 1977): 136. (Originally published in *Aesthetik und Kommunikation* 25 [September 1976].)

2. Laura Mulvey, "Feminism, Film, and the Avant-Garde," *Framework*, no. 10 (Spring 1979): 6. See also Christine Gledhill's account "Recent Developments in Feminist Film Criticism," *Quarterly Review of Film Studies* 3, no. 4 (1978).

3. Laura Mulvey, "Visual Pleasure and Narrative Cinema," *Screen* 16 (Autumn 1975): 18.

4. B. Ruby Rich, in "Women and Film: A Discussion of Feminist Aesthetics," *New German Critique*, no. 13 (Winter 1978): 87.

5. J. Laplanche and J.-B. Pontalis, *The Language of Psycho-analysis*, trans. D. Nicholson-Smith (New York: Norton, 1973), 206.

6. Lea Melandri, *L'infamia originaria* (Milan: Edizioni L'Erba Voglio, 1977), 27; my translation. For a more fully developed discussion of semiotic theories of film and narrative, see Teresa de Lauretis, *Alice Doesn't: Feminism, Semiotics, Cinema* (Bloomington: Indiana University Press, 1984).

7. See Audre Lorde, "The Master's Tools Will Never Dismantle the Master's House" and "An Open Letter to Mary Daly," in *This Bridge Called My Back: Writings by Radical Women of Color*, ed. Chérrie Moraga and Gloria Anzaldúa (New York: Kitchen Table: Women of Color Press, 1983), 96. Both essays are reprinted in Audre Lorde, *Sister Outsider: Essays and Speeches* (Trumansburg, N.Y.: Crossing Press, 1984).

8. "Chantal Akerman on *Jeanne Dielman*," *Camera Obscura*, no. 2 (1977): 118–19.

9. In the same interview, Akerman said: "I didn't have any doubts about any of the shots. I was very sure of where to put the camera and when and why. . . . I *let* her [the character] live her life in the middle of the frame. I didn't go in too close, but I was not *very* far away. I let her be in her space. It's not uncontrolled. But the camera was not voyeuristic in the commercial way because you always knew where I was. . . . It was the only way to shoot that film—to avoid cutting the woman into a hundred pieces, to avoid cutting the action in a hundred places, to

look carefully and to be respectful. The framing was meant to respect the space, her, and her gestures within it" (ibid., 119).

10. Janet Bergstrom, "*Jeanne Dielman, 23 Quai du Commerce, 1080 Bruxelles* by Chantal Akerman," *Camera Obscura*, no. 2 (1977): 117. On the rigorous formal consistency of the film, see also Mary Jo Lakeland, "The Color of Jeanne Dielman," *Camera Obscura*, nos. 3–4 (1979): 216–18.

11. Kaja Silverman, "Helke Sander and the Will to Change," *Discourse*, no. 6 (Fall 1983): 10.

12. Gertrud Koch, "Ex-changing the Gaze: Re-visioning Feminist Film Theory," *New German Critique*, no. 34 (Winter 1985): 144.

13. Sheila Rowbotham, *Woman's Consciousness, Man's World* (Harmondsworth, England: Penguin Books, 1973), p. 28.

14. Claire Johnston, "Women's Cinema as Counter-Cinema," in *Notes on Women's Cinema*, ed. Claire Johnston (London: Society for Education in Film and Television, 1973), 31. See also Gertrud Koch, "Was ist und wozu brauchen wir eine feministische Filmkritik," *frauen und film*, no. 11 (1977).

15. Mary Ann Doane, Patricia Mellencamp, and Linda Williams, eds., *Re-vision: Essays in Feminist Film Criticism* (Frederick, Md.: University Publications of America, 1984), 4.

16. Ibid., 6. The quotation from Adrienne Rich is in her *On Lies, Secrets, and Silence* (New York: Norton, 1979), 35.

17. See Barbara Smith, "Toward a Black Feminist Criticism," in *All the Women Are White, All the Blacks Are Men, but Some of Us Are Brave: Black Women's Studies*, ed. Gloria T. Hull, Patricia Bell Scott, and Barbara Smith (Old Westbury, N.Y.: Feminist Press, 1982).

18. Helen Fehervary, Claudia Lenssen, and Judith Mayne, "From Hitler to Hepburn: A Discussion of Women's Film Production and Reception," *New German Critique*, nos. 24–25 (Fall-Winter 1981–82): 176.

19. Toni Morrison, *Sula* (New York: Bantam Books, 1975), 44.

20. Kathleen Hulser, "Les Guérillères," *Afterimage* 11 (January 1984): 14.

21. Anne Friedberg, "An Interview with Filmmaker Lizzie Borden," *Women and Performance* 1 (Winter 1984): 43. On the effort to understand one's relation as a feminist to racial and cultural differences, see Elly Bulkin, Minnie Bruce Pratt, and Barbara Smith, *Yours in Struggle: Three Feminist Perspectives on Anti-Semitism and Racism* (Brooklyn, N.Y.: Long Haul Press, 1984).

22. Interview in *Women and Performance*, 38.

23. Craig Owens, "The Discourse of Others: Feminists and Postmodernism," in *The Anti-Aesthetic: Essays in Postmodern Culture*, ed. Hal Foster (Port Townsend, Wash.: Bay Press, 1983), 57–82. See also Andreas Huyssen, "Mapping the Postmodern," *New German Critique*, no. 33 (Fall 1984): 5–52, now reprinted in Huyssen, *After the Great Divide: Modernism, Mass Culture, Postmodernism* (Bloomington: Indiana University Press, 1986).

24. Borden's nonprofessional actors, as well as her characters, are very much part of the film's intended audience: "I didn't want the film caught in the white film ghetto. I did mailings. We got women's lists, black women's lists, gay lists, lists

that would bring different people to the Film Forum" (interview in *Women and Performance*, 43).

25. Betsy Sussler, "Interview," *Bomb*, no. 7 (1983): 29.

26. Stephen Heath, *Questions of Cinema* (Bloomington: Indiana University Press, 1981), 167.

27. The script of *Born in Flames* is published in *Heresies*, no. 16 (1983): 12–16. Borden discusses how the script was developed in conjunction with the actors and according to their particular abilities and backgrounds in the interview in *Bomb*.

28. Interview in *Bomb*, 29.

29. Interview in *Women and Performance*, 39.

30. Adrienne Rich, "Compulsory Heterosexuality and Lesbian Existence," *Signs: Journal of Women in Culture and Society* 5 (Summer 1980): 631–60; Monique Wittig, "The Straight Mind," *Feminist Issues* (Summer 1980): 110.

31. Interview in *Women and Performance*, 38.

32. Ibid., 44.

33. See Mary Ann Doane, "Film and the Masquerade: Theorising the Female Spectator," *Screen* 23 (September-October 1982): 74–87.

34. Interview in *Women and Performance*, 44–45.

Bakhtin, Language, and Women's Documentary Filmmaking

Janice R. Welsch

Language—its acquisition as well as its relation to subjectivity, to self-identity and self-realization—has been a central issue in feminist theory and feminist film research and a major concern of the feminist movement during the past twenty-five years. Aware that "language so completely structures our grasp of the world that 'reality' can be seen as an effect of linguistic convention,"[1] feminist artists and scholars have frequently addressed the issues of language and voice.[2] Among them are feminist filmmakers and critics who have experimented with new cinematic and verbal vocabularies and forms and have redefined and broadened the uses of established film discourses. Through their work, filmmakers have allowed women to speak from and to their experiences, developing women's discourses around historical events, contemporary situations, and issues of language itself. Feminist film scholars have stressed the power of naming and of developing our own languages if we are to step beyond patriarchal thinking.[3]

On both the level of theory and practice, of filmmaking and film scholarship, language occupies a pivotal place among feminist issues and concerns. Its critical importance is behind my investigation of Mikhail Bakhtin's account of language. Bakhtin's analysis of dialogism and heteroglossia provides an approach that can contribute to understanding languages and their significance for women as a marginalized social group, as cultural groups distinguished by ethnicity, sexual orientation, class, age, and ability in addition to gender, and as women as individuals. More specifically, Bakhtinian concepts can trigger new insights into how languages, including critical and cinematic languages, can be used to counter the dominant languages of patriarchy and validate feminist discourses.

Bakhtin's concepts of dialogism and the many-languagedness (heteroglossia) of society's diverse cultural groups, as well as of the individuals within those groups, provide a framework for an investigation of women's speech and conversation that underscores their potential political and ideological force and suggests how feminist consciousness-raising films contribute to the realization of that potential. His investigations of language reflect a perspective that can broaden our own, even though he did not explicitly explore the issue of gender. Because "his sympathies are clearly . . . with the marginalized, the oppressed, the peripheralized," his "theoretical grid . . . does not have to be stretched to encompass [us]";[4] it indicates our position vis-à-vis power. While, like many linguists, Bakhtin was aware that "speech is always a way of controlling people's behavior or directing their thinking," he also insisted speech is active, that it can change, a crucial point for women and other marginalized people who want to effect change within any oppressive social structure. Indeed, Bakhtin suggested that the conflict of values between and within social groups, as expressed always and necessarily in dialogue, is what facilitates linguistic change, and ultimately behavioral change.[5] The grounding in ideology and in material reality that Bakhtin insisted upon has a particular appeal because it avoids a split between theory and practice, between abstract constructs and historical realities, or between woman and women, while offering an explanation of the dynamics of speech that invites challenges to the patriarchal status quo.

Bakhtin recognized centripetal forces that move to "unite and centralize verbal-ideological thought" and thus guarantee "a certain maximum of mutual understanding" through the unity of a "correct language."[6] Those forces, operating through a dominant social group that seeks to impose its language throughout society, tend to standardize language and set it as a measure by which society is stratified and status assigned. Within patriarchal societies, women constitute a group whose status is defined and circumscribed by the dominant male population. That population has linked women's languages to emotion as well as to the personal and subjective in contrast to male languages with their orientation toward rationality and public concerns. Women's words have then been dismissed,[7] our credibility and experience limited, and the "integrity of work and life which can only be found in an emotional and intellectual connectedness" denied.[8] To be taken seriously women have often suppressed the emotional aspect of their discourse and have censored the issues they address in public speech, just as other groups have suppressed aspects of their languages, such as accent, dialect, vocabulary, and grammar, considered nonstandard by the dominant group.

However, any unity achieved through the imposition of standardized speech is relative, for even within the dominant group, language is neither one nor static. Languages of power, like other languages, reflect members' differences – differences such as age, profession, ethnicity, and region – and they are always in flux, always open to historical process. At every moment language is informed by the past and by the present, by different ideological and political forces, by diverse social and cultural values, by multiple individual and group identifications, by complex and at times contradictory priorities existing within and between speakers and listeners.[9] The diversity of language occurs naturally and reflects the diversity in society. As defined by Bakhtin, languages are so extensive that individuals and groups are inevitably identified with several and can use one or another according to the particular role and the specific context governing a given moment. Yet, in practice, they are based on reproducible linguistic elements, including words, syntax, and sounds, that provide their common "technical apparatus"[10] and allow us to juxtapose and relate them one to another.[11]

Strong centrifugal forces assure continued diversity of languages and keep languages alive and developing, even while the pull toward a unified language makes itself felt. The impact of those centrifugal forces varies, of course, depending on the amount of resistance they meet. Because patriarchal discursive control has been exercised so pervasively for so long, it has achieved relative stability and is not easily challenged or changed.[12] Within patriarchy, male-identified, male-centered languages do not just valorize male patterns of thought and male perspectives; they often erase women as, for example, in the use of masculine nouns and pronouns to refer to both genders, in Bakhtin's own failure to consider gender differences, and in the male voice-of-authority off-screen narrators typical of traditional documentaries. Patriarchal languages have been presented as essentially neutral, as reflections of the natural order, the implication being that to be genuinely human is to speak a language of patriarchy.[13]

The devaluation of women's languages in personal male/female relationships as well as in public forums has led women to adapt patriarchal languages, but we can persist in attempts to "seize and transform" those languages through dialogue (Bakhtin 293–94). As long as interaction among speakers and listeners takes place, we can do so with the expectation that we will effect change. We can also continue using and developing other discourses that reflect more accurately and positively our own identities and experiences. Among women and other oppressed peoples, opportunities to do so exist. In our own cultural and social groups, we can speak the languages that more accurately reflect our selves; we can use our unofficial discourses to celebrate and explore what we value within our lives and to critique, counter, or contradict what we have been told by those exerting power over us.[14]

The making and screening of women's documentaries offer opportunities for such discourse since many independent, feminist documentaries use language, including film techniques and verbal exchanges, narrative and visual discourses, differently; they address issues of special interest to women and develop the new languages needed to discuss them. Frequently they provide a climate and a situation in which women can focus on their experiences and achievements without pressure to conform to the expectations or dictates of patriarchal authority and without fear of male censure. Offering the empathic milieu of a formal or informal consciousness-raising group, the setting bears directly on how issues are presented and how they are received. The conversational, woman-centered contexts set up, even precipitate, responses oriented toward feminist consciousness, and they facilitate a means of experiencing a meaningful exchange between official, authoritative discourses and women's languages as well as between women's external speech and individual women's inner speech.[15] The establishment of favorable feminist contexts, however, is not simply a matter of providing congenial environments. Context as understood by Bakhtin is more inclusive and far-reaching in its bearing on language; it is central to his conception of language as dynamic and changeable, and, therefore, of major interest to those who want to shape or redirect language use.

As developed by Bakhtin, language's dynamism is its dialogism and its contextual resonance. He was not particularly interested in abstract linguistic systems or grammatical form as such; his focus was on utterance, on the historical-materialist aspects of languages, in what is expressed or articulated at a given moment within a specific set of circumstances (Todorov ix-x, 42–43). Nothing is spoken that is not shaped by the "elastic environment" surrounding the word and its subject/speaker, its object and listener. "Living dialogic threads" (Bakhtin 276) are spun from the word, its history and usage; the subject, her history as well as her social and personal identities; the object or theme, its multiple facets and significance; and the listener/s, her/their history/ies, identities, perspectives, and values. Together those elements, in their complex and varied interaction, compose the context that leads to active understanding and ideological development. Because utterances are "half someone else's," having been structured, always and necessarily, by an anticipated response, they can bring new elements, different perspectives, and "other social languages," into the subject's discourse. When this happens an internal dialogism occurs, making possible new understanding within the subject herself. This intrapersonal exchange exists in tandem with interpersonal dialogue, the former setting up an interaction among various facets of the subject's own social identities and viewpoints as, for example, a professional, a feminist, a sister, a friend, a mother, and the latter creating interaction between the cultures and multiple perspectives of the subject and the listener (Bakhtin 288–300). To lead to growth and creative understanding, this interaction cannot simply become fusion or identification of the self with the other. Within the interaction neither subject, object, nor listener "renounce[s] its self, its place in time, its culture; it does not forget anything" (Todorov 109), but it remains receptive and open to the possibility of altering its perceptions since such openness is a prerequisite for dialogism and growth.

For women making, participating in, or viewing women's documentaries, dialogue can occur between filmmakers and participants or viewers, among the film participants or between them and viewers, among viewers, and within a viewer. These multiple dialogic exchanges are possible because viewers are encouraged to respond to the films and because filmmaking practices are chosen with dialogue in mind. For instance, rather than relying on the seemingly omniscient voice-over of many traditional documentaries, feminist documentarists have often favored interviews and on-screen discussions. In films such as the Iris Feminist Collective's *In the Best Interests of the Children* (on challenges faced by lesbian mothers), Lee Grant's *The Willmar Eight* (about the strike of eight female bank employees), Camille Billops and James Hatch's *Suzanne, Suzanne* (on domestic violence within a middle-class family), and Elena Featherston's *Visions of the Spirit: A Portrait of Alice Walker*, various women become important sources of information and insight as they either interact with the filmmaker or with other women being filmed.

The dialogic process frequently begins earlier with the preparatory research for a film. *Daughter Rite*, for example, while bridging experimental and documentary filmmaking forms, is firmly grounded in documentary practice through the extensive interviews and exploratory discussions that provided Michelle Citron with many of the ideas she pursues in the work. Talking with women about their experiences as daughters and sisters helped her formulate questions her narrator and on-screen interviewees consider. Connie Field was also influenced by extensive interaction with women who had worked in industry during World War II when she made *The Life and Times of Rosie the Riveter*. Before choosing the 5 former "Rosies" who appear in her film she interviewed 100 on videotape, chosen from among 700 who completed written questionnaires. Judging from the overall issue-oriented organization of the film, the on-film interviews were planned to cover clearly defined aspects of the women's experiences that had surfaced in the preproduction questionnaires and video conversations. To continue the dialogues, Field followed the film's credits with an address and an invitation to viewers to write to her about their reactions to the film. Such filmmaker-viewer interaction is also possible because the filmmakers are often present when their films are shown and encourage viewers to discuss the films in light of their own knowledge and experience. In addition, some filmmakers have collaborated on material contextualizing the films' subjects and explaining the conditions of production. Examples include Women Make Movies' "Point of View: Latina Study Guide" that accompanies a series of films and videotapes directed by Latin American women and *Hearts and Hands: The Influence of Women and Quilts on American Society* that filmmaker Pat Ferrero wrote with Elaine Hedges and Julie Silber to complement Ferrero's documentary *Hearts and Hands: A Social History of Nineteenth Century Women and Quilts*. Thus dialogue among women becomes part of film reception as well as filmmaking.

The complex of social and cultural resonances reverberating through the films and among the women in their roles as subjects and listeners inevitably reflects points of difference as well as points of agreement. The task of both speakers and listeners, each person alternately assuming each role, is to evaluate the ideas, insights, and viewpoints offered them in light of their own histories and values. How effectively they do this depends in part on how much speaker-listener or listener-speaker distance they maintain. The genial environment often created for screenings of women's documentaries fosters empathy among speakers and listeners on all levels, but many feminist documentarists try to avoid complete or unthinking identification between themselves, their film subjects, and their viewers.[16] Even in realist documentaries various filmmaking techniques are used to help maintain distance, among them direct address to the audience by the filmmaker or film participants, the filmmaker's visual or verbal interaction with her subjects, and shots reminding viewers, either through images, printed text, or sound, that the film is constructed and offers neither a comprehensive nor completely objective treatment of an issue or situation. Such cinematic distancing must be coupled with a viewer's own critical perspective in order to benefit from the dialogue the film makes possible. Bakhtin suggests that maintaining distance or "finding oneself outside" is not just desirable but essential if dialogic interaction is to lead to growth (Todorov 99). He sees identification and empathy only as an initial step in the process of understanding. They cannot lead to enriching one's self if they amount to duplicating a perspective rather than enlarging one's own. When a person does maintain some distance between her self and the other, she can understand the other and be enriched through the other's unique background and perspectives (Todorov 108–9; Bakhtin 280–82).

While warning against losing one's self in an other, Bakhtin just as strongly insists that a subject can be a subject, an I, only by revealing herself to another, by interacting with an other.[17] Given the silencing of women and the concomitant low self-esteem and limited value many women have experienced within patriarchal structures, Bakhtin's attention to the self, the subject, is significant. That he identifies self-realization with interaction with an other suggests again the value of empathic feminist consciousness-raising groups that validate the experience and words of the individual.

As Bakhtin indicates, the word or utterance seeks a response; the subject, a listener. Bakhtin develops his basic thesis that "[l]ife is dialogical by its very nature," from the perspective of the individual when he insists that "self-consciousness is achieved only through . . . another consciousness." In explaining this, Bakhtin begins with the external, pointing out that no one can see her self, her body in its entirety and that our experience of ourselves as finite beings comes only through an other. He then proceeds to the internal: "All that touches me comes to my consciousness—beginning with my name—from the outside world, passing through the mouths of others. . . . They give me the words, the forms, and the tonality that constitute my first [and subsequent] image[s] of myself." My "very being (both internal and external) is a *profound communication. To be* means *to communicate*" (Todorov 96–97, x–xi): "the subject . . . cannot remain a subject if it is voiceless" (Todorov 18).

Clearly, consciousness-raising groups have functioned as an affirming other for many women participating in them. They have offered women the opportunity to communicate, to enter into conversation with other women who listen, hear, and respond from their own experiences and needs. In speaking they have given their ideas and experiences a validity that strengthens their inner consciousness of themselves and a public status and political resonance that can, and often has, challenged established discourses of power. As Julia Lesage has pointed out, "the self-conscious act of telling one's story as a woman in a politicized yet personal way gives . . . women's conversation . . . a new social force as a tool for liberation."[18] Feminist documentarists have provided a forum for such potentially liberating conversation and exploration by making films that both depict and facilitate personal, politicized conversation among women. Such organic consciousness-raising experiences, such exchanges contribute to the formation of women as women, subjects whose self-consciousness reflects their own gendered experiences as these have been refracted through the experiences of other women.[19]

For feminists, then, the imperative is to speak to one another and then to the rest of society. We need to engage one another in conversation to validate and make our own, our selves; to create the environments that make speaking possible; to listen, and through our listening, provide the "half word" (Bakhtin 293) that facilitates the development of our own languages and fosters deeper self-consciousness. Given our multiple roles within society and the saturation of that society by patriarchal languages, we still need those languages, but having opportunities to speak languages that express what is ideologically meaningful to us as women and understanding the implications of doing so, we put ourselves in better positions to understand the implications of our adoption of patriarchal languages, to more effectively use and adapt those languages, and to lessen their control over us. Since using patriarchal languages means entering into dialogical relation with them, we can also expect to change them, not radically or quickly, but gradually and continually, to effect shifts in meaning that give us greater visibility and equality.[20]

The women's movement initiated a favorable historical moment, an agreeable context in which to affect languages.[21] The feminist documentaries of the late sixties and of subsequent decades that have come out of the movement have helped shift our conversations from the private space of the home to the more public spaces of women's centers, meeting halls, television studios, and classrooms, allowing validation of our selves and of our roles within society. Forums of challenge, inquiry, and celebration, feminist documentaries have given women time and space to speak: to name our oppression, define our concerns, confirm our creativity, celebrate our accomplishments, establish our place in history, share our expertise, and explore our values. Whether offering the distance initially needed to consider traditionally taboo issues or simply articulating some aspect of women's lives, the documentaries are dialogic by virtue of their juxtaposition of feminist perspectives with patriarchal perceptions. Their dialogism is frequently more complex, however, because language itself is complex, the individuals using it are always multifaceted, and the films incorporate cinematic discourses in addition to the dynamics of on-screen conversation, interviews, and commentary.

Frequently, in feminist documentaries, the most immediately apparent dialogic interaction occurs between patriarchal and feminist discourses. Even when not explicit, patriarchal discourses function as a context in which the visual and aural languages of the film are read. In Pat Ferrero's *Quilts in Women's Lives*, for example, the celebration of quilting as an aesthetic and creative activity is filtered through male definitions and evaluations of art because art history as we know it is predominantly the history of male artists. Ferrero's film consists of separate interviews with eight women who share a passion for quilting but who differ in many other aspects of their lives, including age, family, ethnicity, and locale. They differ too in their approaches to quilting and the types of quilts they make. Because they are interviewed individually (with the exception of two sisters), within each segment dialogism occurs between their words and their work, and between the other contextual languages within the exchange. As interview follows interview, however, film viewers can readily relate them dialogically on many more levels, both personal and aesthetic, because of their diversity, without forgetting the dialogism prompted by the implicit positioning of women's art against a male norm.

Feminist validative documentaries,[22] whether chronicling women's achievements in art or in other areas, set up implicit dialogical interaction because of the pervasiveness of patriarchal perspectives and languages. Some feminist documentaries, however, more explicitly and deliberately foster dialogue by exposing and challenging the silences created by patriarchal discourses, silences that have allowed sexual harassment, domestic violence, rape, and incest to be blamed on the victims rather than the perpetrators. Films such as Mary Tiseo and Carol Greenwald's *We Will Not Be Beaten*, Meri Weingarten's *Waking up to Rape*, and Ayoka Chenzira's *Secret Sounds Screaming: The Sexual Abuse of Children* break the silences and counter the myths surrounding such issues. By naming the abuse they help initiate dialogue that is often healing and empowering. In *Secret Sounds Screaming*, for instance, Chenzira juxtaposes the testimony of victims, the insights of trained support personnel, the observations of average citizens, and the haunting slow-motion images of an empty swing in a deserted playground. Through this collage of discourses, she explores the legal, economic, political and cultural, emotional and intellectual aspects of incest and invites viewers to continue the dialogue she has begun.

Women's health concerns, often lost in patriarchally sanctioned silences or co-opted by a male medical establishment, are another reality feminist documentarists have helped articulate and reclaim. Numerous films that present women who share their experiences and explore their health-related rights and responsibilities have given women viewers opportunities to discuss and reassess their own perceptions of and responses to health issues. Among the most interesting and cinematically complex is Kathryn High's *I Need Your Full Cooperation*, a critique of nineteenth-century medical practice and its twentieth-century remnants. High intercuts diverse shots, including fictional film clips, graphically manipulated images, a dramatization of Charlotte Perkins Gilman's "The Yellow Wallpaper," interviews, and split-screen images to provide information and a sense of women's position vis-à-vis a male determination of their needs. The film helps counteract the silence surrounding women's experience of their bodies.

While many feminist documentaries challenge areas of patriarchal silence and co-optation through women's stories and discussion, some confront patriarchal language directly. High's *I Need Your Full Cooperation* is one such film. Connie Field's *The Life and Times of Rosie the Riveter* is another. In her film, Field consciously juxtaposes the official 1940s male discourses of government-sanctioned World War II newsreels and documentaries with the contemporary discourses of five working-class women who were employed in traditionally male jobs during the war. Omniscient off-screen narrators are the principal and official spokesmen heard in the government-approved footage. Their statements, delivered with assurance[23] in grammatically correct Standard English, are particularly authoritative: "Their power resides in [their] possession of knowledge and in [their] privileged, unquestioned activity of interpretation."[24] Speaking from what appears to be incontestable and privileged knowledge and objective understanding, they seem to leave no room for disagreement, discussion, or debate.

When first delivered, these messages spanned a period of four or five years and reflected the patriotic climate generated by the prevailing public discourses of the time.[25] In the 1970s when Field used the material she worked within a significantly different context, one that allowed her to juxtapose the 1940s footage dialogically with 1970s interview footage of former World War II "Rosies." Field's perspective mirrored the insights into women's history and social positioning that came out of the contemporary women's movement; she chose archival film footage, interviewees, and interview questions to convey her feminist perspective.[26] Her strategy was to counter the authoritative narrators with stories by her protagonists, stories of particular incidents that often contradict the official position, stories told with passion and often with humor and always from firsthand knowledge. To many viewers, because of Field's overall structure, the women's unpretentious, personal testimony is far more convincing than the smoothly delivered, imposing, and often patronizing scenario of the Office of War Information (OWI) and newsreel clips. The dialogic interplay of the archival footage with that of the interviews is more multidimensional than this very brief analysis suggests, however. As Bakhtin insists, "language is heteroglot from top to bottom" (219); it is "shot through with intentions and accents," with the history and context of its use.

What first appears to be *the* language of government and industry in *Rosie the Riveter* is actually a polyphony of languages, languages of politics, patriotism, patriarchy, capitalism, racism, and sexism. Connie Field's filmmaking practice also incorporates multiple discourses: those of feminism and unionism, of black women and white, of mothers and of the working class.[27] The opposing languages are expressed through interviews, archival newsreel and OWI footage, photographs, newspaper headlines, magazine articles, songs, animated graphs, fantasy sequences, voice-over narration, the mise-en-scène of specific shots, and, most important, the careful editing of this material. The film's multiplicity of languages increases further through the dialogism between it and its viewers since viewers bring to Field's film feminist and multicultural perspectives shaped by the cultural and socioeconomic movements of the past three decades.

Feminist documentary filmmakers such as Field, High, Chenzira, and the many others who acknowledge women's accomplishments and articulate their experiences, encourage viewers to listen and provide the "half word" that will continue the process of communication and dialogue the women's movement en-gendered. Bakhtin, inasmuch as he posits a dynamic concept of language, provides an impetus for us to develop our own language and to modify patriarchal discourses. He suggests a method of systematically exploring the varied languages of our cultures that will enable us to use those languages more effectively: to understand those that may limit us and to create others that will strengthen us individually and communally. When making or analyzing films, identifying the multiplicity of languages at play positions us to understand the varied levels on which a film communicates and offers the possibility of greater flexibility in choosing or responding to those languages. Although Bakhtin's concept of society's many-languagedness need not be limited to readings of feminist documentaries, the ideas comfortably fit films that are consciousness-raising conversations among women who are seeking their voices. For many women the process leads to empowerment, a validation affirming our place in society while confirming, as well, our potential as capable and productive individuals.

Notes

An earlier version of this essay was read during the Fifth International Bakhtin Conference at the University of Manchester, England. Some of the ideas were also presented at Florida State University's 1987 Literature and Film Conference.

1. Ella Shohat and Robert Stam, "The Cinema after Babel: Language, Difference, Power," *Screen* 3–4 (May-August 1985): 35–36.

2. See, for example, Dale Spender, *Man Made Languages* (Boston: Routledge and Kegan Paul, 1984); Adrienne Rich, *On Lies, Secrets, and Silence* (New York: Norton, 1979); and Mary Daly, *Websters' First New Intergalactic Wickedary of the English Language* (Boston: Beacon Press, 1987).

3. See, for example, B. Ruby Rich, "In the Name of Feminist Film Criticism," this volume; Julia Lesage, "The Political Aesthetics of the Feminist Documentary Film," *Quarterly Review of Film Studies* 3 (Fall 1978): 507–23; and Kaja Silverman, "Dis-Embodying the Female Voice," in *Re-vision: Essays in Feminist Film Criticism* (Frederick, Md.: University Publications of America, 1984).

4. Robert Stam, *Subversive Pleasures: Bakhtin, Cultural Criticism, and Film* (Baltimore: Johns Hopkins University Press, 1989), 231, 234.

5. Gary Saul Morson, "Who Speaks for Bakhtin? A Dialogic Introduction," *Critical Inquiry* 10 (December 1983): 230, and Tzvetan Todorov, *Mikhail Bakhtin:*

The Dialogical Principle, trans. Wlad Godzich (Minneapolis: University of Minnesota Press, 1984), 43. Further Todorov references are indicated within the text.

6. M. M. Bakhtin, *The Dialogic Imagination*, ed. Michael Holquist, trans. Caryl Emerson and Michael Holquist (Austin: University of Texas Press, 1981), 270-73. Further references are indicated within the text.

7. Dale Spender, *Man Made Languages*, 84-85.

8. Adrienne Rich, *On Lies*, 208

9. Although her subject is literary and aesthetic value, in "Contingencies of Value," *Critical Inquiry* 10 (September 1983): 1-35, Barbara Herrnstein Smith explicates a critical theory that, like Bakhtin's analysis of language, valorizes "mutability and diversity," the radically contingent. She states: "We do not move about in a raw universe. Not only are the objects we encounter always to some extent pre-interpreted and preclassified for us by our particular cultures and languages, but also pre-evaluated, bearing the marks and signs of their prior valuings and evaluations by our fellow creatures" (23). Herrnstein Smith's "objects" are markedly similar to Bakhtin's "words."

10. V. N. Volosinov, *Marxism and the Philosophy of Language*, trans. Ladislav Matejka and J. P. Tetunik (New York: Seminar Press, 1973), 99-102. Further references are cited within the text.

11. Ken Hirschkof (Fifth International Bakhtin Conference, University of Manchester, July 15-19, 1991) has challenged Bakhtin's perception of a common plane that allows all languages to be compared. He has suggested that Bakhtin's notion wrongly assumes that all linguistic exchanges are dialogues in which speakers enjoy parity. My own interpretation of Bakhtin's position assumes that equality is not a prerequisite for the juxtaposition of discourses.

12. One indication of how difficult challenging established languages is is evident in the patriarchal co-optation of women's movement discourses. Jean Kilbourne, in her film *Killing Us Softly* and video *Still Killing Us Softly*, provides examples.

13. Ella Shohat and Robert Stam, following Albert Memmi, expand on this idea in terms of colonizer and colonized; they point out that "the mother tongue, which holds emotional impact and in which tenderness and wonder are expressed, is . . . least valued" (54).

14. See Christine Gledhill, "Developments in Feminist Film Criticism," in *Revision*. She approaches the issue of conflicting discourses through the cultural analysis of Tessa Perkins but, like Bakhtin, writes of unofficial discourse grounded in the material and the historical.

15. Bakhtin's concept of dialogism includes speech between individuals and within individuals, consciousness being dependent upon or synonymous with the capacity to verbalize internally and internal dialogization between various values and perspectives being a necessary condition for ideological development (Bakhtin 282; Volosinov 14-15; Stam 65).

16. Cinematic distancing techniques are not unique to feminist documentarians, of course. Numerous avant-garde filmmakers have employed such techniques. See, for example, Teresa de Lauretis's "Rethinking Women's Cinema"; Lisa Cartwright and Nina Fonoroff's "Narrative Is *Narrative*"; Amy Lawrence's "Women's Voices

in Third World Cinema"; and Valerie Smith's "Telling Family Secrets," all in this volume. Formal consciousness-raising groups also incorporate structures that help prevent complete absorption into another's story.

17. In developing this aspect of his social psychology (or philosophical anthropology), Bakhtin puts himself within a long philosophical tradition that posits the I-Thou relationship at the center of individual being. Todorov, in a long footnote, reviews this tradition and cites Bakhtin's place within it. See Todorov, 117–18.

18. Lesage, "Political Aesthetics" 520.

19. See Teresa de Lauretis, *Alice Doesn't: Feminism, Semiotics, Cinema* (Bloomington: Indiana University Press, 1984). In her closely argued analysis of feminism, semiotics, and cinema, she concludes that "feminism has not only 'invented' new strategies, new semiotic contents, and new signs, but more importantly it has effected a habit-change in readers, spectators, speakers, etc. And with that habit-change it has produced a new social subject, women" (185–86). See also her "Rethinking Women's Cinema: Aesthetics and Feminist Theory" in this volume.

20. Feminists are not, of course, the only ones who are trying to alter the dominant languages of our society. Given the stakes–control of language/thought/action/being–and the possibilities, dialogic interaction remains a strong imperative for all marginalized groups.

21. The women's movement, publicly and politically recognized as a movement in the 1960s and 1970s, provided the impetus for feminist movement that is ongoing even while it is currently less visible on some levels and not as clearly identified as a movement. See bell hooks, *Feminist Theory: From Margin to Center* (Boston: South End Press, 1984), chap. 2, esp. p. 29.

22. B. Ruby Rich, "In the Name of Feminist Film Criticism," this volume, suggests the term *validative* for films "about women's lives, political struggles, organizing . . . [s]ince they function as a validation and legitimation of women's culture and individual lives."

23. Bakhtin develops the concept of tone or "intonation," that phenomenon which lies on the border of the verbal and the nonverbal, the spoken and the nonspoken, and which "pumps the energy of the real life situation into the discourse," imparting "active historical movement and uniqueness" (Stam, *Subversive Pleasures*, 44–45).

24. Mary Ann Doane, "The Voice of the Cinema: The Articulation of Body and Space," *Yale French Studies* 60 (1980): 42.

25. See Miriam Frank, Marilyn Ziebarth, and Connie Field, *The Life and Times of Rosie the Riveter* (Emeryville, Calif.: Clarity Educational Products, 1982), esp. 92.

26. Mimi White makes a similar observation in "Rehearsing Feminism" in this volume and points out that Field's juxtaposition of "the past's self-representation in the film's compilation of archival footage with the retrospective individual narratives . . . conveying attitudes toward and memories of the period from a distance of thirty-odd years" is more complicated than the filmmaker acknowledges.

27. At the beginning of the film, Field uses government recruitment posters of anonymous "Rosies" to introduce her interviewees and identify them with the

many women working in industry during World War II; in the process she erases the ethnic and class differences among the women. She later reintroduces these differences as she focuses on the specific experiences of the five women she interviews.

Filmography

Daughter Rite (U.S., 1979). Michelle Citron, 53 min., Women Make Movies.

Hearts and Hands: A Social History of Nineteenth Century Women (U.S., 1987). Pat Ferrero, 63 min., Hearts-Hands Media Arts.

I Need Your Full Cooperation (U.S., 1989). Kathryn High, 28 min., Women Make Movies.

In the Best Interests of the Children (U.S., 1977). Frances Reid, Elizabeth Stevens, and Cathy Zheutlin, 55 min., Women Make Movies.

Life and Times of Rosie the Riveter, The (U.S., 1980). Connie Fields, 65 min., Direct Cinema.

Quilts in Women's Lives (U.S., 1980). Pat Ferrero, 28 min., New Day Films.

Secret Sounds Screaming: The Sexual Abuse of Children (U.S., 1986). Ayoka Chenzira, 30 min., Women Make Movies.

Suzanne, Suzanne (U.S., 1982). Camille Billops and James Hatch, 30 min., Third World Newsreel.

Visions of the Spirit: A Portrait of Alice Walker (U.S., 1989). Elena Featherston, 58 min., Women Make Movies.

Waking up to Rape (U.S., 1985). Meri Weingarten, 35 min., Women Make Movies.

We Will Not Be Beaten (U.S., 1979). Mary Tiseo and Carol Greenwald, 25 min., Transition House.

Willmar Eight, The (U.S., 1979). Lee Grant, 55 min., California Newsreel.

White Privilege and Looking Relations:
Race and Gender in Feminist Film Theory

Jane Gaines

This essay was originally conceived as a challenge to the paradigm that dominated feminist film theory in Britain and the United States for roughly ten years, from 1975 to 1985. Because that paradigm, introduced and developed in the British journal *Screen*, has since lost its exclusive position in the field, the combativeness of the original essay no longer seems appropriate. And yet, debates over the use of psychoanalytic theory have continued, now less heated in film studies than in African and African-American studies.[1] There is another development. Not only is a strong tradition of black feminist literary theory and cultural studies emerging, but we are about to see a parallel development in both critical and creative work on film and video art.[2] One key question remains, however, and I dedicate this reprinting of "White Privilege and Looking Relations" to the consideration of this issue. Yes, more work is being done by Asian, Hispanic, and African-American women. However, has feminist film theory, heretofore written exclusively by white women, shown signs of transformation?[3]

What I want to do here is to show how a theory of the text and its spectator, based on the psychoanalytic concept of sexual difference, is unequipped to deal with a film that is about racial difference and sexuality. The Diana Ross star vehicle *Mahogany* (Berry Gordy, 1975) immediately suggests a psychoanalytic approach because the narrative is organized around the connections between voyeurism and photographic acts and because it is a perfect specimen of the classical cinema, which has been so fully theorized in Lacanian terms. But as I will argue, the psychoanalytic model works to block out considerations that assume a different configuration, so that, for instance, the Freudian-Lacanian scenario can eclipse the scenario of race-gender relations in African-American history, since the two accounts of sexuality are fundamentally incongruous. The danger here is that when we use a psychoanalytic model to explain black family relations we force an erroneous universalization and inadvertently reaffirm white middle-class norms.

By taking gender as its starting point in the analysis of oppression, feminist theory helps to reinforce white middle-class values, and to the extent that it works to keep women from seeing other structures of oppression, it functions ideologically. In this regard, bell hooks criticizes a feminism that seems unable to think of women's oppression in terms other than gender: "Feminist analyses of woman's lot tend to focus exclusively on gender and do not provide a solid foundation on which to construct feminist theory. They reflect the dominant tendency in Western patriarchial minds to mystify women's reality by insisting that gender is the sole determinant of woman's fate."[4] Gender analysis rather exclusively illuminates the condition of white middle-class women, hooks says, and its centrality in feminist theory suggests that those women who have constructed this theory have been ignorant of the way women in different racial groups and social classes *experience* oppression. Many of us would not dispute this. But exactly how should the feminist who does not want to be racist in her work respond to this criticism? In one of the few considerations of this delicate dilemma, Marilyn Frye, in her essay "On Being White," urges us *not* to do what middle-class feminists have historically done: to assume responsibility for everyone. To take it upon oneself to rewrite feminist theory so that it encompasses our differences is another exercise of racial privilege, she says, and therefore all that one can do with conscience is to undertake the study of our own "determined ignorance."[5] One can begin to learn about the people whose history cannot be imagined from a position of privilege.

I recall from graduate school in the late 1970s the tone of feminist film theory as I first heard it – firm in its insistence on attention to cinematic language and strict in its prohibition against making comparisons between actuality and the text. I always heard this voice as a British-accented female voice, and over and over again I heard it reminding me that feminists could only analyze the ideological through its encoding in the conventions of editing and the mechanics of the motion picture machine. This was the point in the history of the field when there were only two texts that had earned the distinction "feminist film theory" (as opposed to criticism), and in the United States we were very aware that they came out of British Marxism:

Claire Johnston's "Women's Cinema as Counter-Cinema," and Laura Mulvey's "Visual Pleasure and Narrative Cinema."[6] In retrospect, we understand that the apparent intransigence of the theory of cinema as patriarchal discourse as it developed out of these essays is the legacy of the Althusserian theory of the subject. From the point of view of Marxist feminism the psychoanalytic version of the construction of the subject was a welcome supplement to classical Marxism; gaining a theory of the social individual, however, meant losing the theory of social antagonism.

The ramifications for feminism would be different on the American side of the Atlantic. The theory of the subject as constituted in language, imported into U.S. academic circles, could swell to the point that it seemed able to account for all oppression, expression, and sociosexual functioning in history. The enormously complicated developments through which European Marxists saw a need for enlarging the capacity of the theory of ideology were lost in translation, so that in the United States we heard that "representation reproduces the patriarchal order." Stuart Hall has described this tendency in both discourse theory and Lacanian psychoanalysis as the opposite of the economism these theories intended to modify – "a reduction upward rather than downward." What transpires in such movements to correct economism is, as he says, "the metaphor of x operates like y is reduced to x = y."[7]

This would happen with a vengeance in the U.S. university scene, where the theory of classical cinema as patriarchal discourse would appear at first quite alone and recently divorced from larger Marxist debates. On campuses where students could not hope to acquire any background in political economy, a film course introduction to the analysis of subjectivity and cinema might well be the only exposure they had to Marxist theory in an entire college career. We must now wonder, however, if the relatively easy assimilation of *Screen* theory into feminist studies in the United States had something to do with the way the radical potential of the theory was quieted with the very use of the psychoanalytic terminology it employed. We further need to consider the warm reception given to high feminist film theory in women's studies circles in terms of the new respectability of academic feminism in the United States, surely signaled by Peter Brooks's statement that "anyone worth his salt in literary criticism today has to become something of a feminist."[8]

Within film and television studies in the United States, the last three years have seen a break with the theory of representation that, it appears, had gripped us for so long. The new feminist strategies that engage with, modify, or abandon the stubborn notion that we are simultaneously positioned in language and ideology are too numerous to detail. In the United States, as in Britain, one of the most influential challenges to this theory posed the question of our reconstitution at different historical moments.

How could the formative moment of one's entry into language be the one condition overriding all other determining conditions of social existence? This question would become especially pertinent as the theoretical interest shifted from the text that produced subjects to the subjects who produced texts; the "real historical subject" became the escape route through which theorists abandoned a text weighted down with impossible expectations.

In the United States, lesbian feminists raised the first objections to the way film theory explained the operation of the classic realist text in terms of tensions between masculinity and femininity. The understanding of spectatorial pleasure in classical cinema as inherently male drew an especially sharp response from critics who argued that this theory canceled the lesbian spectator, whose viewing pleasure could never be construed as anything like male voyeurism. Positing a lesbian spectator would significantly change the trajectory of the gaze. It might lead us to see how the eroticized star body might be not just the object but the visual objective of another female gaze within the film's diegesis–a gaze with which the viewer might identify. Following this argument, Marilyn Monroe and Jane Russell in *Gentlemen Prefer Blondes* are "only for each other's eyes."[9] Two influential studies building on the lesbian reading of *Gentlemen Prefer Blondes* suggested that the lesbian reception of *Personal Best* held a key to challenging the account of cinema as producing patriarchal subject positions, since lesbian viewers, at least, were subverting dominant meanings and confounding textual structures.[10]

Consistently, lesbians have charged that cultural theory posed in psychoanalytic terms is unable to conceive of desire or explain pleasure without reference to the binary oppositions male/female. This is the function of what Monique Wittig calls the heterosexual assumption, or the "straight mind," that unacknowledged structure not only built into Lacanian psychoanalysis, but also underlying the basic divisions of Western culture, organizing all knowledge, yet escaping any close examination.[11] Male/female is a powerful, but sometimes blinding, construct. And it is difficult to see that the paradigm that we embraced so quickly in our first lessons in feminism may have been standing in the way of our further education.

The male/female opposition, seemingly so fundamental to feminism, may actually lock us into modes of analysis that will continually misinterpret the position of many women. Thus, women of color, an afterthought in feminist analysis, remain unassimilated by its central problematic. Feminist anthologies consistently include articles on black female and lesbian perspectives as illustration of the liberality and inclusiveness of feminism; however, the very concept of "different perspectives," while validating distinctness and maintaining woman as common denominator, still places the categories of race and sexuality in theoretical limbo. Our political etiquette is correct, but our theory is not so perfect.

In Marxist feminist analysis, race and sexuality have remained loose ends because as categories of oppression they fit somewhat awkwardly into a model based on class relations in capitalist society. Although some gay historians see a relationship between the rise of capitalism and the creation of the social homosexual, only with a very generous notion of sexual hierarchies–such as the one Gayle Rubin has suggested–can sexual oppression (as different from gender oppression) be located in relation to a framework based on class.[12] Race has folded into Marxist models more neatly than sexuality, but the orthodox formulation that understands racial conflict as class struggle is still unsatisfactory to Marxist feminists who want to know exactly how gender intersects with race. The oppression of *women* of color remains incompletely grasped by the classical Marxist paradigm.

Just as the Marxist model based on class has obscured the function of gender, the feminist model based on the male/female division under patriarchy has obscured the function of race. The dominant feminist paradigm actually encourages us *not to think* in terms of any oppression other than male dominance and female subordination. Thus feminists and lesbians, says Barbara Smith, seem "blinded to the implications of any womanhood that is not white womanhood."[13] For purposes of analysis, black feminists agree that class is as significant as race; however, if these feminists hesitate to emphasize gender as a factor, it is in deference to the way black women describe their experience, for historically, African-American women have formulated identity and political allegiances in terms of race rather than gender or class.[14] Feminism, however, seems not to have heard the statements of women of color who say they experience oppression first in relation to race rather than to gender, and for them exploitation can be personified by a white female.[15] Even more difficult for feminist theory to digest is black female identification with the black male. On this point, black feminists diverge from white feminists in repeatedly reminding us that they do not necessarily see the black male as patriarchal antagonist, but feel instead that their racial oppression is "shared" with men.[16] In the most comprehensive analysis of all, black lesbian feminists have described race, class, and gender oppression as an "interlocking" synthesis in the lives of black women.[17]

The point here is not to rank the structures of oppression in a way that implies the need for black women to choose between solidarity with men or solidarity with women, between race or gender as the basis for a political strategy. At issue is the question of the fundamental antagonism so relevant for Marxist feminist theory. Where we have foregrounded one antagonism in our analysis, we have misunderstood another, and this is most dramatically illustrated in applying the notion of patriarchy. Feminists have not been absolutely certain what they mean by patriarchy: alternately it has referred to either father-right or domination of women, but what is consistent about the use of the concept is the rigidity of the structure it describes.[18] Patriarchy is incompatible with Marxism when used transhistorically without qualification to become the source of all other oppressions, as in the radical feminist theory that sees oppression in all forms and through all ages as derived from the male/female division.[19] This deterministic model, which Sheila Rowbotham says functions like a "feminist base-superstructure," has the disadvantage of leaving us with no sense of movement or idea of how women have acted to change their condition, especially in comparison with the fluidity of the Marxist conception of class.[20]

The radical feminist notion of absolute patriarchy has also one-sidedly portrayed the oppression of women through an analogy with slavery, and since this theory has identified woman as man's savage or repressed Other, it competes with theories of racial difference that understand the black as the "unassimilable Other."[21] Finally, the notion of patriarchy is most obtuse when it disregards the position white women occupy over black men as well as black women.[22] In order to rectify this tendency in feminism, black feminists refer to "racial patriarchy," which is based on an analysis of the white patriarch/master in U.S. history and his dominance over the black male as well as the black female.[23]

I now want to reconsider the film *Mahogany*, the sequel to *Lady Sings the Blues*, in which Diana Ross plays an aspiring fashion designer who dreams of pulling herself up and out of her Chicago South Side neighborhood by means of a high-powered career.

Mahogany functions ideologically for black viewers in the traditional Marxist sense, that is, in the way the film obscures the class nature of social antagonisms. This has certain implications for working-class black viewers who would benefit the most from seeing the relationship between race, gender, and class oppression dramatized. Further, *Mahogany* has the same trouble understanding black femaleness that the wider culture has had historically; a black female is either all woman and tinted black, or mostly black and scarcely woman. These two expectations correspond with the two worlds and two struggles the film contrasts: the struggle over the sexual objectification of Tracy's body in the face of commercial exploitation and the struggle of the black community in the face of class exploitation. But the film identifies this antagonism as the hostility between fashion and politics, embodied respectively by Tracy Chambers (Diana Ross) and Brian Walker (Billy Dee Williams); through them it organizes conflict and, eventually, reconciliation. Intensifying this conflict between characters, the film contrasts "politics" and "fashion" in one daring homage to the aesthetic of "attraction by shock." Renowned fashion photographer Sean McEvoy (Tony Perkins) arranges his models symmetrically on the back stairwell of a run-down Chicago apartment building and uses the confused tenants and street people as props. Flamboyant excess, the residue of capital, is juxtaposed with a kind of dumbfounded poverty. For a moment, the scene figures the synthesis of gender, class, and race, but the political glimpse is fleeting. Forced together as a consequence of the avant-garde's socially irresponsible quest for a new outrage, the political antagonisms are suspended – temporarily immobilized as the subjects pose.

The connection between gender, class, and race oppression is also denied as the ghetto photography session's analogy between commercial exploitation and race/class exploitation merely registers on the screen as visual incongruity. Visual discrepancy is used for aesthetic effect and makes it difficult to grasp the confluence of race, class, and gender oppression in the image of Tracy Chambers. The character's class background magically becomes decor in the film – it neither radicalizes her nor drags her down; instead it sets her off. Diana Ross is alternately weighted down by the glamour iconography of commercial modeling and stripped to a black body. But the *haute couture* iconography ultimately dominates the film. Since race is decorative and class does not reveal itself to the eye, Tracy can be seen as exploited only in terms of her role as a model.

One of the original tenets of contemporary feminist film theory – that the (male) spectator possesses the female indirectly through the eyes of the male protagonist (his screen surrogate) – is problematized in this film by the less privileged black male gaze. Racial hierarchies of access to the female image also relate to other scenarios that are unknown by psychoanalytic categories. Considering the racial categories that psychoanalysis does not recognize, then, we see that the white male photographer monopolizes the classic patriarchal look controlling the view of the female body, and that the black male protagonist's look is either repudiated or frustrated. The sumptuous image of Diana Ross is made available to the spectator via the white male character (Sean) but *not* through the look of the black male character (Brian). In the sequence in which Tracy and Brian first meet outside her apartment building, his "look" is renounced. In each of the three shots of Tracy from Brian's point of view, she turns from him, walking out of his sight and away from the sound of his voice as he shouts at her through a megaphone. Both visual and audio control is thus denied the black male, and the failure of his voice is consistently associated with Tracy's white world publicity image. The discovery by Brian's aides of the Mahogany advertisement for Revlon in *Newsweek* coincides with the report that the Gallup Polls show the black candidate trailing in the election. Later, the film cuts from the *Harper's Bazaar* cover featuring "Mahogany" to Brian's limping campaign where the sound of his voice magnified through a microphone is intermittently drowned out by a passing train as he makes his futile pitch to white factory workers.

"The construction of the sexual self of the Afro-American woman," says Rennie Simpson, "has its roots in the days of slavery."[24] Looking at this construction over time reveals a pattern of patriarchal phases and female sexual adjustments that have no equivalent in the history of white women in the United States. In the first phase, characterized by the dominance of the white master during the period of slavery, black men and women were equal by default. To have allowed the black male any power over the black woman would have threatened the power balance of the slave system. Thus, as Angela Davis explains social control in the slave community, "The man slave could not be the unquestioned superior within the 'family' or community, for there was no such thing as the 'family' provided among the Slaves."[25]

If the strategy for racial survival was resistance during the first phase, it was accommodation during the second phase. During Reconstruction, the black family, modeled after the white bourgeois household, was constituted defensively in an effort to preserve the race.[26] Black women yielded to their men in deference to a tradition that promised respectability and safety. Reevaluating this history, black feminists point out that during Reconstruction, the black male, "learned" to dominate. Thus they see sexism as not original to black communities but more as a plague that struck.[27] One of the most telling manifestations of the difference between the operation of patriarchy in the lives of black as opposed to white women is the way this is worked out *at the level of language* in the formal conventions organizing the short stories and novels by African-American women. Particularly in the work of early writers such as Harriet E. Wilson, Frances E. W. Harper, and Pauline Hopkins, the black father is completely missing, and, as Hazel Carby says, "The absent space in fiction by black women confirms this denial of patriarchal power to black men."[28] The position consistently taken by black feminists, that patriarchy was originally foreign to the African-American community and was introduced into it historically, then, represents a significant break with feminist theories that see patriarchal power invested equally in all men throughout history, and patriarchal form as color blind.

Black history also adds another dimension to the concept of "rape," the term that has emerged as the favored metaphor for defining women's jeopardy in the second wave of feminism, replacing "prostitution," the concept that articulated women's fears in the nineteenth century.[29] The charge of rape, conjuring up a historical connection with lynching, is inextricably connected in American history with the myth of the black man as archetypal rapist. During slavery, white male abuse of black women was a symbolic blow to black manhood, understood as rape only within the black community. With the increase in the sexual violation of black women during Reconstruction the act of rape began to reveal its fuller political implications. After emancipation, the rape of black women was a "message" to black men that could be seen, says one historian, as "a reaction to the effort of the freedman to assume the role of patriarch, able to provide for and protect his family."[30] Simultaneous with the actual violation of black women, the empty charge of rape hurled back at the black man clouded the real issue of black (male) enfranchisement, creating a smoke screen by means of the incendiary issue of interracial sexuality. Writing at the turn of the century, black novelist Pauline Hopkins unmasked the alibis for lynching in *Contending Forces*: "Lynching was instituted to crush the manhood of the enfranchised black. Rape is the crime which appeals most strongly to the heart of the home life. . . . *The men who created the mulatto race, who recruit its ranks year after year by the very means which they invoked lynch law to suppress*, bewailing the sorrows of violated womanhood!"[31] Here is a sexual scenario to rival the oedipal myth: the black woman sexually violated by the white man, but her rape repressed and displaced onto the virginal white woman, and thus used symbolically as the justification for the actual castration of the black man. It is against this historical scenario that I want to reconsider the connotations of sexual looking that at one time in history would have carried with it the threat of real castration against which symbolic castration must surely pale.

Quite simply, then, there are structures relevant to any interpretation of *Mahogany* that override the patriarchal scenario feminists have theorized as formally determining. From African-American history, we should recall the white male's appropriation of the black woman's body that weakened the black male and undermined the community. From African-American literature, we should also consider the scenario of the talented and beautiful mulatta who "passes" in white culture, but decides to return to black society.[32] Further, we need to reconsider the narrative convention of the woman's picture—the career renounced in favor of the man—in the context of black history. Tracy's choice recapitulates black aspiration and the white middle-class model that equates stable family life with respectability, but her decision is significantly different from the white heroine's capitulation since it favors black community cooperation over acceptance by white society. Finally, one of the most difficult questions raised by African-American history and literature has to do with interracial heterosexuality and sexual "looking." *Mahogany* suggests that, since a black male character is not allowed the position of control occupied by a white male character, race could be a factor in the construction of cinema language. More work on looking and racial taboos might determine whether or not mainstream cinema can offer the male spectator the pleasure of looking at a white female character via the gaze of a black male character. Framing the question of male privilege and viewing pleasure as the "right to look" may help us to rethink film theory along more materialist lines, considering, for instance, how some groups have historically had the license to "look" openly while other groups have "looked" illicitly.[33] Phrased differently, does the psychoanalytic model allow us to consider the prohibitions against homosexuality and miscegenation?

Feminists who use psychoanalytic theory have been careful to point out that "looking" positions do not correlate with social groups, and that ideological positioning is placement in a representational system that has no one-to-one correspondence with social experience. While I would not want to argue that form is ideologically neutral, I would suggest that we have overemphasized the ideological function of "signifying practice" at the expense of considering other ideological implications of the conflicting meanings in the text. Or, as Terry Lovell puts it, "While interpretation depends on analysis of the work's signifying practice, assessment of its meanings from the point of view of its validity, or of its ideology, depends on comparison between those structures of meaning and their object of reference, through the mediation of another type of discourse."[34] The impetus behind Marxist criticism, whether we want to admit it or not, is to make comparisons between social reality as we live it and ideology as it does not correspond to that reality. This we attempt to do knowing full well the futility of looking for real relations that are completely outside ideology.

Thus, while I am still willing to argue, as I did in earlier versions of this essay, that we can see the *Mahogany* narrative as a metaphor for the search for black female sexuality, I see something else in hindsight. I would describe this as the temptation in an emerging black feminist criticism, much like an earlier tendency in lesbian criticism, to place sexuality safely out of patriarchal bounds by declaring it outside culture, by furtively hiding it in subcultural enclaves where it can remain its "essential self," protected from the meaning-making mainstream culture. *Mahogany*, then, is finally about the mythical existence of something elusive. We know it through what white men do to secure it, and what black men are without it. It is the ultimate substance to the photographer—Tony Perkins's character—who dies trying to record its "trace" on film. It is known by degree—whatever is most wild and enigmatic, whatever cannot be conquered or subdued—the last frontier of female sexuality. Although it is undetectable to the advertising men who can analyze only physical attributes, it is immediately perceptible to a lesbian (Gavina herself, the owner of the Italian advertising agency), who uses it to promote the most inexplicable and subjective of commodities—perfume.[35] Contrary to the suggestion that black female sexuality might still remain in excess of culture, and hence unfathomed and uncodified, it is worked over again and again in mainstream culture because of its apparent elusiveness, and in this context it is rather like bottled scent, which is often thought to convey its essence to everyone but the person wearing it.

To return to my main point, as feminists have theorized women's sexuality, they have universalized from the particular experience of white women, thus effecting what Hortense Spillers has called a "deadly metonomy."[36] While white feminists theorize the female image in terms of objectification, fetishization, and symbolic absence, their black counterparts describe the body as the site of symbolic resistance and the "paradox of nonbeing," a reference to the period in African-American history when black female did not signify "woman."[37] What strikes me still in this comparison is the stubbornness of the terms of feminist discourse analysis, which has not been able to deal, for instance, with what it has meant historically to be designated as not-human, and how black women, whose bodies were legally not their own, fought against treatment based on this determination. Further, feminist analysis of culture as patriarchal cannot conceive of any connection between the female image and class or racial exploitation that includes the male. Historically, black men and women, although not equally endangered, have been simultaneously implicated in incidents of interracial brutality. During two different periods of African-American history, sexual assault, "symbolic of the effort to conquer the resistance the black woman could unloose," was a warning to the entire black community.[38] If, as feminists have argued, women's sexuality evokes an unconscious terror in men, then black women's sexuality represents a special threat to white patriarchy; the possibility of its eruption stands for the aspirations of the black race as a whole.

My frustration with the feminist voice that insists on change *at the level of language* is that this position can deal with the historical situation described above only by turning it into discourse, and even as I write this, acutely aware as I am of the theoretical prohibitions against mixing representational issues with real historical ones, I feel the pressure to transpose people's struggles into more discursively manageable terms. However, a theory of ideology that separates the levels of the social formation in such a way that it is not only inappropriate but theoretically impossible to introduce the category of history into the analysis cannot be justified with Marxism. This has been argued elsewhere by others, among them Stuart Hall, who finds the "universalist tendency" found in both Freud and Lacan responsible for this impossibility. The incompatibility between Marxism and psychoanalytic theory is insurmountable at this time, he argues, because "the concepts elaborated by Freud (and reworked by Lacan) cannot, *in their in-general and universalist form*, enter the theoretical space of historical materialism."[39] In discussions within feminist film theory, it has often seemed the other way around–that historical materialism could not enter the space theorized by discourse analysis drawing on psychoanalytic concepts. Sealed off as it is (in theory), this analysis may not comprehend the category of the real historical subject, but its use will always have implications *for* that subject.

Notes

Earlier versions of this essay appeared in *Cultural Critique*, no. 4 (Fall 1986), and *Screen* 29 (Autumn 1988).

1. These debates can be traced through the following: Henry Louis Gates, ed., *Black Literature and Literary Theory* (New York: Methuen, 1984); "Critical Fanonism," *Critical Inquiry* 17 (Spring 1991); Homi Bhabha, "What Does the Black Man Want?" *New Formations* 1 (Spring 1987); Stephen Feuchtwang, "Fanonian Spaces," *New Formations* 1 (Spring 1987); Kobena Mercer and Isaac Julien, "De Margin and De Centre," *Screen* 29 (Autumn 1988).

2. See, for instance, Patricia Hill Collins, *Black Feminist Thought: Knowledge, Consciousness, and the Politics of Empowerment* (New York: Unwin Hyman, 1991); Cheryl A. Wall, ed., *Changing Our Own Words: Essays on Criticism, Theory, and Writing by Black Women* (New Brunswick, N.J.: Rutgers University Press, 1989); Michelle Wallace, *Invisibility Blues: From Pop to Theory* (New York: Verso, 1990); Valerie Smith, "Reconstituting the Image: The Emergent Black Woman Director," *Callaloo* 11 (Fall 1988); Martina Attille, "Black Women and Representation," *Undercut*, nos. 14–15 (Summer 1985); Alile Sharon Larkin, "Black Women Filmmakers Defining Ourselves: Feminism in Our Own Voice," and Jacqueline Bobo, "*The Color Purple*, Black Women as Cultural Readers," both in *Female Spectators: Looking at Film and Television*, ed. E. Deidre Pribram (London: Verso, 1988); Karen Alexander, "Fatal Beauties: Black Women in Hollywood," in *Stardom: Industry of Desire*, ed. Christine Gledhill (New York: Routledge, 1991); see also *Black American Literature Forum* 25 (Summer 1991) and *Wide Angle* 13 (July 1991).

3. Consider, for instance, Mary Ann Doane, "Dark Continents: Epistemologies of Racial and Sexual Difference in Psychoanalysis and Cinema," in *Femmes Fatales: Feminism, Film Theory, Psychoanalysis* (New York and London: Routledge, 1991).

4. bell hooks, *Feminist Theory: From Margin to Center* (Boston: South End Press, 1984), 14.

5. Marilyn Frye, *The Politics of Reality* (Trumansburg, N.Y.: Crossing Press, 1984), 113, 118.

6. Claire Johnston, "Women's Cinema as Counter-Cinema," in *Notes on Women's Cinema*, ed. Claire Johnston (London: Society for Education in Film and Television, 1973); Laura Mulvey, "Visual Pleasure and Narrative Cinema," *Screen* 16 (Autumn, 1985): 6–18.

7. Stuart Hall, "On Postmodernism and Articulation: An Interview," *Journal of Communication Inquiry* 10 (Summer 1986): 57.

8. As quoted in Annette Kolodny, "Respectability Is Eroding the Revolutionary Potential of Feminist Criticism," *Chronicle of Higher Education*, May 4, 1988, A52.

9. Lucie Arbuthnot and Gail Seneca, "Pre-Text and Text in *Gentlemen Prefer Blondes*" *Film Reader* 5 (Winter 1981): 13–23.

10. Chris Straayer, "*Personal Best*: Lesbian/Feminist Audience," *Jump Cut* 29 (February 1984): 40–44; Elizabeth Ellsworth, "Illicit Pleasures: Feminist Spectators and *Personal Best*," *Wide Angle* 8, no. 2 (1986): 46–56.

11. Monique Wittig, "The Straight Mind," *Feminist Issues* (Summer 1980): 107–11.

12. Gayle Rubin, "Thinking Sex: Notes for a Radical Theory of the Politics of Sexuality," in *Pleasure and Danger*, ed. Carol Vance (Boston: Routledge and Kegan Paul, 1984), 307.

13. Barbara Smith, "Towards a Black Feminist Criticism," in *The New Feminist Criticism*, ed. Elaine Showalter (New York: Pantheon, 1985), 169.

14. Bonnie Thornton Dill, "Race, Class, and Gender: Prospects for an All-Inclusive Sisterhood," *Feminist Studies* 9 (Spring 1983): 134; for a slightly different version of this essay, see " 'On the Hem of Life': Race, Class, and the Prospects for Sisterhood," in *Class, Race, and Sex: The Dynamics of Control*, ed. Amy Swerdlow and Hanna Lessinger (Boston: G. K. Hall, 1983); Margaret Simons, "Racism and Feminism: A Schism in the Sisterhood," *Feminist Studies* 5 (Summer 1979): 392.

15. Adrienne Rich, in *On Lies, Secrets, and Silence* (New York: Norton, 1979), 302–303, notes that while blacks link their experience of racism with the white woman, this is still patriarchal racism working through her. It is possible, she says, that

> a black first grader, or that child's mother, or a black patient in a hospital, or a family on welfare, may experience racism most directly in the person of a white woman, who stands for those service professions through which white male supremacist society controls the mother, the child, the family, and all of us. It is *her* racism, yes, but a racism learned in the same patriarchal school which taught her that women are unimportant or unequal, not to be trusted with power, where she learned to mistrust and hear her own impulses for rebellion; to become an instrument.

16. Gloria Joseph, "The Incompatible Ménage à Trois: Marxism, Feminism, and Racism," in *Women and Revolution*, ed. Lydia Sargent (Boston: South End Press, 1981), 96; the Combahee River Collective, "Combahee River Collective Statement," in *Home Girls: A Black Feminist Anthology*, ed. Barbara Smith (New York: Kitchen Table: Women of Color Press, 1983), 275, compares their alliance with black men with the negative identification white women have with white men: "Our situation as Black people necessitates that we have solidarity around the fact of race, which white women of course do not need to have with white men, unless

it is their negative solidarity as racial oppressors. We struggle together with Black men against racism, while we struggle with Black men about sexism."

17. "Combahee River Collective Statement," 272.

18. Michele Barrett, *Women's Oppression Today* (London: Verso, 1980), 15.

19. For a comparison between radical feminism, liberal feminism, and Marxist and socialist feminism, see Alison Jaggar, *Feminist Politics and Human Nature* (Totowa, N.J.: Rowman and Allenheld, 1983).

20. Sheila Rowbotham, "The Trouble with Patriarchy," in *People's History and Socialist Theory*, ed. Raphael Samuel (Boston: Routledge and Kegan Paul, 1981), 365.

21. Frantz Fanon, *Black Skin, White Masks*, trans. Charles Lam Markmann (Paris, 1952; reprint, New York: Grove Press, 1967), 161.

22. Simons, "Racism and Feminism," 387.

23. Barbara Omolade, "Hearts of Darkness," in *Powers of Desire: The Politics of Sexuality*, ed. Ann Snitow, Christine Stansell, and Sharon Thompson (New York: Monthly Review Press, 1983), 352.

24. Rennie Simpson, "The Afro-American Female: The Historical Context of the Construction of Sexual Identity," in *Powers of Desire*, 230.

25. Angela Davis, "The Black Woman's Role in the Community of Slaves," *The Black Scholar* (December 1971), 5–6.

26. Omolade, *Powers*, 352.

27. Joseph, "The Incompatible Ménage à Trois," 99; Audre Lorde, *Sister Outsider: Essays and Speeches* (Trumansburg, N.Y.: Crossing Press, 1984), 119 , says:

> Because of the continuous battle against racial erasure that Black women and Black men share, some Black women still refuse to recognize that we are also oppressed as women, and that sexual hostility against Black women is practiced not only by the white racist society, but implemented within our Black communities as well. It is a disease striking the heart of Black nationhood, and silence will not make it disappear.

28. Hazel Carby, " 'On the Threshold of Woman's Era': Lynching, Empire, and Sexuality in Black Feminist Theory," *Critical Inquiry* 12 (Autumn 1985): 276; Harriet E. Wilson, *Our Nig* (1859; reprint, New York: Random House, 1983); Frances E. W. Harper, *Iola Leroy, or Shadows Uplifted* (1892; reprint, New York: Oxford University Press, 1988); Pauline E. Hopkins, *Contending Forces* (1900, reprint, New York: Oxford University Press, 1988).

29. Linda Gordon and Ellen DuBois, "Seeking Ecstasy on the Battlefield: Danger and Pleasure in Nineteenth Century Feminist Sexual Thought," *Feminist Review* 13 (Spring 1983), 43.

30. Jacquelyn Dowd Hall, " 'The Mind That Burns in Each Body': Women, Rape, and Racial Violence," in *Powers of Desire*, 332; See also, Jacquelyn Dowd Hall, *The Revolt against Chivalry* (New York: Columbia University Press, 1979), and Angela Davis, *Women, Race and Class* (New York: Vintage, 1983), chap. 11.

31. As quoted in Carby, " 'On the Threshold of Woman's Era,' " 275.

32. See, for instance, Jessie Fauset, *There Is Confusion* (New York: Boni and Liveright, 1924), and *Plum Bun* (1928; reprint, New York: Routledge and Kegan

Paul, 1983); Nella Larsen, *Quicksand* (1928), and *Passing* (1929; reprint, New Brunswick, N.J.: Rutgers University Press, 1986).

33. Fredric Jameson, in "Pleasure: A Political Issue," *Formations of Pleasure* (Boston: Routledge and Kegan Paul, 1983), 7, interprets Mulvey's connection between viewing pleasure and male power as the conferral of a "right to look." He does not take this further, but I find the term suggestive and at the same time potentially volatile.

34. Terry Lovell, *Pictures of Reality* (London: British Film Institute, 1980), 90.

35. Richard Dyer, "*Mahogany*," in *Films for Women*, ed. Charlotte Brunsdon (London: British Film Institute, 1986), 135, suggested this first about Gavina.

36. Hortense J. Spillers, "Interstices: A Small Drama of Words," in *Pleasure and Danger*, 78.

37. Ibid., 77.

38. Davis, "The Black Woman's Role," 11.

39. Stuart Hall, "Debate: Psychology, Ideology and the Human Subject," *Ideology and Consciousness* (October 1977), 118–19.

The Politics of Film Canons

Janet Staiger

Canon formation in film, as in any other area, can be located in a variety of projects. In film criticism, whether popular or academic, some films will be chosen for extensive discussion and analysis; others will be ignored. In theoretical writing, arguments are buttressed by films cited as examples. In histories, certain films are marked as worth mentioning for one reason or another (e.g., influence, aesthetic significance, typicality). This occurs not only for historiographical reasons (every causal explanation invariably privileges particular linkages or conjunctions), but for practical reasons as well: a history including every film would be trapped by the *Tristram Shandy* contradiction of constantly losing ground to the increasing number of films added daily to the list of those to be covered.[1] Even filmmakers are involved in canon formation. Those films chosen to be reworked, alluded to, satirized become privileged points of reference, pulled out from the rest of cinema's predecessors.[2] As ideal models, these films are given homage or rebelled against.

That canons exist in film studies and that canon formation is political is evident to me.[3] Much less evident are the shifting politics, past and present, of the factors contributing to canon formation. In attempting to identify and characterize some of these factors, as well as their limitations, I will consider films critics, theorists, historians, and filmmakers have chosen for study and why shifts have occurred even over the short period of cinema's existence. In addition, I will be suggesting that escape from canon formation will be difficult. Competition in academia and the film industry reinforces canons and canon making. However, my project is not to encourage a stance of relativity or political pluralism upon recognizing that all canonical projects are political but rather to make the politics self-evident, to find the political centers of particular enterprises for use by feminists and others interested in increasing the diversity of values in our society and culture. For even in revising and decentering dominant canons, new centers appear. My hope is to encourage as knowledgeable, humane, and progressive a choice as possible among the various politics.[4]

The Politics of Admission

Among the earliest writings about cinema were those involved in proving film was an art. This was a politics of opening up the established set of arts to a newcomer – moving pictures. The first film theorists – Vachel Lindsay, Hugo Münsterberg, the French impressionists, and Rudolf Arnheim – as well as early historians, such as Robert Grau and Terry Ramsaye, typify this project. While each of these writers used various tactics, their approaches are characterized by a basic assumption: some moving pictures ought to be included in the group of objects that the cultural elite terms aesthetic. It was a politics of admission, not of redefinition and, hence, not as radical as it might have been. Although the mechanical nature of photography could have provoked a possible decentering and revising of the established characteristics of an aesthetic object (i.e., a human's manipulation and transformation of raw materials into an object whose primary function was an aesthetic effect), the battle plan was, rather, to show that cinema's mechanical nature was inconsequential or, better yet, capable of being overcome through human intervention. As Arnheim would write, "Art begins where mechanical reproduction leaves off."

   Although the overt project may seem only an issue for aestheticians and historians, underlying it were economic and social contexts. For writers such as Grau and Ramsaye the definition of film as art would provide a status and recognition of that medium as a worthy product in the competition for consumers of cultural goods. Raising film to the level of art ensured the attention of a middle-class audience already spending significant sums of money on legitimate theater, vaudeville, novels, music, and reproductions of paintings. Indirectly, then, Grau and Ramsaye's own work as publicists and journalists would be perceived as valuable and worth financial support. For others, such as the French impressionists and Arnheim, the profit advantage was equally at stake. Financing film projects or receiving support for research on the relationship of art and psychology mattered to these people. The apparently value-free discussion of what film-as-art was can thus be related to a self-interest and an economic gain. This is also the case for Lindsay and Münsterberg, both of whom received financial rewards for their theorizing: Lindsay became a film critic for the *New Republic*, and Münsterberg did a series of educational shorts for Paramount.

The social context was also linked to the economic one. The last third of both Lindsay's and Münsterberg's books detail the possible effects that film might have on society, with suggestions about how films could reinforce appropriate social behavior. Such advice provided methods of how a hegemonic culture and economic structure could reproduce itself; again, to the political and economic advantage of a particular group. Thus, the strategy of seeking cinema's admission to the category of art was by no means apolitical; furthermore, its politics were a reinforcement of the status quo.

As a politics of admission, then, these writings took at least three related argumentative strategies. The first strategy might be termed the "essence of art" method. It was argued through a characteristic syllogism with this reasoning: All arts do x; film can do x; therefore film is an art. This fallacious strategy was widely employed, even though what constituted the "x" or "essence" of art differed among the various writers.

A second strategy of the politics of admission is related to the "essence of art" method. It is the "specificity" corollary. Nineteenth-century art criticism included several approaches to comparing the individual arts. One was to follow the historical development of the arts, arguing syntheses of various arts' characteristics in later developing arts. Another emphasized apparently "unique" qualities of the various media, occasionally ranking those features and, thus, the media. This was a particularly important strategy if film was to be seen as a unique art form rather than, say, a simulacrum of theater.

A third strategy for admitting film into the hallowed halls of art might be called the "maturation" ploy. This argument, like the other two, assumes that not all films ought to be characterized as art and that cinema should have taken some time to develop sufficiently so as to produce artful works. Thus, early cinema is relegated to the prehistory of film-as-art in order to mark a point at which cinema has matured adequately to produce artistic works. For many writers, cinema reached its maturity with the technical expertise of D. W. Griffith's cinema, although they are often not too interested in what his films were saying (downplaying the racism in *Birth of a Nation* to point out its commercial success). At least cinema had achieved an ability to form articulate statements and could, thus, create intelligible aesthetic experiences.

All three of these strategies worked together in a general politics of seeking cinema's admission into the category of art. Even if not all films deserved the appellation of an aesthetic object, some films could be singled out as worthy of inclusion. In making these arguments, the earliest critics, theorists, historians, and filmmakers set up various canons of exemplary films, with some regularity among the canons occurring. Since these writers generally accepted dominant notions of art, this near uniformity is understandable even though some variations did exist. Few films before Griffith's features are mentioned, perhaps because of the consistent comparisons of films to other established narrative arts, such as literature and drama; after 1915, feature-length films dominated commercial distribution and exhibition. With the explosion of alternative film practices in the 1920s, European-produced films are cited with as much (and sometimes more) respect as American-made films. Although subsequent writers would still return to these problems of essence, specificity, and maturation, arguments after the 1920s also hinged on issues of greater discrimination among films considered to be artful works. The politics of film canons turned from an emphasis on admission to an interest in selection and finer judgments.

The Politics of Selection

> But on the day when the Philosopher's [Aristotle's] word would justify the marginal jests of the debauched imagination, or when what has been marginal would leap to the center, every trace of the center would be lost. The people of God would be transformed into an assembly of monsters belched forth from the abysses of the terra incognita, and at that moment the edge of the known world would become the heart of the Christian empire, the Arimaspi on the throne of Peter, Blemmyes in the monasteries, dwarfs with huge bellies and immense heads in charge of the library!
>
> — *Umberto Eco*, The Name of the Rose[5]

Between 1915 and 1960, the United States alone produced some 20,000 feature-length narrative films for commercial distribution. Furthermore, other countries such as Japan and, recently, India have exceeded the output of the United States. In purely practical terms, a scholar of cinema cannot study every film made. Selection becomes a necessity and with selection comes a politics of inclusion and exclusion. Some films are moved to the center of attention; others, to the margins. It is particularly in this situation that feminists have been concerned about canons.

Several rationales for selection exist. One is efficiency. A typical strategy of critical writing is assuming that readers are familiar with a certain set of works; thus, a writer does not have to recap a story or extensively analyze every aspect of a text. Rather, a point can be made quickly with allusion to the work as sufficient for the argument. The advantages of this for both the writer and the reader are immense. Once a set of texts is considered institutionalized, referencing those works is economical and brief.

However, such a procedure can lead to the sloppy thinking that these texts are the only or best ones that do whatever is being suggested; whereas, less known or earlier texts might prove as "exemplary." An instance of this is, in fact, what happened as a result of the early canonization of Griffith's works. Griffith's feature films and contemporary publicity (for which he was in part responsible) led some writers to the conclusion that he was the first to achieve a number of technical innovations and, following that, that he was the only one and thus influenced the rest of the industry.

Film historians' recent examination of pre-1915 cinema has seriously questioned the placement of Griffith in the center of cinematic innovation. Some earlier filmmakers and films evince all the devices and functions of those claimed for Griffith. The response, however, has not always been a reanalyzing of Griffith's achievements, but an attempt to redefine what is at stake so that his work remains at the center. The claim now made is that while others may have used such and such a device, Griffith "mastered" its function. For example, in one of the most recent histories, David Cook writes that Porter is "the next major link in the chain between the animated photographs of Edison-Lumière and the fully elaborated cinematic syntax of Griffith."[6] Rather than Griffith's films becoming useful examples among others of the transition to classical Hollywood cinema, they become the master and epitome of early cinema, subordinating and excluding others. Griffith's prestige did cause his work to be influential, but as historians we do not want to repeat an old error and draw from that the claim that Griffith was unique. Efficiency is certainly a commendable excuse for paring down the number of films about which an educated scholar should know. Yet selection for efficiency and practicality can too easily slide into a politics of denigration and exclusion based on the mistaken notion that those films regularly chosen are necessarily unique or superior.

Another rationale for selection relates to a worthwhile goal of creating some order out of the apparent chaos of so many films. Grouping, classifying, and finding typicality are long-honored and traditional pursuits in the acquisition of knowledge. Hence, large numbers of films are more easily handled if certain generalizing characteristics are determined. The idea of "Renaissance painting" or "realist drama" or "American horror films" provides a grip on a large and historically specific group of objects. Yet, often, only a select set of works are given as examples of a group with these becoming not merely typical instances, but exemplaries. Logically, once the characteristics of a grouping are developed, any item in the set ought to be equally valid as an object of analysis. In fact, to prove the validity of the grouping a wide selection ought to be made. A random or unbiased selection might escape normal canonic tendencies, but in actual practice, the tactic has been, instead, to select not on the basis of typicality, but for another rationale.

That third rationale is an evaluative selection, and here politics are most definitely involved. One of the more persuasive justifications for establishing canons based on an evaluative standard comes from Charles Altieri.[7] Altieri argues that readers use aesthetic works as "a set of challenges and models" (40) that allow individuals to interpret themselves and to act responsibly. From that premise, Altieri proposes that a society ought to preserve works that could produce a social or public good. However, as Barbara Herrnstein Smith has argued, any evaluation, including an appeal to the social good, is always reducible to economies of self-interest.[8] Even in attempts to construct value-free systems of judgment, such as art for its own sake, a "long-term profit in enhanced development, behavioral flexibility, and thus biological fitness" (14) suggests that such choices are not interest free. If selections seem natural, inherent, universal, or timeless (and thus socially good), it may well be that individuals' interests have been determined by hegemonic cultural needs and institutions. Challenges to such an "illusion of consensus" will come from the not-yet-acculturated young and from those typified by the hegemonic culture as "uncultivated" or even pathological. Herrnstein Smith writes: "Consequently, institutions of evaluative authority will be called upon repeatedly to devise arguments and procedures to validate the community's established tastes and preferences, thereby warding off barbarism and the constant apparition of an imminent collapse of standards and also justifying the exercise of their own normative authority."[9] Furthermore, canons are not only a fixed part of a library, but also "*binding* upon a group of people."[10] They are not just reference books for analysis; they are supplied to members of a society as models for appropriate or inappropriate behavior, as Altieri desires. Thus, selective choices based on criteria supposedly for the good of society end up being canons supportive of the interests of a hegemonic society, not necessarily in the interests of all segments of that culture or other cultures. Claims for universality are disguises for achieving uniformity, for suppressing through the power of canonic discourse optional value systems. Such a cultural "consensus" fears an asserted "barbarism" and a collapse into the grotesque and monstrous, because it recognizes the potential loss of its hegemony. It is a politics of power.[11]

When Andrew Sarris published *The American Cinema* in 1968, he explicitly appealed to the rationale of evaluative standards for cultural good: "Film history devoid of value judgments would degenerate into a hobby like bridge or stamp collecting, respectable in its esoteric way, but not too revelatory. Or, as has been more the fashion, the collectivity of movies would be clustered around an idea, usually a sociological idea befitting the mindlessness of a mass medium."[12] His decision to rank directors (and, hence, films) was to "establish a system of priorities for the film student"; Sarris was disturbed by "the absence of the most elementary academic tradition in cinema" (27).

Within his program can be detected an attitude typifying Herrnstein Smith's description of the establishment of a cultural preference and centering, suppressing optional methods of selection. Sarris castigates nonevaluative approaches as "degenerate" or prompting an appearance of "mindlessness," perhaps even sacrilegious. I shall return to this, but it is necessary first to underline the eruption of a fear of some kind of threat or disservice to a society if selections are made without regard to some standard of value. As I have already pointed out, selections based on efficiency or typicality can lead to knowledge that may be culturally valuable; in fact, employing a "masterpiece-only" approach can suppress a number of interesting questions about styles, genres, national movements, and the relation between signifying practices and groups of people (as work on cultural studies and ideology has shown). Yet Sarris and the auteur school to which he is linked are not the only advocates of setting up value criteria for the choice of films deemed worth studying. Other groups, likewise, argue that the social good will be achieved with value selections. Thus, the questions are these: By what standards do we make value judgments? What are the political implications of various standards? What ends do these standards promote? How do we, if we are to make selections based on value, choose among the standards? If evaluative standards are for the social good, who determines the social good? Are standards for the society at large, for segments of the society, for individuals? What about those outside a particular hegemonic culture?

The answers to these questions, of course, will depend on personal judgments; the problem, then, is to determine what the politics are of competing value systems. It is not possible here to survey all of the systems. Rather, two major groups will be briefly analyzed: a particular group of auteur critics and a group of writers I call the "ideological" critics. As will become apparent, my personal judgment and politics lie with the latter group; however, I do have reservations about some of the tendencies of the ideological critics' projects.

Auteurism developed in France in the 1950s, spreading later to England and the United States. Although auteurism can be seen as a grouping procedure for films, as others have pointed out, it was more than that. It was also a *politique des auteurs*, of being for some directors and against others. Not just a method of classification and analysis, auteurism was practiced as a politics of evaluation. The evaluative criteria of the French *Cahiers du cinéma* critics who were major advocates of auteurism are of significance to what became a dominant system of judgments. The *Ca-*

hiers' auteurism was launched as part of a plan for reforming the French film industry to allow control of filmmaking by the workers. However, John Hess argues that this group of auteurists was culturally conservative and politically reactionary.[13] The "moral vision" of those films and filmmakers chosen to be praised were ones in which characters reject social values for spiritual ones, as the *Cahiers* critics tried to separate social and political problems from spiritual issues.

Whether or not this is an adequate characterization of this group, as auteurism spread, many auteurist critics tended to suppress historical, class, and social issues.[14] Although each practitioner set her or his own standards of judgments, at least three criteria characterize the group I call "Romantic" auteurists, making their politics evident. These criteria are transcendence of time and place, a personal vision of the world, and consistency and coherence of statement.

Like the *Cahiers* auteurists, the Romantic auteurists seek "universality" and "endurance," which implies a transcendence of history. Sarris, for instance, criticizes those writers who argue that films are related to their historical circumstances, claiming that some of the most interesting films have nothing to do with the period in which they are made (25). Gerald Mast is even more explicit: "The best American films of the present (and of the future), like those of the past, can and will succeed in transcending their immediate temporal, commercial, technological, and cultural limitations."[15] For a Romantic auteurist, the value of a work is claimed to be in its cross-cultural, cross-temporal benefits.

In addition, while a film should have an ability to speak to everyone, it ought to be an expression of an individual's "personal vision of the world." Thus, unique characteristics of an auteur's work are sought. In Sarris's ranking, he consistently describes what constitutes a particular director's thematic and stylistic tendencies. Mast does the same, using a habitual method of comparing and contrasting directors to play one off the other: "Clair was the more ingenious; Renoir the deeper, more perceptive artist" (204). "If John Ford was the sound film's Griffith, Howard Hawks was its Ince" (244). In this procedure, Mast uses a "like *x*, unlike *x*" rhetoric that simultaneously sets up universal sets of qualities while making the auteurs unique, hence special and capable of being ranked.

Finally, the auteur must be consistent and coherent in statement. Sarris writes: "The auteur critic is obsessed with the wholeness of art and the artist. . . . The parts however entertaining individually, must cohere meaningfully" (30). In a way, this is related to the auteur's "personal vision" rather than *visions* of the world. But it also derives from the requirement that the auteur have been touched with an enduring message, not one fragmented by historical, social, or idiosyncratic problems.

Part of the politics of Romantic auteur critics is the elevation of some individuals into an elite group that often takes on religious tones, as if they were members of a spiritual priesthood. Such individuals have an omniscience capable of knowing, yet transcending, the vulgar historical world, an omnipresence of being elected to speak for and to all, and an omnipotence of having been chosen from the beginning. The religious motif is not accidental. Although I sense Sarris is partially jesting in his vocabulary for ranking his auteurs, at the same time, his jest cannot be taken lightly or innocently. He develops images of sincere, humble prophets, raised to sainthood by critics acting as disciples for the cathedral of film art, to whom the masses should pay homage. These icons are the lay person's vade mecum.

The problem with this is not the religious motif, but the implications that knowledge, righteousness, wisdom, and truth are in the hands of a select group. That group provides models for behavior and, hence, has the power to provide standards for every culture and individual. Furthermore, the reason why these auteur statements may seem universal to Romantic auteurists is never broached. If, in fact, Western culture has been hegemonic for some time, our ability to recognize a "universal" statement is questionable. And once "universality" is problematized, role modeling for a social good is put in doubt.

Also distressing is that by using these criteria, the question of *what* is being said is generally ignored. Sarris does not seem to care what gospel is preached as long as it appears universal to him, seems to be a personal statement, is consistent and coherent, and is presented in good faith. Romantic auteurists seldom delve into ideologies of their auteurs' work. Griffith's films may be claimed to transcend their time and place and to indicate a personal and coherent vision, but their racist, misogynist, and reactionary vision can be neatly eliminated from the discussion when historical, social, gender, and political effects are removed from the agenda. Romantic auteurists may respond by arguing that, of course, they do not approve of racism, misogyny, or reactionary politics; yet they do not remove these auteurs from the canon. Rather, the disturbing ideological statements are downplayed to the "higher" goal of finding romantic geniuses.[16] The solution is not, however, to censor such films from our classrooms but to reconsider the criteria that we use for evaluation and the process of evaluation itself.

This is, in fact, what the project of the ideological critics is. This group wishes to evaluate films on the basis of the films' ideological effect. In one sense, many of our more famous (and equally canonized) writers have been implicitly or explicitly interested in the social and historical effect of films on spectators. Siegfried Kracauer, Walter Benjamin, Dziga Vertov, Sergei Eisenstein, and André Bazin analyzed the implications of film form, style, and subject matter as it related to specific historical and social conditions. Each judged films in terms of whether or not they led to progressive or regressive social or political effects. Furthermore, it is significant that each of these theorists and historians had strong connections to Marxism: Kracauer and Benjamin to the Frankfurt School; Vertov and Eisenstein to Soviet Marxism; Bazin to French humanist Marxism.[17] But, as is obvious, the writers' judgments differ because their political systems and understandings do not coincide exactly. Thus, even if ideological critics do overtly raise the criterion of the social effect of a film, they do not escape politics any more than the Romantic auteurists do. Perhaps their saving grace is at least an open acknowledgement of the political nature of their activities. In the last fifteen years, this strand of methodology has been a major opponent of Romantic auteurism, evincing, perhaps, the historical determinants that have caused the general raising of the issues of canon formation across the fields of art and literary criticism.

Although contemporary ideological critics have attacked all of the assertions of Romantic auteurism, one of their frontal lines of battle has been against the criterion of universality.[18] The arguments of Noël Burch and those of feminist film criticism are worth focusing upon, since the contrast between them indicates the diversity as well as similarity of political objectives among the ideological critics. Burch's work can be considered a formalist and romanticist politics for the avant-garde, disguised behind an attack against what he calls the institutional mode of cinema. Thus, in some ways, Burch is connected to those with whom he disagrees. In *Theory of Film Practice* he argues against standard filmmaking practices and for alternative practices.[19] Using a reductive "x, not x" strategy, Burch labels dominant film devices as "literary" and "a 'zero point of cinematic style'" while appropriate alternative practices become truly cinematic as well as "liberating" (15). Using a formalist idea, the "disautomatization of perception," and a post-Romantic concept, "organicity of form," as crucial criteria (the specificity strategy), Burch actually employs New Criticism's ideals of "surface tension, ambiguity, and complexity."[20] In this phase of Burch's work, he attacks the universality claim of Romantic auteurists by providing an Other that he believes is excluded from the canon, while it ought to be the canon instead.[21]

Just at the time of the publication of *Theory of Film Practice*, events in May of 1968 in France helped shift the editorial stance of the *Cahiers du cinéma*. By 1970, *Cahiers* articles were devoted to ideological analyses of cinema, defining dominant filmmaking practices as supporting and reinforcing bourgeois capitalism. The alternative that the *Cahiers* promoted was a selection of films that through their formal procedures made apparent the process of representation and through their political statements explored the exploitation of certain classes and cultures.

Such a political analysis fits in well with Burch's project. By the mid-

1970s, Burch was overlaying his formalism with the *Cahiers'* ideological critique.[22] Now disautomatization is viewed as a contestation of "the validity of the system of codes in force" (41) and a "deconstruction" and "subversion" of dominant codes of representation and narrativity. What was formerly praised as perceptual tension and complexity is now prized as a revelation of false consciousness. Thus, the formal appearance of reflexivity and discourse marks a work as not-*x*, not dominant cinema.

In this new phase of Burch's work, however, formalism still hinders his critique. Disautomatization or reflexivity is sufficient to allow him to include a work in his canon of "masterpieces" (43), no matter what effect the signified of the film produces or what effect the overall formal structure has on the spectator.[23] His initial politics of promoting an Other as truly cinematic can now be doubly fought as a politics against dominant cinema generally labeled as bourgeois with everything else as politically radical. Burch's work (and that of many others who seek only reflexivity and discourse, ignoring their relation to other aspects of a film) falls into a fallacy of reducing formal characteristics to a progressive ideological effect.[24]

Yet Burch's project is directed as well at the claims of universality. He argues that not all historical or cultural groups prize the same formal features, nor do the hegemonic styles and practices of cinema represent a transcendence across time and place. His and others' elevation of alternative practices indicates that segments of a society do not uniformly value the same works. In addition, he does not indicate the political result of canons for economic repression of optional filmmaking practices: avant-garde filmmakers are not funded by Hollywood; nonstandard films have difficulty penetrating capitalist-controlled distribution and exhibition systems. Burch's work effectively criticizes the power of a certain set of films to be viewed as transcending history and cultures; he locates them, instead, within a historically hegemonic practice, reinforcing a particular economic and political structure.

A second site for ideological analyses of films and for a criticism of Romantic auteurists' criterion of universality comes from feminist film criticism. As feminist film critics argue, and Claire Johnston states: "The idea that art is universal and thus potentially androgynous is basically idealist: art can only be defined as a discourse within a particular conjunction—for the purpose of women's cinema, the bourgeois, sexist ideology of male dominated capitalism."[25] Johnston's point is crucial in understanding what feminist criticism offers to our view of canons and canon formation. If a film is claimed to be universal, what the proponents of such a possibility are implying is that the film speaks in the same way to everyone. Not only does this claim wipe out historical, cultural, and social differences, but it denies sexual difference, treating all individuals as uniformly constituted. While the question of an "essential" psychoanalytically constituted characteristic of gender is currently under debate, certainly we recognize the actual dissimilarity of male and female socialization. Small children are routinely taught appropriate "masculine" and "feminine" behavior. Thus, what Johnston is pointing out is that in a generally male-dominated society – and academy – the characteristics of art termed "universal" are more adequately defined as those reinforcing the socialized dominance of the "masculine." Furthermore, if a work of art is raised to canonical status on such a basis, it provides a model for social behavior and, thus, social good. What such a model does is repeat hegemonic notions of gender (and sexual orientation). Furthermore, and more dangerously, because of our present historical situation, the work reinforces the cultural and economic dominance of one gender over the other.

The politics of feminist film criticism in combating such notions has been to point out sexual stereotyping and often misogynist characteristics in works canonized as "universal" by a male-dominated academy. Feminists employing a psychoanalytic framework argue further that such works do not speak to them, or else speak in ways that only perpetuate a masochistic positioning for a spectator. Again, this is an attack on the politics of power of those representing canonized films as universal.

Over the last ten years, feminist criticism in literature as well as in cinema has shifted significantly, and with this change has come varying positions on how to proceed regarding the problem of canons and canon formation. One proposal is to revise the criteria for canon selection so as to include works that previously were marginalized because of male-dominated institutionalizing practices.[26] Such a procedure would then provide a variety of models for society. A second is to employ an ideological critique of the "classics" via a process such as "reading against the grain" and thus expose the assumptions of "authority" and "value" in previously canonized texts.[27] Such a project may fit in well with a "negative hermeneutics," arguing that no single valid interpretation exists. Rather, a number of interpretations is theoretically and actually possible, each with its own center and effects. Likewise, recent reception studies, particularly those focusing on historical communities of readers and interpretative strategies, question the notion of the interpretation of a text, concentrating instead on how institutions and ideologies have established appropriate methods of understanding a work. Thus, the activities of the academy are analyzed, not as universal, but rather as a politics that marginalizes and devalues nonelite reading strategies.

A third approach derives from an analysis that language itself is irrevocably patriarchal, with the feminine linked to a forced association with difference, lack, and absence. The feminine becomes what is heterogeneous. Thus, a feminist canon could be built from the linguistically heterogeneous: items from the avant-garde or any optional practice that challenges "rational" (patriarchal) discourse.[28] Another proposal is to reconsider completely the practice of canonization. If based on evaluative criteria, canons can only repeat a system of exclusion and inclusion.

All of these proposals–revising criteria so as to include marginal works, criticizing present canonical works, constructing a radical other canon, or destroying canon formation itself–pose various theoretical and practical difficulties. Fear of "dwarfs with huge bellies and immense heads in charge of the library" is a strong nightmare for those who assume that selection by their evaluative criteria is necessary for the perpetuation of knowledge and societal good. Yet, as I have argued, other rationales can provide a basis for selection. In addition, selection by evaluation can be made less dangerous to marginalized groups if such a selection is made with an awareness of the politics of the chosen criteria and with a politics of eliminating power of some groups over others, of avoiding centering at the expense of marginalizing classes, genders, sexual orientations, or cultures.

The Politics of the Academy

The politics of film canons, however, does not cease at the level of admission or selection of films. Within a capitalist economy, politics also exists in the film academy. Not only a canon of films exists but also a canon of literature about film and a canon of film methodologies. The significance of this to women, to minorities, to those discriminated against because of sexual preference is apparent. Even if, because of film studies' unusual history and only recent admission into the academy, we have been conscious of these issues, it is appropriate to remind ourselves of them, since we are, in many ways, as entrenched, at least in this regard, as older fields of art. Competition for jobs, for better salaries, for higher professional ranking, for endowed chairs, competition for publishing contracts or research grants hinges on the academic establishing an exchange-value by proving that her or his critical methodology, history, or theory is not only worth financial support but, in an era of a tight economy, worth it more than others are. A student must master not only the canon of films, but also a canon of articles and books, so that he or she can supersede that work and be admitted into the group of professional canon makers and canon analyzers. One rereads canonized works not only for providing another interpretation, but also, usually, to make one's name with a new methodology. One resurrects a film to claim it as an unnoticed masterpiece. One may survey a genre, a national film output, a historical period, or a stylistic group to show how other scholars have misunderstood, simplified it. One applies rigorous analyses of theories and methodologies to indicate fallacious reasoning of predecessors.

All of this is in the pursuit of furthering our knowledge and appreciation of cinema, or of literature, drama, the arts; hence it is valuable to a society. Yet, within an educational system financed through a capitalist economy, academic reputations and economic awards are also at stake. If those involved in making the first film canons did so in a social and economic context, so do we. Furthermore, networks of tastemakers support those who support them. Achieving recognition for marginal approaches is difficult in part because it threatens the center of power. It is not just a question of "dwarfs with huge bellies and immense heads in charge of the library," but "the people of God" transported to the edge of the known world. Thus, as we continue to consider canons and canon making, we would be naive to ignore the existence of a politics of the academy. Yet we cannot accept a political pluralism or relativity that would allow some to support a reactionary or conservative politics that reinforces the present domination of some by others. The questions, then, are, What politics do we support? If we wish to eliminate a politics of power, how do we do that? And what does that mean in terms of those films we choose to study and how we study them?

Afterword

Response to this essay stimulated the following clarification of its ideas about pluralism and the relation of the spectator, film, and reality.   The reason for rejecting pluralism develops out of my underlying assumption that a utopia would be a society in which no member had power or wished to have power over another. (Pluralists probably would not argue with that.) The difficulty with a pluralist stance as it is practiced is that it often takes a "neutral" or a "wait and see" attitude, an attitude that has its own political consequences. If all members of a society held this philosophy in both thought and action, I would have less trouble with it. However, as we know, they do not. Rather, some individuals wish to impose their beliefs on others and are willing to use violence to achieve this. The pluralist, consequently, must tolerate, for example, fascism because those individuals who hold such a belief have a right to hold it. Or homophobics who harass gays and lesbians. Or prolifers who bomb abortion clinics to stop what they consider to be murder.

I likewise reject the idea that the only practical alternative to pluralism is to follow a party line. Such a notion would lead me into a contradiction: accepting the power of a party to dictate my beliefs and actions. In rejecting pluralism, we can still discuss these problems from a middle ground – a ground where some lines are drawn while others are left for further investigation. For example, as mentioned above, at least four positions regarding canons can be located within feminist film criticism, which implies that knowing the feminists' (not to mention the ideological critics') party line would be difficult, if not impossible, since none exists.

The ethical, logical, and political problems involved are complicated. Thus, my concluding question (What politics do we support?) was not a rhetorical but a real question. In addition, one of my points was that our current answers to this question are implicit in our teaching practices. The study of film is not an experience isolated from our moral and political lives, although sometimes pedagogical methods might imply this.

The question of the spectator/film/reality relation also occurs. Many writers, in examining readers and reception of texts, can be categorized as more or less falling into either a "text-activated" or "reader-activated" model. The former assumes the text controls or provides all the factors for the reader's response, while the latter argues that an individual reader makes whatever meaning results. I have serious difficulties with both extremes. For the text-activated model a variety of "ideal" readers are postulated: the "undifferentiated" reader (no gendered or socialized sex, no class, cross-cultural); the "normative" reader (invariably male, heterosexual, white, Western); the "harmonious" reader (one who agrees fully with the text); or the "historically synchronous" reader (a perfect reader at the time of the text's original appearance). The undifferentiated and normative reader positions are particularly unacceptable because they smooth over actual differences and issues of power. Both the harmonious and the historically synchronous readers freeze interpretations, depoliticizing them by making them unavailable for alternative or current use. On the other side, the reader-activated model ignores the force of widespread ideologies, psychoanalytical constructions, and the roles of institutions (such as the academy) to set up appropriate interpretative strategies. Such a model can easily slide into an illusion of freedom—we make our own meanings (the transcendental subject).

Thus, my notion of the reader is that her response is a complex combination of differences, including how she chooses to use a text in relation to notions of reality. We do treat "art" differently than we treat reality. Yet, as with art, we experience and interpret everyday events. We use both types of experiences and interpretations in a process of continual adjustment and change. Furthermore, in order to make an art object meaningful, we employ (through comparison and contrast) our sense of reality. Perhaps we can never fully put our experience of an art work into a (coded) response, but, then, our cognitive comprehension of our experiences of reality is as incomplete.

The questions are, do we use these experiences and attendant meanings wisely or foolishly, consciously or unconsciously? Moreover, what art objects are retained and made accessible for us to provide these experiences? (And which ones destroyed by intent or neglect?) Hence, the issue of spectator/film/reality returns to the politics of film canons. Our evaluative procedures relate to our interpretative strategies; interpretative strategies result from how we are constructed as subjects and which interpretative strategies we learn. What art works we have available are a product of these causes. Canons are "inevitable" only as a consequence of prior choices. This is not a question of shepherds leading sheep but making sure all of us are shepherds (of whatever variety) and none of us sheep. Thus, the issue of the politics of film canons is one of consciously (as far as possible) choosing methods of interpreting the experience of films so as to improve our human condition. It is one of teaching our students strategies (not interpretations) and the implications of those strategies. Such a move from the "what" to the "how" and "why" may help toward removing our authority as teachers and the power of film canons.

Notes

This essay is a shortened and revised version of the essay that appeared in *Cinema Journal* 24 (Spring 1985): 4–23, and my response to Gerald Mast and Dudley Andrew in 25 (Fall 1985): 61–65. I encourage readers to review the originals. I would like to thank the following people who provided very helpful criticism and ideas for this essay: Melinda Barlow, Guiliana Bruno, Lucille Chia, Leger Grindon, Kathy Sharpe, and Harald Stadler.

1. Although written histories of cinema are the more obvious place of canon formation, archival practices are just as prone to this, with perhaps more potent implications in terms of what films are available for study. Christopher Phillips suggests that we interrogate the structure of archives in terms of their rules of formation and classification and their systems of exclusion. "A Mnemonic Art? Calotype Aesthetics at Princeton," *October* 26 (Fall 1983): 62.

2. See Robert von Hallberg's remarks that the institution of academics was not the first (or the only) site of canon formation. "Editor's Introduction," *Critical Inquiry* 10 (September 1983): iv.

3. Canons and canon formation have recently been the site of much critical attention in literary studies. Most notable is *Critical Inquiry*'s September 1983 issue. In his introduction, von Hallberg defines a canon in terms of its political implications, although he argues that political determinations may not be able to account totally for the phenomenon.

4. This is not to imply that our choices are totally free. Unconscious determinants limit to some extent the ability to choose.

5. Umberto Eco, *The Name of the Rose*, trans. William Weaver (New York: Warner Books, 1984), 78–79.

6. David A. Cook, *A History of Narrative Films* (New York: Norton, 1981), 19–20. Also, see in particular p. 59.

7. Charles Altieri, "An Idea and Ideal of a Literary Canon," *Critical Inquiry* 10 (September 1983): 37–60.

8. Barbara Herrnstein Smith, "Contingencies of Value," *Critical Inquiry* 10 (September 1983): 1–35.

9. She continues, stressing the use of pathology to characterize deviations from standards: "The particular *subjects* who compose the members of the [authoritative] group are of sound mind and body, duly trained and informed, and generally competent, all other subjects being defective, deficient, or deprived– suffering from crudenesses of sensibility, diseases and distortions of perception, weaknesses of character, impoverishments of background-and-education, cultural or historical biases, ideological or personal prejudices, and/or undeveloped, corrupted, or jaded tastes" (18).

10. Gerald L. Bruns, "Canon and Power in the Hebrew Scriptures," *Critical Inquiry* 10 (March 1984): 462.

11. Although I will focus on the politics of these criteria, evaluative standards include other criteria than universality or social good, among them: beauty; complexity; what someone would have wished to have written (Roland Barthes, *S/Z: An Essay*, trans. Richard Miller [New York: Hill and Wang, 1974], 4); and "unsettling" texts (Stanley E. Fish, "Literature in the Reader: Affective Stylistics" [1970; reprinted in *Reader-Response Criticism*, ed. Jane P. Tompkins (Baltimore: Johns Hopkins University Press, 1980), 88]).

12. Andrew Sarris, *The American Cinema: Directors and Directions, 1929–1968* (New York: E. P. Dutton, 1968), 20.

13. John Hess, "La Politique des auteurs," pt. I and pt. II, *Jump Cut*, no. 1 and no. 2 (May-June 1974 and July-August 1974): 19–22 and 20–22; John Hess, "Auteurism and After: A Reply to Graham Petrie," *Film Quarterly* 27 (Winter 1973–74): 28–37.

14. Auteurism does not necessarily lead to this. Structuralist or psychoanalytic critics have used it for other purposes.

15. Gerald Mast, *A Short History of the Movies*, 3d ed. (Indianapolis, Ind.: Bobbs-Merrill Educational Publishing, 1981), 450.

16. Cook, for example, calls Griffith a "muddleheaded racial bigot" but overshadows this with declaring him cinema's "first legitimate poet" and his achievement as "unprecedented in the history of Western art, much less Western film" (59). Romantic auteurism is not a "universal" system of literary criticism. Literary criticism itself has sought a variety of objectives in its work. Jonathan Culler points this out: "The notion that the task of criticism is to reveal thematic unity is a post-Romantic concept, whose roots in the theory of organic form are, at the very least, ambiguous. . . . Nor has discourse on literature always been so imperiously committed to interpretation. It used to be possible in the days before the poem became pre-eminently the act of an individual and emotion recollected in tranquility, to study its interaction with norms of rhetoric and genre, the relation of its formal features to those of the tradition, without feeling immediately compelled to produce an interpretation which would demonstrate their thematic relevance" *Structuralist Poetics* (Ithaca, N.Y.: Cornell University Press, 1975), 119.

17. On Bazin's political allegiances, see my *"Theorist, yes, but what of?" Iris* (France) 2, no. 2 (1984): 99–109.

18. The criticisms against the personal vision and consistency criteria are related to the arguments of semiology, Marxism, psychoanalysis, and deconstructionism in which the individual is viewed as a contradictory construction of language codes, economic determinants, and psychoanalytic forces.

19. Noël Burch, *Theory of Film Practice*, trans. Helen R. Lane (1969; reprint, New York: Praeger Publishers, 1973).

20. See, for example, pp. 15–37. A concise statement from which these terms are taken is Jerome T. McGann, "The Religious Poetry of Christina Rossetti," *Critical Inquiry* 10 (September 1983): 129.

21. Sarris and other Romantic auteur critics do concentrate on narrative films to the exclusion of other organizational patterns, but nothing in Romantic auteurism prevents its application to other films, and, in fact, criteria of universality, personal vision, and consistency have been a standard approach to evaluating avant-garde film. In addition, at this point Burch is privileging formal effects over analysis of ideological effects. On Romantic auteurism criteria as applied to nonnarrative cinema, see Michael Selig, "Toward a History of the Cinematic Avant-Garde: The Romantic Impulse in Writings on Experimental Film," unpublished paper, Society for Cinema Studies Conference, Los Angeles, June 1982.

22. Noël Burch and Jorge Dana, "Propositions," trans. Diana Matias and Christopher King, *Afterimage* (England), no. 5 (Spring 1974): 40–66.

23. Also see Noël Burch, "Porter, or Ambivalence," trans. Tom Milne, *Screen* 19 (Winter 1978–79): 91–105; Noël Burch, *To the Distant Observer: Form and Meaning in the Japanese Cinema* (Berkeley: University of California Press, 1979).

24. It is difficult to believe that only and all discursive, nonzero degree stylistic devices are politically progressive. See, for example, moments of reflexivity in Hollywood films, particularly comedies and musicals. A more intensive analysis of the avant-garde that considers formal features in relation to subject matter, overall structure, and the context of the film's conditions of existence will reveal a sufficient number of examples of conservative and even reactionary politics to question the equation "Form equals politics." Finally, through such an argument, Burch ends up reducing a reader's response to surprise or disruption, discounting and ignoring other cognitive, affective, and unconscious activities during the reception of a film. On the latter point, see Stanley Fish's argument against Michael Riffaterre's "deviation theory" of poetics in "Literature in the Reader," pp. 92–99.

25. Claire Johnston, "Women's Cinema as Counter-Cinema" (1973; reprinted in *Movies and Methods*, ed. Nichols), 214.

26. See, for example, Lawrence Lipking, "Aristotle's Sister: A Poetics of Abandonment," *Critical Inquiry* 10 (September 1983): 61–81.

27. See Christine Froula, "When Eve Reads Milton: Undoing the Canonical Economy," *Critical Inquiry* 10 (December 1983): 321–47; Judith Fetterley, *The Resisting Reader: A Feminist Approach to American Fiction* (Bloomington: Indiana University Press, 1978); Judith Mayne, "The Woman at the Keyhole: Women's Cinema and Feminist Criticism," in *Re-vision: Essays in Feminist Film Criti-*

cism, ed. Mary Ann Doane, Patricia Mellencamp, and Linda Williams (Frederick, Md.: University Publications of America, 1984), 49–66.

28. See Mary Ann Doane, Patricia Mellencamp, and Linda Williams, "Feminist Film Criticism: An Introduction," in *Re-vision*, 1–17. (The writers reject this approach, however.)

Part II

Practice

To Be Seen but Not Heard: *The Awful Truth*

Diane Carson

In the final scene of *The Philadelphia Story* the imperious Tracy Lord (Katharine Hepburn) happily parrots lines spoken for her by her ex- and soon-to-be husband, C. K. Dexter (Cary Grant). By the end of *His Girl Friday* the assertive Hildy Johnson (Rosalind Russell) bursts into tears and babbles about being afraid Walter Burns (Cary Grant) doesn't want her anymore, as she struggles awkwardly with their luggage. In *Twentieth Century* Lily Garland (Carole Lombard) raves, whimpers, sobs, stomps, and frantically kicks her feet in answer to Oscar Jaffe's (John Barrymore) melodramatic behavior, then she collapses, speechless. In *It Happened One Night*, the last time Ellie Andrews (Claudette Colbert) and Peter Warne (Clark Gable) occupy a motel room, Ellie retreats to her side of the "walls of Jericho" and cries herself to sleep, rebuffed by Peter after articulating her desire for his idyllic, romantic dream.

There's more. In *My Man Godfrey* Irene Bullock (Carole Lombard) babbles hysterically, behaves like an irritating child, and indulges in crying jags and emotional outbursts, continually throwing herself at a debonair, dignified Godfrey (William Powell). Her cruel sister, Cornelia (Gail Patrick), much more the match for Godfrey, crumbles under his kindness, her aggressive outspokenness replaced with tears. In *Nothing Sacred* Hazel Flagg (Carole Lombard) is a crying, whining, punching bag; in *Bringing up Baby* Susan Vance (Katharine Hepburn) makes unfathomable, illogical pronouncements. And in the conclusion of *The Lady Eve*, Eve/Jean

(Barbara Stanwyck) sums up these women's dilemma best when she tells Hopsie/Charles (Henry Fonda), "Don't you know you're the only man I ever loved . . . don't you know I waited all my life for you, and then talked too much!"

Within all of these classic screwball comedies,[1] these celebrated "comedies of equality,"[2] assertive, high-spirited women defy the patriarchal system that seeks and gains their physical and verbal submission. And yet, these women's "disruptive excess"[3] poses so substantive a threat that their expressions and actions engender extreme retaliatory strategies intended to defuse their power. Always romantically linked with a commanding male, these women, nonetheless, temporarily confront oppression and enthusiastically model subversive, rebellious behavior. Although we may read the films as presenting animated women only to denigrate their defiance, the vitality of their joyful rebellion resists facile dismissal. The screwball comedy genre, then, invites a potentially productive reassessment from a contemporary feminist perspective.

To be sure, as screwball comedies inevitably and inexorably pursue conservative agendas, men conquer these verbally adept women by revealing the nonsensical nature of loquacious ramblings, by meeting and topping their verbal aggression, or by co-opting their speech and silencing them. As defenders of patriarchy, authoritative male characters question, refute, and ridicule women's speech as anarchic while they "typically scold, lecture, admonish, or preach . . . [mimicking] rational persuasion."[4] But with "a disproportionate emphasis on women's voices as the *source* of textual anxiety,"[5] the repudiation of these verbally proficient women may not be entirely successful.

Instead of convincingly discouraging confrontation and providing a safety valve for cathartic release, as the classic Hollywood agenda would like, selected scenarios encourage a reconceptualization of social and political relations. Even with screwball comedies' allegiance to woman's containment, "through the gaps, the fissures and incongruities of the films there is a fascinating dramatization of the . . . ideal of sexual democracy as well as its shying away from its consequences."[6] These films, then, want to have it both ways: joyous rebellion and a status quo securely in place. They flirt with danger: despite all attempts to repress them, these defiant women clearly exceed their subordinate positions.

Reaffirmation of the current inequitable system demands visual as well as verbal evidence. Feminist scholars have, for years now, recognized the specular objectification of the woman and, more recently, have turned their attention to the role of voice in reinforcing the primacy of the body.[7] On the most basic level, the synchronization of body and voice confine the woman to "the safe place *of* the story [as well as] safe places *within* the story. . . . Both constituents of the surveillance system – visual and auditory – must be in effect for it to be really successful."[8] We must admit that, within Hollywood narratives, women's enunciation will be unable to materially transform this inequity into full female empowerment.[9] But since "[t]he opposition between the surveillant gaze and the disruptive (excessive or insistent) voice constitutes the structure of these ambivalent texts,"[10] I argue that these classic films entertain such a troubled, interanimated discourse that they conclude indeterminately, unable to convincingly reinforce dominant ideology. In other words, the diverse ways in which the outspoken woman challenges and confronts, subverts and questions the established patriarchal norm reveal a heteroglossic dialogic that resists closure.

Since oppression fosters rebellion, at decisive moments within screwball comedies the transient overthrow of the male dominance inspires a carnivalesque giddiness that characterizes relief from tyranny. To be sure, the woman's temporary rebellion and her feisty resistance are a pale shadow of the liberating, regenerating spirit of the medieval carnival that Bakhtin celebrates in *Rabelais and His World*.[11] Even so, the exhilaration we feel in watching screwball comedies testifies to the therapeutic power of laughter, the pleasure in defying "all that oppresses and restricts. . . . Laughter contains something revolutionary. . . . Only equals may laugh."[12] And these couples demonstrate their rightness for each other by stepping outside constraining societal roles. "What is suspended [in carnival] is hierarchical structure and all the forms of terror, reverence, piety, and etiquette connected with it – that is, everything resulting from socio-hierarchical inequality or any other form of inequality among people."[13] And so, even though the woman often reveals the inadequacy of her verbal mastery; even though in her witty repartee she is shrill, imploring, and halting, confused and confusing; even though analysis of her speech reveals her "auditory insufficiency";[14] her unprecedented challenge forces male retaliation into the open and creates an arena of playful abandon that, however temporarily, questions the status quo.

The primary emphasis is on language, one area in our society in which women have often been credited with "natural" aptitude. To defuse the potentially significant threat posed by articulate women, these films perform a deft sleight of hand. They redefine female utterance as something tangential to rational (that is, male) discourse. As Silverman notes in discussing woman's enunciation in general, the woman is "associated with unreliable, thwarted, or acquiescent speech . . . the male subject has privileges conferred upon him by his relationship to discourse, the female subject is defined as insufficient through hers."[15] The woman's verbal adeptness is regarded as sometimes enigmatic, sometimes indecipherable, but always threatening. As a counterstrike, the man will physically and/or verbally embarrass, ridicule, or, through a host of strategies, strive to intimidate the woman into surrender.

Despite screwball comedies' emphasis on verbal exchanges, the physical components must not be ignored. When the woman does temporarily grasp verbal power, physical retaliation often strives to undermine her ascendancy.[16] In relegating the woman to her subservient position, screwball comedies find excuses for numerous scenes that include physical abuse. While pratfalls, blows, bumps, and physical lack of coordination are staples of slapstick, these more "sophisticated" comedies usually eschew such humor. And yet the films find opportune moments and means for putting "pushy" women in their place. The central male character spanks the woman (*It Happened One Night*), knocks her out with a punch (*Nothing Sacred*), kicks her (*The Awful Truth*), jabs her with a pin (*Twentieth Century*), throws her under a shower (*My Man Godfrey*), or pushes her over with a solid hand to the face (*The Philadelphia Story*). In the latter film, Tracy Lord becomes inebriated, is carried semiconscious from the pool, apologizes repeatedly, and cries because of her alienating "magnificence," as it is labeled in the film. In *My Favorite Wife* Irene Dunne proclaims her independence and flops into a pool. Eve (*The Lady Eve*) runs hysterically from Hopsie's snake, Susan (*Bringing up Baby*) destroys David's brontosaurus, and, as previously noted, numerous women are reduced to tears: Hildy, Hazel, Tracy, Ellie, Irene, Cornelia, and Linda (*Holiday*).

Equally telling, in the screwball comedies that involve significant gender reversals, especially *The Lady Eve* and *Bringing up Baby*, the man finds himself physically humiliated. In the former, an apple, dropped by Eve, clunks Hopsie on the head. He trips over Eve's outstretched leg and, later, over a sofa, has a platter of roast beef dumped on him, upsets a tray whose contents drop on his head, falls in semi-slow motion into sloppy mud, and bungles incompetently on many other occasions. In *Bringing up Baby*, David falls on his top hat, has the tails ripped off his coat, has his clothes stolen so he must don Susan's frilly, white negligee, and, in the final scene, cannot prevent his life's work, a dinosaur skeleton, from toppling. When the narrative portrays the man as operating from a passive, "feminine" mode, he suffers indignities similar to those visited upon the outspoken woman. As pervasive as the pattern is, little attention is paid to this punishing of the female body, for in these scenes clever dialogue slyly distracts us from taking the abuse seriously. We're meant to laugh at the slapstick antics *and* enjoy the verbal wit.

Where women are concerned, the physical reprisals have consequences that reach beyond humorous moments. They function to disrupt and usurp the power of her voice. The message is clear: stay in your place. As Peter Warne says to Ellen Andrews's father at the end of *It Happened One Night*, "What she needs is a guy that'll take a sock at her once a day

Screwball comedies find opportune moments to physically abuse women. Wally (Fredric March) punches Hazel (Carole Lombard) in *Nothing Sacred*.

whether she has it coming to her or not . . . She's my idea of nothing." And then he admits he loves her. Physical retaliation will keep her in line, her verbal assertiveness notwithstanding. Or, as Tracy says to Dexter (*The Philadelphia Story*), "I don't know anything anymore." To which he replies, "Well, that sounds very hopeful, Red. That sounds just fine."

The Awful Truth

As a representative example, *The Awful Truth* reveals clearly the ideological work necessary to control women. Called "the definitive screwball comedy – and the purest of all such films" and "the best, or the deepest, of the comedies of remarriage,"[17] *The Awful Truth* (1937) epitomizes the genre's strengths and weaknesses. The original 1921 play by Arthur Richman proved so popular on Broadway that Hollywood filmed it twice before the Depression.[18] The 1937 film version stars Irene Dunne as Lucy Warriner and Cary Grant as Jerry Warriner. As the film opens, Jerry, who pretends he has just completed a trip to Florida, discovers that Lucy is not dutifully awaiting his return, as he expects. When she does arrive with her voice teacher, Armand Duvalle (Alexander D'Arcy), her explanation of an overnight stay necessitated by a car breakdown elicits disbelief from Jerry. Lucy soon echoes his dismay when she sees "California" stamped on his oranges brought from Florida. They agree to begin divorce proceedings: a marriage is over without trust, here equated with sexual fidelity.

The remainder of the film consists of both Lucy's and Jerry's flirtations with other suitors (Dan Leeson and Barbara Vance, respectively) as well as with each other. One significant scene involves Lucy and Jerry running into each other at a nightclub and Jerry's date, Dixie Belle Lee, performing a semirisqué song. By film's end, the entirely predictable reunion occurs.

Perhaps in part because the original play was written before the Depression, *The Awful Truth* lacks this genre's characteristic pseudoclass conflict. It must be noted in passing that whatever the gender warfare, in all of the classic screwball comedies, class divisions never present insurmountable hurdles to romantic union,[19] thus ducking a critical variable in our society's hierarchical structuring of gender, race, and class. In *It Happened One Night*, the upper-class Ellie sacrifices no material wealth in choosing Peter, though money, or lack thereof, introduces several complications along the way. Similarly, *My Man Godfrey* deftly sidesteps the issue by establishing Godfrey's blue-blood heritage. *Holiday* endorses commonsense, "real people" values while asserting the ease of any smart man making a killing in the stock market. *His Girl Friday* and *Nothing Sacred* present professional men with no significant class commentary, and the illusion of a classless society is reinforced in *Bringing up Baby*, *The Philadelphia Story*, and *The Lady Eve*. The trappings of the rich offer a fantasy of plenitude for Depression Age and contemporary audiences, but deference to upper-class status goes beyond this erasure of class differences. Working-class representatives and less sophisticated, less urbane individuals consistently provide comic relief, including the only supporting role for an African American in these films, the bootblack in *Nothing Sacred*. In *The Awful Truth* we laugh at Dixie Belle Lee (Joyce Compton) and Dan Leeson (Ralph Bellamy) for their lack of refinement, while the indulgence of the upper class slips by without comment.

Distracting us from these issues, *The Awful Truth*'s appeal resides in the vitality of the dialogue, in the verbal exchanges between the feisty Lucy Warriner and her domineering, suspicious husband, Jerry. Lucy disrupts and undermines the legal system, law enforcement, and the very sense of language itself, its ability to communicate clearly, distinctly, formally. Her disturbances build momentum until the final, anarchical scene.

The film begins with discord and Lucy and Jerry's verbal skirmishes reveal the inability of language to negotiate their misunderstandings. When Lucy enters with her voice teacher, Armand, her obvious high spirits, despite assurances that nothing happened, give Jerry compelling evidence for his suspicions. Her verbal protestations are discounted because she *looks* much too cheerful. Appearance speaks louder than words; the visual gains primacy over the spoken; an attempt to contest the visual regime fails. In the nightclub encounter, several scenes later, Dixie sings "My Dreams Have Gone with the Wind," as wind effects blow her skirt high in the air, exposing her legs and frilly underpants. She embarrasses Jerry ("her date"), Lucy, and Dan, though this Oklahoman also enjoys the number. Lucy uses Dixie's routine to her advantage. Late in the film, intent on stealing Jerry away from his fiancée, Barbara Vance, Lucy parodies Dixie's act, and thereby wins Jerry back. Notably, visual spectacle dominates these scenes, and Lucy gains power by presenting herself as such.

Several other provocative verbal-visual juxtapositions are significant. Lucy has, appropriately enough, a male voice teacher, and she appears physically most composed and in command as she sings Italian in a recital, ironically suggesting a joyful abandon that can be experienced only by leaving the constraints of her own native language for the apparent freedom of another, and Italian, in particular, enjoys a special cachet as full of abandon. In contrast, when she sings "Home on the Range," she is accompanied by the cacophonous singing of Dan Leeson, who slaps her abusively on the back, emblematic of the unpleasant aggressiveness of American English and her discomfort with it. "Where nary is heard a discouraging word" ironically contrasts with the domestic discord dramatized in the opening scene and further marks this song as a colloquial, male, cowboy song.

The legal system becomes implicated in the attempt to wrestle the truth from deceptive appearances and assertions, to restore order (a plot twist in several other screwball comedies as well). In three scenes in *The Awful Truth* Lucy challenges the patriarchal legal system and those who enforce its codes. Immediately after deciding to divorce, Lucy calls her and Jerry's lawyer to start proceedings. His paternalistic replies to Lucy contrast with his increasingly curt dismissal of his wife, calling attention to the hypocrisy of his public versus private persona. Most significantly, he first tells his wife to "please be quiet, will you?" This escalates to a more irritated response, "Will you shut your mouth," and, when she reminds him a third time how much he hates for his meal to get cold, he snaps, "Will you shut your big mouth. I'll eat when I get good and ready, and if you don't like it, you know what you can do. So shut up." While his wife implores him from the background, the lawyer, front and center of the composition, sweetly reassures Lucy that "Marriage is a beautiful thing." His order to his wife, his increasingly ruder attempts to silence her, unmasks the dichotomous strategies for controlling women. One is institutionalized control—marriage—which the Warriners' lawyer represents; the other is the personal use of intimidation to silence a specific woman. Although disparate in their tone, both intend the same result: male control.

A carnivalesque challenge to legal authority dominates the next scene but also establishes Lucy's verbal inadequacy. Lucy and Jerry appear in Chancery Court to agree to the conditions of their divorce (to be finalized in sixty days) and to determine the fate of Mr. Smith (Asta), their dog and substitute child. Lucy's replies to the judge and her questions are characterized by inordinate rambling, silly half laughs, and non sequiturs. Court is clearly an arena in which the precise use and definition of words exceed her verbal ability, or at least her customary use of language. As she tells the judge the story of her and Jerry's simultaneously finding Mr. Smith at a pet shop, the judge registers irritation, frustration, and disbelief at Lucy's blather. The scene, while amusing, shows the inappropriateness of her use of language in a court of law, a male-dominated realm, one in which women are not "heard." Her half-suppressed giggles and sighs, her expressive and exaggerated physical movement undermine her authority and dignity. In addition, her costume, especially a bizarre hat, increases the silliness of her presentation.

To rescue himself from Lucy's illogical, muddled ramblings, the judge decides to let Mr. Smith choose his own fate. Lucy wins by cheating, teasing Smittie with a toy mouse hidden in her hand muff. She entices him into her arms and wins custody, just as physical enticement will lure Jerry back to her arms late in the narrative. In both instances, words fail but physical seduction works; the visual wins over the verbal.

So untrustworthy is language that fully half the statements made throughout *The Awful Truth* are ambivalent or "polite" lies, and our attention is regularly directed to them. Dixie Belle Lee has changed her name, Lucy tells Dan his poems are "really wonderful," Lucy asserts to Aunt Patty that she really cares about Dan and is ready to marry him, Jerry asserts Lucy's virtues to Dan's "Ma" with such faint praise that it's clear her reputation has suffered from rumors, and Jerry, at Lucy's prompting, tells Barbara Vance that Lucy is his sister. (Lucy acknowledges the dominant male position when she tells Jerry not to let Barbara push him around.) Feeling constrained by a language that undermines truth, defies her logic, and frustrates clear communication, not surprisingly Lucy retreats to making a physical spectacle of herself to win Jerry back. In Hollywood films, for women this is a familiar and predictable reassertion of body over speech. What Lucy must resort to, humorous as it is, demonstrates the "truth" of women in society, to be seen, not heard.

Other strategies strive to ensure women's subjugation. It isn't sufficient to reduce Lucy's diatribes to noise (as her court scenes do), to dismiss the truth when she speaks it (in the opening discussion with Jerry), or to place her utterances squarely within the threatening territory of verbal anar-

Lucy's (Irene Dunne) dunce hat and language undermine her dignity in a court of law in *The Awful Truth*.

chy. As would be expected from the preceding discussion, throughout *The Awful Truth* embarrassment or physical pain accompanies Lucy's unsuccessful attempts to rebound from her breakup with Jerry. Both are red-faced when Dixie sings her suggestive song, while Dan surreptitiously enjoys it, delighted at the immodest, farcical display. Jerry quickly turns the tables, tricking Dan and Lucy onto the dance floor. He gleefully watches Lucy humiliated by Dan's dancing as she is kicked and stepped on. Jerry then pays the band to repeat the song to prolong Lucy's misery. In one reaction shot, Jerry addresses the camera with such ecstatic joy that Stanley Cavell uses this picture on a pretitle page of his book *Pursuits of Happiness*, writing, "This man, in words of Emerson's, carries the holiday in his eye; he is fit to stand the gaze of millions." We too are clearly meant to find this enormously enjoyable and humorous. Some of us don't, since Jerry's gaze communicates male rapture at woman's mortification.

Lucy shares Jerry's discomfort in ways he never shares hers. Even when Jerry comes to apologize for the recital fiasco, Lucy's hiding Armand in her bedroom distracts us from Jerry's sheepish apology, redirecting the humor to Lucy's dilemma. Similarly, when Dan comes to Lucy's apartment to deliver his witless poem, Jerry hides behind the door. Lucy "punishes" him with a door bouncing off Jerry's nose. But Jerry's revenge surpasses

Lucy's clever command of the situation. Jerry tickles Lucy with a pencil (an appropriate phallic tool), causing her to erupt in uncontrollable, inappropriate bursts of laughter. Power struggles and libidinal undercurrents define these scenes and clearly tilt the balance toward Jerry's dominance. His patriarchal command–he can disrupt as well as control–undermines Lucy's independence and composure, though her spunky playfulness, her refusal to submit, still delights us.

Near the conclusion of the film the law, in the person of two motorcycle policemen, intervenes once more. Again carnivalesque delight in the overthrow of authority drives the scene. Lucy and Jerry have just left the Vances, heading for Aunt Patsy's cabin in the woods, when the police stop them. After she releases the brake and rolls the car into a ditch, Lucy bums a ride from the motorcycle police, determined to get away from the civilization to which she cannot yet be reconciled. She romps on the motorcycle handlebars, bouncing up and down, repeatedly setting off a siren with her bottom. Surely this woman is cause for sounding alarms until she is removed from society, until she relinquishes her masquerade, until she acquiesces to the submissive, seductive role.

At the cabin, away from society's restraints, the wind takes over, a cat tries to keep the door between Lucy's and Jerry's rooms closed, Aunt Patsy's clothes don't fit Lucy, and the restrictive world of nightclubs, parlors, apartments, athletic clubs, and homes exists far away in dramatic contrast. During their last exchange, Jerry awkwardly straddles the doorway between their two rooms in a striped nightshirt, visually suggesting his temporary lack of phallic power. Quite carefree in his nightshirt, lacking male attire, he struggles to regain control and dominance. He's in liminal territory: sporting a compromise between male and female clothes, within minutes of a finalized divorce and, therefore, between independence and marriage.

During the exchange, we see Lucy on her back in bed, tucked under a quilt, seductively teasing Jerry. But, her body hidden, her anarchic use of language takes center stage and challenges Jerry to regain ascendancy. A convoluted, nonsensical exchange follows in which Lucy's apparently contradictory logic defies Jerry's rational approach, though he quickly learns to accommodate it.

JERRY: "In half an hour we'll no longer be Mr. and Mrs. (*pause*) Funny, isn't it?"

LUCY: "Yet, it's funny that everything's the way it is on account of the way you feel."

JERRY: "Huh?"

LUCY: "Well, I mean if you didn't feel the way you do, things wouldn't be the way they are, would they? I mean, things could be the same if things were different."

JERRY: "But, uh, things are the way you made them."

LUCY: "Oh, no. No, things are the way you think I made them. I didn't make them that way a'tall. Things are just the same as they always were, only you're the same as you were too, so I guess things'll never be the same again. Ahh. Good night."

JERRY: "Good night."

JERRY goes to his adjoining room but returns shortly.

LUCY: "You're all confused, aren't you?"

JERRY: "Umm-hmm. Aren't you?"

LUCY: "No."

JERRY: "Well you should be, because you're wrong about things being different because they're not the same. Things are different, except in a different way. You're still the same, only I've been a fool. Well, I'm not now. So as long as I'm different, don't you think that, well, things could be the same again, only a little different, huh?"

LUCY: "You mean that, Jerry? You're sure. No more doubts?"

Throughout their exchange, surface dissonance disrupts the "sense" communicated. In the pauses, Jerry learns the game and plays it well. In essence, he usurps and dismantles Lucy's verbal anarchy. He collapses difference and sameness, ignores apparent illogical thought, and represses a confusing disruption of intelligibility.

In co-opting Lucy's "logic," in using her own words, Jerry completes the transaction. He's taken her utterance and gained her acquiescence. Lucy's not inconsequential victory is in forcing Jerry to reconstitute his power in her terms, which he readily learns to do. He assimilates meaning even when it means moving into a foreign territory, her room, her "sense." Lucy has relinquished her voice, the source of textual anxiety, to Jerry.

Typically, screwball comedies depict the verbally dexterous woman as less appealing than the visually arresting one. In so doing, they reveal the slippery surface of language established by a patriarchal society that must constantly struggle to maintain semantic and physical dominance. While women's attempts at authoritative utterance are undermined physically as well as verbally, strategies to recuperate women into a femininity that couples seductiveness and appeal with acquiescence or silence fail to erase the subversive possibilities for the feminist viewer, so transparent are those efforts, so delightful is the rebellion.

Screwball comedies yield an ambivalent pleasure for the feminist critic. The social agenda remains: to defuse any threat posed by women who physically or verbally reject the roles patriarchy prescribes, to sustain an inequitable system. Nevertheless, within these confines, an oppositional reading finds cause for celebration. The energetic, outspoken woman's exclusion from power reveals a need for systematic regeneration and the overthrow of restrictive hegemony. Patriarchy's retaliatory response to her challenge, the physical and verbal hostility, forces repression into the open and makes it vulnerable to examination and rejection. Whatever the narrative strategy, women's voices will continue to be heard, will retain a subversive force, and will continue to open up possibilities for movement in the direction of a more equitable society.

Notes

This article draws upon the theory and examples elaborated in my dissertation, *A Feminist Reinterpretation of Screwball Comedies: 1934-1942.* I have benefited from discussions with generous colleagues, especially Willis Loy, my coeditors, Kevin Sweeney, David Shumway, Bill Costanzo, Robin Bates, Brenda Wineapple, Phyllis Mael, Tom Hemmeter, Peter Brunette, and the late, and very missed, Linda Singer.

1. Screwball comedies are generally considered as those films with fast-paced, witty repartee revolving around a couple humorously at odds with each other and, as frequently, social and gender expectations. The classic period extended from at least 1934 through 1942.

2. A theme implicitly or explicitly addressed in numerous discussions of screwball comedies. See, for example, Bruce Babington and Peter William Evans, *Affairs to Remember: The Hollywood Comedy of the Sexes* (New York: Manchester University Press, 1989); Wes D. Gehring, *Screwball Comedy: A Genre of Madcap Romance* (New York: Greenwood, 1986); James Harvey, *Romantic Comedy in Hollywood, from Lubitsch to Sturges* (New York: Knopf, 1987); Elizabeth Kendall, *The Runaway Bride: Hollywood Romantic Comedy of the 1930's* (New York: Knopf, 1990); Thomas Schatz, *Hollywood Genres: Formulas, Filmmaking, and the Studio System* (New York: Random House, 1981); David Shumway, "Screwball Comedies: Constructing Romance, Mystifying Marriage," *Cinema Journal* 30 (Summer 1991): 7-23; Ed Sikov, *Screwball: Hollywood's Madcap Romantic Comedies* (New York: Crown, 1989); and Katherine Solom Woodward, *The Comedy of Equality: Romantic Film Comedy in America, 1930-1950* (Ann Arbor, Mich.: UMI Dissertation Services, 1988).

3. Luce Irigaray, *This Sex Which Is Not One,* trans. Catherine Porter (Ithaca, N.Y.: Cornell University Press, 1985), 78.

4. Shumway, "Screwball Comedies," 13.

5. Amy Lawrence, *Echo and Narcissus: Women's Voices in Classical Hollywood Cinema* (Berkeley: University of California Press, 1991), 5.

6. Babington and Evans, *Affairs to Remember,* 13.

7. In addition to Lawrence, cited above, see, for example, Mary Ann Doane, "The Voice in the Cinema: The Articulation of Body and Space," *Yale French Studies*, no. 60 (1980): 67–79; Stephen Heath, "Body, Voice," *Questions of Cinema* (Bloomington: Indiana University Press, 1981), 176–93; and Kaja Silverman, *The Acoustic Mirror: The Female Voice in Psychoanalysis and Cinema* (Bloomington: Indiana University Press, 1988).

8. Silverman, *The Acoustic Mirror*, 164.

9. The woman threatens to move out of her assigned role, to disrupt the narrative in ways modeled in many recent, experimental narratives, several Yvonne Rainer films, Bette Gordon's *Empty Suitcases*, Sally Potter's *Thriller*, and many other avant-garde works.

10. Borrowing from Dale M. Bauer's observation concerning several written texts, in *Feminist Dialogics: A Theory of Failed Community* (Albany: State University of New York Press, 1988), 2.

11. Mikhail Bakhtin, *Rabelais and His World*, trans. Helene Iswolsky (Bloomington: Indiana University Press, 1984).

12. Ibid., 92.

13. Robert Stam, *Subversive Pleasures: Bakhtin, Cultural Criticism, and Film* (Baltimore, Md.: Johns Hopkins University Press, 1989), 21.

14. Ibid., 11.

15. Silverman, *The Acoustic Mirror*, 131.

16. As William Everson notes in "Screwball Comedy: A Reappraisal," "Basically, the Screwball Comedy is a Battle of the Sexes – often a physical battle, since sex itself was taboo, and those energies had to be diverted into fisticuffs between men and women, manhandling and pratfalls," *Films in Review* 34 (December 1982), 578–84.

17. See Gehring, *Screwball Comedy*, 110; Harvey, *Romantic Comedy*, 234; and Stanley Cavell, *Pursuits of Happiness: The Hollywood Comedy of Remarriage* (Cambridge, Mass.: Harvard University Press, 1981), 231.

18. Columbia assigned the film to one of the best comedic directors in the business, Leo McCarey. During rewrites, Dwight Taylor changed the couple's name from Satterly to Warriner, which sounds remarkably like "warring-her." McCarey and the husband and wife team that took scriptwriting credit under her name, Vina Delmar, collaborated on final revisions until June 15, 1937, six days before shooting began.

19. Shumway, "Screwball Comedies," 13–14.

The Marrying Kind: Working-Class Courtship and Marriage in 1950s Hollywood

Judith E. Smith

In this essay I examine a set of films made in Hollywood in the 1950s, *The Marrying Kind* (1952), *Marty* (1955), *The Catered Affair* (1956), and *The Bachelor Party* (1957). These films merit attention because they shifted the boundaries of popular discourse celebrating domesticity and marriage in the 1950s by representing the limits of working-class privacy, autonomy, and consumption as these conflicted with normative expectations of intimacy and romance.

This popular discourse about marriage appeared in magazines and advice books as well as films, interpreting the postwar demographic shift to earlier marriage and early and frequent child rearing as an expanded commitment to an ideal nuclear family, housed in modern suburbs, freed from obligation to kin and neighbors, devoted to higher standards of personal pleasure and romantic intimacy. Working-class ethnic traditions of familial obligation and homosociability were less visible in these discussions, which appeared primarily in media aimed at the middle class. When acknowledged, these traditions were posed as obstacles to marital intimacy and privacy for young men and women. The popular discourse about marriage acknowledged tension between women and men over the goals of domesticity and intimacy, but these were often represented as women's desperation to marry and raise children and men's reluctance to be tamed by domesticity. Focusing on this formulaic battle between the sexes masked the new kinds of stresses and strains generated by the heightened emphasis on heterosexual romance, higher expectations of home owning and household consumption, and by the increased isolation and exclusivity with which women in postwar suburban housing developments were raising their children.[1]

These films were part of a post-World War II genre of working-class realism, characterized by distinctive class and ethnic markers instead of Hollywood's ordinary presentation of homogeneous classlessness. Filmed in black and white with mostly unknown actors on location where working-class people lived and worked, these productions claimed an aura of "authenticity" beyond what moviegoers expected from mainstream Hollywood movies. But unlike a film such as *On the Waterfront* (1954), in which the working-class setting provided a framework for exploring the links between work, politics, and betrayal, these films explore the dynamics of class-inflected family life, particularly the tensions between male power and autonomy and familial needs and constraints.[2] The way these films constructed the meaning of class had special significance in the postwar period, when memories of successful collective gains from wartime labor militance and the unprecedented postwar strike wave competed with new inducements to see oneself as part of the middle class via new government-funded education and suburban housing benefits. Popular culture everywhere seemed to become more homogeneous, with foreign language newspapers, theaters, and social halls declining and distinctive class patterns of leisure and expenditures disappearing.[3]

A discourse about marriage figured prominently in several prior genres of Hollywood film, although none of these gave particular focus to the tensions between class constraints and romantic intimacy. A narrative focus on courtship and reconciliation characterized the screwball comedies of the 1930s and 1940s. Even though much of the action in these comedies took place on the normative class terrain of Hollywood fantasy where wealth flowed as freely as champagne and witty repartee, visual references to the 1930s economic crisis and class differences between the romantic leads did illuminate the boundaries of carefree affluence. Women's films in the 1930s and 1940s also explored marital relationships in a firmly middle-class setting, but here the focus was on the primacy of emotionality and attachment, often revolving around the grandeur of women's sacrifice. As women's films evolved into family melodramas in the 1950s, the psychodynamics of the middle-class family interaction overshadowed themes of sacrifice, and any exception to unlimited affluence largely disappeared. In the shadowy and dark world of postwar *film noir*, sexuality and sexual power were central narrative themes. Women often appeared as seductresses whose sexuality was fatal, although on occasion the fatal danger emanated from men.[4] By the 1950s, the playful and sophisticated partnerships of Colbert and Gable, Lombard and Powell, or

Hepburn and Tracy, and the obsessive dangerous passion of Stanwyck and MacMurray, Turner and Garfield, and Hayworth and Ford gave way to the flatter, more cardboard battle of the sexes as enacted by Hollywood's "foremost romantic couple" of the decade, Doris Day and Rock Hudson.[5]

One Day-Hudson vehicle, *Pillow Talk* (1959), can serve as a representative example of mainstream Hollywood romantic comedies in the 1950s. *Pillow Talk* was a stylish box office hit shot in lavish color with plush sets and gorgeous fashions. The film's comic premise revolves around Jan's need for sexual awakening within marriage (which will confirm her adulthood) and Brad's need to avoid marital domesticity's encroachment on masculine sexual prerogatives. These positions are enunciated in exchanges of dialogue, written by Stanley Shapiro and Maurice Richlin:

> MAID: If there's anything worse than living alone—it's a woman saying she likes it.
>
> JAN: Why, I have a good job, a lovely apartment—I go out with nice men to fine restaurants, parties, the theater—what am I missing?
>
> MAID: Ma'am, when you have to ask, you're missing it.

Compare this to Brad's emasculation anxiety:

> "Before a man gets married, he's like a tree in the forest. He stands there, independent, an entity unto himself. And then he's chopped down. His branches are cut off—he's stripped of his bark—and he's thrown into the river with the rest of the logs. Then this tree is taken to the mill— and when it comes out, it's no longer a tree. It's the vanity table, the breakfast nook, the baby crib, and the newspaper that lines the family garbage can."

Pillow Talk's final tracking shots of Brad in a hospital maternity ward show the couple's acquisition of the decade's most highly touted reward for her sexual and his domestic transformation.

Jan and Brad have no economic constraints, no families—there is nothing standing in the way of their romance except misunderstanding, mistaken identities, and their opposing stances on the link between domesticity and sexuality, all of which can be neatly resolved by the end of the film. The absence of economic constraints is represented in the film's presentation of consumerist affluence. From the establishing shots of office skyscrapers and penthouse apartments, the locale of *Pillow Talk* is the Manhattan of purchasable pleasure. This abundance is reiterated in a variety of transformations—Jan's constant wardrobe changes, each outfit set off by matching accessories coordinated with colors in the set design, and Brad's various personas, which he changes nearly as frequently. In the world of *Pillow Talk*, a suitor of Jan's tries to get her attention by presenting her with a new model sports car as an encouragement to go out with him. He is unsuccessful (apparently, money can't buy love, at least not with such explicitness) but no one faults him for trying. Jan and Brad do work—she's an interior decorator, he's a Broadway songwriter—but their work is so tied up with consumption that it is practically indistinguishable from it. Any potential conflicts for Jan between career and marriage are resolved almost before they can even surface, since Jan's work is practically identical to the work of suburban domesticity. The audience also knows that her commitment to her work is only temporary because her interest in it has been linked to her virginal innocence concerning sexual pleasure.

There are only a few oblique references to class or ethnicity in *Pillow Talk* and they work as stereotypical class, racial, or ethnic foils to Jan's sexual reluctance. Jan's maid, played by Thelma Ritter, comes to work drunk. Presumably because she is working class, she is open to physical abandon and thus advises Jan to give up her middle-class prudery and respond to Brad's sexual appeal. One of Brad's playboy girlfriends has a French accent and another speaks with a southern drawl; these presumably explain why they are sexually available and attractive to him. When Brad and Jan go out to a nightclub, Jan joins an African-American woman torch singer at the piano for a song. Stereotypically signaling open sexuality, the African-American singer in this instance is toned down in order to foreground Day as a singer. The parallel between her restraint and Jan's momentary abandon at the microphone helps to narrow the distance between Brad's sexual experience and Jan's sexual naïveté, a drawing together that is necessary for the eventual triumph of the couple.

This construction of marital tension suppresses many other kinds of issues that divided men and women. Like most Hollywood films, *Pillow Talk* shows courtship rather than marriage—getting the guy/girl rather than sustaining a relationship. Color, art and set design, music, cinematography—all contextualize the relationship in a world of gorgeous and limitless abundance. The films I want to discuss, *The Marrying Kind, Marty, The Catered Affair, The Bachelor Party*—were shot in black and white, sets and costumes intended to invoke scarcity and limits rather than abandon and plenty. They offered spectators an increased possibility for identifying with the view of real life they approximated on the screen. They, too, open with establishing shots of New York City, but instead of office suites and penthouse apartments we see divorce court, a butcher in his shop, a driver in his taxi paying a toll, a window looking out from cramped postwar public housing. While films such as *Body and Soul* (1947), *Force of Evil* (1948), and *On the Waterfront* were shot using the dark and shadowy cinematography of the *film noir* style to evoke their criticism of the injustices of capitalist power and the corruptibility of individuals, these films are shot in an almost documentarylike style, bringing ordinary daily lives and particularly ordinary heterosexual relationships into scrutiny. Here the obstacles to romance are both interpersonal and social. The problem is how to claim the space for romance in a world with competing familial and economic demands; how to sustain a marriage without enough room, money, or time for pleasure, and without much experience with emotional intimacy as the popular psychologists extolled it.

These films were shaped by writers who had grown up in ethnic and working-class communities and were familiar with stories of traditional marriages in which family considerations were paramount, distance between male and female social worlds was taken for granted, and hard work sometimes gave way to affection. As adults in the 1930s and 1940s, they inhabited a landscape where the heterosexual couple was supposed to be autonomous and self-determining, where marital connections, if fueled by love and romance, promised sexual and emotional intimacy, and where sex and pleasure were everywhere on display in advertisements and films, advice columns and paperback book covers. Their films are rooted in the tensions between these competing notions of marriage. Although the narrative in each of these films is resolved in favor of the heterosexual couple rather than the claims of extended kinship networks, and although romantic heterosexual intimacy triumphs in them over homosociability and friendship, romance, family responsibilities, and economic constraints themselves coexist very uneasily.

The Marrying Kind, like *Pillow Talk*, is framed by a schema of irreconcilable differences between the sexes.[6] But each aspect of this difference is colored by a sense of constraint rather than unlimited individual possibility. Written by prize-winning Broadway playwright and director Garson Kanin and his wife, the successful actress Ruth Gordon, from self-described backgrounds of "working people," they meant their screenplay to be the story of an ordinary marriage.[7] The film begins by showing us that romance is fragile as the camera pans divorce court. Like *Pillow Talk*, the locale is Manhattan, but *The Marrying Kind* shows us a different Manhattan. A series of flashbacks reveals the relationship unfolding, not in designer interiors and ritzy nightclubs, but at a drive-in movie, a cheap honeymoon in Atlantic City, a small apartment in postwar public housing, the post office where the husband works as a machine fixer. Each location situates the characters in modest and ordinary public space and implicitly uses the ordinariness to contrast with romantic expectations that are disappointed for the characters as well as for the viewers.

The film narrative is itself constructed by the difference between women and men's experience of their shared married lives. After an argumentative exchange between opposing lawyers and partisan family members, each trying to outshout the other, the female divorce court judge invites the couple by themselves into her chambers to hear their sto-

The Marrying Kind (1952): Domestic discord between Florence Keefer (Judy Holliday) and Chet Keefer (Aldo Ray). Photograph courtesy of the Academy of Motion Picture Arts and Sciences.

ries, pronouncing that there are always "three sides to every story, yours, his and the truth."[8] The film is then organized by a series of flashbacks narrated by voice-overs of either the husband (Aldo Ray) or wife (Judy Holliday), telling his or her experience of what we see on screen. At first the viewer enjoys the humorous dissonance between each character's verbal recollection and what appears on the screen (what the judge might call "the truth"), later experiencing the diverging interpretation and memories (although normal and inevitable) as the fundamental cause of their breakup. This dissonance has privileged the spectator, placing the spectator in alliance with the female judge, in a position to assess the "truth," presumably against the judicial convention of assigning guilt or innocence.

Economic constraints widen the rift generated by the sexual divide and gendered distance between the husband and wife. The first shots of their married life together contrast sharply with the lush interiors in *Pillow Talk*, exposing the barrenness of their furnished apartment, the limits of their consumption, and the divide between them: the camera pans one table, two chairs, a radio cabinet, and a lamp in the living room, two box springs on the floor, a lamp, and a prominent alarm clock in the bedroom.

As in *Pillow Talk*, their unsatisfied longings are distinctly at odds, but their concerns are very different from *Pillow Talk*'s sexuality/domesticity debate. The wife wants intimacy and connection: "Well, I always thought if I ever got married the thing I'd never be anymore was lonesome. It's a funny thing, you can even be in the same bedroom with a husband and he seems to be worrying and thinking about different things except you." The husband expresses his connection in taking on the pressure to provide for her. "But the different things are always for you," the husband, Chet, interrupts. "The kind of love they got in books and movies, that's not for people. You've got to be more realistic." Although she wants companionship, she also feels constrained by their limited resources. He feels unrelenting pressure to make good or to invent something that will make them rich, assuming that the things he can then give his wife and family are what matter and what they really want. A number of the incidents in the film suggest the ways that each one's indecisiveness and lack of self-confidence, bred by their sense of the limitations placed on them by their lack of education and class prerogatives as well as their economic constraints, keep them from being able to either gain financial security or come closer to sharing their dreams. The husband never resolves the conflict between his ambition and the pressures he feels to provide and the kinds of work he can get with its limited pay and even more limited autonomy. When an accident puts the husband temporarily out of work, the wife returns to the job she held before marriage, suggesting the possibility that the wife's competence can flourish only when her husband is down.

Kin and friends in this film pose alternatives to the heterosexual couple that eventually serve to enforce its boundaries. The wife's family aspires to a standard of middle-class ownership and consumption of glamour and excitement that constantly highlights the husband's lack of economic autonomy and power. The husband's family provides the counter example of traditional working-class marriage: stuck in the old neighborhood, supported by work that is steady but has no room for advancement, surrounded by loyal if intrusive kin, and cemented by affectionate love without romance or style. The husband's friend, jovial coworker, and buddy in the early scenes of dating is transformed into the lonely bachelor during the film, his presence at their dinner table serving to reinforce the primacy of the couple over single life.

The film ends with a new, more forgiving marriage contract that the wife and husband tentatively propose. Their remarriage vows reframe the problems in their marriage as a communications problem, and in effect their telling their stories to the judge has approximated the husband's proposal for fixing their marriage: "Maybe if we could have gotten together in the right way and talked everything over." But very little has actually been resolved. This interpersonal solution, which functions to sidestep the other issues raised, seems insubstantial and inadequate given the deep pain of the class constraints and the gendered divide the film has revealed. The film fails to narrow the distance between the husband's and wife's emotional lives, or to reconcile the wife's growing economic resourcefulness with her husband's chronic economic inadequacies. In contrast to *Pillow Talk* where material and personal transformations abound, there is explicit pessimism about the possibility of change.

The way that *The Marrying Kind* is structured to expose the distance between husband and wife provides unusual space for expounding the wife's point of view. Her concerns are as poignantly illuminated as his; her dissatisfactions are as fully a challenge to the success of the marriage as his. The marriage relationship they implicitly seek is genuinely a partnership, not the more conventional bargain where her efforts are directed toward supporting his self-development.

The Marrying Kind is also unusual for the clarity with which it specifies a class location poised between the promise of middle-class expansiveness and the disappointments of working-class constraints. Kanin and Gordon were trying for an uncharacteristic verisimilitude in the film; as Kanin spelled it out in a letter to Cukor, "Its aim is realism, its tone is documentary rather than arty, its medium is photography rather than caricature. I think it is the closest we have ever come to 'holding the mirror up to nature.'"[9] The film's narrative incidents eloquently illuminate the tensions between romance and everyday strains, between intimacy and the incessant demands of child care, between consumer dreams and suburban standards of family life and the pressures of immobility at work and limited income. The dissonance in the narrative resolution recapitulates this tension because the representation of the strains on the marriage is more compelling than the final resolution. The film's unadorned black-and-white cinematography and the modest character of the locations shown construct a view of New York City as a place of limits, of obstacles, of sharp conflict between dreams of the good life and realities of the hard life.

The Marrying Kind's low box office proceeds and uneven critical response suggest that its unusual form and content were probably confusing to audiences who found the film difficult to categorize. If audiences expected Judy Holliday to reprise her comedic role as *Born Yesterday*'s dizzy blonde Billie Dawn, for which she had won the 1950 Academy Award for best actress, they must have been disappointed by the serious depths her character explored in *The Marrying Kind*. In the bittersweet story the characters had to confront real tragedy as well as mundane daily life. The dialogue was witty and literate, but class constraints positioned the characters as naive and unsure. Most reviewers found the characters disagreeable, too contentious, once married, too naturalistic.[10] The recognition of familiar problems did not seem to compensate for the disappointing lack of accustomed cinematic pleasure and may have been too dissonant a challenge to the mystique of opportunity, mobility, and rosy domesticity that constructed the norm in the 1950s.

Paddy Chayefsky's 1950s films were more popular with audiences, especially *Marty* and *The Bachelor Party*, suggesting that he was better able to balance the appeal of realistic recognition with conventional cinematic pleasure.[11] These films of Chayefsky all appeared initially as live television plays. From its earliest broadcasts, television was associated with "realism" because of its ability to train a camera on a specific action as it was unfolding and transmit it in real time; its "liveness" was identified as its most distinguishing feature. The experimentation in television's early years to find the broadcast material most suitable to its particular capabilities had opened up considerable program time to live presentations of original drama, churned out for the insatiable weekly schedule by a group of young playwrights firmly committed to dramatizing contemporary issues within the stylistic conventions of realism.[12] Chayefsky's television drama played a major role in popularizing a realistic drama of everyday life, where interior and psychological realism could make use of television drama's technical limitations: low budgets, minimal sets, and modest costuming, over-the-shoulder close-ups, more dollying than in film because live television couldn't have as many camera setups, and predominantly close and medium shots.[13] The claustrophobic settings and shot compositions of television drama were extremely well suited to intimate drama. As one reviewer of the time commented, "The secret of television's hypnosis is that it gives you an illusion of actuality and of prying into the private lives of your fellows."[14]

Marty, The Catered Affair, and *The Bachelor Party* clearly owe a debt to their live television drama origins. Shot in black and white on location in Manhattan and the Bronx, the films evoke a sense of place and class as characters meet in crowded apartments, stairwells, subway trains, the Automat, and neighborhood bars. In all three films, enmeshed family dynamics are established quickly through repetitive dialogue and are reiterated in shots heightening claustrophobia, framed so that the camera and audience look from the outside into cramped spaces. These three films together situate the process of courtship, negotiations over the wedding, and the reevaluation of married life itself in the context of lives embedded in family and kinship obligations, constrained by scarcity of money and competing claims on what little there is. Although each narrative is resolved in favor of the 1950s version of romantic intimacy, dissonances remain powerful because the tensions between homosociability and heterosexuality, the broader claims of family and community, and the sanctity of the couple are not so easily resolved. As in *The Marrying Kind*, the representations of distance between male and female worlds, of the unceasing grind of married life and parenthood without enough money, and of the strangeness of such close physical proximity without shared experience or connection are much more compelling than the requisite Hollywood resolutions in favor of married love and companionship as the source of life's meaning.

In *Marty*, the main obstacle to marriage between Marty, the butcher (Ernest Borgnine), and Clara, the schoolteacher (Betsy Blair), is his reluctance. But male reluctance to marry is fundamentally different in the world of *Marty* than in the world of *Pillow Talk*. In *Marty*, this reluctance is weighted down by the opposition of family, friends, and neighbors, all of whom value marriage within the context of maintaining loyalties and obligations to them. To marry Clara means Marty must reject the claims of ethnicity and choose the heterosexual couple and its intimacy over commitment to the extended family, and in opposition to male friendship and camaraderie, which the movie frames as immature and latent homosexual male bonding. Marty's final choice of his schoolteacher is made to seem all the more dramatic because of his narrow escape, on the one hand, from oppressive and restrictive responsibilities to his mother and aunt, and on the other, from the desultory pastimes of immature nonmarried life.

Women's agency in *Marty* is somewhat obscured. Clara is much less well defined as a character than the female lead in either *Pillow Talk* or *The Marrying Kind*. She works as a teacher, but, as was the case with Doris Day's interior decorator, when single women appeared in Hollywood movies in the 1950s, the autonomous potential of career and self-definition were made invisible by a focus on incompleteness and lack of fulfillment. She is socially diffident and, before meeting Marty, has been attentive to her father in a way that the film psychologizes as immature. Camera angles emphasize her slightness; makeup defines her as pale and thin-lipped. She is costumed as prim and repressed, with a little bow at her collar. Although *Pillow Talk*'s Day is meant to be glamorous and *Marty*'s Blair is meant to be plain, they both represent an assumed link between virginity/prudery and powerlessness. Clara does try to control the pace of their sexual contact, and she does voice opposition to the domestic consensus when she tells Marty's mother that she doesn't "think a mother should depend so much upon her children for her rewards in life." But Marty's interest in her overwhelms her initial social reluctance, and from then on she is willing to position herself passively, waiting by the phone for his call. There is no indication of how a relationship between them might integrate her questioning of domesticity and her acceptance of passivity.[15]

By the end of the film, Marty and Clara are left hanging in that promising netherworld where the decision to marry has solved the narrative dilemmas while the viewer doesn't actually have to imagine an actual ongoing relationship. The stakes are high – cut off from family and friends, all of their expectations for personal happiness and social contact must be met by the couple. But by not showing the marriage itself, the film is able to successfully balance recognizable (and unresolved) dilemmas in working-class life with Hollywood's conventional promise of happiness ever after, signaled by the upbeat opening and closing score. The film's enthusiastic reception benefited from an expensive, innovative, and very carefully orchestrated publicity campaign, part of which was designed to attract critics and art-house audiences by stressing *Marty*'s non-Hollywood black-and-white realism, and part of which depended on promotions through butchers' unions and special previews for bootblacks and beauticians who were thought to have credibility with local working-class audiences.[16]

The Catered Affair, adapted by Gore Vidal from Chayefsky's television play and directed by Richard Brooks, uses family conflict over the plans for a wedding as a dramatic but ultimately surmountable obstacle to romantic love. Family members take positions according to their own concerns as to whether the young couple should be joined at a big public ritual affirming family ties and community norms or a small private event celebrating the autonomous couple. By the end of the film, heterosexual romance is once again triumphant. The daughter and her fiancée's true love has been restored by their reclaiming their original private wedding plans and thus regaining self-determination. The boarding bachelor uncle, pushed by his exclusion from the small wedding to rethink his marital situation, has given in to a proposal of marriage from his elderly card-playing widow companion, seeing this as his final chance for domestic happiness in his own home. Most significant in terms of screen time, the mother has confronted the ways that the circumstances of her own arranged marriage and subsequent familial responsibilities had blinded her to the feelings of her husband and their potential for a romantic connection. The closing shots of the movie are of the mother choosing her relationship with her husband rather than the company of kin and children, and his arm tentatively encircling her.

Although MGM tried to pitch the film as a celebration of romance and marriage, the dissonance between the cramped and dismal familial enmeshment in the Bronx tenement and the promise of "happily ever after" was too powerful for the film to support this ideological formulation. As in *The Marrying Kind*, the obstacles to ordinary people's romance turned out to be too ordinary to allow viewings for pleasure and too mundane to sustain a love story. The *New York World-Telegram and Sun*'s reviewer, Alton Cook, argued that an audience could not believe that "a loveless marriage of two decades can suddenly turn to bliss."[17] The narrative resolution could not successfully contain the painful dissonances the film uncovered.

The Bachelor Party, directed, like *Marty*, by Delbert Mann, represented another attempt to contextualize the obstacles to love on a tight budget, and, like *The Catered Affair*, focused squarely on marriage itself rather than courtship. Establishing shots track a vista of high-rise apartments and then move through an apartment window to the couple inside, who are thinking through the impact of the wife's unplanned pregnancy on their marital intimacy as well as on their upward mobility, certain to be checked if she has to quit her job and he give up his night-school accounting course. Their crisis is contextualized as he joins his office buddies at a bachelor party that inevitably sets off questioning the pleasures of married life. Dimly lighted, noisy, smoky restaurants and bars are the setting for the married men's bleak discourse about companionate intimacy, sparked by anguished questioning from the groom-to-be about what his upcoming marriage will entail:

> "Most of the time, Arnold, you don't even see her. You're away working. You come home, she fixes you supper. Then one of you washes the dishes. Then if you're not tired, you can go to the movies or visit somebody. Or you watch TV."

The groom's response reveals how sexually closed off he is as he questions the need for even this level of companionship: "But I do that now with my mother." At the party, the mood of questioning and uncertainty spreads to all the guests, giving way to tawdriness and even sordidness as the night wears on and the men search desperately for the big time they have been promising the bridegroom and themselves. The delights of promiscuous revelry are revealed to be lonely and fumbling sex without love, and as the sun comes up on the city, the married men and the prospective groom reaffirm their commitment to matrimony.

Women's voices are almost completely silenced in *The Bachelor Party*. Certainly the power of the drama lies in the men's self-discovery. As in *Marty* and *The Catered Affair*, the best marriage has to offer women is a supporting role to men's quest for affirmation and self-knowledge. Still, the film contains one extremely noteworthy scene that sets up a conversation between two women to contrast with the men's stag posturing. Here the pregnant wife, alone with her sister-in-law, tries to evaluate the impact of the impending child on her marriage. The wife is dreamy about her pregnancy, but her sister-in-law powerfully challenges the domestic ideal by proposing that an abortion might be better for the marriage than the pressures of early child bearing without enough money or the choice between children and upward mobility. The problem is still framed in terms of pleasing men: the sister-in-law can only question child bearing because of her fear that her attending to their young children caused her husband to have extramarital affairs. But even this challenge cannot hold up against the force of 1950s pronatalism: "I've wanted this baby. I've wanted it for a long time. It's the only thing I've ever asked of Charlie." As in *Pillow Talk*, questioning the quality of marital intimacy will be resolutely silenced by attempting to cement heterosexual bonds with child bearing.

Despite its conventional ideological stance, *The Bachelor Party* was packaged and promoted as sexually explicit. The film's mention of pregnancy and abortion and the scenes of men viewing stag films and picking up a prostitute were reframed as mature subject matter, probably aimed at emulating the successes of European art films in American movie houses and, like them, exploiting sex as a way of sharpening the distance between film and television.[18]

The Bachelor Party was successful at the box office, but an apparent gender divide among reviewers suggests that women and men may have had different responses to the film. Women critics showed only "lukewarm interest" while men were "enthusiastic."[19] Middle-class women audiences who had committed themselves to lives as mothers and housewives in the 1950s may not have wanted to confront the bleakness of the challenge to the domestic ideal, especially not as part of a precious night out. Again, many critics articulated dissatisfaction resulting from the tension between the problems opened up by the film narrative and the lack of conviction of its resolution. The *Cue* reviewer found the film so "grimly real that it lacks conviction in its last reel hurry-up reconciliation scene, a scene which after too much gloom, comes too late, too fast, and with too little persuasion."[20] Like *The Marrying Kind* and *The Catered Affair*, *The Bachelor Party* was more successful in dramatizing the strains on ordinary people's marriages than in promoting the successes. Lingering and tender close-ups, vows of love, and sweet, triumphant music couldn't reconstruct a convincing romantic resolution because romantic successes shaded too easily into dishonesty in films that attempted honest scrutiny of the problems that beset ordinary marriages. The distance between women and men, once acknowledged, could not be narrowed even with the screen power of a Hollywood embrace; the varieties of women's agency could not be contained within the supporting roles allotted to them.

The Marrying Kind, Marty, The Catered Affair, and *The Bachelor Party* did indeed contribute to contemporary discourse about marriage and domesticity, and within certain limits they rearticulated the issues in terms of class and ethnic constraints. Offering a counterpoint to a film such as *Pillow Talk*, these films show scarcity instead of abundance; they suggest that people occupy identities that are firmly grounded in class and ethnic backgrounds rather than endlessly shifting personas that go only as deep as a costume change; and they do so, most important, by constructing a world where men and women are much less confident about being able to come together to spark romance or sustain intimacy without enough money and with too many demands from children, parents, and kin. In the end, the films fundamentally revise the formulaic battle of the sexes. Instead of opposing women as tamers and men as tamed, they construct a world where women's longing for intimacy was often liable to be disappointed and where their loyalties to men were in competition with other responsibilities. They also constructed a world where men's lack of status and autonomy at work heightened what they demanded of their families and where intimacy with male peers was much more familiar than closeness with women. Too often in the films, women's stakes in these choices were less visible than those of men. But when the films were effective in questioning the possibility of romance and the enticements of domesticity, they had the potential to tap into the deeper pain of unsatisfied longings experienced by women with diverse class and ethnic backgrounds.

Not surprisingly, the values of romantic intimacy triumph in each film, but over and over, the films' conventional narrative resolutions in favor of heterosexual romance and intimacy were not able to convincingly contain the problems provoked by social and economic challenges to marital pleasure, nor could they stylistically resolve the tensions between the grimness of "realist" sets and locations with audience expectation of conventional Hollywood cinematic pleasure. Narrative resolutions tended to feature individual mobility and heterosexual privacy, reframing class boundaries as permeable by means of style and consumption, even while still acknowledging the painful lack of independence, autonomy, and compensation available from working-class employment. By popularizing psychological jargon about maturity and utilizing psychological rather than social explanations, the films privilege the authority of the experts and diminish the credibility of the characters' own self-understanding or social analysis. Still, repressed conflict, anxiety, and skepticism about domesticity worked its way into the films at least enough to question the common characterization of the 1950s as domestic celebration.

Notes

I want to thank those colleagues who commented on various versions of this essay presented in 1990 at the History Department at the University of California at Berkeley, the Graduate History Colloquium at the University of California at Davis, and the American Studies Association meeting in New Orleans. Special thanks to Sharon Strom, for first encouraging me to read and write about film and to see *The Marrying Kind*.

1. Steven Mintz and Susan Kellogg, *Domestic Revolutions: A Social History of American Family Life* (New York: Free Press, 1988); Elaine Tyler May, *Homeward Bound: Families in Cold War America* (New York: Basic Books, 1988); John D'Emilio and Estelle B. Freedman, *Intimate Matters: A History of Sexuality in*

America (New York: Harper and Row, 1988); Barbara Ehrenreich, *The Hearts of Men: American Dreams and the Flight from Commitment* (Garden City, N.J.: Doubleday, 1983).

2. John Hill, *Sex, Class and Realism: British Cinema 1956–1963* (London: British Film Institute, 1986).

3. Roland Marchand, "Visions of Classlessness, Quests for Dominion: American Popular Culture, 1945–1960," in *Reshaping America: Society and Institutions, 1945–1960*, ed. Robert Bremner and Gary Reichard (Columbus: Ohio University Press, 1982), 163–90. Ethnic working-class situation comedies appearing on national network television consistently attempted to resolve ethnic and class-specific dilemmas with individual mobility and commodity purchase. George Lipsitz, "The Meaning of Memory: Family, Class, and Ethnicity in Early Network Television Programs," *Camera Obscura* 16 (1988): 79–116.

4. Thomas Schatz, *Hollywood Genres: Formulas, Filmmaking, and the Studio System* (Philadelphia: Temple University Press, 1981), 150–85; Stanley Cavell, *Pursuits of Happiness: The Hollywood Comedy of Remarriage* (Cambridge, Mass.: Harvard University Press, 1981); Elizabeth Kendall, *The Runaway Bride: Hollywood Romantic Comedies of the 1930s* (New York: Knopf, 1990); Andrea Walsh, *Women's Films and Female Experience* (New York: Praeger, 1984); Mary Ann Doane, *The Desire to Desire: The Woman's Film of the 1940s* (Bloomington: Indiana University Press, 1987); Christine Gledhill, ed., *Home is Where the Heart Is: Studies in Melodrama and the Woman's Film* (London: British Film Institute, 1987); Jackie Byars, *All That Hollywood Allows: Re-reading Gender in 1950s Melodramas* (Chapel Hill: University of North Carolina Press, 1991); Marcia Landy, ed., *Imitations of Life: A Reader on Film and Television Melodrama* (Detroit, Mich.: Wayne State University Press, 1991); E. Ann Kaplan, ed., *Women in Film Noir* (London: British Film Institute, 1978).

5. Schatz, *Hollywood Genres*, 170–71. Douglas Sirk cast Rock Hudson as a romantic hero in the family melodramas he made during the 1950s for Universal, using Hudson's screen persona as an icon of masculinity to call attention to film's own artifice (245–56, esp. 250). It is possible that the choice of Hudson for *Pillow Talk* (produced by Ross Hunter, who was also Sirk's producer at Universal) may have been similarly ironic, especially in the context of his presumed ability as a homosexual to "act out" masculinity. Or the casting may simply have reflected the fact that Hudson was the biggest box office star of the late 1950s and early 1960s.

6. Brandon French drew attention to this film and its unusual focus on gender difference in her discussion in *On the Verge of Revolt: Women in American Films of the Fifties* (New York: Ungar, 1978), 12–34.

7. As Kanin and Gordon described their backgrounds in 1952, "We come from working people." Kanin's parents were Russian immigrants; his father was a tinsmith and later an alternately successful and failed builder, his mother a buttonhole maker. Gordon's father was variously described as a sea captain, a factory worker, and a foreman. The Gordon-Kanin team had unusual control over their scripts because they never wrote under contract and because their director and friend George Cukor filmed their scripts as written. In contrast with *Adam's Rib*, which concerns marital issues provoked by wealthy husband and wife lawyers

(Tracy and Hepburn) taking opposite sides in a court case, this marriage story (showcasing Holliday, a New York Jewish actress from the lower-middle class) was very consciously set in a milieu of economic limitations and constraints. See letters between George Cukor and Garson Kanin and Ruth Gordon in the George Cukor Collection, Special Collections, Library of the Academy of Motion Picture Arts and Sciences; Kanin and Gordon clippings files, AMPAS.

8. Kanin locates the source of the judge's pronouncement as his father's "fruity Yiddish" advice, "Remember, mein gold, there are three sides to every story: yours and his and the truth." Garson Kanin, *Tracy and Hepburn: An Intimate Memoir* (New York: Primus, 1988), preface.

9. Letter from Garson Kanin to George Cukor, September 9, 1951, George Cukor Collection, AMPAS.

10. Nineteen fifty-two reviews consulted in trade papers, Los Angeles and New York daily newspapers, and national weekly and monthly news magazines.

11. Chayefsky was the son of two Russian-Jewish emigrants who had come to the United States as adolescents and met at Coney Island. His father worked as a milkman, became the owner of a dairy in the 1920s, and went bankrupt in 1930, finally regaining some financial security as a manager of a creamery in the late 1930s. Helen Dudar, "A Post Portrait: Paddy Chayefsky," *New York Post*, January 4–7, 1960, in the Paddy Chayefsky Collection, box 1, folder 3, "Biographical Clippings, 1953–1972," at the Wisconsin State Historical Society. Both *Marty* and *The Bachelor Party* were among the top-grossing films of the years in which they were released, according to the charts in the annual *Variety* anniversary editions. As a writer, Chayefsky bargained for unusual control over his scripts in his contract with independent production company Hecht-Hill-Lancaster and also had the advantage of having his scripts filmed as written by friend and former television drama director Delbert Mann.

12. On early television drama, see Eric Barnouw, *The Tube of Plenty* (New York: Oxford University Press, 1975), 154–66; Michael Kerbel, "The Golden Age of Television Drama," *Film Comment* 15 (July-August 1979): 12–19; Kenneth Hey, "*Marty*: Aesthetics vs. Medium in Early Television Drama," in *American History/American Television*, ed. John J. O'Connor (New York: Ungar, 1983), 95–133.

13. On the constraints of live television drama, see Tad Mosel's foreword to *Other People's Houses: Six Television Plays* (New York: Simon and Schuster, 1956), ix-xi; Tad Mosel, "In Search of the Untouched Moments of Life," *New York Times*, December 10, 1989; Fred Coe, "TV Drama's Declaration of Independence," *Theater Arts* 38 (June 1952): 29–31, 87–88; Gore Vidal, "Television Drama, ca. 1956," *Theater Arts* 40 (December 1956): 65–66, 85–86; Ring Lardner, Jr., "TV's New 'Realism': Truth sans Consequences," *Nation* 181 (August 13, 1955): 132–34. For a critical analysis of television's realism, see David Barker, " 'It's Been Real': Forms of Television Representation," *Critical Studies in Mass Communication* 5 (March 1988): 42–56; Lynn Spigel, "Installing the Television Set: Popular Discourses on Television and Domestic Space, 1948–1955," *Camera Obscura* 16 (January 1988): 11–46.

14. The quote is from Robert Hatch's discussion of the teleplays in his review of the film *The Bachelor Party* in *Nation*, April 27, 1957: 379.

15. Brandon French also called attention to this aspect of the film in her chapter on *Marty* in *On the Verge of Revolt*, 84–91.

16. The promotion for *Marty* cost just a little more than the film itself – $350,000 compared with $343,000. Author's interview with Delbert Mann, Los Angeles, March 3, 1986; author's interview with Walter Seltzer, Los Angeles, March 4, 1986; *New York Times*, September 11, 1955, and September 14, 1955; "The Promotion of *Marty*," *Time*, March 19, 1956.

17. Promotion included featuring the wedding dress in the summer issue of *Modern Bride*; *Seventeen* magazine's selection of the film as the picture of the month for July 1956; and schemes for drive-ins to offer their screen areas for real weddings to take place before picture showings. MGM pressbook for *A Catered Affair*, 12, 15–17, USC Cinema-Television Library. Other reviewers echoed Cook's concerns in "*Catered Affair* at Victoria," *New York World-Telegram and Sun*, June 15, 1956; for example, Bosley Crowther, "Screen: *A Catered Affair*," *New York Times*, June 15, 1956; "*A Catered Affair*," *Cue*, June 16, 1956.

18. Legion of Decency ratings, in box 9, folder 10: *Bachelor Party*, clippings, 1954–57, of the Paddy Chayefsky Papers, Wisconsin State Historical Society; articles on the struggle with the MPAA over *Bachelor Party* ads in *Variety*, April 10, 1957; *Variety* (daily), April 27, 1957; MPAA files on *The Bachelor Party*, AMPAS.

19. Philip Hartung, "Long Night's Journey into Day," *Commonweal*, April 12, 1957: 35.

20. For example, *Cue*, April 13, 1957; *Variety* (daily), February 15, 1957.

Contradiction and Viewing Pleasure: The Articulation of Racial, Class, and Gender Differences in *Sayonara*

Gina Marchetti

Over the last twenty years or so, feminism has foregrounded the issue of gender for film scholarship, making this type of analysis an acceptable part of the discipline. However, feminist film scholarship has too often ignored the important ways in which race, ethnicity, class, sexual preference, and other differences figure in analyses of gender. The fact that gender difference never exists in a vacuum is sometimes lost in studies that treat gender as the single determining factor within film analysis. As Jane Gaines has pointed out in her essay "White Privilege and Looking Relations: Race and Gender in Feminist Film Theory," the isolation of gender relations blinds feminist film criticism to other kinds of oppression:

> Since it has taken gender as its starting point in the analysis of oppression, feminist theory has helped to reinforce white middle-class values, and to the extent that it works to keep women from seeing other structures of oppression, it functions ideologically. . . . The dominant feminist paradigm actually encourages us *not to think* in terms of any oppression other than male dominance and female subordination.[1]

Sayonara (directed by Joshua Logan, based on a novel by James A. Michener, 1957), for example, could be looked at solely in terms of its treatment of gender differences; however, that reading would miss the complicated way in which the text treats gender in relation to class, race, and nation. Since *Sayonara* expressly deals with issues of gender, racial, and national identity, the ideological operations of the text, the ways in which it both takes up and denies social inequalities, can be seen even more clearly to be determined not by gender alone.

Sayonara: From War to Romance

Sayonara deals with a love affair between Major Lloyd Gruver (Marlon Brando), a pilot serving in the Korean War, and Hana Ogi (Miiko Taka), a star of the all-female musical company Matsubayashi. Other interracial relationships parallel this principal one – for example, the relationships between Gruver's Anglo-American fiancée, Eileen Webster (Patricia Owens), and a Kabuki performer, Nakamura (Ricardo Montalban), and between an enlisted man serving under Gruver, Joe Kelly (Red Buttons), and his Japanese wife, Katsumi (Miyoshi Umeki).[2]

Sayonara makes a statement against racial intolerance within the context of postwar U.S.-Japanese relations. Like *The Teahouse of the August Moon, Japanese War Bride, Cry for Happy*, and other films featuring interracial love affairs in postwar Japan, *Sayonara* uses romance as a metaphor for interracial/intercultural understanding. As such, it can be seen as another entry in a long Hollywood tradition of social problem films that use melodrama and romance to concretize (but also personalize, individualize, and often trivialize) broader social or political concerns.

At first glance, *Sayonara*'s sympathetic treatment of interracial romance appears to be a move toward increased liberalization on the part of a film industry whose production code had strictly outlawed representations of miscegenation just a few years before. When looked at more closely, however, the film presents a far more contradictory picture of race, culture, and sex than might first appear to be the case. In fact, *Sayonara* features a series of narrative transpositions that serve to obscure a good deal of the film's apparent social criticism. Through these narrative twists, the film manages to voice and then ignore ideological contradictions by transforming them into more distant, but related, problems. According to Roland Barthes's analysis of classical realist narratives in *S/Z*,[3], plots are usually driven forward by a series of such transpositions, which create narrative interest, obscure ideological contradictions, and lead to an eventual narrative closure that promises to resolve both narrative and, symbolically, ideological conflicts in one movement.

Sayonara begins this narrative process with war, which stands in this text as the extreme form of cultural, national, and racial intolerance being criticized. A title reads "Korea 1951," setting the tale during the Korean War. Although *Sayonara* seems to ask to be read as an antiwar film, the reality of the Korean War and the controversy it generated are quickly dismissed.[4] Early in the film, Gruver, apparently disillusioned with American involvement in Korea, mumbles that one of the pilots he shot down that day had a "face." This is the film's only real reference to the actual morality of war, and, rather than take the Korean War as a historical event in its own right, the film instead chooses to only quietly question war in general by allowing Gruver to comment on the humanity of his enemy.

Further, *Sayonara* very quickly places the Korean War at an even greater distance. During a medical exam, a doctor announces that Gruver will be transferred to Kobe, in occupied Japan, at the request of his future father-in-law, General Webster. Leaving Korea behind, narrative interest moves to Japan, to a *post*war setting, where issues involving war, morality, and the nature of the enemy have an even greater temporal and emotional distance. The narrative problematic also shifts from war to romance, obscuring the issue of war in the process, but still making the romantic relationships involved understandable only through a reference to war and the definition of racial otherness.

However, the Korean War is not the only "structuring absence"[5] that kicks *Sayonara*'s plot into operation. In order to understand the impact the film had in 1957, it seems necessary to look at the operation of ideology within the text against the backdrop of American history and the pressing social issues of the day.

Although *Sayonara* begins as a statement on war, peace, and American militarism, it very rapidly shifts to the issue of race and sexuality. More than either Korea or World War II, civil rights is closest to the emotional heart of the film and, certainly, more recently on the minds of its 1957 audience. In *"The Searchers*: An American Dilemma,"[6] Brian Henderson notes that although John Ford's *The Searchers* deals with relations between Native Americans and white settlers, the power of the text and the problems it treats relate more to the controversy surrounding blacks and civil rights in the mid-1950s than to Native Americans and the threat of interracial sexuality in the post-Civil War era. *Sayonara* seems to have a similar relationship to the civil rights movement. Like Ethan Edwards, Lloyd Gruver is a southerner, a military man, who represents conservative southern values. Supposedly, both characters are meant to stand for a South in transition. Still, neither film deals with racism in a contemporary context.

However, even though the reference is oblique, this preoccupation with issues of racial separation and sexuality actually blurs *Sayonara*'s antiwar message. By dealing with race and war simultaneously, the text sidesteps any direct confrontation of either issue. Instead, it teeter-totters between both issues.

Moreover, *Sayonara* complicates even this issue. At one point, Gruver chastises his subordinate Kelly for threatening to give up his American citizenship in order to marry Katsumi. Kelly then challenges Gruver's love for Eileen: "Perhaps you don't feel as strongly about your girl as I do about mine." At this point, the text twists away from the theme of racial tolerance to a questioning of gender identity and heterosexual romance. If American identity as "good, pure, righteous, and white" had been put in doubt by Hiroshima, the Korean War, and the civil rights movement, then it had been put in doubt, too, as male by the entry of women into the American work force in unprecedented numbers during World War II. If *Sayonara* is about racial tolerance and understanding, it is also about keeping women in their "place" as wives and mothers.

Romeo and Juliet in Japan: Transcendent Love and the Ideology of Romance

Any critique *Sayonara* may make of war, racism, or militarism is very firmly held in check by the text's very conservative treatment of romance. Within Western thought, from stories of courtly love during the Middle Ages to nineteenth-century bourgeois Romantic notions of love as the key to personal salvation,[7] there has been an important link between social criticism and the dually forbidden and transcendent nature of romantic love. Standing outside laws and conventions that forbid it, romantic love acts as a corrective to social norms that are seen as restrictive, irrational, inhumane, intolerant, or hypocritical. However, even though the notion is linked to social criticism, it also quiets that criticism by placing it in the realm of individual eccentricity. Rather than calling for sweeping social change, romantic love calls only for a bit of tolerance. Further, since romantic love is so often linked to death and tragic ends of various sorts, that social critique is usually viewed as a hopeless cause even before the tale begins.

Romantic love also has its profoundly conservative side – a side keenly felt in *Sayonara*. Linked to the "natural" expression of deeply held feelings, romantic love makes a case for heterosexual coupling, and usually marriage, as the fulfillment of all desires and needs. Even more than national or racial boundaries, patriarchal ideology mystifies gender lines as beyond culture, "genuine," ahistorical, and immutable. If *Sayonara* questions national and racial boundaries on one level, it also affirms and solidifies very conservative notions of gender identity and sexuality on another.

In fact, perhaps more than anything else, *Sayonara* deals with the definition of heterosexual love and places it indirectly but clearly opposite homosexuality, which the text presents as alluring, but ultimately "unnatural" and "perverse." The threat it poses to traditional, patriarchal definitions of gender manifests itself in three ways: (1) through the expression

Any political critique is held in check by a conservative treatment of romance.

of female sexuality outside the realm of male control, (2) through the questioning of the definition of masculinity and its link to war and the military, and (3) through the challenge Japanese theatrical conventions involving cross-dressing pose to gender boundaries.

By introducing Gruver as a man in moral crisis because of a barely voiced suspicion that the Korean War is unjust, *Sayonara* implicitly places Gruver's identity as a man in crisis. Until he meets Hana Ogi, Gruver appears to be drained of power, of masculine potency. Instead of openly saying this identity crisis is linked to male identity and war, however, *Sayonara* puts the blame on women—namely, Gruver's fiancée, Eileen. For example, she confronts him directly about his future plans and asks him why he is not more passionate about their relationship: "Haven't you ever felt like grabbing me and hauling me off to a shack somewhere?" Clearly threatened by Eileen's questions, Gruver defends traditional marriages, the military, and sexual restraint.

The scene that immediately follows features Kelly and Katsumi's wedding, with Gruver in attendance as the best man. Unable to speak English, quiet and still, Katsumi stands in marked opposition to Eileen. Gruver speaks to Katsumi quietly and slowly, as one might to a child, and, at the conclusion of the ceremony, he kisses her lightly on the mouth. Katsumi smiles and blushes. Unlike Eileen, Katsumi is not openly sexual, but passive, dependent, and childlike.

The film holds Katsumi up as a paragon of female virtue. Later, she is shown performing her domestic tasks – cooking, serving guests, bathing her husband – cheerfully and quietly. Her devotion to Kelly is all-consuming and unquestioning. At one point, Katsumi even contemplates self-mutilation, a questionable eye operation, in order to please her husband by "fooling" the authorities into thinking she is white. Kelly beats her for this stupid idea, exercising his control over her body and her identity. Gruver steps between them and quiets Katsumi paternalistically by telling her "not to do it again." Despite the unpleasantness, he clearly envies Kelly his devoted wife.

If *Sayonara* calls for tolerance on the part of the viewer to accept this interracial marriage, the text also seems to be warning American women to take a lesson from Katsumi's passivity and devotion. After all, Katsumi keeps her man, while Eileen loses hers. Moreover, although *Sayonara* attempts to criticize racism, the film, as it shores up traditional gender definitions, also sticks to accepted stereotypes about Asians, particularly Asian women, as passive, childlike, and servile.[8]

Structurally, the text situates Hana Ogi between the active Eileen and the passive Katsumi. As the narrative unfolds, however, Hana Ogi moves away from the independence and sexual expression represented by Eileen to the more traditional, servile, domestic role represented by Katsumi. The film presents Gruver as "saving" Hana Ogi from the excesses of her own culture, which permits women in certain circumstances to live apart from and independently of men. Gruver puts her in touch with her "true" nature, that is, her desire for a "normal" domestic life and children.

Although Katsumi does represent the "ideal" woman, there is another side to *Sayonara*'s vision of Japanese gender relations. If Katsumi stands for the everyday domestic aspect of Japanese sexual conventions, then Hana Ogi represents the larger-than-life theatrical world of Matsubayashi, where ordinary gender definitions do not apply in the same way, a world that is coded as "perverse" within the text. Likely based on the Takarazuka Young Girls' Opera Company,[9] Matsubayashi is a musical theater in which all the roles are played by women.

Hana Ogi plays the star of Matsubayashi, famous for her portrayal of male roles. When Gruver first sees her, Hana Ogi is on her way to the theater, dressed in boyish drag, wearing knickers, a turtleneck sweater, and a felt hat with a long pheasant plume. She dramatically stands out from the other women, who are dressed in kimonolike uniforms of various colors. A fan gives her a white cock, which further accentuates her association with a transgressive, but beautiful, androgyny. Gruver is mesmerized. He stands in awe of the ultimate personification of forbidden love; not only is Hana Ogi a member of an enemy nation, a different race, and part of a theatrical troupe that absolutely forbids its members to marry or even date, but she is also in drag, a male impersonator who conjures up an even more forbidden homoeroticism.

However, the transgressive potential of Gruver's romance with Hana Ogi very quickly ebbs. After a sequence in which Hana Ogi, always in drag, silently rejects Gruver's advances on a daily basis, she finally agrees to meet her persistent admirer at Kelly and Katsumi's. When Gruver enters the room where she is waiting, he is dumbfounded. Kneeling at a low table, eyes downcast, dressed in a woman's kimono, Hana Ogi's gender has visibly changed. No longer coded in the text as "male," as an androgyne, she has become a woman, and it is not surprising that this scene should mark the beginning of Gruver and Hana Ogi's love affair.

Hana Ogi both apologizes for her rude behavior and for hating Americans. Here, gender change and submission to American authority coincide. If the film is ostensibly an indictment of American racism and militarism, then, very conveniently, the tables turn in this scene. Just as the woman apologizes for stepping outside her gender and snubbing the advances of a man, the nation also symbolically apologizes for what the film supposedly seeks to condemn in American society, that is, racism and intolerance. By projecting bigotry back onto the object of prejudice, the film's critical bite softens yet again.

Conveniently, Gruver's love affair with Hana Ogi restores three important power hierarchies that the text had placed in crisis–between the East and the West, nonwhites and whites, and women and men. It is somewhat ironic that Gruver learns racial tolerance through the sexual subjugation of a woman, who sacrifices her independence for his enlightenment. The didactic point of the narrative blurs, and the viewer may begin to wonder if, by putting Hana Ogi back into her proper "place" as a woman, Gruver is not also symbolically putting the racial and national other into its "place" as subordinate to white America.

Hana Ogi performs her last musical number in the film dressed as a Japanese bride mounted on a white horse. Visually, even before Gruver appears to talk her into marriage, he has won her, "saved" her from the "perverse" celibacy and androgyny of the Matsubayashi stage. In the climactic scene that follows, Gruver tells Hana Ogi that they have an obligation to have children, and when, at the film's conclusion, Hana Ogi makes a statement to some reporters about her future, she reiterates this by saying emphatically that she feels she and Gruver must have children.

The issue of the Korean War never resurfaces. The survival of Hana Ogi and Gruver's romance brings all narrative and, symbolically, social conflicts and contradictions back into balance. Narrative closure reaffirms gender, racial, and cultural norms with little variation.

Loose Ends: Subplots and Unsolved Social Conflicts

Although the social criticism promised by *Sayonara* really fizzles out in the resolution of the main plot line, the film's two principal subplots involving interracial romances remain more problematic. Kelly and Katsumi's constant harassment by racists within the military and eventual double suicide point to a possibly more biting denunciation of American racism, military injustice, and class bias. Similarly, Eileen's realtionship with Nakamura indicates that the gender questioning squelched by Gruver's pursuit and conquest of Hana Ogi may not have been completely obliterated through the operation of patriarchal ideology within the text.

The two relationships present unanswered narrative questions. The first revolves around why Kelly and Katsumi commit suicide, while for Hana Ogi and Gruver death never comes up as a possible solution to their dilemma. The other narrative question involves whether Nakamura's relationship with Eileen is platonic or not. Through these two unresolved dilemmas, the narrative opens up a certain space for a possible ideological interrogation of class and gender shut off by the main plot.

Throughout *Sayonara*, Kelly is coded as "working class"–that is, an Irish ethnic from the East, an enlisted man under the command of Gruver. In contradistinction to Kelly's working-class roots, Gruver represents the aristocratic old South, West Point, military privilege, and power. Kelly openly questions the military hierarchy and vocally critiques its institutionalized racism. However, his criticisms are never actually articulated as "antimilitary" or "antiwar." He remains personally loyal to Gruver, his immediate superior, even after Gruver rather viciously opposes Kelly's marriage, calling his fiancée a "slant-eyed runt." As Gruver changes from a virulent bigot to a supporter of interracial romance, the military, too, symbolically "cleans its house."

Flamboyant and theatrical, Gruver and Hana Ogi are placed at a considerable distance from the more mundane problems facing the working-class couple, Kelly and Kasumi. Clearly, Gruver, despite his relationship with a Japanese woman, still has certain privileges that Kelly does not have–namely, money. Although never expressed as such in the text, it is implied that Kelly and Katsumi are doomed because they simply do not have the financial resources to go against the system and live out their lives as a slap in the face to bigotry and racism. Gruver and Hana Ogi do have this privilege.

Conveniently, *Sayonara*, conservatively articulating the truism that forbidden interracial love leads to tragedy, allows the working-class couple to sacrifice themselves to make the drama of the upper-class couple more poignant. Narratively, then, the double suicide makes aesthetic, if not logical, sense. It also keeps in play an ideologically conservative attitude toward race within a fantasy that purportedly condemns racism.

Eileen's relationship with Nakamura also opens up certain ideological complications closed off in the rest of the film. She loses her "man" implicitly because she is not as "feminine" as Japanese women, but her relationship with Nakamura opens up some potentially subversive possibilities for reading gender as other than eternally fixed and for looking at interracial sexuality in a different light. In and of itself, any relationship between a man of color and an Anglo-Saxon woman is more threatening to the status quo than the obverse relationship. Within American popular thought, the Anglo-American female stands for hearth and home, the continuation of white-defined and dominated culture. If stolen or seduced away from white men, she implicitly represents a challenge to white male identity and authority. Not only does she challenge the truism that white American culture is superior to all others, she also challenges male authority by asserting herself as a woman, who chooses to look outside the confines of her own culture for sexual expression.

Sayonara indicates that Eileen is fascinated by Nakamura because he is a Kabuki performer, a "male actress," able to play both female and male roles. Just as Hana Ogi magically transcends gender boundaries in Matsubayashi, Nakamura performs with the "grace of a woman and the power of a man." However, *Sayonara* keeps this couple at a distance from each other as well as the viewer. Although clearly enamored of Nakamura, Eileen takes every opportunity to proclaim her love for Gruver. The exact nature of the relationship remains obscure. Certainly, too, the fact that Nakamura's part is played by a Latin (Ricardo Montalban) rather than an Asian actor further removes the threatening racial aspect of the fantasy, while keeping a certain exoticism at its core.

Despite this, the fact that a romance between Nakamura and Eileen is even hinted at opens up the possibility for another reading of the strictly conservative rendering of gender roles the film presents in its main plot. By choosing a relatiohsip with a man of another race and an "enemy" nation, Eileen asserts her autonomy in a way that Gruver could never accept. Moreover, the free gender movement and sensuality that the Kabuki theater promises also allow for the potentially disruptive expression of female desire. All these possibilities, however, are only hinted at and then dropped. Through this marginalization of alternate class and protofeminist discourses, *Sayonara* remains quite conservative in its treatment of both gender and class differences.

Conclusion

Romance ironically makes *Sayonara* a profoundly conservative film despite its seemingly genuine plea for peace and racial tolerance. Moving from war to race and subsuming both issues within the sexist ideology of romance weds a call for change to the reaffirmation of male – and, by implication, American – domination of the racially, ethnically, and sexually Other.

While contradictions within the text open up possible alternate readings, these possibilities are marginalized within subplots. However, these contradictions must not be trivialized. Although ostensibly a critique of racism sugar-coated by a Romeo and Juliet love story, *Sayonara*, also exists as a historical document that illustrates how the dominant ideology deals with social and cultural change by both acknowledging and squelching it. The text implies that Gruver and Hana Ogi ultimately live happily ever after as man and wife, but the rumblings of class and gender inequalities heard within the film's subplots cannot be wrapped up as neatly.

In terms of feminist film criticism, this analysis of *Sayonara* points to the importance of understanding the complexity of Hollywood's treatment of gender. Going beyond a view of patriarchal ideology as simply molding women's thought to conform to a society that takes male domination as a given, this type of analysis helps the feminist film critic look at possible sites of resistance within Hollywood texts, sites of potentially subversive pleasures, as well as sites where new alliances across class, ethnic, and racial boundaries can be explored.

Notes

1. Jane Gaines, "White Privilege and Looking Relations: Race and Gender in Feminist Film Theory," *Cultural Critique*, no. 4 (Fall 1986): 61, 66. Emphasis in the original.

2. Another interracial relationship between Captain Bailey (James Garner) and Fumiko (Reiko Kuba) is also featured in *Sayonara*; however, it is not in any way foregrounded within the plot.

3. Roland Barthes, *S/Z: An Essay* (New York: Hill and Wang, 1974).

4. In 1948, Korea, which had been under Japanese rule, was divided at the thirty-eighth parallel. In 1950, after the withdrawal of American troops in the south following the withdrawal of Soviet troops in the north, North Korea, supported by the newly established People's Republic of China, crossed the dividing line in an attempt to reunify the country. United Nations troops, predominantly American, came to the aid of the Republic of Korea in the south. President Truman was able to manage UN involvement because the Soviets were boycotting Security Council meetings at the time. The Cold War mindset that surfaced after World War II now found concrete expression on the battlefield. Eventually, a truce was

reached under Eisenhower, and the country remains divided along the thirty-eighth parallel to this day. Controversy surrounding the war came from various sources: some thought it was illegal because no formal declaration of war ever existed, others condemned any United States involvement in foreign civil wars, and still others thought it unwise to support the notoriously corrupt South Korean government, believing unification under the Communists to be inevitable. The U.S. Left, assailed by the HUAC hearings and all the concurrent problems associated with the Cold War domestically, was unable to organize any clear opposition to the war.

5. The editors, *Cahiers du cinéma,* "John Ford's *Young Mr. Lincoln,*" in Bill Nichols, *Movies and Methods* (Berkeley: University of California, 1976), 493–529.

6. Brian Henderson, *"The Searchers*: An American Dilemma," *Film Quarterly* 34 (Winter 1980–81): 9–23.

7. See, for example, Kate Millett, *Sexual Politics* (New York: Avon, 1969).

8. John W. Dower, *War without Mercy: Race and Power in the Pacific War* (New York: Pantheon, 1986).

9. Ian Buruma, *Behind the Mask* (New York: Meridian, 1984).

Tears and Desire: Women and Melodrama in the "Old" Mexican Cinema

Ana M. López

The melodrama has been a crucial site for the interrogation of many of the categories utilized for the contemporary study of the cinema and for debates over questions of genre, narration, ideology, subjectivity, and representation.[1] Above all, however, film melodrama has been one of the most important areas for the development of feminist film criticism. Long considered a "feminine" mode because of its insistent attention to the domestic sphere and related emotional issues, the melodrama – especially that subset of the genre known as the "woman's film" and ostensibly addressed to female audiences – has proven to be a productive area for the investigation of the representation of women, female subjectivity, and desire, gendered critical categories, and the role of women as cultural producers and consumers.[2] Emerging in the context of the 1960s-70s rediscovery and reassessment of the classical Hollywood cinema and the 1970s-80s boom in feminist scholarship, this investigation of the melodramatic mode was limited, until very recently, to the study of the Hollywood melodrama and its relationship to U.S. society, ideology, and patriarchy. However, recent studies exploring the historical and international inscription of women and melodramatic representation (in cinemas as diverse as German Weimar films, French films of the 1920s and '30s, the *bourekas* films of 1970s Israeli cinema, and the commercial 1950s Hindi cinema)[3] have begun to delineate the complex lines of historical and cultural affiliations that link and differentiate the social functions of the melodramatic in specific moments of Western and non-Western societies. Above all, the investigation of the gendering of subjects in melodramatic representation in non-U.S. societies has forced scholars to confront conflicting, historically specific claims of national, ethnic, and gender identity.

Within this context, I want to explore the placement of women in Mexican film melodramas of the 1940s and 1950s and its relationship to Mexican society. Rather than present a content-based description of the "types" of women represented (virgins/mothers versus whores, for example) or summarize clichéd plot resolutions,[4] I am concerned with the interrelations among patriarchal Mexican society, women's place in Mexican culture and national identity, and film production and consumption. Emphasizing the different articulations of gender and subjectivity in a society formed by colonization and marked by a history of violence and discontinuity, I attempt to link the history of the classical Mexican cinema melodrama with Mexican society, to trace the inscription of the melodramatic alongside the social positioning of women, and to highlight moments when conflicting voices and needs visibly erupt into the cinematic and social spheres.

The Melodrama and the Latin American Cinema

As has been extensively detailed elsewhere, the melodrama, along with music and comedy, became synonymous with the cinema in Latin America after the introduction of sound.[5] Taking advantage of Hollywood's temporary inability to satisfy the linguistic needs of the Latin-American market, local producers used the new technology to exploit national characteristics. Argentina took on the tango and its melodramatic lyrics and developed the tango melodrama genre in the early 1930s. Similarly, Mexico made the melodrama a central genre of the sound cinema after the success of *Santa* (1931, Antonio Moreno), an adaptation of a well-known melodramatic novel by Federico Gamboa about an innocent provincial girl forced into urban prostitution and redeemed only in death.[6]

Furthermore, the rapid establishment of a specific Latin-American star system heavily dependent on radio and popular musical entertainers gave rise to melodramas with at least one or two musical performances to heighten a film's "entertainment value." Starring singers-turned-actors, narratives about entertainers sprinkled with performances became *de rigueur*. Thus Libertad Lamarque's suffering mothers always also sang, Pedro Infante could weep over his little black child with the popular song "Angelitos Negros" ("Little Black Angels") in the film of the same title, and Ninón Sevilla could vent her sexual anger and frustration dancing wild rumbas in the *cabaretera* (brothel) films of the 1950s. In these and other films, the narrative stoppage usually generated by performances was reinvested with emotion, so that melodramatic pathos emerged in the moment of performance itself (through gesture, sentiment, interactions with the audience within the film, or simply music choice). And in a film such as *Amor en las Sombras* (*Love in the Shadows*, 1959, Tito Davison), which featured ten complete performances in less than two hours' screen time, music and song rather than dramatic action propel the narrative.

Despite this diversity, however, two basic melodramatic tendencies developed between 1930 and 1960: family melodramas that focused on the problems of love, sexuality, and parenting, and epic melodramas that reworked national history, especially the events of the Mexican Revolution. Although the two categories are somewhat fluid, with some family melodramas taking place in the context of the Revolution and its aftermath, I shall be concerned primarily with the operations of the former. The revolutionary melodramas are perhaps as significant for the development of a gendered "Mexican" consciousness as the family ones, but I am interested in analyzing the cinematic positioning of women within the Mexican domestic sphere, and the ideological operations of the family melodramas provide us with privileged access to that realm. Set in quintessential domestic spaces (homes or similar places) that, as Laura Mulvey says, "can hold a drama in claustrophobic intensity and represent . . . the passions and antagonisms that lie behind it,"[7] the family melodramas map the repressions and contradictions of interiority and interior spaces – the home and unconscious – with more urgency than is possible within the cathartic large-scale action of revolutionary dramas.

The Melodrama, Women, and Mexico

The melodramatic is deeply embedded in Mexican and Hispanic culture and intersects with the three master narratives of Mexican society: religion, nationalism, and modernization. First of all, Hispanic culture carries the burden of its Christianity, which, as Susan Sontag argues in *Against Interpretation*, is already melodramatic – rather than tragic – in structure and intention. In Christianity, as Sontag says, "every crucifixion must be topped by a resurrection," an optimism inimical to the pessimism of tragedy.[8] Furthermore, the staples of the family melodrama – sin and suffering abnegation – are essential components of the Christian tradition: Sin allows for passion and, although it must always be punished, passion, after all, justifies life.

Perhaps most significantly, the melodrama always addresses questions of individual (gendered) identity within patriarchal culture and the heart of Mexico's definition as a nation. In Mexico, questions of individual identity are complicated by a colonial heritage that defines woman – and her alleged instability and unreliability – as the origin of *national* identity. The Mexican nation is defined, on the one hand, by Catholicism and the Virgin

Guadalupe, the Virgin Mother and patron saint, and, on the other, by the *Chingada*, the national betrayal of Doña Marina – also known as La Malinche or Malintzin Tenepal – the Aztec princess who submitted to Cortez and handed her people over to the conquistadores.[9] As Cherríe Moraga succinctly puts it,

> Malinche fucked the white man who conquered the Indian peoples of Mexico and destroyed their culture. Ever since, brown men have been accusing her of betraying her race, and over the centuries continue to blame her entire sex for this "transgression."[10]

Raped, defiled, and abused, Malintzin/Malinche is the violated mother of modern Mexico, *la chingada* – the fucked one – or *la vendida* – the sellout. As Octavio Paz explains in *The Labyrinths of Solitude*, Malinche's "sons" (*sic*), the Mexican people, are "the sons of La Chingada, the fruits of a rape, a farce."[11] Thus the origins of the nation are located at a site – the violated mother – that is simultaneously an altar of veneration and the place of an original shame. The victim of a rape, Malinche/La Chingada, mother of the nation, carries the guilt of her victimization. Deeply marked by this "otherness," Mexican national identity rejects and celebrates its feminine origins while gender identity, in general, is problematized even further. To be Malinche – a woman – is to be a traitor, the great whore-mother of a bastard race. The melodramatic became the privileged place for the symbolic reenactment of this drama of identification and the only place where female desire – and the utopian dream of its realization – could be glimpsed.

Mexico's colonial heritage – first Spanish and most recently North American – also affects the social functions of the melodrama. Colonialism always implies a crisis of identity for the colonial subject, caught between the impulse to imitate the colonizer and the desire for an always displaced autonomy. Like Caliban in Shakespeare's *Tempest*, the colonized must use the colonizer's "words" – the imported cinematic apparatus – and learn the colonizer's language before he or she can even think of articulating his or her own speech: "You taught me language and my profit on't is I know how to curse." Just as in Brazil the parodic *chanchada* genre can be seen as a response to the impossibility of thinking of a national cinema without considering the Hollywood cinema as well as Brazil's own underdevelopment, in Mexico, melodrama's excess explicitly defies the Hollywood dominant:

> Since there can be no nostalgic return to pre-colonial purity, no unproblematic recovery of national origins undefiled by alien influences, the artist in the dominated culture cannot ignore the foreign presence but must rather swallow it and recycle it to national ends.[12]

As Carlos Monsiváis has said, "If competition with North America is impossible artistically or technically, the only defense is excess, the absence

of limits of the melodrama."[13] Thus the melodrama's exaggerated signification and hyperbole – its emphasis on anaphoric events pointing to other implied, absent meanings or origins – become, in the Mexican case, a way of
cinematically working through the problematic of an underdeveloped national cinema.

The melodrama is also formally and practically linked with the specific
trajectory of Mexican national identity and the significance of the Revolution for the nation-building project. If we agree with Peter Brooks that the
melodrama is "a fictional system for making sense of experience as a
semantic field of force" that "comes into being in a world where the traditional imperatives of truth and ethics have been violently thrown into
question,"[14] then we should not be surprised by the cultural currency of
the melodrama in post-Revolutionary Mexico. In the midst of the great social upheavals of this period, the country seemed ungovernable and the
city an unruly mecca: the Revolution changed the nature of public life,
mobilized the masses, shook up the structures of the family without changing its roots and, as Monsiváis says, "served as the inevitable mirror where
the country recognized its physiognomy." The Revolution may not have
"invented" the Mexican nation, but "its vigor, for the first time, lent legendary characteristics to the masses that sustained it."[15] In other words, the
Revolution created a new class – the new urban poor soon to be a working
class – whose willpower, roughness, and illiteracy became insistently visible in the formerly feudal national landscape.

The Revolution also further problematized the position of women in
Mexico. Women had fought alongside the men and had followed the troops
cooking, healing, and providing emotional and physical solace, either as
legitimate wives, lovers, or paid companions. Known generally as *sol-
daderas*, these women formed the backbone of an incipient feminist movement that emerged after the Revolution. Yet as Jean Franco argues in
Plotting Women,

> The Revolution with its promise of social transformation encouraged a
> Messianic spirit that transformed mere human beings into supermen and
> constituted a discourse that associated virility with social transformation
> in a way that marginalized women at the very moment when they were,
> supposedly, liberated.[16]

Precisely when the nation created itself anew under the aegis of Revolutionary mythology and its male superhero redeemers, women were, once
again, relegated to the background, and in cultural production – especially
in national epic allegories – represented as a terrain to be traversed in the
quest for male identity. Simultaneously, while the new secular state ostensibly promoted women's emancipation to combat Catholicism and its al-

leged counterrevolutionary ideology,[17] Mexico found itself caught in the wheels of capitalist modernization.

The new class created by the Revolution – an increasingly mobile, urban, migratory class of male and female workers – was entertained by the popular theater (*teatro frívolo* or *género chico*) before it found the cinema, but after the coming of sound, Spanish-language movies became the principal discursive tool for social mapping. While the *género chico* and its carnivalesque ribaldry[18] attracted a socially but not sexually mixed audience, the cinema was family entertainment and, by design and by commercial imperatives, broader based. By the late 1930s and through the 1940s and 1950s, the national cinema granted access not only to entertainment, but also to vital behaviors and attitudes: "One didn't go to the cinema to dream, but to learn."[19] There was not much room here for the carnivalesque celebration that continued to take place in the *teatro frívolo*: the cinema helped transmit new habits and reiterated codes of behavior, providing the new nation with the common bases and collective ties necessary for national unity. In fact, the cinema helped make a new post-Revolutionary middle class viable.

If it is indeed true, as Monsiváis says, that film melodramas served this kind of socializing function, what exactly were the lessons they taught women? How did the melodrama mediate the post-Revolutionary crisis of national and gendered identity and its subsequent institutionalization? Rather than blindly enforce or teach unambiguous high moral values, stable codes of behavior, or obedience to the patriarchal order, the family melodramas staged specific dramas of identity that often complicated straightforward ideological identification for men *and* women without precluding accommodation. However, the melodrama's contradictory play of identifications constituted neither false communication nor a simple lesson imposed upon the people from above. Rather, these films addressed pressing contradictions and desires within Mexican society. And even when their narrative work suggests utter complicity with the work of the Law, the emotional excesses set loose and the multiple desires detonated are not easily recuperated.

The narratives of the Mexican family melodrama deal with three principal conflicts: the clash between old (feudal, *porfirian*) values and modern (industrialized, urban) life, the crisis of male identity that emerges as a result of this clash, and the instability of female identity that at once guarantees and threatens the passage from the old to the new. These conflicts are played out in two distinct physical and psychic spaces – the home, a private sphere valorized and sanctified by the Law, and the nightclub, a barely tolerated social space as liminal as the home is central. Only marginally acceptable, the nightclub is nevertheless the part of the patriarchal public sphere where the personal – and issues of female subjectivity, emotion, identity, and desire—finds its most complex articulation in the Mexican melodrama.

The Home: Mothers, Families, and Their Others

Although Mexican patriarchal values insist on the sanctity of the traditional home (as an extension of the "fatherland" blessed by God), the extended families in them are rarely well adjusted precisely because of the rigidity of the fathers' law and in spite of the saintliness of the mothers. In Mexico, the family as an institution has a contradictory symbolic status as a site for the crystallization of tensions between traditional patriarchal values (especially the cult of machismo) and modernizing tendencies and as a source of maternal support and nurturing the secular state could not replace.[20] This ambivalence is clearly evidenced in the deployment of the Mexican cinema's so-called mother obsession. Although it is undoubtedly true that the Mexican melodrama's fascination with saintly mother figures can be traced to the deeply conservative social impulses of the post-Revolutionary middle classes, who countered their insecurity over the legitimacy of their status with aggressive nationalism and an obsessive attachment to traditional values, how this mother obsession is worked out in the melodrama complicates any assessment of the politics and social mapping of such representations.

Director Juan Orol and the actress Sara García created the archetypal mother of the Mexican melodrama in *Madre Querida* (*Dear Mother*, 1935), the heart-wrenching story of a young boy who goes to a reformatory for arson and whose mother dies of grief precisely on the tenth of May (Mother's Day in Mexico). Over the next decades, García played suffering, self-sacrificing mothers in countless films such as *No Basta ser Madre* (*It's Not Enough to Be a Mother*, 1937), *Mi Madrecita* (*My Little Mother*, 1940), and *Madre Adorada* (*Beloved Mother*, 1948). However, despite their self-acknowledged narrative focus on mothers and their positioning of the mother as the central ideological tool for social and moral cohesion, these and other films ostensibly glorifying mothers as repositories of conservative family values were clearly maternal melodramas rather than women's films. This distinction, invoked by E. Ann Kaplan in her discussion of Hollywood 1920s and '30s melodramas,[21] is significant for Mexican cinema, because it helps to distinguish between films that focus on male oedipal dramas and films that more self-consciously address female spectators. Indeed, one could argue that despite their focus on mothers, these family melodramas are patriarchal rather than maternal because they attempt to preserve patriarchal values over the sanctity of the mother. In attempting to reinforce the patriarchy their narrative logic breaks down: the moral crisis created in these films revolves around the fathers' identity and not the mothers', whose position is never put into question.

In *Cuando los hijos se van* (*When the Children Go Away*, 1941, Juan Bustillo Orol), for example, a rigid provincial family is torn asunder by the father's (Fernando Soler) inability to see the true characters of his sons or to recognize their mother's (Sara García) more sensitive assessment of their characters. Influenced by the "bad" son, the father banishes the "good" son to the city, while the mother, with her unerring maternal instinct, never doubts his integrity and is ultimately proven right by the narrative: the banished son returns a popular radio star and saves the family from a bankruptcy engineered by his sibling. Despite the narrative's obvious privileging of the mother's sight, the film attempts to shore up a patriarchal family structure threatened not only by the patriarch's inability to see, but by the other world lying outside the patriarch's control: Mexico City, emblem of modernization and progress, and the modern and highly pleasurable world outside the family. The film attempts to idealize the family as a unit whose preservation is worth all sacrifices, even death, but its suggestion that the familial crisis is caused by the father's blindness and irrational rigidity, especially when compared to the mother's unerring instinct, puts in question the very patriarchal principle it seeks to assert.

Mothers may have a guaranteed place in the home as pillars of strength, tolerance, and self-abnegation – in other words, as oedipal illusions – but outside the home they are prey to the male desires that the Mexican home and family disavow. As a foil to the mother's righteous suffering and masochistic respect for the Law, men, especially father figures, are self-indulgent and unable to obey the moral order. It is their desire – unleashed because of maternal asexuality – that most threatens and disturbs the stability of the family and its women. While denying desire within the family, outside it is a compelling and at times controlling force. Thus a variant of the family melodrama focuses on the impossible attraction of "other" women: the "bad" mothers (*las malas*), the vamps, the mistresses.

While Sara García portrayed the archetypal good mother, María Félix depicted her opposite, the *mala mujer* (bad woman): the haughty, independent woman, as passionate and devilish as the mothers are asexual and saintly. The titles of Félix's films clearly reveal her star persona: *Doña Bárbara* (Fernando de Fuentes, 1943), *La Mujer de Todos* (*Everyone's Woman*, Julio Bracho, 1946), *La Devoradora* (*The Devourer*, Fernando de Fuentes, 1946), *Doña Diabla* (Tito Davison, 1949). *Doña Bárbara*, her third film, most clearly defined this persona.[22] After being brutally raped as a young girl, Bárbara becomes a rich independent landowner – la Doña – who enjoys despoiling and humiliating others, especially men. She exults in her power and discards lovers and even her own daughter easily, exhibiting neither pity nor shame and relishing her hatred. Despite her power, Bárbara, like most of Félix's characters, is simply the vampiresque flip side of the saintly mothers of the family melodramas. Easily classified as antifamily melodramas insofar as they reject the surface accoutrements of the patriarchal family, ultimately her films forcefully reinscribe the need for the standard family. Despite titles focusing on the female character, Félix's films are male-centered narratives, where the specular pleasure lies with the woman (and her masquerades of masculinity), but the narrative remains with a male protagonist. Even in *Doña Bárbara*, the principal narrative agent is Santos Luzardo, a young man (Julián Soler) who challenges la Doña's power when he refuses her seduction. The film is more concerned with how he defeats Bárbara than with Bárbara's point of view or her downfall. Bárbara remains unknowable, an enigma given a sociological raison d'être – the rape – and the face of a goddess, but whose subjectivity and desires remain unknown. As a star, Félix could not embody female desire, for she was an ambivalent icon, as unknowable, cold, and pitiless as the mother figure was full of abnegation and tears.[23] Her presence is simply an echo of the dangers of desire for men rather than its realization for women.

Woman's Desire on the Margins of the Home

In general, only two kinds of Mexican melodramas were structured around woman's identity and presented from a female point of view: the fallen-but-redeemed-by-motherhood women's films and the *cabaretera* subgenre. Each type also had its prototypical female star: whereas the former films most often starred Dolores del Rio or, somewhat later, Libertad Lamarque, two stars whose characters suffered copiously for their meager sins and relished child obsessions without equal, the latter were epitomized by the sexy *rumberas* portrayed by Cuban actress Ninón Sevilla. Since neither Lamarque nor Sevilla are Mexican, the relative independence achieved by Lamarque's characters and the sexual wantonness of Sevilla's could be distanced as foreign otherness even when the actresses portrayed Mexican women. However, Mexican-born del Rio began her career in Hollywood, and, unlike the other two, was always considered a great actress, the *grande dame* of the Mexican cinema, whose face would acquire mythical status as *the* archetype of the moral and physical perfection of the indigenous woman.

Lamarque, singer and Argentine stage and movie star, acquired a tango-inspired star persona after successfully competing for screen time with singing idol Jorge Negrete in Luis Buñuel's *Gran Casion* (1946). Neither matriarchal mother, vampish other, nor a symbol of indigenous purity, Lamarque was most often a prototypically innocent fallen woman who also sang professionally. In *Soledad* (*Solitude*, Tito Davison, 1948), for example, Lamarque plays a young orphaned servant (Argentine!) tricked into a false marriage by the family heir, made pregnant, and abandoned but finally successful as an entertainer.

Despite their innocence, however, Lamarque's characters fall uneasily into the prevailing stereotypes of the Mexican cinema. In her best films, where she portrays entertainers with tragic pasts or fates, the need to position her simultaneously in relation to family life and to public life as a performer complicates the affirmation of standard social structures and woman's position vis-à-vis the private and public spheres. Her status as a respectable performer – and the incumbent independence of a salary, relationships outside the domestic sphere, and the adoring gaze of diegetic audiences – destabilizes her identity as a hopeless mother. Thus *Soledad* is unable to sustain the figurative melodramatic signification of its initial scenes (for example, prefiguring the falsity of the wedding ceremony via ominous mise-en-scènes and the *coup de theatre* of a candle blown out by violent wind when the couple first embrace) and depends increasingly on Soledad's voice rather than her silence to unravel its melodrama. Told from her point of view and, by film's end, literally dependent on her voice, the melodrama of *Soledad* ends appropriately with her long lost daughter's anguished cry of recognition: "Mother!" But by now Soledad is far more than "just a mother" and remains an outstanding model of self-sufficiency.

The Cabaret: *Rumberas* and Female Desire.

Whereas Lamarque's characters are usually tricked or forced by circumstances into successful careers as singers while all they really want to be is wives and mothers, Ninón Sevilla and other *cabareteras* (María Antonieta Pons, Leticia Palma, and Meche Barba) present a different problematic. Much more sordid, their fates and entertainment activities project a virulent form of desire onto the screen. Nowhere else have screen women been so sexual, so willful, so excessive, so able to express their anger at their fate through vengeance. As François Truffaut (under the pseudonym Robert Lacheney) wrote in *Cahiers du cinéma* in 1954,

> From now on we must take note of Ninón Sevilla, no matter how little we may be concerned with feminine gestures on the screen or elsewhere. From her inflamed look to her fiery mouth, everything is heightened in Ninón (her forehead, her lashes, her nose, her upper lip, her throat, her voice). . . . Like so many missed arrows, [she is an] oblique challenge to bourgeois, Catholic, and all other moralities.[24]

Albeit uneasily, Lamarque's sophisticated performers could be narratively recuperated within an expanded domestic sphere, but Sevilla's excessively gendered gestures engaged melodramatic tropes beyond the point of hyperbole. Thus with Sevilla, the performative excess of the "musical/performance melodrama" reaches its zenith and the boundary between performance and melodrama disappears entirely.

The most virulent of Sevilla's *cabaretera* films was Alberto Gout's 1952 *Aventurera* (*Adventuress*). The plot is extraordinarily complicated and evidence of the excess associated with such films. Elena (Ninón Sevilla), a happy bourgeois girl, is left destitute when her mother runs away with a lover and her father commits suicide. Unable to find a job, she is tricked into a Juarez brothel, drugged, and gang-raped. Eventually, Elena becomes the star/prostitute of the nightclub, but she is so unruly that the madam (Andrea Palma) hires a thug to scar her in punishment. She runs away, becomes a nightclub star again, and meets and seduces Mario (Ruben Rojo), only to discover that his high-society mother is the madam of the Juarez brothel. After many other melodramatic twists and murders, the film finally ends with Mario and Elena supposedly free of their family traumas and about to enjoy a normal family life. The film's resolution imposes an end to the story, but it cannot contain the excess of signification circulated by the film: the malevolence of Andrea Palma's icy glance as she watches Elena's first tastes of champagne through an ominously barred lookout, Sevilla's haughty cigarette-swinging walk around the cabaret, her lascivious drunken revelry during her own wedding party, the sevenfold multiplication of her image while she sings "Arrimate cariñito" (Come Closer Little Love") in a Juarez nightclub. This excess is narrative and visual, for the plot is only as excessive as Elena's own physical presence, the sum of Sevilla's exaggeratedly sexual glance, overabundant figure, extraordinarily tight dresses, rolling hips, intemperate laughter, and menacing smoking. This excessive performance functions not so much as a parody of a mimetic performative ideal, but as an oblique affirmation of the gender identity that a mimetic repetition elides. Unlike the asexual mother figures of Garcia, the suffering mothers of Lamarque, or the frozen sculptural beauty of María Félix's temptresses, Sevilla is made of flesh and blood, a bundle of unrepressed instinctive desires. If, as Judith Butler argues, the performative gesture "as a certain frozen stylization of the body" is the constitutive moment of feminine gender identity,[25] Sevilla—like a drag queen—melts the style. Her moral provocation is much greater than the admonitions provided by the narrative.

This provocation is not, however, as straightforward as it might seem. In Mexico, the prostitute as emblem of desire, necessary evil, and mother of the nation (Malinche/Malintzin) has a prominent place in national cultural history. Prostitution might indeed be the oldest profession everywhere, but rarely have prostitutes been the preferred subject of so many popular culture texts as in Mexico. What we see in the *cabaretera* films of

Ninón Sevilla in *Aventurera* epitomizes the "excess" of the *cabaretera* films.

the late 1940s and 1950s is the culmination of a complex process in which the figure of the prostitute–albeit cloaked with the shameful aura of Maliche–became the site of a serious challenge to the *porfirian* moral order and an emblem of modernity.

Officially regulated and socially shunned, the post-Revolutionary prostitute and her spaces–the brothel, assignation house, and cabaret–had a distinct social function: they offered men a place to escape from the burdens of home and saintly wives and to engage in uninhibited conversations and the ambivalent pleasures of the flesh. Mexican culture always celebrated the myth of the prostitute, but in the 1920s the prostitute also assumed a different iconic status in the wildly popular romantic visions of singer-composer Agustín Lara. Idealized and simultaneously romantic and perverse, the prostitute of Lara's songs was not pitied for falling from grace. Lara's popular songs embodied a fatalistic worship of the "fallen woman" as the only possible source of pleasure for modern man.[26] Though at first considered scandalous (and prohibited in schools by the Mexican Ministry of Public Education), Lara's audacious songs were quickly absorbed as a new popular culture idiom, the exaltation of the Lost Woman.[27]

By the late 1940s,[28] the cinema had completely assumed Lara's vision of the prostitute as an object of self-serving worship and his songs were the central dramatic impulse propelling the action of many *cabaretera* films. Thus, for example, *Aventurera* is clearly inspired by a song of the same title (sung by Pedro Vargas in the film):[29]

> Sell your love expensively, adventuress
> Put the price of grief on your past
> And he who wants the honey from your mouth
> Must pay with diamonds for your sin
> Since the infamy of your destiny
> Withered your admirable spring
> Make your road less difficult,
> Sell your love dearly, adventuress

Lara's songs idealized woman as a purchasable receptacle for man's physical needs–the ultimate commodity for modern Mexican society–but also invested her with the power of her sexuality: to sell at will, to name her price, to choose her victim. Nevertheless, as Monsiváis says, his songs also made the object of pleasure, once used, abstract:

> The deified prostitute protects the familiar one, exalts the patriarchy, and even moves the real prostitute herself to tears, granting a homey warmth to its evocation of exploited lives.[30]

In literature, in the songs of Agustín Lara and others, and finally in the cinema, the prostitute and the nightlife of which she is an emblem became an anti-utopian paradigm for modern life. The exaltation of female desire and sin and of the nightlife of clubs and cabarets clearly symbolized Mexico's new (post-World War II) cosmopolitanism and the first waves of developmentalism. The *cabaretera* films were the first decisive cinematic break with *porfirian* morality. Idealized, independent, and extravagantly sexual, the exotic *rumbera* was a social fantasy, but one through which *other* subjectivities could be envisioned, other psychosexual/social identities forged.

But the *rumbera* is not a simple model of resistance. When analyzed as part of a specific process of neurotic determinations[31] and in the context of the suffering mother, the emerging image of female subjectivity is deeply contradictory and without an easy resolution. In fact, it is a fantasy. As Ninón Sevilla with much self-awareness explains to her lover in the *cabaretera* film *Mulata* (Gilberto Martínez Solares, 1953), the impossible challenge of female identity is the insecurity of "never knowing whether a man has loved me or desired me." Not that one is necessarily preferable to the other – she can be either the wife *or* the sexual object – but that Mexican society insists that they are mutually exclusive.

Notes

Research for this essay was made possible, in part, by grants from the Mellon Foundation and the Roger Thayer Stone Center for Latin American Studies at Tulane University. Parts of this essay have appeared in "Celluloid Tears: Melodrama in the 'Old' Mexican Cinema," *Iris*, no. 13 (Summer 1991), and in *Mediating Two Worlds*, ed. Ana López, John King, and Manuel Alvarado (London: British Film Institute, 1992).

1. See, for example, Christine Gledhill, "The Melodramatic Field: An Investigation," in *Home is Where the Heart Is: Studies in Melodrama and the Woman's Film*, ed. Christine Gledhill (London: British Film Institute, 1987), 5–39; Robert Lang, *American Film Melodrama: Griffith, Vidor, Minnelli* (Princeton, N.J.: Princeton University Press, 1989); and Rick Altman, "Dickens, Griffith, and Film Theory Today," *South Atlantic Quarterly* 88 (Spring 1989): 321–59.

2. See, for example, the essays collected in Christine Gledhill, ed., *Home is Where the Heart Is*, and Mary Ann Doane, *The Desire to Desire: The Woman's Film of the 1940s* (Bloomington: Indiana University Press, 1987).

3. Patrice Petro, *Joyless Streets: Women and Melodramatic Representation in Weimar Germany* (Princeton, N.J.: Princeton University Press, 1989); Maureen Turim, "French Melodrama: Theory of a Specific History," *Theater Journal* 39 (October 1987); Ginnette Vincendeau, "Melodramatic Realism: On Some French Women's Films in the 1930s," *Screen* 30 (Summer 1989); Ella Shohat, *Israeli Cinema: East/West and the Politics of Representation* (Austin: University of Texas Press, 1989); Ravi Vasudevan, "The Melodramatic Mode and the Commercial Hindi Cinema," *Screen* 30 (Summer 1989).

4. For this kind of analysis, see Carl J. Mora, "Feminine Images in Mexican Cinema: The Family Melodrama; Sara García, 'The Mother of Mexico'; and the Prostitute," *Studies in Latin American Popular Culture*, 4 (1985): 228–35.

5. This period of the Latin-American cinema has generated much solid historical/archival research. For Mexico, see especially Emilio García Riera, *Historia Documental del Cine Mexicano*, 10 vols. to date (Mexico City: Ediciones Era, 1969), and Moises Viñas, ed., *Historia del Cine Mexicano* (Mexico City: UNAM/UNESCO, 1987). In English, see Carl J. Mora, *Mexican Cinema: Reflections of a Society, 1896–1980* (Berkeley: University of California Press, 1982). For a succinct and well-informed comparative historical analysis of this period in English, see John King, *Magical Reels: A History of Cinema in Latin America* (London: Verso, 1990).

6. Although the Mexican cinema would not take off on an industrial scale until the 1936 international success of the *comedia ranchera* (ranch comedy) *Allá en el Rancho Grande (Out on the Big Ranch*, Fernando de Fuentes), melodramatic films were a staple from the 1930s through the 1960s. Aided by U.S. wartime policies (and U.S. resentment of Argentina's neutrality), the Mexican cinema thrived during the war and immediate postwar periods, producing 124 films in 1950, the majority of which were melodramas. I am using the term *melodrama* here loosely, for the Mexican cinema (and other Latin American cinemas, especially Brazil's and its *chanchadas*) proved extraordinarily adept at generic mixing. I use the word *melodramatic* in its broadest sense, as a structuring principle of expectations and conventions against which individual films establish their uniqueness as singular products, while recognizing that the term has a different currency in Latin America than in the United States or Europe.

7. Laura Mulvey, "Melodrama in and out of the Home," in *High Theory/Low Culture*, ed. Colin MacCabe (New York: St. Martin's Press, 1986), 95.

8. Susan Sontag, "Death of Tragedy," *Against Interpretation* (New York: Dell, 1966), 132–39.

9. An Aztec legend claimed that Quetzalcoatl, a feathered serpent god, would come from the East to redeem his people on a given day of the Aztec calendar, which, coincidentally, was the same day (April 21, 1519) that Cortez and his men (fitting the description of Quetzalcoatl) landed in Vera Cruz. Thus Malintzin Tenepal became Cortez's translator, strategic advisor, and eventually mistress, believing that she was saving her people. This is how recent scholarship has reinterpreted the 400-year-old legacy of female betrayal, the founding moment of the Mexican nation. See Nancy Alarcón, "Chicana's Feminist Literature: A Re-Vision Through Malintzin/or Malintzin: Putting Flesh Back on the Object," in *This Bridge Called My Back: Writings by Radical Women of Color*, ed. Cherríe Moraga and Gloria Anzaldúa (New York: Kitchen Table: Women of Color Press, 1983).

10. Cherríe Moraga, "From a Long Line of Vendidas: Chicanas and Feminism," in *Feminist Studies/Critical Studies*, ed. Teresa de Lauretis (Bloomington: Indiana University Press, 1986), 174–75.

11. Octavio Paz, *The Labyrinths of Solitude: Life and Thought in Mexico* (New York: Grove Press, 1961), 85.

12. João Luiz Vieira and Robert Stam, "Parody and Marginality: The Case of

Brazilian Cinema," *Framework*, no. 28 (1985), reprinted in *The Media Reader*, ed. Manuel Alvarado and John O. Thompson (London: British Film Institute, 1990), 96.

13. Carlos Monsiváis, "Reir Llorando (Notas Sobre la Cultura Popular Urbana)," in *Politica Cultural del Estado Mexicano*, ed. Moises Ladrón de Guevara (Mexico City: Ed. GEFE/SEP, 1982), 70.

14. Peter Brooks, *The Melodramatic Imagination* (New Haven, Conn.: Yale University Press, 1976), xiii, 14–15.

15. Monsiváis, "Reir Llorando," 27.

16. Jean Franco, *Plotting Women: Gender and Representation in Mexico* (New York: Columbia University Press, 1989), 102.

17. However, women did not win the right to vote in national elections until 1953.

18. The *género chico*, or *teatro frívolo*, was a vaudevillelike theatrical genre that developed in neighborhood playhouses and tents. While the bourgeois theater staged classical melodramas from Spain and France that outlined the parameters of decent behavior and exalted heightened sensibilities in perfect Academic Spanish, the *género chico* thrived with popular characters and satire. Carnivalesque in the Bakhtinian sense, it included in its repertory taboo words and gestures and popular speech while exalting the grotesque and demanding a constant interaction between players and audience. See Ruth S. Lamb, *Mexican Theater of the Twentieth Century* (Claremont, Calif.: Ocelot Press, 1975), and Manuel Manón, *Historia del Teatro Popular de Mexico* (Mexico City: Editorial Cultura, 1932).

19. Carlos Monsiváis, "El Cine Nacional," in *Historia General de Mexico*, vol. 4 (Mexico City: El Colegio de Mexico, 1976), 446.

20. See Jean Franco, "The Incorporation of Women: A Comparison of North American and Mexican Popular Narrative," *Studies in Entertainment: Critical Approaches to Mass Culture*, ed. Tania Modleski (Bloomington: Indiana University Press, 1986).

21. E. Ann Kaplan, "Mothering, Feminism, and Representation: The Maternal in Melodrama and the Woman's Film 1910–40," in *Home is Where the Heart Is*, 123–29.

22. For an extensive analysis of María Félix's career and star persona, see Paco Ignacio Taíbo, *María Félix: 47 Pasos por el Cine* (Mexico City: Joaquín Mortiz/Planeta, 1985).

23. See Carlos Monsiváis, "Crónica de Sociales: María Félix en dos tiempos," in *Escenas de Pudor y Liviandad* (Mexico City: Grijalbo, 1981), 161–68.

24. Robert Lacheney, *Cahiers du cinéma*, no. 30 (1954); cited by Emilio Garcia Riera, *Historia Documental del Cine Mexicano*, vol. 4, 132–34, and Jorge Ayala Blanco, *La Aventura del Cine Mexicano* (Mexico City: Ediciones Era, 1968), 144–45.

25. Judith Butler, "Lana's 'Imitation': Melodramatic Repetition and the Gender Performative," *Genders* 9 (Fall 1990): 6.

26. "The Perverted One"

> To you, life of my soul, perverted woman whom I love
> To you, ungrateful woman
> To you, who makes me suffer and makes me cry

I consecrate my life to you, product of evil and innocence
All of my life is yours, woman
I want you, even if they call you perverted.

27. As Eduardo Galeano summarizes it in *Century of the Wind*, "Lara exalts the Lost Woman, in whose eyes are seen sun-drunk palm trees; he beseeches Love from the Decadent One, in whose pupils boredom spreads like a peacock's tail; he dreams of the sumptuous bed of the silky-skinned Courtesan; with sublime ecstasy he deposits roses at the feet of the Sinful One and covers the Shameful Whore with incense and jewels in exchange for the honey of her mouth" (New York: Pantheon, 1988), 110.

28. As Jorge Ayala Blanco indicates, in a few months between 1947 and 1948 alone, precisely coinciding with the Mario Rodríguez Alemán *sexenio*, over twelve *cabaretera* films were produced. See *La Aventura del Cine Mexicano*, 137.

29. The Lara song "Aventurera" had already been featured in the 1946 María Félix film *La Devoradora* (Fernando de Fuentes). At the time, Lara and Félix were enjoying a much-publicized, albeit short-lived, marriage, and he ostensibly wrote the song explicitly for her.

30. Carlos Monsiváis, *Amor Perdido* (Mexico City: Ediciones Era, 1977), 60.

31. John Hill. *Sex, Class and Realism: British Cinema 1956–1963* (London: British Film Institute, 1986).

Missing in Action: Notes on Dorothy Arzner

Beverle Houston

The problem of Dorothy Arzner. The assumption has been this: her work will display something exceptional in handling the Hollywood machinery of obsessive, pervasive examination of sexual difference, since she is "the only woman . . . to build up a coherent body of work within the Hollywood system."[1] The questions have been these: (1) What are her (unique? uniquely woman's?) strategies in handling genre, narrative, character, spectator relations? (2) How can she be not simply added to a list of "important people in film history" but positioned in a history of film that is a theory of the structure and development of its institutions and practices? But, as Claire Johnston also points out, we cannot at the same time "ignore the political importance of the real role women have played in the history of cinema."[2] Thus, the work of this essay is twofold: first, to make yet another (crude) insistence on the fact of Arzner's existence and, second, to examine four of her films in terms of the specular practices of classical cinema.

Despite film festivals, feminism, interviews, articles, retrospectives, and the like, Arzner remains largely invisible. No mention of her is to be found in "little" books such as the A. S. Barnes series item *Hollywood in the Thirties*. Nor is there a single mention in a huge volume such as Ron Haver's *David O. Selznick's Hollywood*,[3] despite the fact that the book covers in some detail three of the four studios where Arzner made films while Selznick was there. Rather than listing once again the facts of her career that should make mandatory her inclusion in such works, let me focus on one aspect of her practice within the studios that has received little attention and that is particularly significant in relation to the Haver omission.

Arzner was a starmaker. She took Fredric March from the stage for his first important role (in *The Wild Party*, 1929). From her stage success in *Girl Crazy*, Arzner cast Ginger Rogers in one of her first screen roles as Doris Blake in *Honor among Lovers* (1931). Rosalind Russell was a bit player at MGM before Arzner chose her for the lead in *Craig's Wife* (1936) over Harry Cohn's objections. After Katharine Hepburn's success in *A Bill of Divorcement* (1932), she is said to have been slotted into Tarzan-type jungle movies, and Arzner is reported to have recruited Hepburn for *Christopher Strong* (1933) from a studio treetop. In a *Photoplay* article from the period, Adela Rogers St. John raises the question of whether Hepburn would turn the first hit (*Divorcement*) into a career or "join the ranks of those who have made one great hit and then drift into mediocrity." St. John decides that it depends largely on the second picture: "The public would go to see that second picture. . . . But whether they would go to see the third and fourth would depend on its success. . . . What should they do to insure her future? They sent for Dorothy Arzner."[4] Yet in the lengthy section on Hepburn in the Haver book, her career is presented as if she went directly from *Divorcement* to *Morning Glory* (1933), as if *Christopher Strong* did not exist. Hence the continuing need for a feminist rewriting of film history at this level, at the same time that Arzner's contribution must be understood in a theoretical structuring of that history.

It has been argued that certain contradictions between the masculine (patriarchal, dominant) and the feminine discourses, certain narrative and other ironic ruptures in a number of her films create open spaces where the spectator may begin to construct a progressive reading.[5] Predictably, it has been counterargued that such work on the part of the (probably feminist) reader has no real force against the text's framing and recuperation of female subjectivity as fetishized concealment of male castration.[6]

Within this context, it is the second task of this essay to examine four of Arzner's films: *Honor among Lovers*, *Christopher Strong*, *Craig's Wife*, and *Dance, Girl, Dance* (1940) in terms of certain moments of specular crisis that actively interrogate the convention of spectator relations structured by the institution of "classic Hollywood cinema" within which Arzner was working. In ways that are not entirely consistent or parallel, but which are always working within the problematic of spectator relations, three of these films offer refusals: the (male) spectator is denied access to the spectacle, as embodied in the woman. The fourth, *Craig's Wife*, closest to the woman's film as that genre would later be fully developed, denies the viewer access, not to the woman but to what she sees as she herself pursues an aggressive act of looking. This refusal needs to be understood in terms of a different viewing process that might be hypothesized for the female spectator of this genre—an issue I will return to later.

The claim being made here for the effect of these interventions on Arzner's part is quite modest. Certainly it is true, as Jacquelyn Suter argues in her *Camera Obscura* article on *Christopher Strong*, that a "systematic rethinking of the entire terms of narrative logic (as in *Jeanne Dielman*) may allow the feminine to express itself more forcefully" (148). However, this seems oddly irrelevant to the problem of Dorothy Arzner, which consists in the question: Was the Hollywood hegemony so total that no contradictions, no interventions, no openings at all were possible—to make or to recognize? Current understanding of ideological formations would not seem to support this view. Although we might share Suter's caution about overemphasizing the significance of "isolated interruptions" in the dominant discourse, these interruptions in specular processes, in the flow of images offered to be looked at, in the act of seeing itself, seem disruptive, contradictory, distancing enough to have altered the spectator's smooth relation with narrative and image even then, as certainly they now do for the feminist viewer. Fetishistic replacement is threatened, and these moves in some measure reply to the ongoing questions about Arzner: Did she refuse, rethink, reformulate *any* elements of classic cinema, in whose history she is so repeatedly and insistently denied the place that may be understood in terms of these very interventions?

In all four films, for most of the narrative, the central woman resists the conventions of sexual difference narrativized in the plot in that she asserts a will to subjecthood, an insistence on initiating and carrying out her own projects and pursuing her own desires, rather than taking her place as part of the projects of men and as object of their desires. The position of the resisting woman is always undermined near the end. In three of the films, the couple/family is restored or maintained, though at the price of the central woman's life in *Christopher Strong*. In *Craig's Wife*, the couple fails and the central woman is punished. But even at the point of the narrative recuperations, at the level of enunciation (where the absent author may express an assertive or contradictory presence), the woman exhibits a final refusal, offers a statement of the unpleasure or intolerability of these narrative containments, from her point of view *as subject*, in resistance to the plot itself. In these specular disruptions, Arzner's move is to deny the viewer the very thing he (and she) came to the movies to get—a field of things to be looked at.

In the beginning of *Honor among Lovers*, Claudette Colbert, the secretary, stands in for her boss (Fredric March) at a board meeting where she persuades the other members to accept her absent boss's point of view. Though she is empowered to speak only through him, she soon reverses conventional difference in earnest. Resisting March's advances—he doesn't offer marriage–she weds someone who is economically and morally beneath her, and takes him home to *her* apartment, where she must make room for his belongings and his body. *She* even makes the traditional joke: "Alone at last." He becomes a success with the help of some business sent his way by March. This allows the couple to enter into the traditional sexual roles of the upper class, but only superficially. Her husband makes a bad business deal and loses March's money as well as his own. She herself is, of course, established as partly guilty for acting on her own desires, for she has willfully chosen the wrong sexual partner and she actively desires her husband's material success. "What a pretty pair of crooks we are," her husband tells her. "You were glad enough to take everything." Yet despite this indictment, the Colbert character continues to initiate activity. Now she offers herself to March in exchange for his lost money. March emphatically rejects this last effort to use her sexuality as a subject, for her own purposes, telling her: "Don't you understand. I loved you . . . wanted and dreamed of you as mine, entirely mine–not standing there *offering* yourself . . . I'll write you a check."

As March lays out with unusual explictness the terms of the sexual difference deal, Colbert turns away from the camera and hides her face–a move that this star of stars would never make unless specifically directed to do so. Thus, while the narrative is so precise about how the exchange must be carried out at the level of film as a system of exchanged looks, there is a resistance to the very role Colbert has just been forced to accept. Arzner's direction at this moment asserts that the Colbert character is in conflict with the demands the plot has put on her. The film further insists, however, on narrativizing her return to her "normal" role by making her husband so awful that she must finally relinquish him as her project and take her place as Fredric March's project. But the ending, while reinforcing the latter's control of her, does underline power relations as those of seeing by casting his "proposal" as a visual prescription: "Wasn't it the south of France we decided you ought to see?"

Christopher Strong works out a complex set of sexual difference issues involving virginity, marriage, motherhood, and career. As in a number of Arzner's films, the clothing codes are extremely important. As the aviator Cynthia Darrington, Katharine Hepburn wears jodhpurs and boots, that old upper-class costume for a woman performing men's activities. As Christopher Strong's mistress, she wears chiffon and discreet glitter. The transition between these roles is especially well marked by an astonishing "moth" costume in gold lamé, which instantly defines her body rather than her career as the new site of her identity.

Yet in contradiction, after this shift Hepburn hides her face in a number of key scenes. After her and Strong's first declarations of love, the camera searches insistently for her facial expression, which is denied at some length while she lowers her head and keeps it down. When she announces her intention to return to flying, she again hides her face; as she writes her suicide note, her face is dimly lighted and as impassive as a mask–she looks like someone else. Finally, she returns to jodhpurs and the world of aviation, choosing to die rather than to live out her pregnancy–the clearest mark of sexual difference and one that would require the destruction of an already constituted couple/family. During the wild, suicidal descent of her airplane, her face is completely hidden by an oxygen mask, which she rips off only a second or two before the final explosion. In all of these visual evasions, there is no hint of teasing or even of fragmenting the woman's body as in the postlovemaking sequence where only her hand is revealed. Rather, there is a denial of the viewer's pleasure in knowing the woman's pain or happiness as the narrative implies its possible excess and as the face might reveal it. This foregrounded refusal reminds the viewer that he is being denied his usual privileged position in the Hollywood cinema-viewing machine.

In *Dance, Girl, Dance*, the relations among sexual difference, the role of mother right and father right, the functions of various kinds of dance within culture, and identifications between voyeurs within the film and in the viewing audience are most explicitly developed. Judy (Maureen O'Hara), the aspiring ballerina, resists the impressario Steve Adams (Ralph Bellamy) as a lover and as a means of access to the world of dance. She wants classical ballet, which is linked to the timelessness of her "Morning Star" choreography and to Madame Basilova, the woman as model and mentor. At one point, Madame Basilova, who typically wears shirt, jacket, and necktie, puts on a ridiculous, veiled "feminine" hat to go out into a world that structures and reads identity by these signs. It is her intention to bring Judy to Steve Adams and provide her access to the world she ostensibly wants, but Madame B. is run over in the street. As the only one who has ever seen Judy act out her inward-turning fantasy of ballet (which she sees only by peeking–by concealing her own watching), and as the one who encourages Judy, Basilova herself cannot survive entry into the world of sexual difference and must be killed to stop her influence over Judy, to move Judy away from the world of secrecy and timelessness. Yet when Judy finally does enter the office of Adams's modern dance company, she herself only peeks at their rehearsal and flees, running back to the secrecy of her private dancing and to the inappropriate and inaccessible married man that she continues to prefer to Steve Adams, whom for no apparent reason she cannot stand.

Judy can be read as resisting movement out of the world of the woman as "other," as being lost in a presymbolic, nameless space. Thus it is possible to see her visual resistance as negative, linked to a failure of "maturation," as Kay and Peary suggest in an early article.[7] Yet at the same time, to enter the world of modern dance, the world of audiences, the world of Steve and culture, is to enter the world of objectification and patriarchal dominance, as is exaggerated in the sequence involving burlesque, the other extreme along the continuum of dance/woman as fetishized spectacle. Judy, as stooge to Lucille Ball's "oomph girl" stripper, angrily chastises the men in the audience for looking at herself and Bubbles as their wives would never permit. Yet what about the middle register of looking that women must/do permit? How is she to reprimand Steve, who looks lovingly at her legs, or the audience of his dance troupe, who will look at her as "artiste"—both audiences she is supposed to desire? In fact, the acquisition of this second audience is the motor of the narrative, and her acceptance of Steve is its inevitable final recuperation.

Yet in the end, as Steve finally enfolds her in his fatherly arms and tells her what a foolish girl she was to resist this easy love and career, he represents the denial of all her own choices, however wrongheaded, and her submission to her cultural position as spectacle. At this moment of what the narrative insists is her fulfillment, her face reveals both tears and a kind of horror. Judy is disgusted to be trapped sexually, to be refathered, as it were, or even first-fathered after Madame Basilova. Thus the gaze of the father and lover, of the several audiences of the modern dance, the burlesque, and of the film itself are all become one here, condensed into the single gaze that Arzner has Judy refuse in her final gesture. She lowers her head slightly, and the huge black hat that she is so oddly wearing for this interview completely obscures the audience's field of vision. Again the character resists at the visual level the narrative recuperation in a move that signals the transgressing, enunciating presence of the typically absent author.

A strange and powerful concentration on issues of seeing is also central to *Craig's Wife*, but in a very different way. It is common to say that this film is about a woman obsessed with housekeeping, but this is true primarily in the sense of *keeping* her house, that is, in the sense of Harriet Craig's wild desire to retain possession of the house against the apparently imagined danger that she might lose home and security through desertion by her husband (as happened to her mother before her). These fears cause her to eavesdrop on her husband's phone calls, spy on his relations with a neighbor woman, accuse him of the will to infidelity, and torment her servants. Thus her obsession with the physical maintenance of her house is an expression of her obsession with staving off the threat of its loss. In "The 'Woman's Film': Possession and Address," Mary Ann Doane identifies a subset of the woman's film as the "paranoid woman's film" where the "paradigmatic woman's space—the home—is yoked to dread, and a crisis of vision."[8] The danger in such films almost always comes from the husband, and usually involves the threat of murder, but Harriet Craig's fear in this film serves a similar function in that it situates the woman as aggressive wielder of the gaze, pursuing some investigation in which certain unknown elements involving the home are at stake for her.

As Doane further points out, the woman is de-eroticized as agent rather than object of the gaze. But this peculiar reversal does not institute the woman as a controlling subject: instead, the narrative reveals that the "process of seeing [is] designed to unveil an aggression against itself" (72). Thus these films involve a fantasy of masochistic suffering for the woman, where her aggressive gaze is often to be read as a sign of illness. In *Craig's Wife*, the specular de-eroticizing of the woman is further narrativized by Harriet Craig's refusal of her husband's advances and by her apparent displeasure in his very presence, to such an extent that it opens a contradiction in relation to his apparent love and desire for her; it is difficult to imagine how both those attitudes can coexist. The film further narrativizes the perverse economy of the gaze by making Harriet Craig into a "controlling woman," one whose fear is cast in the form of an unnatural will to hold sway over the household and its inhabitants. Near the end of the film, her husband lectures about the presumptuousness of herself and "millions like her" who dare try to control their husbands. Then, having provided this narrative basis, the film brings Harriet a fate more terrible than her worst fears; she keeps the house, but her husband and everyone else who lives there go away. It is shown once more that to get what she desires–the house, in this case–is the worst possible fate for the woman. It was not the loss of her house but the loss of love–abandonment by the man–that was the true threat. The woman is shown again to be wrongheaded in her desire as well as in her fear. Willing/desiring itself is shown to be completely self-defeating and, as I shall show later, its very fulfillment leads to the loss of its real object. The fantasy of the suffering woman (as Doane suggests, presented for the consumption of the female audience) is now fully available. Doane also suggests, in relation to Freud's studies of paranoia and masochism, especially the essay "A Child Is Being Beaten," that, unlike the man, the woman frequently stands outside her own masochistic fantasy. She no longer seeks sexual participation but assumes the position of spectator, whose goal is merely the development of the fantasy itself. The female cinema spectator is also thus disembodied. Doane continues: "The cinema, a mirror of control to the man, reflects nothing for the woman, or rather, it denies the imaginary identification which, uniting body and identity, supports discursive mastery" (79). Thus, the woman who directs the aggressive, paranoid gaze does not do so as a controlling subject, and does not provide such a subject as object for identification by the woman spectator.

This denial of the relation between the gaze-when-wielded-by-the-woman and mastery is developed in a highly excessive way in *Craig's Wife*.

Suddenly, the last several moments of the film are devoted to prolonged shots of Harriet Craig looking – almost directly into the camera – at the empty house she now occupies. During this extended looking, *there are no reverse shots whatsoever*. We never see anything of what Harriet Craig is looking at. Instead, we get only cuts to shots of her looking from different angles. We are denied the primary mechanism of suture and of mastery through identification. There is no position left for the field of things seen. Like Adèle H., who doesn't recognize her lover when she sees him in the streets of Barbados, Harriet is shown to be utterly absorbed in her paranoid fantasy of scrutiny/investigation/suffering. The whole world is effaced, and there is only Harriet Craig looking-but-failing-to-possess. The woman who looks possesses nothing, yet she continues to look defiantly, so that we understand that to look is her crime. It is also true that the wide-open stare of her eyes invokes the medical discourse – surely this must be the gaze of a madwoman, made such by the perversity (the unnaturalness) of using her own eyes.

Yet the excess with which this position is developed through the prolonged absence of reverse shots, together with the transgression of the rule that the audience never be addressed directly, makes spectators uneasy: it violates the prohibition against making the audience aware of the exchange of glances in which it is involved. Although Harriet's looking is now a substitution for all other aspects of participation, we may have some sense of its *continuation* as a hint of defiant subjectivity. We may be reminded of what we are doing as spectators and why it feels so good to do it. In its very excess, the final sequence refuses to smooth over entirely "the contradictions which necessarily arise in attributing the epistemological gaze to the woman" (Doane, 80).

What, then, is it possible to say about Dorothy Arzner, the enunciator of these films, the absent one who has used so oddly the basic givens of the cinematic institution in which she was so uniquely situated? The claims being made here are very modest. When sitting in a theater audience without being able to see (either as classic spectator-in-mastery, or in relation to a woman who is blind to what she looks at), some spectators may be forced into recognizing that seeing is facilitated from somewhere – enunciation must be wielded to make images available. Thus it is a source of enunciation – a director, an editor – who must be taken as the source of these odd contradictions. For the film viewer who is unsettled into awareness of the differences between narrative and image, between the promise and the denial of the field of images, and of the excess perpetrated through these systems – for such a viewer, this author is marked by forms of disruption that sometimes result in making images absent, not allowing the film to be seen. Thus the presence of this author is signaled through a kind of absence-made-active. Her position as enunciator is offered not so much as a personal source or site of a certain kind of seeing, like the work of Orson Welles or Ingmar Bergman. Instead, this only woman who ever occupied such a place in the history of cinema – who is herself repeatedly suppressed from the scene of history – often seems to construct that place as the location of subversion, a place from which to resist the classical cinema's primary function of presenting things to be looked at rhythmically, with uninterrupted pleasure. Instead, ironically, her characters and her enunciation from time to time insist on that which the male spectator fears most – that there is, in fact, nothing to be looked at. An absence that can mark the woman's displacement from active subjectivity may also perhaps be read as a gesture of defiance.

Notes

1. Claire Johnston, "Dorothy Arzner: Critical Strategies," in *The Work of Dorothy Arzner: Towards a Feminist Cinema*, ed. Claire Johnston (London: British Film Institute, 1975), 1.

2. Johnston, "Critical Strategies," 2.

3. Ronald Haver, *David O. Selznick's Hollywood* (New York: Alfred A. Knopf, 1980).

4. *Silver Screen*, December 1933, 23.

5. See Johnston, "Dorothy Arzner: Critical Strategies," and Pam Cook, "Approaching the Work of Dorothy Arzner," in *The Work of Dorothy Arzner*; see also Claire Johnston, "Women's Cinema as Counter-Cinema," in *Notes on Women's Cinema*, ed. Claire Johnston (London: Society for Education in Film and Television, 1973), reprinted in *Movies and Methods*, ed. Bill Nichols (Berkeley: University of California Press, 1976).

6. Jacquelyn Suter, "Feminine Discourse in *Christopher Strong*," *Camera Obscura*, nos. 3-4 (Summer 1979): 135-50.

7. Karyn Kay and Gerald Peary, "Dorothy Arzner's *Dance, Girl, Dance*," *The Velvet Light Trap*, no. 10 (Fall 1973): 26-31.

8. Mary Ann Doane, "The Woman's Film: Possession and Address," in *Revision: Essays in Feminist Film Criticism*, ed. Mary Ann Doane, Patricia Mellencamp, and Linda Williams (Frederick, Md.: University Publications of America, 1984), 69-70.

Is China the End of Hermeneutics?; or, Political and Cultural Usage of Non-Han Women in Mainland Chinese Films

Esther C. M. Yau

Introduction

The Cultural Revolution in China in the 1960s has a convoluted history yet to be properly understood.[1] After 1979, the People's Republic opened its doors to international capitalism and put an end to the social forces generated by the monumental mass movement. However, to a whole generation of Chinese, and especially the Han people sent to the countryside, the experience of the Cultural Revolution was and still is important in the context and the collective unconscious of the 1980s and the 1990s.

In the West, efforts to construct China as an object of knowledge and as the "non-Western Other" are often limited by the tendency to interpret China's experiences according to liberal agendas (or conservative, or radical ones, for that matter);[2] by the benign but nonetheless narcissistic character of the venture; by dulled awareness of the slippery nature of cross-cultural articulations; and by the West's long-standing ignorance about ethnic differences in China, which takes "Chinese" for a single racial category.

From the perspective of Western self-critique, we need to be suspicious of claims that purport to recognize "the rich values of an ancient oriental civilization" or to acknowledge "those cultural differences which enable us [i.e., Western investigators] to learn something," assuming knowledge as a basis of superiority. Indeed, ventures into the still-unchartered "Third

World" areas are becoming fashionable but no less questionable, as are generous inclusions of women of color within global (feminist or otherwise) definitions of liberation and sexuality. Many of these cross-cultural pursuits, prefaced by ritualistic self-critique, are oblivious to the neocolonial character of the ways they theorize the Others' differences.[3] Readiness to accept "experts" who pay only lip service to historical and local specificities, and whose pro-forma apologies are complemented by uncritical use of native sources as truth, further attests to a troubling Western tolerance of superficial scholarship concerning the "Third World."

This essay, which examines the appropriation of national minorities in Chinese cinema, does not intend to seek out the recuperative values of underrepresented groups as an alternative to the Confucian-based dominant Han Chinese culture. Rather, the purpose is to critique the appropriation and subjugation of minority cultures within the national boundary. Edward Said's *Orientalism* (1978) has stimulated many similar discussions concerning the ways aspects of non-Western societies have been interpreted and integrated into nationalistic and ethnocentric formulations of Western knowledge.[4] Said's critique is invoked here to reflect on our participation in a similar process as we encounter the Other. China, according to the still-prevailing logic that equates the "First World" with the Self, is perceived by the West as the Other (and more so since the Chinese government crushed the 1989 public outcry for self-determination); however, when it comes to marginalizing minority cultures and creating the exotic, the dominant races and classes in China and the West are similarly culpable. Through reflection on the analogy, critiquing Chinese films' subjugation of the national minorities (as the "third realm" within China) could be inverted, so that reading the Other is turned into a confrontation with the Self.

Context

To condense centuries of history into a brief narrative, one begins arbitrarily. The Han and their *huaxia* civilization of the northern plains of China rose from the battlefields. In different dynasties, the Han emperors and their army fought the surrounding tribes and countries as they established territorial domination and claimed mandate from heaven. Etymology marks the Han's self-centering efforts. The term *Zhongguo* literally means "the middle kingdom." The four most common terms for the surrounding tribes are *nu*, which shares the same character with "slave"; *di*, which is composed of the hieroglyph "animal" and "fire"; *yi*, which uses the character that means, in one context, "to flatten by destruction"; and *man*, which includes an ideogram "insect" in the character and denotes "uncivilized savages."[5] Thus, by defining the tribal Others as less than human, the

Han have positioned themselves in the center of intelligence and cultural superiority. The supremacy of the Middle Kingdom's civilization was preserved at the expense of soldiers at war and beautiful courtesans dispatched as part of diplomatic *he fan* gifts to "keep peace with the aliens." In the years when the Mongolians ruled over China, the Han maintained that the inner strength of their culture would eventually bleach and convert the non-Han emperors.

By comparison, the modern, socialist version of Han cultural hegemony was apparently more benign. In the early 1950s, the People's Republic of China (PRC) government acknowledged that fifty-five nationalities lived in the country with the Han as the majority (approximately 94 percent of the entire population). The Common Program of 1949 and the Constitution of 1954 prohibited discrimination against the fifty-four non-Han nationalities officially named *shaoshu minzu* ("national minorities").[6] National unity and regional autonomy were dual goals in the Common Program, which dictated that "all national minorities [should] have freedom to develop their dialects and languages, to preserve or reform their traditions, customs, and religious beliefs."[7] The program also committed the government to attend to the minorities' economic and cultural well-being, and to be more flexible with the *xiongdi minzu* (brother nationalities).

The Soviet-inspired PRC's national/ethnic policy (*minzu zhengce*) of the 1950s attributed the reasons for inequality to uneven regional economic development. While Chairman Mao Zedong criticized Han chauvinism and stressed Socialist brotherhood, the government's long-term objectives stressed national unity and defense, appropriation of resources (notably minerals) in the "autonomous regions," elimination of local elites, and institutionalization of ethnic differences. Regional demands for self-determination were suppressed, silenced, or transformed by the mandate of integrating all nationalities within China.[8] Defined as *"national* minorities," non-Han peoples who refused to comply with the government would be labeled political segregationists. As "national *minorities,"* they were offered a contract without end—with terms arranged like those of a traditional marriage in which the bride (as the "minor") had no freedom to refuse but hoped to prosper by getting along. Overt and covert assimilation pressures kept transforming the sociocultural character of the "national minorities." In other words, military, organizational, and discursive forms of violence helped sustain the official-national constructions of unified struggle, harmonious coexistence, and cultural diversity.

The "National Minorities" Genre

From 1949 to 1965, the state-financed studios produced more than fifty feature films about the Mongolians, Tibetans, Kazakhs, Uighurs, Koreans,

Dais, Miaos, Yis, Bais, and other "national minorities."[9] The productions involved non-Han consultants, interpreters, performers, and crew members. At the same time, Han control measures were omnipresent in every film: Han performers played national minorities' roles; slogans written in the Chinese language appeared in the scenes; a male Han cadre present in every story judged political and folk matters; and the government's agendas informed the narrative strategies. Together, the films purportedly represented the minorities' revolutionary struggles but subtly implemented nationalizing policies and constituted a special genre in China's postrevolutionary cinema.

The use of women as rhetorical figures in the national minorities genre was consistent with the Party's discursive use of women in general. Non-Han female protagonists, played by Han actresses, were set up as role models to suture narrative and visual interests with political functions. Ostensibly minority and actually Han, the performers with their mixed identities addressed both non-Han and Han viewers. Not surprisingly, only the strong and healthy bodies dressed in exotic costumes were selected as couriers of political messages. In films such as *Five Golden Flowers* (*Wuduo jinhua*, 1959) and *The Red Flower of Tienshan* (*Tienshan de honghua*, 1963), these women worked, sang, danced, suffered, and struggled in ways that whetted the Han viewers' voyeuristic interests in "primitive" cultures.[10] Inevitably, spectacles of beautiful and spontaneous women drew attention to themselves and provoked escapist fantasies. Thus, through attractive "minority" female protagonists, the didactic and the escapist functioned simultaneously, though probably more didactically for the non-Han spectators and more as escape for the Han ones.

The national minorities films invariably set up a triangular relationship that consisted of non-Han men and women and a Han cadre through which sexual transgression was negatively correlated with ethnic leadership. Among native elite men were oppressive slave owners, landlords, and Guomindang sympathizers who either raped or abused the powerless native women. While regional/ethnic authority was sexualized and constructed as male aggressiveness, compliance with Han socialism was presented as female vulnerability in need of Han official intervention as male chivalry. The virtuous minority woman, a Han supporter, has ethical and familial reasons for supporting the Party—a logic based on Confucian priorities. In short, good minority women were strategically produced to incriminate native men who resisted the government's regional policies. This nexus of ethnic, gender, and moral organization constituted the dominant paradigm of interethnic relations in the national minorities films from 1949 to 1965 and revealed the character of intra-national "brotherhood."

Contrary to their prowomen stance, the films betrayed sadist interests in non-Han cruelty directed toward female protagonists. For example, in

The Dai Doctor (*Moyadai*, 1960) a young Dai mother is punished and burned as a witch by the lustful tribal lord who failed to rape her; later, the superstitious villagers set fire to the family hut to expel both her husband and daughter. In *Visitors over Ice Mountains* (*Bingshan shang de laike*, 1963), a Tajikh woman—an impersonator and spy—is murdered by the Guomindang sympathizers in her own tribe. In *The Red Flower of Tienshan*, a Kazakh woman is whipped and later abandoned by her husband, who opposes her leading role in organizing the people's commune. These and other scenes of torture and killing underscore the Other's violence for purposes of discrediting the nationalist government, undermining non-Han men's power, winning women's empathy, and making charges against minority dissidents. Moreoever, the "ethnic" characteristics of the violent acts consolidate the popular (mis)perception of the national minorities as "uncivilized."

Aside from political functions, non-Han women on screen provided an exclusive site for sexuality that was not addressed in other films. In most postrevolutionary films, Confucian morality continued to make the self-sacrificial mother the bearer of Han civilization and to condemn sexuality outside the institutions of reproduction and economic production. Moral and sexual crimes were often conflated with political crimes. The Party's attitude toward desire was codified in the calculated shrouding of women's sexual appeal on screen through costume, lighting, camera angles, and acting styles. Consequently, positive female Han types appeared uniformly and predictably virtuous. While most films observe rigid codes of female representation, the national minorities genre, which occupies a lower status in the hierarchy of Han postrevolutionary art, was sometimes spared by the strictest censorship of desire and sexuality and "licensed" to elaborate on beautiful and "exotic" female bodies. "Erotic excesses" invoked in scenes featuring national minority women acknowledged desires and smuggled them through Confucian and Party taboos, though, inevitably, they did not seriously threaten the codes of Han sexual propriety. In this manner, they also helped sustain both a segregationist logic and the austere codes of the hard-core revolutionary genres.

Significantly, the few early women directors working in the 1950s were just as faithful in executing Party prerogatives as their male counterparts and provided no distinctive "female" voices in the postrevolutionary cinema. So far, only two films of the genre have been identified as being co-directed by women working with senior male colleagues: *Menglongsha Village* (*Menglongsha*, 1960) and *Eagle of the Plains* (*Caoyuan xiongying*, 1964). Since these films are similar to others in the genre, female directors' gender identity does not appear to be significant. *A Blade of Grass on the Kunlun Mountains* (*Kunlun shanshang yikecao*, 1962), a low-budget film directed by a woman director, Dong Kena, is, however, an exception. The film depicts the initial disappointments, frustrations, and struggles of two Han women who assisted male Han truck drivers working in the Qinghai-Tibetan Plateau. The film advocates self-sacrifice and devotion in the face of harsh living circumstances, in line with the general call for perseverance in the early 1960s when the country was suffering from famine and from withdrawal of Soviet support. Dong Kena worked entirely within the sociopolitical parameters and did not question frontier development. Still, the film underplays the role of the male Han cadre (a deceased husband, he appears only briefly in a flashback), and it suggests that it was his widow's persistence and the companionship she offered to the newcomers that mattered in this unromantic frontier. Inadvertently, the film provides alternative insights into what it meant for the Han to be "settling happily" in the border provinces. Not a national minorities film, Dong's heroic portrayal of workers of the "autonomous regions" nevertheless makes an intertextual comment on the Han's frontier mentality. Still, the film does not question the politics of the national minorities genre, and Han ethnocentrism remains unaddressed.

Post-Cultural Revolution Introspection and Sacrificed Youth

In the post-Cultural Revolution "New Era" (which ended in about 1989), the government's modernization policy was accompanied by more autonomy given to filmmakers. Nevertheless, since the earlier, "classical" national minorities films did not challenge Han biases, more recent and "depoliticized" versions of non-Han cultures were not free of ethnocentric tendencies either. Still subjected to state censorship, films could not portray the national minorities' independence movements or the extent of harm done to them during the Cultural Revolution—these matters remained more or less oral history.[11] Of the many films that addressed the implications of the Cultural Revolution, only several reenacted the Han's traumatic "exile" to the autonomous regions and took pains to present the non-Han's cultural superiority. The ethnocentric tendencies in these films, which pursued cultural (and obliquely political) self-examination, suggest a complex introspective process.

Sacrificed Youth (Qingqun ji, 1984), an acclaimed film based on an award-winning novella written by Zhang Manling, who worked with the Dai nationality during the Cultural Revolution, is an example of the Han's self-critical efforts. Zhang Nuanxin, the film's director, was born in Inner Mongolia and is a graduate of and has been a lecturer at the Beijing Film Academy since 1958. Both Han women had lived in the border provinces, both were college-educated in Beijing, and both use the ethnographic mode for personalized narratives.

Zhang Manling's There Exists a Beautiful Place (You yige meili de *difang*) is semiautobiographical. It depicts in flashbacks the psychological changes within a young Han woman, Li Chun, who, during the Cultural Revolution, was dispatched from the city to work and live with the Dai natives in a Yunnan village. The narrative dramatizes the inner fears and anomie of a seventeen-year-old separated from her own Han community and drawn toward the friendly but unfamiliar Dai people, who live like the Thai. Li Chun's eagerness to observe and to mimic the Dai ways of living is motivated by political and survival needs (what the government required of the rusticated youths), by her own competitive character (especially with Yibo, the prettiest and most capable of the Dai girls in the village), and by her desire for a comforting acceptance badly needed since her own family members were forced apart by persecutions. In order to liberate herself from a homogeneous political upbringing and to explore a new identity, she puts on Dai clothes and becomes increasingly aware of her sexuality.

Li Chun's efforts to free herself from her Han background strains against the repressive mechanisms she has internalized. Dage, the son of her host family, a hunter and a brick maker, is infatuated with her but patiently awaits her initiative. However, the unstated reasons of class difference and interracial taboos sustain her distance from Dage. Her reluctance to give up her Han intellectual identity accounts for her friendship with Renjia, a Han youth whose fate is similar to hers but who is skeptical of the native life-style. As the novella maintains these split and repressed sexual interests without acknowledging their problematic nature, Li Chun's dilemma in the Han-Dai encounter is resolved by a narrative ploy: she comes under suspicion for money lost in the host family and, although the misunderstanding is clarified later, she leaves the village. (In the film version, Dage gets drunk and, venting his jealousy, beats Renjia.) In any case, a pretext is given that motivates Li Chun to move to another area. After many years, she returns to the city and enters college. But there is a mud-rock slide in the Dai village that hosted her, and Renjia is buried under it. At the end, educated and in her thirties, she regrets her ultimate separation from the perpetual youthfulness of the Dai. In her dreams, however, she remembers the lush green and the ever-flowing waters.

The novella presents positive and intimate details of Dai culture from a Han perspective. Li Chun is initially drawn to the Dais, while she has reservations about the Han. To a Han girl used to civil surveillance, an involuntary "exile" to Yunnan actually means gaining warm and trustful friends and protection from political strife. Yet, the romanticized Han-Dai relationship comes to an impasse when Li Chun's inability to become the Other is dramatized via the traditional (and sexist) device by which she has to choose between two men to signify identity and inscribe her loyalties. In other words, the novella suffers from its unconscious adoption of the dominant patriarchal perspective that prevents a woman from defining herself outside the restrictive realm of the family and heterosexuality. Li Chun's inevitable return to Han culture at the end, therefore, fulfills Han ethical prerequisites; but, sadly, she lives in a different form of "exile" as she has to give up the vibrant "non-Han" part of herself.

The novella's sentimental descriptions of Yunnan and the Dai natives are beautifully visualized in filmic terms by Zhang Nuanxin. Zhang shot her second film on location using the country's standard of a 3.5-to-1 shooting ratio, with a small budget from the Youth Studio of the Beijing Film Academy. *Sacrificed Youth*, a lyrical piece that set an important precedent for personal filmmaking long submerged in the self-effacing 1950s aesthetic practices, subtly expresses a middle-aged woman's sense of emotional loss. Through Li Chun's self-examination, Zhang shows that the naive notion of "beauty" had been distorted by repressive indoctrination and that a conceptual and visual restoration of that "beauty" is possible via a process of self-critique and inspiration from the (preliterate) rural southwestern Dai culture.

In a discussion of her directorial intentions, Zhang Nuanxin summarized the Han woman's (and her own) dilemma:[12]

> Amidst the cultural conflict between the Dai civilization (that which is primitive, sincere, befitting to human nature) and the Han civilization (that which is modern, partly hypocritical, and distorting to human nature) lies the tragedy of Li Chun. She was awakened, but it made her feel even more painful. The clearer she knew, the more she felt her youth slipping away during the turmoil, and getting buried within the concepts which bind many.

Zhang added that she was composing "an ode to the passing away of the youth of a whole generation of people." That is, her own generation, which spent its thirties during the Cultural Revolution, is "sacrificed youth." Nevertheless, the film does not confront the Han's mutual destruction during those years that led to the deaths of many; instead, it offers an intellectual audience disturbing cultural insights without trespassing political taboos.

Zhang Nuanxin's adaptation mixes reality and fiction, ethnography and memory, and the dramatic and poetic forms of realism. The subtle style and narrative ambiguity underscore the flow of Li Chun's consciousness. Zhang Nuanxin also experimented with practices new to the Mainland Chinese at the time, including shooting in sync sound, setting up elaborate long takes, filming in extremely low light situations, and sensitively handling tones in a potentially monotonous subtropical environment. By asking the Dai people in Yunnan to play themselves, Zhang created what she calls "a real challenge to the professional Han actress who was trained to perform before the camera in more conventional ways." She also invited suggestions from the Dai people and welcomed improvisations from the 102-year-old Dai granny, who first encountered film on this occasion, and who turned out the best "performance" among the cast. Back in Beijing, she accepted her colleagues' suggestion to use dramatic shock as a concluding device, and reedited the ending, which now gives the impression that the whole Dai village has been eliminated by the mud-rock slide. In these various ways, Zhang Nuanxin actualized her notions of a modernized film language and ethnographic sensibilities, though, regrettably, she was not fully aware of the ideological implications of the film's new ending.[13]

Like most Han directors and some ethnographic filmmakers, Zhang Nuanxin's observation-participation techniques serve the ideology of artistic creation. Zhang recalled the hours and mileage the crew had spent on location reconnaissances, since many areas in Yunnan had been subjected to development and "they no longer look like they used to." Obviously, Zhang's thematic obsession with untainted nature obscured her perception of the everyday effects of Han presence on the Dai land, which keep jumping out as images "unsuitable" for her film. For, as the ideas about the Dai are beautiful, so their reality must be beautiful, too. Accordingly, the poetic, culturally introspective, and humanist film seeks out the Dai's primitive and positive virtues only; while the natives, like other national minorities, face the modern problems of colonization and deprivation. Thus, when the ideology of artistic reconstruction has replaced that of political didactics in the post-Cultural Revolution era, the objectifying processes are not automatically removed. A Han youth commented on the film's aesthetic project, "I know what it really means to be living in the beautiful borders and I do not need the intellectuals to tell me."[14] Yibo, the prettiest Dai girl in the film, acted on a similar attitude by leaving the village to join a cultural troupe after the filming.

In *Sacrificed Youth*, the prominent aspects of Dai life and culture are earthy, agrarian, and sensuous—qualities that feed into the bourgeois appeal of the film. The exotic connotations of the images are enhanced by the indigenous sounds of the Dai conversations, music, and songs, which create a subtropical ambience alluring to Han Chinese and Westerners alike. (Zhang told an American that most Chinese have never visited the Sino-Burmese border, and she had the Western audience in mind when she shot the film.)[15] Again, unconsciously, a "third realm" within China is "colonized" by well-intentioned Han artists and becomes a part of a "new Chinese cinema" that is being launched on an orbit of international marketing (hence indirect global colonization?) as well.

International glamour notwithstanding, privileges in cross-cultural encounters prove to be hard to give up. Still, for such encounters to be meaningful to the privileged, the latter must experience humility and learn; however, the experience remains superficial if the privileged refuse to give up their superior, centered positions. Such superficial experiences abound in fictional and ethnographic texts that depict figures that cross the racial and cultural boundaries. In relation to *Sacrificed Youth*, I shall focus on two different narcissistic articulations by identifying the tropes of "cultural disguise" and "familial projection" in two notable instances in which the Han woman undergoes psychological and emotional changes.

Earlier, in order to be included in the Dai girls' work team, Li Chun puts on a tight blouse and a long purplish sarong dress. Her attractive feminine figure, previously hidden by the grayish Maoist uniform, emerges, noted by musical accompaniment, and becomes a pleasurable site for gazes from within the diegesis and from offscreen. Instantaneously, the social relationships within the film work for Li Chun's benefit: Ya gives her a silver waistband and treats her as a family member; the arrogant Yibo admits her into the work team; and Renjia (the Han youth) and Dage (the Dai man) are attracted to her. In short, she gains full access to cultural-sexual exchange. While the Dai girls' difference initially displaces Li Chun's superiority, her adoption of Dai ways and mores, which has enlightened her, has also brought immense and immediate rewards. Evidently, the "superior" cultural figure's respect for the Other's difference enables the former to regain confidence and become the center of minority attention.

To describe the erotic power newly discovered when she discards the Maoist uniforms, Li Chun says in the voice-over that she is "like the Ash Maid [meaning Cinderella] in the fairy tale who has put on crystal shoes." The allusion to a Western fairy tale reveals the Han-Dai encounter as at once imagined in a narcissistic and romantic manner and legitimized by a fantastic (Western) figure.[16] What gives the Han character and viewers the pleasure of enlightenment is not just a departure from asceticism, but also the fantastic ability of a single Han body to take up and sustain two different cultural codes, one dominant and the other complementary. The experience turns out to be one of "cultural disguise"–a Han intellectual adopts a Dai identity and knows the Other from the inside, while power relations remain unchanged. That is, respect for the Dai turns into appropriation for the Han's benefit. Such a "cultural disguise" in this and other contexts enriches the privileged travelers, legitimizes their authority as "minority experts," and masks their appropriation of minority strengths as genuine facilitation of cross-cultural exchange.

The narcissism in the Han-Dai encounter, however, should also be considered alongside the dilemma of the female Han intellectual. That is, the personal voices in the text need to be historicized. After Ya's death, there are four sequences before the film comes to an end. They include Li Chun's mourning in whitish gray, a Dai funeral in fiery red climaxing in the cremation of Ya, a grayish gigantic mud-rock slide that erases all the traces of

Dai life, and a lingering visual caress of the subtropical region in orange tones accompanied by the theme song. While the previous scenes have been carefully conceived with psychological nuances, realistic colors, and ethnic details, these four sequences have a different syntax and style – extremely condensed, almost abstract in quality, and highly charged, they reorder iconic codes to produce distinctive changes in tonal scheme and emotional expression. It is at the film's very end that the death of the Dai granny, the burial of the Dai village, the passing away of Li Chun's youth, and the mourning for all the losses are chained tightly together. Together, they enact an emotional rupture that calls for further analysis of the film's oblique expression of a Han woman's bind in ways that cannot be further repressed or delayed by the film's narrative and aesthetic concerns.

Undoubtedly, the film deploys a surrogate mother as linchpin to the success of the Han-Dai encounter. In the body of Ya, the director found the perfect ethnographic realization: a real Dai offering the most genuine (m)otherly expressions to verify the film's sincerity, and an ideal maternal figure that naturalizes the Han's demands for a good mother who guarantees the productivity and prosperity of the household.[17] The Dai community's openness and warmth contrast the Han's destructive behavior during the Cultural Revolution. The "familial projection," a romanticizing gesture, also offsets the film's apparent engagement with a different, autonomous, and sexual identity and reinscribes the Dai (as it does the Han) into a Confucian familial order. This inability to affirm any feminine existence outside the familial definition is indeed troubling. In as consciously self-critical a film as Sacrificed Youth, the imposition of a Han social-ethical scheme nevertheless reenacts the repressive mechanism that the film sets out to criticize and reveals its ideological fixation despite its conscious objectives. Moreover, projecting oneself on the Other, as the film uses the mythical Dai figure Ya for Han self-location, is ethnocentric indeed. Such inability to perceive or act outside one's ideological inscription despite having gained insights from the Others underscores ethnocentrism as a stubborn blind spot of the mind that may generate colonizing moves in cross-cultural encounters.

In a text as overdetermined by repressive cultural norms and by revisionist efforts of the early 1980s as Sacrificed Youth, the ending sequences finally come to an eruption. Even so, it was the death of Ya and her funeral as a spectacle of fire that provide "pretexts" or metonymic ways to articulate the feelings that Han women (the character used as an agent for both the writer and the director) have contained inside themselves for many years. Yet, even so, the pressures to prioritize the culture and the family rather than oneself have taken effect, so that this intimate moment of feminine self-revelation is tactfully placed, almost invisibly, within the "important scenes" of the mother's death and the mud-rock slide's ruthless destruction of Dai life. This "diminution" matches the choice of the "national minorities genre" for expression, though the film has taken crucial steps to avoid the clichéd images of the non-Han people. Still, as the middle-aged Li Chun cries in front of the overwhelming and silent site of the mud-rock slide, a deeply personal voice emerges that cannot be explained by the diegesis. This articulation of loss figured by a perpetual deprivation of contact with the spontaneous Dai can be historicized by relating it to the regrets of Han women who for years live within the binds of the Han political culture.

Ultimately, a sincere and deeply personal voice comes out in *Sacrificed Youth*'s representation of the Self: Chinese socialism as political culture has perpetuated a patriarchal dogma that trains women how to dress, behave, and think, and it produces forms of power they must learn to live in, especially since the demands of male leaders have influenced the men in their own families. What is repressed in the film's criticism of Han culture, then, is the criticism of sociopolitical ethics that keeps burdening the representation of the Self and Other. The discourses on cultural introspection and female sexuality in *Sacrificed Youth*, complicated and contradictory as they are, constitute the fabric of a fictional Dai ethnography that is indeed suitable for our hermeneutic reading of the Han.

Concluding Remarks

When the relationship of domination and subordination remains unchanged, a better knowledge of the Other can become a form of rhetorical violation toward the Other viewed as an object of study. Thus, there is no consolation except that which is found in self-critical silence.[18] But a silence as refusal to colonize and to be colonized is very difficult when advanced forms of colonial discourse hardly pause in their benign global advancements in knowledge making.

Notes

1. Tsou Tang, *The Cultural Revolution and Post-Mao Reforms: A Historical Perspective* (Chicago: University of Chicago Press, 1986).

2. Roland Barthes noted that "China . . . defeats the constitution of concepts, themes, names. . . . [O]ur knowledge is turned into a figment of the imagination: the ideological objects that our society constructs are silently declared impertinent. It is the end of hermeneutics." Roland Barthes, "Well, and China?" *Discourse* 8 (Fall-Winter 1986–87): 117, an English translation of "Alors, la Chine?" privately published in Paris, 1975.

3. See Gayatri Chakravorty Spivak's "French Feminism in an International

Frame," in her *In Other Worlds: Essays in Cultural Politics* (New York: Routledge, 1988), 134–53.

4. Edward Said, *Orientalism* (New York: Pantheon, 1978).

5. Southern China was traditionally the place of exile for the banished official class from the north.

6. See chap. 3, sec. 4 of *The Constitution of the People's Republic of China* (Beijing: Foreign Language Press, 1983).

7. Article 53 in "The Common Program," adopted by the First Plenary Session of the Chinese People's Political Consultative Congress on September 29, 1949. *China Digest*, Oct. 5, 1949.

8. Thomas Herberer, *China and Its National Minorities: Autonomy or Assimilation?* trans. Michel Vale (New York and London: M. E. Sharpe, 1989).

9. Those who can read Chinese may look at the synopses of feature films in *Zhongguo yishu dianying bianmu (1949–1979) (A catalog of Chinese artistic films [1949–1979])*, vols. 1 and 2, China Film Archive and China Art Research Institute Film Research Center (Beijing, 1981).

10. Paul Clark also discusses the uses of "national minorities" in *Chinese Cinema: Culture and Politics since 1949* (Cambridge, Mass.: Cambridge University Press, 1987).

11. The Chinese always use informal and orally circulated knowledge to bypass formal and official prohibition. See Thomas Herberer, *China and Its National Minorities*, 23–29

12. Zhang Nuanxin, "Director's Comments on *Sacrificed Youth*," *Dangdai Dianying (Contemporary Cinema)* 5 (1985): 134–36.

13. The quotes in this and the next paragraph are cited from personal interviews with Zhang Nuanxin in Beijing, February and March 1988.

14. Personal discussion with Yao Xiao-meng in Beijing, February 1988.

15. See Zhang's comments in George Semsel's interview published in *Chinese Film: The State of the Art in the People's Republic* (New York: Praeger, 1987), 124–28. Videocassette copies of *Sacrificed Youth* can be purchased from within the United States by contacting China Video Movies Distributing Co., 1718 Broadway, Redwood City, CA 94063; (415) 366-2424.

16. Although an old Chinese "Cinderella" story existed in about A.D. 850–860 (translated by Arthur Waley in *Folk-Lore* 58 [March 1947]: 226–13), Zhang Nuanxin's reference to the "Ash Maid" in *Sacrificed Youth* treats the wonder tale figure as a Western one.

17. See Chu Tung-tsu's *Han Social Structure*, vol. 1, *Han Dynasty China* series, ed. Jack L. Dull (Seattle and London: University of Washington Press, 1972).

18. Both Edward Said's "Intellectuals in the Post-Colonial World" and Gayatri Chakravorty Spivak's "Can the Subaltern Speak?" address the dilemma of the postcolonial intellectual.

The Production of Third World Subjects for First World Consumption: *Salaam Bombay* and *Parama*

Poonam Arora

I

The recent trend toward the inclusion of non-Western films made by women in film and gender studies and in cultural studies courses is a clear indicator that such texts are increasingly being regarded as resources that, upon investigation, will yield evidence of relations of power, especially those pertaining to gender, within unfamiliar cultures. In other words, such films are often read as feminist ethnographies.[1] This tendency is problematic for two reasons. On the one hand, it is important to remember that filmic texts from non-Western cultures are implicated in the regimes of specatatorship that cinema has universally instituted, and that feminist film theory has so extensively analyzed. On the other hand, the discipline of ethnography itself has come under serious scrutiny because of, among other things, poststructural anxiety about the difficulty of "language and/as representation."[2] Can films made by women documenting their own cultures resolve this double impasse? My analysis of two fiction films made by Indian women—*Salaam Bombay!* (1988) by Mira Nair and *Parama* (1987) by Aparna Sen—will attempt to answer whether such indigenous, feminist ethnographies can provide a window on "native" cultures, and on the gender dynamics operative within them, to Western viewers.

Both films are made by Indian women and, thus, both invert the traditional paradigm wherein the ethnographer is male and speaks from within

293

a stronghold of patriarchal authority. However, there is an important distinction to be made between the two films' approach to ethnography. *Salaam Bombay!* advertises itself as an indigenous account of Indian culture: its appeal results precisely from its ability to produce the Indian subject in terms dictated by the representational codes of the West. By contrast, *Parama*, through its attention to culturally specific structures of representation, which compete within the text to produce the "Indian housewife," comprises a feminist critique of the notion of an indigenous ethnography. In fact, *Parama* constitutes a critique of the type of ethnography for which *Salaam Bombay!* serves, in my argument, as the model. However, *Parama*'s attempt to reinstate a "third" perspective raises the question of who is qualified to "read" the film's sophisticated analysis of the gender dynamics at work within a middle-class, urban, Indian milieu.

II

> Insiders studying their own cultures offer new angles of vision and depths of understanding. Their accounts are empowered and restricted in unique ways.[3]

When in 1988 *Salaam Bombay!* made the circuit of art theaters and film societies in Europe and America, it got more media attention than any other Indian film seen recently in the West. The film, shot on location in the streets of Bombay, foregrounds the fact that it is an indigenous ethnography: within the text itself, it is the point of view of Chaipau, a young Indian boy who becomes implicated in the city's drug trade and prostitution, that structures the narrative and provides the audience with a point of entry into the narrative. At a metatextual level, the film is an account by an insider – Mira Nair, the Indian woman director – studying her own culture and offering to the West a relatively undiscovered "angle of vision." The authenticity of the film's representation of social ills such as child labor and prostitution within Indian society is corroborated at both levels. Audiences unfamiliar with the Indian social context are likely to see the situation depicted in the narrative as a typical Third World predicament, a reading encouraged by the film's much publicized commitment to donating a portion of its revenues to the very street children it portrays. The question of whether this constitutes a genuine commitment to a worthy social cause or is merely cynical "advertising" is beside the point. Either way, its gesture toward the "real" street children who provide the model for the film's representation supports the film's ethnographic claims.

However, while *Salaam Bombay!* purports to depict the realities of Bombay street life, it is unsuccessful on two levels. First, the film's utter failure to address the nuances of cultural specificity means that, despite the veneer of documentary realism, "Bombay" as locale functions merely as a representative, and therefore interchangeable, Third World city anywhere, and Chaipau, as protagonist, functions as any oppressed Third World subject. Second, the film works to establish the absolute and untraversable distance between the events depicted and the secure, unimplicated position of the First World viewer, of whom sympathy alone is demanded. What the film refuses is the "realization that there is a Third World in every First World, and vice versa."[4] Despite the use of the Bombay drug trade as setting within the film (which signals again and again, albeit inadvertently, the economic interdependence of First and Third World) the ethnography fails to deconstruct the simplistic polarization of First and Third World socioeconomic contexts as well as the multiplicity of viewing positions that may be taken from within each context.

My point is that just as the production of texts such as *Salaam Bombay!* renders voiceless its marginal subjects, an urban center such as Bombay, in its turn, may be equally hegemonic vis-à-vis other cultures. Sweet Sixteen, the young girl kidnapped from Nepal and up for sale in the flesh trade of Bombay, is perhaps the most glaring example of the film's refusal to elucidate for the nonnative viewer the complex social and political conditions that have led to the girl being kidnapped from Nepal and brought to Bombay. However, the film refuses to process an inter-reference between these two cultures, ignoring the nuances of cultural specificity.

If we strip the film of its racial component, doesn't it become just another story of urbanization, with the city, as anywhere in the postcapitalist world, operating as the arena for corruption, economic underdevelopment, and exploitation? I want to stress that *Salaam Bombay!* continues to represent the Third World subjects merely as the Other. Thus the characters in the film have generic names – "Chaipau" in Bombay dialect means any errand boy who brings tea; "Chillum," the name of the petty drug pusher, literally is the pipe used to smoke pot; "Sweet Sixteen" must be approximately that age – and they serve a generic function, positioned solely as the recipients of the viewer's sympathy, serving as one-dimensional symbols of the degradation rampant within the Third World. Even a viewer who does not follow the dialect will not miss the point that these characters have generic names: when the protagonist loses his job at the tea shop, the next errand boy is called Chaipau too. Likewise, when Chillum, the first drug pusher, dies, another one takes not just his place but his name as well. However, a viewer who is familiar with the dialect further follows the implications of the protagonist's actual name, which is Krishna. Lord Krishna, as every Hindu knows, had made a promise to his devotees in the Bhagavad Gita that he would be reborn as the savior whenever the land of Bharat (the mythic name of India) is plagued by irreligion and corruption. Thus whereas from one viewing position the film is a documentary on deprivation and exploitation, from another it could be an ironic comment on the faith of the Hindu.

The irreconcilable difference between these two viewing positions is further heightened by the film's representation of woman-as-commodity. The Western viewer cannot appreciate the implications of Sweet Sixteen's Nepalese background and consequent transportation to India. This viewer has no way of knowing that for sociopolitical fringe cultures such as Nepal, Sikkim, Sri Lanka, Tibet, Bangladesh, and a host of others, a city such as Bombay carries all the charge of a First World center of commerce and power, attracting capital and raising the aspirations of the under-privileged much as any First World center would do. Sweet Sixteen is mute and therefore disempowered in this city, because for her it is a foreign city whose language she has yet to learn. Thus Sweet Sixteen as prostitute becomes a metaphor for the commodification of the woman in any postcapitalist urban context and the film fails to locate her in her historical and cultural specificity.

Likewise, despite the prominence of drug trade as social and economic backdrop in the narrative, the film fails to establish the complex inter-dependence of First and Third Worlds in the arena of drug traffic. In the film Bombay is a veritable stock exchange of illegal drugs. Here consumers, producers, and middlemen are all engaged in haggling, insider trading, or brokering the best possible deal. Unlike in other international markets, in the contemporary bazaar of illegal drugs it is hard to determine who is more disempowered, the buyer or the seller of drugs. For the first time in the history of capitalist expansion, the consumers with the buying power are also disempowered because of what they buy. This addiction-consumption has established an interdependence between societies that consume narcotics and societies that produce them, such that it is hard to determine which of the two is the perpetrator of oppression and which is the victim. The drug trade has dislocated the more traditional relations of polarity between the developed and the underdeveloped parts of the global economy. It may be argued that societies that are poor in capital and technological know-how are making up for this impoverishment through the power of drug trade and narco-terrorism. Thus constituencies such as First World and Third World no longer signify the valency of economic and political power that they did until recently. The sequence in *Salaam Bombay!* where the local pusher, Chillum, sells drugs to an American tourist is illustrative of the fluidity of international geopolitics. However, despite this brief irruption into the text of the dynamism of a more contemporary economic reality, the film conforms to a system of representation that is predicated on an anachronistic specularity, a regime where the Third World is constructed for, and subject to, the gaze of the First World.

Salaam Bombay!, then, despite its "indigenous" nature, produces, processes, and packages a simplistic version of Third World subjectivities such that these may more readily be consumed at First World tables. It is clear evidence that the "indigenity" or otherwise of even a feminist and non-Western ethnographer no longer guarantees the representation's political acuteness. Indeed, cross-cultural borrowing, as indicated in Nair's use of Western codes of cinematic representation, has rendered obsolete the very notion of indigenity. As Haile Gerima indicates, "Under the scrutiny and supervision of neo-colonialism, imposed by the value judgment of the Western cultural barometer, most fall prey to an exhausted convention of Euro-centric cinema language."[5] However, this is not to argue for a return to a more "authentic," Third World system of representation. Rather, to dramatize that the "experience" of the other as mediated and indeed constructed through the discourse of the ethnographer is the precursor of considering new ways of articulating that subjectivity. Paul Willemen has, however, pointed to some of the difficulties involved in such a project:

> A pessimist might argue that the deeper a film is anchored in its social situation, the more likely it is that it will be "secondarized" [i.e., read for its authorial artistry rather than for its political point] when viewed elsewhere or at a different time unless the viewers are prepared to interest themselves precisely in the particularities of the socio-cultural nexus addressed, which is still a very rare occurrence.[6]

Such difficulties force a consideration of the effects of this new articulation in the place of its reception. Critiques of ethnography, whether from anthropology or from cultural studies perspectives, have been preoccupied with an investigation of the ethnography's (non)approximation to the truth of its subject, a preoccupation reflected in the inordinate attention given to the position of the ethnographer with respect to the culture being represented. This has overshadowed consideration of the equally crucial and related problem: that of the effects of the ethnography – as itself a discursive system – in the places of its reception. Even within a text such as *Salaam Bombay!*, which (as I have pointed out) is not deeply anchored in its social situation, ignorance of such factors as Indian/Nepalese economic relations means that even with all the best intentions the Western viewer will not be able to deconstruct the film's representations in the way I have done here. Aparna Sen's film *Parama* dramatizes this difficulty further, as its conscious attempt to reinstate a "third" perspective only runs up against the probability of its noncomprehension outside of Indian circles.

The plot of *Parama* concerns an Indian photographer living in New York who is commissioned by *Life* magazine to do a photo feature on the

Indian housewife, for which project he chooses Parama as his subject. The film foregrounds the photographer's consciousness of his First World audience and his presentation of subjects in terms capable of being read by the readers of *Life* magazine. Further, the photographer sees the Indian woman as unindividuated, selfless, tradition-bound, and disempowered; hence he attempts to empower Parama by convincing her to change her life-style and her ambitions. In other words, Parama comes under the photographer's liberal tutelage. She is schooled in individualism and encouraged to develop her neglected musical talent and express her sexuality, even if that may take her outside marriage. The photographer promises Parama that at the end of her schooling the two of them will travel across America in a small trailer, stopping in small towns where she will give sitar recitals, and he accompany her on the tabla. After preparing this itinerary, which is not merely geographic but also psychological, the photographer leaves India, not to return again. The intimate photographs, however, do return to India. Published in *Life*, they split open the cocoon of secrecy within which the affair had developed. Parama is ostracized by her community and suffers an emotional breakdown.

The use of the photographer figure enables Sen to mount a critique of the ethnographic project: despite the photographer's indigenity, he misconstrues Parama from the very beginning. Indeed, this is conditioned by the very terms of his project—to do a feature on the "Indian housewife"—for the very concept of housewife is alien to the Indian context. In order to speak the language of his audience, that is, readers of *Life* magazine, he superimposes the bourgeois, modernist notion of "housewife" onto a cultural context that is still largely prebourgeois. The housewife is a position in a nuclear family, but the subject that he studies is located in an extended family: two very different structures. The *mise-en-cadre* of the photographer's close-ups of Parama, showing her playing the sitar or adorning herself, not only differentiate her from other women but wrench her apart from her family and her community, both of which are crucial and defining contexts for the Indian woman. If anything, the traditional Indian woman should have been positioned in large family portraits rather than in intimate close-ups. Hence, the film foregrounds the fact that ethnography is never a mere "writing up" of cultural accounts and demonstrates, instead, that the ethnographic intervention tends to disturb and restructure some very delicate and tenuous systems of meaning in the culture under analysis. In this instance, the gaze of the indigenous investigator not only tends to fetishize its subject but also precipitates a psychic and familial crisis in the particular social context. Thus, the photographer's isolation of Parama in close-ups preempts as well as leads to her lonely, defenseless, and confused position in the film's narrative.

The photographer continues his (mis)construal by attempting in his photographs to convey what he sees as the Indian woman's disempowerment. The film, however, contests that reading by showing that power lies with another woman, the mother-in-law, who is the real nucleus of power in the extended, Hindu family. The photographer, having chosen to not explore the mother-in-law's relation to Parama and other women in the family, is unable, therefore, to locate this nucleus of power. Meanwhile, the film itself contains innumerable scenes and situations involving these familial dynamics. Even before we are introduced to Parama, we see the mother-in-law seated on a raised stool and surrounded by other women sitting on the floor, a mise-en-scène that parallels the positioning of Durga (the goddess of power in Hindu mythology), with whose huge and ornate image the film begins. In the opening sequence, the family is engaged in the festivities that celebrate the goddess's annual visit to her devotees. Like the goddess, the mother-in-law is bestowing her favor by coming to live with Parama, the daughter-in-law, who, she tells the other women, takes very good care of her. Thus if the film duplicates the photographer's ironic positioning of Parama against the backdrop of the image of Durga, it is to direct the greater irony at the photographer/ethnographer himself.

The photographs of Parama intended for *Life* magazine are first shown to the viewer in the sequence where the photographer shows a selection of his slides from the war in Lebanon, his encounter with the primitives of Papua and New Guinea, and his sojourn in a secluded Greek monastery to a gathering of Parama's family. What becomes evident in this display and later corroborated by the more intimate poses published in *Life* magazine is that Parama's photographs, like the others in his slide collection, function as "postcards" that pretend to straddle two cultures: the one they capture and the one they are addressed to. Like the trophies of the colonizer, they certify to the "territorial spread" of the traveler, giving him the occasion to say, "I have seen this," "I know this," and, most important, in the context of the photograph of an exotic, denuded woman, "I have possessed this!"[7] The photographer emerges as the "brown sahib," a pseudo-Westerner. Historically, the brown sahib was the native who was educated and trained to be the mediator between the colonial ruler and the native population. His loyalties were and still are to the colonial power. If, as Gayatri Spivak points out, the British had taken upon themselves the responsibility of liberating Indian women from oppression by their own men, the brown sahib—in this case the ethnographer—faithfully carries out the duties of his absent master.[8]

Sen's film enacts the process whereby the Third World subjects are constructed by other Third World subjects for consumption by audiences elsewhere. It does so by positioning the woman in a discursive structure, the extended family, which pulls against the very different structure in which the photographer places her, the "housewife as bourgeois individual."

Parama is ironically positioned against the image of Durga.

Once again, however, questions about the competency of the audience to read this dual construction arise: How can the viewer, unfamiliar with the structure of Hindu families, read this filmic text? Needless to say, such a viewer regards the photographer as an "insider" who has access to physical and cultural spaces that would surely be out of bounds for a foreigner. As a friend of the family, the photographer is expected to follow the honor code; as a guest he can request anything of his hosts and indeed he requests a lot when he asks to photograph a woman of the family. Under these circumstances, the photographer is ideally qualified to be the "indigenous ethnographer," and since the Western audience is eager to gain entry into a hermetically closed field, it is only too willing to access it via the photographer. It is possible, then, that a large section of the Western audience retains the point of view of the photographer and his photographic text as a helpful guide for viewing the filmic text, without doubting the reliability of the ethnographer or the authenticity of his cultural representations. Many Western viewers are apt to miss entirely the ethnographic critique, the "Third" aspect of this film.

When the photographer takes Parama under his liberal tutelage and encourages her self-expression and individuality, postenlightenment audiences are reassured that the ethnographic intervention, rather like the colonial intervention of the British, is justified. Few viewers are likely to set aside their liberal ideologies to acknowledge that individualism is a nonconcept in Hindu philosophy as well as in Indian society. In Hinduism, one's subjectivity is defined by one's *bhumika*, what translates as one's familial and social role. Thus Parama is addressed as daughter-in-law, sister-in-law, wife of a maternal uncle, wife of a paternal uncle, mother, or wife. The photographer is the only one who refuses to recognize her various other roles and insists on calling her by her first name; an act that not only disregards the sanctity of familial relations, but also tears the fine fabric of that society. At another level, this is precisely what his photographic close-ups had done—separated the woman from the context that defines her.

Parama's worst punishment for being unfaithful to her husband is not that she is turned away, deprived of money, or treated cruelly in any physical way. Instead she is relieved of her role as mother, as wife, as daughter-in-law, and even as mistress over the servants of the household. In fact, her image at the end (after she has undergone an operation for a skull injury), dressed in white, with hair cropped close to her head and wearing no jewelry or even the mandatory dot on her forehead, which in traditional India is a sign of a woman's married status, is unmistakably the image of a widow. Represented as a widow, Parama is thus possibly one of the most disempowered of women in Hindu society. Parama subconsciously acknowledges this as her fate when she repeatedly dreams of her widowed aunt who had been kept locked up because she had had an affair with a man after her own husband had died. Ultimately, Parama's breakdown is precipitated by her vision of her aunt escaping from a mental institution and being dragged back by nurses dressed in Western-style skirts, jackets, and caps.

If part of the photographer's project was to give expression to Parama's repressed sexuality, the film shows his error, for in the Indian context this is impossible for the woman. At the end, indigenous patriarchy and an alien system of cure, that is, psychoanalysis (to which considerable social stigma is attached in India), collude to discipline female desire. Both her analyst and her family members try to convince Parama that her extramarital affair has been a disease of the mind. This is an interesting move on the part of Sen. For, although Indian patriarchy earlier refused to acknowledge Western discursive systems such as individualism, self-determination, and sexual liberation, it feels no compunction about using a Western system of cure as a disciplinary technology. What is more, the only way Indian society can safeguard itself against the threat of alien intervention is by making the woman acknowledge her guilt.

Parama disavows all guilt, for she has subconsciously equated her relationship with the photographer to the most celebrated and erotic couple in Hindu mythology, Radha and Krishna. Like Parama, Radha is older than Krishna, she is married to another man, and her relationship with

Krishna never materializes into marriage. Parama unconsciously models herself on Radha by choosing to play *raag Bahar* on the sitar. The musical composition is virtually synonymous with the romance of Radha and Krishna; its mood is passion, its season is spring, and the time most appropriate for its playing is the middle of the night. Earlier in the film, the photographer gains Parama's confidence when he finds for her the leaves that grew outside her window when she was a child. Throughout the film, Parama tries to remember the name of the leaves. At the exact time that she disavows guilt for her sexual encounter the name finally comes to her: *Krishna Pallavi*, the plant of Krishna. Under the influence of the romantic musical composition, reawakened guiltless sexual desire and the mythological stories of Radha and Krishna told to her in her childhood become metonymically related.

It is important to remember here that the aesthetics of classical Indian music as formulated in the *Natya Shastra*[9] are imbued with certain narrative qualities. If Parama shows the subjectivity of the Indian woman virtually torn in the tug-of-war between the native culture, which must maintain its structures of power by resisting foreign intervention, and the ethnography that smuggles in a Western value system, Parama escapes both, to some extent, by constructing herself according to a different discursive system – that of myth. It is the consistent use of variations of the *raag Bahar* in the music score of Parama that signals this mythic level and its implications to the viewer.

However, if competing discursive structures attempt to "produce" Parama in terms congruent with their own needs, only to have her escape in the end to a mythic realm where her sexual "excesses" find legitimate expression, the question again arises about the extent to which viewers, unversed in Hindu mythology and untrained in classical Indian aesthetics, can read this text. If the text has attempted to create a new kind of ethnography by examining competing structures of representation and creating a polyphony of cultural voices, this polyphony is inaudible to large sections of the audience. The filmmaker's difficulty in reaching different sections of her audience, both at home and abroad, is echoed by Teshome Gabriel's comments on the reception of "Third Cinema" in a Western context:

> The difficulty of Third World films of radical social comment for Western interpretation is the result a) of the film's resistance to the dominant conventions of cinema, and b) of the consequence of the Western viewers' loss of being the privileged decoders and ultimate interpreters of meaning.[10]

Although this loss of position is only to be welcomed, the difficult question remains of how then women filmmakers from the Third World can problematize gender relations within their indigenous context and still not fall into the easy dichotomies of self and other that are inherent to the traditional ethnographic venture.

The two films I have considered raise questions of audience reception in a particularly urgent way. Nair's *Salaam Bombay!*, although a film by a woman from the Third World, presents a simplistic and stereotypical version of Bombay and its inhabitants: the irony is that this type of representation is precisely the kind most easily "read" by, and accessible to, mainstream Hollywood audiences. Unfortunately, then, the question of the audience cannot be brushed aside as yet another instance of Eurocentrism precisely because the West as cultural forum "has disproportionate influence." Homi K. Bhabha indicates the paradox of this situation: "An Indian film about the plight of Bombay's pavement-dwellers [*Salaam Bombay!*] wins the Newcastle Festival which then opens up distribution facilities in India. The first searing expose of the Bhopal Disaster is made for Channel Four [a British television station]. . . . An archival article on the important history of neotraditionalism and the 'popular' in Indian cinema sees the light of day in *Framework*."[11]

By contrast, my analysis of Aparna Sen's *Parama* emphasizes the film's deconstruction of the authority of the indigenous ethnographer. Its simultaneous forging of a new kind of ethnography comprises a demonstration of how structures of representation compete to produce the Indian woman within her social context. Within this new kind of ethnographic venture, however, questions of audience reception are again inevitable. As a sophisticated investigation of competing structures of representation—Western ideas of individuality versus the Indian notion of *bhumika;* Western psychoanalysis versus Hindu mythology and the narratives of Indian classical aesthetics—the issue is raised as to who has the competence to "read" this investigation. Certainly not the average cinemagoer untrained in Indian aesthetics or philosophy. It is no wonder then that Aparna Sen has made the film with two different endings. The one seen in conservative Indian constituencies shows Parama "cured," reconciled to her husband and returned to her family after having admitted her guilt in psychoanalysis. The film seen in the West and, I should add, in Westernized Indian circles, shows the woman committed to finding her independence although not knowing how exactly to go about it. Thus, the hegemony of Indian society sees patriarchal order reestablished, and Western society feels gratified that the other has been "civilized." Each has seen what it wanted to see.

If films by women filmmakers from the Third World are being unselfconsciously deployed as ethnographic tools for the representation either of their cultural contexts or of the construction of gender in that culture, I hope my discussion of *Salaam Bombay!* and *Parama* sounds a cautionary note. In the ultimate analysis, Mira Nair's *Salaam Bombay!* fails to challenge the representations of India that already inundate the Western media. And even though Aparna Sen's *Parama*, from the point of view of a Third World woman filmmaker, is a pointed critique of traditional ethnography's inalienable implication with ethnocentrism and patriarchy, it cannot go much further than posing the problem.

Notes

1. A longer version of this paper, "Culturally Specific Texts, Culturally Bound Audiences: Ethnography in the Place of Its Reception," *Journal of Film and Video*, no 43 (Spring-Summer 1991), coauthored with Katrina Irving, discusses in more detail the recent theoretical debates about ethnography.

2. Paul Smith, "Writing, General Knowledge and Postmodern Anthropology," *Discourse* 11 (Summer 1989): 160.

3. James Clifford, introduction to *Writing Culture: The Poetics and Politics of Ethnography*, ed. James Clifford and George E. Marcus (Berkeley: University of California Press, 1986), 9.

4. Trinh T. Minh-ha, "Introduction," *Discourse* 8 (1987): 3.

5. Haile Gerima, "Triangular Cinema, Breaking Toys, and Dinknesh vs. Lucy," in *Questions of Third Cinema* ed. Jim Pines and Paul Willemen (London: British Film Institute, 1989), 77.

6. Paul Willemen, "The Third Cinema Question: Notes and Reflections," in *Questions of Third Cinema*, 9.

7. Malek Alloula, *The Colonial Harem* (Minneapolis: University of Minnesota Press, 1986), 4.

8. Gayatri Spivak, quoted by Barbara Harlow in the introduction to *The Colonial Harem*, xviii.

9. The sacred book of Hinduism that deals with Sanskrit aesthetics.

10. Teshome Gabriel, "Toward a Critical Theory of Third World Films," in *Questions of Third Cinema*, 38–39.

11. Homi K. Bhabha, "The Commitment to Theory," in *Questions of Third Cinema*, 113.

Note: *Parama* is available from Atlantic Video and *Salaam Bombay!* from October Films. See distributors' list.

Portrait(s) of Teresa:
Gender Politics and the Reluctant Revival of Melodrama in Cuban Film

Julianne Burton-Carvajal

> The social presence of a woman is different in kind from that of a
> man. . . . Men act and women appear. Men look at women. Women
> watch themselves being looked at. This determines not only most rela-
> tions between men and women but also the relation of women to
> themselves. [Women turn themselves] into an object – and most partic-
> ularly an object of vision: a sight.
>
> *– John Berger,* Ways of Seeing

> Men are men and women are women, and even Fidel can't change
> that!
>
> *(Maternal wisdom from* Portrait of Teresa)

The Cuban Image, Michael Chanan's unmatched account of film in Cuba
before and particularly after the rise of Fidel Castro, ends with a puzzling
omission. Since his chosen chronological frame takes his account through
the end of the 1970s, one can't help but wonder why Chanan excludes *Portrait of Teresa* (Pastor Vega, 1979), arguably the most significant film of
that period, preferring instead to conclude his account with Sara Gómez's
One Way or Another, which was completed in 1975, though not released
until the end of the decade. Perhaps Chanan's omission is a tacit acknowledgement that *Portrait of Teresa* represents a turning point in
Cuban filmmaking, taking earlier themes to their apparent limit and exem-
plifying the generic and stylistic shifts that would characterize Cuban
filmmaking in the subsequent decade.

In one sense, *Portrait of Teresa* can be viewed as a de facto sequel to
part III of Humberto Solás's monumental epic *Lucía* (1969), in its resolute
and courageous depiction of the strains and contradictions of personal life
in proletarian Cuba nearly two decades after the third Lucía acquired
literacy and, with it, a sense of her own autonomy. Despite the disconcert-
ing duplication of actor Adolfo Llauradó, who plays the third Lucía's husband, Tomás, as a veritable dinosaur of machismo, and then reappears in
an only marginally advanced guise as Teresa's husband, followers of
Cuban cinema would have to wait more than a decade for another feature
film willing to pose issues of gender (in)equality in such a candid and un-

compromising manner. If *Lucía* put women's experience at the center of processes of historical change to a degree that had not been seen before in Cuban film, and if *Memories of Underdevelopment* (Tomás Gutiérrez Alea, 1969) offers a still unmatched portrayal of the predatory sexuality exemplified by too many privileged males in the 1960s, and if Sara Gómez's *One Way or Another* began to suggest the social and personal advantages of a more introspective, feminine-influenced masculinity, *Portrait of Teresa* still represents a high point in Cuban cinema's attempt to address if not redress gender inequity.

Neither Vega's own subsequent *Habanera* (1984) nor Tomás Gutiérrez Alea's, *Up to a Certain Point* (1983), made in open homage to Gómez's *One Way or Another*, succeeds in advancing the scope of the gender debate as aired in Cuba. In fact, both subsequent films seem to represent a step backward in terms of their gender politics. Although the marital breakup in *Habanera* (which features the same pair of actors as *Portrait of Teresa*) is again occasioned by the husband's infidelity and attempt to lead a double life, his behavior is called even less to account than in the earlier domestic (melo)drama. The class shift in the later film, the couple's status as professional rather than working class, is the pretext for the elaboration of a psychoanalytic discourse that focuses on almost exclusively feminine neuroses. The overall effect, disconcertingly, is of a kind of Cuban "yuppie" film in which the social, historical, and political contexts are almost completely subsumed by claustrophobic and obsessive individual angst. *Up to a Certain Point*, in which the plot again revolves around an extramarital and this time also cross-class affair, reverts to a treatment of the working-class female as "other," removing her at the end of the film to a distant city through the (hackneyed) poetic symbolism of a bird in flight. Because both of these later features make such a show of their "good intentions" in the gender department, their ultimate inability to advance the discourse is particularly striking, retrospectively enhancing the significance of *Portrait of Teresa* as the high point in the (predominantly heterosexual, predominantly male-authored) national cinematic exploration of gender issues. An alternative direction, allowing for a more profound exploration of female subjectivity, did not make itself evident until the 1990 release of *Mujer transparente*, a compilation of five short features directed primarily but not exclusively by women under the general supervision of Humberto Solás.

Pastor Vega began making documentaries in 1961.[1] *Portrait of Teresa* was his first feature-length fictional film.[2] His documentary formation suggests that he would not take a word such as *portrait* lightly. The word implies a passive (or at least stationary) subject, a certain possessiveness of vision, a simultaneous interpretation and appropriation. It presupposes a portraitist and simultaneously implicates an undefined spectator.

More fluid than a depiction in poetry or prose, a static photograph or oil painting, a filmed "portrait" is a dynamized assembly of scenes and events in which the nominal subject is not always present or, if present, is not always the primary focus. What the film "says" at the level of dialogue and action constitutes only one stratum of meaning – a stratum always open to differing interpretations. What is omitted from the story is potentially as significant as what is included. Additional and potentially conflicting meanings are embedded in the myriad decisions that determine style and form. The various aspects of the film's *facture* that combine to compose the "portrait" in question also constitute a kind of practice, encoding in a more layered manner the explicit themes of the film: in this case, the theory, practice, and ideology of sex/gender relationships in a society attempting socialist transformation – a society that was in fact enjoying what would retrospectively prove to be its high point in terms of economic and political achievement at the particular historical juncture during which *Portrait of Teresa* is set (the film was both set and shot in 1978).

The opening and closing shots bracket the film with two very different still portraits of Teresa. The precredit sequence opens with a slow track-in on a woman and children along a cement promenade with the ocean as backdrop. Still in long-shot, the camera pans with the kids as they move toward a refreshment stand, then cuts to a man readying a viewfinder camera. Looking up, he calls, "Teresa!" The camera cuts to a close-up of her from the back, looking seaward. She instantly turns her head in response to her husband's call, solemn and only mildly startled. Her flowing black hair, tousled by the wind and her own abrupt movement, partially conceals her features. The frame freezes as the film's title appears superimposed on this image.

The film ends with another freeze-frame portrait of Teresa, again in the open air. By this time, the family unit has been rent asunder by Teresa's dual rejection of the "double shift" (full-time responsibilities at work with no concomitant modification of household responsibilities) and the double standard. The context is not a weekend family outing but the pedestrian-congested workaday streets of downtown Havana. Teresa's luxuriant hair, established from the film's opening as an emblem of her sexuality, is here totally concealed under a white silk scarf tied Afro-Cuban style around her head. The transition from loud street music whose lyrics parody the life she is leaving behind ("Te-re-sa, sweep the floor! Te-re-sa! Te-re-sa!") to more reflexive instrumental strains that echo the opening music prepares us for a final shot of her, purposeful and confident, in marked contrast to the husband who, though once in control, now tracks her at a distance, disoriented and unsure. As Teresa walks resolutely toward the camera, the background crowd disperses and goes increasingly out of focus until her head dominates center screen and, echoing the opening sequence, the frame freezes the final time.

Her husband's initial portrait stripped her of her social context, silhouetting her against sky and sea in a decontextualizing, romantic image. The final portrait, in contrast, isolates her against a sea of faces, retaining her social context while particularizing her within it. Her image is not being "captured" by her husband as a "portrait of the eternal female, privatized, a glamour-magazine cliché stripped of her social context to enhance her desirability."[3] No longer the passive, stationary subject, she is being instantaneously (and only temporarily) "frozen" in her resolute movement forward by *another* portraitist—invisible, omniscient—who works in a more dynamic medium. It is significant that in this final freeze-frame Teresa does not face the camera head-on as she did in the opening shot but looks off to one side. No longer looking at herself being looked at, she has ceased to be defined by the "vision" of husband, parent, or social convention.

Framed by these two "snapshots" is a more dynamic portrait, constituted by the detailed depiction of Teresa's life with family, friends, and fellow workers. The film's accessible, quasi-documentary style, compelling acting, and candid presentation of marital strains and the fits and starts of change when personal consciousness lags behind social policy elicited enthusiastic popular response in Cuba and abroad. Reactions in Cuba, though impassioned, were not uniformly positive. *Portrait of Teresa* reportedly catalyzed countless domestic crises and unleashed weeks of heated debate in newspapers and magazines, on radio, television, and street corners. Half the adult population in Havana, the setting of the film, had seen the movie within the first six weeks of its release and, apparently, few viewers declined to take sides in the confrontation between "sacred" family tradition and women's need for self-realization.

During the preceding decade, Cuban leaders had given priority to the "revolution within the revolution," attempting to educate for and legislate sexual equality in the home as well as the workplace, in the bedroom as well as the kitchen. The Cuban Family Code, promulgated in 1974 after widespread public discussion and debate, was the spearhead of this effort, requiring equal participation by both partners in domestic chores and child rearing, and stipulating that women are entitled to the same sexual prerogatives as men. Although equality can be formally legislated, the legislation obviously cannot be effectively enforced in the most private arena of personal life, where change, when it occurs, is always fragmentary, disorganized, and uneven. *Portrait of Teresa* reduces the scale of that nationwide campaign to the more intimate proportions of a single household, a single couple, without abstracting them from the larger social context in which they live and work.

Although the components of Teresa's personal crisis and the setting in which it is played out are carefully established, although the portrait is intimate enough to reveal both bedroom battles and the relentless tedium of her morning housework, Teresa seems somehow elusive. Essentially limited to reacting rather than acting on her own initiative and accessible to us only through overt response rather than through inner thoughts, dreams, or fantasies, Teresa remains partially inscrutable—just as certain crucial components of her life remain unknown. Repeated close-ups of her—pensive, withdrawn, dejected—bear the burden of communicating her subjectivity and inner struggle.

There is another reason why the portrait of Teresa seems strangely incomplete. The title of the film is arguably a telling misnomer. Discussing issues of gender (in)equality with Cubans of both sexes on several occasions during the period represented in the film, I was struck by the consistency of their insistence that the politics of sexuality do not divide into women's issues and men's. Instead they expressed the belief that the lowest common social denominator is not one sex "abstracted" from the other but both sexes together as the basic interactional unit: *la pareja*, the heterosexual couple. Despite its title, Vega's film seems to be in fact not so much a challenge to as a validation of this position. Although it claims to present a portrait of Teresa, what the film actually constructs is a portrait of a *couple*, Teresa *and* Ramón—or at best a portrait of Teresa *in terms of* her relationship to Ramón, very much as *Lucía*, a decade earlier, had chosen to draw its female characters in relation to one male with whom they chose to partner. This would explain why *Portrait of Teresa* follows the events of Ramón's work and personal life as closely as it does Teresa's. It can even be argued that the film presents *more* details of Ramón's life, since we witness the inception, development, and decline of his extramarital affair, whereas Teresa's possible intimacy with coworker Tomás constitutes the biggest enigma of the film. Instead of following Teresa's subsequent development as an autonomous being, the film ends with the end of the marital relationship. On the one hand, this vested interest in a nonexclusionary focus testifies to an admirable recognition of interpersonal dialectics, while on the other it privileges nuclear, heterosexual units and deflects criticism directed at the male gender. As long as social inequities guarantee that women have a greater stake in self-realization within the *pareja* than men, this formulation will continue to obfuscate as much as it illuminates. The final rift between Teresa and Ramón is provoked precisely by the latter's inability to grasp, much less respond adequately to, Teresa's repeated query, referring to his infidelity, "What if I had done the same thing?"

The more one interrogates Teresa's portrayal, the more disquieting omissions, contradictions, and biases come to light. Teresa's decision to reject the reconciliation proposed by Ramón hinges on two factors: her determination to challenge the double standard by turning the tables on traditional sexual mores that encourage philandering in the male while demanding charity as well as chastity from the female and the "support" she says she has derived from friends during the crisis. Viewers are left somewhat puzzled about which friends she is referring to in this conversation with her cousin Charo since she seems in fact extremely isolated throughout the film.[4]

When her friend Sonia, visiting Teresa at home, tells her, "Not everyone has your luck, with a husband who loves you and lends a hand," Teresa does nothing to counter this misrepresentation of her "ideal" marriage, preferring to change the subject and suffer the painful irony in silence. Bernal, plant manager and benevolent father figure, is removed and patronizing. More of a counselor than a genuine friend, he is capable of cutting off Teresa's account of her problems in the service of "more important" business. Both her mother and her divorced cousin Charo advocate adherence to the double standard that Teresa is determined to reject, thus intensifying her isolation. After her separation from Ramón she is also narratively severed from her three sons, who, though they remain with her, subsequently appear in the film only when motivated by the imminent or actual presence of their father.

Only one candidate remains to provide the friendship that sustains Teresa: Tomás, her coworker and collaborator in organizing the amateur dance group of textile workers that is the locus of her political activity and creative energy and (because of the long hours it involves) the initial bone of marital contention. His devotion is conveyed most tellingly by a silent vigil he keeps beside the depressed, nearly catatonic Teresa on a park bench. There are only two indications that their friendship entails more than political dedication, parallel creative interests, and platonic camaraderie: a shared cigarette at a dance rehearsal and, more important, Tomás's reaction when Teresa informs him of their group's invitation to perform in national competition. "Today I *can* kiss you, can't I?" he asks confidently, implying a prior history of forestalled attempts and suggesting that from his point of view *she* is the real prize to be won by this collective effort. In striking contrast to the explicit scenes of Ramón and his girlfriend trysting on the beach or on her parents' brocade couch, narrative ellipses "edit out" the exact nature of Teresa's relationship to Tomás. It is not inconsequential that this ellipsis replicates the social attitude that the film purportedly criticizes: that extramarital sexual intimacy is tolerable, even encouraged, for men but inconceivable for women.[5]

It is also troubling to note that the stimulation and satisfaction Teresa derives from her "extracurricular" work are largely referred to rather than represented. The locker-room argument over the needles, which be-

gins the film, is clearly not an example of the charismatic leadership qualities that the avuncular Bernal, in a later sequence, attributes to Teresa.
Here she bitterly and aggressively denounces her coworker for putting
commitments to friends and family above her obligations to the collective
cultural effort. The next scenes show Teresa at work fitting a costume. Instead of encouragement or praise, her efforts are met with friendly deri-
sion; the general consensus is that the costume looks ridiculous. Later
Tomás, presumably her coequal in authority, chides Teresa for disrupting
his rehearsals with *her* fittings.

Although we repeatedly see her sullen, despondent, desperate on camera, scenes that contribute to the growth of Teresa's self-esteem are comparatively few. News of the dance group's invitation to perform in national
competition is undercut by Tomás's inappropriate response and counter-
balanced by the jubilant celebration at the TV technicians' school where
Ramón, having won a prized post in Santiago, is awarded his diploma.
Teresa's television appearance after her dance group wins the competition
should be her crowning triumph. Yet the unctuous emcee (played without
prompting by TV personality German Pinelli) manages to rob her of this
satisfaction by turning the appearance into a pretext for his own ludicrous
sexism. All substantive questions are directed to Tomás, while Teresa is
politely relegated to the status of decorative object of contemplation, gal-
lantry, and, finally, suspicion: shouldn't the husband of such an attractive
woman be on his guard? Although the sequence serves a progressive function in the critique of the mass media, which is one of the dominant themes
of the film, it also reinforces the image of Teresa as relatively passive and
defenseless outside the domestic sphere. In all these sequences, the activities that Teresa associates with her self-realization are consistently belit-
tled or depicted as laced with tension and strain rather than deserved
satisfactions.

Although the film calls into question both the "double day" and the double standard, its structure implies an artificial separation between the two.
Once Teresa and Ramón have separated, the focus shifts from questions
of the double day to the morality of women's sexual freedom. The suggestion, however guarded, that Teresa's problems could be solved by relating
to another, more "evolved" man poses an individual, private solution to
what is clearly a social as much as a personal problem.

Except for the mother-in-law's exclamation "Thank God you have all
boys!" the film circumvents the issue of the socialization of the next generation. Its unchallenged affirmation of *mother-right* and the marked and disproportionate separation of labor in parenting implicitly condone the perpetuation of traditional sex/gender dynamics. The very existence of a film
such as this one politicizes the issues of domestic life, but except for one
workers' assembly where poor child-care facilities are discussed as a public

problem, the forum for addressing issues of sexual equality *within the film* remains the private, domestic sphere.

Ironically, Teresa's work at home, on the job, and as a political activist in the cultural sphere all vindicate the ancient Hispanic adage "For the woman, needle and thread." She is a textile worker by day, a costume designer and seamstress after hours. One of the most overdetermined images of her domestic entrapment has her, once again, at her sewing machine, framed through the vertical bars of her living room window. In the first line of dialogue, Teresa asks a coworker, "Did you bring the needles?" It seems that Teresa's will to "find herself" inevitably entails the "womanly" emblems of needle and thread.

Ramón's work is the vehicle that allows Vega to offer the intimate glimpses into contemporary Cuban domestic life, which are one of the film's most innovative aspects. His job as a TV repairman offers him mobility, relative independence, and broad social exposure. Teresa's work, voluntary as well as salaried, keeps her within the walls of the textile plant. Without the interest in documenting varieties of domestic life, Ramón might well have been scripted as a factory or construction worker, but it is hard to imagine Teresa having been assigned a job that would give her a mobility similar to Ramón's.

Although Ramón makes certain gestures toward lending Teresa a hand around the house (he clears his plate from the table in one sequence, takes the kids off to school in another), actually performing "woman's work" seems, in the view of both spouses, altogether outside his role. When his mother gives him instructions for making dinner, he says he'll "just pick up a bite on the street." When Teresa lets him know that if he walks out the door, he's leaving for good, she signals the break by tearing his clothes out of the closet and threatening to throw them out the front door. "Let *another woman* wash these for you!" she cries, missing the chance to challenge him to do his own laundry and indicating how deeply ingrained concepts of "women's work" are in *both* sexes.

These problems of characterization and concept must be balanced against the film's bold initiative and substantial achievements. *Portrait of Teresa* adopts a critical stance toward contemporary Cuban society, displaying the kind of refreshing candor that characterized the most intriguing Cuban films of the 1960s and '70s. Here the critical commentary ranges from good-humored barbs (a man jostled off an overflowing bus, an argument over equivalences at the seaside beer stand, power failures and poor telephone connections) to serious and perhaps even urgent warning signs of social malaise (the round-the-clock dependency on cigarettes, the pervasive domestic discord and psychological stress in a cultural setting where women as well as men are portrayed as extremely guarded despite their putative gregariousness, and the pointed references to wife battering).

When asked about the genesis of the film, Vega cites a psychological study done by the Academy of Sciences on the crisis of traditional (pre-Socialist) family structures in Socialist Cuba.

As suggested earlier, the film reserves the brunt of its criticism for the mass media—women's magazines of superficial scope, "schlocky" popular music (domestic or imported), and, in particular, television. Denunciation of the latter's role as pacifier and mindless escape hatch is crystallized in the numerous sequences that expose that medium's continuing cultivation of archaic female stereotypes in equally "archaic" melodramatic forms. Early in the film, Teresa arrives home from a late rehearsal to find two neighbor women watching TV in her living room while Ramón, feeling neglected and resentful, does a slow burn in the bedroom. The voice-over strains of the tearjerker—"I am going to confront you with all the strength of my soul!"—are in explicit contrast to the suppressed passions of the barely deflected bedroom confrontation. In a later scene, Ramón, waiting for payment, is forced to watch with a mesmerized housewife while an actress in early-nineteenth-century frills gushes over her erring lover's sagacity in winning her forgiveness by offering "una sencilla rosa." When Ramón later makes the same peace offering to Teresa, our twentieth-century heroine tosses the flower out the window in exasperation and disgust.

In its survey of contemporary Cuban home life, *Portrait of Teresa* offers a revealing cross-section of kinds and classes of Cuban housing and family structure: the modest but cheerful bungalows of Teresa and Ramón's neighborhood, the modern high-rise apartment blocks of Alamar, the spacious colonial patio of Teresa's mother's house, the decrepit shack of the inhospitable man with his arm in a cast, the plush appointments and generous proportions of the nineteenth-century mansion where Ramón's girlfriend lives with her parents. A persistent housing shortage encourages shared housing: Teresa's mother has taken in her divorced niece and her children, apparently in exchange for housekeeping services; after walking out on Teresa, Ramón moves back in with his mother.

The stylistic eclecticism and experimental mixture of modalities that characterize earlier Cuban films as thematically and formally diverse as *Memories of Underdevelopment, The First Charge of the Machete, Bay of Pigs,* and *One Way or Another* have only distant echoes here in the incorporation of the "rival" medium, television. The formal resonance of these now-classic films is here replaced by a system of primarily verbal resonances. The script is subtly structured by repetitions and transformative echoes of past exchanges. The effect is to suggest a kind of closed world while at the same time affirming the possibility of transformative regeneration of meaning when the same phrases are echoed in a new context.

After she defiantly drops the unwashed dinner dishes in the trash can, Ramón asks Teresa in solicitous tones, "What has happened to you?" Unwilling to take exclusive responsibility for her predicament, she immediately fires the question back at him. After their separation, Ramón drops in unexpectedly as Teresa and their eldest son are dancing to the music of a TV show. Both use the same phrase—"It just came to me all of a sudden, right Tony?"—to conceal their real motives (for her dancing and his visit) from one another. When Ramón expresses his desire for her, Teresa becomes sullenly coquettish, defiantly hurling another of his previous embittered accusations back at him with each advance he makes.

In their culminating exchange, which begins in a cafeteria and ends, pointedly, in front of a bridal shop, Teresa claims the right to be as unforgiving of his infidelity as he would be of hers. She has to ask half a dozen times what he would do if the tables were turned; from his obtuse point of view, she seems to be positing the inconceivable. Echoing the dual morality espoused earlier by Teresa's cousin, her mother, and his own, Tomás insists, "It is not the same. Things are different for a man. It is never the same." Teresa repeats his phrase, transforming it into a question, before turning on her heel and walking out of the cafeteria. Increasingly alarmed as the import of her suggestion begins to dawn on him, Ramón chases her down the street and, in front of mannequins in coming-out dresses and wedding gowns, demands, "Tell me the truth! What have you done, Teresa?" In one final repetition, she reminds him firmly before she disappears into the crowd, "Remember, it's not the same." The tables are turned on the level of discourse as well as social convention.

The foregoing arguments suggest that the gender ideology expressed in *Portrait of Teresa* is a two-edged sword or—"tailoring" the metaphor to the symbol-system of the film—a needle with an eye on each end. Explicitly and implicitly, *Portrait of Teresa* exposes all the contradictions of sexual politics in Cuba, including the potential inadequacy of "an eye for an eye" as a strategy for righting traditional imbalances between the sexes.

Portrait of Teresa conforms to the classic pattern that permeates Western visual culture from Renaissance painting to contemporary advertising and pornography: the erotic identification of the male spectator is facilitated by the mode of presentation of the female protagonist and further enhanced by the comparative unworthiness of her mate or suitor. In this sense, reconsidering the connotations of the film's title, *Portrait of Teresa* is both a portrayal of a relationship in dissolution and a "portrait" of a particular and yet also intentionally "typical" woman (in the Marxian sense) that replicates traditional appeals to the appropriative instincts of an implicit male spectator at least as much as it challenges them. Yet this implicit complicity with a male spectator is probably less obvious and more constructive in the Cuban context. It can, in fact, be viewed as a subtle form of subversion of sexist attitudes, since on the terms established by the film, an erotic identification with Teresa entails both an acceptance of her candid deglamorization and a concomitant reconsideration of those prized masculine traits to which Ramón–a "progressive" man by Cuban standards–so tenaciously clings.

The ending of the film also strikes a potentially subversive chord, in the context of sexual politics in Cuba. It offers an inspiring confirmation–*not* of the centrality of *la problemática de la pareja*–but of one woman's need and determination to make it on her own. Her final resolve and newfound independence constitute a strong statement in the context of contemporary Cuban sexual politics–a statement that is only slightly undercut by the viewer's uncertainty as to whether or not she has already constituted herself as part of another couple.

Portrait of Teresa signals a significant shift in postrevolutionary Cuban cinematic discourse. With this film, the melodramatic mode, so ardently rejected by those who wished to create a genuinely "revolutionary" cinema,[6] resurfaces. If the references to melodrama appear at first to be ironic or parodistic, embedded as they are in a filmmaker's complacent critique of television, this ironic dimension barely conceals the film's own recourse to melodramatic modalities, a recourse that, retrospectively, may seem to be driven by incipient frustrations in the sociopolitical as well as interpersonal spheres.

Perhaps the principal achievement of the movement that became known as the New Latin American cinema, always the recipient of broad support from Cuban cultural institutions, was the fusion of documentary and fictional modalities in ways that posed profound formal and epistemological challenges.[7] Surely the Cuban filmmakers, with their early and enduring emphasis on documentary, were central to this tendency. One might argue, in fact, that the primacy accorded to documentary occluded melodrama in Cuban cinematic discourse of the 1960s and 1970s, and that, by the end of the latter decade, that is, twenty years into the revolution, the kinds of personal and political tensions that could not effectively be addressed in the genre-defying modes initially favored by the members of the Cuban Film Institute (ICAIC)–or, for that matter, in the society at large–began to surface as melodramatic expression even through the vehicle of a film that ostensibly–perhaps defensively–satirized melodramatic forms. In an unpublished article on political melodrama and Jesús Díaz's *Lejanía* (*The Parting of the Ways*, 1985) in which she reconsiders the subversive potential of melodrama in the dual context of Western theoretical constructions and Cuban cinematic practice, S. Travis Silcox

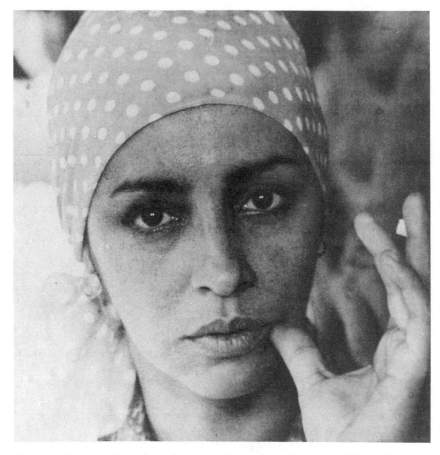

A portrait of actress Daysi Granados during the shooting of *Portrait of Teresa*. Production still courtesy of Cinema Guild.

writes, "It seems logical that dramatic and literary representations from embattled and marginalized countries, like Cuba, would move toward the excess and solace of the melodramatic mode." Her work, which builds upon writings by Ana López and Carlos Monsiváis as well as by Peter Brook, Christine Gledhill, and Janice Radway, emphasizes the oscillation inherent in melodramatic forms, which can both defuse sites of conflict and reinscribe traditional values while at the same time preparing viewers to cope more effectively with actual processes of social change.

Reconsidered more than a decade later, *Portrait of Teresa* retains both much of its appeal and much of its initial importance because it links two diverse moments—and, ultimately, two divergent philosophies—of Cuban and Latin-American filmmaking. *Portrait of Teresa* leaves behind the kind of deconstructive experimentation with cinematic form that prevailed up through *One Way or Another* and *The Other Francisco* (Sergio Giral, 1975), instead referring quite openly to the allure of the once-disparaged "perfect cinema" of Hollywood-style production values and sunset-bathed television commercials. Focusing on contemporary domestic issues in a home-and-workplace setting, and invoking individual neurosis and depression as the product of recalcitrant social problems, the film both perpetuates and challenges—in the figure of shop boss Bernal—the embracing of paternalistic authority so pervasive in Cuban cinema that even Sara Gómez's feature, as celebrated by Western feminists, could not or would not eschew it. Finally, parodying television's reliance on "outdated" melodramatic forms, *Portrait of Teresa* rather slyly revives the domestic melodrama, transforming it into an engine of political controversy.

Notes

1. These include *Men of the Cane Fields* (1965), *The Song of the Tourist* (1967), *Viva la República* (1972), *Panama: The Fifth Frontier* (1974). The medium-length *De la guerra americana* (*Of the American War*, 1969) is an early attempt at fictional filmmaking.

2. The project of assessing *Portrait of Teresa* by examining precisely what kind of portrait it constitutes takes on an added dimension in light of the fact that the subject of director Vega's "portrait" (Daysi Granados as Teresa) is, offscreen, his wife. (The three boys in the film are the couple's own.)

3. B. Ruby Rich, "*Portrait of Teresa*," *Jump Cut*, no. 2 (May 1980).

4. The absence of any reference to an organized women's movement is striking, since one of the major concerns of the twenty-year-old Federación de Mujeres Cubanas (FMC) has been to bring women into the work force and help them cope with the problems that arise from their full "integration" into society.

5. According to Vega, "If we'd made it definite that she'd had an affair, [Cuban] viewers would simply have said she deserved what she got. They're still too attached to traditional attitudes when it comes to extramarital sex. And we wanted people to hear *all* of what Teresa says, not just what she says about sex" (taken from background sheet on *Portrait of Teresa*, distributed by Unifilm).

6. The dismissive, censorious attitude that characterized Enrique Colina and Daniel Díaz Torre's "Ideología del melodrama en el viejo cine latinoamericano" (*Cine cubano*, 1972) still prevails in recent debates such as those conducted around the 1930s-'40s retrospective at the 1991 Havana film festival.

7. See part III of my *The Social Documentary in Latin America* (Pittsburgh, Penn.: University of Pittsburgh Press, 1990).

Rehearsing Feminism: Women/History in *The Life and Times of Rosie the Riveter* and *Swing Shift*

Mimi White

The Life and Times of Rosie the Riveter (1980) and *Swing Shift* (1983) both deal with women's experience during World War II, a period that saw an unprecedented number of women entering the work force and a temporary change in the sexual division of labor as women were recruited for work in a wide range of industries. One of the films is an independently produced documentary, the other a Hollywood fictional narrative. In light of their respective modes of production one might expect the films to be quite different. However, while they are by no means identical, they significantly adopt a similar perspective on the events they treat.

The films share a common reference period, focusing on the "unusual" positions and opportunities available to women during the war, and are hardly singular in turning attention to women working in World War II. On the contrary, there exists a vast body of material dealing with the same events in the same period, constituting an emergent historical tradition.[1] In this context the films extend a body of discourse, elaborating on the investigation of a specific aspect of women's past in a popular medium. Both films evince an awareness of the preoccupations of this "tradition," signaling their own status as historical narratives in a number of ways.

The signs of history—marker dates, period documents, and so forth—are incorporated in both films to authenticate the narratives of working women. Stylistically and narrationally this material identifies the narrativized events as "past" and as "having really happened." The radio

318

broadcast announcing the Japanese attack on Pearl Harbor and the official entry of the United States into World War II is replayed in both films. *Rosie the Riveter* uses a variety of archival footage, newspaper headlines, and popular songs from the period. *Swing Shift* offers glimpses of period film clips and restages/rewrites material from the newsreels as dramatic scenes. The inclusion of this sort of archival material does not simply serve as a neutral sign of authenticity and pastness. Rather, in both films it is seen to construct and address a representation of "woman," a representation subsequently confirmed and/or belied by the films' respective heroines.

With their connections to an extrafilmic body of historical discourse and use of period media documents as constructions of a specific historical (narrative) setting, the films cannot escape the function of metatexts: they construct their own images and meanings in and for a present of production as they incorporate and comment on images and meanings cited from the past. The narratives they construct and positions they make possible (for viewers and for understanding events of the past) are inevitably caught up in preexisting networks of discourse. And while their narrative strategies are very different, the narrational perspectives engaged in the confrontation between past and present in both films – a historical perspective and the founding terms of narrativization – are remarkably similar.

In this context an examination of these particular contemporary texts (contemporary with us, with the production of this paper) may help clarify issues of historical writing and rewriting specifically with regard to questions of women's history and feminist history (not always, or necessarily, the same thing). The analysis proceeds from the assumption that a closer look at *Rosie the Riveter* and *Swing Shift* will help focus on issues that arise from the conjunction of history, cinema, and feminism.

The Life and Times of Rosie the Riveter alternates between period documents and interviews conducted in the film's "present" with five women (three black, two white) who worked in various branches of the war industry between 1942 and 1945.[2] The period footage is compiled from an array of sources; this is apparent in the editing and confirmed by the film's end titles with its long list of archival sources. But only a few of the clips are specifically identified in the film. Otherwise, in the absence of differentiation, the film suggests that the sources are equivalent, conveying in concert the unified self-image of a culture entreating women to enter the "silent army" of defense plant workers; offering a rosy view of the nature and conditions of this work; and finally urging women to cede their jobs to returning veterans and to resume more appropriate feminine roles as wives and mothers.

The interviews supplement this "official" representation of women's work and working women as it is compiled in the film from period sources. Embedded in the traditions of oral history and women's documentary filmmaking,[3] they give a voice to individuals and views repressed in the more conventional channels of information dissemination. Through the representation of individuals of the silent army we get an alternative account of the period, one that undermines the authority, truth, and unity carried by the period footage. For example, a newsreel offers a picture of middle-class housewives sacrificing afternoon card gamees to enter the work force out of a sense of patriotic duty. But all five of the women in the interviews speak of working before and after the war, needing the income to support their families, of work as economic necessity. In another period documentary a factory official, the (female) Supervisor of Women Employees, describes the workplace as safer than the home. We then hear stories from the women in the interviews of dangerous working conditions and accidents in the factories. A newsreel clip on day-care facilities that allow mothers to work without worrying about their children is followed by tales of women regretfully leaving their children with parents in another state, or sending them to boarding school.

Two discourses thus confront each other, an array of period documents, and an array of contemporary narratives about the past. They speak of the same period and the same events in an asymmetrical opposition. The period documents come to be seen as a cultural mythology, manipulative fantasy, when filtered through the individual experiences recounted by the women in the interviews. And each range of discourse, although plural in sources (a variety of archival footage, a variety of individual stories) is seen as basically unified in its diversity. The film's "multiple" discourse is a function of this confrontation between two relatively unified bodies of discourse. If no "one" can speak/represent the truth of history, or represent the whole picture, the film's power comes from its ability to compile or assemble an adequate series of representations to construct two discrete poles of coherence and unity.

We are given on the one hand the past's version of its own truth or, more appropriately, a contemporary version of the past's self-representation in the film's compilation of archival footage. On the other hand the interviews give us a presumably superior truth in the "real working women" who tell us their stories. But these individual narratives are all retrospective accounts, conveying attitudes toward and memories of the period from a distance of thirty-odd years. And they are offered as a counter to the traditional historical documentation without questioning that the perspectives in the present of recounting may only be available as a present truth about the past. Indeed the very possibility of expressibility may be a function of this temporal distance.

For example, near the end of the film one of the women describes the postwar shift in women's status. The society, she says, wanted babies and women who were psychologically prepared to assume this reproductive function. "We all wanted babies, and that's okay. But we gave up everything for that. We gave up everything." This expression of loss stands in stark contrast to the previous discussion of wartime work as providing expanded personal and economic opportunities for women. But the clear terms of a tradeoff—babies or everything, domestic roles or the new woman, reproduction or production—are recognized from the perspective of the seventies. This expression of a decisive either/or situation, confronting women individually and collectively, caps off the film's examination of women's experience during the war with an air of nostalgia: lost opportunity, crushed hopes, wrong choices. But such a perception is definitive only from the vantage of retrospection; a decisive choice or final loss can be identified only in relation to a closed sequence of events.

This is not to challenge the sincerity of the stories we hear, or the genuineness of the women's lived/remembered experience. Rather, the key issue is how the film implements these stories in contrast to the period documents without questioning or examining their disparate determinations. The film requires temporal distance as the founding condition of its own discourse. Indeed, the differentiation of past from present, the assertion of temporal demarcation to define this gap, is the a priori and effectivity of historical discourse. As Michel de Certeau explains, in the very process of addressing the past, history signals a differential relation between past and present that in turn functions to constitute a social-historical identity:

> If on the one hand history functions by expressing the position of one generation in relation to previous ones by saying: "I am not that," it always affects this affirmation with a no less dangerous complement which makes a society avow: "I am other than I want and determined by that which I deny." It attests to an autonomy and a dependence whose proportions vary according to the social milieux and political situations where it is elaborated.[4]

The identity constructed through the operations of history is necessarily contradictory; it emerges and is defined on the basis of a past that is simultaneously excluded and preserved. This act of demarcation/affiliation is carried out on the basis of representations that mediate past and present. (The representations are *in* the present but not *of* the present.) In the case of *Rosie the Riveter* it is precisely this distance that enables the compilation of archival source footage and that determines that the women speak as they do. But the film also represses this distance as an active principle informing its structure.

More precisely, the implication of a break, a boundary, of terms of demarcation, is figured in the opposition between two temporally discrete bodies of discourse (past/present) while the specification of the division is absent. A change has occurred: the present has incorporated and surpassed the past. But the historical "moments" of the filmic discourse are presented as an abstract before and after, implying that the break – the transformation allowing recognition of and regret over decisive loss and passed opportunities – must be somewhere between 1946 and the mid-seventies, a "somewhere" that remains unrepresented and unexplored in the film. The differential determinations of its two arenas of discourse – past/present, male-generated discourse/female-generated discourse – are through alternation construed as an absolute value difference: patriarchal myth/feminist truth. Women's history and the feminist perspective on women's past experience are thereby seen as the rewriting of a previous discourse – a relatively unified set of representations – from the vantage of a relatively unified set of current beliefs/positions in the spirit of progress.

In many ways *Swing Shift* stands as the complementary inverse of *Rosie the Riveter*. Kay Walsh (Goldie Hawn), the protagonist of *Swing Shift*, is not the "real working woman" ignored by the dominant media of the war era, but is instead the ideal subject addressed therein, the fictional spectator (and fictional character) constructed by the documentary discourse. We are first introduced to Kay and her husband, Jack, on the eve of the United States' entry into World War II. Their marriage is presented in terms of emphatic, conventional domesticity. Kay's clothing and her behavior with Jack code her as an infantilized housewife; he returns home from a hard day of work to shower as she, in her white anklets and little-girl dress, fetches his beer and cuddles in his lap.

When the United States declares war on Japan, Jack immediately enlists in the Navy. We see Kay, left to fend for herself, alone in a movie theater watching a newsreel about the need for women in defense work. Soon thereafter she applies for a job at a local aircraft plant, conceding to another woman applicant, "My husband would kill me if he knew what I was doing." Initially bumbling and insecure on the job, Kay learns to stand up to the male bullies in the factory who think that women do not belong there, masters mechanical skills so well that she can repair home appliances, and finally averts a fatal accident in the factory, leading to her promotion to leadman.

As Kay undergoes this transformation, narrative attention is focused on her relationship with Lucky (Kurt Russell), her supervisor in the factory. He persistently asks her out and she refuses at first but finally succumbs to his advances/charms and embarks on a full-scale affair. In this way the film suggests that Kay's growth and independence is manifested in both the public and private sphere. But in concentrating on the latter it clearly circumscribes the terms of this independence. The key to Kay's success as a "new woman" lies in replacing the support of one male with that of another. The affair ends when Jack comes home on an unannounced leave and discovers his wife's involvement with Lucky. His unease with her job success is exponentially compounded by the affair. Indeed his acknowledgment/recognition of the affair is initiated through the agency of her success in the workplace. He finds her factory uniform and asks who the "leadman" is. She feebly explains that *she* is the leadman, which is in fact the case. Yet the shirt, emblazoned with her job title, is clearly the condensed locus of the dual transformation–professional and personal– effected by her wartime experience. Still, Kay does not actively or consciously choose one man over the other. In love with both of them, she decides (as much out of guilt as anything) to reinstate behavior in line with her marriage vows, and Lucky leaves town with a group of musicians.

With the end of the war Kay and her women friends lose their jobs as the normative order of postwar domesticity is reinstated. However, the final scene indicates that the reassertion of aggressive patriarchal dominance, a force that is always present but loosened during the war, is not totally or simply embraced. At a party with her former coworkers, Kay and her husband circulate. The women, all married, enthuse over the different hors d'oeuvres being served and the wonderful new household appliances; the men discuss new housing developments. Kay seems surprisingly uninvolved in the proceedings. As most of the couples dance contentedly, Kay signals to her closest friend, Hazel, to meet her outside. They tearfully embrace as Kay asks, "Well, we showed them. Didn't we?" The film ends with a freeze-frame on an overwhelming note of loss, nostalgia.

Kay Walsh may not be an ideal of feminist independence, but is singled out in her feeling/knowledge that the impending postwar order of things will deny the sense of achievement afforded by the war. Whatever limitations are imposed on Kay as a narrative character, the film traces her path from ordinariness to extraordinariness embodied in her singular moment of nostalgic despair. If at the start of the film she ideally responds to the media appeal for housewives to enter the work force, at the end she is unwilling to assume the role of ideal subject of a similar but reversed media campaign and to graciously or happily return to the home.

This conclusion is in one sense typical of the constitutive ambiguity at work in a number of recent films;[5] it is simultaneously conservative and progressive. The film can unproblematically return its case of working women characters to the household *and* suggest that the terms of its own narrative stability are not unequivocally acceptable or untroubling. This narrational position, and the specific nature of the film's equivocal resolution, are made possible because it is *historical* narrative. What begins to emerge here is the same structure of history that was seen in *Rosie the Riveter*, history as founding narrational perspective and repressed distance.

This appropriation and disavowal of historical distance is clear from the outset as the film's first narrative scene opens with a superimposed title: Dec. 6, 1941. A few scenes later a second similar title appears: Sunday, Dec. 7, 1941. These titles generate narrative suspense as (and only if) the viewer recognizes the meaning of these dates. This is not anytime, anywhere, or even a generalized past, but the day before and the day of the Japanese attack on Pearl Harbor. But this is a prospective narrative device that can be reconstructed only as recognized retrospectively, even as it used to engage an audience in the otherwise unknown and unfamiliar fates of the film's fictional characters. The truth of history as it is known in the present is thus the founding alibi of narrative involvement in *Swing Shift*.

A similar but more elaborate structure informs the film's concluding scene. The return to domesticity as the impending state of affairs (in the terms of the fiction) can be justified as the dominant historical truth, but only when the period is reviewed from a distance of nearly forty years. In 1983 the postwar introduction of suburban housing projects and new consumer appliances does not merely signify a change of address or some abstract conception of a "higher standard of living" but connotes a whole social and cultural regime with specific implications for women. Once again we confront the problem of the temporal break constituting historical perspective and allowing a retrospective reevaluation of events defined as past, closed. The film assumes that a viewer will grasp the implications of the fiction's impending sociocultural regime, or at least promotes this as one important (if potential) interpretive position, as postwar marriages and consumerism are the prevalent topic of conversation in the final scene. At the same time it does not investigate/specify how or when this perception takes hold. The truth of the past is held up in the light of current terms of understanding as an abstract before and after; postwar life was understood (indeed misunderstood) one way "then," but we understand it (correctly) another way "now."

This distance is redoubled and conflated with the representation of at least one character, Kay, who is dissatisfied with the state of things at the end of the film. Her attitude suggests—perhaps even requires—a clear image of the fiction's imaginary future, "The Fifties," and it implies more crucially that she shares values that come from somewhere even beyond the fifties. She not only "knows" what is coming, but also knows that this future (imaginary, implied) is undesirable. (If the dominant mentality/ideology of the film's narrational perspective matched that of the fifties, or matched the terms in which we currently understand "The Fifties," one would not expect such a clear expression of dissatisfaction.) Kay embodies a position that is retrospectively projected onto her by the film so that she can prospectively anticipate our present. Thus the film can offer a conservative resolution for its construction of the past, relying on "truth to history" as an alibi, and can simultaneously hint at a way out that leads directly to the present and to liberal feminist ideology. In doing so however, the film does not allow Kay to project the rise of feminism in the sixties, but instead expresses this "out" in the narrative form of her immediate nostalgia.

It is in light of this process of construction that it is possible to identify a common structure of history at work in both *Swing Shift* and *Rosie the Riveter*. The past is construed as a closed sequence of events with a clear beginning, middle, and end. In the case of these two films the narrative sequence is clearly focused, 1941–1945. This period is seen from a later point in time that narrationally asserts its teleological superiority. A contemporary feminist consciousness is an a priori condition of the films' respective narrational postures, and the opportunity lost in the past is expressed from the perspective or opportunity regained. However, this split perspective – a distance repressed – is manifested differently according to the conventions of documentary film on the one hand and narrative film on the other.

The clear delineation of two discourses in *Rosie the Riveter* – period footage and interviews – is displaced but reproduced in *Swing Shift*, where it is manifested in the interaction between narrative development (the construction of imaginary characters and events of their lives) and the narrational perspectives that can only be a function of retrospective projection. This includes not only the opening and closing sequences described above, but encompasses also the film's restaging of sequences from period newsreels, sometimes duplicating scenes included in the compilation footage of *Rosie the Riveter*.

For example, *Rosie the Riveter* presents footage of training films and promotional documentaries comparing various factory jobs to more traditional household tasks. This material is dramatized in *Swing Shift* as the factory boss describes specific jobs to new women employees with similar kinds of metaphors; riveting is like sewing. In fact, in relation to conventional filmic coding, *Swing Shift*'s opening title sequence literally enacts the move from "documentary" to "fiction," as it opens with a series of black-and-white photographs representing the period and dissolves into color footage only with the first dramatic scene. This does not authenticate the film's events in relation to a "real" past, but in relation to a familiar body of filmic and photographic material from the past, including the film *Rosie the Riveter* and its archival footage.

In terms of the two filmic narratives, the past offered a series of irreconcilable choices. In general, the choice was between new possibilities and more conventional, restrictive life-styles for the various female protagonists. More specifically, this is defined as jobs/families, work/nonwork, "men's" work/"women's" work, production/reproduction, independence/dependence, and in *Swing Shift* lover/husband. But the loss entailed in this structure of absolute choice is projected into the past with the implication that the options, as real and compatible, are recoverable and recovered in the present. The way in which the choices are (re)activated in the interim remains absent. "Before" the choices are incompatible; "after," or now, they are reclaimed. But before and after what?

The synchronic structure embodied by the films' logic of choice is projected as diachronic progression: then/now, before/after, past/present. Through this temporal-historical sleight of hand the past can be closed and can become the basis for representing the present as a terrain of unlimited opportunity. The past is thus a nonidentical mirror for the present: "we" have reenacted the struggle and have succeeded where "they" have failed. The narrational logic in both cases hinges on a tacit scheme of progress and hierarchical development in the face of an absent break, absent because it may indeed be impossible to finally articulate the boundary that constitutes our difference from that which is represented as past in the films.

In both films then the historical perspective is the alibi for including certain materials from the past that are in turn the pretext for asserting mastery and superiority over the past as that which can be contained by the present. Historical perspective confers authority on the instance of production in the present: the narrated events of the past are not only true, but also inferior. This is not simply a conclusion achieved through the "work" of the films as textual systems, but also the stance that determines their use of history, documents, and events from the start – the meeting of prospective and retrospective strategies of narration and the joining of the supposedly antithetical positions of historicism and antihistoricism. History is at once a determined sequence of past events that really happened and a discursive practice that serves knowledge in and for the present as a function of specific social and political ideologies.

The investment in the study of women's status during World War II makes sense from the perspective of contemporary feminism, as something on the order of a rehearsal for the present. But to engage or activate this period as a closed sequence of events is to diffuse the political force of this representation. The attention per se suggests a degree of self-recognition within the past, but the terms of its representation refuse to push the implications of this self-recognition. The possibility of a call to struggle and self-examination is muted by the narrative and narrational containment offered by both films, and this in spite of the metatextual and substructures and split discursive perspectives they offer.

World War II becomes a dream scenario for feminist theory and history, the deficient mirror of the present, a past that can now and only now be written with a different ending. However, as wish fulfillment this scenario elides the contradictions within both the past and present. Contradiction, a process, is rewritten as a set of irreconcilable choices in the past and as the superior achievement of the present over the past. The question that emerges is whether and how a feminist historical understanding can embrace a model of complex, heterogeneous determinations and sustain political effectivity. At a minimum it must be possible to conceive of a history that negotiates the relation between past and present in terms that address and activate the constitutive contradictions of the various temporal sites that compose the particular history being narrated. The very conception of historical process and temporal relations may also be reconstrued. For example, nonhierarchical models of causality would shift the focus of attention to intersecting discursive and temporal schemes that inflect one another and exert interdependent pressures. From this perspective, the contemporary understanding of World War II as a period of new opportunities for women in the labor force might be seen as the effect of unresolved issues and contradictions in women's current status rather than as an unfulfilled but closed sequence, merely a stage en route to a fulfilled present. Concomitantly, more supple and subtle notions of textual ideology and social ideology must be developed.[6]

Swing Shift and *The Life and Times of Rosie the Riveter* bring these issues into focus in a particularly pointed way. To acknowledge the embedded metatextual substructures and double temporality at work in both films is to allow the possibility of a (presumably progressive) split in identification. And there is clearly something to be gained in giving a voice to women and turning attention to a period of women's achievement, however provisional. At the same time, to trace the constitutive limits of the films' historical conception is to imply conservative containment. The point is not to conclude by identifying the films in an ideological typology, but to initiate a consideration of the constitutive contradictions that inform present feminist historical perspectives.

In part this involves a reexamination of reigning conceptions of textual ideology. But it is also necessary to question more aggressively how and why we appropriate particular histories. The forties as a site of overdetermined historical investigation is an obvious case in point, expressed as feminist fascination with World War II as a lost possibility on the one hand and with *film noir* as the simultaneous displacement of and retribution for the provisional independence afforded by the wartime economy on the other.[7] In this context, and with this emphasis, the rest of cinema is reduced to pale ordinariness, though echoes of contradictory and ambiguously progressive practices remain in the work of select, privileged genres and directors (e.g., the fifties melodramas of Douglas Sirk or Vincente Minnelli). Otherwise, the thirties and the fifties as periods of social activity and cultural signification are by and large represented as "merely" the normative reign of dominant patriarchal ideology.

This fascination is not strictly scholarly but is becoming progressively institutionalized and generalized, embodied, for example, in the revival of "Rosie the Riveter" as a feminist popular cultural icon and in the revival/rewriting of *film noir* in contemporary cinema (e.g., *Against All Odds* [1984], *Body Heat* [1981], *Blood Simple* [1984]). The developing historical tradition focused on the forties both contributes to this revival and curiously ignores its own contradictory and complex extrication in the events presented as distant and closed. In the face of *this* strategy and use of history, what is needed is a reconceptualization of historical process and historical writing that can simultaneously confront this extrication and grant to the past its otherness. This seemingly paradoxical proposal is necessary if past Rosies are to function as more than our disadvantaged if heroic predecessors to confirm/position us as the inheritors of a determined and rosier future—only to become the ground of another closed sequence of past events.

Notes

1. A very partial listing of work in this vein includes Karen Anderson, *Wartime Women* (Westport, Conn.: Greenwood Press, 1981); Susan M. Hartmann, *The Home Front and Beyond* (Boston: Twayne, 1982); Susan M. Hartmann, "Prescriptions for Penelope: Literature on Women's Obligations to Returning World War II Veterans," *Women's Studies* 5 (1978): 223–39; Paddy Quick, "Rosie the Riveter: Myths and Realities," *Radical America* 9 (July-October 1975): 115–31; Leila J. Rupp, *Mobilizing Women for War* (Princeton, N.J.: Princeton University Press, 1978).

2. It should be noted that the film's "present" is in fact relatively dispersed and unstable, both in theoretical terms and more specifically in terms of its actual production; research, filming, and postproduction were carried out over a number of years.

3. Discussion of these traditions in feminist documentary filmaking are found in Julia Lesage, "The Political Aesthetics of the Feminist Documentary Film," *Quarterly Review of Film Studies* 3 (Fall 1978): 507–23; Sonya Michel, "Feminism, Film, and Public History," *Radical History Review*, no. 25 (1981): 47–61; and Bill Nichols, "The Voice of Documentary," *Film Quarterly* 34 (Spring 1983): 17–30.

4. Michel de Certeau, *L'Ecriture de l'Histoire* (Paris: Gallimard, 1975), 59 (my translation).

5. Julia Lesage discusses the ending of *An Unmarried Woman* (1978) in terms

that are relevant here in "The Hegemonic Female Fantasy in *An Unmarried Woman* and *Craig's Wife*," *Film Reader*, no. 5 (1982): 83–94. *Romancing the Stone* (1984) is another recent film, released at about the same time as *Swing Shift*, that resolves itself in terms of constitutive ambiguity, though in this case the equivocation is whether one takes the end as "really" fulfilling in terms of the same old "ideology of true love" or as blatantly and self-consciously fictional.

6. On this latter point, similar arguments are advanced in relation to readings of genre texts in a number of articles in *Screen* 25 (January-February 1984). In particular, see Jane Feuer, "Melodrama, Serial Form, and Television Today," 4–16; Annette Kuhn, "Women's Genres," 18–28; and Barbara Klinger, " 'Cinema/Ideology/Criticism' Revisited: The Progressive Text," 30–44.

7. While there is an extensive body of critical work on *film noir*, an exemplary collection of essays is available in E. Ann Kaplan, ed., *Women in Film Noir* (London: British Film Institute, 1978).

"A Queer Feeling When I Look at You": Hollywood Stars and Lesbian Spectatorship in the 1930s

Andrea Weiss

Boldly claiming to "tell the facts and name the names," in July 1955 *Confidential Magazine* embarked on telling "the untold story of Marlene Dietrich." The exposé reads, "Dietrich going for dolls," and goes on to list among her many female lovers the "blonde Amazon" Claire Waldoff, writer Mercedes de Acosta (rumored to be Greta Garbo's lover as well), a notorious Parisian lesbian named Frede, and multimillionaire Jo Carstairs, whom *Confidential Magazine* dubs a "mannish maiden" and a "baritone babe."[1]

The scandal sheet may have shocked the general public by its disclosures, but for many lesbians it only confirmed what they had long suspected. Rumor and gossip constitute the unrecorded history of the gay subculture. In the introduction to *Jump Cut*'s 1981 Lesbian and Film issue, the editors begin to redeem gossip's lowly status: "If oral history is the history of those denied control of the printed record, then gossip is the history of those who cannot even speak in their own first-person voice."[2] Patricia Meyer Spacks in her book *Gossip* pushes this definition further, seeing it not only as symptomatic of oppression but actually as a tool that empowers oppressed groups: "[Gossip] embodies an alternative discourse to that of public life, and a discourse potentially challenging to public assumptions; it provides language for an alternative culture."[3] Spacks argues that through gossip those who are otherwise powerless can assign meanings and assume the power of representation. Her concept of gossip as the reinterpreting of materials from the dominant culture into shared private values could also be a description of the process by which the gay subculture in the United States in the early twentieth century began to take form.

Something that, through gossip, is commonplace knowledge within the gay subculture is often completely unknown on the outside, and if not unknown, at least unspeakable. It is this insistence by the dominant culture on making homosexuality invisible and unspeakable that both requires and enables us to locate gay history in rumor, innuendo, fleeting gestures, and coded language – signs I will consider as historical sources in order to examine the importance of the cinema, and certain star images in particular, in the formation of lesbian identity in the 1930s.

By the time her "unspeakable" sexuality was spoken in *Confidential Magazine*, Marlene Dietrich was no longer a major star. She had not yet stopped making movies, but she was not a major box office draw in the United States, and would soon return to the European cabaret stage on which she began. The appeal of her sophistication, her foreign accent, and exotic, elusive manner had been replaced by a new, very different kind of star image, that of the 1950s all-American hometown girl, exemplified by Doris Day and Judy Holliday. Had the article been published in the 1930s when Dietrich was at her peak, it may well have cut her career short. The Hollywood studios went to great lengths to keep the star's image open to erotic contemplation by both men and women, not only requiring lesbian and gay male stars to remain in the closet for the sake of their careers, but also desperately creating the impression of heterosexual romance – as MGM did for Greta Garbo in the 1930s.[4]

But the public could be teased with the possibility of lesbianism, which provoked both curiosity and titillation. Hollywood marketed the suggestion of lesbianism, not because it intentionally sought to address lesbian audiences, but because it sought to address male voyeuristic interest in lesbianism. This use of innuendo, however, worked for a range of women spectators as well, enabling them to explore their own erotic gaze without giving it a name, and in the safety of their private fantasy in a darkened theater. Dietrich's rumored lesbianism had been exploited in this way by Paramount's publicity slogan for the release of *Morocco* (Josef von Sternberg, 1930): "Dietrich – the woman all women want to see."[5] This unnaming served to promote intrigue while preventing scandal. Lesbians may well have suspected, for example, that Mercedes de Acosta and Salka Viertel were great loves in Greta Garbo's life, but the "general public" only remembered that she once agreed to marry John Gilbert. Interestingly, Garbo used to answer Gilbert's many proposals of marriage with "you don't want to marry one of the fellows."

What the public knew, or what the gay subculture knew, about these stars' "real lives" cannot be separated from their star images. For this reason I am not concerned with whether the actresses considered here were actually lesbian or bisexual, but rather with how their star personas were perceived by lesbian audiences. This star persona was often ambiguous and paradoxical. Not only did the Hollywood star system create inconsistent images of femininity, but these images were further contradicted by the intervention of the actress herself into the process of star image production. Certain stars such as Katharine Hepburn, Marlene Dietrich, and Greta Garbo often asserted gestures and movements in their films that were inconsistent with the narrative and even posed an ideological threat within it.

In the famous scene from *Morocco*, Amy Jolly (Marlene Dietrich), dressed in top hat and tails, suddenly turns and kisses a woman on the lips. She then takes her flower and gives it to a man in the cabaret audience (Gary Cooper). This flirtation with a woman, only to give the flower to the man, is a flirtation with the lesbian spectator as well, and a microcosm of the film's entire narrative trajectory. The film historian Vito Russo has written of this scene, "Dietrich's intentions are clearly heterosexual; the brief hint of lesbianism she exhibits serves only to make her more exotic, to whet Gary Cooper's appetite for her and to further challenge his maleness."[6] But if we bring to the scene the privileged rumor of Dietrich's sexuality, shared by many lesbians when the film was first released but denied to the general public (until *Confidential* so generously supplied it in the 1950s), we may read the image differently: as Dietrich momentarily stepping out of her role as femme fatale and "acting out that rumored sexuality on the screen."[7]

Not only rumor but also the scene's cinematic structure allowed for lesbian spectators to reject the preferred reading (as described by Vito Russo above) in favor of a more satisfying homoerotic interpretation. Amy Jolly's performance – her singing a French song in Dietrich's inimitable voice and her slow, suave movements across the stage – is rendered in point-of-view shots intercut with the two contending male characters. Yet when her song is finished and she steps over the railing separating performer and audience, the image becomes a tableau. When Amy Jolly looks at the woman at the table, she quickly lowers her eyes to take in the entire body – to "look her over"; she then turns away and hesitates before looking at the woman again. The sexual impulses are strong in this gesture, impulses that are not diffused or choked by point-of-view or audience cutaway shots. Dietrich's gaze remains intact.

Furthermore, in the scene's concluding gesture of giving the flower to Tom Brown (Gary Cooper), she inverts the proper heterosexual order of seducer and seduced. Her costume, the tuxedo, is invested with power derived both from maleness and social class, a power that surpasses his,

Dietrich posed in a top hat and tails; her star persona was often ambiguous and paradoxical.

as represented by his uniform of a poor French legionnaire. While he is "fixed" in his class, she is able to transcend momentarily both class and gender. This fluidity and transcendence of limitations can be seductive for all viewers, male and female; for lesbian viewers it was an invitation to read their own desires for transcendence into the image. Richard Dyer has pointed out that "audiences cannot make media images mean anything they want to, but they can select from the complexity of the image the meanings and feelings, the variations, inflections and contradictions, that work for them."[8]

In the 1930s this process of selection was especially important for lesbian spectators because they rarely saw their desire given expression on the screen. By providing larger than life cultural models, Hollywood stars exercised a captivating power over the public; for lesbian spectators struggling to define their sexual identities and with virtually no other models within the ambient culture, this power must have been intensely persuasive and attractive. Aspects of certain star images were appropriated by the growing number of women who began to participate in the emerging urban gay subculture and played an influential role in defining the distinctive qualities of that subculture.

The early 1930s, of course, were the worst years of the Great Depression, and any discussion of the emergence of the gay subculture in this period must specify that it was largely metropolitan, middle class, and white. Antony James's claim in "Remembering the Thirties" that "it was a wonderful time to be in New York, to be young and to be gay" clearly didn't hold true for everyone.[9] But even individuals scraping by on shoestring budgets often saved for the Saturday matinee. And for those who could not afford the box office, the marquees, posters, and magazine covers made Hollywood stars into household images. Stars served as cultural models for a large spectrum of homosexuals across America, not just for those able to participate in the developing urban gay communities.

This fledgling gay subculture of the 1930s consisted of people who as yet lacked enough self-consciousness to see themselves as belonging to a minority group. Unlike racial and ethnic minorities, they grew up in households where their parents not only didn't share their lifestyle but actively fought it with the help of the law, psychology, religion, and sometimes violence. For a people who were striving toward self-knowledge, Hollywood stars became important models in the formation of gay identity.[10] The subtexts of films also provided the opportunity to see in certain gestures and movements an affirmation of lesbian experience—something that, however fleeting, was elsewhere rarely to be found, and certainly not in such a popular medium. This affirmation served to give greater validity to women's personal experience as a resource to be trusted and drawn upon in the process of creating a lesbian identity. Richard Dyer summarizes this process by claiming that "gays have had a special relationship to the cinema," because of isolation and an intensified need to use the movies as escapism, because the need to "pass for straight" elevated illusion to an art form, or because the silver screen was often the only place our dreams would ever be fulfilled.[11]

As Vito Russo points out in *The Celluloid Closet*, the film *Queen Christina* (Rouben Mamoulian, 1933) has met in the past some of these needs even though the lesbianism of the real-life queen is not overtly depicted. He writes, "In *Queen Christina*, Garbo tells Gilbert that 'it is possible . . . to feel nostalgia for a place one has never seen.' Similarly, the film *Queen Christina* created in gay people a nostalgia for something they had never seen onscreen."[12] Greta Garbo herself complained that the Hollywood version of Christina was too glamorous and that Swedes who saw the film would expect a more realistic depiction. But despite Swedish audiences' expectations or Garbo's protests, her director insisted that Christina be glamorous and fall in love with a man.[13] Through her performance, however, Garbo was able to compensate for what was omitted from the script, giving her portrayal sufficient sexual ambiguity so that her movements, voice, and manner became codes for lesbian spectators.

The scene in which Queen Christina kisses Countess Ebba on the lips obviously expresses sexuality, but there are other visual clues here that also allow for a lesbian reading. For example, the process of getting dressed into male attire seems to be a daily ritual for Queen Christina and her manservant, their movements are so coordinated. Because of this, the scene doesn't appear as a transvestite reversal, in which a woman transforms herself into a man, but rather that of remaining a woman while rejecting the dominant codes of femininity, a process "naturalized" by the ease with which it is done. Within this scene, Christina's little story about Molière, who says that marriage is shocking, reverses the sentiment thus far spoken in the film that the queen's not marrying is shocking. For viewers privy to the gossip about Garbo's relationship with the film's screenwriter, Salka Viertel, the inclusion of Molière's comment about enduring the idea of sleeping with a man in the room can easily be seen as a lesbian joke. Finally, the interaction between Queen Christina and Countess Ebba relies on sexual innuendo within their dialogue and gestures, revealing the desire of the two women for each other and their frustration in having duty and responsibility interfere with that desire.

In another key scene, the chancellor tries to impress upon Christina the importance of marriage as a duty. After she responds by saying, "I do not wish to marry, and they can't force me," there is a long silent take of her face, and she resumes with, "The snow is like a wild sea. One can go out and be lost in it, and forget the world, and oneself." This famous close-up on Garbo's face encourages the viewer to identify with the character's longing, as Andrew Britton pointed out, "to make the spectator's experience of Garbo's face the analog of Christina's experience of the landscape."[14] In addition to this erotic contemplation of Garbo's face, her romantic choice of desire over duty could have special resonance for lesbians who were struggling to make a similar choice in their own lives. When the chancellor warns her that "you cannot die an old maid," her response is ironic but with serious overtones: "I have no intention to, Chancellor; I shall die a bachelor." In this final statement she is no longer pleading to be understood, but has closed the debate by appropriating male language in the way she has appropriated male clothing to claim her power.

Such an act had far different meaning in the 1930s than it would have today: appropriating male language or values was not male-identified antifeminist, but rather the opposite. Carroll Smith-Rosenberg, describing the New Woman of the 1930s, writes: "They wished to free themselves completely from the considerations of gender, to be autonomous and powerful individuals, to enter the world as if they were men. Hence they spoke with male metaphors and images."[15] When viewed in this historical context, one finds that although its director attempted to purge the story of Queen Christina from the taint of lesbianism, the subtext left itself wide open to possible lesbian readings.

Film theorist Mary Ann Doane defines the position assigned to the female spectator by the cinema as a "certain over-presence of the image – she *is* the image."[16] This female spectator position lacks sufficient distance from either voyeurism or fetishism, the two forms of looking on which visual pleasure is based, according to contemporary film theory. The notion of a feminine "overpresence" draws on the Freudian argument that women do not go through the castration scenario that demands the construction of a distance between men and the female image. To simplify a complex argument, Doane finds that the theoretical female spectator's pleasure in the cinema can take the form of masochism in overidentification with the image, or of narcissism in becoming one's own object of desire, or it may be possible, by reinserting the necessary distance, for the woman's gaze to master the image. This distance can be achieved through two kinds of transformation, which Doane identifies as transvestism and masquerade. Female transvestism involves adopting the masculine spectatorial position; female masquerade involves an excess of femininity, the use of femininity as a mask, which simulates the distance necessary for the pleasure of looking.[17]

Whether or not one accepts the psychoanalytic model, alone it cannot account for the different cultural positioning of lesbians at once outside of and negotiating within the dominant patriarchal modes of identification. Since the psychoanalytic approach can see lesbian desire only as a function of assuming a masculine heterosexual position, I believe that other, non-psychoanalytic models of identification must be called upon that could account for the distance that makes possible the pleasure the female image offers the lesbian spectator.

The Motion Picture Code of 1934 prohibited references to homosexuality in the cinema, resulting in a dearth of images that can be considered lesbian. Since lesbian images have been chronically absent from the screen, and were even prior to the reign of the code, it is questionable whether lesbians would enter into the spectatorial position of "over-presence," of overidentification with either a virtually nonexistent lesbian image or a pervasive heterosexual female one. When a star or her character *can* be considered lesbian, she is usually exoticized, made "extraordinary" either by the star quality of the actress or by the power given to the character (or in the case of *Queen Christina*, both). In this way the star system often served to distance lesbian spectators from the "lesbian" star or character. Identification involves both conscious and unconscious processes and cannot be reduced to a psychoanalytic model that sees sexual desire only in terms of the binary opposition of heterosexual masculinity and femininity; instead it involves varying degrees of subjectivity and distance depending upon race, class, and sexual differences. For white working-class lesbians in the 1930s, for example, across huge gulfs of experience, glamorous upper-class white heterosexual star images often held tremendous appeal. For women of color, spectatorship was further problematized by the central role assigned to whiteness in standards of femininity and glamour, but it is possible that racial difference worked to create erotic fascination while also hindering identification with the star image.[18] Although not much evidence exists to clarify fully these questions, it is clear that for a lesbian who perceived herself as "butch," identification did not require what film theorist Laura Mulvey has called a "masculinization of spectatorship" in order to connect with the male star, he who controls the action and has a power that for two hours and thirty-five cents she could appropriate.[19] For a "femme" the problem of spectatorship was also complex and remains largely a matter of speculation.

An identification process thus complicated by different cultural and psychosexual positioning places lesbians outside of conventional gender definitions, as a gender in-between, which partially explains the attraction to certain androgynous qualities in the cinema. Lesbians who were fascinated with *Morocco* and *Queen Christina* when these films were first released spoke endlessly of the allure of their "ambiguity," a quality that carries great appeal among people who are forced to live a secret life.[20]

The sexually ambiguous, androgynous qualities that Marlene Dietrich and Greta Garbo embody found expression in the emerging gay subculture of the 1930s. Garbo and Dietrich were part of the aristocratic, international lesbian set that was this subculture's most visible and influential component; as such they played a role in defining the meaning of androgyny for the small, underground communities of lesbians across the country who saw their films and heard about them through rumor. Writing about the use of androgyny in images by lesbian artists and writers of the period, Flavia Rando has observed, "In an atmosphere heavy with repressive theories, androgyny offered women struggling to create a lesbian identity a possible alternative framework for self-definition."[21] Rando has found that for lesbians Romaine Brooks and Natalie Barney, androgyny represented a spiritual transcendence of human limitations.

But while sexual androgyny was embraced as a liberating image by some (especially more privileged) lesbians, it came to have a different, less positive meaning within the dominant culture. Androgyny began to be associated in the early twentieth century with the "mannish lesbian," a concept developed by sexologists, particularly the Austrian Richard von Krafft-Ebing, as an expression of sexual and social deviance, of degeneration and pathology. The historian Carroll Smith-Rosenberg has described this "mannish lesbian" image as that of "a sexually atavistic and ungovernable woman, associated with the 1920s bar culture and with European decadence."[22] Certainly Dietrich and Garbo on some level evoked this, Dietrich in her films and Garbo in the mystique that surrounded her personal life.

Dietrich's image is virtually inseparable from the bar culture setting or from the decadent cabaret stage; even the film *Blonde Venus*, a radical departure for her in that she plays a poor, devoted, and selfless mother rather than an independent woman, has her performing some of her most outrageous cabaret acts to support her poor son. Although as a cabaret singer in *Blonde Venus* Dietrich gives many performances, she appears in male attire—a white tuxedo—for the act only once: immediately after she has been rejected by her husband and has had her son taken away from her. Because she has been portrayed as an unfit mother, and is now without husband or child, her status as an unnatural woman is confirmed by her cross-dressing.

Garbo in *Queen Christina* and Dietrich in *Morocco* and *Blonde Venus* each evoke aspects of Smith-Rosenberg's description of the "mannish lesbian" of the 1920s and 1930s as "sexually powerful, yet ultimately defeated and impotent."[23] Yet their androgynous qualities held a sexual appeal that the "mannish lesbian" did not. Although they function within the narrative as a sexual threat that must be contained, their appropriation of male clothing (while retaining female identity), their aloof and inscrutable manners, and their aggressive independence provided an alternative model upon which lesbian spectators could draw. This model was an appealing departure both from heterosexual images of femininity and from the images of deviance that pervaded the medical texts.

Other Hollywood films of the 1930s also utilized this double-edged image that was at once subversive and confirming of the social order: the 1933 film *Blood Money* features Sandra Shaw in tuxedo with monocle, a contemporary lesbian fashion; Katharine Hepburn dons male attire and assumes the independence and privilege of men in both *Christopher Strong* (1933) and *Sylvia Scarlett* (1936); and the original German film, *Viktor and Viktoria* (1933) was closely followed by its British version, *First a Girl* (1935), both of which featured a woman who "passed" as a homosexual man while projecting an image with lesbian overtones. Such recurring appearances in the early 1930s of this cross-dressing image are not mere coincidences, but embody crucial historical debates that had begun to move from the pages of scientific journals and women's private diaries into public discourse. The 1920s had seen the publication of Radclyffe Hall's *The Well of Loneliness*, the censorship of which "caused great upheavals in the American judicial system, spilling out into the newspapers and becoming a topic of conversation for people across America."[24] The lesbian-themed play *The Captive* created a sensation on Broadway. The debates over changing definitions of gender and sexuality in the early twentieth century were now fought out over the terrain of popular culture.

The cinema as the most widespread and powerful form of popular entertainment became an especially important battleground. The films addressed here are those that are stretched and pulled by struggles between images of powerlessness and power, between the dominant cinema's metaphor of sexual deviance and the inverting of this metaphor by female stars—who brought to it a strong sexual appeal that the "mannish lesbian" lacked, and by lesbian spectators—who appropriated cinematic moments and read into them their own fantasies. And particular images generate meanings that are in conflict with their function within the narrative; poignant lesbian moments are constricted by the demands of heterosexual narrative closure. Thus, while the endings of both *Morocco* and *Queen Christina* can be viewed as affirming the heterosexual contract, it is also possible that lesbians found pleasure in these resolutions, partly because the endings are relatively open, permitting a range of interpretations, and partly because the heterosexual relationships they promote are still considered unacceptable (for reasons of class and status); they are not the socially sanctioned relationships that the characters have been encouraged to choose.

The endings of both *Morocco* and *Queen Christina* are complex and ambiguous. The romantic image of Amy Jolly following her man into the desert does not necessarily affirm the heterosexual social order. Queen Christina's choice to relinquish the throne in order to marry the Spanish

Garbo's inscrutable face contradicts the aims of narrative closure.

Ambassador can be viewed more as an action to escape the narrow confines of her life of duty than as a heterosexual triumph. Moreover, since the Ambassador dies before they are united, Christina is left alone to search for something she has not yet known. Amy Jolly and Queen Christina actually become more liminal and marginal in the films' conclusions, rejecting their past, their nationality, and their social position. Although each character can be viewed as having made the ultimate sacrifice in favor of a man, in doing so they've moved outside of the culture in which the heterosexual contract is constructed and maintained. In *Morocco*, Amy Jolly moves through the city's gate into the expanse of the desert, leaving her shoes behind in the sand, strong visual symbols for this departure from her culture. Queen Christina leaves on a ship, standing alone as its figurehead, her inscrutable Garbo face contradicting the aims of narrative closure. While heterosexual viewers might have found an affirmation of heterosexuality in the films' resolutions, lesbians could perceive the scenes as moving away from and rejecting the heterosexual social order.

Film theorist E. Ann Kaplan has argued that "to appropriate Hollywood images to ourselves, taking them out of the context of the total structure in which they appear, will not get us very far."[25] We need to understand how the discourse of the dominant cinema works to contain the most threatening aspects of women's sexuality by using lesbianism as its boundary. The moments in *Queen Christina* and *Morocco* that have poignancy for lesbians are only fleeting, transitory moments; they simply suggest what might be and then are snatched away by their incorporation into and co-optation by the discourse of the dominant cinema. Still, historical lesbian spectators have been able to appropriate these cinematic moments that seem to offer resistance to the dominant patriarchal ideology and to use these points of resistance and the shared language of gossip and rumor to, in some measure, define and empower themselves. As such, the cinema's contribution toward the formation of lesbian identity in the early twentieth century should not be underestimated.

In *The Celluloid Closet*, Vito Russo quotes the *Herald Tribune* review of *Queen Christina* when it first appeared: "What do facts and theories matter? Christina, to all those who see Garbo's film, will always be the lovely girl who fell in love with the Spanish Ambassador in the snow, and no amount of professional research will ever change her."[26] For lesbian spectators who saw Garbo's film in the early 1930s, however, Queen Christina will always be the lovely girl who dressed in male attire and refused to marry, and no amount of heterosexual cover will ever change her.

Notes

An earlier version of this essay appears in my book, *Vampires and Violets*, and is reprinted here with the permission of the publisher, Jonathan Cape Ltd. The original essay includes an analysis of Katharine Hepburn's title role in *Sylvia Scarlett* (1936).

1. Kenneth G. McLain, "The Untold Story of Marlene Dietrich," *Confidential Magazine* 3 (July 1955): 22.

2. Edith Becker, Michelle Citron, Julia Lesage, and B. Ruby Rich, "Lesbians and Film: Introduction," *Jump Cut*, nos. 24–25 (March 1981): 18.

3. Patricia Meyer Spacks, *Gossip* (New York: Alfred A. Knopf, 1985), 46.

4. Andrew Britton, *Katharine Hepburn: The Thirties and After* (Newcastle upon Tyne, England: Tyneside Cinema, 1984), 16.

5. Cited in the "Morocco" program notes of the D. W. Griffith Film Center screening, May 13, 1976.

6. Vito Russo, *The Celluloid Closet* (New York: Harper and Row, 1981), 14.

7. Becker et al., "Lesbians and Film," 18.

8. Richard Dyer, *Heavenly Bodies: Film Stars and Society* (New York: St. Martin's Press, 1986), 5.

9. Antony James, "Remembering the Thirties," in *The Yellow Book*, 7. On file at the Lesbian Herstory Archives, New York City.

10. This experience of living a "double life" in the 1930s was a common theme expressed in a series of interviews conducted by the *Before Stonewall* Film Project, on file at the Lesbian Herstory Archives, New York City.

11. Richard Dyer, ed., *Gays and Film* (London: British Film Institute, 1977), 1.

12. Russo, *Celluloid Closet*, 65.

13. Rebecca Louise Bell-Metereau, *Hollywood Androgyny* (New York: Columbia University Press, 1985), 74.

14. Britton, *Katharine Hepburn*, 11.

15. Carroll Smith-Rosenberg, "The New Woman as Androgyne: Social Disorder and Gender Crisis, 1870–1936," in *Disorderly Conduct* (New York: Oxford University Press, 1985).

16. Mary Ann Doane, "Film and the Masquerade: Theorizing the Female Spectator," *Screen* 23 (September-October 1982): 78.

17. Ibid.

18. A black lesbian, recalling the movie stars that were important to her growing up in Chicago in the 1950s, looked back to films of the 1930s, especially *Morocco*: "I was just enthralled with Dietrich. . . . She has a sustaining quality about her that I know has turned on thousands of women in this world. I can't say I identified with her. I wasn't thinking in terms of black and white in those days. . . . [It was just] lust, childhood lust, I'm sure."

19. Laura Mulvey, "Afterthoughts on 'Visual Pleasure and Narrative Cinema' Inspired by *Duel in the Sun* (King Vidor, 1946)," *Framework*, nos. 15–17 (1981): 12.

20. Unpublished interviews with (Ms.) Christopher Sitwell and Karl Bissinger, on gay life in the 1930s, May 1988.

21. Flavia Rando, "Romaine Brooks: The Creation of a Lesbian Image" (unpublished paper).

22. Smith-Rosenberg "New Woman," 282.

23. Ibid.

24. Andrea Weiss and Greta Schiller, *Before Stonewall: The Making of a Gay and Lesbian Community* (Tallahassee, Fla.: Naiad Press, 1988), 24.

25. E. Ann Kaplan, "Is the Gaze Male?" in *Powers of Desire: The Politics of Sexuality*, ed. Ann Snitow, Christine Stansell, and Sharon Thompson (New York: Monthly Review Press, 1983), 314.

26. Russo, *Celluloid Closet*, 66.

The Hypothetical Lesbian Heroine in Narrative Feature Film

Chris Straayer

Feminist film theory based on sexual difference has much to gain from considering lesbian desire and sexuality. Women's desire for women deconstructs male/female sexual dichotomies, sex/gender conflation, and the universality of the oedipal narrative. Acknowledgment of the female-initiated active sexuality and sexualized activity of lesbians has the potential to reopen a space in which straight women as well as lesbians can exercise self-determined pleasure.

In this article, I am concerned mainly with films that do *not* depict lesbianism explicitly, but employ or provide sites for lesbian intervention. This decision is based on my interest in the lesbian viewer and how her relationship to films with covert lesbian content resembles her positioning in society. In textual analyses of *Entre Nous* and *Voyage en Douce* – two French films that seemingly oblige different audiences and interpretation – I demonstrate how, rather than enforcing opposite meanings, the films allow for multiple readings that overlap. I use the term *hypothetical* to indicate that neither the character's lesbianism nor her heroism is an obvious fact of the films. I articulate a lesbian aesthetic that is subjective but not idiosyncratic.

In particular, I examine two sites of negotiation between texts and viewers, shifts in the heterosexual structure that are vulnerable to lesbian pleasuring: the lesbian look of exchange and female bonding. I place these in contrast to the male gaze and its narrative corollary, love at first sight.

I then examine the contradictions that arise when the articulation of non-heterosexual subject matter is attempted within a structure conventionally motivated by heterosexuality. Finally, the question inevitably raised by women-only interactions – "Where is the man?" – inspires a radical disclosure of sex as historically and socially constructed and a redefinition of subjectivity.

Feminist Film Theory: Gender, Sexuality, and Viewership

Within the construction of narrative film sexuality, the phrase *lesbian heroine* is a contradiction in terms. The female position in classical narrative is a stationary site to which the male hero travels and on which he acts. The relationship between male and female is one of conquest. The processes of acting and receiving are thus genderized.[1]

There can be no lesbian heroine here, for the very definition of lesbianism requires an act of defiance in relation to assumptions about sexual desire and activity. Conventional filmic discourse can accommodate the lesbian heroine only as a hero, as "male." Yet maleness is potentially irrelevant to lesbianism, if not to lesbians.

The lesbian heroine in film must be conceived of as a viewer construction, short-circuiting the very networks that attempt to forbid her energy. She is constructed from contradictions within the text and between text and viewer, who insists on assertive, even transgressive, identifications and seeing.

The Hollywood romance formula of love at first sight relies on a slippage between sexuality and love. Sexual desire pretends to be reason enough for love, and love pretends to be sexual pleasure. While sexual desire is visually available for viewers' vicarious experiences, sexual pleasure is blocked. By the time the plot reaches a symbolic climax, love has been substituted for sex, restricting sex to the realm of desire. So structured, love is unrequited sex. Since this love is hetero-love, homosexual viewers are doubly distanced from sexual pleasure.

The sexual gaze as elaborated in much feminist film theory is a male prerogative, a unidirectional gaze from male onto female, pursuing a downward slant in relation to power. In contrast, the lesbian look that I describe requires exchange. It looks for a returning look, not just a receiving look. It sets up two-directional sexual activity.

Considerable work by feminist film theorists has attempted to articulate operations of looking in narrative film texts and film spectatorship. In "Visual Pleasure and Narrative Cinema," Laura Mulvey described how the patriarchal unconscious has structured classical cinema with visual and narrative pleasure specifically for the heterosexual male viewer, gratifying his narcissistic ego via a surrogate male character who condones and relays the viewer's look at the woman character and providing him voyeuristic pleasure via a more direct, nonnarrative presentation of the woman as image (rather than character). Woman's erotic image elicits castration anxiety in the male viewer, which is eased by visual and narrative operations of fetishism and sadism. As Mulvey states, "None of these interacting layers is intrinsic to film, but it is only in the film form that they can reach a perfect and beautiful contradiction, thanks to the possibility in the cinema of shifting the emphasis of the look."[2]

Although Mulvey's article remains invaluable in addressing patriarchal dominance as the ideological status quo formally enforced by/in the mainstream cinema/text, it does not account for other sexual forces and experiences within society. Mulvey's arguments have been constructively elaborated, revised, and rebutted by numerous other feminist film theorists. However, much of this work has brought about an unproductive slippage between text and actuality that presses this exclusive patriarchal structure onto the world. This excludes the reactions of "deviant" participants in the film event from theory's discursive event. Even though the spectator's psychology is formed within a culture that collapses sexual/anatomical difference onto gender, the same culture also contains opposing factors and configurations that generate a proliferation of discourses that instigates actual psychological diversity. It is this diversity rather than cinema's dominant ideology that we must examine in order to deconstruct the alignment of male with activity and female with passivity.

In a later article, "Afterthoughts on 'Visual Pleasure and Narrative Cinema' Inspired by *Duel in the Sun*," Mulvey suggests that female viewers experience Freud's "true heroic feeling" through masculine identification with active male characters, a process that allows this spectator "to rediscover that lost aspect of her sexual identity, the never fully repressed bedrock of feminine neurosis." With her "own memories" of masculinity, a certain "regression" takes place in this deft "trans-sex identification" and, like returning to her past daydreams of action, she experiences viewer pleasure. Nevertheless, "the female spectator's phantasy of masculinisation is always to some extent at cross purposes with itself, restless in its transvestite clothes."[3]

Such a confusion of clothing with sex, and of both with desire for action, accepts the limitations of sex-role stereotyping in the text. True, such desire on the part of female viewers usually requires identification with male characters, but this is a limitation of mainstream cinema, not a "regression" on the part of women.

By not addressing mechanisms of gay spectatorship, the above scheme denies such pleasure or suggests that it is achieved from the heterosexual text via transvestite ploys. Mainstream cinema's nearly total compulsory heterosexuality does require homosexual viewers to appropriate heterosexual representations for homosexual pleasure. However, the "transvestite" viewer-text interaction described by Mulvey and others should not be confused with gay or bisexual viewership.

Mary Ann Doane understands this cross-gender identification by female viewers as one means of achieving distance from the text. In "Film and the Masquerade: Theorizing the Female Spectator," she argues that, because woman's preoedipal bond with the mother continues to be strong throughout her life (unlike man's), the female viewer – unless she utilizes specific devices – is unable to achieve that distance from the film's textual *body* that allows man the process of voyeurism: "For the female spectator there is a certain over-presence of the image – she *is* the image. Given the closeness of this relationship, the female spectator's desire can be described only in terms of a kind of narcissism – the female look demands a becoming."[4] As a result, woman overidentifies with cinema's female victims, experiencing a pleasurable reconnection that is necessarily masochistic. Because her body lacks the potential for castration, "woman is constructed differently in relation to the process of looking."[5]

Doane goes on to describe an alternate strategy for women to overcome proximity and mimic a distance from the(ir) image – the masquerade of femininity: "Above and beyond a simple adoption of the masculine position in relation to the cinematic sign, the female spectator is given two options: the masochism of over-identification or the narcissism entailed in becoming one's own object of desire, in assuming the image in the most radical way. The effectivity of masquerade lies precisely in its potential to manufacture a distance from the image, to generate a problematic within which the image is manipulable, producible, and readable to woman."[6]

The primary question that followed Mulvey's "Visual Pleasure and Narrative Cinema" was, How can women's film viewing pleasure be understood? Although subsequent feminist film theory drawing on psychoanalysis successfully opened up that field for feminist purposes and raised significant new questions, the answers it has provided – elaborations of particular processes of masochism and transvestism – remain only partially sufficient to the original question. Much of this work has circumvented a crucial option in female spectatorship by avoiding the investigation of women viewers' erotic attraction to and visual appreciation of women characters.[7] Further work needs to examine how viewers determine films as much as how films determine viewers. And, care should be taken that the theorized transvestite or bisexual viewer does not inadvertently suppress the homosexual viewer.

Eroticizing Looks between Women Characters

Visual exchanges between same-sex characters typically are nonsexual. The challenge becomes to eroticize these looks. This is the goal of the homosexual viewer who brings her/his desires to the heterosexual raw material and representational system of the text. Occasionally she/he collaborates with texts to excavate subtexts and uncover ambivalence in the patriarchal "order." Since the heterosexual structure of the gaze is already established as sexual, it can be built on to accomplish an erotic homosexual look.

Independently structured glances between women, however, are outside conventional definition, and therefore threaten. The ultimate threat of eye contact between women, inherent in all scenes of female bonding, is the elimination of the male. Any erotic exchange of glances between women requires counterefforts to disempower and de-eroticize them.

I now will focus on two films, both open to lesbian readings, that are interesting for their similarities and differences. *Voyage en Douce* (Michele Deville, 1980) is an erotic art film, bordering on "soft porn," about two women who take a trip to the country together. They exchange fantasies and flirtations, then return home to their male partners. *Entre Nous* (Diane Kurys, 1983) is also about the interactions between two women, but their relationship leans ostensibly toward the buddies genre. They too take a trip away from their husbands. The women demonstrate growing mutual affection and, at the film's conclusion, they are living together. Although the two films appear opposite—one pseudolesbian soft porn serving a male audience, the other feminist and appealing to a female audience—this dichotomy is deconstructed once viewers are actively involved.

Voyage en Douce is particularly interesting in relation to looking because, instead of resolution, it attempts sustained sexual desire. According to the conventions of pornography, the erotic involvement of two women functions as foreplay for a heterosexual climax. This does not happen in *Voyage en Douce*. Erotic looking and flirting between women is thematic in this film. The lesbian desire this stimulates is accentuated by a hierarchical looking structure that mimics the male gaze. Throughout the film, a blonde woman, Helene, played by Dominique Sanda, is the more active looker and the text's primary visual narrator. It is primarily "through her eyes" that sexual fantasies are visualized on the screen. When taking nude photographs of her brunette companion, Lucie, played by Geraldine Chaplin, a camera prop "equips" Helene/Sanda for this male role.

Helene is also the primary pursuer in the narrative, while Lucie functions to stimulate, tease, and frustrate that desire. The film's episodic

Erotic looking, flirting, and photographing occur between Helene (Dominique Sanda) and Lucie (Geraldine Chaplin) in *Voyage en Douce*.

structure – another convention of pornography – alternates between the women's individual sexual stories and fantasies and their erotically charged interactions. Helene pampers and grooms Lucie, appreciates her visually, and verbally reassures her about her beauty and desirableness. This serves to build both a generalized sexual desire and a more specific lesbian desire. In both cases, a series of narrative denials and delays establishes an "interruptus" motif. Early in the film, there is a point-of-view shot of a look from Lucie at Helene's breast, which Helene quickly covers. Later, when Helene purposely exposes her breast to excite Lucie, Lucie is not responsive. When photographing Lucie, Helene encourages her to remove her clothes. Lucie does so hesitantly and coquettishly, but, when Helene attempts to take the final nude shot, she is out of film.

In several scenes Helene and Lucie exchange unmediated glances, as do the two women characters in *Entre Nous* – Lena, played by Isabelle Huppert, and Madeline, played by Miou Miou. Such exchanges, which occur primarily within two-person shots, gain sexual energy from the women's physical proximity and subtle body contact. The fact that two women share the film frame encourages this lesbian reading, that is, the women are consistently framed as a "couple." This visual motif provides a pleasurable homosexual content that is frustrated by the plot.[8] However, the absence of a shot-reverse-shot, reciprocal point-of-view pattern in these two-shots excludes the viewer from experiencing the looking.

In *Entre Nous*, the reciprocal point-of-view shot sutures the viewer into the looking experience.

Thus, the viewer's identification with the women's looking is necessarily more sympathetic than empathic.

In *Entre Nous*, the addition of a mirror to such a shot establishes a second internal frame. The reciprocal point-of-view exchange achieved between these two simultaneous frames—a two-shot of the women looking at each other through the mirror—allows the viewer to be sutured into the looking experience, while also experiencing the pleasure of seeing the two women together. It is notable that during this shot, the women are nude and admiring each other's breasts.

A similar construction occurs temporally instead of spatially when, in a sequence in the garden, the camera temporarily identifies with the look and movement of Lena (Huppert) approaching Madeline (Miou Miou) through a subjective tracking shot and then holds steady while Lena enters the frame. The viewer is carried into the women's space via an identification with Lena's look, then observes their embrace from an invited vantage point. This is followed by a shot of Madeline's father and son watching disapprovingly—a look from outside. Standing together, hand in hand, these two males foreground the generation missing between them—Madeline's husband. Hence their look both acknowledges and checks the dimensions of the women's visual exchange.

Voyage en Douce also contains abundant mirror shots, some of which similarly conduct visual exchanges between the characters, while others seem to foreground hierarchical erotic looking. In particular, several mirror shots occur in which the two women examine Lucie's image while Helene compliments and/or grooms her.

Female Bonding in Film

What becomes evident from these examples is that when one searches for lesbian exchange in narrative film construction, one finds a constant flux between competing forces to suggest and deny it. As with sexuality in general, efforts to subdue lesbian connotations can stimulate innovations. Female bonding and the exchange of glances between women threaten heterosexual and patriarchal structures. When female bonding occurs in feature narrative film, its readiness for lesbian appropriation is often acknowledged by internal efforts to forbid such conclusions.

Conceptually, female bonding is a precondition for lesbianism. If women are situated only in relationship to men or in antagonistic relationship to each other, the very idea of lesbianism is precluded. This partially explains the appreciation lesbian audiences have for films with female bonding. So often has female bonding stood in for lesbian content that lesbian audiences seem to find it an acceptable displacement at the conclusions of such "lesbian romances" as *Personal Best* (1982, Robert Towne) and *Lianna* (1982, John Sayles).

The widespread popularity of *Entre Nous* among lesbian audiences is attributable to basic narrative conditions, which are reiterated throughout the film. Most important is female bonding. The film begins with parallel editing between Lena's and Madeline's separate lives. This crosscutting constructs audience expectation and desire for the two women to meet. Once they have met, the two women spend the majority of screen time together. Lesbian viewers experience pleasure in their physical closeness. Although lesbianism is never made explicit in the film, an erotic subtext is readily available. The specific agenda held by lesbian viewers for female bonding warrants an inside joke at the film's conclusion when Lena and Madeline are finally living together. In the "background" a song plays: "I wonder who's kissing her now. I wonder who's showing her how."

The development of Lena and Madeline's relationship stands in sharp contrast to the development of Lena's marriage. During World War II, she and Michel are prisoners in a camp. He is being released and is allowed to take a wife out with him. He selects Lena by sight alone.

In many ways, female bonding is the antithesis of love at first sight. While love at first sight necessarily de-emphasizes materiality and context, female bonding is built upon an involvement in specific personal environments. Furthermore, the relationship acquires a physical quality from the presence of personal items that, when exchanged, suggest intimacy. Women frequently wear each other's clothes in both of these films. Body lotion and love letters pass between Lena and Madeline as easily as do cigarettes.

Such bonding activity between women suggests an alternate use for the feminine masquerade. This mutual appreciation of one another's feminine appearance, which achieves intimacy via an attention to personal effects, demonstrates the masquerade's potential to draw women closer together and to function as nonverbal homoerotic expression that connects image to body. This "deviant" employment of the feminine masquerade is in contradistinction to Doane's elaboration of it as a distancing device for women.

The primary threat of female bonding is the elimination of the male. The unstated but always evident question implicit in such films – "Where is the man?" – acknowledges defensive androcentric reactions. Its underlying presence attempts to define female bonding and lesbianism in relation to men. Publicity that accompanies a distribution print of *Voyage en Douce* from New Yorker Films describes the film as "What women talk about when men aren't around." In *Entre Nous*, scenes approaching physical intimacy between the two women are juxtaposed with shots signaling the lone male. Depicting female bonding as the exclusion of men moves the defining principle outside the women's own interactions. The lesbian potential, an "unfortunate" by-product of the female bonding configuration, must be checked.

The Male Intermediary

One way to interfere with female bonding is to insert references to men and heterosexuality between women characters. In *Entre Nous*, Madeline and Lena spend a considerable portion of their time together talking about their husbands and lovers. For example, they jointly compose a letter to Madeline's lover. Reassuring references to offscreen males, however, remain a feeble attempt to undermine the visual impact that the women together make.

To be more effective, the interference needs to be visual in order to physically separate the women's bodies and interrupt their glances. Male intermediaries are common in films with female bonding. In *Entre Nous*, when Lena and Madeline are dancing together in a Paris nightclub (which opens with a *male* point-of-view shot of Madeline's ass), two male onlookers become intermediaries by diverting the women's glances and easing the tension created by their physical embrace.

Voyage en Douce literally places a male between the two women. The soft porn approach of *Voyage en Douce* relies on titillating the male viewer with lesbian insinuations. Ultimately, however, female characters must remain available to male viewers. In one scene, Helene verbally instructs a young male, placed between the women, on how to kiss Lucie. The inexperienced boy reinforces the male viewer's sense of superior potency – the male viewer is represented but not replaced. In this scene the boy connects the two women as much as he separates them. It is Helene who is sensitive to Lucie's pacing and is manipulating her desire. The boy is an intermediary. Helene's vicarious engagement, however, is confined to the realm of desire. The actual kiss excludes her.

Often, as in the following example from *Entre Nous*, the connection that an intermediary provides is less obvious. Lena is on her way to meet Madeline in Paris when she has a sexual encounter with an anonymous male. A soldier who shares her train compartment kisses and caresses her. Later, while discussing this experience with Madeline, Lena "comes to realize" that this was her first orgasmic experience. The scene on the train reasserts Lena's heterosexuality. At the same time, this experience and knowledge of sexual pleasure is more connected to her friendship with Madeline, via their exchange of intimate information, than to her heterosexual marriage of many years. In fact, it is Madeline who recognizes Lena's described experience as an orgasm and identifies it to her. Because the film cuts away from the train scene shortly after the sexual activity begins, the film viewer does not witness Lena's orgasm. Had this train scene continued, her orgasm might have approximated, in film time, the moment when Madeline names it – and Lena gasps. In a peculiar manner, then, Madeline is filmically credited for the orgasm. Likewise, Lena's excited state on the train, her predisposition to sexual activity, might be read as motivated by her anticipation of being with Madeline.

A male's intrusion upon female bonding, then, is just as likely to homoeroticize the situation as to induce corrective heterosexuality. In *Entre Nous*, it is Lena's jealous husband who gives language to the sexual possibilities of their friendship. By calling the women's boutique a "whorehouse," he foregrounds the erotic symbolism that clothing provides. When he calls the women "dykes," he not only reveals the fears of a jealous husband but confirms the audience's perceptions.

While I would not go so far as to equate these two films, it would be naive to dismiss *Voyage en Douce* simply as a "rip-off" of lesbianism for male voyeuristic pleasure while applauding *Entre Nous* as "politically correct" lesbianism. In their different ways, *Entre Nous* does just as much to stimulate lesbian desire as does *Voyage en Douce*, and *Voyage en Douce* frustrates it just as much as *Entre Nous* does. The two films exhibit similar tensions and compromises. As far as any final commitment to lesbian-

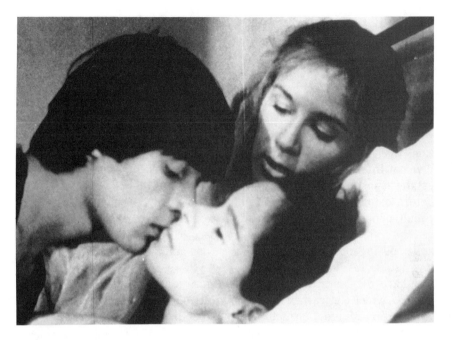

In *Voyage en Douce*, the actual kiss excludes Helene and confines her to the realm of desire.

ism, *Entre Nous* is no more frank than is *Voyage en Douce*. Lesbian reading requires as much viewer initiation in one film as the other.

One could argue that any potential lesbianism in *Voyage en Douce* is undermined by heterosexual framing in early and late scenes with Helene's male partner. Another interpretation of this framing device, however, sends conclusions in a different direction. Early in the film, Lucie crouches outside Helene's door. Helene sees Lucie through the railing under the banister as she climbs the stairs to her apartment. When Lucie declares that she is leaving her male partner, Helene takes her into her apartment, where they plan a vacation together. At the film's conclusion, the two women return to Helene's apartment. Then Lucie decides to go back to her husband, but Helene decides to leave hers again. Inadvertently, Helene locks herself out of the apartment without her suitcase. Instead of ringing the doorbell, she crouches in Lucie's earlier position as the camera moves down the stairs to observe her through the railing. One can read this shot as portraying the prison of heterosexuality or domesticity – as a cul-de-sac. Or one can read this pattern as indicating a cyclic structure.

Helene's display of lesbian desire throughout *Voyage en Douce* qualifies her as a hypothetical lesbian heroine as much as the women in *Entre Nous*.

Ultimately, these characters' lesbianism remains hypothetical and illusory because of their isolation. The acknowledgment of lesbian desire does not, in either film, acknowledge the *condition* of lesbianism within culture.

To summarize, *Voyage en Douce* and *Entre Nous* are narrative films that exist by right of a language informed by heterosexuality. However, because they are about women's relationships, they also challenge the conventions of this language. The contradictions that result from their use of a heterosexual system for nonheterosexual narratives give rise to innovations that interact with audience expectations to create multiple and ambivalent interpretations. The focus on two women together threatens to establish both asexuality and homosexuality, both of which are outside the heterosexual desire that drives mainstream film and narrative. Therefore, simultaneous actions take place in the text to eroticize the women's interactions and to abort the resulting homoerotics. These very contradictions and opposing intentions cause the gaps and ambiguous figurations that allow lesbian readings.

I have demonstrated three such figurations: the erotic exchange of glances, which contrasts with the unidirectional, hierarchical male gaze articulated by Mulvey; eroticized female bonding, which utilizes the feminine masquerade to achieve closeness, contrasting the use and purpose of the masquerade described by Doane; and the oppositely sexed intermediary who both separates and connects the same-sexed couple, accomplishing both heterosexuality and homosexuality within the contradictory text. These structures neither replace nor compromise the heterosexual film text and event recognized and analyzed in previous feminist film theory, but rather offer additions and alternatives to account for homosexual viewership and desire.

Revising Binary Sexual Ideology

As a woman, the lesbian is defined and situated in culture as opposite to man, as a lack. The lesbian's physical/sexual interactions, however, insist on a different presence that operates outside male determination. It is her womanness, not her lesbianism, that confines her within the patriarchal formation of femininity. Therefore, were lesbians able to situate themselves as another sex, that is, as nonwomen (and nonmen), they could theoretically create a defining model to which men are irrelevant.[9]

In his introduction to *Herculine Barbin: Being the Recently Discovered Memoirs of a Nineteenth-Century French Hermaphrodite*, Michel Foucault contrasts the allowance of free choice and the coexistence of sexes within one body in the Middle Ages, to the medical/legal relegation of the hermaphrodite to a single "true" sex in the eighteenth century:

Do we *truly* need a *true* sex? With a persistence that borders on stubbornness, modern Western societies have answered in the affirmative. They have obstinately brought into play this question of a "true sex" in an order of things where one might have imagined that all that counted was the reality of the body and the intensity of its pleasures.

For a long time, however, such a demand was not made, as is proven by the history of the status which medicine and law have granted to hermaphrodites. Indeed it was a very long time before the postulate that a hermaphrodite must have a sex—a single, true sex—was formulated. . . .

Biological theories of sexuality, juridical conceptions of the individual, forms of administrative control in modern nations, led little by little to rejecting the idea of a mixture of the two sexes in a single body and consequently to limiting the free choice of indeterminate individuals. Henceforth, everybody was to have one and only one sex. Everybody was to have his or her primary, profound, determined and determining sexual identity; as for the elements of the other sex that might appear, they could only be accidental, superficial, or even quite simply illusory.[10]

Foucault's insights challenge the very "obvious" criteria used not only to delineate the sexes but to limit their number to two. By denying evidence of sexual continuums and conceptually precluding a more complex sexual variance in favor of a system of binary opposition, arbitrary and enforced standards for assignment of both sex and sexual behavior are made to seem adequate, primary, and natural.

No attempt to delineate clearly between two "true" sexes has been successful. The exceptions and ambiguities in anatomical and physiological assignments become even more pervasive when considering secondary sex characteristics, hormones, chromosome patterns, and behaviors. Erasing the hermaphrodite from our consciousness allows male and female terms to appear unambiguous and definite. In effect, the hermaphroditism existing within each of these terms is dismissed.

If we understand male and female sexes as constructs, we must ask ourselves what investment empowers them. Certainly within classic narrative film, the language/expression/momentum of heterosexual desire relies precisely on this particular system of binary opposition.

Within contemporary psycholinguistic thought, the subject is always male. Because of her different psychological development and relationship to the mother, the female remains more strongly connected to the prelanguage imaginary. Any "I" she speaks is constructed for her by the male principle, just as female is defined not from itself but as male's other.

Lesbian sexuality generates an identity that is *not* defined by an opposition to maleness. Thus the lesbian (of a lesbian) remains outside the male-female polarity. She demonstrates a radical possibility for attaining subjectivity through activity that asserts personal meaning and is understood via similarities as much as differences.

Lesbian "deviance" refutes the all-encompassing "natural" power of the male-female opposition as defining principle. Lesbianism demands a new operation of subjectivity in which active desires, pleasures, and other specific declarations of identity construct a field of multiple entry points. Within this new operation, a heterosexual woman's active sexuality would not be consumed but empowered. Rather than enforcing two "true" sexes, which allow one (male) subject, we must recognize the power of individual activities, in this case sexualities, to assert subjectivity.

I am not merely suggesting that sexual preference be added to anatomy as a determiner of the subject position, but rather that individual activity and assertion can construct subjectivity. Thus, for example, the experience and assertion of one's ethnic or racial identity would be acknowledged as an authentic subject component.

The proposal that lesbians might abandon the female "position" without adopting maleness uncovers an historical investment in and enforcement of a system of two sexes as well as two genders. This consistent maintenance of an historical construct explains the overloaded significance of the question "Where is the man?" in response to relationships between women and/or lesbians. It raises the ultimate importance of investigating lesbian aesthetics.

Notes

1. See Teresa de Lauretis, *Alice Doesn't: Feminism, Semiotics, Cinema* (Bloomington: Indiana University Press, 1984), especially the "Desire in Narrative" chapter.

2. Laura Mulvey, "Visual Pleasure and Narrative Cinema," *Screen* 16 (Autumn 1975): 17.

3. Laura Mulvey, "Afterthoughts on 'Visual Pleasure and Narrative Cinema' Inspired by *Duel in the Sun* (King Vidor, 1946)," *Framework* 15–17 (1981): 13.

4. Mary Ann Doane, "Film and the Masquerade: Theorizing the Female Spectator," in *Femmes Fatales: Feminism, Film Theory, Psychoanalysis* (New York: Routledge, 1991), 22. See also Doane's "Masquerade Reconsidered: Further Thoughts on the Female Spectator," also in *Femmes Fatales*.

5. Ibid., 80.

6. Ibid., 87.

7. Such an investigation was called for more than a decade ago by Michelle Citron, Julia Lesage, Judith Mayne, B. Ruby Rich, and Anna Marie Taylor. See their discussion in "Women and Film: A Discussion of Feminist Aesthetics," *New German Critique* 13 (Winter 1978): 83–107.

8. See Lucie Arbuthnot and Gail Seneca, "Pre-text and Text in *Gentlemen Prefer Blondes*," *Film Reader* 5 (Evanston, Ill.: Film Division/School of Speech,

Northwestern University, 1982): 13–23. Arbuthnot and Seneca describe the pleasure afforded the lesbian viewer by such framing-together of women characters.

9. Although my own position differs from hers on some points, Monique Wittig is the foremost contemporary theorizer of a lesbian "third sex." See her "One Is Not Born a Woman," *Feminist Issues* 1 (Winter 1981), and "The Category of Sex," *Feminist Issues* 2 (Fall 1982), for her arguments that oppression constructs sex, that the concept of lesbian is beyond the categories of sex, and therefore that "lesbians are not women." For a useful discussion of Wittig's antiessentialist materialism, see Diana Fuss, *Essentially Speaking: Feminism, Nature, and Difference* (New York: Routledge, 1989), 39–53.

10. Michel Foucault, introduction to *Herculine Barbin: Being the Recently Discovered Memoirs of a Nineteenth-Century French Hermaphrodite*, trans. Richard McDougall (New York: Pantheon Books, 1980), vii–viii.

A Call for Militant Resistance

bell hooks

In 1988 I was invited by the Malcolm, Rodney, Biko Collective in Toronto to speak at an event commemorating the day black South African women assembled en masse in Pretoria to protest against pass laws, to protest against apartheid. Although I was honored by the invitation (it was one of the rare times radical black men on the Left have organized a feminist lecture and urged black women to speak), I expressed uncertainty about whether I was the right person for the occasion. I felt that I did not know enough about the history of apartheid in South Africa or the particular circumstances of black women there. Even after I confessed my limitations, they urged me, "Sister, come and speak, we need your words." I agreed to come, saying that what I had to offer was a message from the heart of solidarity in struggle, from African-American women to black South African women. After reading intensively about the situation of black women in South Africa, I chose to talk about the way sexism informs the system of apartheid, the gendered nature of the assault on black people, particularly about the disruption of family life, about black women working as domestics in white homes. My talk was called "We Know How Our Sisters Suffer." It did not begin with South Africa but with my memories of growing up in the apartheid black American South, memories of black women leaving the racially segregated spaces of our community to work in white homes. As I spoke these memories, repeating often a line that runs through *Freedom Charter*, a work documenting aspects of the black liberation movement in

South Africa–"Our struggle is also a struggle of memory against forgetting"–black South African women in the audience responded. They knew firsthand what I was describing. They heard in my words a commonality of experience–a link between the African-American past and the contemporary struggle against white supremacy that unites us.

A piece I wrote for *Z* magazine in January 1988 on white supremacy began with a declaration of solidarity between black Americans and black South Africans, stating that we share a common struggle rooted in resistance–the fight to end racism and white supremacist domination of black people globally. After my article was published, several white left academic colleagues let me know that it was misguided–that they did not agree with the idea that the United States is a white supremacist society. These colleagues have made their academic fame writing about race–interpreting black folks, our history, our culture. They no longer supported my intellectual efforts after the publication of this piece. For me it was a militant piece, voicing ideas many black folks hold but dare not express lest we terrify and alienate the white folks we encounter daily. White and black folks alike told me this piece was "too extreme." Whatever its form, black militancy is always too extreme in the white supremacist context, too out-of-order, too dangerous. Looking back at the history of black liberation struggle in the United States one can see that many glorious moments, when our plight was most recognized and transformed, when individuals black and white sacrificed–put their lives on the line in the quest for freedom and justice–happened because folks dared to be militant, to resist with passionate commitment. I often tell students who have no memory of this time to look at footage of civil rights struggle, at those old photographs (remember the ones of the young black and white women and men sitting at the Woolworth counter?) and they will see that the sacrifice and the suffering endured.

Confronting the profound, life-threatening nihilism that has a choke hold on masses of black people today, strangling us so that we cannot engage in effective protest and resistance, I ponder not so much where that spirit of militancy has gone, but the way in which it sustained and nurtured our capacity to struggle. Some folks may have heard resignation in that prophetic sermon when Martin Luther King, Jr., declared that he had been to the mountaintop and received a vision–for many of us it was a militant message. We heard him testify that he had found reconciliation on that mountaintop, the understanding that black liberation struggle was worth the sacrifice, that he was ready to give his life. Although not heard by many, playwright Lorraine Hansberry echoed this militancy when she wrote in 1962, "The condition of our people dictates what can only be called revolutionary attitudes." Countering white criticisms of "black power" and militant opposition to racism, Hansberry declared: "Negroes must concern themselves with every single means of struggle: legal, illegal, passive, active, violent and nonviolent. They must harass, debate, petition, give money to court struggles, sit-in, lie-down, strike, boycott, sing hymns, pray on steps – and shoot from their windows when the racists come cruising through their communities."

The statement she makes that has most urged me on in moments when I feel too tired to struggle is the militant reminder that "the acceptance of our present condition is the only form of extremism which discredits us before our children." Hansberry was one of the many black artists, writers, thinkers, and intellectuals of her day who were not ashamed to link art and revolutionary politics, who were not afraid to speak out publicly against white imperialism in Africa.

A similar militancy can be seen in Euzhan Palcy's antiapartheid film, *A Dry White Season*. It is a work that explores the emergence of critical consciousness from the standpoint of black folks engaged in militant resistance to apartheid and a white liberal father and son who become radicalized struggling on behalf of the oppressed. The film's focus on a white family disturbed many progressive viewers who did not want to see another film about a white man becoming radical, particularly one made by a black woman filmmaker. As clichéd and boring as this representation may be for some folks, it is certainly a representation of whiteness that disrupts that status quo, one that challenges the white spectator to interrogate racism and liberalism in a far more progressive way than is normally seen in mainstream cinema. How many films show white men acting in solidarity with the oppressed to resist white racist domination? Why is it that so many reviews saw this representation as uninteresting, as though it is a common sight? Talking about "cold war liberalism" in a 1960s forum on "The Black Revolution and the White Backlash," Hansberry stressed that

> radicalism is not alien to this country, neither black nor white. We have a great tradition of white radicalism in the United States – and I never heard Negroes boo the name of John Brown. Some of the first people who have died so far in this struggle have been white men. . . . I don't think we can decide ultimately on the basis of color. The passion that we express should be understood, I think, in that context. We want total identification. It's not a question of reading anybody out; it's a merger . . . but it has to be a merger on the basis of true and genuine equality. And if we think that it isn't going to be painful, we're mistaken.

Palcy's film is the cinematic exploration of a white liberal's realization of what authentic solidarity with the oppressed demands, yet this powerful dimension of the film has received little attention. The reality that the continued racism of Hollywood and the culture of white supremacy dictates that masses of people are more likely to watch a film about South Africa that has a compelling story line centralizing white folks does not diminish the radical subversive element in the film. And one of those features is the complex representation of "whiteness." The story of a white liberal acquiring a radical consciousness is a needed representation for many indifferent or uncertain white folks who do not know that they have a role to play in the struggle to end racism.

Yet liberals are not all alike in this film. As the cynical lawyer who has presumably been through what Ben du Toit is going through, Marlon Brando offers us another perspective, and the radical white female journalist and her supportive father give us yet another take. Concurrently, what contemporary film has depicted white female complicity in the perpetuation of white supremacy as clearly as Palcy's film? White supremacy is a family affair, not a mere spectacle of patriarchy.

Even though Palcy faced constraints that undoubtedly forced her to deradicalize her vision, *A Dry White Season* has many subversive cinematic moments. Again and again whiteness is interrogated, exposed, problematized in ground-breaking ways. One such moment happens when Ben transgresses the boundaries of white supremacy by the seemingly unimportant gesture of publicly embracing Emily, the black wife of the murdered gardener, Gordon. Right then the film poses critical questions about the intersection of race and gender, about sexuality and power, that are rarely addressed in cinema. Palcy explores the question of whether a white male who chooses to give up his privilege and work on behalf of the oppressed who struggle against racism does not as a consequence challenge the system of patriarchal male power. Ben du Toit must turn his back on the patriarchal birthright that is the husband's legacy, offered him as a necessary initiation rite. It is this gesture that proves he is worthy of black solidarity. To use Adrienne Rich's phrase, he must be "disloyal to civilization," and thus Palcy, whether consciously or unconsciously, links the struggle to end racism with feminist struggle, suggesting that any authentic white male challenge to white supremacy threatens the structure of white patriarchy. Few white feminists have acknowledged that the struggle to end racism challenges and disrupts white supremacist patriarchy, even though it is now commonplace for feminists to acknowledge the importance of race. Privileged phallocentric white women in Palcy's film want to keep intact their luxurious lifestyles and actively support white supremacist patriarchy. Representations of white womanhood in the film do not allow the viewer to overlook race and class and see these characters as "just women."

Again and again in *A Dry White Season* Palcy suggests that it is not one's race, gender, class, or circumstance that determines whether or not one will have a radical political standpoint. Exploited black people are as reluctant to participate in resistance struggle as paralyzed whites such as Ben du Toit. Like him, they must choose radical political commitments, and the power of that choice will be indicated by the sacrifices and risks taken to fulfill those commitments.

Although black people in the film share a common plight, they do not share a common understanding of their situation. They are not all radicalized. Palcy shows radical critical consciousness to be a learned standpoint, emerging from awareness of the nature of power and domination that is confirmed experientially. That is why the black children assume a primary role, questioning their parents, resisting the status quo. Many viewers allowed their dissatisfaction with the focus on white people to blind them to the powerful representations of black militancy. When has a Hollywood film shown black characters fiercely resisting white supremacy? What recent films by black filmmakers, Hollywood movies or independent productions, explore meaningful black resistance to white supremacy? Perhaps it is this cinematic standpoint that caused the public's lukewarm reception to *A Dry White Season*. Coming out of a theater in the Midwest, I heard white folks telling the people in line not to see the film because it was "too violent." Did too violent mean that the good white hero dies and the revolutionary black male hero lives?

It is not just the leading characters who are militant in the film. The most powerful dramatization of black militancy involves minor characters who are rarely mentioned in reviews. Yet their actions disrupt the idea that black liberation struggle can take place only if there is an inspired individual messianic (preferably male) leader. Two memorable scenes challenge this assumption. One occurs with the dramatization of the Soweto demonstration, where black schoolchildren were brutally murdered by police. Sophie Tema, a black woman journalist, gave the world the first eyewitness account of this event. Palcy reenacts this gesture through her retelling. Audiences watch as two black girls run from the police. The little one is brutally shot and her older sister stands facing her oppressors saying, "You killed my sister, kill me too!" This scene is utterly subversive, one of the most radical cinematic representations of black militancy. The direct gaze she gives the camera and her oppressors lets us know that she is not a victim. She stands in the midst of slaughter, not silent, but able to bear witness through speech, able to talk back. What young black girl watching this scene would not be awed and inspired by the courage on the older sister's face? Even though her little sister has been murdered as sacrifice, she lives to bear witness and to go forward in struggle. She remembers. This scene may have had little impact on viewers in this society who pay no attention to the affairs of little black girls, yet I wanted every black girl struggling to resist racism to see it—to be able to hold it in the mind's eye, placing it alongside all the passive sexist/racist portraits of black girl-hood that abound in the mass media.

Another unpredictably subversive scene takes place in the courtroom. There, it is not Marlon Brando's performance that grips the audience but that of the black male messenger who takes the witness stand ostensibly to provide testimony that will cover up the evils of white supremacy, that will deny the torture and violence against black people. When he rebels, audiences are not only surprised, they are overwhelmed. It is scenes such as this one that make *A Dry White Season* a successful thriller. But I was thrilled by the portrayal of resistance. Again, it was a resistance that demanded sacrifice. Militant rebellion has its price. The scene is no less powerful because it is utopian. Perhaps in these less than militant times we need to imagine the possibility of resistance anew; for what we cannot imagine will never happen. The messenger's actions are a call for militant resistance.

That spirit of militant resistance is most personified in the character of Stanley, played by South African Zakes Mokae. I first saw Zakes in a Fugard play. Talking with him about his performance, about the situation in South Africa, I was struck by the aura of calm that emanates from him. It is this calmness in the face of struggle that the character Stanley consistently conveys. Throughout the film he is the *rational* revolutionary strategist. We see his emotional vulnerability only when Emily dies, a scene that suggests that even the most militant spirit can be broken. Stanley can achieve his revolutionary goals only with collective support. It is Ben's support that sustains him during that difficult moment. Who can argue with the film's message that white people should assume a major role in the fight against racism and white supremacy and that black people should militantly resist?

It took Palcy five years to make this film. With this film she dares viewers to confront the current situation in South Africa. This is the fulfillment of the radical promise of the film, that it will both awaken and renew interest in the struggle against apartheid, that it will make us remember – "Our struggle is also a struggle of memory against forgetting." Anyone who does not hear the call for militant participation in black liberation struggle that this film conveys has missed its most important message.

After my talk in Toronto, I met with black South Africans to eat and dialogue. Sitting near me was Mangi, a young black male. I was impressed by his knowledge of black liberation struggles globally and his sophisticated understanding of feminist politics. I saw reflected in him the hope of a decolonized, liberated black mind. That night he talked of life in exile away from his mother and sister. In exile he is safe, alive, well, and critically conscious. Yet I hear in his voice the longing for an intimacy and family and community that are lost. The black family and community are torn asunder in *A Dry White Season*. That is the reality for most black families in South Africa. African Americans share this plight. Our families and communities are in crisis. Can we face that crisis with militancy, with the passionate will to resist and commitment to struggle that will lead to transformation in our lives and in society? Sick and dying, Lorraine Hansberry continued to interrogate her political commitment, asking: "Do I remain a revolutionary? Intellectually—without a doubt. But am I prepared to give my body to the struggle or even my comforts?" Palcy's film also poses that question. Who will answer?

Aspects of Black Feminist Cultural Ideology in Films by Black Women Independent Artists

Gloria Gibson-Hudson

> When images of African-American women are depicted on the screen by someone outside our culture, it is a projection of that filmmaker's mind—not an expression of our reality. The films I make are from a Black aesthetic and from an African-American woman's reality.
>
> *Julie Dash*

Black women independent filmmakers are emerging as one of the most vibrant, influential groups of contemporary cultural artists. Through their interpretations of black women's racial, sexual, and class status in white society, and of the sexism prevalent in the black male community, these "cultural storytellers" provide new perspectives on varied personal, sociocultural, and emotional relationships of black women's communities. Specifically, their works, drawn from the diverse experiences of black women's lives, promote exploration of self, attack racial polarity, instill racial and female pride, and encourage individual and collective activism.

Focusing on three representative films, *Hair Piece: A Film For Nappy-Headed People* (Ayoka Chenzira, 1984), *Illusions* (Julie Dash, 1983), and *Losing Ground* (Kathleen Collins, 1982), this analysis demonstrates (1) how past and present attitudes and behaviors toward black women have helped formulate certain tenets of the black feminist movement; (2) how selected films function within a black feminist cultural ideology to communicate aspects of African-American female sociocultural identity; and (3) how elements of a black feminist cultural ideology in films can serve as a catalyst to promote audience introspection and change.

Black Feminist Cultural Ideology

Art does not develop in a vacuum; its metamorphoses result from a melding of personal/cultural history, values, and norms. Moreover, art communicates a specific ideology derived from one's sociocultural identity. Bill Nichols states, "Ideology is how the existing ensemble of social relations represents itself to individuals. It proposes obviousness, a sense of 'the way things are' within which our sense of place and self emerges."[1]

Deborah Gray White explains the implications of this concept of ideology formation to the oppression of African-American women from the earliest days of slavery: "Black in a white society, slave in a free society, women in a society ruled by men, female slaves had the least formal power and were perhaps the most vulnerable group of antebellum Americans."[2] Their experience as female slaves contributed to their lack of self-identity as historical racism and the racial polarization of the sexes continues to define the "place" of black women in society despite the women's movements.

The ideology of black women's art developed in response to the complexities of black women's interpersonal relationships. Given the history of black women and their invisible or negative position within the dominant white patriarchal society, black women artists frequently infuse their work with didactic messages exposing racial and sexual inequities by pointing to aspects of their lives that are lost in the stereotypes and narrow roles allotted them in the mass media.[3]

Black feminist scholar Michele Wallace notes, "It is necessary to realize that the voices of black feminism in the U.S. emerge today from a long tradition of structural 'silence' of women of color within the sphere of global knowledge production."[4] African-American women filmmakers collectively as well as individually voice their personal and cultural realities based on "the shared belief that black women are inherently valuable, that [their] liberation is a necessity not as an adjunct to somebody else's but because of [their] need as human persons for autonomy."[5] Stemming from black feminism the philosophical core of which is the desire for complete recognition and understanding of black women's life experiences as valuable, complex, and diverse, the films of black women function as a cultural microcosm. They provide narratives that relate to historical occurrences and conditions, beliefs and values that are germane to black women. Consequently, their cinematic frames challenge decades of "structural silence" levied against African-American women.

Although black feminist cultural ideology manifests itself within film narratives in several ways, I want to concentrate on only two components: first, the eradication of racial and sexual distortion and myths concerning black womanhood.[6] The silver screen has consistently presented grossly distorted, patriarchal visions of black women since its inception. From *Birth of a Nation* (D. W. Griffith, 1915) onward, the character, morals, and physical stature of black women have been maligned in white cinema. In addition, while a few black male filmmakers have incorporated women's issues into their works, for the most part they have not unraveled the historical tensions that have contributed to a lack of self-fulfillment experienced by many black women.[7] Therefore, a dire need exists to dispel myths and "half-truths."

The second means by which black feminist cultural ideology manifests itself in films is through characterizations of black women conceived and projected by black women filmmakers themselves. Most important, the images are situated within a cinematic context to explore black women's sociocultural identity and the environmental forces that have shaped their self-concepts. As the narratives progress the filmmakers underscore the psychological maturation and self-awareness the characters undergo as their personal and/or cultural consciousness is transformed. From these films emerge black women characters that represent "cultural" heroines whose qualities of "heroism" exemplify the values of black women artists.

Perhaps the most dynamic element utilized by these women to restructure and convey the complexity of black women's existence is narrative theme, especially when understood as a concept within a cultural milieu. Viewed as chronicles of African-American experiences, theme becomes a powerful and indispensable agent to dramatize the characters' consciousness-raising process. Black women independent filmmakers hope that all audiences will understand how the characters' maturation and subsequent empowerment on the screen can function to strengthen their own personal knowledge and consciousness.

Hair Piece: A Film for Nappy-Headed People

Hair Piece: A Film for Nappy-Headed People is a hilarious animated satire that traces historically the "hair problem" among black people and questions the relationship between beauty and ethnicity. *Hair Piece* goes beyond a discussion of black hairstyles and fads to an examination of the cultural values that have accompanied those hairstyles. Chenzira's film functions as an important work because, "on the one hand it shows a political commitment and an ideological lucidity, and is on the other hand interrogative by nature, instead of being merely prescriptive."[8]

Chenzira, in the opening sequence, uses voice-over to communicate the value system operating before the black power movement. The narrator equates "bad" nappy hair with unattractiveness and charges that it is a major contributing factor in black women's inability to attract men or find and keep a job. Clearly the standard of beauty was constrictive, dictated by white "mainstream" society. Long, straightened hair was the imposed icon and many black women and men believed conformity to or an approximation of white standards would translate into social acceptance in white America.

Music reinforces the voice-over's message. The film begins with a blues melody to punctuate the dilemma of nappy hair and to capture the low self-esteem ingrained into the fiber of black consciousness. Still, as the voice-over and blues accentuate the feelings of inferiority that shackled many African Americans, Chenzira's visual images portray diversity among the penciled faces of black women moving across the screen, faces only. The visual complexity is intensified as she integrates photographed faces of black women, once again faces without hair. The women are noticeably different shades of "black," subtly pointing out that although African-American women share "blackness," their individual stories may contain unique experiences based on skin color and hair texture.[9]

The animated character begins her yarn. "For years there have been many approaches used by colored women, Negro women, and black women in dealing with what is commonly referred to as the 'hair problem.' " Thus Chenzira grounds her script within a historical context as the labels "colored," "Negro," and "black" convey different cultural icons and an evolving self-awareness. Colored is a label that conjures up the image of subservience, but the Negro, especially the "New" Negro of the Harlem Renaissance, suggests assertion, polite assertion of one's rights, and black connotes strength and aggression as black people demanded and fought for their freedom in the sixties. Thus the "hair problem" reflects historical eras, the politics of black America, and issues of self-identity, self-esteem, and cultural awareness.

The animated narrator then briefly discusses Madame Walker and the Afro hairstyle. While the narrator delivers these lines, animated women wearing natural hairstyles move across the screen. They are followed by a still of Angela Davis displaying her powerful Afro symbolizing resistance and liberation. On the soundtrack, James Brown bellows, "With yo bad self, say it loud, I'm black and I'm proud."

Through the film Chenzira briefly surveys the solutions African Americans have ingeniously adopted to disguise or eliminate the true nature of their hair, including wigs, permanents, and the straightening (hot) comb. In the sequence highlighting perms the "male-sounding narrator" begins to "preach" about the miracle of permanents. His rhetorical style imitates the speech/song mode of the black folk preacher. However, the dream of long hair, promised by the *white* cream to *colored girls*, turns into a nightmare as the female animated character returns to report that she had a

Hair in the full beauty of its own rebelliousness, from *Hair Piece: A Film for Nappy-Headed People.*

perm and her hair performed for a while, but then fell out. Once again, the dream is deferred and feelings of despair and unattractiveness resurface.

In the final scene, however, Chenzira dramatizes that exploration and affirmation of self can bring about a keener sense of one's personal and cultural identity. The narrator states, "If you have problems with your hair, perhaps the comb you use was not designed with your hair in mind." She continues over a still photo of black women wearing "natural" hairstyles including Afros, cornrows, and dreadlocks, "Perhaps now it's time to allow your hair to come into the full beauty of its own rebelliousness." During this climactic scene, the "cute" narrator's voice modulates to a powerful delivery, singing, "Give me something real, something that won't fade in the light of day," and the comical one-dimensional cartoon imagery transforms into a still photo of "real" black women wearing natural hairstyles.

Hair Piece functions as participatory, not escapist, art. Two levels of involvement emerge. First, black audience members laugh and "talk" to the film characters. In many cases, however, the laughter is a mask for suppressed anxiety or pain. Consequently, the second level of participation becomes personal confrontation. As the laughter fades, audience members begin thinking and discussing aspects of self-awareness and self-definition that reveal the film's function as a catalyst for introspection. The emphasis on filmmaking and film viewing shifts from an activity of entertainment to one of personal growth and pride while audiences follow Chenzira's identification of damaging, erroneous myths and attitudes about African-American identity and then affirms and celebrates black womanhood and African-American beauty.

Illusions

Like Chenzira's, Julie Dash's keen sense of racial and sexual oppression provides the undergirding structure for her film *Illusions*. Set during World War II, the black-and-white work examines various levels of illusion, including that which surrounds racial identity and the presentation of history. "This story is about Mignon Dupree, a black woman who appears to be white; Ester Jeeter, a black woman who is the singing voice for a white Hollywood movie star; and the power and the use of the film medium—three illusions in conflict with reality."[10] Dash dramatizes how the film industry, perhaps more than any other institution, has sown seeds of racism and sexism. Individually and collectively, one-dimensional stereotypes have promoted "homogeneous" imagery ignoring diversity. Dash demonstrates that film has the potential to become an influential mechanism to document and communicate black history, women's history—to be an inclusive history rather than continue to be illusionary, presenting a dysfunctional misrepresentation of reality.

Dash's goal to "demythify and demystify" cinema is presented in the opening credits. The film title is overlaid in white over a coiled reel of black film. In the following frames a shining, twirling white object moves from the background to the foreground in a sea of black. It appears to be an Oscar, the symbol of cinematic excellence. The female narrator's voice begins, "In the beginning was not the shadow, but the act and the province of Hollywood is not action but illusion."[11]

Illusions, however, functions as more than an attack upon Hollywood. It seeks to alert audience members to the seductive influence of cinema as it promotes "shadows" rather than the "acts" by denying or ignoring the diversities of black life. Dash is careful not to generalize, but specifically singles out Hollywood cinema, thereby establishing lines of demarcation between Hollywood and independent productions.

After a brief clip of newsreel footage from World War II, Dash presents the setting of the film, National Studios, and the central character, Mignon Dupree. Her suit is black and white, sculpted to depict a "double V."[12] Throughout the film Dash ingeniously colors *Illusions* with black and white —black-and-white film stock, a black-on-white, white-on-black suit, black *or* white woman. As the audience is presented with a full view of Mignon, the camera reveals another symbolic prop. She wears a hat with a veil.

In *Illusions*, Mignon wears a symbolic hat with a veil.

The veil or mask is a recurring symbol incorporated in black film and literature. It was scholar W. E. B. DuBois, however, who almost a century ago attempted to penetrate the psychological dimension of the veil, stating, "The Negro is born of a veil, and gifted with second sight in this American world—a world which yields him no true self-consciousness but only lets him see himself through the revelation of the other world."[13] The veil of Mignon Dupree functions not only as a shield that masks her true identity, but also as a barrier she must eventually overcome. Transcending the veil becomes the broader issue Dash addresses.[14]

Mignon is determined to structure her "visibility" by communicating realistic objectives for the film industry, although her boss, Mr. Forrester, is strictly concerned with finances. Her present assignment is to salvage their current film production, in which the audio and visual elements are out of sync. They cannot reshoot because the white singer is out of the country entertaining military troops. The solution is to bring back Ester Jeeter, the black singer who performed the original soundtrack, to perform a reverse lip sync.[15]

As Ester carefully watches the screen to match word for word the white singer's lip movements, Mignon appears distressed, seemingly convinced that now the visual imagery is out of sync. Her face fills with anguish at the gross appropriation of Ester's talent. Dash then divides the screen into three parts to juxtapose illusion with reality – at the top of the screen the white singer, in the foreground Ester, and in the center a reflection of the white technician in the sound booth. They all appear to be in close physical proximity to each other, but actually they are quite distant in the realization of their contribution "to the shadow."

After Ester saves the film, Mignon calls her mother. It is from this conversation that audience members gain greater insight into her ambition and true identity. Mignon explains that she wants more out of life and does not conform to the "traditional" mold of a woman. This line of discussion is interrupted by an apparent question from her mother regarding her racial disguise. Mignon replies, "They didn't ask and I didn't tell them." Dash then moves the camera in for a close-up shot of a small poster on the wall of the phone booth. It reads, "I am *so* an American – no matter what race, creed, or religion." Ironically, the poster has some, but not full, relevance to Mignon and Ester. Once again the dream is deferred.

The perplexity of Mignon's life intensifies in the next scene as she brings contract papers for Ester to sign. She immediately recognizes Mignon's true racial identity and embraces her as a sister. Ester functions as a pivotal character in Mignon's life. Their relationship develops and strengthens as they fantasize about goals and aspirations they fear will never materialize. Although both women are wounded by racism, they use each other as a support system. The two women illustrate how female bonding can ultimately provide self-healing and inner strength. Moreover, their relationship dramatizes that "for women, the need and desire to nurture each other is not pathological but redemptive, it is within that knowledge that real power is rediscovered."[16] Mignon's and Ester's relationship serves as a symbol of and a paradigm for female bonding.

In the final scene of *Illusions*, Lieutenant Bedsford discovers Mignon's true racial identity. Because of her heightened self-esteem, Mignon has the personal strength to "fight back." She proudly admits she is *not* ashamed of her race. Mignon then delivers a searing indictment against the film industry and biased, inaccurate historical accounts, stating, "I never once saw a film showing 'my boys' fighting for this country. Your scissors and paste methods have eliminated my participation in the history of this country."

As the camera moves in for a close-up shot Mignon is symbolically seated behind Mr. Forrester's desk. A voice-over reveals her heightened consciousness. "We would meet again, Ester Jeeter and I, for it was she who helped me see beyond shadows dancing on a white wall; to define what I had already come to know, and to take action without fearing. Yes, I wanted to use the power of the motion picture, for there are many stories to be told and many battles to begin."

Illusions presents a holistic image of an African-American woman and the effects of her social and cultural environment. Despite negative circumstances, Mignon emerges as a heroine. Dash molds a character who is not afraid to face her fears. Mignon recognizes the social forces that she must combat, and she also recognizes and values genuine friendship. These attributes closely conform to those Claudia Tate ascribes to heroines created by black women writers.[17]

Dash's film conforms to and promotes the concepts of black feminist cultural ideology. She uses film as a context in which to reexamine history, reminding audiences that "scissors and paste" are sometimes used to erase the contributions of African Americans, while at other times their talents are exploited or expropriated. Dash's cinematic reinterpretation of history articulates not a chronology of facts, but a period in the developing consciousness of two African-American women. The eradication of "illusion" and the presentation of "authenticity" regarding racial identity and the effects of history become the dominant message of the film. *Illusions*, however, is not a film of despair and despondency. The spiritual center, the very essence of the film, communicates the power of self-awareness and maturation.

Losing Ground

Kathleen Collins's film *Losing Ground* continues the theme of self-affirmation. Collins, however, produces a cinematic narrative that examines the importance of self-definition to the maturation process. Creatively she dramatizes the concept that change results from introspection and from an awareness that external stimuli such as sociocultural history, values, and norms have an impact upon the perception of self.

Briefly recounted, *Losing Ground* explores a black woman professor's quest for a more complete identity. Collins summarizes her persona: "She is an exceptionally intelligent woman, in many ways trapped by her intelligence – trapped into not being able to explore other areas of herself." Sara Rogers, a philosophy professor, is married to an artist who is outgoing and sometimes irrational. She is the antithesis of her husband.

Collins seeks to dramatize the transition of a woman from "emotional frigidity" to self-awareness and empowerment. The path to this "new self" for Sara is subsequently realized through searching for ecstasy and embracing her own psyche. Initially, however, Sara views herself strictly as a professional to the extent that she denies certain aspects of her own "womanhood." Consequently, in some ways she emulates personality traits generally attributed to men: she is analytical, cold, and sterile. Collins conveys this by employing medium shots throughout the film. These revealing shots capture Sara's personal environment and her disengaged interactions within it. For example, the audience first meets Professor

Rogers as she is lecturing to her class on existentialism. Most class members fight to stay awake or rock to the beat of their walkman. Amusingly, however, she rambles on with her lecture on the existential movement.

Dr. Rogers's class must prepare an analysis of Jean-Paul Sartre's play *No Exit* (1944). Yet, paradoxically, it is Sara who personifies the quest for existentialism as she wrestles with the meaninglessness of her life. Sara's present "realm of existence" consists of her sterile life as an intellectual and a wife – both personally unfulfilling. So she embarks on a mission to intellectually research the notion of ecstasy, a concept that implies the ability to *feel* emotional exaltation.

As a scholar she searches meticulously for concrete facts on her research topic by visiting the library, her mother, the church, and a spiritual reader. As she explores her topic, Sara actually yearns, not for information on ecstasy, but for the experience of ecstasy. She subsequently discovers that she has lost touch with her own spiritual essence. It is not until she conducts an introspective analysis of herself that the impetus to seek what she is missing surfaces.

A series of incidents and conversations precipitate Sara's awakening from "emotional somnambulism." The culmination of her quest for self-affirmation occurs, however, when she believes her husband Victor is having an affair with his Puerto Rican model. She then decides to star as "Frankie" in a student's film project entitled "Frankie and Johnny." This is Sara's first step in confronting her emotionless state. Paralleling the song's lyrics, her frustration with herself and Victor builds to a climax when Victor vigorously flaunts his relationship with the model:

> SARA: There you go taking your thing out in front of me. It's uncalled for, for you to sling your little private ecstasies in my face.
>
> VICTOR: This is not one of your classes, don't lecture to me.
>
> SARA: Don't fuck around then! Don't you take your dick out like it was artistic – like it's some goddamn paint brush. Maybe that's what's uneven – that I got nothing to take out.

Sara has been suffering in silence, but no more. On the one hand she is jealous of Victor's ability to experience ecstasy and is angered at the means by which he achieves it. Sara questions if ecstasy is achieved only by "taking something out." Is it strictly a male privilege? Collins captures the irony in Sara's life. She feels emotionally fragmented and frustrated by restrictions she has placed on herself. In her thoroughly exasperated state she calls her mother on the way to the film set.

> SARA: I'm on shaky ground.
>
> MOTHER: That's not the kind of feeling you'd like.

SARA: That's what Victor loves about me; that there's no chaos any-where.

MOTHER: That's the quality in you that even I admit to counting on.

SARA: Mama . . . (*silence*)

Sara has functioned as a dependable "pillar" for her students, mother, and husband – a pillar that now crumbles under severe pressure. She must determine how she will resolve her personal relationship with her mother, her husband, and, most important, herself.

Collins employs a blues folk ballad and the film-within-a-film technique to conceptualize Sara's emotional experience. "Frankie and Johnny" serves as a microcosm of Sara's world. It becomes the "stage" in which Sara explores her inner self through a film exploring someone else's experience. Most important, the "Frankie and Johnny" blues ballad resides in the oral tradition of black folklore and music and within the film to elucidate aspects of the overall cinematic narrative.[18] In addition, the blues ballad has historically functioned as a vehicle to confront life on a personal basis as it explores intimate situations in detail. The blues provides the ideal cultural context for Sara's examination of self and transforming consciousness because the text and structure in many instances represent a cultural icon communicating sexual empowerment.[19]

Sara, like Frankie, rebels. In the final scene of *Losing Ground*, the student director is filming the climactic scene of "Frankie and Johnny." Sara is dressed as Frankie, low-cut top, skirt with a slit, hair down and blowing in the wind. As the director gives final instructions, Victor arrives at the set. In this provocative scene, Frankie points the gun to kill her lover, Johnny. On another level, it is Sara pointing the gun at Victor and her previous life. Collins uses a medium close-up shot to allow the audience to experience the mental anguish Sara is undergoing. As the saxophone plays the theme music of "Frankie and Johnny," the student director shouts out, "OK, Frankie . . . raise the gun . . . take your time and when it feels right . . . blow him away."

Frankie fires, Johnny falls. As the bullet explodes it is Sara's previous psychological state that is shattered to reveal a new person. Paradoxically, Sara fires and Victor also symbolically falls. Collins moves the camera to a close-up of Victor's face, also filled with anguish. They both understand that if their relationship is to survive, there must be change. Collins moves the camera back to Sara, still pointing the gun. She ends the film with stark, naked silence – only the reverberation of the gunshot is heard. If, when, and how Sara and Victor will mend their relationship is not answered. The only clear message is that Sara has discovered something about herself that was previously lost.

Collins dramatizes a concise message—introspection is the path to empowerment. In an article published posthumously, she admits, "While I'm interested in external reality, I am much more concerned with how people resolve their inner dilemma in the face of external reality."[20] *Losing Ground* encourages women to develop the inner resources they need to cope with greater social forces. Furthermore, it conforms to the basic principles identified by Jan Rosenberg in what she terms "feminist issue films": "The themes in issue films delineate the shared, socially structured limitations, oppression, and discrimination which women suffer as a group. The recordings of such experiences are compressed cinematic simulations of the consciousness-raising process."[21] Collins's objective is to uncover perplexing ironies demonstrating that "through conflict we get to see something about people, and realize something about them and ultimately about ourselves."[22]

Synthesis

In one sense, *Hair Piece, Illusions,* and *Losing Ground* are three very different films because the experiences of black women in America are not homogeneous. Collins and Dash focus on highly privileged women, certainly middle class; Chenzira is more pluralistic and inclusive and transcends class. Sara's identification with Frankie and Mignon's with Ester take them out of upper-class privilege. The films demonstrate that differences existed and exist in the lives of African-American women and in the lives of the filmmakers translating everyday experiences into cinematic narratives.

On another level, however, striking similarities among these films suggest a cinematic message forged from common ingredients of black womanhood. Moreover, aspects of black feminist cultural ideology, which provide the undergirding structure contributing meaning, stem from a shared sociocultural history. Consequently, one of the major threads that permeates black feminist cultural ideology and the films of Dash, Chenzira, and Collins is the need for women to understand themselves in the totality of their sociocultural environment.

Chenzira, Dash, and Collins demonstrate that confrontation with self and others, is, in fact, intrinsic to growth and inner strength. As the film characters confront their problems, they, in essence, help eradicate prescribed images of self and they forge their own unique self-definition. Thus these films dramatize the resilience of black women who seek creative solutions as they confront and overcome personal and historical tensions.

These films also demonstrate that women should function as reflectors for one another. That is, in their reciprocal relationships they should be able to share their feelings, insights, and fears. Sisterhood and female bonding become important ingredients for survival. Therefore, these films, and others, function as participatory art suggesting a paradigm for personal and collective introspection and activism. Unlike mainstream film, which frequently promotes a "living happily ever after" formula, films by black independent filmmakers frequently isolate the necessary personal skills needed to interpret and confront issues in everyday life with the hope that a heightened sense of self will lead to individual and collective empowerment.

Each of the films presented here addresses the multiplicity of life's issues that converge with African-American women's historic and contemporary experience. Cinema becomes a form of expression that allows filmmakers to present their personalized vision of culture. Most often, black women independent filmmakers select themes that highlight sociocultural issues, not only promoting education, but also personal awareness and activism. Black in a white world, woman in a man's world, Dash, Chenzira, and Collins affirm their existence and present and control their image, thereby dignifying "blackness" and "womanhood."

Notes

I would like to thank the following scholars for their generous and faithful help: Elizabeth Hadley Freydberg, Phyllis Klotman, Adrienne Livingston, and Gayle Tate. Special thanks to my husband, Dr. Herman Hudson, for his comments, encouragement, and support.

1. Bill Nichols, *Ideology and the Image* (Bloomington: Indiana University Press, 1981), 1.

2. Deborah Gray White, *Ar'n't I a Woman: Female Slaves in the Plantation South* (New York: W.W. Norton, 1985), 15.

3. See the following for discussions of how black women's music and literature convey poignant sociocultural messages. Billie Barlow and Lisa Miller, "Women's Music: Activism and Artistic Expression," *Iris: A Journal about Women*, no. 15 (Spring-Summer 1986); Barbara Christian, "Trajectories of Self-Definition," in *Conjuring: Black Women, Fiction, and Literary Tradition*, ed. Marjorie Pryse and Hortense J. Spillers (Bloomington: Indiana University Press, 1985).

4. Michele Wallace, *Invisibility Blues: From Pop to Theory* (New York: Verso, 1990), 242.

5. Combahee River Collective, "A Black Feminist Statement," in *This Bridge Called My Back: Writings by Radical Women of Color*, ed. Cherríe Moraga and Gloria Anzaldúa (New York: Kitchen Table: Women of Color Press, 1983), 212.

6. Because black women's cinema still exists in a developmental stage as an emerging tradition, new and dynamic theoretical foci to analyze the films are at an equally embryonic phase. Several approaches such as "womanist perspective," "black feminism," "Afrocentric feminism," and "Third World feminism" are beginning to surface in the analysis of black women's film. See Mark A. Reid, "Dialogic

Modes of Representing Africa(s): Womanist Film," *Black American Literature Forum* 25 (Summer 1991): 375–88; "Black Feminism and Media Studies," upcoming issue of *Quarterly Review of Film and Video*; Trinh T. Minh-ha, "Questions of Images and Politics," in *When the Moon Waxes Red: Representation, Gender, and Cultural Politics* (New York: Routledge, 1991).

7. The following films by black men address the complexity of black women's lives: Haile Gerima's *Bush Mama*, Billy Woodberry's *Bless Their Little Hearts*, and Bill Gunn's *Ganja and Hess*.

8. Trinh T. Minh-ha, *When the Moon Waxes Red*, 149.

9. Intraracial prejudice is addressed in *Color* by Warrington Hudlin and Denise Oliver and *School Daze* by Spike Lee.

10. *Black Camera: Catalog for the Black Filmmaker Foundation*, (New York, 1982), 11.

11. This statement is a direct quote from Ralph Ellison's *Shadow and Act* (New York: Random House, 1964), 276.

12. The double V philosophy was promoted by many blacks during World War II. Blacks fought for victory in Europe against fascism. They felt that this monumental effort would subsequently result in victory at home against racism.

13. W. E. B. DuBois, *The Souls of Black Folk* (Chicago: A. C. McClurg, 1903), 7.

14. Trinh T. Minh-ha gives a slightly different interpretation of the veil: "If the act of unveiling has a liberating potential, so does the act of veiling. It all depends on the context in which such an act is carried out. [To replace the veil] is to reappropriate [one's] space or to claim anew difference, in defiance of genderless hegemonic standardization" (151). It should be noted that Mignon never replaces the veil in the film, but she does defy hegemonic, patriarchial standardization.

15. Ester's voice is really that of Ella Fitzgerald. Dash adds another level of illusion, only with a cultural foundation.

16. Audre Lorde, "The Master's Tools Will Never Dismantle the Master's House," in *This Bridge Called My Back*, 98.

17. See *Black Women Writers at Work* (New York: Continuum, 1988), xxiv.

18. See Kathryn Kalinak, "Music as Narrative Structure in Hollywood Film" (unpublished Ph.D. diss., University of Illinois, 1982), 2.

19. Hazel Carby, "It Jus Be's Dat Way Sometime: The Sexual Politics of Women's Blues," *Radical America* 20, no. 4 (1986): 21.

20. David Nicholson, "A Commitment to Writing: A Conversation with Kathleen Collins Prettyman," *Black Film Review* 5 (Winter 1988–89): 12.

21. Jan Rosenberg, *Women's Reflections: The Feminist Film Movement* (Ann Arbor: UMI Research Press, 1983), 55.

22. Nicholson, "Commitment to Writing," 14.

Selected Video/Filmography

Anita Addison: *The Secret Space* (1981); *Savannah* (1989), 30 min.; *Sound of Sunshine, Sound of Rain* (1983). Addison Productions.
Madeline Anderson: *Integration Report I* (1960), 24 min.; *I Am Somebody* (1970), 30 min. Indiana University.

Camille Billops: *Suzanne, Suzanne* (1982), 25 min.; *Older Women and Love* (1988), 28 min.; *Finding Christa* (1991), 55 min. Women Make Movies.

Carroll Parrott Blue: *Varnette's World: A Study of a Young Artist* (1979), 26 min.; *Conversations with Roy deCarava* (1984), 28 min.; Smithsonian World Series: Nigerian Art–Kindred Spirits (1990), 58 min. Produced by WETA and the Smithsonian Institute. First Run.

Ayoka Chenzira: *Flamboyant Ladies Speak Out* (1982), 30 min.; *Hair Piece: A Film for Nappy-Headed People* (1984), 10 min.; *Secret Sounds Screaming: The Sexual Abuse of Children* (1986), 30 min.; *Five out of Five* (1987), 7 min.; *Zajota and the Boogie Spirit* (1989), 20 min. Women Make Movies.

Kathleen Collins: *The Cruz Brothers and Miss Malloy* (1980), 54 min.; *Losing Ground* (1982), 86 min. Mypheduh Films.

Julie Dash: *Four Women* (1978), 7 min.; *Illusions* (1982), 34 min.; *Praise House* (1991), 30 min.; Women Make Movies; *Daughters of the Dust* (1991), 30 min. Kino International.

Zeinabu irene Davis: *Crocodile Conspiracy* (1986), 13 min., *Recreating Black Women's Media Image* (1987), 28 min. Third World Newsreel. *Cycles* (1989), 17 min.; *A Powerful Thang* (1991), 58 min. Women Make Movies.

Elena Featherston: *Visions of the Spirit: A Portrait of Alice Walker* (1989), 58 min. Women Make Movies.

Alile Sharon Larkin: *Your Children Come Back to You* (1979), 27 min.; *A Different Image* (1982), 51 min. Women Make Movies. *Miss Fluci Moses: A Video Documentary* (1987), 22 min.; *Dreadlocks and the Three Bears* (1991), 12 min. Alile Productions.

Michelle Parkerson: *But Then She's Betty Carter* (1980), 53 min.; *Gotta Make This Journey: Sweet Honey in the Rock* (1983), 58 min.; *Storme: Lady of the Jewel Box* (1987), 21 min. Women Make Movies.

Telling Family Secrets: Narrative and Ideology in *Suzanne, Suzanne* by Camille Billops and James V. Hatch

Valerie Smith

During the past twenty years or so, black feminist writers have turned their attention increasingly to the family, broadly defined, as a site at which black women and children suffer the varied and conjoined effects of racist and patriarchal exploitation. Nineteenth-century black feminist theorists such as Anna Julia Cooper and Ida B. Wells denounced the large-scale cultural racism and sexism that impeded black women's access to the franchise, education, and the professions, but said little about the ways in which misogyny and patriarchy shaped the domestic lives of black women. Early- to mid-twentieth-century black women writers of imaginative literature such as Jessie Fauset, Zora Neale Hurston, and Nella Larsen articulated some of the ways in which the institution of marriage limited the options available to black women. But as Deborah E. McDowell and Patricia Hill Collins, among others, have indicated, only in recent years have writers such as Toni Morrison, Audre Lorde, Alice Walker, Angela Davis, Gayl Jones, Ntozake Shange, Michele Wallace, bell hooks, and Pearl Cleage mounted more trenchant and explicit critiques of black women's vulnerability to domestic violence.[1] Increasingly, they have addressed as well what Shange calls the "conspiracy of silence" that constructs as disloyal or antimale any black feminist attempt to name the vulnerability of black women to abuse at the hands of black men.[2] Although this kind of secrecy is at least partly an overcompensation for mainstream associations of black masculinity with immorality and violence, Hill Collins is right to equate this silence with "the bond of family secrecy that often pervades dysfunctional families," thereby enabling the abuses to continue.[3]

This group of black feminist writers thus replaces narratives of black consensus and unity, predicated on women's silence, with narratives of disruption and dissent. They reconceptualize the idealized notion of a monolithic black community; as such they interrogate the family romance upon which this notion of community relies.[4]

In her recent essay "Reading Family Matters," McDowell likewise situates within the context of a family romance the virulently misogynist response on the part of some black male critics to the work of some black feminist writers. Offering a detailed critique of certain reviews of the work of Wallace, Shange, Morrison, Jones, and Walker, McDowell shows that these writers have been excoriated since the mid-seventies for exposing male abuses within "the family," be it the nuclear family or the broader black community. McDowell suggests that to the extent that these writers belie the family romance—"the story of the Black Family cum Black community headed by the Black Male who does battle with an oppressive White world"[5]—they are represented by certain male critics as traitors to the race who are overly influenced by the white feminist agenda. To the extent that within their texts they problematize the status of the nuclear or racialized family, they are constructed as errant daughters by some members of the black literary establishment.

Such criticism notwithstanding, it is of course crucial that black feminists continue to shatter the secrecy that surrounds the issue of domestic violence within black communities. As Judith Lewis Herman, Lorde, Linda Gordon, Wallace, hooks, Davis, and many others have argued, naming the prevalence of domestic violence within any racial group or economic class profoundly threatens public consciousness and patriarchal values.[6] Naming domestic violence constitutes a refusal to mask the ways in which ideologies of race, class, and gender conspire to subjugate women who are physically, economically, or psychologically vulnerable.

To borrow Kimberle Williams Crenshaw's formulation, within the context of domestic violence, the intersectionality of racial and gendered hierarchies makes itself evident.[7] Precisely because of the complex cultural and psychopathological forces that enable domestic violence to continue, it is an area sorely in need of feminist interventions. Black feminist interventions are especially critical in analyzing domestic violence within black communities, since they illuminate the specific impact of constructions of blackness upon the abuse to which men submit women. By this light, black feminist analyses of the nexus of classism, misogyny, and racism might enable a discourse around black domestic violence that constructs black men simultaneously as victims of racism and perpetrators of physical abuse; that locates individual responsibility within the context of oppressive cultural circumstances and conditioning; that explores the sexualization of race and class oppression; that examines the subtle mechanism of black women's own internalized self-loathing; and that critiques constructions of masculinity and femininity more broadly. Continued silence, by contrast, perpetuates the circumstances that allow the abuses to continue and isolates both victims and victimizers alike.

Many readers are familiar with black feminist theoretical and "literary" critiques of black women's victimization within heterosexual domestic configurations. Black feminist directors are no less concerned with breaking the silence around women's exploitation, but their work is less widely accessible than is that of their counterparts who work in the medium of print. *Suzanne, Suzanne*, independently produced and directed by Camille Billops and James V. Hatch, provides a compelling example of the nature of black feminist cinematic work that addresses the issue of domestic violence.[8] A 16mm black-and-white documentary shot in 1977 and released in 1982, the film places the narrative of physical and drug abuse in a specific family within the context of a more expansive critique of the nuclear family. The demystification both of this family and of the idea of the middle-class family is achieved within the context of a nonfiction film that repeatedly destabilizes the status of the truth. In this discussion of the film I examine how *Suzanne, Suzanne*'s interrogation of the space between "the real" and "the fictional" functions within the film's critique of a specific family and the myth of the normative, nuclear family.

The extracinematic circumstances that led to the production of *Suzanne, Suzanne* remind us that no documentary is ever "true" or "objective;" "the truth" is inevitably constructed. Billops and Hatch undertook this film intending it to be the story of Billops's niece Suzanne Browning's battle against drug addiction. During the course of their interviews with Suzanne and other relatives, the story of Suzanne's and her mother's—Billops's sister Billie's—experiences of abuse emerged. The film that was to situate Suzanne as a recovered drug addict thus became additionally, if not instead, an exploration of the suffering to which women are vulnerable in the nuclear family. The filmmakers then constructed an implicit narrative forged from sequencing, crosscutting, and the interpolation of still photographs and footage from home movies that identifies domestic violence as a major factor in Suzanne's addiction.

The film begins with a still photograph of Brownie (the abusive husband and father) lying in repose in his coffin. First in a voice-over and then on camera, Suzanne reflects on her turbulent and ambivalent relationship with her father. In the opening sequence, Suzanne's comments are crosscut with her mother's on-camera reflections about her own profoundly mixed feelings about her late husband. Throughout much of the film, in scenes shot in and around the family home in Los Angeles, Suzanne, Billie,

Michael (their respective son and brother), and the grandparents answer Billops's questions about topics such as the importance of fashion and beauty to the women in the household; Suzanne's addiction and criminal behavior; and Brownie's abuse of his wife and daughter. The characters for the most part speak to Billops, the codirector and interviewer. However, in two powerful scenes that occur late in the film, Billie and Suzanne talk to each other in a highly stylized context. In these scenes, the two women appear to achieve some recognition of the relationship between their experiences of abuse.

The film is composed of at least three different representational modes: twenty-five still photographs; eight clips from Bell & Howell home movies taken by Walter ("Mr.") Dotson, Billie's and Billops's stepfather; and the frame of the film, which includes the interviews and the music and possesses the authority of sound.[9] By negotiating the relationship among these three modes through juxtaposition and crosscutting, the filmmakers produce their cinematic narrative as well as the critique that underlies that narrative.

In an interview with playwright-director George C. Wolfe, Billops says that she and Hatch "could not arrive at what the film was about until [she] told their editor . . . about Mr. Dotson's home movies." She continues: "These were the missing pieces that gave the film its focus. . . . [The home movies] gave the family a history."[10] The footage and photographs certainly function to place the characters within a generational, class, and regional context. They also produce much of the narrative tension in the film, by prompting questions about how the beaming young girl shown at age eight becomes the adult addict, how the seemingly stable family becomes fractured.

What is perhaps most striking about these interpolated images is their familiarity. Several of them fix moments that have become ritualized within the construction of the nuclear family: pictures of Brownie smiling, embracing his children; footage of the family off to church in their Sunday best; a photograph of the dead Brownie lying in repose in his open coffin; footage of Billie holding Camille's infant daughter, Christa—all establish the family in familiar middle-class respectability. These pieces of documentary evidence thus memorialize a picture-perfect family, one whose history might be reconstructed out of the photographic record of public events: holiday celebrations, deaths, births, and so on.

And yet, it is precisely the familiarity of these images that the film contests. If viewers were to rely solely upon spoken critiques of the family romance, we would perhaps be less likely to consider our own implication in what Annette Kuhn calls "the signification process."[11] However, the silent record of the still photographs and the home movies encodes a subtext of family stability and safety that viewers interpret and that Billops and

Hatch's film challenges. The juxtaposition of Suzanne's and Billie's stories with the images from the family history prompts viewers to question both the process by which we attribute meanings to images as well as the explanatory power of certain rituals. Perhaps more important, the use of these materials enables the film to address at once the psychopathology of this particular family as well as the nature of the oppressive cultural weight that the image of the nuclear family bears.

The inequitable distribution of power within the nuclear family that, taken to its outer limits, allows husbands to tyrannize their wives and children is here the most obvious cause of the family's circumstances and Suzanne's addiction. However, the internalized effects of the commodification of women's bodies within a gendered and racialized hierarchy are shown to have produced substantial psychological damage as well. The world of fashion and beauty culture as represented in the film clearly provided an opportunity for women to control their labor and express their creativity: Billie and her mother, Alma, share a gift for sewing and fashion design; both love the opportunity for self-display that performing in fashion shows allows. These activities are thus to some degree emancipatory; however, they contribute to a climate in which the value of women and children is located in their appearance and objectification.

Within the film, Michael, Suzanne's brother, is assigned value both because of his status as only son and eldest child, and also because he has inherited what the family considers his mother's good looks. He is introduced as Suzanne's "handsome brother," and he appears grooming his oversize moustache in the bathroom mirror three of the times he is evident in the film. Clearly delighted with his appearance, he grows and waxes a moustache that is a virtual parody of itself, and takes pride in the comments his mother wrote in his baby book. Suzanne, on the other hand, says that she grew up believing herself to be ugly. She inherited Browning, not Billops, features—what she calls "puffy eyes, sorta set back into the head." The still photographs suggest that her sense of being unattractive may bear a particular racial valence, for she has broader features, coarser hair, and darker skin than does her mother. While Michael can delight in the pride Billie took in his good looks, Suzanne recalls the humiliation of being considered less attractive than her mother.

In the scene, Billie applies makeup to Suzanne's face while the two of them discuss issues having to do with their respective appearances. Visually and discursively, this scene dramatizes the extent to which Suzanne may have felt betrayed by her mother. This scene recalls its earlier counterpart in which Billie applies makeup to her mother Alma's face while both are facing the camera. The two women are positioned in that earlier instance—Billie bending over Alma's shoulder to apply her blush—so that both may be introduced to the viewer. In the latter scene, however, which focuses explicitly on the issue of appearance, Suzanne's face is turned away, hidden, from the camera while her mother, facing the camera, applies her makeup. The staging of this scene allows greater access to Billie's confident subjectivity while concealing and thereby reinforcing Suzanne's expression of her self-loathing. Furthermore, it provides a visual counterpart for the story Billie and Suzanne recount during the scene.

The two women describe the reactions of Suzanne's friends upon meeting Billie:

> BILLIE: In the very beginning, I didn't really pay that much attention to it. But then, later on, I began to watch Suzanne's face when she would say to her friends, "I want you to meet my mother." And they'd say, "Oh, how do you do Mrs. Browning?" And then they'd turn and say, "Well, what the hell ever happened to you?" And that would just really get to me. I didn't like it, because they were making too much of a comparison. And I realized at that time that Suzanne did not like that at all.

> CAMILLE BILLOPS: Suzanne, did you believe that?

> SUZANNE: What they were saying? Sure. You know, I knew it. Because when I looked at my mom . . . you know my mother was beautiful . . . you know she's still a beautiful woman. You know, I got a really big complex from that. I thought I was extremely ugly.

By the standard of physical attractiveness, Suzanne always loses to her mother, her self-esteem always negated. Billie seems strikingly unaware of the destructive power of her investment in appearance. Her secondhand disapproval of Suzanne's friends' response to her exposes her insensitivity—she noticed that the comparison between her daughters' and her own looks was inappropriate only when she perceived Suzanne's pain, when she realized that "Suzanne did not like that at all." It is striking as well that on the heels of Suzanne's admission that she felt less attractive than her mother, Billie boasts about having entered the Mrs. America contest of 1979. The sequencing here—the makeup scene, Billie's displaying of her beauty pageant photograph, Michael's grooming of his moustache—exemplifies the nature of the causal links that the filmmaker sought to establish and suggests a closer connection between mother and son than that between mother and daughter. The staging and sequencing in these scenes exemplify the ways in which the filmmakers impose a specific interpretation upon the experiences described.

Mr. Dotson's Bell & Howell home movies enact the commodification of women and children that Billops and Hatch's film critiques. Virtually all of the footage from these films centers on women and children, under the proprietary, controlling gaze of the male—the absent father—behind the camera. Displayed in Easter finery or in scenes of domestic delight, they are signs of the family's, particularly the father's, achievement.

Suzanne, Suzanne, however, is the product not of the father behind the camera but of a daughter with her partner/codirector and cinematographer. Here, women and children are not silent collaborators within a family romance. Rather, they speak in response to questions that Billops poses or that they pose themselves. Moreover, while cinematographer Dion Hatch, like Mr. Dotson, is not visible within this film, Billops, one of two producer-directors, is both audible and, more important, visible. Twice she appears standing side by side in the mirror with Michael. The image of a woman with braids and a faint but discernible moustache, standing beside a man waxing his moustache, also deconstructs conventional standards of beauty that the film problematizes elsewhere.[12]

Billops's appearance in the mirror reminds the viewer of the constructedness of the film and the cinematic process. It is also a figure for the black feminist intervention within the family romance. Simultaneously director and subject, relative and observer, insider and outsider, she occupies the position from which the multiple manipulations of parents, sons, and daughters are visible.

Camille Billops's liminal role as both subject and observer is evident at the juncture of cinematic and extracinematic discourse. Within the film, Billops appears in Bell & Howell footage as the young mother of an infant daughter, Christa. As these scenes appear, Camille and this same daughter, now an adult, sing the title song, which Christa composed. However, as Billops and Hatch's most recent film, *Finding Christa* (1991), recounts, the space between birth and duet is occupied by a narrative that is, in its own way, as disturbing as Suzanne's. Christa's father is absent from these scenes not because he is behind the camera, but because he has abandoned his family. In the years between birth and duet, Billops, a single mother, determined that she was unable to care for Christa adequately and gave her up for adoption when the child was four years old. The choices enacted in this extracinematic narrative further critique the images of motherhood and family enshrined within the Bell & Howell home movies; the narrative of this fragmented family anticipates the story told in *Finding Christa*.

Through juxtapositions and the multiple interrogations of its material, the story that *Suzanne, Suzanne* tells problematizes the potentially destructive nature of the middle-class nuclear family; the film's discourses work to dismantle the image of the ideal family created by the photographs and home movies. Indeed, the inclusion of these materials in the film interrogates their very status as evidence. However much one might wish to read photographic images as denotative—signs of what really existed—they too are fictive constructs; like the techniques of cinematic or literary realism, they represent a body of conventions that privileges par-

Suzanne and Billie preparing for their exchange at the end of *Suzanne, Suzanne*.

ticular ideological positions. The shot of Alma and her granddaughters going off to church – the one in an elegant suit, the other in dresses with crinoline slips – memorializes an eminently readable image of family harmony, recalling the popular conception of the ostensibly religious nuclear family: the family that stays together because it prays together. Given the subtext of family violence, however, this Bell & Howell moment suggests the central role of performance and imitation in the ways that families, like individuals, construct their identities.

These considerations about the place of performance within real life, and about the artificiality of documentary evidence, shape the ways we interpret the two scenes between Billie and Suzanne that are set in a darkened room, with the two women, shot from midchest up, simultaneously facing the camera.[13] This darkened space provides an alternative to the domestic locations used for the rest of the film – rooms that recall the past history of family relations. In striking contrast to the scenes that are shot in and around Alma and Walter Dotson's Los Angeles home, these dark, stark, partially scripted scenes are constructed as pivotal and self-consciously dramatic. In this setting, the relationship between mother and daughter is altered dramatically.

Billops says that Hatch provided Suzanne with a list of questions to ask her mother in these scenes. One such question is the one with which

Suzanne begins: "Do you love me?" By providing Suzanne with a list of questions, Hatch and Billops allow her to assume the role of interviewer. But at some point, Billops says, Suzanne began to ask her own questions, assuming the role of both interviewer and director. This recollection is confirmed by the transcript of unused footage from an interview in which Suzanne admits that she used this occasion to ask some of her own questions:

> BILLIE [BB]: I knew that in the very beginning it was going to stir up something, but I thought, well Suzanne and I, we have never really talked. . . . I didn't know what was going to happen. . . . Yesterday . . . the last thing I ever wanted to do was to cry. . . . I didn't know that she was going to ask me about did I know what it felt like to be on death row. . . .
>
> SUZANNE: . . . It wasn't Jim. . . . I told you Sunday, I have questions – of my own. You know, there's like a lot of things that come to my head. You know, and I wanted an answer. . . . I was there to ask some of those things.

Up until the exchange between Billie and Suzanne that we see in the film, the family members have, for the most part, answered the questions that are asked of them. But here Suzanne takes advantage of the context to address her own nagging concerns. And Billie uses the occasion to tell her own story. When Suzanne asks, for instance, if she'd like to know what it was like to wait on death row, Billie doesn't really respond to her, but rather explains both to herself and to her daughter why she would retreat into the shower whenever Brownie came home, answering the question she had posed indirectly earlier in the film.[14]

The staging of these scenes calls attention to their artificiality even as their sheer emotional power bestows upon them a quality of authenticity. I am tempted to read these scenes as "real" at the moment when Suzanne asks if Billie's beatings were like being on death row. At this point, Billie's head shifts and her facial expression changes, apparently signaling a recognition of their shared circumstances. Not only were both victims of physical violence, but both also endured the psychological terror of imagining and awaiting each instance of Brownie's abuse. The sense of process evident here is coded as being more authentic than the communication that occurs in the rest of the film. But the very fact that the film exists within a frame that questions "the real" renders such a determination problematic. These scenes in the darkened space suggest minimally, however, that to the extent that domestic relations are captured (if not fabricated) in our interactions with private as well as public media, they might be reconstituted as well through the intervention of the artificial.

I have considered here ways in which the intersectionality of black feminist analysis inflects this narrative of domestic violence. *Suzanne, Suzanne* constitutes a cinematic discourse that interrogates a host of interconnections, those between cultural circumstances and individual responsibility, documents and ideology, truth and artificiality, and, indirectly, racism and misogyny. The film seeks to disrupt the facade of orderly respectability that depends upon the conspiracy of silence within the family. Yet nowhere is the tension between the disruptive power of the cinematic process and the seductive power of the family romance more powerful than at the end of *Suzanne, Suzanne*, where the film appears to satisfy viewers' desire for closure and healing.[15]

In the second of the "staged" scenes between Suzanne and Billie, Suzanne partially faces her mother and tells her about one particular beating when Brownie whipped her until she bled. This description is particularly harrowing, yet Billie seeks to recuperate Brownie's behavior by reassuring Suzanne that she was her father's favorite. Billie's explanation pales when contrasted with this vivid account; the juxtaposition reveals the price narrators and viewers alike pay for narrative closure and the sentimentalization of family.

Notes

I wish to thank Marianne Hirsch, Clyde Taylor, Richard Yarborough, Linda Dittmar, Diane Carson, and Janice Welsch for their advice and help as I wrote and revised this essay. I am especially grateful to Camille Billops and James V. Hatch, without whose advice and encouragement I could never have undertaken this project.

1. Deborah E. McDowell, "Reading Family Matters," in *Changing Our Own Words: Essays on Criticism, Theory, and Writing by Black Women*, ed. Cheryl A. Wall (New Brunswick, N.J.: Rutgers University Press, 1989), 75–97; Patricia Hill Collins, *Black Feminist Thought: Knowledge, Consciousness, and the Politics of Empowerment* (Cambridge, Mass.: Unwin Hyman, 1991).

2. Interview with Claudia Tate quoted in Hill Collins, *Black Feminist Thought*, 187. A recent example of this kind of silencing occurred during the recent confirmation hearings of Supreme Court Justice Clarence Thomas. Various African-American women and men believed that Professor Anita Hill was disloyal to the race for submitting Thomas to public scrutiny (and potential humiliation) by accusing him of sexual harassment. The misogyny of this response is evident in the presupposition that his embarrassment is considered inherently more damaging to African Americans than is the continued abuse Professor Hill allegedly underwent.

3. Ibid.

4. I draw here on Marianne Hirsch's version of Freud's definition of the family romance. Hirsch writes that "the family romance is the story we tell ourselves about the social and psychological reality of the family in which we find ourselves

and about the patterns of desire that motivate the interaction among its members. . . . The notion of family romance can thus accommodate the discrepancies between *social reality* and *fantasy construction*, which are basic to the experience and the institution of family." See Marianne Hirsch, *The Mother/Daughter Plot: Narrative, Psychoanalysis, Feminism* (Bloomington: Indiana University Press, 1989), 9–10.

5. McDowell, "Reading Family Matters," 78.

6. Judith Lewis Herman, *Father-Daughter Incest* (Cambridge, Mass.: Harvard University Press, 1981); Audre Lorde, *Sister Outsider: Essays and Speeches* (Trumansburg, N.Y.: Crossing Press, 1984); Linda Gordon, *Heroes of Their Own Lives: The Politics and History of Family Violence* (New York: Penguin Books, 1988); Michele Wallace, *Black Macho and the Myth of the Superwoman* (New York: Dial Press, 1978); Wallace, *Invisibility Blues: From Pop to Theory* (New York: Verso, 1990); bell hooks, *Thinking Feminist, Thinking Black* (Boston, Mass.: South End Press, 1989); hooks, *Yearning: Race, Gender, and Cultural Politics* (Boston, Mass.: South End Press, 1990); Angela Davis, *Women, Race, and Class* (New York: Vintage Books, 1993); Davis, *Women, Culture, and Politics* (New York: Random House, 1989).

7. Kimberle Williams Crenshaw, "Demarginalizing the Intersection of Race and Sex: A Black Feminist Critique of Antidiscrimination Doctrine, Feminist Theory and Antiracist Politics," *The University of Chicago Legal Forum*, 1989: 139–67.

8. Another example is *Secret Sounds Screaming: The Sexual Abuse of Children* (1985) by Ayoka Chenzira.

9. Theresa L. Johnson produces this numerical breakdown in her unpublished essay "*Suzanne, Suzanne*: Oral History in a Visual Frame."

10. George C. Wolfe, "Camille Billops," *A Journal for the Artist* 6 (Spring 1986): 27.

11. Annette Kuhn, "Textual Politics," in *Issues in Feminist Film Criticism*, ed. Patricia Erens (Bloomington: Indiana University Press, 1990), 250.

12. I am grateful to Elizabeth Gregory for calling this detail to my attention.

13. Leo Spitzer first and then other viewers have remarked to me that the artificiality of this scene is heightened by the fact that the positioning of Billie and Suzanne within the frame recalls a similar scene within Ingmar Bergman's *Persona*.

14. Earlier in the film Billie says, "No matter what time it was, . . . the minute I heard [Brownie's] car door slam, I knew that he was drunk. So immediately, I'd get up and go get in the shower and cut the water on. I don't know what the water was doing for me, but I think it gave me time to compose my thoughts so I would have an answer for him, because I didn't know what he was going to say."

15. I thank Patricia Schechter for this observation.

The Articulating Self: Difference as Resistance in *Black Girl, Ramparts of Clay,* and *Salt of the Earth*[1]

Linda Dittmar

In the straightforward, biological and acoustical sense, voices are our birthright. Most of us are born with the necessary organs and are served well by them through lifetimes of speaking, groaning, laughing, crying, or singing. But once we think of "voice" as a vehicle of human utterance – of expressed opinion, judgment, and will – the notion of birthright holds little sway. That is, once we think of vocal articulation as a symbolizing activity people use to interpret experience and negotiate their access to well-being, the important issue turns out to be not our innate ownership of this tool but our ability to use it. In this respect our voices are a function of political circumstances as well as individual identities. As instruments with which we position ourselves or are positioned by others in society, our voices have far-reaching personal and political implications. They sway and argue, reason and bully, or josh and convince within social institutions that allocate and reallocate wealth, dignity, and power. Our voices are tools, then, sometimes even weapons, that serve us ill or well in our struggles.

This said, it is striking that representations of vocal articulation have received so far only intermittent attention in film studies. In part this may be attributable to the seduction of images and the *jouissance* of the gaze, both of which have proved irresistible magnets for film scholarship in recent years. Certainly there are other historical reasons for this omission, including film's origin in photography and its development as an image-based and originally "silent" medium, the circumstances surrounding its conversion to sound technology, and its investment in playing a realistically corroborative part in relation to the visual track. Too often we set aside the constructed and coded aspects of the soundtrack as mere attributes of a supposed actuality. Speech, in this view, is just a vehicle for what is being said, music is just atmospheric, and ambient sounds merely authenticate what we see.

Still, despite this resistance, important scholarship concerning the soundtrack and filmic renditions of the voice have nonetheless emerged. Included here are formative studies by Pascal Bonitzer and Mary Ann Doane, Sarah Kozloff's and Claudia Gorbman's respective work on voice-overs and narrative film music, and Kaja Silverman's and Amy Lawrence's feminist readings of the female voice.[2] Although this scholarship generally skirts questions of difference other than gender, the thrust of all this work has been to foreground representations of speech as signifying practices and, thus, to open up a space for extending this kind of inquiry to other communities of speakers.

Ella Shohat and Robert Stam as well as several authors included in this volume take on this project, situating speech and its reception within the crisscrossings of difference in race, ethnicity, nationality, social class, and gender. As they demonstrate, films are anything but monolingual. Rather, they register the "prodigality of tongues," which, following Bakhtin, they see as an arena for the clash of differences.[3] This approach urges us to think of filmic representations of individual speakers as occurring across an array of social relations that include gender but are not limited to it. Thus, "the articulating self" of my title is hardly a solitary being pursuing her own trajectory of personal development. Inscribed within the play of power, she is an individual whose access to and manner of articulation are shaped by her social position.[4] Most important, how films represent such individuals in relation to their social as well as personal identities encodes listening attitudes on our part, too. In particular, we need to be aware of how commercially produced films appropriate politically specific markings of linguistic difference – Latino, African-American, or gay, for instance – in order to diminish certain speakers in relation to an implicit hegemonic norm. Such appropriations have a colonizing effect when they use pacing, registers, and fluency of speech, as well as dialects and regionalisms and even impediments such as hesitations or lisps to establish connotations of disability and inferior status.

Women, in this regard, find themselves doing double duty when they are made to function both as members of the designated Other and as carriers of a supposedly female incapacity. When this happens, their filmic treatment tends to encode their problematic relation to speech as integral to their gender and, on top of that, as constrained by their position within race, class, ethnicity, and the like. Accordingly, the following discussion of *Salt of the Earth*, *Black Girl*, and *Ramparts of Clay*, all made outside the normal venues of commercial production and distribution (U.S. 1954; Senegal 1966; Algeria-France, 1972, respectively), uncovers the ideological effects of female articulation and links it explicitly to other political issues. These are frankly oppositional films. They are committed to dramatizing the politics of emergence as involving interrelated struggles, and they usually focus on women's relationship to articulation as a signifying trope that guides us toward a critical reading of narrative and character. Challenging mainstream cinema's efforts to disguise and naturalize ideology, they construct oppositional representations and, thus, pose alternative ways of understanding our political present and envisioning our political future.

As we shall see, the overall effect of these films' strategies is to make it difficult for spectators to drift into the uncritical reception that mainstream cinemas make so inviting. In part they do so through their subject matter, in that they interweave considerations of gender with different kinds of Otherness from an explicitly political perspective. Encouraging attention to their female protagonists' positions within imperialism, colonialism, racism, and class oppression, they foreground the need for a dialectical understanding of interrelated struggles for social justice. But they also do so through narrative procedures that urge awareness of discourse itself as one way cultural diversity is implicated in unequal power relations. Modeling for the audience the effort to transcend discursive gaps, they encourage a reception that strives to understand and support the disempowered Other as a speaking subject. For all their obvious differences in history, geography, culture, and political content, their comparative reading usefully situates feminism in relation to socialist and antiracist discourses of emergence.

Given this emphasis on discourses of emergence, it is important to note that access to voice does not necessarily translate into power, or vice versa. After all, women are audible and even fluent in "talking pictures," even if their disruption of male-defined reason in screwball comedies, their exclamatory excess in melodrama, the subordination of their speech to image, or the near absence of authoritative female voice-overs often cast women's speech as corporeal, subjective, and unreliable.[5] In face of such practices, silence can indeed be a positive value. As feminist cinemas of the 1970s and 1980s show, silence can also be oppositional. It can signal a holding of oneself apart, a resistance that cherishes one's inviolability. When emphasized, it can displace conventional notions of audibility and fluency and encourage audiences to listen in new ways and discover new, hitherto unsuspected, modes of eloquence and assertion. At the same time, the moment one renames silence as muteness, the valuation of this concept changes. What at first seemed a sign of strength in adversity turns into erasure. Clearly at issue here is not the absence of sound but a value-laden relationship between articulation and presence, notably as it bears on women's position within society. Ultimately, at stake for women is the interaction of silence, speech, and dignity as it conveys defeats and triumphs.

This interaction works itself out interestingly in *Black Girl, Ramparts of Clay*, and *Salt of the Earth* precisely because their soundtracks provide a key to understanding women's particular repression and emergence in relation to other decolonizing struggles. *Black Girl* concerns a young Senegalese governess, Diouana, who leaves her home, culture, and a close male friend (or fiancé) in order to accompany her white employers when they return to France. Once in France, the film focuses on the family's indifference to Diouana and on her isolation and increasing depression as these lead her eventually to suicide. *Ramparts of Clay* concerns an unnamed young woman in a remote North African desert village who is rebelling against the constraints of her position as a single, orphaned, and dowryless woman within a strictly patriarchal society. While both films probe the relation between isolation and freedom, this woman's marginality yields more complex options that Diouana's. She is an exile within a social structure that cannot accommodate her with dignity, but she is also a free agent, living within her own culture and capable of personal and political resistance. Although the film ends with her suicidal escape into the desert, it also shows her teaching herself to read and using her initiative to support the men's strike in the local quarry. *Salt of the Earth* concerns a shift in gender-role expectations as it occurs within a largely Mexican-American community once the women start participating in the local miners' strike. Central here is Esperanza – a married housewife, pregnant, and mother of two – whose emergence from gendered subservience to personal autonomy is made possible through the reeducation the strike brings to the community as a whole.

A comparative reading of these films reveals various shared characteristics: all three are feature-length films directed by men and focused on female protagonists; all three concern disempowered people (Senegalese, Berber, and Mexican-American, respectively) eking out a meager living in a racist world marked by the lingering effects of a colonial past; all three treat their female protagonists with considerable respect and compassion; and each situates its protagonist's struggle for personal autonomy as a woman within a larger context of economic, territorial, and racial conflict. Especially significant to the present discussion is the fact that, in addition, each film depicts a woman whose voice is muted by social repression. The Berber woman barely speaks, Diouana sinks into silence once in France, and Esperanza reclaims her voice only once she enters a world larger than the domestic one. Although *Salt of the Earth* ultimately breaks out of verbal and political paralysis in ways that the other two films do not, a comparative reading suggests that all three films link the tensions between silence and utterance to a broader investigation of dignity, autonomy, and community in ways that ultimately empower women.

Diouana's silence in *Black Girl* goes beyond a language barrier caused by exile. In this film, female muteness functions semiotically. Registering Diouana's increasingly painful alienation, it builds a case, scene by scene, against her exploitation – as a woman, as an African, and as a servant – within a supposedly postcolonial context that proves merely a variant on colonial power relations. The film conveys this through procedures that are short on narrative and visual pleasure. The black-and-white photography is plain, the pace is slow, and the plot lacks drama. Acoustically, the film defines Diouana's situation by contrasting the lively Senegalese music and her originally easygoing relation to language in Dar with the harsh speech and jarring urban noises of France, making dissonance replace ease. Like the mask that she reclaims from her employers in a symbolically eloquent gesture of resistance, the film's stylistic rendition conveys judgment, which the human voice withholds. While the film casts Diouana's progression toward suicide as inexorable, its treatment of that suicide registers her unspoken anger and, thus, metaphorically reclaims her absent voice from oblivion. Significantly, this suicide is not an act of despair. Although it does reflect a defeat, in terms of African beliefs it also signifies that Diouana sends her spirit back home to the *omphalo*, the spiritual center.[6]

In contrast, *Ramparts of Clay* does not assign its protagonist's silence an immediate cause. This woman, young by Western standards, has ahead of her a lifetime spent outside the communal rituals that allow adult married women in her society at least a measure of matriarchal power. On those occasions the film shows her repeatedly standing apart and silenced by this exclusion.[7] Although there is much in this film that argues for anger and indignation on this woman's behalf, the way it presents itself is ultimately contradictory, perhaps because the director (Bertucelli) and other crew members of this French-Algerian coproduction are outsiders to the society and gender issues that are their subject matter. Visually, the film's striking color photography and relish in the Other invoke an orientalism that tends to mystify, not challenge.[8] Acoustically, the film's very spareness complements its orientalism. The desert sounds, selectively recorded ambient sounds, and the near absence of speech suggest an acoustical emptiness that mirrors the romance of the land's open expanse. However, unlike the visual treatment, the sound track also functions symbolically. Its lacunas invite a heightened listening that underscores the fact that there is almost nothing to be heard and that what can be heard is symbolically overdetermined. The distant call to prayer, a monotonous hammering at the quarry, or the crunching of soldiers' boots on gravel mark the institutional boundaries of this woman's life (religion, capital, and military government), while the prolonged wails of the unoiled well pulley – a surrogate for the protagonist's voice – encode her anguish and desolation.

In these two films female muteness is clearly based in anger. The women's proud bearing and their growing refusal to play the roles assigned them within their social order assert resistance. Both films recalcitrantly withhold from viewers the intimacy of articulation. They provide us with no explanation, no catharsis. Letting their silent protagonists remain as inaccessible to us as they are to the people who have power over them, they construct for spectators viewing positions closely allied with those of the oppressors. They treat us as the enemy, the one who cannot be trusted. *Black Girl* further underscores this point by starting the narrative in media res, toward the end of the plot, and then backtracking to uncover the reasons for Diouana's suicide. Positing through this frame an inquiring mode aligned with the white husband's somewhat concerned but ultimately removed and uncomprehending viewpoint, the film turns its back on Western viewers much as Diouana does on her employers. Its refusal to provide us with easy explanations insists that we, like Diouana's employers, are responsible for our insights, empathies, and political positions.

Ramparts of Clay is less confrontational. Introducing the narrative with a quotation from Frantz Fanon and concluding it with a shot that redirects the camera from the narrative to the filmmaking situation (showing the helicopter from which the woman's disappearance is filmed and making us strain to see her fast-dwindling figure), this film encourages a detached, analytic, and even bemused reception. Its point-of-view shots may align us with the protagonist, but its fascination with the geographic and ethnographic Other is an outsider's. Once again we find ourselves unable to bridge the gap between our position and what lies behind her silence, though this time the effect is less confrontational, more pleasurable. The viewing position offered to us is a familiar one – that of the Western tourist.

While these differences say much about these films' different political perspectives and ideological effects, both films evince admiration for the strength and inviolability of their protagonists, and an awareness that in these two cases silence registers resistance. Not accidentally, this resistance concerns the combined effects of colonial, racial, economic, and patriarchal institutions. Society clearly devalues these protagonists as women, and especially as women outside material reproduction, but it also devalues them economically and racially. In *Black Girl* the white post-colonials' assumption of their race and caste hegemony is blatant, but even in *Ramparts of Clay*, which concerns no outsiders, a Western-oriented government presence sustains the racial and caste agendas of the recent colonial past. *Black Girl* dramatizes this residue of colonialism by stressing the whites' blindness to anything Diouana might know or represent apart from her instrumentality as an African servant. They fail to appreciate the symbolic gift she makes them of a mask, and, ignoring her fluent knowledge of French, they criticize her to their guests in front of her, thus excluding her from their hegemonic sphere of linguistic privilege.[9] *Ramparts of Clay* alerts us to this by framing its account in Fanon's quotation concerning the postcolonial extension of colonialism, and by stressing the powerful outsider position of Western-identified bureaucrats and military men who make forays into the village to record data, dispense meager pay, and repress the strike.[10]

Both films, then, situate women's silence within this configuration of oppressions, and each treats this silence as a resisting stance that asserts one's autonomous presence in the world. In both cases silence is not irrevocable. Rather, it occurs in women whose strength and capacity for intelligent reflection and eloquence are established as preceding their eventual erasure, and it alludes to resistance more than to defeat. Indeed, *Ramparts of Clay*'s intermittent use of the unaccompanied, raw-timbered, and forcefully punctuated voice-over singing of a well-known female Algerian performer, Taos Amrouch, as a leitmotiv makes this admiration for female articulation explicit. Silence, both films register, is a willed assertion of difference, a deliberate refusal to enter into dialogue within social institutions that preclude equal exchange.

Significantly, in both films resistance to Western incursions includes also a linguistic clash between the colonizing language, French, and the indigenous languages. As Shohat and Stam have already argued, in *Black Girl* the interplay of French and Senegalese replicates the relation of the colonized to the colonizer. It makes verbal inaccessibility become the arena for the exercise of power on the one hand, resistance on the other. Access to language proves not just a natural ability, a birthright, but an acquisition subject to politics. *Ramparts of Clay* not only shares this view but occasionally uses Arabic without subtitles to further defamiliarize language for Western audiences. In so doing it situates the struggle between the colonized and colonizer in the auditorium itself. Treating Arabic (itself, ironically, a colonizing language in North Africa) as the linguistic norm, it casts Western audiences into the role of outsiders. These strategies bring us back to the questions of reception and access discussed above. "Access" in this instance means our access to characters, to language, and finally to understanding. Seen politically, this notion of access is intertwined with

considerations of power, exchange, and appropriation in both gender relations and other political contexts.

Although *Salt of the Earth* was made on another continent and years
earlier than the preceding two films, it is useful to consider it in relation
to them because both its political concerns and its discursive strategies at
once echo and recast theirs. Produced in the United States at the height
of the Cold War's "Red scare," this film is anchored in distinctly different
historical and political debates than those at work in Senegal and the
North Mughreb of the 1960s and 1970s. It is a McCarthy-era, counter-
Hollywood film concerning labor struggles, capitalism, and ethnic prejudice in a largely Mexican-American mining community in New Mexico. Es-
pousing a Socialist perspective officially designated "subversive" by the
U.S. government, its preoccupations are local and historically specific.[11]
Black Girl and *Ramparts of Clay*, on the other hand, concern a different
agenda. Made during a period of heightened critiques of Western colonialism, notably in Africa, they posit support for contemporary independence
movements specific to their region.

While a comparative reading of this heterogeneous film cluster cannot
trace chronological developments or propose a theory of geographic or cultural contiguities, it does argue for a cross-cultural perspective that illuminates interrelated themes and cinematic strategies. Seen globally, the
particular circumstances that made *Salt of the Earth* a bold maverick in
United States film history do not preclude comparison to other films that
emerged out of clearly different contexts but that also address related
questions of social justice. On the contrary, this film's use of a woman's narrative consciousness as a guide to its reception, its making her and other
women's problematic relation to articulation serve as a trope for gender
relations, its situating each gender within a broader critique of race, ethnicity, and social class in a postcolonial context, and its doing so by engaging spectators in a deciphering activity geared to promote ideals of equality echo the preoccupations of the preceding films and recast them more
optimistically.[12]

Salt of the Earth shares with *Black Girl* and *Ramparts of Clay* the view
that political oppression is sustained by myths of supposedly essential and
therefore insurmountable inequalities among races, sexes, classes, and
ethnicities. Like them, its project is to reclaim such myths from their unex-
amined state and propose a more egalitarian way of thinking about oppression and social justice. It also shares with them a critique of the postcolonial condition, in that it focuses on a Mexican-American community
that bears the residual scars of economic and national displacement under
Spanish, then Anglo, conquest in the Southwest. In all three films the very
notion of "post" colonialism proves a misnomer. For even in liberated coun-

tries with redrawn borders, myths of the inherent inferiority of indigenous people continue to benefit neocolonial ruling elites in a direct line of descent from the old colonial powers. But unlike *Black Girl* and *Ramparts of Clay*, *Salt of the Earth* foregrounds possibilities for recovery. It does so by proposing a more hopeful view of female agency and political solidarity. Its narrative tells of a successful miners' strike and of women's pivotal role in bringing about the union's victory and linking that victory to feminist gains in the domestic sphere. It also does so through its treatment of language. Like the preceding two films, it starts off by establishing a disempowered female speaker and a problematic audience reception, but, unlike them, it goes on to reclaim both. Here the protagonist's and the audience's growing access to articulation and comprehension support the plot's optimistic faith in collective action in the fullest sense.

Starting off by representing Esperanza, the framing voice-over narrator and protagonist, as linguistically and physically disempowered, the film dramatizes her increasing competency in action and language. Moreover, starting off by placing its spectators in the position of uninformed outsiders whose auditory relation to her voice is impeded by her difficulties both as an English-speaking Latina and as a self-effacing woman, the film gradually gives its spectators (notably the initially excluded Anglos) access to comprehension and solidarity. In so doing, *Salt of the Earth* challenges standard practice. Its use of Esperanza's retrospective voice-over signals a female coming-of-age narrative within a tradition usually reserved for men, but its casting her as a debased narrator who lacks linguistic fluency denies her the authority usually granted her male counterparts.[13] Visually coded as a diffident woman, worn, pregnant, and drab, the film's opening sequence imbues her first few words as our voice-over guide with awkwardness and uncertainty: "How shall I begin my story that has no beginning?" she asks. Heard against a backdrop of desolate visuals, the groping quality of this opening sequence defines Esperanza's poverty, ethnicity, and familial position as interlocking oppressions.

Yet for all the discomfort the film initially constructs for its viewers (especially for those watching it from a middle-class Anglo perspective), Esperanza's retrospective narration, her vivid recollections, and her clear grasp of a watershed political development in her community and in the labor movement make her voice-over compelling. In part, her authority derives from the content of her account: from the inherent importance of the events narrated and from the obvious gains made by her own and other women's growing activism. In addition, this authority derives from her manner of narration: it is direct, factual, truthful, and purposeful. Finally, and most important, her authority grows in relation to the film's mounting validation of her linguistic difference as a Mexican-American speaker. In short, her voice-over constructs personal authority through the emergence of political consciousness, analysis, and action. That *Salt of the Earth* manages to do that even as it positions viewers as outsiders is a measure of its success in reclaiming and recasting linguistic and cultural difference as an opportunity for building alliances.

Most immediately this success is attributable to the film's overall conformity to the standard Hollywood practice of securing a compelling plot and appealing protagonists, and to its use of the cinematographic conventions Hollywood has taught us to accept as a realist record. But the film's subversion of Hollywood's conventions makes it doubly interesting. Ultimately it had to move audiences to respect, not just pity, a denigrated community, to embrace a political position that contemporary national myths demonized as subversive, and to accept women as equal partners in defining society's political and economic as well as familial character. In terms of these goals, the film's production outside the studio system, in exile and in the face of considerable efforts to block it, proved a boon. Its on-location shooting in a New Mexico mining community, its mixture of professional and nonprofessional actors, and the close collaboration that took place between the filmmakers and the grass-roots labor movement imbue it with a documentary quality that elicits identification and solidarity precisely because its authenticating effects coincide with strong commitment to this community.[14]

The respect and clarity *Salt of the Earth* ends up according Spanish and Spanish-accented English, both traditionally denigrated in Hollywood films, also argue for this commitment. Instead of severing the protagonists from the Latino and the Anglo linguistic communities, as is the case in the two preceding films, it normalizes linguistic difference and honors Mexican-American identity and culture. Thus, when it refrains from subtitling the Spanish used during the union's debate, it empowers the speakers and disables Anglo listeners. But the film also helps such listeners reenter the Latino discourse by having English-speaking characters participate in the debate and by letting Latino characters educate their Anglo counterparts about their heritage (e.g., when Esperanza's husband, Ramon, stresses the equality between Benito Juárez and George Washington as "fathers" of their respective countries). At issue is less the audience's ability to follow every utterance than its recognizing the nature and rights of diverse cultural and political communities. By challenging the Anglos' discursive hegemony and by granting Mexican Americans access to eloquence, self-knowledge, and political power, the film poses bilingualism as yet another arena for self-claiming.

Women are pivotal to this proposition. The local miners' political radicalization and the solidarity it attracts regionally and nationally are bound up in their wives' entry into political activism and in the changing gender roles that follow this development. The turning point occurs when a court injunction forbids the miners from picketing. As the wives replace their husbands on the picket line, a transfer of responsibilities and power takes place. The women venture into the public spheres of the union hall, the picket line, and prison, while the men are forced into the private sphere of kitchens and laundry lines. The film shows such shifts in autonomy, assertiveness, and political power as fraught with uncertainty for both sexes. The plot justifies them tactically as key to the strike's success and morally as necessary to an egalitarian and cohesive labor movement. At the same time, the film's linguistic subtext affirms this process by linking women's emergent articulation to their emergent power as Latina activists allied with their Anglo sisters.

Salt of the Earth dramatizes this progression through changes it depicts in Esperanza's and other women's manner of speaking. They all start off as laconic, halting, and elliptic. Their speech is cramped into very simple syntax and limited vocabulary, and it lacks connectives and transitions. Early on in the film, the self-deprecating quality of Esperanza's voice-over continues; she does not dare complete a thought or provide a connection between ideas. Her effort to persuade her husband of the justice of the women's demands is weakened by ellipses and conditionals: "But if your union . . . if you're asking for better conditions . . . why can't you ask for decent plumbing, too?" (p. 9). Shortly afterward, when the women first venture into the masculine preserve of the union hall, their language retains the same painful hesitations, ellipses, and subjectives. The "ladies," we learn, are necessarily dependent on men's authority and goodwill:

SAL: Yes? You ladies have an announcement?

CONSUELO (*haltingly*): Well—it's not an announcement, I guess. The ladies wanted me to . . .

VOICE FROM THE FLOOR: Louder!

SAL: Consuelo, will you speak from over here?

Painfully, self-consciously, CONSUELO moves toward Camera in foreground. She faces the men [and us] and begins again, nervous but trying to speak louder.

CONSUELO: The ladies have been talking 'bout sanitation . . . and we were thinking . . . if the issue is equality, like you say it is, then maybe we ought to have equality in plumbing too . . .

CONSUELO'S VOICE: I mean, maybe it could be a strike demand . . . and some of the ladies thought it might be a good idea to have a ladies' auxiliary! Well, we would like to help out . . . if we can.   (25)

But as the women forestall the strike's defeat by "manning" the picket line, and once they find themselves fighting scabs, blocking cars, standing up to physical and verbal abuse, and hauled off to prison, they replace verbal diffidence with assertion—most vocally in prison, where, fifty strong, they launch into earsplitting demands for food, beds, and formula for Esperanza's baby. On the line, in the union hall, and at home, the women come into their own not just as individuals but as a group. Their very clothes change; we now see them wearing pants and checkered lumberjack jackets. But it is mainly their new verbal certainty that is so striking— their ability to speak as men's equals. In keeping with its collective agendas the film does not single out any one character as a heroic instance of such emergence. Esperanza is simply one among many. We know her more intimately, but the film embeds her struggles and empowerment in communal experience and solidarity. At one point, when Ramon is about to hit her in frustration over her autonomy, she stands up to him, defiant and unflinching: "That would be the old way," she says. "Never try it on me again—never" (p. 82). After months of shared defeats and successes, the "me" of this sentence clearly stands for "us."

Salt of the Earth is clearly more affirming of women's ability to reclaim control of their voices and destinies than either *Black Girl* or *Ramparts of Clay*. In part it accomplishes this by linking feminism to other ideals of equality and justice, thus making a convincing case for inclusive alliances. But it also does so by reclaiming the concept of difference and turning it into a constructive force. Difference, in this treatment, starts off as the nexus of inequities and clashing interests but becomes the bedrock of alliances and parity. Validating women's voices in particular as they engage in cultural production, and suffusing these voices with growing conviction and assertiveness, *Salt of the Earth* dramatizes Zinc Town's move toward marshaling its discourse in opposition to capitalism, sexism, and cultural colonialism. *Black Girl* and *Ramparts of Clay*, in contrast, cannot offer women an analogous communal role. Their protagonists are shown as solitary individuals, cut off from a women's community and from a broader context of shared political struggle. Both their linguistic repression as women and the linguistic dissonance built into these two films' narratives mainly convey anger and protest. Thematically and linguistically they elicit empathy and indignation but leave obscure the possibility of resistance and productive struggle. Seen historically, this obscurity is not surprising. Both the politically focused development *Salt of the Earth* accords its women and the politically diffuse trajectory *Black Girl* and *Ramparts of Clay* accord their women are based in historic actuality. The one testifies to specific attainments made possible by a long history of articulated social struggle; the other two testify to an as yet not fully articulated sense of women's place within complex processes of social transformation.

Perhaps what is especially poignant about *Salt of the Earth* in this respect is how utopian it proved to be. Although it is based on a real-life incident, the victorious note on which it ends was short-lived. Neither at work nor at home have we attained the parity for homemakers and wage earners that this film presents as plain common sense. Seen from a feminist perspective, at issue are not just men's efforts to exclude women from a particular union hall or the picket line – in this case Zinc Town's – but from the workplace in general. In this respect, these women's emergence into their autonomy, activism, and voice is not the end of the struggle. While this issue is extraneous to *Salt of the Earth*'s narrative, the film's focus on ways male-dominated unions essentialize femininity and thus represent it as antithetical to unionism and as lacking in class consciousness highlights a gender conflict that the United States' labor movement is yet to resolve.[15]

Still, these misgivings concern a broader historic trajectory than the particular one *Salt of the Earth* dramatizes. After all, the utopian yearnings it stirs have their origin in gains made locally and, as it turned out, under unique circumstances. Neither the victory this film represents nor the setbacks that attended it can serve as a blueprint for our future. Rather, it opens up for audiences a horizon of possibilities. It stresses the need to understand oppression as an interlocking system of injustices, it singles out the female voice and its problematic reception as a paradigm for this political thinking, and it locates in that voice's agency a potential for resistance and self-claiming. In all these respects *Salt of the Earth* at once recapitulates the preoccupations of *Black Girl* and *Ramparts of Clay* and heads elsewhere. Sharing their use of female articulation as a trope for a complex set of power relations, it moves beyond the protest their renditions of women's solitary voices inscribe to propose, instead, a politically motivated and communally sustained basis for female agency.

Notes

1. Parts of this essay draw on shorter treatments of the films under discussion: "Dislocated Utterances: The Filmic Coding of Verbal Difference," *Iris: La Parole au Cinema (Speech in Film)* 3, no. 1 (1985): 91–97, and "Voices at the Margin," in *Double Vision: Perspectives on Gender and the Visual Arts*, ed. Natalie H. Bluestone (forthcoming, Associated University Presses).

2. Pascal Bonitzer, *Le Regard et la Voix* (Paris: Union Générale d'éditions 1976), and "The Silence of the Voice," in *Narrative, Apparatus, Ideology: A Film Theory Reader*, ed. Philip Rosen (New York: Columbia University Press, 1986), 319–34; Michel Chion, *La Voix au cinema* (Paris: Editions de l'etoile, 1982); Rick

Altman, "Moving Lips: Cinema as Ventriloquism" *Yale French Studies* 60 (1980): 67–79; Mary Ann Doane, "The Voice in the Cinema: The Articulation of Body and Space," ibid., 33–50; Claudia Gorbman, *Unheard Melodies: Narrative Film Music* (Bloomington: Indiana University Press, 1987); Sarah Kozloff, *Invisible Storytellers: Voice-Over Narration in American Fiction Film* (Berkeley: University of California Press, 1988); Kaja Silverman, *The Acoustic Mirror: The Female Voice in Psychoanalysis and Cinema* (Bloomington: Indiana University Press, 1988); Amy Lawrence, *Echo and Narcissus: Women's Voices in Classical Hollywood Cinema* (Berkeley: University of California Press, 1991).

3. Ella Shohat and Robert Stam, "The Cinema after Babel: Language, Difference, Power," *Screen* 26 (May-August 1985): 35–58.

4. Linda Alcoff, "Cultural Feminism versus Poststructuralism: The Identity Crisis in Feminist Theory," *Signs: Journal of Women in Culture and Society* 13, no. 3 (1988): 405–36.

5. See Silverman's "Body Talk," in *The Acoustic Mirror*, 42–71; Kozloff's "Gender," in *Invisible Storytellers*, 99–101; and Mary Ann Doane's "Paranoia and the Specular," in *The Desire to Desire: The Woman's Film of the 1940s* (Bloomington: Indiana University Press, 1987).

6. Clyde Taylor, "Two Women," in *Journey across Three Continents*, ed. Renee Tajima (New York: Third World Newsreel, 1985), 28–31. See also Robert Stam and Louise Spence, "Colonialism, Racism, and Representation: An Introduction," *Screen* 24, no. 2 (1983).

7. *Ramparts of Clay* adapts segments of Jean Duvignaud's *Change at Shebika: A Report from a North African Village* (Austen: Texas University Press, 1977), based on a ten-year sociological study of a Tunisian Village. The film's protagonist is a composite of two unmarried women described in this study–a nineteen-year-old orphan who disappeared in the desert and a young woman whose attacks of "the fevers" at once marginalized her and cast her in the role of a "seer."

8. Edward W. Said, *Orientalism* (New York: Vintage, 1978). At issue is a complex discourse that marshals a series of interests (geographic, sociological, psychological, philological, aesthetic, and so on) through which the Occident has maintained its hegemony over the Orient–notably, the Islamic Near East–in Said's work. Also Assia Djebar, "Forbidden Sight, Interrupted Sound," *Discourse* 8, Special Issue: "She, the Inappropriate/d Other" (Winter 1986-87): 39–56.

9. Shohat and Stam, "After Babel," 54.

10. Frantz Fanon, *The Wretched of the Earth* (New York: Evergreen 1968; first French edition 1961). Bertucelli provides the following excerpt without further citation: "In fact, the bourgeois phase in the history of underdeveloped countries is a completely useless phase. When this caste has vanished, devoured by its own contradictions, it will be seen that nothing new has happened since independence was proclaimed and that everything must be started again from scratch."

11. The credits for *Salt of the Earth* included a number of blacklisted professionals and labor activists. Michael Wilson and Deborah Rosenfelt detail the political efforts to block its production and distribution in *Salt of the Earth* (Old Westbury, N.Y.: Feminist Press, 1978). This volume includes the film's script. For further background information see Francis R. Walsh, "Hollywood's Labor Films:

1934-1954," in *The Popular Perception of Industrial History*, ed. Robert Weible and F. R. Walsh (Lanham, Md.: University Publishing Associates, 1989), 237-53. Larry Ceplair and Steven Englund, *The Inquisition in Hollywood* (Berkeley: University of California Press, 1979). See also Stephen Mack and Barbara Moss's documentary film *A Crime to Fit the Punishment* (1983, 46 min., distributed by First Run/Icarus Films, New York).

12. While this discussion singles out gender, the myriad political interconnections at work across these and similar films can be traced through Sembene's oeuvre, interviews with Bertucelli, and in the documents relating to *Salt of the Earth* cited above.

13. Margo Kasdan, "'Why are you afraid to have me at your side?' From Passivity to Power in *Salt of the Earth*," in *The Voyage In: Fictions of Female Development*, ed. Elizabeth Abel, M. Hirsch, and E. Langland (Hanover: University Press of New England, 1983), 258-69.

14. Linda Williams, "Type and Stereotype: Chicano Images in Film," in *Chicano Cinema: Research, Reviews and Resources*, ed. Gary D. Keller (New York: Birmingham, 1985), 59-63. The opposite occurs in *Ramparts of Clay*, where an "orientalist" approach to ethnography compromises the film's authenticity.

15. For a detailed discussion of these and related issues, see Ava Baron, "Gender and Labor History: Learning from the Past, Looking to the Future," in *Work Engendered: Toward a New History of American Labor*, ed. Ava Baron (Ithaca, N.Y.: Cornell University Press, 1991), 1-46; Nancy A. Hewitt, " 'The Voice of Virile Labor': Labor Militance, Community Solidarity, and Gender Identity among Tampa's Latin Workers, 1880-1921," ibid., 142-67; Brandon French, "Introduction: The Transitional Woman," in *On the Verge of Revolt: Women in American Films of the Fifties* (New York: Ungar, 1978), xii-xxiv.

Women's Voices in Third World Cinema

Amy Lawrence

Recent feminist film theory has been concerned with the way women's voices have been constructed by mainstream cinema so as to reenforce certain ideological assumptions about the roles of women and men. Most of this work, however, has centered on United States and European production, whether classical or experimental. Trinh T. Minh-ha's 1989 film *Surname Viet, Given Name Nam* redefines the terms of the discussion by actively examining issues of voice, gender, and language in a space located precisely between the United States and the Third World. Issues of synchronization, central to the representation of women's voices in Hollywood films, are complicated by questions of language and made problematic by having actresses in California literally "give voice" to the transcribed and translated testimony of women still in Vietnam. By considering this film and its theoretical context, we can begin to reopen and redefine the relationship between the cinematic representation of women's images/voices on the one hand and the construction of a female subject on the other, and to unravel some of the issues tangled in the terms *United States/Third World, feminist, woman's voice/women's speech, synchronized sound, subjectivity,* and *talking heads* – all of which come into play when a woman in a film speaks.

Feminist Theory and Sound

In traditional-style narrative film, the synchronization of image and voice is sacrosanct. In "Ideology and the Practice of Sound Editing and Mixing," Mary Ann Doane argues that the primary purpose of the flawless "invisible" synchronization of voice and image is to obscure the medium's "material heterogeneity"—to mimic a unified and coherent text out of the mass of technology and technicians required to make a sound film.[1]

The ideal of a coherent, unified text mirrors the fantasy of a coherent, unified spectator, and in "The Voice in Cinema: The Articulation of Body and Space," Doane expands her argument to focus on the goal behind classical sound film's sleights of hand. She argues that the conventions of sound reproduction, together with invisible editing and narrative transparency, work to create the illusion of a unified source of audiovisual information. The body of the film becomes a "fantasmatic body," the text demonstrating a kind of self-sufficiency where images and sounds seem to be internally (even organically) generated by the fictional world of the film. This process helps "sustain the narcissistic pleasure derived from the image of a certain *unity, cohesion, and hence, an identity* grounded by the spectator's fantasmatic relation to his/her own body."[2] Sound perspective and "techniques which spatialize the voice and endow it with 'presence' guarantee the singularity and stability of a point of audition, thus holding at bay the potential trauma of dispersal, dismemberment, difference."[3] For Doane, the purpose of classical cinema's construction of sound is to reassure the spectator that "he" is a stable and unified subject, a subjectivity forever indebted to and inseparable from the institution that creates it.

In *The Acoustic Mirror*, Kaja Silverman argues that disguising the work that goes into sound/image production not only guarantees the cohesiveness of *any* subject, but also specifically shores up male subjectivity. Classical cinema's "denial of its material heterogeneity" (the "effacement of work . . . [characteristic] of bourgeois ideology") is for Silverman merely one of a series of displacements enacted by cinema to lessen the anxiety of the male subject, for whom the "potential trauma of dispersal, dismemberment, and difference" held at bay by "invisible" sound editing techniques is castration.[4] These "displacements follow a precise trajectory" from the original "loss of the object" (in the accession to language), "to the foreclosed site of production, to the representation of woman as lacking. These orchestrated displacements," she argues, "have as their final goal the articulation of a coherent male subject."[5]

Feminist film theory has traditionally focused most of its attention on the last category—the representation of woman as lack. Silverman shows how this is communicated not only through the image of woman's body as fetishized object of the male gaze but through the construction of the woman's voice. While synchronization of the man's voice and image marks the traditional beginning of sound film with *The Jazz Singer* in 1927, Silverman shows how, when women's voices are linked to their bodies through synchronization of sound and image, women are threatened paradoxically with silence, that is, erasure of their subjectivity. Using a selection of films from the 1940s, Silverman shows how women's voices are narratively taken away from them, held within the diegesis and out of their control. In these films, female characters are no longer subjects but bodies that can be made to signify only through the masculine agency of doctors, lawyers, and others. The male characters wrench sounds out of women through techniques such as hypnosis, sodium pentathol, or torture, and then interpret or make meaning out of the sounds "they" have produced. Synchronization in such circumstances not only contains women within the diegesis of the film, barring them from the realm of enunciation "outside" the narrative (a position reserved for the male subject), but at its most chilling "[identifies] the female voice with an intractable materiality" and alienates the female subject from the meanings "produced" by her own voice.[6]

For Silverman, the only way for the woman's voice to escape "that semiotics, [that] obliges the female voice to signify the female body, and the female body to signify lack" is to be disembodied.[7] The woman's voice thus "escapes that anatomical destiny to which classical cinema holds its female characters."[8]

For all its estimable sophistication, the danger of Silverman's argument is its susceptibility to oversimplification: synchronization as automatically bad and "asynchronization," or the disembodied voice, as always potentially good for women.

I would like to reopen the issue of synch by focusing on a film that radically problematizes the synchronization of women's voices and images. In doing so, the film puts into question the "unity, coherence," and "presence" assumed of a synchronized image and voice as well as the unity, coherence, and presence of a stable viewing subject. I shall argue that in Trinh T. Minh-ha's film the synchronized voice points not to a singular cohesive female subject but to a more complicated conception of subjectivity as multiple, shifting, and communal—pointing not only to the psychological but to the social heterogeneity of a talking head. For this more complex conception of subjectivity, it is important to keep in mind Teresa de Lauretis's definition of subjectivity: "A woman, or a man, is not an undivided identity, a stable unity, 'consciousness,' but the term of a shifting series of ideological positions. Put another way, the social being is . . . an always provisional encounter of subject and codes at the historical (therefore changing) intersection of social formations and her or his personal history."[9] The question, then, is how can the synchronization of image and voice render such a complex subject readable in a film text?

Western Feminism and the Third World

Before looking at the film's representation of Third World women in translation and in transition, it is necessary to examine the ways contemporary Western feminism initially failed in its attempts to engage in a true dialogue with the feminism(s), texts, and people from other cultures. Among the primary questions to be addressed are the following: How do we discuss Third World film without defining a monolithic "other" and without imposing our own Western feminist agendas? And how do we discuss voice in relation to language and gender in an other, or multi-, cultural context? As a Western academic feminist, how do I avoid defining or limiting the reading of Trinh's film? I shall argue that *Surname Viet, Given Name Nam* is already a text that examines issues of voice, gender, and language from a space located precisely between the United States and the Third World. Given its prominent use of direct address (which I shall discuss later), the film is itself initiating a dialogue with its audience. This is one response.

In an article entitled "Under Western Eyes: Feminist Scholarship and Colonial Discourses," feminist writer Chandra Talpade Mohanty points out the ways American feminist attempts to promote an idea of "universal sisterhood" have ended up romanticizing women of other cultures, obscuring differences, and illustrating Western feminism's power to define.[10] "Woman," as Western feminism has pointed out, is not a universal term transcending histories or cultures; it is socially constructed, and culturally and historically defined. By homogenizing and systematizing the oppression of women in the Third World, Mohanty argues, Western feminism positions "woman" and the "Third World Woman" as stable categories.[11] She states that "the production of the 'Third World Woman' as a singular monolithic subject in . . . (Western) feminist texts" is an act of discursive colonization, a "mode of appropriation and codification" whereby the other is restricted to certain stereotypical roles that reaffirm the Western feminist/colonizer as the sole possessor of political consciousness and knowledge.[12]

Mohanty traces the way the "average" Third World woman is described again and again in feminist works on the Third World as "ignorant, poor, uneducated, tradition-bound, domestic, family-oriented, victimized, etc. This . . . is in contrast to the (implicit) self-representation of Western women as educated, modern, as having control of their own bodies and sexualities, and the freedom to make their own decisions."[13] In this system, women of the Third World are defined "in terms of their *object status* (the way in which they are affected or not affected by certain institutions and systems)," that is, as victims with needs or problems but not choices – a discursive strategy that denies Third World women both political consciousness and, more important, agency.[14]

The term *Third World* was originally coined as a means of constructing a coalition among postcolonial states, unifying a disparate group into a cohesive identity neither Soviet block nor U.S.-influenced.[15] The Third World encompasses countries in Asia, Africa, the Middle East, Central and South America, the Pacific, India – in other words, nearly all the world. When using the term *Third World* one is always faced with the question "Who uses this term, and for whom?" This is crucial because "Third World" has been appropriated by much of Western discourse to mean something quite different from the political and economic self-determination implicit in its origin. Instead it is used as synonymous with poverty, destabilized governments, and underdevelopment; "Third World" has become the multiply-stigmatized Other to "our" unified subjectivity.

The primary danger of the concept of a "Third World Woman" is traditional Western humanism's tendency to project its own fears and desires onto an Other. But Mohanty recognizes more subtle risks inherent in the very desire for unity represented by the self-identification "Third World." In privileging sameness over difference, material differences between cultures can be suppressed. Mohanty reiterates the importance of Bernice Johnson Reagon's distinction between "coalition" and "home."[16] For Reagon, "home" is a "nurturing space" based on "sameness of experience, oppression, culture, etc." but which "ultimately provide[s] an illusion of community based on isolation and the freezing of difference."[17] Coalition, on the other hand, is founded on a strategic "cross-cultural commonality of struggles" where a community is formed as part of a political strategy. In "Feminist Politics: What's Home Got to Do with It?" Mohanty and Biddy Martin note that "The assumption of, or desire for, another safe place like 'home' is challenged by the realization that 'unity' – interpersonal as well as political – is itself necessarily fragmentary, . . . struggled for, chosen, and hence unstable by definition."[18]

Speaking as a subject whose own unity or identity is necessarily "fragmentary, struggled for, chosen, and hence unstable" isn't easy. Mohanty describes how the speech of the stereotypical Third World Woman has been privileged in Western feminist works as that of "truth teller." In this conception women transcend history as well as cultural indoctrination and consequently possess "a privileged access to the 'real,' [and] the 'truth' " (both singular).[19] (Mohanty refers specifically to Robin Morgan's work in the anthology *Sisterhood Is Global*.)[20] She finds a potentially more helpful definition of a global women's community that does not deny difference(s) among women in Reagon's work. Instead of positing a community of women who exist outside of a "man-made" history and who almost unconsciously and inevitably tell the Truth, this elected community "is forged on the basis of memories and counternarratives, not on an ahistorical universalism."[21] What women say is thus implicated in history and culture; what provides common ground are the positions women take discursively in relation to specific goals. This is an active and a conscious construction of community (and identity) through the use of language, the positioning of self and other, of community and resistance, as opposed to the passive ahistorical victim or "Truth teller."

As we'll see, the positions available to Third World women in constructing themselves and possible communities through language differ from those available to Western feminists. In her concept of a "politics of location," Adrienne Rich states that "a place on the map is also a place in history."[22] What you are is determined to an extent by "where" you are (in geography as much as history).[23] But this location is not stable, monolithic or beyond change. Feminism itself is an intervention in the Western humanist tradition. As members of a postcolonial society or as refugees from Vietnam living in the United States, the characters in Trinh T. Minh-ha's *Surname Viet, Given Name Nam* exist between cultures and between languages.[24] Mohanty avers that the "movement *between* cultures, languages, and complex configurations of meaning and power [has] always been the territory of the colonized."[25] For those fighting colonization as for the refugee, community as well as identity becomes a matter of choice, alignment, a series of choices played out in the film in the relation between women's voices and women's speech. It is this relationship between cultures, languages, identity, and gender *as exemplified by the representation of the voice* that I wish to examine in Trinh's film.

Surname Viet, Given Name Nam

The first section of the film presents a series of Vietnamese women describing conditions in postwar Vietnam. As they do so, their words appear at times, written either before the image begins or directly over it. Interspersed with the carefully staged testimonies are segments of black and white archival footage from prewar Vietnamese life with excerpts from Vietnamese folk songs on the soundtrack as well as voice-over commentary by the filmmaker. The second half of the film reveals that the women of the first section have been played by actresses selected from Vietnamese émigrés living in the United States. While the women's speech in the first section of the film is given in halting, heavily accented English, the "real" women in the second part speak subtitled Vietnamese and are presented in a *vérité* cinematic style. It is the distances between image, voice, and language in the seemingly contradictory first and second halves of the film I want to focus on here.

All the women in the film confront what it means to speak as a woman, a historical experience that is lived through the body and which is at the same time a culturally constructed position. Even within a traditional culture, however, woman's identity is not fixed but fluid. One maxim we hear on the sound track is that before marriage a woman is a lady, during marriage she's a maid, and when old and husbandless, a monkey.

The narrator underscores how even within the most traditional patriarchal cultures there has always been a parallel history of resistance. Folk tales or popular novels such as *The Tale of Kieu* detail the suffering women have endured trying to fit the ideal roles prescribed for them. However, women's attempts to speak from a position of authority have been appropriated as metaphors for national struggle and women's authorship of important literary works denied, especially when they address topics deemed unacceptable for a woman, such as sexuality or war. Trinh comments, "Each government has its own interpretation of Kieu. Each has its peculiar way of using and appropriating women's images."

Women's relations to their voices are constructed by culture as well. Of the "four virtues . . . required of women" in Vietnamese tradition, the third, *Ngon*, applies to voice and speech. A woman, we're told, is required "to speak properly and softly and never raise [her] voice–particularly in front of the husband or his relatives." Women's speech can be countenanced only for certain purposes and to the husband's advantage. As Linda Peckham notes, "the very act of speech is self-effacement."[26]

In the first half of the film, the Vietnamese women who directly address the camera speak English. Many postcolonial films and books raise the sensitive issue of language and decolonization. For instance, in Ousmane Sembene's *La Noire . . . (Black Girl,* 1966) the title character, Diouana, seems restricted to a life as a domestic because of her inability to speak the fluent French of her employers; however, a more psychologically devastating trap is that of the colonial thinking that privileges the European over the African, epitomized by Diouana's thinking in French. Sembene has since begun to make films in Wolof, but replacing the language of the colonizer with an original "native" language does not automatically eradicate colonized thought, nor is an "original" language always easy to locate. In countries such as India, where many different languages exist over a large area, the language of the colonizer may serve as a universal second language enabling the speaker to avoid the political conflicts involved in privileging the language of one indigenous group over another. In countries whose histories include more than one colonizer–for instance, the Dutch and the British in South Africa, or France and the United States in Vietnam, one of the foreign languages may be chosen as a tool of resistance—especially if the other is the language of the state.

A possible reason the women do not speak Vietnamese is because for them, as for the film, there is no "Vietnam." There is a traditional culture founded on Confucian and Chinese influence, colonized by France ("French Indochina"), engulfed in civil war fanned by the United States ("North Vietnam, South Vietnam"), and restructured as a single nation by a Communist government. Each stage had its own internal resistances, contradictions, and ruptures. Under the Communist government, silence becomes these women's strategy of resistance. When some of the women are officially commanded to speak against themselves in reeducation camps, they distance themselves from language through the mechanical repetition of writing. One relates how, when ordered "to produce and periodically update 'a resume of [her] past life,' . . . she simply recopied it verbatim each time she was required to submit it."[27]

The use of English in the film emerges as multiply determined. It suggests first a conscious address to an English-speaking audience; resistance to the official government line epitomized by the government's language; a consciously political alienation from their "own" country and culture. This last gap between subject and language in particular breaks any simple equivalence between women of the Third World and "home" or their so-called native lands: that women of the Third World are automatically and unproblematically representative of their cultures. For survival, these women consciously select or construct a highly negotiated identity both "at home" and as speakers addressing a non-Third World audience.

As each woman speaks, her accent foregrounds the *effort* of speech, separating the speaker from the language she speaks. Grammatical mistakes and unfamiliar cadences underscore the constructedness of this address, as when ex-Party member Thu Van says, "I am deeply rebelled." The extreme close-up of the right half of her face as the camera bisects her makes us aware of the effort and artifice of this self-conscious construction of words, and of the fact that the film's representation of Thu Van must always be incomplete. Silverman argues that accents in Hollywood films limit the speech of a female character by calling attention to the grain of the voice and the body, thus containing her firmly within the diegesis and making her subject to the control of male characters.[28] Here I would argue that accents locate women in history, in "the politics of location."[29] What an accent deprives its speaker of is the unlocatable timeless universality of Man in the humanist sense, such a concept of subjectivity encouraging an illusion of unproblematic wholeness and domain these women make no claims to.

In her writing as well as her film work, Trinh insists that subjectivity is never homogeneous but "multiple and shifting,"[30] a conception of identity similar to the politics of location but one where the location sits on shifting ground. In *Woman, Native, Other* she describes writing as "a practice located at the intersection of subject and history."[31] For the writer-filmmaker who is Third World-identified and who considers herself a "multiply organized, unstable, and historically discontinuous" subject,[32] "I is not unitary, [just as] culture has never been monolithic."[33]

One of the techniques Trinh uses to foreground the distance between the women and English is to print their words across the frame like a barrier in scenes throughout the first half of the film. This is done in different ways. The first time we see it, parts of the women's speech are printed against black before the women appear. As they speak, we wait to hear them say the words we've read. In later scenes, the entire screen is filled with words so that the viewer's relationship to the film becomes fragmented between image, graphics, and sound track. We can choose to listen, to read quickly and then listen, to read as we hear, or to use the written words as a backup when the spoken words become difficult to understand. As we do so, we discover that the transcription is almost always at variance with some part of the spoken text. The position of native English speakers, I would argue, is one of acute self-consciousness – the insider confronted, distanced from "our" "own" language. The use of titles also calls attention to the fact that the women could speak Vietnamese and simply be subtitled. The double presentation of English, however, insists on the difference between spoken language and written – which is precisely the voice, rhythms, and accents of speech versus the declamatory authority of the printed word. The message written on the screen is one thing; the slow and difficult delivery of it exists in time, insisting on history, person, and geography, establishing the women as conscious, active, *and* Other.

In *Surname Viet* language is spoken, transcribed, and translated, yet the narrator states that translation betrays the spirit, the letter, and the aesthetics of what was said. With the best of intentions, the speaker's act of speech when translated has been taken over, tamed, colonized. A more interesting issue, though, is that of self-translation. Speaking, for an exile, is a matter of constant self-translation, "the transcription of a new culture onto one's very being while still speaking the language of the original."[34] For Trinh, translation "graft[s] several languages, cultures and realities onto a single body," the body becoming the site for multiple identities.[35] Seen the first way, the self-translated speaker would be colluding in her own colonization. However, as heterogeneous and shifting subjects, the women cannot be accused of betraying a more authentic "inner self" in their struggle to speak English over Vietnamese.

Linda Peckham points out how in the traditional "talking heads" documentary "interviews are conducted and reconstructed according to

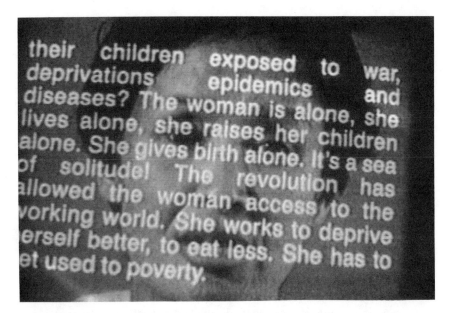

The screen filled with words and images fragments the viewer's relationship to *Surname Viet, Given Name Nam.*

this sense of articulation [as] . . . reflecting and embodying 'truth' value."[36] This kind of documentary privileges language over image and makes simplistic and reductive assumptions about subjectivity and its relation to cinema that have important ramifications when the speaking subject is a Third World woman. Once again the Third World Woman becomes Truth-Teller, without self-consciousness or the ability to shape her story.

Peckham finds that the constructedness of the film's image precisely mediates between testimony and any conception of presence. Visually, the women are fragmented by the camera through close-ups of hands and body parts or seen in long shots and long takes, one as long as twelve minutes, that fix them in static compositions of dramatic symmetry. Absence, she argues, is built into the "artifice of style and form," its exaggeration "a disturbing demarcation of an abyss between the camera and the woman, the viewer and the experience."[37] The use of the long take charts the passage of time and implicitly of space between the woman "here" before us and the events in Vietnam.

Equally important is the mediation between language and voice. "It is when we recall that the speaker is an actress, a substitute, a 'fake,' that the interview style becomes . . . subversive—for the artificial subject points to the absence of the 'real' speaker, an absence that suggests intern-

ment, censorship and death, as well as the survival of a witness, a record—
a history."[38]

The use of actresses to read the translated testimony of the "real" Vietnamese women is the most radical choice of the film, blurring traditional
boundaries between documentary and fiction, and more important, the association of synchronized speech and subjectivity. Halfway through the
film Trinh reveals that the women of the first half have been actresses
reading scripted roles. *Surname Viet* is not a "talking heads" documentary
but an acted adaptation of another author's book of interviews with women
in Vietnam (published in French).[39] On the sound track, Trinh tells how
she then interviewed 150 women to find the 5 who act in the film. These
women are then seen in California discussing the "roles" they played. The
act of translation on which the entire first half of the film is based, then,
is Trinh's translating the Vietnamese women's testimony from French
into English, which the actresses then play out as they illustrate or realize
the first essential of exile existence: self-translation into another language,
another culture, even, as a woman, another body.

The use of actresses, literally putting one person's words into another
body, seemingly undermines the traditional documentary's construction of
speech-as-subjectivity where sync "proves" an essential link between im-
age/soundtrack/being. In doing so, *Surname Viet* would seem to complicate the relation between language and referent: these women are mouth-
ing someone else's words, words that have already been translated by a
third party. Given all these mediations, how can one locate what we're being told? Where is the truth-value? I would argue that *Surname Viet* does
not devolve into a simple deconstructionism and actually resists being
positioned as such a text by Western audiences because of the moral
claims invoked by the women's self-presentation as witnesses. The relation between language and a referent cannot be dismissed given the political context of testimony and the women's claims to linguistic agency as
seen in their attempts to communicate the "truth" of a political reality as
well as the truth of personal experience.

The use of actresses does not undermine this project. On the contrary,
as Peckham says, the "artifices of [the film's construction] are used [para-
doxically] to *augment* the reality of a woman's story"[40]; using actresses
constructs a new way of thinking about women's synchronized speech. The
actresses choose to contribute their voices and images to embody the
words of other women with whom they share a cultural and political history. Unlike actresses in Hollywood films, whose voices are appropriated
for patriarchal ends and who in effect are made to speak against themselves, the actresses in Trinh's film take on the words of others as their
own in an act of community, the refugee women living in San Francisco

and Berkeley electing to carry the words of sisters in struggle to an American audience.

In the film's second half, the women who played the "characters" in the first half speak "as themselves" in Vietnamese. Each of the women, none of whom is a professional actress, mentions how she accepted a role in the film despite her community's disapproval of singers and cinema actresses. The use of Vietnamese notwithstanding, the traditional beliefs are no longer internalized. "Home," as Bernice Johnson Reagon says, is simply something they've outgrown.

The use of a *cinéma vérité* style, coming after the highly posed scenes of the first half, cannot be read as a simple relapse into documentary realism. As narrator, Trinh states that "by choosing the most direct and spontaneous form of voicing and documenting, I find myself closer to fiction," fiction being the illusion of an unproblematic and unfragmented cohesiveness.

However, if the film does have a problem, it is in its reticence about confronting the issue of speaking Vietnamese in California, of the presence of the Third World within the United States. On the one hand, Trinh's stance toward the Vietnamese women in America avoids the tragic or melodramatic overtones of "exile." On the other hand, an American audience can comfortably situate the film along a traditional Cold War axis with "the commies" as the bad guys and America as the land of the free. There are no racist incidents directed against Vietnamese immigrants, no poverty or unemployment. All of the women have nice jobs and the teenage daughter of one woman is a particularly forceful example of becoming American without tears.[41]

Modern Western ideology has been defined as "valorizing . . . the individual as an autonomous moral being" while "neglect[ing] or subordinat[ing] the social whole."[42] What Trinh does in her construction of the women's voices in *Surname Viet* is disrupt our perception of the "individual as autonomous moral being" in order to refocus our attention on the women as part of a wider social context. When one woman speaks, there are three superimposed: the witness, the translator, the actress. When the actresses speak "as themselves," we "see" them through or in relation to the women they've played, the country they've come from, and the country they're in. No woman speaks from a single place, including Trinh. Each woman is plural, in transition, in process, to use Kristeva's term.[43] They transform their bodies into the site from which the other can speak, not in a mystical, transcendental sense, but historically and politically.[44]

Trinh problematizes the classically transparent link between voice and language, image and speech, in order to undermine film's presentation of the Third World woman as "witness to Reality." This does not mean that the women in the film cannot speak the truth or take a political stand. The truth-value of their testimony rests not on Third World woman as Truth-teller, nor on *cinéma vérité*'s "myth of an essential core, of spontaneity and depth as inner vision," nor on bourgeois conceptions of personal experience as proof of a cohesive subjectivity, but on faith in women as politically conscious social agents forming coalitions with other women in shifting communities of resistance.[45]

Notes

1. Mary Ann Doane, "Ideology and the Practice of Sound Editing and Mixing," in *The Cinematic Apparatus*, ed. Teresa de Lauretis and Stephen Heath (New York: St. Martin's Press, 1980), 47.

2. Doane, "The Voice in Cinema: The Articulation of Body and Space," ed. Rick Altman, *Yale French Studies*, no. 60 (1980): 45.

3. Ibid.

4. Doane, "Ideology," 47.

5. Kaja Silverman, *The Acoustic Mirror: The Female Voice in Psychoanalysis and Cinema* (Bloomington: Indiana University Press, 1988), 10.

6. Ibid., 61.

7. Ibid., 168.

8. Ibid., 130.

9. Teresa de Lauretis, "Through the Looking Glass," in *The Cinematic Apparatus*, 187.

10. Chandra Talpade Mohanty, "Under Western Eyes: Feminist Scholarship and Colonial Discourses," *boundary* 2 (Spring-Fall 1984): 333-58.

11. Ibid., 334-35.

12. Ibid., 333.

13. Ibid., 337.

14. Ibid., 338.

15. In an article in the *New York Times*, Flora Lewis writes that "the idea of a 'third world' . . . was generated at the 1955 Bandung conference" and "reinforced at the 1961 non-aligned summit conference in Belgrade." The term's original "purpose was to reject the polarization of the world into blocs led by the U.S. and the Soviet Union, to map a third way, and to spur decolonization" ("Words and Work," *New York Times*, January 18, 1985: 27).

16. Bernice Johnson Reagon, "Coalition Politics: Turning the Century," in *Home Girls: A Black Feminist Anthology*, ed. Barbara Smith (New York: Kitchen Table: Women of Color Press, 1983), 356-68.

17. Mohanty, "Feminist Encounters: Locating the Politics of Experience," *Copyright* 1 (Fall 1987): 38-39.

18. Biddy Martin and Chandra Mohanty, "Feminist Politics: What's Home Got to Do with It?" in *Feminist Studies/Critical Studies*, ed. Teresa de Lauretis (Bloomington: Indiana University Press, 1986), 208-9.

19. Mohanty, "Feminist Encounters," 35.

20. Robin Morgan, "Planetary Feminism: The Politics of the 21st Century," in *Sisterhood Is Global: The International Women's Movement Anthology* (New York: Anchor Press/Doubleday, 1984), 1–37.

21. Mohanty, "Feminist Encounters," 40.

22. Adding, "within which as a woman . . . I am created and trying to create" (Adrienne Rich, *Blood, Bread, and Poetry: Selected Prose 1979–1985* [New York: W. W. Norton, 1986], 212).

23. Martin and Mohanty note that the "claim to a lack of identity or positionality" is a colonialist gesture of the West's "based on privilege, on a refusal to accept responsibility for one's implication in actual historical or social relations, on a denial that positionalities exist or that they matter, the denial of one's own personal history and the claim to a total separation from it" ("What's Home . . . ?" 208). The result of this gesture, according to Martin, Mohanty, and Minnie Pratt, is "cultural impersonation," taking on "the identity of the Other in order to avoid not only guilt but pain and self-hatred" (Minnie Bruce Pratt, "Identity: Skin Blood Heart," in *Yours in Struggle: Three Feminist Perspectives on Anti-Semitism and Racism*, ed. Elly Bulkin, Pratt, and Barbara Smith [Brooklyn, N.Y.: Long Haul Press, 1984], 207).

24. If "a place on the map is a locatable place in history," Trinh is all over the map, moving from Vietnam to Paris, Berkeley to Dakar, framed as her current project "India/China" suggests by the unique colonial conjunction of the place known as French Indochina, otherwise known as Vietnam. Her refusal to be restricted to an "insider" position as the West's authority on Asia by making films originally about Africa is something she discusses in her article "Not You/Like You: Post-Colonial Women and the Interlocking Questions of Identity and Difference," *Inscriptions* 3–4 (1988).

25. Mohanty, "Feminist Encounters," 42.

26. Linda Peckham, "*Surname Viet, Given Name Nam*: Spreading Rumors and Ex/Changing Histories," *Framework* 2, no. 3 (1989): 32.

27. Peckham, "Spreading Rumors," 32.

28. Silverman, *Acoustic Mirror*, 49.

29. While it is important to remember that this is a fictionalized re-creation of reality (an enactment of a documentary), the accents are not "acted." They attest to the *speaker's* "otherness" or distance from the language she speaks, and by one remove, to the *character's* distance or absence from the world of the speaker (the United States) and the world of the film. This accent is one that links Trinh herself, through her voice-over narration, to the actresses/characters in the film.

30. Deborah Gordon, "Introduction," *Inscriptions* 3–4 (1988): 2.

31. Trinh T. Minh-ha, *Woman, Native, Other: Writing Postcoloniality and Feminism* (Bloomington: Indiana University Press, 1989), 6.

32. De Lauretis, "Displacing Hegemonic Discourses: Reflections on Feminist Theory in the 1980s," *Inscriptions* 3–4 (1988): 141.

33. Trinh, "Not You/Like You: Post-Colonial Women and the Interlocking Questions of Identity and Difference," ibid., 76.

34. Peckham, "Spreading Rumors," 35.

35. Ibid. For Peckham, "translation is a truer image of the interpenetration of textualities that occur in an individual."

36. Ibid., 33.

37. Ibid.

38. Ibid.

39. Mai Thu Van, *Viet Nam, une peuple, des voix* (Paris: Pierre Horgy, 1983).

40. Peckham, "Spreading Rumors," 33, my emphasis.

41. It has also been pointed out that the film does not directly address contemporary *Vietnamese* political issues either, including the invasion of Cambodia, the boat people, and their exploitation by pirates. The latter may indeed be alluded to by the slow-motion, grainy black-and-white footage of people in boats that recurs throughout the film and is especially privileged by being placed near the beginning and the end. The ambiguous beauty of these images situates them in the realm of poetry (where they are undeniably powerful) but at the same time limits their ability to serve as references to specific political events.

42. Aihwa Ong, "Colonialism and Modernity: Feminist Re-presentation of Women in Non-Western Societies," in Gordon, *Inscriptions*, 86, referring to Louis Dumont's *Essays on Individualism: Modern Ideology in Anthropological Perspective* (Chicago: University of Chicago Press, 1986), 279–80.

43. See Toril Moi, ed., *The Kristeva Reader* (New York: Columbia University Press, 1986), esp. 13 and 88–123.

44. This argument takes Rick Altman's concept of "ventriloquism" (the illusion of synchronization that the image produces the sound) a step further ("Moving Lips: Cinema as Ventriloquism"). To quote Edward Branigan, in this film, synchronization itself forms the foundation for "a staging of a documentary about *voices and bodies which are absent*" (my emphasis). At once we move into the realm of Metz's "imaginary signifier," where the essential cinematic illusion of presence signifies a profound absence. I would argue that Trinh rewrites this absence as a *political* absence of the exile, of those left behind, and of the exclusion from historical consciousness of women's experience of both exile and abandonment. I am also indebted to Kaja Silverman for her provocative reading of the film's presentation of the body, raised in discussion at the Sound Symposium, Iowa, April 1990.

45. Trinh, "Not You/Like You," 77.

Her Image Fades as Her Voice Rises

Lis Rhodes and Felicity Sparrow

Often during the Day, Joanna Davis (U.K., 1979), 15 min.
A House Divided, Alice Guy (U.S., 1913), 13 min.
The Smiling Madame Beudet, Germaine Dulac (France, 1922), 35 min.
Light Reading, Lis Rhodes (U.K., 1978), 20 min.

Sitting with her at the table, talking, her hands poised over the typewriter. The words in our minds turning between description and analysis – to write the image, or to write about an image. This will be a subjective gathering of threads of meaning, drawing attention to the spaces between four films that are dense with connections and difference. Seen thus, the program becomes a fiction in itself; a looking at – a listening to – the relationships between the filmmakers – their stories – avoiding false isolation, the separations determined by history as it is written – as it has been read – to mean meanings other than HERS.

We shall try to make explicit the links and fractures between four films made by four women whose lives and work belong to different times and different places – different languages even – but whose voices are placed within similar constraints. We all experience these constraints, but most women are allowed no time or space to reflect upon them.

Daughter of a publisher, I had read widely and remembered a fair amount. I had done a bit of amateur theatricals and thought that one could probably do better. Arming myself with courage, I timidly proposed to Gaumont that I write one or two sketches and have them acted by friends. If anyone could have foreseen the course of development this would take, I would never have got this permission. My youth, my inexperience, my sex, all would have conspired against me. . . . However I obtained this permission, on the express condition that it didn't interfere with my secretarial duties.[1]

The idea came from the experience of sharing a kitchen with two men. Through realising, over a period of time, specific things that they didn't notice, I was able to crystallise my own response to particular tasks, particular parts of this room. . . . I discovered several areas (often very small) within the kitchen that I was very aware of becoming dirty and enjoyed–or rather was urged–to clean. I developed a special relationship to these 'corners'; I enjoyed the materials that constituted them and felt the repetitive cycle of things becoming dirty–the way each part became dirty and the different methods of cleaning. I became more aware of this in myself as I realised that the men had no understanding for it. Why? Was it education? My conditioning as a woman? Was it to do with me in particular? Or is it just part of 'women's nature?[2]

Traces made, traces removed; a woman is caught midsentence often during the day. The traces of sound from the radio, as a newscaster's voice surfaces and sinks in a burble of music, remain peripheral, outside and obscured by the unnaturally foregrounded sounds of tea being poured and bread being cut repeatedly throughout the film. *Often during the Day* opens with a series of still images of a kitchen, photographs that have been delicately hand-tinted by the filmmaker. A woman's voice is heard describing a particular kitchen space, through its geography–every minute detail of which she is familiar with–and through the various activities taking place within it. The room is referred to as the center of the house and the voice describes the traces left by the users of the kitchen (the spatterings of food left on the floor around the saucer after the cat has finished eating–the little pieces of hair washed from a razor after a man has finished shaving). She reflects on the tasks of cleaning and repair, the "small unnecessary" tasks, the caring for a space.

When we first constructed the sink there was a gap between the enamel part and the wooden drawers that support it. The gap worried me because I saw water trickled through on to the things in the drawers. The others didn't notice, or didn't mind, and it took me several months to do anything about it.[3]

The attention given to a domestic space that Joanna Davis speaks of seems to avoid a strict definition of housework–the unpaid servicing that that usually implies–and centers on her pleasure. It is a pleasure that is expressed in relation to certain surfaces and textures, "the way each part became dirty," and the placings of things. A different pleasure–the satisfaction of a job being done–is described by another voice, a man's, reading extracts from the testimonies of women's reflections on housework as catalogued in *The Sociology of Housework*.[4] This conflict–can pleasure be pleasing if that pleasure is seen as oppressive?—is expressed by the filmmaker through images showing the continual violation of her feelings for the space. In the final shot of the film, a long continuous take, the tea is poured; the bread is cut; an arm reaches across a woman's body to reach the butter. *She* refolds the paper carefully after he has used it. Their consumption leaves traces: a scattering of crumbs on the surface of the table, the stain of tea leaves on the draining board. Disturbed by the crumbs, she interrupts her meal to wipe them up.

This sense of impingement is confirmed by the quotations from *The Sociology of Housework*, which rest within the film as uneasily as the news from Armagh and the song "Dancing in the City." The printed words emerge from a thin veil of tissue paper with an authority of which Joanna Davis is extremely wary. Perhaps it is to enforce this distance from her own experience that a man's voice reads the passages, just as the women quoted are defined by the men they are married to: carpenter's or lorry driver's wife. The implication is that the male voice is placed outside of the experience of the female filmmaker, within the parameters of sociological research.

In *Often during the Day* the woman is not socially placed by a particular man. Thus the issues of sexual and economic control are recognized, rather than suffered, and the historical determinates that underlie her feelings of pleasure and anxiety in relationship to domestic tasks can be analyzed.

It is here that one of the central issues connecting the films is raised and can be clearly seen in the different positioning of the women in *Often during the Day* and the two earlier films. For Mme Beudet it is not only the institution of marriage, but also the collusion of the Catholic church in reinforcing that institution, that is questioned. In *A House Divided*, Alice Guy approaches the domestic relationship as a civil bargain—the external social control being secular rather than divine. The marital relationship of the couple is represented by the "house." The "divine" is privatized as romantic love, and now forms the fragile foundations of the "house."

The bourgeois home depicted in *A House Divided* has already developed the characteristics of the industrialized family; separate supposedly equal spheres of work, the woman within the home, the man outside. A similar division of work is apparent in the office between the husband and his secretary. Thus the women are established as financially dependent, and their work is primarily concerned with providing service for the husband. A misunderstanding, an assumption of mutual infidelity, shakes the foundation of the home—the house divides into silence. Communication between the wife and the husband is a series of notes—a nice use of intertitles—carefully stored in a jar in the kitchen. The wife refuses to service the husband. The marriage bargain is broken and the humor in the film asserts itself. A "new legal agreement" must be arranged. Only now

A House Divided places the woman squarely within the home.

can the wife reclaim her identity and independence; she deletes the words *your wife* at the end of a letter and signs her own name (albeit her name by marriage). By contrast, the cheerful independence of the unmarried secretary is established early on—surely Alice Guy must have directed those office scenes with glee, remembering when she herself was secretary to Leon Gaumont.

The film plays upon the women's independence within dependency, and the husband's apparent independence—though, left to himself, he is incapable of even deciding whether or not to wear a raincoat! However, for Alice Guy, rationality overcomes doubt, the divided house can be restored to unity—the infidelities are no more than misunderstandings. The contract is reestablished, romantic love can reassert itself. The yawning chasms of prejudice and oppression determining a woman's position within marriage—so accurately portrayed by Germaine Dulac ten years later—were not part of Alice Guy's pragmatic optimism and trust in "equality."

To Alice Guy, it was obvious that

> there is nothing connected with the staging of a motion picture that a woman cannot do as easily as a man, and there is no reason why she cannot completely master every technicality of the art. The technique of the drama has been mastered by so many women that it is considered as much her field as a man's and its adaptation to picture work in no way

removes it from her sphere. The technique of motion picture photography, like the technique of the drama, is fitted to women's activities.[5]

The tradition of narrative film that Alice Guy initiated in 1896 with her first film, *La Fée Aux Choux*, appears to be drawn from the theater. She used sets and actors to represent visually the only form of cultural expression in which women were allowed to play a major part—the writing of fiction. "Writing was a reputable and harmless occupation. The family peace was not broken by the scratching of a pen. No demand was made upon the family purse. For ten and six pence one can buy paper enough to write all the plays of Shakespeare—if one has a mind that way.[6]

Alice Guy's determination and optimism were shared by many women at the time in their fight for equal education, better working conditions, and the vote. However, this energy was rapidly dissipated by the outbreak of the war, the ensuing nationalism, and economic depression. The old patterns began repeating themselves. Guy's husband, Herbert Blaché, took over the production company in 1914. With him in control outside producers were brought in and she was forced out of the picture. She finally gave up going to production meetings because "Herbert said I would have embarrassed the men who wanted to smoke their cigars and spit in peace while discussing business.[7]

Imprisoned in Dependency; or, The Violence of Meaning

The cinema can certainly tell a story, but you have to remember that the story is nothing. The story is surface. The seventh art, that of the screen, is depth rendered perceptible, the depth that lies beneath the surface; it is the musical ungraspable. . . . Plot film or abstract film, the problem is the same. To touch the feelings through the sight and, as I've already said, to give predominance to the image. . . . The image can be as complex as an orchestration since it may be composed of combined movements of expression and light.[8]

Six years before writing these words Germaine Dulac made *The Smiling Madame Beudet*. Its plot, the surface, is simple, as a reviewer was to say sixty years later: "Madame Beudet is married to a bombastic idiot, refuses to go to the opera with him, dreams up the nearly perfect murder and, when it fails, gets away with it because of Monsieur Beudet's lack of imagination."[9] The film's intensity, its visual impact and depth of feeling are achieved through an orchestration of emotive gestures and facial expressions. Often described as the first feminist film, we share Madame Beudet's (and Germaine Dulac's) point of view throughout—her "voice," although silent, can only be that of the first person singular, as in *Often during the Day*.

"*In a quiet provincial town* . . . Madame Beudet is isolated; . . . *behind the peaceful facades*" she is trapped. Her gaze through the window is blocked by the view of the prison opposite; inwardly she sees the reflection of that institution in her wedding ring. Locked within the niceties of a middle-class marriage she struggles to maintain her sanity. The interior space of her home is constantly reflective of Madame Beudet's mental restriction; her gestures and expressions, constantly juxtaposed with those of her husband, are reflective of her emotional suffocation. The placing of a vase of flowers becomes symbolic of conflicting sensibilities, the key to her piano the control of her means of expression. Her book of poetry provides a way for her to retreat into herself and her desires. Baudelaire, Debussy, and the ghostlike apparition of a male tennis player stepping out from the pages of a magazine are her only cultural reference points. But even these are impinged upon by the distorted face of Monsieur Beudet. Escape is impossible. Outside, the institutions of justice and religion have sealed and sanctified her dependency. Inside "it was in this accumulation of other men's thoughts and experiences that she looked for affirmation of identity."[10] She is excluded; even the running of the house is in her husband's hands; she is held accountable. Monsieur Beudet's obstructive and destructive presence occupies both her physical and mental space. With the loss of space she cannot act. In the absence of action she remains without response. She is shown looking at herself–alone with her own reflection–framed in a triple mirror.

In case we need more clues, Germaine Dulac shows the completeness of Madame Beudet's mental decapitation: as Monsieur Beudet tears the head off her ornamental doll, an intertitle reads, "[A] doll is fragile . . . a bit like a woman." And he puts the head in his pocket. A fine symbol of men's idea of femininity and how this can be manipulated and used against women–they can be handled, idolized, and popped away . . . so the cigar smokers can spit in peace and continue to exclude women from the "real" business and understanding of life. However, close-ups of Madame Beudet's face earlier in the film show her awareness of, and resignation to, Monsieur Beudet's stupidity. He thinks she knows nothing about Faust, that women have no minds of their own (which is probably true when their heads are forcibly removed). Her expression shows that she knows the story and recognizes it as one of male dominance and female dependency. The bitterest moment of the film–the center of the argument–is when he thinks she is suicidal. He is incapable of considering the possibility that she intended the bullet for him: "*How could I ever live without you?*" She is caught in *his* emotional dependency. She knows but cannot act. The ending portrayed in *A House Divided* Germaine Dulac cannot accept. The happy conclusion reflected in the mirror, "theater," to her, is a facade that the priest and Monsieur Beudet accept; the film ends with Madame Beudet's

Madame Beudet alone with her own reflection framed in a triple mirror.

back to the camera while the two men greet each other and indicate their
collusion and her exclusion.

"*In the quiet streets, without horizon, under a low sky . . . united by
habit.*" Thus *The Smiling Madame Beudet* ends where it begins, unsmil-
ingly. The provincial town is the scene of her imprisonment; behind the facade of habit is the scene of her attempts to escape. But the escape, the
analysis of her situation, remains private to her, voiced in her fantasies.
She cannot change her situation however clearly she understands it.

> in her own voice she cried
> the end cannot be confused with the end that ended
> somewhere—but not here
> not here at the beginning . . . [11]

Light Reading could be picking up the thread of Madame Beudet's
story, the voice could be hers after seeing herself on film sixty years later.
She has in the meantime been granted the right to vote; film can now record her spoken words and we can hear them. As for her image . . . that
has gone. Sixty years of film and television and advertising have much to
answer for.

> Who turned the light away
> the light away from her
> she will not be placed in darkness
> she will be present in darkness only to be apparent
> to appear without image
> to be heard unseen . . .
> her hands reach out
> she could only glimpse the shadow
> the faint reflection of the fading image
> stumbling on the traces of her knowing
> sinking in the ruts of her experience
> slipping amongst the shadows of her story
> she couldn't reach herself . . . [12]

The film begins in darkness as a woman's voice is heard over a black screen. "She" is spoken of as multiple subject—third person singular and plural. Her voice continues until images appear on the screen and then is silent. In the final section of the film she begins again, looking at the images as these are moved and replaced, describing the piecing together of the film as she tries to piece together the tangle of strands of her story.

The voice is questioning, searching. She will act. But how? Act against what? The bloodstained bed suggests a crime . . . Could it be *his* blood—was that the action denied to Madame Beudet? No answers are given, after the torrent of words at the beginning all the film offers are closed images and more questions . . . Is it even blood on the bed, what fracture is there between seeing and certainty? Could it be *her* blood—rape/murder of the mind, of the body, of both? Her image has gone. If there has been a crime, "she" might still be victim . . . How can a crime of such complexity and continuity be "solved"? The voice searches for clues, sifting through them, reading and rereading until the words and letters (in themselves harmless enough) loom up nightmarishly, no longer hung on the structure of language.

> the violence of sequence tears at the threads of her thoughts
> the folds of light fade into deep shadows
> the sense of her dreams is disturbed by the presence
> of a past not past
> a past that holds her with fingers sharpened on logic
> nails hardened with rationality
> cutting the flow of her thoughts
> forcing her back within herself
> damned by the rattle of words
> words already sentenced
> imprisoned in meaning . . . [13]

The clues suggest it is language that has trapped her, meanings that have excluded her, and a past that has been constructed to control her. Do we have to delve into history and reappropriate it? Perhaps there are other ways, such as examining the scene of the crime as we're told in detective fiction. But magnifying the stain on the bed reveals only a blur, measured with a ruler, but that doesn't add up to much. She's forced back within herself and her own thoughts; she begins again cautiously:

> she watched herself being looked at
> she looked at herself being watched
> but she could not perceive herself
> as the subject of the sentence . . . [14]

Madame Beudet's light reading can neither provide escape nor reflect her own thoughts and desires. In *Light Reading*, Lis Rhodes recognizes that dead end. She searches for other clues and other means of finding her own reflection. But she seems to be framed everywhere she looks: the cosmetic mirror gives her back only part of her image, photographing herself in a mirror gives her back another. There are fragmented images, multiple images, and shadowy photographs, but they remain as enigmatic and implacable as the stain on the bed. The images (snapshots of a past) are torn up and rearranged, leaving gaps that she tries to measure with letters and figures—fragments.

Where do we begin? There is the past, always, which we can reread, reframe, just as we can try to replace Alice Guy and Germaine Dulac. But it's not just a question of balancing out the injustices: "There is nothing connected with the staging of a motion picture that a woman cannot do as easily as a man"—it goes deeper than these crimes of exclusion and unequal opportunities.

"She stopped the action . . . "

Gertrude Stein said,

> And now she wrote
> and now mountains do not cloud over
> let us wash our hair and stare
> stare at mountains . . . [15]

Her words, quoted, are like a light refrain running through the threads of meaning in *Light Reading*'s monologue; and the thought of her there, so solidly, in the past and now . . . *Light Reading* ends with no single solution. But there is a beginning. Of that she is positive. She will not be looked at but listened to:

> *she begins to re-read*
> *aloud*

She is not alone, in speech, she can begin to find reflections of herself outside of herself. Nobody can say anything unless someone is listening. And we can't act without response . . .

> I read to you and you read to me and we both read intently. And I waited for you and you waited for me and we both waited attentively. I find knitting to be a continuous occupation and I am full of gratitude because I realise how much I am indebted to the hands that wield the needles.[16]

> LIS: Do you think we've written what we meant to write? I mean is what we've written *fiction*?

> FELICITY: We've shifted the "facts" . . . but they needed shifting–like my carpet they gather dust–and that begins to obscure the patterns that make facts mean . . .

> LIS: Arguing all the way round to here . . . sitting with her at the table–still talking–We wrote this together–she wrote on light reading–and we both wrote on the other three.

Notes

1. Alice Guy, *Autobiographie d'une Pionniere du Cinéma* (Paris: Denoel/ Gonthier, 1976). Alice Guy is referring to her request to Gaumont to make her first film after having seen the Lumière Brothers' films documenting trains coming into stations, military parades, and the like. Gaumont's firm at the time was primarily concerned with the manufacture of cameras and projectors, but with the success of this first fiction film he readily allowed his secretary to continue her directorial work. She became head of productions for Gaumont until her departure for the United States in 1907 and marriage to Herbert Blaché. In Fort Lee, New Jersey, she founded her own production company, Solax, which was successful until its folding in 1914. *A House Divided* was a Solax production and is one of half a dozen of her short films to have been preserved–none of her features have survived, despite their popularity at the time. In 1923 she returned (divorced) to France, where she remained until her death in 1968.

2. Joanna Davis (from a conversation with Lis Rhodes and Felicity Sparrow, 1978).

3. From *Often during the Day*.

4. Ann Oakely, *The Sociology of Housework* (London: Martin Robertson, 1974).

5. Alice Guy, "A Woman's Place in Photoplay Productions," *Moving Picture World*, July 11, 1914.

6. Virginia Woolf. "Professions for Women," in *Death of the Moth* (1942).

Reprinted in *Virginia Woolf: Women and Writing*, ed. Michele Barrett (London: Women's Press, 1979).

7. Alice Guy, *Autobiographie d'une Pionniere du Cinéma.*

8. Germaine Dulac, "Visual and Anti-Visual Films" *Le Rouge et Le Noir* (July 1928). Reprinted in *The Avant-Garde Film: A Reader of Theory and Criticism*, ed. P. Adams Sitney (New York: Anthology Film Archives, 1987).

9. Helen MacKintosh, *City Limits*, March 16, 1982.

10. P. D. James, *Innocent Blood* (London: Sphere Books, 1981).

11. From *Light Reading*.

12. Ibid.

13. Ibid.

14. Ibid.

15. Gertrude Stein, "Sonatina followed by Another." The entire poem is reprinted in *Bee Time Vine* (New Haven, Conn.: Yale University Press, 1953).

16. Ibid.

A Jury of Their Peers: Marleen Gorris's
A Question of Silence

Linda Williams

In a now-classic article of feminist criticism, Elaine Showalter argues for a theory of women's writing based on a model of the specific and "self-defined nature of female cultural experience." Borrowing from feminist historian Gerda Lerner and anthropologists Shirley and Edwin Ardener, Showalter points out that women's culture is not so much a subculture as a dual perspective of living and participating in a dominant male culture with boundaries that overlap, but do not entirely contain, the non-dominant, "muted" culture of women. She thus views male and female experience as two overlapping circles with much of the woman's muted circle falling within the boundaries of the dominant circle but with a small crescent of experience that she dubs, following Edwin Ardener, a "wild zone" or "no-man's-land" of woman's culture that is entirely off-limits to men. Where women know the male crescent, if not through personal experience, at least through myth and legend, men have no experience or knowledge of the female crescent precisely because there is so little women's art known to men.[1]

The explicitly feminist artist thus faces a dilemma: whenever she attempts to speak and validate the mysterious "wild" zone of woman's experience she runs the risk of making a leap to a mythic level of female identity conceived outside the limits of all existing language, all "known" reality. Yet not to run this risk is to remain trapped within the limits of patriarchy's definition of what it knows: man as subject, woman as other.

My purpose is not to bemoan the limitations of this dilemma—which are inescapable—but to see how an exemplary work of feminist film art negotiates its difficulties.[2]

The problem, as I see it, is that once an explicit work of feminist art begins to press the "muted" "wild zone" of woman-specific consciousness to speak, it may speak too clearly in facile parables rather than in aesthetically rich language. In this case, the tension inherent in the feminist revision of patriarchal language becomes mere reversal: black becomes white, passive women become Amazonian guerrillas; and the gorgon Medusa grows beautiful and laughs. But if, as Showalter and others have noted, women's culture must inevitably envelop the social, literary, and cultural heritages of both the muted female and the dominant male groups, if women really have a "double-voiced discourse," "inside two traditions at once," or if, as B. Ruby Rich puts it in a slightly different context, women are the "ultimate dialecticians,"[3] then we need feminist texts that can reveal this duality, this tension in the often unspoken contradictions between the dominant and the mute.

More than any other feminist film of the last decade, Marleen Gorris's 1982 Dutch film, *A Question of Silence*, seems to me to avoid the pitfalls of a facile or utopian feminist revision while speaking eloquently from within the still "muted" experiences of its three women protagonists. The film is about the spontaneous and unmotivated murder-mutilation of a male boutique owner by three women shoppers. They commit the crime after one of them—a near catatonic housewife—is caught shoplifting a dress. Instead of meekly returning the garment as the smug male owner seems to expect, Christine stubbornly shoves it back in her bag. Two other women watch with interest this spectacle of an obviously guilty woman refusing to act guilty. They come to her defense and then, slowly, deliberately, join in her offense, taking garments themselves.

What follows is a gradual escalation of an initial crime against property into the ritual mutilation and murder of a male scapegoat. We see almost none of the actual violence of this scene—just enough to know that hangers, clothes racks, and ashtrays serve as weapons. The bulk of the film is the investigation into this crime by a court-appointed woman psychiatrist. The investigation culminates in a hearing on the sanity of the defendants in which the psychiatrist, much to the annoyance of the court, declares the women sane.

The three women cannot or will not explain why they committed the crime. During the investigation, the psychiatrist earnestly attempts to find the psychosocial explanations for their acts. But each woman resists the imposition of a clinico-juridical discourse that would explain her crime by judging her mad, then leave her to grow truly insane in the clean, brightly lighted panopticon that is the Dutch penal system. The psychiatrist must finally agree that they are three "very ordinary women." The only way to "read" this crime, she learns, is to see it as proceeding from that portion of women's culture and experience that is truly not known to men. Her investigation thus leads her directly into Showalter's wild zone.

Showalter's first method of understanding the wild zone of female culture is to visualize it as a place—a "no-man's-land"—where women congregate. There are few such places outside the home, but a woman's dress shop is certainly one of them. Although the psychiatrist could never argue the point in a court of law, it is clear that the crime could not have taken place in a more male-defined space; nor could it have taken place in that space if the shop owner had been a woman. Neither fact can be used to excuse the crime, but both are important to its women readers. For only in this space could the women let out the rage and defiance they did not even know was in them, only in this space could Christine channel her rage into action, and only in this space could Annie and Andrea identify with this rage, own it, and finally share in its expression as well.

Showalter's second method of understanding the wild zone is through the experiences women share. In the film three scenes stand out from the jigsaw puzzle of flashbacks elicited by the psychiatrist's interviews. Each contains a relatively insignificant detail that takes on meaning only in relation to its similarity to the other women's common experiences. These details could never be mentioned in a court of law or even among the women themselves should they find a way to talk to one another. Nor does the psychiatrist ever speak of them. Yet they are there in the full visual rendering of experience by which cinematic flashback can sometimes belie the specific memories of its reminiscers.

Each has to do with coffee or tea. Coffee first appears innocuously enough in an early scene depicting a bit of banter between Annie, the overweight and jolly waitress, and a male customer in the café where she works. The customer calls out for a refill and jokingly adds the insult that a few more steps couldn't hurt Annie's ample figure. She laughs heartily and serves the coffee, even as the police enter to pick her up for the crime that has not yet been revealed to us. The incident is unremarkable except in retrospect, in relation to the accumulated rendering of the experiences of all three women, each of whom is insulted and put in her place through some aspect of her conventional role as server, but not customer. In retrospect, Annie's laughter will come back to haunt both the audience and Janine, the psychiatrist.

A second, more pointed, scene shows Andrea, the efficient executive secretary, at work at a board meeting with her boss and several male advisors. When asked about a detail of their overseas investments, Andrea answers with slightly more command of the facts than befits a mere secretary. The advice is not taken kindly by her boss. But he takes his revenge indirectly, first, by growing irritated at the sound her spoon makes stirring her coffee – one of his advisors even stays her hand – and second, by taking the advice of this same male advisor, who recommends the opposite of Andrea's plan. It is clear that the issue is not her ability to give sound advice, but the fact that a mere secretary has stepped out of her role as discreet notetaker and coffee server to do so.

In this prolonged scene built upon the noise of a coffee cup and spoon, we begin to read the small indignities of women's lives. These indignities could never be offered in a court of law as justification for the rage unleashed in the boutique, but they nevertheless clearly present humiliations other women can understand. But it is finally through Christine's eerie silence that we come to experience the ultimate indignity of women's lives. Christine stands in her kitchen amid the chaos of three children and a hurried husband who is about to leave her holding just the saucer, as if she were a table. Through the social determination of a life that has asked her only to serve, Christine has become an inanimate thing. "It is no wonder she has stopped talking," explains Andrea, in one of the film's few moments of direct explanation, "no one was listening."

Each of these humiliating incidents is experienced by a woman alone, in a space that does not seem to belong to her even if, as in the case of Christine's kitchen, it should. There is no other woman to recognize or name the experience. As it occurs, the woman does not appear able to name it herself. The shared aspects of women's experience represented by the film are thus entirely forms of negative alienation, while the only instances of shared experience occur at the scene of the crime and later in the courtroom. Although the film certainly could have contrived to make the spatial and experiential aspects of women's wild zone coincide in an easy parable of feminist solidarity, I think it is important that it does not. A comparison to a work that does just that is instructive.

Susan Keating Glaspell's 1917 short story, "A Jury of Her Peers," has recently entered the canon of feminist literature.[4] Like Gorris's film, the story concerns a female murderer and a male victim. A farmer's wife, Minnie Foster, is arrested for the strangulation murder of her husband. Minnie's story is never told directly, but it is pieced together by two groups of male and female investigators. While the sheriff and county attorney vainly search her house and barn for clues to the motive, their wives, relegated to the space of kitchen and parlor, do some unofficial investigating of their own. They discover ample motive for Minnie's crime in her husband's systematic destruction of all life and beauty in her world. They decode the poverty of the house, the stove that doesn't draw, the patchwork of her wardrobe, the broken neck of her canary, and her presumed reaction to this cruelty in sewing that goes awry, chores that are left undone, and finally her revenge, the strangulation of her sleeping husband.

As the female jury of peers comprehends the significance of each piece of evidence, they systematically destroy it, erasing clues to Minnie Foster's guilt. As Annette Kolodny has noted in an article on the story, their reading thus amounts to a complete reordering of "who, in fact, has been murdered . . . what has constituted the real crime in the story."[5] Even more revealing than their ability to read the deeper nature of the crime is their immediate sense of their own participation in it: "Oh, I *wish* I'd come over here once in a while! . . . That was a crime! Who's going to punish that?"[6]

Kolodny's major point about the story is that the women readers of the crime expand the literal male reading into a larger, figurative, understanding of its modus operandi: strangulation. The male reading sees only that a man is strangled, that his wife is the likely suspect, and that they themselves are the expert readers of the evidence; the female (figurative) reading sees the many ways in which a woman's life has been strangled, that the husband is the likely suspect, and that they themselves are the true investigators into the crime. Their very expertise lies in their ability not to judge from on high but to act, as Carol Gilligan has shown with respect to the "moral development" of women in general, as an empathic jury of peers sensitive to extenuating circumstances.[7]

Thus, in Kolodny's terms, women are the better readers of other women's literal and figurative truths because of their shared experiences. The two women in Glaspell's story are able to make Minnie Foster's kitchen and house "speak" in her defense when she herself cannot or will not speak. The story even implies that they help her to beat the rap as well. For Kolodny, "A Jury of Her Peers" is a parable of female reading and solidarity that speaks its parable of the unique ability of women to read the supposed "insignificance of kitchen things." But I am concerned that the elevation of such parables to the status of key texts within the emerging canon of feminist art may have a simplistically utopian influence on the sort of work we begin looking for from feminist artists. Much as the tale satisfies as an example of table turning, I think it would be a mistake to take it as the sort of feminist revision most called for now. What interests me instead are not the remarkable similarities between Glaspell's story and Gorris's film, but their illuminating differences.

In "A Jury of Her Peers," the feminist moral has been facilitated by the congruence of Showalter's first two categories of the unique cultural experience of women: the spatial and experiential. The isolated experiences of each housewife are able to emerge when two of them get together in the kitchen and parlor of a third woman. Only in this no-man's-land are these first two women able to reorder the significance of the third woman's experience.

In Gorris's film, however, the separation between the spatial and experiential aspects of the wild zone of women's cultural experience emphasizes the very real difficulty women have in finding the places where they can speak their experience to one another. Thus, where Glaspell's reversal of the initial patriarchal terms of judgment is facilitated by the convergence of the spatial and experiential realms, Gorris's film separates these realms and thus separates the women from one another. There is no positive way for them to articulate what they nevertheless begin to know that they share. The violence of the crime and the negative disruption of laughter in the courtroom are their only forms of speech.

The viewer of the film, like the internal reader-investigator within the film, cannot base her reading on a simple reversal of an initial male judgment. Instead, she must engage in a deeper and more complicit process of identification with mute and wild zones of experience that are not yet known and that certainly may not help her to beat the rap of male judgment. What is missing from Glaspell's story and Kolodny's criticism, then, is the third aspect of Showalter's wild zone: its "metaphysical" or "imaginary" side. Showalter writes,

> If we think of the wild zone metaphysically, or in terms of consciousness, it has no corresponding male space since all of male consciousness is within the circle of the dominant structure and thus accessible to or structured by language. . . . In terms of cultural anthropology, women know what the male crescent is like, even if they have never seen it, because it becomes the subject of legend (like the wilderness). But men do not know what is in the wild.[8]

The genuine sense of excitement and danger generated by the two screenings of Gorris's film I have attended might be partly explained by the film's demonstration that women do not necessarily know what is in "the wild" either. For the film suggests that the most genuinely heroic moment of feminist consciousness consists in a woman's decision to cast her lot with an identity that has not yet been spoken and that cannot as yet speak itself. Unlike Glaspell's story, there is no neat parable, no pat reversal of judgment that can metaphorically explain the crime. There is only a radical silence erupting into violence when the women first get together, and erupting into laughter when they meet again.

This laughter occurs when the male court begs Janine the psychiatrist for at least a "tentative provisional diagnosis" that would make the job of categorizing the crime as simple insanity easier. Janine refuses to declare the women insane; she even goes on to insist that the sex of the victim and his position as owner of the boutique are important factors precipitating the crime. To counter this, the prosecutor argues a ridiculous parallel: the crime could just as well have been perpetrated by three male shoppers on a female shop owner. Annie the waitress is the first to laugh. Soon Christine and Andrea join in, as do various female spectators, including a chorus of four silent women whom we recognize as also having been present at the scene of the crime. Finally, Janine laughs too.

Raucous, disruptive laughter achieves the recognition and solidarity among women that Janine's earnest attempts at communication had failed to achieve. When the laughing women are ordered to leave the court so that the trial might proceed in their absence, a pregnant moment ensues as the significant female actors—Janine, the three defendants, and the four silent witnesses—all converge at the center of the courtroom, a low railing and a pit between them. They repeat looks of recognition that had occurred the first time the defendants had been led into the pit. But that first look of recognition served merely to reveal Janine's awareness of a silent bond between the defendants and the chorus of women spectators. By the time of this second look, Janine's laughter has spoken her solidarity with these silent women. She has joined the "high-heeled army of Furies" referred to by the prosecution at the very moment they are led, like the Furies of Aeschylus, out of the light, down into the bowels of the earth.

But the film does not end on this note of solidarity. It ends, rather, on a moment of suspension between the known world of patriarchal light and the unknown world of matriarchal shadow. In the parking lot outside the courtroom, as Janine's husband angrily honks his car horn for Janine to come, she once again encounters the chorus of silent witnesses to the crime. Janine turns to look at them, and on this look the frame freezes. The spatial, experiential, and metaphysical realms of female difference are recognized in her look, though they still have not been spoken.

A *Question of Silence* offers no neat parables, no pat reversals, no clear motives, and, most important, no clear language that states women's truths. It offers a silence that questions all language, a laughter that subverts authority, a judgment that never gets pronounced. In all of this it does not so much work to *revise* its underlying patriarchal myth of the irrationality of women as it reopens all the questions supposedly solved by such a myth. In the final play of Aeschylus's *Oresteia*, a female chorus of "Furies" is sold out in the first court of law by a male-identified goddess who is always for the male. Sweet-talked by Athena, the Furies go quietly to their new home beneath the earth, making way for the progress of the city-state and its new codes of justice. Repressed and renamed, the "Eumenides" now mask the ancient war between the sexes symbolized by Clytemnestra and Agamemnon's cycle of revenge.

Gorris's film returns to this war and to the original matriarchal power repressed by this myth. Where the male myth gets rid of the unsightly, raucous Furies by stage-managing a quiet exit, Gorris restages this descent into the bowels of the earth in a feminist revision that transforms her Furies' original rage into subversive laughter. These Furies exit convulsed by the absurdity of a male reason that cannot understand women. Like Cixous's Medusa—who was also part of a monstrous sisterly trio—they have been revised. But although they are laughing, Gorris has not simply changed the monstrous into the beautiful, the negatives into positives, the repressive ending into a liberatory one. In fact, the film does not so much revise the *Oresteia* with a female-defined happy ending as it reopens all the questions supposedly solved by Athena's original judgment against women. Like "A Jury of Her Peers," it asks what real judgment of women by women might be. But unlike Glaspell's story, it does not proceed to perform that judgment itself. The language of such judgment, it suggests, does not yet exist.

The power of *A Question of Silence* as feminist art thus lies in its resistance of all the male paradigms by which female deviance has been understood, in its insistence on the wildness of women's cultural experience and, finally, in its refusal to narrate the positive, utopian identity of women.

Notes

1. Elaine Showalter, "Feminist Criticism in the Wilderness," *Critical Inquiry* 8 (Winter 1981): 179–205.

2. The fundamental dilemma addressed by Showalter's essay is that of all feminist attempts to define the difference of women without falling into ahistorical models of the biological, linguistic, or psychic nature of that difference. Her solution is to move beyond these first three models to a fourth: a cultural model of women's difference that has the advantage both of being more general and of taking the social context as primary to the others. But in naming the y crescent of female experience a "wild zone" that has no parallel to the male crescent x, Showalter herself runs the risk of reessentializing woman's experience in the social. She argues, for example, that this wild zone is unique to women and unknown to men. Although I realize there are inevitable problems in seeking a solution to essentialist qualities in feminist art by invoking a theory that itself has recourse to an essentialist position, I also recognize that the most important question about this art may not be whether it makes some sort of leap beyond the constraints of patriarchal language and thought, but how it goes about doing so.

3. See Michelle Citron, Julia Lesage, Judith Mayne, B. Ruby Rich, and Anna Marie Taylor, "Women and Film: A Discussion of Feminist Aesthetics," *New German Critique* 13 (Winter 1978).

4. Susan Glaspell, in *American Voices, American Women*, ed. Lee Edwards and Arlyn Diamond (New York: Avon Books, 1973), 359–81.

5. Annette Kolodny, "A Map for Re-Reading: Or Gender and the Interpretation of Literary Texts," *New Literary History* 11 (Spring 1980): 462.

6. Glaspell, *American Voices*, 378.

7. Carol Gilligan, *In a Different Voice: Psychological Theory and Women's Development* (Cambridge, Mass.: Harvard University Press, 1982).

8. Showalter, "Feminist Criticism," 200.

Part III

Course Files

Feminist Film Theory/Criticism in the United States

Janice R. Welsch

Feminists have, as Teresa de Lauretis has suggested, been "willing to begin an argument," to challenge the intellectual, philosophical, ideological status quo of our patriarchal society in order to redefine our world. The argument begun, however, is "not only an academic debate on logic and rhetoric," but "also a confrontation, a struggle, a political intervention in institutions and in the practice of everyday life."[1] This perspective underlies the approach to feminist film criticism adopted here and has governed my choice of texts as well as structure.

Feminist film theory has grown out of two diverse phenomena of the past three decades: the women's movement and an intensification of interest in theory among film scholars. The women's movement and the feminist theory of that movement have prompted many film scholars to adopt feminist perspectives that in turn have influenced the questions they have posed in their film research. Yet the search for answers has often led to the philosophical and critical work of male semioticians, structuralists, psychoanalysts, and Marxists, rather than to the work of feminist thinkers and activists. However, feminist writings have influenced film scholars and continue to remind us of the need to transcend the false dichotomy between research and political action, for feminism involves, as de Lauretis indicates, political commitment as well as academic argument.

To acknowledge feminist film theory's ties with the women's movement, this introductory but upper-level course begins with a unit based on

Hester Eisenstein's *Contemporary Feminist Thought* and bell hooks's *Feminist Theory: From Margin to Center*. Together they give an overview and analysis of feminist issues as they have been articulated, developed, and debated since 1970 by women in the United States. A study of developments within film theory follows, with Kaja Silverman's *The Subject of Semiotics* anchoring the discussion of semiotic, structuralist, and psychoanalytical texts that have become the bases for much current feminist film criticism, and Terry Eagleton's brief but lucid *Marxism and Literary Criticism* furnishing a focal point for a consideration of Marxist contributions to contemporary film criticism. The remaining course unit focuses on essays by feminist film scholars who represent different theoretical approaches. Texts include documentary, experimental, and/or feature fiction films that are listed at the end of each unit.

Readings

De Lauretis, Teresa. *Alice Doesn't: Feminism, Semiotics, Cinema*. Bloomington: Indiana University Press, 1984.

Unit One: Feminism – 1970 to the Present

This unit analyzes the three phases of feminist writings and debates Eisenstein has outlined in *Contemporary Feminist Thought*. The first phase was characterized by "an analysis of sex roles as a mode of social control" (xi) and reflected Kate Millett's articulation of the concept of patriarchy, a key concept in subsequent feminist theory, including feminist film theory. Inherent in the concept is the assumption that the male is Subject, the female, Other (de Beauvoir). To understand and refute the idea that this order is natural, feminists distinguished biological sex roles from social gender roles and examined how the oppressive role identified with women originated and was perpetuated (Janeway, *Man's World, Woman's Place*; Firestone, *The Dialectic on Sex*). They explored, in consciousness-raising groups, the impact of male control on their lives and validated their own experiences, redefined the personal as political, and celebrated the "commonality underlying the diversity of women's experience" (Eisenstein, 38; Shulman, "Sex and Power").

Eisenstein suggests the second phase of development within feminist theory sought to account for women's designation as "different" (from men), to examine the origins of that difference, and to reevaluate the traits identified with female difference. Critiques of sex-role stereotyping (Chesler, *Women and Madness*), of heterosexuality (Bunch, "Not for Lesbians Only"; A. Rich, "Compulsory Heterosexuality"), and of motherhood (A. Rich, *Of Woman Born*; Dinnerstein, *The Mermaid and the Minotaur*;

Chodorow, *The Reproduction of Mothering*) followed. At the same time explorations of female psychology and of woman-identified experiences provided positive alternative views of women's differences (Radicalesbians, "The Woman-Identified Woman"; Miller, *Psychoanalysis and Women*).

In a third phase of feminism, Eisenstein examines the intensification of woman-centered analyses that at times led to a feminist essentialism, and/or an insistence on female superiority and an advocacy of separatism. In her final two chapters she proposes a way around the essentialist impasse through realignment with the political Left and with Marxism; a balancing of psychological and socioeconomic questions; and reevaluation of difference (among women) to take into account "specificities of race, class, and culture" (as women of color, including bell hooks, Barbara Smith, and Cherríe Moraga and Gloria Anzaldúa had been demanding).[2]

These ideas have figured prominently in subsequent feminist theory. The recognition and celebration of differences among women as a central tenet of contemporary feminist thought provides the underlying assumption of bell hooks's *Feminist Theory*. Defining difference in terms of ethnic identification and class, as well as gender, hooks challenges feminists to examine sexist oppression in relation to racist and economic oppression and to redefine the parameters of feminist movement in light of the experience and insights of women of color. She offers a valuable corrective to a feminism narrowly identified with the concerns of white middle-class academics as she explores perspectives of women of color on issues of family, work, education, violence, and political alliances and allegiances.

Texts

Eisenstein, Hester. *Contemporary Feminist Thought*. Boston: Hall, 1983.
hooks, bell. *Feminist Theory: From Margin to Center*. Boston: South End Press, 1984.

Films Documenting Women's Consciousness-Raising and Redefinitions of Themselves

Comedy in Six Unnatural Acts, A (U.S., 1975). Jan Oxenberg, 26 min., Iris Feminist Collective. A satirical look at lesbian stereotypes.
Growing up Female: As Six Become One (U.S., 1971). Julia Reichert and James Klein, 60 min., New Day Films. Examination of how traditional women's roles are perpetuated.
Home Movie (U.S., 1972). Jan Oxenberg, 12 min., Iris. An autobiography on film.
I Am Somebody (U.S., 1970). Madeline Anderson, 28 min., First Run/Icarus. Chronicle of 500 black women's unionization efforts.
In the Best Interests of the Children (U.S., 1977). Frances Reid, Elizabeth Stevens,

and Cathy Zheutlin, 53 min., Women Make Movies. Study of lesbian mothers
and their children.
Nana, Mom, and Me (U.S., 1974). Amalie Rothschild, 47 min., New Day. An explo-
ration of women's intergenerational relationships.
Quilts in Women's Lives (U.S., 1980). Pat Ferrero, 28 min., New Day. A celebra-
tion of women's creativity.
Susana (U.S.-Argentina, 1980). Susana Munoz Velarde, 25 min., Women Make Mo-
vies. A lesbian relationship seen in the context of family expectations.
We Will Not Be Beaten (U.S., 1979). Mary Tiseo and Carol Greenwald, 25 min.,
Transition House. A discussion by victims of domestic violence.

Readings

Brownmiller, Susan. *Against Our Will: Men, Women and Rape*. New York: Simon
and Schuster, 1975.
Chesler, Phyllis. *Women and Madness*. Garden City, N.Y.: Doubleday, 1972.
Chodorow, Nancy. *The Reproduction of Mothering: Psychoanalysis and the So-
ciology of Gender*. Berkeley: University of California Press, 1978.
Daly, Mary. *Gyn/Ecology: The Metaethics of Radical Feminism*. Boston: Beacon,
1978.
De Beauvoir, Simone. *The Second Sex*. Translated by H. M. Parshly. New York:
Knopf, 1953.
Dinnerstein, Dorothy. *The Mermaid and the Minotaur: Sexual Arrangements
and Human Malaise*. New York: Harper, 1977.
Donovan, Josephine. *Feminist Theory: The Intellectual Traditions of American
Feminism*. New York: Ungar, 1985.
Dworkin, Andrea. *Pornography: Men Possessing Women*. New York: Peri-
gee/Putnam's, 1981.
Eisenstein, Zillah R., ed. *Capitalist Patriarchy and the Case for Socialist Femi-
nism*. New York: Monthly Review Press, 1979.
Firestone, Shulamith. *The Dialectic of Sex: The Case for Feminist Revolution*.
New York: Bantam, 1970.
Griffin, Susan. *Pornography and Silence: Culture's Revenge against Nature*. New
York: Harper, 1981.
Janeway, Elizabeth. *Man's World, Woman's Place: A Study in Social Mythology*.
New York: Dell, 1971.
Malson, Micheline R., et al., eds. *Feminist Theory in Practice and Process*. Chi-
cago: University of Chicago Press, 1989.
Miller, Jean Baker. *Toward a New Psychology of Women*. Boston: Beacon, 1976.
Millett, Kate. *Sexual Politics*. Reprint. New York: Avon, 1971.
Moraga, Cherríe, and Gloria Anzaldúa, eds. *This Bridge Called My Back: Writings
by Radical Women of Color*. New York: Kitchen Table: Women of Color Press,
1983.
Newton, Judith, and Deborah Rosenfelt, eds. *Feminist Criticism and Social
Change: Sex, Class and Race in Literature and Culture*. New York: Methuen,
1985.
Ortner, Sherry. "Is Female to Male as Nature Is to Culture?" *Women, Culture and*

Society. Edited by Michelle Z. Rosaldo and Louise Lamphere. Stanford, Calif.: Stanford University Press, 1974.

Rich, Adrienne. *Of Women Born: Motherhood as Experience and Institution.* New York: Norton, 1976.

——. "Compulsory Heterosexuality and Lesbian Existence." *Signs: Journal of Women in Culture and Society* 5 (Summer 1980): 631–60.

Smith, Barbara, ed. *Home Girls: A Black Feminist Anthology.* New York: Kitchen Table: Women of Color Press, 1983.

Spender, Dale. *Man Made Language.* Boston: Routledge and Kegan Paul, 1980.

Unit Two: Film Theory

Sandwiching a study of Kaja Silverman's *The Subject of Semiotics* between discussions of feminist theory and specific feminist film analyses presents a challenge. However, Silverman's presentation, given the complexity of the material, is exceptionally clear and well ordered and lends itself to inclusion in a course in feminist theory, not only because of its synthesis of semiotics and psychoanalysis, but also because of its attention to sexual difference. Silverman begins her study with a brief history of semiotics, emphasizing first recognition of the human subject as a sign, as a product of language, and then, the complexity and heterogeneity of signification networks. A Freudian-based investigation of the relations between signifying processes and the unconscious follows. Silverman then turns her attention to "The Subject" and from there moves to a discussion of suture, the process by which films position viewers as subjects. As part of this discussion she examines several possibilities for feminist challenges to the subject positions designated for women in classical narrative cinema.

Eagleton, in *Marxism and Literary Criticism,* lays out the basic tenets and questions central to Marxist criticism, like Eisenstein, bringing a materialist perspective to aesthetic issues. Elements of Marxism that Eagleton highlights and that Marxist feminists have incorporated into their own theory include an awareness of history as a material context informing all aspects of life; recognition of ideology as the values and perspectives that determine our perception of ourselves and of our relationships to and within society; and the realization that the present capitalistic (and patriarchal) organization within most industrial countries is not "natural" or unquestionable but changeable.

Texts

Eagleton, Terry. *Marxism and Literary Criticism.* Berkeley: University of California Press, 1976.

Silverman, Kaja. *The Subject of Semiotics.* New York: Oxford University Press, 1983.

Films through Which Issues of Sexuality and Suture Can Be Explored

Gilda (U.S., 1946). Charles Vidor, 114 min., Kit Parker.
Lola Montes (France, 1955). Max Ophuls, 110 min., Films, Inc.
Marnie (U.S., 1964). Alfred Hitchcock, 129 min., Swank.
Psycho (U.S., 1960). Alfred Hitchcock, 109 min., Swank.

Unit Three: Feminism, Film Theory, and Feminist Film Criticism

Limiting the number of articles included presents the principal challenge of this final unit. Feminist theory and criticism continues as one of the richest veins of contemporary film scholarship, and a course that strives to survey the field will inevitably demand difficult choices. My own choices have been determined by (1) the prominence certain critics or works have achieved, (2) the desire to balance semiotic/psychoanalytic and "realist"/materialist perspectives, and (3) a commitment to represent women of diverse cultures. In addition, I've incorporated essays that survey and critique the state of feminist film criticism since such studies point to the political self-consciousness of feminist criticism and incisively delineate the underlying theoretical assumptions of individual works.[3]

To begin, Julia Lesage, in "Feminist Film Criticism: Theory and Practice," alerts us to the comprehensiveness of film as a process that encompasses the social milieu, the filmmaker, the film itself, the production and distribution systems, and the audience, identified singly and collectively as film spectator(s) and as ideologically shaped member(s) of particular segments of society. Discussion of the film-spectator relationship can lead to the consideration of Laura Mulvey's article "Visual Pleasure and Narrative Cinema."

Already encountered in Silverman's chapter "Suture," "Visual Pleasure" provides a controversial center from which much subsequent study, both complementary and contradictory, has radiated. Based on psychoanalytical theory and positing the female figure within film as an erotic spectacle, Mulvey suggests that "pleasure in looking has been split between active/male [subject/voyeur] and passive/female [object/spectacle]" roles (11) that reflect the male dominance characteristic of patriarchal society generally. Mulvey grounds her position in an understanding of the oedipal phase as critical in the establishment of male subjectivity, with its concomitant positioning of woman as lack and as object of the male gaze.

In "Film and the Masquerade—Theorising the Female Spectator" and "The Woman's Film: Possession and Address" Mary Ann Doane expands the exploration of the idea of film spectatorship, and like Mulvey, bases her analyses in Freudian/Lacanian psychoanalytic theory and semiotics. In

"Masquerade" Doane examines the possibility of producing an active female spectator position for characters in or viewers of classical narrative cinema (e.g., *Now Voyager* and *Leave Her to Heaven*), suggesting that attempts by female characters to appropriate the look are inevitably thwarted. In "The Woman's Film," Doane investigates the "viewing process triggered by the 'woman's film'" and finds the aims of the male-identified classic narrative structure contradictory to those of texts that focus on female subjectivity (*Secret beyond the Door, Rebecca, Gaslight,* and *Caught*).

Doane suggests that within the woman's film, "the economics of female subjectivity" lead to an identification of the female position with masochism and the disassociation of the female spectator from her own sexuality. Her object-relations analysis contrasts with Gaylyn Studlar's very different exploration of masochism grounded in Gilles Deleuze's *Masochism: An Interpretation of Coldness and Cruelty*. Studlar redirects attention away from the Freudian/Lacanian emphasis on the oedipal/mirror phase in psychological development to the oral period of infancy, a period when the mother is the most important figure of identification and of masochistic pleasure. The mother/the woman is thus placed in an influential and authoritative role that allows Studlar to redefine visual pleasure and the cinematic gaze in terms of the plenitude and pain of the preoedipal stage. Studlar supports her analysis, as Mulvey does, via references to several von Sternberg-Dietrich films. Kaja Silverman also invokes classical narrative film (*Lola Montes, Marnie, Snake Pit,* and *A Woman's Face*) when she shifts from image to voice in "Dis-Embodying the Female Voice" and shows how female speech and language are controlled and used to reinforce woman's patriarchally defined role. But Silverman moves to New German Cinema and avant-garde films made by women and indicates how those filmmakers challenge traditional uses of the female voice, explicating films such as Yvonne Rainer's *Journey from Berlin/71*.

The 1978 discussion among Michelle Citron, Lesage, Judith Mayne, B. Ruby Rich, Anna Marie Taylor, and the editors of *New German Critique* ("Women and Film: A Discussion of Feminist Aesthetics") contrasts sharply with the theoretical psychoanalytic and semiotic criticism presented to this point in unit three. The discussion focuses more directly on women's experiences within history and reflects political concerns similar to those Eisenstein expresses. In "Visibility and Feminist Film Criticism," Mayne links the validation of women's experience to increased visibility of women within history and suggests rereading history as encompassing both the public/male realm and the private/female sphere. This means "reading against the grain" (Silvia Bovenschen quoted by Mayne), a strategy reassessing films and film forms identified with patriarchy from a feminist perspective, for example, adapting realist documentary to raise consciousness and redefine the public domain.

Feminist psychoanalytic critics have been far more supportive of feminist avant-garde films than of realist documentarians, arguing for a radical departure from patriarchally identified film methodologies. Differences in emphases, approaches, and commitment are not always as clear cut as this division implies. Still, divergences certainly exist, and the "Introduction" to *Re-vision* as well as Gledhill's "Developments in Feminist Film Criticism" focus on divergent appraisals of feminist film criticism. Through carefully considered arguments they advocate either psychoanalytic/semiotic (*Re-vision*) or material/historical (Gledhill) feminist film theory and practice. Ironically, despite their advocacy of disparate perspectives, the *Re-vision* editors and Gledhill, like Eisenstein, conclude their analyses with discussions of "difference." Whether theoretically posited as an aspect of our understanding of subjectivity (*Re-vision*) or as a politically motivated call to acknowledge women's diverse material conditions (Gledhill), the concept of difference is clearly a potential point of convergence for the two lines of feminist film criticism.

Such a convergence is evident in de Lauretis's essay "Aesthetics and Feminist Theory: Rethinking Women's Cinema." She begins with an overview of the work done so far and then suggests we now go much further and rethink "women's cinema as the production of a feminist social vision" that attends to "*the differences among women*" (164), differences of ethnicity, class, culture, sexual orientation, age, education, and language.

Jump Cut has consistently published feminist criticism that acknowledges differences among women, including articles on films about lesbian lifestyles and analyses of work by and about women of color. The March 1981 issue, for example, features a special section on lesbians and film. The introduction outlines the functions of lesbian images in mainstream cinema as well as the issues surrounding lesbian filmmaking practices, while B. Ruby Rich's analysis of Leontine Sagan's *Maedchen in Uniform* and Citron's discussion of "The Films of Jan Oxenberg" examine some of those issues in terms of specific films. Lesage's critique of Sara Gomez's *One Way or Another*, "Dialectical, Revolutionary, Feminist," in the May 1979 *Jump Cut*, brings attention to Third World filmmaking, and Loretta Campbell's March 1989 "Hurting Women" reviews films by Camille Billops (*Suzanne, Suzanne*) and Christine Choy (*To Love, Honor, and Obey*).

Alile Sharon Larken ("Black Women Film-makers Defining Ourselves") and Kathleen Collins ("A Commitment to Writing: A Conversation with Kathleen Collins Prettyman") point to the necessary intersection of gender, ethnicity, and class issues for women filmmakers of color whether they work in fiction or documentary. Jacqueline Bobo takes up the issue of Hollywood representation of African Americans in *"The Color Purple*: Black Women as Cultural Readers" and shows how black women have used Steven Spielberg's mainstream text to strengthen themselves individually and collectively.

The introduction and first chapter ("Critical Subjectivity") of Mary Gentile's *Film Feminisms* provide a further synthesis of the work of feminist film critics and her "Directions for Feminist Film" an additional perspective on the future of women's cinema. Like de Lauretis, Gledhill, and the *Re-vision* editors, and the critics presenting minority perspectives, Gentile focuses on difference as an essential and pivotal concept for feminist film theory that is grounded in *all* individuals. Such a focus calls not only for "a willingness to see multiple intention, multiple perspectives, and to entertain multiple readings of a particular text," but also to "actively [entertain] contradiction within and around the work" (9), with the aim being "not to construct a whole and single world, but to suggest the multiplicity of possibility and the recognition that these possibilities exist simultaneously" (67).[4] With that in mind, multiple readings of a film already mentioned, a film Gentile discusses (*A Question of Silence* or *The All-Round Reduced Personality/Redupers*, for example), or a film explicitly presenting cross-cultural or Third World perspectives (*Black Girl, Portrait of Teresa, Bagdad Cafe, Girl from Hunan*, and *Yaaba* come immediately to mind) could close the course while inviting continuing analysis and dialogue.

Texts

Becker, Edith, Michelle Citron, Julia Lesage, and B. Ruby Rich. "Lesbians and Film: Introduction." *Jump Cut*, nos. 24–25 (March 1981): 17–21.

Bobo, Jacqueline. *"The Color Purple*: Black Women as Cultural Teachers." In *Female Spectators: Looking at Film and Television*, edited by E. Deidre Pribram, 90–109. New York: Verso, 1988.

Citron, Michelle. "Films of Jan Oxenberg: Comic Critique." *Jump Cut*, nos. 24–25 (March 1981): 31–32.

Citron, Michelle, Julia Lesage, Judith Mayne, B. Ruby Rich, and Anna Marie Taylor. "Women and Film: A Discussion of Feminist Aesthetics." *New German Critique* 13 (Winter 1978): 82–107.

De Lauretis, Teresa. *Technologies of Gender*. Bloomington: Indiana University Press, 1987.

Doane, Mary Ann. "Film and the Masquerade – Theorising the Female Spectator." *Screen* 23 (September-October 1982): 74–87.

——. "Masquerade Reconsidered: Further Thoughts on the Female Spectator." *Discourse* 11 (Fall-Winter 1988–89): 42–54.

——. "The 'Woman's Film': Possession and Address." In *Re-vision: Essays in Feminist Film Criticism*, edited by Mary Ann Doane, Patricia Mellencamp, and

Linda Williams, 67–82. Frederick, Md.: University Publications of America, 1984.

——. Introduction to *Re-vision*, 1–17.

Gentile, Mary. *Film Feminisms: Theory and Practice*, 3–24, 63–85. Westport, Conn.: Greenwood Press, 1985.

Gledhill, Christine. "Developments in Feminist Film Criticism." In *Re-vision*, 18–48.

Larkin, Alile Sharon. "Black Women Film-makers Defining Ourselves: Feminism in Our Own Voice." In *Female Spectators*, 157–73.

Lesage, Julia. "Feminist Film Criticism: Theory and Practice." In *Sexual Strategems: The World of Women in Film*, edited by Patricia Erens, 144–55. New York: Horizon, 1979.

——. *"One Way or Another*: Dialectical, Revolutionary, Feminist." *Jump Cut*, no. 20 (May 1979): 20–23.

Mayne, Judith. "Visibility and Feminist Film Criticism." *Film Reader*, no. 5 (1982): 120–24.

Mulvey, Laura. "Visual Pleasure and Narrative Cinema." *Screen* 16 (Autumn 1975): 6–18.

Nicholson, David. "A Commitment to Writing: A Conversation with Kathleen Collins Prettyman." *Black Film Review* 5 (Winter 1988–89): 6–15.

Rich, B. Ruby. *"Maedchen in Uniform*: From Repressive Tolerance to Erotic Liberation," *Jump Cut* nos. 24–25 (March 1981): 44–50. Reprinted in *Re-vision*, 100–30.

Silverman, Kaja. "Dis-Embodying the Female Voice." In *Re-vision*, 131–49.

Smith, Valerie. *Callaloo* 11 (Fall 1988): 711–17.

Studlar, Gaylyn. "Masochism and the Perverse Pleasure of the Cinema." In *Movies and Methods, Volume II*, edited by Bill Nichols, 602–21. Berkeley: University of California Press, 1985.

Films

All-Round Reduced Personality/Redupers, The (Germany, 1977). Helke Sander, 98 min., West Glen Films.

Bagdad Cafe (U.S., 1988). Percy Adlon, 91 min., New Yorker Films.

Black Girl (Senegal, 1965). Ousmane Sembene, 60 min., New Yorker.

Blonde Venus (U.S., 1933). Josef von Sternberg, 97 min., Museum of Modern Art (MOMA).

Born in Flames (U.S., 1983). Lizzie Borden, 90 min., First Run/Icarus. Fiction depicting women's revolutionary activity in New York.

Caught (U.S., 1949). Max Ophuls, 88 min., Kit Parker.

Color Purple, The (U.S., 1985). Steven Spielberg, 155 min., Swank.

Daughter Rite (U.S., 1979). Michelle Citron, 53 min., Women Make Movies. On mother-daughter and sister relationships.

Different Image, A (U.S., 1982). Alile Sharon Larkin, 51 min., Black Filmmaker Foundation.

Gaslight (U.S., 1944). George Cukor, 114 min., Swank.

Girl from Hunan (China, 1986). Xie Fei and U Lan, 99 min., New Yorker.

Girltalk (U.S., 1987). Kate Davis, 85 min., Kate Davis. Documentary about runaway teens.

Hearts and Hands (U.S., 1987). Pat Ferrero, 63 min., Ferrero Films. Nineteenth-century United States history through quilts of the era.

Illusions (U.S., 1983). Julie Dash, 34 min., WMM-Black Filmmakers Foundation. Exploration of black women's identity in the world of Hollywood illusion.

Inside Women Inside (U.S., 1978). Christine Choy and Cynthia Maurizio, 28 min., Third World Newsreel. Documentary about women in prison.

Jeanne Dielman, 23 Quai du Commerce, 1080 Bruxelles (France, 1975). Chantal Akerman, 198 min., New Yorker.

Journey from Berlin/1971 (U.S., 1980). Yvonne Rainer, 125 min., MOMA. Experimental exploration of the personal versus the political.

Leave Her to Heaven (U.S., 1945). John M. Stahl, 110 min., Films, Inc.

Life and Times of Rosie the Riveter, The (U.S., 1980). Connie Field, 65 min., Direct Cinema. Women's World War II contributions to industry.

Losing Ground (U.S., 1982). Kathleen Collins, 86 min., Mypheduh. Fictional depiction of an African-American female professor's search for a fuller life.

Maedchen in Uniform (Germany, 1931). Leontine Sagan, 87 min., Films, Inc.

Morocco (U.S., 1930). Josef von Sternberg, 92 min., Swank.

No Longer Silent (Canada, 1986). Loretta Deschamps, 56 min., International Film Bureau. On the discrimination experienced by women in India.

Now, Voyager (U.S., 1942). Irving Rapper, 117 min., Swank.

One Way or Another (Cuba, 1974). Sara Gomez, 78 min., New Yorker. Combines documentary and fiction to portray female-male relationships in Cuba.

Portrait of Teresa (Cuba, 1979). Pastor Vega, 115 min., New Yorker.

Question of Silence, A (Holland, 1982). Marleen Gorris, 92 min. First Run (video only).

Rebecca (U.S., 1940). Alfred Hitchcock, 130 min., Kit Parker.

Sambizanga (Angola, 1972). Sarah Maldorer, 102 min., New Yorker. Fictional account of Angolan woman's political education.

Secret beyond the Door (U.S., 1948). Fritz Lang, 98 min., Kit Parker.

Snake Pit, The (U.S., 1948). Anatole Litvak, 108 min., Films, Inc.

Surname Viet, Given Name Nam (U.S., 1989). Trinh T. Minh-ha, 108 min., Women Make Movies.

Suzanne, Suzanne (U.S., 1982). Camille Billops and James Hatch, 30 min., Third World. Documentary about domestic violence in middle-class black family.

Ties That Bind, The (U.S., 1984). Su Friedrich, 55 min., Women Make Movies. A daughter's exploration of her mother's life in Nazi Germany.

To Love, Honor, and Obey (U.S., 1980). Christine Choy, 55 min., Third World Newsreel. On domestic violence.

Woman's Face, A (U.S., 1941). George Cukor, 105 min., Swank.

Yaaba (Burkina Faso, 1989). Idrissa Ouedraogo, 90 min., New Yorker.

Readings

Bergstrom, Janet, and Mary Ann Doane, eds., "The Spectatrix." *Camera Obscura*, no. 20–21 (May-September 1989): 5–372. Special issue on the female spectator.

Campbell, Loretta. "Reinventing Our Image: Eleven Black Women Filmmakers." *Heresies* 16 (1983): 58–62.

De Lauretis, Teresa. "Guerilla in the Midst: Women's Cinema in the 80s." *Screen* 31 (Spring 1990): 6–25.

Del Gaudio, Sybil. "The Mammy in Hollywood Film." *Jump Cut*, no. 28 (April 1983): 23–25.

Doane, Mary Ann. *The Desire to Desire: The Woman's Film of the 1940s*. Bloomington: Indiana University Press, 1987.

Erens, Patricia and Marian Henley, eds. *College Course Files*. UFVA Monograph no. 5. River Forest, Ill.: UFVA, 1985.

Fischer, Lucy. *Shot/Countershot: Film Tradition and Women's Cinema*. Princeton, N.J.: Princeton University Press, 1989.

Gaines, Jane. "White Privilege and Looking Relations: Race and Gender in Feminist Film Theory." *Screen* 29 (Autumn 1988): 12–26. (Reprinted here.)

Helprin, Sarah. "Writing in the Margins." *Jump Cut*, no. 29 (February 1984): 29–30.

Kaplan, E. Ann. "Feminist Film Criticism: Current Issues and Problems," *Studies in the Literary Imagination* 19 (Spring 1986): 7–20.

Kuhn, Annette. *Women's Pictures: Feminism and Cinema*. Boston: Routledge and Kegan Paul, 1982.

Lesage, Julia. "Feminist Documentary: Aesthetics and Politics." In *Show Us Life: Toward a History and Aesthetics of the Committed Documentary*, edited by Thomas Waugh, 223–51. Metuchen, N.Y.: Scarecrow, 1984.

Lorde, Audre. "The Master's Tools Will Never Dismantle the Master's House." In *This Bridge Called Our Backs: Writings by Radical Women of Color*, 98–101. New York: Kitchen Table: Women of Color Press, 1983.

Mayne, Judith. "Feminist Film Theory and Criticism." *Signs: Journal of Women in Culture and Society* 11 (Autumn 1985): 81–100.

Modleski, Tania. *The Women Who Knew Too Much*. New York: Methuen, 1988.

Mulvey, Laura. *Visual and Other Pleasures*. Bloomington: Indiana University Press, 1989.

Penley, Constance, ed. *Feminism and Film Theory*. New York: Routledge, 1988.

Pribram, E. Deidre, ed. *Female Spectators: Looking at Film and Television*. New York: Verso, 1988.

Silverman, Kaja. *The Acoustic Mirror: The Female Voice in Psychoanalysis and Cinema*. Bloomington: Indiana University Press, 1988.

Notes

An earlier version of this course file appeared in the *Journal of Film and Video* 39 (Spring 1987): 66–82.

1. Teresa de Lauretis, *Alice Doesn't: Feminism, Semiotics, Cinema* (Bloomington: Indiana University Press, 1984), 3.

2. The term *race*, as it is generally used, is problematic and contributes to the continuing credence given to divisions that have no scientific basis. Speaking and writing of "ethnicity, class, and culture" is not only accurate but also shifts our dis-

cussions to a more productive plane and illustrates again the importance of names and naming. See B. Ruby Rich, this volume.

3. Except for Christine Gledhill's "Developments in Feminist Film Criticism" (a 1978 article that Gledhill updated in 1984 for inclusion in *Re-vision*), I have avoided articles that Phyllis Mael includes in her AFI/UFVA Course File. However, a number of those essays are particularly relevant to the present course and could be reviewed or incorporated into it. They include Claire Johnston's "Women's Cinema as Counter-Cinema," Julia Lesage's "The Political Aesthetics of the Feminist Documentary Film" (an article that is part of her later study, "Feminist Documentary: Aesthetics and Politics"), and Linda Williams and B. Ruby Rich's "The Right of Re-Vision: Michelle Citron's *Daughter Rite.*"

4. Contradiction is increasingly being recognized among feminist theorists as a given. For further discussion of the concept, see Malson, Newton and Rosenfelt, de Lauretis (*Technologies* 1–30), and Mayne ("Feminist Film Theory and Criticism").

Women Filmmakers

Diane Carson

Both in front of and behind the camera, women have actively participated in film production since its inception in 1895, however unacknowledged their creative and technical contributions have been in the white, male-dominated industry. This course counters the misconception, fostered by many film texts and college courses, that women seldom directed, produced, edited, or wrote significant cinematic works. It does so by affirming the historical scope of women's filmmaking and by examining noteworthy selections. This introductory course's objectives are to analyze alternative as well as conventional images crafted by women and to establish the breadth and depth of women's substantive contributions to cinematic history.

This course plan briefly surveys more than nine decades of films in several categories: live action and animation, fiction and nonfiction, narrative and experimental. It includes studio-generated and independent work, American and foreign productions. After a brief introduction, approximately equal time should be allotted units one and two, which chronicle the silent and early sound periods, respectively. Unit three needs more time because numerous contemporary films provocatively address issues of race and class, spectatorship and reception, concerns that should arise in all film history courses.

In each unit, a commitment to represent diverse directorial styles, subject matter, and cultures has guided the selection process. Some attention has been given the most prominent directors, especially those whose films are readily available. But because this risks establishing or reinforcing a woman's canon, an outcome no more desirable for women's films than for men's, alternatives are encouraged, especially from work by women in China, India, Africa, Mexico, and other non-European countries.

This course encourages, then, a reassessment of film history. It interrogates Hollywood's hegemony by focusing on images of women, by women, and it directs our attention to the personal, political, and ideological investment in representation: the attitudes women endorse, the roles women play, and the stereotypes they reinforce or challenge. Since presenting films in chronological order helps reveal the sociohistorical changes they reflect or resist, this course uses that organization rather than thematic groupings.

Complementing the films, the readings challenge dominant mainstream representation from a feminist perspective, suggest alternative reception strategies, and provide close readings of selected works. The essays collected in part I of this anthology offer an introduction to several analytical approaches; they survey the theoretical bases of feminist film study from psychoanalytic and Marxist perspectives to historical and canonical considerations, from the influence of Althusser, Bakhtin, semiotic and poststructuralist theory to the politics of narrative construction, especially as informed by issues of race, class, age, and sexual preference. Consideration of the development and diversity, complementarity and dissonance of feminist film criticism should establish a productive framework from which to approach the following.

Readings: See the essays in part I of this anthology.

Unit One: The Early Years: Silent Films

This unit dispels the erroneous impression that women worked little, if at all, in the earliest days of film history. For a corrective to this inaccuracy, see especially Ally Acker's and Annette Kuhn's encyclopedic books listing, as Acker's subtitle states, *Pioneers of the Cinema, 1896 to the Present.* The following is a small selection of the many possible choices.

Recent research suggests that the first woman director, Alice Guy Blaché (born 1873), is arguably the first person, male or female, to put a narrative on the screen in her 1896 filmed fairy tale *La Fée aux Choux* (*The Cabbage Fairy*). The most powerful woman executive at the time, Guy Blaché owned her own studio, the Solax Corporation, from 1910 to 1914. Although most of her approximately three hundred silent films have been lost, those remaining testify to her technical innovations, her breakthroughs in character development (especially in supporting roles), and the impressive coherence of her plots.

Equally noteworthy is Lois Weber, born in 1881 in Pennsylvania. Originally a film actress, she produced, wrote, starred in, and began directing films in 1913, becoming the highest-paid director in the field in 1916. As famous at the time as D. W. Griffith or Cecil B. deMille, she formed Lois Weber Productions in 1917 and, in the course of her career, made almost four hundred films. Technically and thematically progressive, Weber's films illustrate her creative, compassionate response to social problems: birth control and abortion, prostitution and racism, child labor and capital punishment. Several of her films were banned, so powerful were her statements for their time.

This unit can move next from America to France, to an impressionist film widely acknowledged as one of the premier avant-garde works: *The Smiling Madame Beudet* (1923). French director Germaine Dulac, a leading radical feminist, edited the journal of the French suffragette movement, wrote for two other feminist journals, and in 1915 formed Delia Film, devoted to highly inventive work. In *Beudet*, Dulac manipulates the image using superimpositions, dissolves, and slow motion to express the frustrated mental state of Madame Beudet, who is trapped in a stultifying, bourgeois marriage. In contrast to Guy Blaché's and Weber's more conventional narratives, Dulac firmly anchors her story in Madame Beudet's subjective point of view. All three of these directors' films repeatedly illustrate their technical and narrative expertise and their imaginative use of the medium.

At the same time, Anita Loos (born 1888) wrote prolifically for film (over one hundred scripts between 1912 and 1915), working in the teens with D. W. Griffith and in later years at MGM. From *The New York Hat* (1912, Mary Pickford) to *San Francisco* (1936), *The Women* (1939), and *Gentlemen Prefer Blondes* (1953), based on her 1925 novel, Loos wrote worldly, witty dialogue for assertive women who, in general, refuse to conform to expectations.

In addition, during this unit we should mention films promoting women's suffrage, for women made rousing cinematic statements as early as the 1910s. These films, produced to persuade the moviegoing public of the justness of the suffragette cause, include Jane Addams and Dr. Anna Shaw in *Independent Votes for Women* (1912), Sylvia Pankhurst and Harriet Stanton Blatch in *Eighty Million Women Want . . . ?* (1913), and *Your Girl and Mine* (1914). Marjorie Rosen chronicles this history in *Popcorn Venus*.

We should also recognize Lotte Reiniger, born in Berlin in 1899, the first person to create "a fully animated feature from 1923 to 1926" (Acker 241), ten years before Disney. In Germany's Golden Age, Reiniger created a new animation technique, backlighting paper cutouts to create silhouettes. With her mechanical expertise, she designed a multiplane camera capable of separating foreground from background to effect perspective, and she experimented with sliced wax and sand on backlit glass. After moving to England in the mid-1930s, Reiniger made numerous films for children based on nursery rhymes and fairy tales.

Finally, at least passing note should be made of Cleo Madison's *Her Defiance* (1916), for its "open defiance of thematic taboos and its avoidance of a stereotypical portrayal of women" (*MOMA* catalog 49). Equally important is Esther Shub, the originator of the compilation documentary with *The Fall of the Romanov Dynasty* (1927), which expertly presents historical reenactments. This unit's narrative, experimental, documentary, and animated films testify, then, to the contributions in style and content of early women filmmakers. Readings noted here give historical background and careful visual analysis of chosen films from feminist perspectives.

Films

The Blot (U.S., 1921). Lois Weber, 110 min., Budget, EmGee, MOMA. A wife who steals for her sick daughter.

Canned Harmony (U.S., 1912). Alice Guy Blaché, 12 min., EmGee. A daughter tricks her father so she can marry the man she wants.

Chapter in Her Life, A (U.S., 1923). Lois Weber, 87 min., EmGee. The relationship between a child and adults.

Eighty Million Women Want . . . ? (U.S., 1912). Unique Film Company, 75 min., Kit Parker. Suffragette film.

Fall of the Romanov Dynasty, The (USSR, 1927). Esther Shub, 101 min., MOMA. Compilation documentary.

House Divided, A (U.S., 1913). Alice Guy Blache, 13 min., EmGee. A misunderstanding and its resulting separation of husband and wife.

New York Hat, The (U.S., 1912). Script by Anita Loos, 10 min., Budget, EmGee, Kit Parker, MOMA, et al. Mary Pickford, subject of a scandal when a minister buys her an expensive hat.

Reiniger shorts (1934–1970). Fifteen shorts from 11 to 17 minutes, MOMA. Classic myths and fairy tales, silhouette animation.

Smiling Madame Beudet, The (France, 1923). Germaine Dulac, 35 min., Budget, EmGee, Kit Parker, MOMA, et al. A frustrated housewife imagines her husband's murder.

Too Wise Wives (U.S., 1921). Lois Weber, 90 min., EmGee. Jealousy, love and marital boredom.

Readings

Acker, Ally. *Reel Women: Pioneers of the Cinema, 1896 to the Present.* New York: Continuum, 1991.

Blaché, Roberta, and Simone Blaché, trans. *The Memoirs of Alice Guy Blaché.* Edited by Anthony Slide. Metuchen, N.J.: Scarecrow, 1986.

Erens, Patricia, ed. *Sexual Stratagems: The World of Women in Film.* New York: Horizon Press, 1979. Articles on Blaché and Shub, et al.

Flitterman-Lewis, Sandy. *To Desire Differently: Feminism and the French Cinema.* Urbana: University of Illinois Press, 1990.

Heck-Rabi, Louise. *Women Filmmakers: A Critical Reception.* Metuchen, N.J.: Scarecrow, 1984.

Kay, Karyn, and Gerald Peary, eds. *Women and the Cinema: A Critical Anthology.* New York: Dutton, 1977. Especially "Alice Guy Blaché: Czarina of the Silent Screen," by Peary; "Woman's Place in Photoplay Production," by Blaché; and "Germaine Dulac: First Feminist Filmmaker," by William Van Wert.

Kuhn, Annette, ed., with Susannah Radstone. *Women in Film: An International Guide.* New York: Fawcett Columbine, 1990.

Norden, Martin F. "Women in the Early Film Industry," *Wide Angle* 6, no. 3 (1984): 58–67, and other essays in this issue on "Feminism and Film."

Rosen, Marjorie. *Popcorn Venus: Women, Movies & the American Dream.* New York: Coward, McCann and Geoghegan, 1973.

Russett, Robert, and Cecile Starr. *Experimental Animation.* New York: Da Capo. 1988.

Slide, Anthony. *Early Women Directors.* New York: A. S. Barnes, 1977.

Unit Two: The Sound Period: The Thirties through the Fifties

During the early sound period, women filmmakers again contributed landmark works to film history. German directors proved particularly influential, endorsing either progressive or reactionary courses. In the latter category is Leni Riefenstahl (German, born 1902) for her infamous documentary *Triumph of the Will* (1935). A powerful propaganda piece, *Triumph* bestows heroic status on Hitler via effective editing rhythms, low angle shots, and resounding audio bombardment alternating with near religious silence. Thea von Harbou (born 1888) wrote for the German cinema at the same time, scripting two of Fritz Lang's Dr. Mabuse films and working actively for the legalization of abortion. Von Harbou's scripts protest the fascist mind-set, though, curiously and unfortunately, her essays and novellas extol the virtues of the German nation and prescribe the role of women as supporting helpmates. She also chose to stay in Hitler's Germany.

The work of Leontine Sagan (born 1899) contrasts sharply with von Harbou's and Riefenstahl's. Joseph Goebbels banned her *Maedchen in Uniform* (1931) for its harsh criticism of authoritarianism, but *Maedchen* is now more celebrated for its radical subtext. Its exploration of lesbianism in a girls' boarding school startles with its deftly confrontational psychodrama, which posits a sensitive humanism to counteract fascism. *Maedchen* also illustrates Sagan's manipulation of light and shadow, her integration of superimpositions, and her complex metaphors and symbols.

An excellent comparison can be made between Sagan and Dorothy Arzner (born 1900), the only woman editor and director who moved from silent to sound films while working within the Hollywood studio system. Responsible for seventeen feature films from 1927 to 1943, Arzner articulated a subversive feminism that invites consideration of spectator positioning and of interpretative strategies such as "reading against the grain." Arzner pushes the passive, voyeuristic viewer into a self-reflexive, critical position as her assertive women confront and expose society's repressive roles. Note Beverle Houston's article in this anthology on Arzner's disruption of specular conventions.

If time allows, this unit can include an informative contrast between Arzner and Ida Lupino (born 1918), Hollywood actress, screenwriter, producer, and director. While Lupino does not possess Arzner's incisive feminist vision or technical expertise, Lupino's films address relevant social topics, especially issues of women's self-esteem and ambition, disillusionment and alienation.

This unit concludes with a study of Maya Deren (born 1917), called the mother of the underground film, and Shirley Clarke (born 1925), an experimental film and video maker. A poet, journalist and left-wing activist in the 1930s, Deren made six short films between 1943 and 1958, the best known being *Meshes of the Afternoon* (1943). In *Meshes*, Deren fashions a meditation on identity, sexuality, and the dislocations of dreams. Haunting halftones and wooden percussion sounds reinforce the eeriness created through slow-motion images, slow pans, canted angles, subjective shots, and disjunctive edits. Deren's lyrical dance films precede Shirley Clarke's improvisation in the same area, notably, Clarke's choreographed, abstract studies such as *Bridges Go Round* (1958) and *Skyscraper* (1959). Clarke uses jazz as inspiration for her films' rhythms and emphasizes the musical connections with black culture, especially her *cinéma vérité*-inspired work in *The Connection* (1961), *The Cool World* (1963), and *Portrait of Jason* (1967). Her compassionate attention to unresolved problems—to drugs, to society's treatment of African Americans, and to dashed hopes and dreams—links her artistically unique cinema to the pioneering women activists studied in Unit One. Her work also sets the stage for our movement into contemporary women's cinema and its concern with class, race, and gender issues.

Films

Bigamist, The (U.S., 1953). Ida Lupino, 80 min., Ivy. A man with a career-minded wife marries another woman.

Bridges Go Round (U.S., 1958). Shirley Clarke, 16 min., MOMA. An abstract rendering of the bridges that encircle Manhattan.

Christopher Strong (U.S., 1933). Dorothy Arzner, 77 min., Films, Inc. A daring aviatrix (Katharine Hepburn) has an affair with a married man, becomes pregnant, and commits suicide.

The Connection (U.S., 1961). Shirley Clarke, 103 min., New Yorker. On drug addiction.

The Cool World (U.S., 1963). Shirley Clarke, 104 min., Zipporah. A realistic portrayal of blacks that was improvised in Harlem.

Dance, Girl, Dance (U.S., 1940). Dorothy Arzner, 89 min., Films, Inc. Artistic versus exhibitionistic dancing and the voyeurism of audiences.

Hard, Fast, and Beautiful (U.S., 1951). Ida Lupino, 76 min., Ivy. An ambitious mother and her tennis champion daughter who opts for love.

Maedchen in Uniform (Germany, 1931). Leontine Sagan, 69 min., Film Images; Films, Inc. Friendship, eroticism, repression, and humanism in a girls' boarding school.

Meshes of the Afternoon (U.S., 1943). Maya Deren, 18 min., EmGee, Kit Parker, MOMA, et al. Avant-garde meditation on dreams, psychological states, and identity.

Olympia: The Diving Sequence (Germany, 1938). Leni Riefenstahl, 6 min., MOMA. A short sequence from her documentary on the 1936 Berlin Olympics (total running time more than 3 hours).

Outrage (U.S., 1950). Ida Lupino, 97 min., Ivy. Personal and public reaction to a woman's rape.

Portrait of Jason (U.S., 1967). Shirley Clarke, 105 min., New Yorker. The dramatic monologue of a black male prostitute who dreams of life as an entertainer.

Skyscraper (U.S., 1959). Shirley Clarke, 20 min., MOMA. Building a skyscraper to jazz tempo.

Triumph of the Will (Germany, 1935). Leni Riefenstahl. 120 min. and 42 min. versions, Budget, EmGee, Kit Parker, MOMA, et al. Documentary of the 1934 Nuremberg Party Congress, glamorizing Hitler.

Readings

From unit one: In Erens, see essays on Arzner, Deren, Dulac and Riefenstahl, and Sagan. See also Heck-Rabi, Kay and Peary, Kuhn, Rosen, and Van Wert, plus:

Clark, Veve A. "Signatures." In *The Legend of Maya Deren*, vol. 1, part 1, edited by Veve A. Clark, Millicent Hodson, and Catrina Neiman. New York: Anthology Film Archives, 1984.

Johnston, Claire, ed. *The Work of Dorothy Arzner: Towards a Feminist Cinema.* London: British Film Institute, 1975.

Kaplan, E. Ann. *Women and Film: Both Sides of the Camera.* New York: Methuen, 1983.

Kuhn, Annette. *Women's Pictures: Feminism and Cinema.* London: Routledge and Kegan Paul, 1982.

Mayne, Judith. *The Woman at the Keyhole: Feminism and Women's Cinema.* Bloomington: Indiana University Press, 1990.

Mulvey, Laura. *Visual and Other Pleasures.* Bloomington: Indiana University Press, 1989 (on avant-garde).

Rabinovitz, Lauren. *Points of Resistance: Women, Power and Politics in the New York Avant-Garde Cinema, 1943–71.* Urbana: University of Illinois Press, 1991.

Sitney, P. Adams. *Visionary Film: The American Avant-Garde 1943–1978.* 2d ed. Oxford: Oxford University Press, 1979.

Unit Three: Contemporary Women Filmmakers: The Sixties to the Present

So many possibilities exist within this unit that making choices proves extremely difficult. Most gratifying of all, the diversity of ethnic and national cinemas available means that a rich multicultural perspective can be achieved. Note, for example, the women directors and films discussed within articles in this anthology: Esther Yau's analysis of mainland Chinese films, Poonam Arora's critique of two East Indian narratives, Mimi White's comparison/contrast of *Rosie the Riveter* and *Swing Shift*, Gloria Gibson-Hudson's discussion of several African-American women directors, Valerie Smith on *Suzanne, Suzanne*, bell hooks on Euzhan Palcy's *A Dry White Season*, Amy Lawrence on Trinh T. Minh-ha's *Surname Viet, Given Name Nam*, Lis Rhodes's and Joanna Davis's work discussed by Rhodes and Sparrow, Linda Williams on *Question of Silence*, and the course files in this section by Janice Welsch, Elizabeth Hadley Freydberg, Frances Stubbs and Freydberg, Julia Lesage, and Chris Straayer. Although women still hold fewer than 10 percent of the production jobs, through the past three decades women directors have fashioned exemplary films that disrupt ideological formulas and expectations. The following discussion singles out only a few of their valuable, unique contributions.

Continuing with the chronological approach, several pacesetters should be mentioned, even if time does not permit screening their work. Mai Zetterling, an established Swedish stage and screen actress, turned to directing narrative features and documentaries in the 1960s. Feminist concerns and issues of class dominate her work. Zetterling's feminist perspective compares favorably to that of France's leading woman director, Agnés Varda. Called the mother of the French New Wave, Varda began her filmmaking career in 1954, first receiving international attention for *Cleo from 5 to 7* (1962). While her later films seem more overtly feminist, the early ones also critique mainstream images (see Flitterman-Lewis).

An outstanding French actress turned director is Jeanne Moreau, whose *Lumière* (1976) self-reflexively raises the issue of the representation of actresses in film and on stage. Like Arzner's *Dance, Girl, Dance*, *Lumière* challenges our voyeuristic, spectatorial positioning. An informative comparison/contrast can be pursued with several other European women directors, especially those working in the New German Cinema: Jutta Brueckner, Ulrike Ottinger, Helke Sander, Helma Sanders-Brahms, Alexandra von Grote, and Margarethe von Trotta. Emerging in the 1970s and 1980s, encouraged to a large extent through subsidies granted by German government and television, these German directors explicitly address the intersection of personal and national politics through deeply moving explorations of women's contemporary lives.

Dutch writer-director Marleen Gorris's *A Question of Silence* (1982) has also crafted a powerful statement about sexism in modern society. A woman psychiatrist must determine the mental states of three women who, unacquainted with one another, murder a boutique owner. A cross section of society, these characters reveal the pervasiveness of the oppressive system: lower to upper class, bedroom to boardroom. Technically, Gorris's film also subverts the status quo; it contains few shot reverse-shot compositions, infrequent close-ups, only two point-of-view shots, and arrhythmic editing. Further, the fractured narrative, which reveals the murder in flashbacks accompanied by discordant sound, refuses to sentimentalize the story. (See Williams's essay in part II of this anthology).

Another film, this time American, shifts our point of view to that of a central investigative woman: Bette Gordon's *Variety* (1983). The central young woman, who sells tickets at a Times Square porn theater, reverses the usual gender roles. The woman becomes the bearer of the gaze, the pursuer, and the interrogator of her own and others' sexual fantasies. Gordon's earlier work, *Empty Suitcases* (1980), can move the class back into experimental terrain. In this semiautobiographical work, Gordon fractures coherent narrative and separates voice from image, focusing on a significant theoretical concern: to what extent can disruption of synchronized voice and image empower women, releasing them from their scopophilic entrapment?

Sally Potter's *Thriller* (1979) also uses the disjunction between voice and image to contest the usual representation of women. A reconstruction of Puccini's opera *La Bohème* from a feminist perspective, Potter critiques the role of woman as romantic victim, using several motifs and strategies, including a black Mimi and a white Mimi. Potter interrogates woman's place in narrative, her role as commodity, and our pervasive racism. Sound is of paramount importance. As in *A Question of Silence*, laughter is liberating and distancing. In *Thriller*, its repeated use as disembodied sound destabilizes the image and encourages us to consider women's representation in art in general and in opera in particular.

Similarly, American filmmaker Yvonne Rainer, who began with the minimalist/structuralist movement, fashions multilayered, intertextual works. Replete with filmic and societal indictment, her *The Man Who Envied Women* (1985) reveals the vacuous constructs that pass for romance, thinking, and conversation. Rainer's film can precede a selection from Belgian director Chantal Akerman. *Jeanne Dielman, 23 Quai du Commerce, 1080 Bruxelles* (1975) in particular demands patience with its 3 hours, 17 minutes running time, which requires us to change our usual viewing habits. Its minimal content, deliberate pacing, distant camera positions, and sparse editing pattern flaunts technical and narrative conventions in this story of an unemotional murder by an ordinary housewife. By refusing to sensationalize the subject matter or to titillate the viewer, Akerman's understated approach reveals much about mainstream cinema's voyeuristic exploitation of women.

Pursuing this topic, the class might now turn its attention to films by African-American women. In *Illusions* (1983) Julie Dash dramatizes the dilemma of a studio executive passing for white and a black singer who dubs the voice of a white star (see Gibson-Hudson's article in part II of this anthology). Dash's first feature, *Daughters of the Dust* (1991), celebrates African culture, the oral tradition, and the Gullah dialect. Stunningly beautiful, it presents a turn-of-the-century gathering on an island off the Georgia coast; the occasion is the exodus to the mainland of most of the Peazant family. Also noteworthy are Kathleen Collins's feature film *Losing Ground* (1982), Alile Sharon Larkin's *A Different Image* (1979), Ayoka Chenzira's animated satire *Hair Piece: A Film for Nappy-Headed People* (1985), and Zeinabu Davis's *Cycles* (1989) and *A Powerful Thang* (1991). To avoid repetition and a lengthy list of films appropriate for this unit, I again call attention to the informative discussion in Gibson-Hudson's essay in part II and the two course files addressing this topic in this course file section. The study of African-American women not only adds important voices and insights to this course but also throws earlier Hollywood films into a different relief, revealing even more the restrictive assumptions guiding studio production.

Other ethnic women directors and their work could also be discussed at this time. Possibilities are Trinh T. Minh-ha, Vietnamese; Pam Tom, Chinese American; Midi Onodera, Japanese American; Ngozi Onwurah, African British; Xie Jin, Chinese; and so many others (see Acker). Their films have become much more readily available; see especially the catalogs of the individuals and companies listed on the distributors' pages.

We should also include a discussion of the significant contributions made by documentaries and pseudodocumentaries (see, in particular,

Janice Welsch's article on Bakhtin and documentaries in part I of this anthology). Michelle Citron has made two experimental films in mock *cinéma vérité* style. In *Daughter Rite* (1979) two actress-sisters discuss their mother's identity and their own sibling rivalry. In *What You Take for Granted* (1983) Citron stages interviews with women in nontraditional jobs and weaves in a story line involving a worldly-wise truck driver and a middle-class doctor. Noted experimental filmmaker Su Friedrich translates autobiographical elements into emotionally powerful vignettes in *The Ties That Bind* (1984) and *Sink or Swim* (1990), and Vanalyne Green also transforms autobiographical material into imaginative documentaries in *Trick or Drink* (1985) and *A Spy in the House That Ruth Built* (1989). For contrast, *The Life and Times of Rosie the Riveter* (1980), *With Babies and Banners: Story of the Women's Emergency Brigade* (1978), *Union Maids* (1977), and *Hearts and Hands* (1987) serve as exemplary representatives of more traditional documentaries that also provide substantive historical information.

Finally, this unit can conclude in several ways. My preference is with both playful and serious animated films. In light of the preceding, a particularly good film is *Interview* by Caroline Leaf and Veronika Soul, a pseudodocumentary that uses the unique animation of these artists to celebrate their friendship. Other animators to choose from include Emily and Faith Hubley, Carol Clement, Sally Cruickshank, Susan Pitt, Joanna Priestley, and Kathy Rose. Their forceful, often ironic, frequently scathingly satirical images provide a summary of previous discussions and a wonderful last laugh. It is gratifying that more choices now exist than we can manage in our study and that, at last, women filmmakers may receive their due for the enormous contributions they have made throughout film history.

Films

The easiest way to find these and other recent works is to examine the catalogs of the rental/sale companies listed on the distributors' pages, especially Black Filmmakers Foundation, California Newsreel, Canyon Cinema, CrossCurrent Kino International, New Day Films, Women Make Movies, and Zipporah. In the interest of space, only a few films are listed here.

Cleo from 5 to 7 (France, 1962). Agnés Varda, 90 min., Corinth.
Daughter Rite (U.S., 1979). Michelle Citron, 53 min., Women Make Movies.
Daughters of the Dust (U.S., 1991). Julie Dash, 113 min., Kino International.
Germany Pale Mother (Germany, 1980). Helma Sanders-Brahms, 123 min., New
    Yorker.
Girls, The (Sweden, 1968). Mai Zetterling, 100 min., New Line.
Illusions (U.S., 1983). Julie Dash, 34 min., Women Make Movies.

Interview, The (Canada, 1980). Caroline Leaf and Veronika Soul, 13 min., Women Make Movies.

Jeanne Dielman, 23 Quai du Commerce, 1080 Bruxelles (France, 1975). Chantal Akerman, 198 min., New Yorker.

Lumière (France, 1976). Jeanne Moreau, 85 min., Films, Inc.

Surname Viet, Given Name Nam (U.S., 1989). Trinh T. Minh-ha, 108 min., Women Make Movies.

Thriller (U.S., 1979). Sally Potter, 45 min., Women Make Movies.

Variety (U.S., 1983). Bette Gordon, 97 min., Kino International.

Readings

In addition to Erens, Flitterman-Lewis, Heck-Rabi, Kaplan, and Kuhn, see *Afterimage, Black Film Review, Camera Obscura, Jump Cut, Screen,* and *Wide Angle.*

Brunsdon, Charlotte, ed. *Films for Women.* London: BFI Publishing, 1986.

Erens, Patricia, ed. *Issues in Feminist Film Criticism.* Bloomington: Indiana University Press, 1990.

Klotman, Phyllis Rauch, ed. *Screenplays of the African American Experience.* Bloomington: Indiana University Press, 1991.

Rainer, Yvonne. *The Films of Yvonne Rainer.* Bloomington: Indiana University Press, 1990.

Women of Color: No Joy in the Seduction of Images[1]

Elizabeth Hadley Freydberg

The films introduced in this course are primarily political. Many are independent, some are documentary, and a few are features, but all are intended to enlighten the student about the cultural, social, and political experiences of women of color. The groups included are limited to those who are either the creators or the subjects of the film, those that present honest, positive images of the women. Suggested film titles are organized by the group portrayed in the film, rather than by a traditional subject classification. The impetus driving these films is informed by holistic autobiography. In addition, since these women have a frame of reference firmly rooted in oral tradition, histories, stories, and events are frequently narrated in a nonlinear pattern.

By reading the works of group members, in conjunction with screening their fiction and nonfiction films, the student will develop a more holistic view of these women and their cultures. Many of the issues addressed in the alternative films and readings are volatile. Students will be intellectually challenged and encouraged to compare, contrast, and question prevailing images against more diverse, complex, and authentic images of women of color. Because institutions have varied budget limitations, and because film accessibility may vary with time, more films and readings are presented below than can be assigned in one course. Although the bibliographic materials may limit formal discussion to a particular ethnic group, the majority contain structural or theoretical statements applicable to the study of all women of color.

Bibliography

Allen, Paula Gunn, ed. Introduction to *Spider Woman's Granddaughters: Traditional Tales and Contemporary Writing by Native American Women*, 1–25. New York: Fawcett Columbine, 1989.

Anzaldúa, Gloria. "Bridge, Drawbridge, Sandbar or Island: Lesbians-of-Color Hacienda Alianzas." In *Bridges of Power: Women's Multicultural Alliances*, edited by Lisa Albrecht and Rose M. Brewer, 216–31. Philadelphia: New Society Publishers, 1990.

hooks, bell. *Yearning: Race, Gender, and Cultural Politics*. Boston: South End Press, 1983.

Lindsay, Beverly, ed. Introduction to *Comparative Perspectives of Third World Women: The Impact of Race, Sex, and Class*, 1–22. New York: Praeger Publishers, 1980.

Moschkovich, Judit. "–But I Know You, American Woman." In *This Bridge Called My Back: Writings by Radical Women of Color*, edited by Cherríe Moraga and Gloria Anzaldúa, 79–84. New York: Kitchen Table: Women of Color Press, 1983. This and many other articles in this anthology are relevant throughout this course.

Miller, Randall M., ed. *The Kaleidoscopic Lens: How Hollywood Views Ethnic Groups*. Englewood, N.J.: Jerome S. Ozer, Publisher, 1980.

Filmography

Voice of Our Own (Canada, 1988). Premika Ratman and Ali Kazimi, 25 min., Shadowcatcher Productions. Excellent analysis of the intersection of race and gender and their function as tools of oppression among women.

Unit One: Aboriginal Women

This unit takes a first step toward eradicating our ignorance about the indigenous people of Australia. The representative films indicate that the concerns of Aboriginal women parallel those of other women of color. They are stereotyped in the media by the dominant culture, sexually exploited by white men, economically exploited by white people, have their children taken away from them, and, like Native Americans, are dispossessed of their homelands. *A Change of Face* uses interviews with actors, producers, and directors in the media to reveal the entrenched racial and ethnic prejudices of powerful white media decision makers. The camera satirically exposes the sexual exploitation of aboriginal women by white males in urban Australia in *Nice Coloured Girls*. *My Survival as an Aboriginal*, a film written and directed by an aboriginal woman, is the story of a family displaced from their fertile land and their efforts to survive on barren reservations. *Night Cries* features an aboriginal woman in psychological conflict as her antipathy and affection emerge while she nurses her dying adopted white mother.

Bibliography

Brady, Maggie. "Indigenous and Government Attempts to Control Alcohol Use Among Australian Aborigines." *Contemporary Drug Problems* 17 (Summer 1990): 195.

Haas, Sandra K. "An Outward Sign of an Inward Struggle: The Fight for Human Rights of the Australian Aborigine." *Florida International Law Journal* 5 (Fall 1989): 81.

"Oral History No More." *Asiaweek* 16 (August 10, 1990): 32, 49+.

Watson, Sophie, ed. *Playing the State: Australian Feminist Interventions*. New York: Verso, 1990.

Filmography

A Change of Face (Australia, 1988). Tracey Moffatt, 30 min., Women Make Movies.

My Survival as an Aboriginal. 55 min., Serious Business.

Nice Coloured Girls (Australia, 1987). Tracey Moffatt, 17 min., Women Make Movies.

Night Cries (Australia, 1990). Tracey Moffatt, 19 min., Women Make Movies.

Unit Two: African Women

In contrast to the semiclad primitives on the commercial movie screen, the films recommended in this section show African women of courage, dignity, and integrity, especially as freedom fighters in the struggle against apartheid. While the films represent women who claim specific national and tribal heritages, nearly all refer to several commonalties of African neocolonialism: how intervention from an outside culture wreaks havoc with the balance of an entire society; how black women's leadership played a role in reclaiming or forging a sane cultural framework; and how white women acquiesce in the continuing oppression of African women. As a whole and individually, these films challenge the Eurocentric notion that African "matriarchs" sanction irresponsible male behavior, thereby weakening or destroying the cornerstone of any social structure, the family.

In addition, these films resist two of the most seductive features of commercial Hollywood films on Africa, and South Africa in particular. They avoid the lush cinematography of entertainment films, and they consciously avoid audience identification with a Bildungsroman white character whose ambivalent moral transformation, however slight, becomes the centerpiece of the film. The films present raw, real, and disturbing images.

Bibliography

Bruner, Charlotte H., ed. *Unwinding Threads: Writing by Women in Africa*. London: Heinemann Educational Books Ltd., 1983.

Marks, Shula, ed. *Not Either an Experimental Doll: The Separate Worlds of Three South African Women*. Bloomington: Indiana University Press, 1988.

Mirza, Sarah and Margaret Strobel. *Three Swahili Women: Life Histories from Mombasa, Kenya*. Bloomington: Indiana University Press, 1989.

Filmography

Maids and Madams: Apartheid Begins in the Home (South Africa, 1986). Mira Hamermesh, 52 min., Filmakers Library. The symbiotic relationship between white women and the system of apartheid in their prevalent exploitation of black maids.

Mama, I'm Crying: Patience Turns to Activism in South Africa (South Africa, 1987). Joyce Seroke and Betty Wolpert, 52 min., Filmakers Library. The different worlds of two friends, a black woman and a white woman, both from Johannesburg; also shows impatient youths prepared to die for their freedom.

Reassemblage (Senegal, 1982). Trinh T. Minh-ha, 40 min., Women Make Movies. Documentary filmmaking and ethnographic cultural representations of underdeveloped Senegal.

Sambizanga (Angola, 1972). Sarah Maldoror, 102 min., New Yorker Films. A woman's transformation into a political activist during the search for her imprisoned husband.

Sidet: Forced Exile (U.S.-Sudan, 1991). Salem Mekuria, 60 min., Salem Mekuria. Three Sudanese women surviving the ordeal of being African women refugees.

South Africa Belongs to Us (South Africa, 1980). 35 min., California Newsreel. Interviews with five antiapartheid leaders who risked their lives by illegally appearing in this film.

You Have Struck a Rock! (South Africa, 1981). 20 min., California Newsreel. Women's narratives reveal their courage campaigning against passbooks required by South African apartheid.

Unit Three: Asian Women

The films in this unit represent several distinct groups that compose Asian people: Filipina, Japanese, Asian-Indian, Chinese, and Vietnamese women. The range of individuals and cultures demonstrates clearly that Asians are not a monolithic group. In addition, differences among Asian peoples in their original homelands and among Asians who live in the United States are explored.

Preconceived notions of the docile, sexually accommodating Asian woman are challenged and dispelled by women's outspoken statements of anger about these images and their corrective descriptions. These films further present the intersection of sexism and racism. A number of the films explore dimensions and meanings of intergenerational conflict: how competing cultural expectations exacerbate tensions between young people and their elders and short-circuit one of the most powerful defenses against racism. Finally, some of the films seek to correct the glaring silences in American history and in American notions of world history.

Bibliography

See Moraga and Anzaldúa and the following:

Chow, Crystal. "Sixty Years on the Silver Screen: Asian Americans." *Rice: The Premier Asian-American/Pacific Rim Magazine* (September 1988): 11–41.

Chow, Esther Ngan-Ling. "The Development of Feminist Consciousness among Asian American Women." *Gender and Society* 1 (1987): 284–99.

Hirata, Lucie Cheng. "Free, Indentured, Enslaved: Chinese Prostitutes in Nineteenth Century America." *Signs: Journal of Women in Culture and Society* 5 (1979): 3–79.

Jen, Gish. "Challenging the Asian Illusion." *New York Times* August 11, 1991, sec. 2.

Oehling, Richard A. "The Yellow Menace: Asian Images in American Film." Miller, 182–206.

"Some of China's Women Directors." *China Screen* 1 (1986): 10–11.

Wakatsuki, Houston, and James D. Houston. *Farewell to Manzanar: A True Story of Japanese American Experience during and after World War II Internment.* New York: Houghton Mifflin, 1974.

Wong, Nellie, Merle Woo, and Mitsuye Yamada. "Three Asian American Writers Speak out on Feminism." Available from: Radical Women, 2661 Twenty-first Street, San Francisco, CA 94110.

Yung, Judy. "A Bowlful of Tears: Chinese Women Immigrants on Angel Island." *Frontiers: A Journal of Women Studies* (Summer 1977).

Filmography

Asian Heart (Philippines, 1987). Kaerne Film, 38 min., Filmakers Library. European men in search of docile, self-effacing, subservient women resort to mail-order brides from the Philippines.

Dim Sum (A Little Bit of Heart) (U.S., 1985). Wayne Wang, 88 min., Orion Classics. A strained relationship between mother and daughter provoked by the struggle to maintain Chinese customs in a Western land.

Displaced View, The (Canada, 1988), Midi Onodera, 52 min., Women Make Movies. A Japanese granddaughter searching for her identity, beginning at the internment camps of World War II.

Gabriela (Holland-Philippines, 1988). Trix Betlam, 67 min., Women Make Movies. The activities of an influential women's group of nuns, students, farm and factory workers, artists, prostitutes, and housewives instrumental in Ferdinand Marcos's defeat.

India Cabaret (India, 1986). Mira Nair, 60 min., Filmakers Library. Exposes diametric codes of conduct imposed upon women by looking at the lives of nightclub strippers in Bombay through the women's eyes.

Knowing Her Place (India-U.S., 1990). Indu Krishnan, 40 min., Women Make Movies. Filmed in India and the United States addressing myriad conflicts immigrant women confront in family and society.

Living on Tokyo Time (U.S., 1986). Steven Okazaki, 83 min., A Farrallon Films Production. Youthful experiences of the cross-cultural conflict between traditional Japanese and Japanese Americans.

Made in China: A Search for Roots (U.S.-China, 1986). Lisa Hsia, 30 min., Filmakers Library. A Chinese-American youth searches for her roots in China, where her American behavior conflicts with tradition.

Mitsuye and Nellie: Asian American Poets (U.S.). 60 min., Light-Saraf Films. A Chinese and a Japanese woman share memories of their lives as immigrants in the United States through poetry, photographs, and film footage of Japanese life in a World War II internment camp.

Slaying the Dragon (U.S., 1987). Deborah Gee, 58 min., NAATA/CrossCurrent Media. Challenges and destroys the derogatory images of Asian women perpetuated in American television and films.

Surname Viet, Given Name Nam (U.S., 1989). Trinh T. Minh-ha, 108 min., Women Make Movies. Contradicts Vietnamese stereotypes with archival footage and interviews and documents women's involvement in the resistance movement.

To Be Ourselves (U.S., 1984). Asian Women United and Wing Productions, 60 min., Wing Productions. Radical Asian women of diverse backgrounds share their experiences growing up Asian and female.

Two Lies (U.S., 1989). Pam Tom, 25 min., Women Make Movies. Portrays generational, cultural, and self-image discord between mother and daughter.

Unit Four: Latina Women

The films on Latina women cover a diversity of national groups, including peoples living in their original homeland and those who have immigrated to the United States. Those set within the United States, like those about Asian women, focus with particular energy on the conflict between older, more traditional values and those of more assimilated young people. They also examine the rationale for immigrants esteeming the United States as a land of opportunity, in spite of its hardships and racism.

Those films set outside the United States, like those about African countries, are frequently concerned with the aftermath of imperialism—specifically, the United States' interventionist foreign policy. Challenging the image of Latin cultures as dominated by aggressive men, all the films portray women as responsible, active participants, whether in earning a family's livelihood or in a country's revolutionary struggle.

Bibliography

Christensen, Edward W. "The Puerto Rican Woman: A Profile." In *The Puerto Rican Woman*, edited by Edna Acosta-Belen, 51–63. New York: Praeger, 1979.
Ferree, Myra Marx. "Employment without Liberation: Cuban Women in the United States." *Social Science Quarterly* 60 (1978): 35–50.
Gómez, Alma, Cherríe Moraga, and Mariana Romo-Carmona. *Cuentos: Stories by Latinas*. New York: Kitchen Table: Women of Color Press, 1983.
Hadley-Garcia, George. *Hispanic Hollywood: The Latins in Motion Pictures*. New York: Citadel Press, 1990.
Keller, Gary D., ed. *Chicano Cinema: Research, Reviews, and Resources*. Binghamton, N.Y.: Bilingual Review Press, 1985.
Mason, Terry. "Symbolic Strategies for Change: A Discussion with the Chicana Women's Movement." In *Twice a Minority: Mexican American Women*, edited by Margarita B. Melville, 95–108. St. Louis, Mo.: C. V. Mosby, 1980.
Melville, Margarita B. "Selective Acculturation of Female Mexican Migrants." In *Twice a Minority*, 155–63.
Nieto, Consuelo. "The Chicana and the Women's Rights Movement: A Perspective." *Civil Rights Digest* 6 (1974): 36–42.
Pettit, Arthur G. *Images of the Mexican-American in Fiction and Film*. College Station, Tex.: A & M University Press, 1980.
Woll, Allen L. "Bandits and Lovers: Hispanic Images in American Film." Miller, 54–72.

Filmography

Black Women of Brazil (Mulheres Negras) (Brazil, 1986). Silvana Afram, 25 min., Women Make Movies. Music and religion are the foundations for self-affirmation against racial oppression.
Chela: Love, Dreams and Struggle in Chile (Chile, 1986). Lars Palmgren, 48 min., Filmakers Library. A Chilean teenager's experience demonstrates how poverty and government oppression radically politicize the young.
How Nice to See You Alive (Que Bom Te Ver Viva) (Brazil, 1989). Lucia Murat, 100 min., Women Make Movies. The experiences of eight Brazilian political prisoners who survived torture and imprisonment during a military coup.
I Am Not a Common Woman (Yo No Soy una Qualquiera) (Argentina, 1989). Maria Cristina Civale, 20 min., Women Make Movies. Debunks the stereotype of women as whores.
Kiss on the Mouth, A (Beijo na Boca) (Brazil, 1987). Jacira Melo, 30 min., Women Make Movies. The experience of Brazilian prostitutes from their perspective of poverty, family, clients, racism, police intimidation, and violence.
Los Dos Mundos de Angelita (The Two Worlds of Angelita) (U.S., 1982; Spanish/English). Jane Morrison, 73 min., First Run/Icarus. A nine-year-old's story of her family's emigration from Puerto Rico to a New York barrio in search of an improved existence.
Love, Women and Flowers (Colombia, 1988). Marta Rodriguez, 58 min., Women Make Movies. The toxic environment and oppressive conditions endured by

60,000 women workers in the flower industry of Colombia that retails to the United States and Europe.

Pregnant with Dreams (Prenadas de Suenos): Fourth Feminist Encuentro (Mexico, 1988). Julia Barco, 48 min., Women Make Movies. An inside glimpse into the fourth Encuentro Feminista Latinamericano y del Caribe that brought together more than 1,200 Latin American women in 1987.

Troubled Harvest (Mexico, 1990). Sharon Genasci and Dorothy Velasco, 30 min., Women Make Movies. Documentary on women migrant workers, features an interview with Dolores Huerta, cofounder of the United Farm Workers Union.

Unfinished Diary (Canada-Chile, 1982). Marilu Mallet, 55 min., Women Make Movies. Chilean émigré Mallet living in French-speaking Canada explores the profound cultural silences she experiences as a Chilean, an artist, and a woman.

Weaving the Future: Women of Guatemala (Guatemala-Mexico, 1988). Sonia Gonzalez, 28 min., Women Make Movies. The first film by and about Guatemalan women's contribution to rebuilding their country, produced by a collective of exiled Guatemalan women filmmakers living in Mexico.

Unit Five: Lesbians

Mainstream films present stereotyped lesbian images. Positive films on white lesbians are underfunded and underdistributed; economic restrictions attendant upon sexism and homophobia restrict their number. Lesbians of color are presented either negatively or not at all. Those who want to present positive images of lesbians of color encounter racism from white lesbians, as filmmakers, critics, or fellow artists who demonstrate racist insensitivity. Straight people of color may be unsupportive because of their sexism and homophobia and because of a conservatism born of an unwillingness to fight negative images on all fronts simultaneously. The films included in this unit seek to persuade viewers of the right and ability lesbians of color have to live healthy, normal lives.

Bibliography

See Moraga and Anzaldúa and the following:

Allen, Paula Gunn. "Beloved Woman: The Lesbians in American Indian Cultures." *Conditions* 7 (1981).

Azalea: A Magazine by and for Third World Lesbians. Available from Azalea, c/o Joan Gibbs, 306 Lafayette Ave., Brooklyn, NY 11238.

Baetz, Ruth, ed. *Lesbian Crossroads.* New York: William Morrow, 1980.

Bataille, Gretchen M., and Charles L. P. Silet. *The Pretend Indians: Images of Americans in the Movies.* Ames: Iowa State University Press, 1980.

Brown, Linda J. "Dark Horse: A View of Writing and Publishing by Dark Lesbians." *Sinister Wisdom* (Spring 1980).

Clarke, Cheryl. "The Failure to Transform; Homophobia in the Black Community."

In *Home Girls: A Black Feminist Anthology*, edited by Barbara Smith, 197–208. New York: Kitchen Table: Women of Color Press, 1983.

Cornwell, Anita. "Three for the Price of One: Notes from a Gay Black Feminist." In *Lavender Culture*, edited by Karla Jay and Allen Young, 466–76. New York: Harcourt Brace Jovanovich, 1979.

Gibbs, Joan, and Sara Bennett, eds. *Top Ranking: A Collection of Articles on Racism and Classism in the Lesbian Community*. Brooklyn, N.Y.: February Third Press, 1980.

Hidalgo, Hilda, and Elia Hidalgo Christensen. "The Puerto Rican Lesbian and the Puerto Rican Community." *Journal of Homosexuality* (Winter 1976–77).

Jones, Brook. "Cuban Lesbians." *Off Our Backs* (October 1980).

"Lesbians and Film." *Jump Cut*, nos. 24–25 (March 1981).

Moraga, Cherríe, and Amber Hollibaugh. "What We're Rollin around in Bed With: Sexual Silences in Feminism, A Conversation toward Ending Them." *Heresies* 12 (Spring 1981).

Smith, Barbara. "The Truth That Never Hurts." In *Third World Women and the Politics of Feminism*, edited by Chandra Mohanty Talpade, Ann Russo, and Lourdes Torres, 101–29. Bloomington: Indiana University Press, 1991.

Vida, Virginia, ed. *Our Right to Love*. Old Tappan, N.J.: Prentice-Hall, 1978.

Wong, Christine. "Yellow Queer," from "An Oral History of Lesbianism." *Frontiers* (Fall 1979).

Woo, Merle. "Letter to Ma." In *This Bridge Called My Back: Writings by Radical Women of Color*, edited by Cherríe Moraga and Gloria Anzaldúa, 140–47. New York: Kitchen Table: Women of Color Press, 1983.

Filmography

African American

Dreams of Passion (U.S., 1989). Aarin Burch, 5 min., Women Make Movies. A romantic relationship between two black Women.

Storme: The Lady of the Jewel Box (U.S., 1987). Michelle Parkerson, 21 min., Women Make Movies. Storme DeLarverie, former emcee and male impersonator, with the legendary Jewel Box Revue–America's first integrated female impersonation show.

Tiny and Ruby: Hell Divin' Women (U.S., 1988). Greta Schiller and Andrea Weiss, 30 min., the Cinema Guild. The story of an enduring professional and love relationship between Tiny Davis, jazz trumpeter, and Ruby Lucas.

Asian

Flesh and Paper (India-U.K., 1990). Pratibha Parmar, 26 min., Women Make Movies. The creative works of Indian Lesbian poet and writer Suniti Namjoshi.

Latina

Not Because Fidel Castro Says So (*No Porque Lo Diga Fidel Castro*) (Cuba, 1988). Graciela Sanchez, 13 min., Graciela Sanchez. Explores homosexuality and homophobia in Cuba through interviews with lesbians, gay men, and straight people.

Susana (U.S.-Argentina, 1980). Susana Munoz Velarde, 25 min., Women Make Movies. Autobiographical portrait of an Argentinean lesbian who leaves her country to pursue aspirations contrary to her cultural upbringing.

Interracial

The Mark of Lilith (U.K., 1986). Bruna Fionda, Polly Gladwin, Isiling Mack-Nataf, 32 min., Women Make Movies. Fictional film of a positive experience between a black lesbian, who is researching the adoption of goddesses from one culture to another, and a white vampire.

Domestic Bliss (U.K., 1984). Joy Chamberlain, 52 min., Women Make Movies. Made-for-British-television soap opera of a lesbian's life.

Just Because of Who We Are (U.S., 1986). Heramedia Collective, 28 min., Women Make Movies. The many faces of societal homophobia, including physical abuse and degradation by church and state.

Night Visions (Canada, 1989). Marusia Bociurkiw, 55 min., Women Make Movies. Targets racism and homophobia and delineates the experiential differences of black and white women.

Native American

Honored by the Moon (U.S., 1990). Mona Smith, 15 min., Women Make Movies. Native Americans have a special place for gays and lesbians, as mediators—in some tribes.

Her Giveaway: A Spiritual Journey with AIDS (U.S., 1987). Mona Smith, 22 min., Women Make Movies. Carole Lafavor, member of the Ojibwe tribe, activist, mother, and registered nurse with AIDS, uses traditional beliefs and healing customs to contend with illness.

Unit Six: Native American

Within mainstream United States iconography, the Native American woman is twice captive in her own land—once as a woman and once as a subject of the United States government's reign of terror. The films included in this section challenge the devaluation of Native American cultures by reclaiming old customs and values as vital, unbroken traditions. They depict the mechanisms for their transmission from generation to generation, with special attention to the role women play as resources in preserving cultural knowledge. Native American women filmmakers also use the new medium of cinema to extend the range of oral traditions. Other films focus on ongoing political and activist struggles and document the contemporary problems of living in a racist society, both on a reservation and in an urban setting, and the effects of alienation and fragmentation experienced by many Native Americans.

Bibliography

See Moraga and Anzaldúa and the following:

Allen, Paula Gunn. *The Sacred Hoop: Recovering the Feminine in American Indian Traditions*. Boston: Beacon Press, 1986.
——, ed. *Studies in American Indian Literature*. New York: Modern Language Association, 1983.
Bataille, Gretchen, and Charles L. P. Silet. "The Entertaining Anachronism: Indians in American Film." Miller, 36–53.
Jennings, Francis. *The Invasion of America: Indians, Colonialism, and the Cant of Conquest*. New York: W. W. Norton, 1975.
Swann, Brian, and Arnold Krupat, eds. *I Tell You Now: Autobiographical Essays by Native American Writers*. Lincoln: University of Nebraska Press, 1987.
Thornton, Russell. *American Indian Holocaust and Survival: A Population History since 1492*. Norman: University of Oklahoma Press, 1987.
Witt, Shirley Hill. "Native Women Today: Sexism and the Indian Woman." In *Female Psychology: The Emerging Self*, edited by Sue Cox, 249–59. Chicago: Science Research Associates, 1976.

Filmography

American Indian in Transition, The (U.S.). J. Michael Hagopian, 22 min., Atlantis Productions. An Indian mother shares her dreams and talks about reservation life, family, and tribal discord.

Annie Mae: Brave-Hearted Woman (U.S., 1981). Lan Brookes Ritz, 84 min., Brown Bird Productions. A narrative on the work and murder of Annie Mae Aquash, a Micmac activist involved in Wounded Knee II.

Navajo Talking Picture (U.S., 1986). Arlene Bowman, 40 min., James Mulryan. An estranged Navajo filmmaker attempts to rediscover the traditional life-style of her grandmother.

Season of Grandmothers, A (U.S., 1975). 25 min., Circle Films. Grandmothers who tell stories and raise children during the winter–their storytelling season.

Why Did Gloria Die? (U.S., 1975). Bill Moyers, 27 min., Indiana University Audio Visual Center. After leaving the reservation to seek a better life, Gloria Curtis, a Chippewa woman, died of hepatitis at age twenty-seven, the disease a by-product of urban blight.

Unit Seven: Caribbean

Caribbeans cannot be categorized as "Asian" or "African" or "Latin," or any of the labels that United States nomenclature finds convenient. The Caribbean islands and northerly portions of South America that were colonized by the Spanish, English, French, Dutch, and Danish encompass the Dominican Republic, Puerto Rico, Haiti, Guyana, Trinidad, Jamaica, Anguilla, the Virgin Islands (Saint Croix, Saint Thomas, Saint John), Martinique, Barbados, and Cuba. Thus, while individual citizens of the various countries in the Caribbean may identify their heritage as Asian, or African, or Latin, it is impossible to classify a film about the region as deriving solely from one or the other. Because of its location, and the history it shares with Latin-American nations, the political perspectives of such a film will resemble those of Latin films by women living outside the United States, yet its internal structures of race and class and the position women occupy within those structures have a unique history.

Bibliography

See Moraga and Anzaldúa and the following:

Bryan, Beverley, Stella Dadzie, and Suzanne Scafe. "Self-consciousness: Understanding Our Culture and Identity." In *The Heart of the Race: Black Women's Lives in Britain*, 182–239. London: Virago Press, 1986.

Justus, J. B. "Women's Role in West Indian Society." *The Black Woman Cross-Culturally*, edited by F. E. Steady. London: Sahenkman Public, 1981.

Williams, E. *From Columbus to Castro: The History of the Caribbean 1492–1969.* New York: Vintage, 1984.

Filmography

Miss Amy and Miss May (Jamaica, 1990). Cynthia Wilmot, 40 min., Women Make Movies. Two improbable friends, Amy Bailey, daughter of a prominent black family, and May Farquharson, daughter of a wealthy planter, and their fights for women's rights in Jamaica.

Sugar Cane Alley (Martinique, 1983). Euzhan Palcy, 106 min., DEC/Canada. Feature film about a young boy living with his grandmother, who encourages him to become a writer.

Sweet Sugar Rage (Jamaica, 1986). Honor Ford-Smith, Harclyde Walcott, and the Sistren Theatre Collective, 42 min., Women Make Movies. Documents the exploitation and horrendous conditions endured by women workers in the Jamaican sugarcane fields.

Unit Eight: Interracial Alliances and Concerns

These films present the opportunity either for use as a supplement to the above sections or as a unit in their own right. They cover the alliances that *Stand Together* and *What Would You Do?* demonstrate among women as well as issues that cut across race lines.

Filmography

Coffee Coloured Children (U.K., 1988). Ngozi A. Onwurah, 15 min., Women Make Movies. Self-esteem and identity crises of mixed-race individuals growing up in the north of England.

Juxta (U.S., 1989). Hiroko Yamazaki, 29 min., Women Make Movies. A Japanese-

American woman's effort to comprehend her life in two cultures and the effect of racism on mixed-race children of Japanese women and American servicemen.

Perfect Image? (U.K., 1989). Maureen Blackwood, 30 min., Sankofa Film and Video Collective. Satirizes black and white concepts of beauty from the colonial era to the present.

Stand Together (U.K., 1977). London Newsreel Collective, 52 min., Third World Newsreel. Documents how the 1976 group of primarily Asian and West Indian women's demands for workers' rights provoked the largest demonstration of laborers in England's history.

What Could You Do with a Nickel? (U.S., 1982). Cara DeVito and Jeffrey Kleinman, 26 min., First Run/Icarus. The founding of the first U.S. domestic workers' union by two hundred black and Hispanic women in the South Bronx.

General Bibliography

Dearborn, Mary V. *Pocahontas's Daughters: Gender and Ethnicity in American Culture*. New York: Oxford University Press, 1986.

DuBois, Ellen Carol, and Vicki L. Ruiz, eds. *Unequal Sisters: A Multicultural Reader in U.S. Women's History*. New York: Routledge, 1990.

hooks, bell. *Ain't I a Woman: Black Women and Feminism*. Boston: South End Press, 1981.

——. *Feminist Theory: From Margin to Center*. Boston: South End Press, 1984.

Hull, Gloria T., Patricia Bell Scott, and Barbara Smith, eds. *All the Women Are White, All the Blacks Are Men, but Some of Us Are Brave: Black Women's Studies*. Old Westbury, N.Y.: Feminist Press, 1982.

Lindsay, Beverly, ed. *Comparative Perspectives of Third World Women: The Impact of Race, Sex, and Class*. New York: Praeger, 1980.

Lorde, Audre. *Sister Outsider: Essays and Speeches*. Trumansburg, N.Y.: Crossing Press, 1984.

Mohanty, Chandra Talpade, Ann Russo, and Lourdes Torres, eds. *Third World Women and The Politics of Feminism*. Bloomington: Indiana University Press, 1991.

Personal Narratives Group, eds. *Interpreting Women's Lives: Feminist Theory and Personal Narratives*. Bloomington: Indiana University Press, 1989.

Trinh T. Minh-ha. *Woman, Native, Other: Writing Postcoloniality and Feminism*. Bloomington: Indiana University Press, 1989.

Note

1. Title inspired by a statement made by Mignon Duprée in Julie Dash's *Illusions* (1983).

Black Women in American Films: A Thematic Approach

Frances Stubbs and Elizabeth Hadley Freydberg

The image of blacks in American films appeared before African Americans themselves were allowed on movie sets – behind or in front of the camera. Blacks were presented as one-dimensional stereotypes, their lines scripted by whites and performed by whites in blackface. These stereotypes derived from American popular culture and were created "to entertain by stressing Negro inferiority" (Bogle 4). As introduction to this course, students should view *Black Shadows on a Silver Screen* (1974), an historical overview of blacks in American cinema from *Birth of a Nation* to World War II. The instructor can use this film concurrently with readings from Bogle and Leab to place the filmic image of black women in historical context. Because the concept of stereotype will be central to much of the course discussion, students should also view *Ethnic Notions* (1987) and read the Allport and King articles to augment their understanding of how images support the prevailing attitudes of the dominant culture. All other readings in this unit provide a foundation for the entire course through articles on black feminism and basic texts on feminist film theory.

Students of film and feminist film theory should already be aware of the absence of substantive discussion of black films and African-American characters in most film history textbooks. A similar disregard is evident in the rarity with which mainstream books and articles on theory and criticism use black films to advance an analysis, and a cursory look at the syllabi in any film studies department will reveal that black films are rarely included in mainstream film courses. Thus, in addition to teaching students black film history and encouraging them to think critically about racial, sexual, and class differences, "Black Women in American Films: A Thematic Approach" offers students an opportunity to examine challenging cultural and social issues that the black female presence interjects in reference to film theory. Students can test black feminism and feminist film theory as methods for examining the complex interplay of race, gender, identity, class, and caste, issues basic to both feminist theory and black feminism.

Bibliography

Allport, Gordon W. *The Nature of Prejudice.* 1954. Reprint. Cambridge, Mass.: Addison Wesley, 1981.

Bogle, Donald. "Black Beginnings: From Uncle Tom's Cabin to Birth of a Nation." In *Toms, Coons, Mulattoes, Mammies and Bucks: An Interpretive History of Blacks in American Films*, 3–18. New York: Continuum, 1989.

Bowser, Pearl. "The Sexual Imagery and the Black Woman in American Cinema." In *Black Cinema Aesthetics: Issues in Independent Black Filmmaking*, edited by Gladstone L. Yearwood, 42–51. Athens: Ohio University Center for Afro-American Studies, 1982.

Combahee River Collective, The. "A Black Feminist Statement." In *All the Women Are White, All the Blacks Are Men, but Some of Us Are Brave: Black Women's Studies*, edited by Gloria T. Hull, Patricia Bell Scott, and Barbara Smith, 13–32. Old Westbury, N.Y.: Feminist Press, 1982.

Cripps, Thomas. "Definitions." *Black Film as Genre*, 3–12. Bloomington: Indiana University Press, 1978.

———. *Slow Fade to Black: The Negro in American Film, 1900–1942.* New York: Oxford University Press, 1977.

Giddings, Paula. *When and Where I Enter: The Impact of Black Women on Race and Sex in America.* New York: William Morrow, 1984.

hooks, bell. "Continued Devaluation of Black Womanhood" and "The Imperialism of Patriarchy." In *Ain't I a Woman: Black Women and Feminism*, 51–86. Boston: South End Press, 1981.

Joseph, Gloria. "The Incompatible Ménage à Trois: Marxism, Feminism, and Racism." In *Women and Revolution*, edited by Lydia Sargent. Boston: South End Press, 1981.

King, Mae C. "The Politics of Sexual Stereotypes." *The Black Scholar* (March-April 1973): 12–23.

Klotman, Phyllis Rauch. *Frame by Frame: A Black Filmography.* Bloomington: Indiana University Press, 1982.

———, ed. *Screenplays of the African American Experience.* Bloomington: Indiana University Press, 1991.

Leab, Daniel. *From Sambo to Superspade: The Black Experience in Motion Pictures.* Boston: Houghton Mifflin, 1975.

Mapp, Edward. "Black Women in Films." *The Black Scholar* 4 (1973). Reprinted in Summer 1982: 36–40.

Smith, Barbara. "Toward a Black Feminist Criticism." In *All the Women Are White, All the Blacks Are Men, but Some of Us Are Brave*, edited by Gloria Hull, Patricia Bell Scott, and Barbara Smith, 157–75. Old Westbury, N.Y.: Feminist Press, 1982.

Filmography

Black Shadows on a Silver Screen (U.S., 1976). Steven York, 55 min., Lucerne Films.

Ethnic Notions (U.S., 1987). Marlon Riggs, 56 min., California Newsreel.

Unit One: Maids, Mammies, and Matriarchs

The stereotype of the mammy, born out of slave plantation lore and concretized in American literature, has been popularized in such films as *Birth of a Nation* (1915), *Gone with the Wind* (1939), *Imitation of Life* (1934 and 1959), and *The Member of the Wedding* (1952). Critics of popular culture assert that the mammy image satisfies a need in the white psyche to believe that their loyal, devoted "servant" not only recognizes and accepts the superiority of the whites but also supports the maintenance of such hierarchy. Like the "faithful soul" in *Birth of a Nation*, the mammy is usually a large, desexed, smiling, joyous, earthbound, jolly creature, often good-naturedly cantankerous and devoted to the care and protection of her white family—even to the neglect of herself and her own family.

In preparation to viewing the films in this unit, the class should review the term *stereotype* and carefully distinguish it from *stock character* in order to fully appreciate the racial nature and the injurious effect of the former. As shown in *Black Shadows on a Silver Screen*, the mammy figure defends the white family in *Birth of a Nation*, and *Brown Sugar: Part II* contains several examples of the maid/mammy type. Two premier artists, Hattie McDaniel and Louise Beavers, built their careers playing maids, and Hattie McDaniel won an Oscar as Best Supporting Actress for her role as the maid in *Gone with the Wind* (1939). The class should look for variations of the stereotype, and thus the instructor may want to select a film featuring Hattie McDaniel and another with Louise Beavers. The films and the readings in this section should generate discussion about how the maid/mammy image buttressed the far-reaching consequences of this negative perception of black women as innately servants.

Because a master/servant relationship is prevalent in all these films, they can be conveniently discussed from a Marxist/feminist perspective, but with the added intricacy of race. These films address issues of ambiguous racial and class boundaries that allow women to become "sisters," social equals because of a common gender, the status of white women living outside of acceptable social norms (e.g., *I'm No Angel*, 1933) or in unusual circumstances (e.g., both versions of *Imitation of Life*) engendering a kind of "equality of marginality" with their maids, who are marginal because of their race. Surrogate motherhood and the interaction between blacks and whites (e.g., Hattie McDaniel/Jean Harlow in *Saratoga* (1937), Ethel Waters/Julie Harris in *Member of the Wedding*) also deserve analysis.

Bibliography

See pertinent sections of Allport and Bogle and the following:

Davis, Angela. "Reflections on the Black Woman's Role in the Community of Slaves." *The Black Scholar* (December 1971): 2–15.
DelGaudio, Sybil. "The Mammy in Hollywood Film: I'd Walk a Million Miles for One of Her Smiles." *Jump Cut* 28 (1983): 23–25.
Harris, Trudier. *From Mammies to Militants: Domestics in Black American Literature*. Philadelphia, Pa.: Temple University Press, 1982.
Jerome, V. J. "The New Stereotype." In *The Negro in Hollywood Films*, 22–29. New York: Masses and Mainstream, 1950.

Filmography

A Raisin in the Sun (U.S., 1961). Daniel Petrie, 128 min., Budget.
Birth of a Nation (U.S., 1914). D. W. Griffith, 105 min., Budget.
Brown Sugar: Eighty Years of America's Black Female Superstars (U.S., 1985). Donald Bogle, 4 hrs. Documentary series for PBS.
Gone with the Wind (U.S., 1939). Victor Fleming, 222 min., Films, Inc.
Judge Priest (U.S., 1934). John Ford, 80 min., Films, Inc.
Little Colonel, The (U.S., 1935). David Butler, 80 min., Films, Inc.
Long Walk Home, The (U.S., 1990). Richard Pearce, 95 min., Miramax.
Member of the Wedding, The (U.S., 1952). Fred Zinnemann, 91 min., Budget.
Nothing Sacred (U.S., 1937). William Wellman, 85 min., Kit Parker.
Saratoga (U.S., 1937). Jack Conway, 94 min., Films, Inc.
Show Boat (U.S., 1951). George Sidney, 108 min., Budget.
Yes, Ma'am (U.S., 1982). Gary Goldman, 48 min., Filmakers Library.

Unit Two: The Mulatto Woman – Color and Caste in American Films

Like the mammy stereotype, the tragic mulatto in film has been appropriated from American literature and popular culture. Unlike its literary counterpart, however, the screen's tragic mulatto has been almost exclusively female. Hollywood depicts her as "tragic" because she is unable or unwilling to accept her marginal, inferior status in society. In prototypical films, these women cannot accept that no matter how light their skin, they are black and therefore not entitled to certain rights and privileges. They suffer because they cannot reconcile their desires with societal expectations. These films dictate that the mulatto's happiness depends upon her contentment with her status as a black person.

The mulatto stereotype provides a context for the discussion of a number of issues, including W. E. B. DuBois's concept of double consciousness, attitudes toward miscegenation, and attitudes toward passing for white. Both versions of *Imitation of Life* present white women and black women who work and live together in a distinct, symbiotic relationship; they offer a rich context for discussion of how class, caste, race, gender, and identity intersect. *Lost Boundaries* (1949), *Pinky* (1949), and both *Imitation*s address the sensitive issue of "passing." The class should discuss how the harsh realities of racial climate and socioeconomic milieu can motivate one to take extreme measures to "pass," given its consequences—alienation of relatives and friends, fear of exposure, rejection by a loved one.

Black independent filmmakers have also dealt with the issue of color and caste in the black community. The silent all-black-cast film *Scar of Shame* (1927) viewed with background readings by Gaines and Cripps offers perspectives on the caste and class systems and their function in the black community. This is the subject of Julie Dash's *Illusions* (1982), Warrington Hudlin and Denise Oliver's *Color* (1983), and Spike Lee's *School Daze* (1988). Dash's film is in many ways the more artistically and aesthetically interesting because it challenges several levels of illusions—the illusion of various art forms as well as color, race, and identity and the assumptions we make about people based solely on skin color.

Bibliography

See pertinent section of Bogle and Cripps and the following:

Berzon, Judith R. *Neither White nor Black: The Mulatto Character in American Fiction.* New York: New York University Press, 1978.

DuBois, W. E. B. *The Souls of Black Folk.* 1903. Reprint. New York: A Signet Classic, 1982.

Gaines, Jane. "The Scar of Shame: Skin Color and Caste in Black Silent Melodrama." *Cinema Journal* 26 (Summer 1987): 3–21.

Johnson, Albert. "Beige, Brown or Black." *Film Quarterly* 1 (Fall 1959): 39–42.

Laurel, Jeanne Phoenix. "*Imitation of Life*: Motherhood by Proxy." In *Double Veil: Cross-Racial Characterization in Six American Women's Novels, 1909–1948,* 122–57. Bloomington: Indiana University, 1990. Dissertation.

Selig, Michael E. "Contradictions and Reading: Social Class and Sex Class in *Imitation of Life*." *Wide Angle* 10 (1988): 13–23.

Walker, Alice. "If the Present Looks Like the Past, What Does the Future Look Like?" In *In Search of Our Mothers' Gardens: Womanist Prose,* 290–312. New York: Harcourt Brace Jovanovich, 1983.

Filmography

Color (U.S., 1982). Warrington Hudlin, 30 min., Black Filmmakers Foundation.
Illusions (U.S., 1983). Julie Dash, 34 min., Women Make Movies.
Imitation of Life (U.S., 1934). John M. Stahl, 90 min., Universal.
Imitation of Life (U.S., 1959). Douglas Sirk, 124 min., Universal.
Lost Boundaries (U.S., 1949). Alfred L. Werker, 99 min., Warner Bros.
Pinky (U.S., 1949). Elia Kazan, 100 min., Twentieth Century-Fox.
Scar of Shame (U.S., 1927). Frank Peregin, 90 min., Kit Parker Films.
School Daze (U.S., 1988). Spike Lee, 114 min., Columbia.

Unit Three: Black Women in Musicals

Although not above reproach, the black musical subgenre places the black woman at center stage, restoring much of the vitality, energy, and sexuality stripped away in the stereotype of the mammy and the mulatto. These films provided black and white audiences with women admired for their beauty and musical talent: renowned musical powerhouses Ethel Waters, Lena Horne, and Hazel Scott, among others.

Short films such as *St. Louis Blues* (1929), Duke Ellington's *Symphony in Black* (1935), and *Boogie Woogie Dream* (1942), as well as features, *Stormy Weather* (1943) and *Cabin in the Sky* (1943), showcase celebrated black musicians. Allen L. Woll contends that some musicals featuring black artists presented a positive alternative devoid of the usual stereotypical characters. For example, Hattie McDaniel and Willie Best performing "Ice Cold Katie" in *Thank Your Lucky Stars* (1943) were not maid and butler, but woman and soldier (Woll 123). Still, Hollywood ignored demands for integration in 1940s musicals that featured black and white performers, preferring instead to promulgate segregation by devising ridiculous measures to separate the singing and dancing blacks from the singing and dancing whites. Further attempts to resolve the parody of race and segregation in a presumably democratic society included the creation of two all-black musicals, *Cabin* and *Stormy*, that embraced all the conventions of standard "white" musicals, but without white performers (Woll 123).

Cripps writes that despite their showcase purpose, many of the early musicals, most notably Roth's *Yamacraw* (1930), Duke Ellington's *Symphony in Black*, King Vidor's *Hallelujah* (1929), and *Way Down South* (1939), depict the discord between two momentous forces in the black American experience, namely, "the cohesive, rural, familial life of the South and the contentious, fractious life of the Northern ghetto" (Cripps 77). Many of these films portray the black woman in both environments.

The class should discuss the dialectics of good and evil, religion and sexuality, the urban and the rural, as well as how these films give expression to the romance and courtship rituals of African-American men and women. Rivalry between women, motivated by their attraction to men, as well as the good-girl, bad-girl syndrome in *Hallelujah, Carmen Jones* (1954), and *Cabin in the Sky* (1943), are all women's issues important to these films. Viewing *Carmen Jones* can engender a controversial discussion around the portrayal of black woman as sex object and as promiscuous tramp. Whereas some feminists perceive this character as a liberated, independent, self-identified woman, many black feminists and critics of black film identify Carmen as yet another negative stereotype. The real lives of these black movie heroines—Dorothy Dandridge, Ethel Waters, Lena Horne, Bessie Smith, Pearl Bailey, and others—were in many ways far more interesting and, in some instances, far more tragic than the roles they played; they triumphed and sometimes failed as they struggled against the incredible odds of racism and sexism.

Bibliography

Again, see Bogle, Cripps, and the following:

Beaton, Welford. "Hallelujah." In *American Film Criticism*, edited by Stanley Kaufmann, 228–30. New York: Liveright, 1972.
Hansen, Miriam. "Pleasure and Ambivalence, Identification: Valentino and Female Spectatorship." *Cinema Journal* 25 (1986): 6–32.
Woll, Allen L. "Separate but Equal: Blacks in Wartime Musicals." In *The Hollywood Musical Goes to War*, 121–31. Chicago: Nelson-Hall, 1983.

Filmography

Cabin in the Sky (U.S., 1943). Vincente Minnelli, 100 min., MGM.
Carmen Jones (U.S., 1954). Otto Preminger, 107 min., Twentieth Century-Fox.
Hallelujah (U.S., 1929). King Vidor, 107 min., MGM.
Porgy and Bess (U.S., 1959). Otto Preminger, 138 min., Columbia.
Stormy Weather (U.S., 1943). Andrew Stone, 77 min., Twentieth Century-Fox.

Unit Four: The Black Woman in Her Family

It is useful to consider whether social science perspectives of the black family are reflected in the various film texts. Among them, the most pervasive and adversarial toward black women is the controversial concept promulgated by "The Moynihan Report" (1965), in which Daniel Patrick Moynihan defined the black family as a dysfunctional unit encumbering the advancement of all African Americans because of the matriarchal structure of its households. Response to Moynihan's report was so intense and overwhelmingly negative that a second phase focusing on "the strengths of Black families" emerged in the study of the black family (Staples xi). More recently, social scientists have implicated socioeconomic forces such as unemployment among black males, imbalanced gender ratios, and misguided public policies as obstacles confronting the black family. The readings by Billingsley, Gutman, Ladner, and Stack will help dispel misunderstandings about the black family.

The films in this unit introduce images of the black woman that are in many ways atypical of the stereotypical images in unit one. These women work as maids, but the traits of the maid/mammy stereotypes are rarely present, and while only a small portion of the action focuses on the workplace, significantly, most of these women work outside the home. Viewing *A Raisin in the Sun* along with reading "Lorraine Hansberry, the Complete Feminist" and "Myth of the Black Matriarch" is an excellent starting place for this unit. The issue of the black matriarch will most certainly surface and should be examined in conjunction with the Claudine (*Claudine*) and Octavia (*The Sky Is Grey*) characters.

Sounder, Claudine, and *The Sky Is Grey* provide opportunities for discussion of women functioning as heads of households. Absentee fathers/husbands enlarge the significance of the relationship between mother and son. Mother-daughter relationships are important in *Raisin, Claudine, Black Girl*, and *God's Stepchildren*, while *The Learning Tree* and *To Sleep with Anger* (1990) present the rare opportunity of seeing a black mother in a nuclear family setting. Other films evoke the issue of the dichotomy of the southern rural experience in *Nothing but a Man* and the northern urban experience in *Diary of a Harlem Family* and *Bless Their Little Hearts*.

Bibliography

Billingsley, Andrew. *Black Families in White America*. 1968. Reprint. New York: Simon and Schuster, 1988.

Edelman, Marian Wright. "The Black Family in America." White, 128–48.

Franklin, Clyde W. "Black Male-Black Female Conflict: Individually Caused and Culturally Nurtured." Staples, 106–13.

Franklin, John Hope. "A Historical Note on Black Families." In *Black Families*, edited by Harriette Pipes McAdoo. 2nd ed., 23–26. Newbury Park, Calif.: Sage Publishing, 1988.

Gutman, Herbert G. *The Black Family in Slavery and Freedom 1750–1925*. New York: Vintage Books, 1977.

Hill, Robert. *The Strengths of Black Families*. New York: Emerson Hall, 1971.

Ladner, Joyce. *Tomorrow's Tomorrow: The Black Woman*. New York: Doubleday, 1971.

Martin, Elmer P., and Joanne Mitchell Martin. *The Black Extended Family*. Chicago: University of Chicago Press, 1978.

Moynihan, Daniel Patrick. "The Negro Family: The Case for National Action." In *The Moynihan Report and the Politics of Controversy*, edited by Lee Rainwater and William L. Yancy, 39–124. Cambridge: Massachusetts Institute of Technology, 1975.

Rich, Adrienne. "The Problem with Lorraine Hansberry." *Freedomways* 19 (1979): 247–55.

Stack, Carol B. *All Our Kin: Strategies for Survival in a Black Community.* New York: Harper and Row, 1974.

Staples, Robert. *The Black Family: Essays and Studies.* 3rd ed. Belmont, Calif.: Wadsworth, 1986.

Wilkerson, Margaret B. "Lorraine Hansberry: The Complete Feminist." *Freedom-ways* 19 (1979): 235–45.

Filmography

A Raisin in the Sun (U.S., 1959). Daniel Petrie, 128 min., Budget.

Black Girl (U.S., 1973). Ossie Davis, 107 min., Swank.

Bless Their Little Hearts (U.S., 1984). Billy Woodberry. 90 min., Black Film-makers Foundation.

Claudine (U.S., 1974). John Berry, 92 min., Twentieth Century-Fox release of a Third World Cinema production, in association with Joyce Selznick and Tina Pine.

Diary of a Harlem Family (U.S., 1968). Gordon Parks, 20 min., Kit Parker.

Five on the Black Hand Side (U.S., 1973). Oscar Williams, 96 min., United Artists.

God's Stepchildren (U.S., 1937). Oscar Micheaux, 65 min., Budget.

Learning Tree, The (U.S., 1969). Gordon Parks, 107 min., Kit Parker.

Nothing but a Man (U.S., 1963). Michael Roemer, 92 min., Du Art Film Labs.

Sky Is Grey, The (U.S., 1972). Stan Lathan.

Sounder (U.S., 1972). Martin Ritt, 106 min., Twentieth Century-Fox.

To Sleep with Anger (U.S., 1990). Charles Burnett, Samuel Goldwyn Company.

Unit Five: Abused Women and Children

Violence against women and children is a universal problem of critical proportion. The research and scholarly writing on the topic are extensive, some focusing specifically on violence against black women and children. The instructor should select enough readings to dispel any myth that the abuse of women and children is endemic to certain races and/or social classes and should stress that the films in this unit are indicative of a will-ingness on the part of some black people to address the issue through a popular medium. These films may elicit intense emotional reactions; all deal with various degrees of sexual, physical, and psychological abuse.

Bibliography

Canaan, Andrea R. "I Call up Names: Facing Childhood Sexual Abuse." White, 78–81.

Cleage, Pearl. *Mad at Miles: A Blackwoman's Guide to Truth.* The Cleage Group, 1990. (To order, call 800/325-6524.)

Fortune, Marie M. *Sexual Violence: The Unmentionable Sin.* New York: Pilgrim Press, 1983.

Hollies, Linda H. A Daughter Survives Incest: A Retrospective Analysis." White, 82–91.

Stuart, Andrea. "The Color Purple: In Defence of Happy Endings." In *The Female Gaze: Women as Viewers of Popular Culture,* edited by Lorraine Gamman and Margaret Marshment, 60–75. Seattle, Wash.: Real Comet Press, 1989.

White, Evelyn C., ed. *The Black Women's Health Book: Speaking for Ourselves.* Seattle, Wash.: Seal Press, 1990.

Filmography

Color Purple, The (U.S., 1985). Spielberg, 154 min., Warner Bros.

Secret Sounds Screaming: The Sexual Abuse of Children (U.S., 1986). Ayoka Chenzira, 30 min., Women Make Movies.

Straight out of Brooklyn (U.S., 1991). Matty Rich, Universal.

Suzanne, Suzanne (U.S., 1982). Camille Hatch Billops and James Hatch, 26 min., Black Filmmakers Foundation.

Unit Six: Black Women behind the Camera

Invisibility, coupled with a stereotyping in the majority of the occasional roles in which blacks did appear, fueled black independent filmmaking. Given the proliferation of negative images of blacks created by whites in the film industry, Murray asserts that blacks have a responsibility to rescue their filmic images through the "correction of white distortions, the reflection of black reality, and (as a propagandizing tool) the creation of a positive black image" (xiv). Black independent filmmakers such as Julie Dash, Michelle Parkerson, Alile Sharon Larkin, and Haile Gerima continue to articulate these objectives as the driving force in their work.

Black independent filmmakers, a loosely connected group—most trained at the University of California-Los Angeles or New York University—arrived in the 1970s. Their political values and their cultural roots, however, belong to a continuum that extends back to pioneers such as Oscar Micheaux, the Johnson brothers, and Spencer Williams. Michelle Parkerson's statement that "our presence behind the camera as directors, producers, writers, and technicians reverses a cinematic legacy of long-suffering mammies, sepia exotics and tortured mulattoes," confirms that these aspirations survive in the works of black women filmmakers (Parkerson 110). These filmmakers have only begun to tell the numerous stories of black women that *must* be told—stories that have been both covertly and overtly neglected in the United States "script."

Bibliography

Campbell, Loretta. "Reinventing Our Image: Eleven Black Women Filmmakers." *Heresies* 16 (1983): 58–62.

Cripps, Thomas. "Black Film as Genre" and "Definitions." In *Black Film as Genre*. Bloomington: Indiana University Press, 1978.

Larkin, Alile Sharon. "Black Women Film-makers Defining Ourselves: Feminism in Our Own Voice." In *Female Spectators: Looking at Film and Television*, edited by E. Deidre Pribram, 157–73. New York: Verso, 1988.

Murray, James P. *To Find an Image: Black Film from Uncle Tom to Super Fly*. Indianapolis, Ind.: Bobbs-Merrill, 1973.

Parkerson, Michelle. "Did You Say the Mirror Talks?" In *Bridges of Power: Women's Multicultural Alliances*, edited by Lisa Albrecht and Rose M. Brewer, 108–117. Philadelphia, Penn.: New Society, 1990. Also includes a comprehensive list of black women filmmakers.

Filmography

Daughters of the Dust (U.S., 1991). Julie Dash, 113 min., Kino International.

A Different Image (U.S., 1979). Alile Sharon Larkin, 51 min., Black Filmmakers Foundation.

A Minor Altercation (U.S., 1977). Jackie Shearer, 30 min., Women Make Movies.

Gotta Make This Journey (U.S., 1983). Michelle Parkerson, 60 min., National Black Programming Consortium and Nguzo Saba Films.

Hair Piece: A Film for Nappy-Headed People (U.S., 1984). Ayoka Chenzira, 10 min., Women Make Movies.

Illusions (U.S., 1983). Julie Dash, 34 min., Women Make Movies.

Killing Time (U.S., 1981). Fronza Woods, 5 min., Black Filmmakers Foundation.

Losing Ground (U.S., 1982). Kathleen Collins, 86 min., Mypheduh Films, 48 Q Street NE, Washington, DC 20002.

Older Women and Love (U.S., 1987). Camille Billops and James Hatch, 26 min., Women Make Movies.

On Becoming a Woman: Mothers and Daughters Talking Together (1987). Cheryl Chisholm, 90 min., Women Make Movies.

Latin American and Caribbean Women in Film and Video

Julia Lesage

A course on Latin American women's film and video should challenge many of the premises of national cinema or women's cinema courses as they are usually taught. Ideally it should not only provide students with new information and ethnographic sensitivity, but it should also lead them to articulate concepts of gender and ethnicity in new ways.

The course as a whole will deal with how race, gender, and nation are *represented*, and with how these representations are denied or deployed internationally. It places in perspective and challenges institutional power and hegemonic discourse. It allows new connections to be drawn between media representations, social structures, intercultural communication strategies, and each individual's own cultural identity. The teacher should be aware of how women students and students of color in the class might want to use this material to affirm and build their own sense of gender and ethnic identity. Optimally, the course material and the interaction the teacher sets up between the students can lead to an awareness of how everyone constructs themselves through others and how a dialectical juxtaposition of identities and traditions can provide an alternative, liberating way to learn.

For background material, a teacher can consult extensive feminist scholarship from and about women's lives internationally. She can also expand the scope of class discussion of just one or two works by inviting local people from an ethnic community or subculture represented in a film or tape to see and discuss it with the students. In my own experience teaching women's studies classes, I have found that Latina mothers and daughters, with the mother often foreign-born, effectively present Latin American women's issues to a class, as do women who are Salvadoran refugees living in sanctuary, or who are Latina community or labor organizers in the United States. One of the issues that will become clear from such face-to-face encounters with immigrants from Latin America is that race and ethnicity are not processes uniformly or simply experienced by people of color.

In South America the term *Latin* is a synthetic term, as is the word *Indian*. Not everyone in South America speaks Spanish. Furthermore, Latin America has had a diversity of peoples since before the Spanish conquest. After the conquest, in some countries the indigenous population was decimated; in others, indigenous cultures and languages have remained a strong force. Native peoples do not refer to themselves as "Indians" but rather as "the people." Some countries had a slave trade and now have large black populations with an African heritage. Caribbean culture is distinct from Latin culture, although both share a common historical trajectory because of imperialism. And from the Spanish conquest to the present, one country, Puerto Rico, has never had independence from a foreign power.

U.S. television presents a lot of information about other countries, but almost all "foreign images" on television are distorted, reduced, and filtered. This course must begin by teaching students what there is to gain by challenging usual sources of information and seeking out alternative ones. Such alternative sources most obviously include works by Latin-American filmmakers and writers. They also include material from politically engaged artists and writers opposing U.S. imperialist intervention in Latin America, works that some students might originally be disposed to dismiss as biased.

Readings about Latin-American women from the discipline of social studies offer students not only information but also analytic structures. Understanding social structures provides a sophisticated basis for analyzing hegemonic media's representations of the "other" or for evaluating self-representations from an underrepresented group. Economic and social structures are determining factors in people's lives, and understanding these factors explains much about what lies under the surface of phenomena and images. The media in the United States almost always eschew presenting structure. In contrast, teaching social and historical concepts regularly plays a large part in courses on national cinema or women's cinema (e.g., when feminist film criticism analyzes the social, psychological, and media structures that derive from and reinforce compulsory heterosexuality [Adrienne Rich]). In this course, the teacher and the readings provide social analyses of women's lives in Latin America.

After the class sees each film, the teacher should encourage the students to deal with the complexities of that given social situation. In this sense, each film is only a case study. The teacher will probably need to rely on outside readings to explain the social and historical circumstances in each country since the differences in the structures shaping women's lives from one country or part of a country to another are not self-evident.

As students learn more about social processes in Latin America, they can deal more critically with and even challenge the "accuracy" of the tapes and films seen in class. The teacher should systematically raise the following issues: To what degree do these media makers know the lifeways and language of the people filmed? How well does a film translate the systems of meaning that lie behind and within what that film shows: that is, the meanings inherent in everyday practices, body language, expressions of feeling, and other cultural forms? I say "translate" advisedly, for not only is accurate translation of foreign language film and video crucial, it is also always a goal that can only be approached. Verbal and social translations always simplify, seek to impose order, generalize, and blur or miss something.

There is also a disadvantage in looking at a culture mainly in terms of structure. Such an approach downplays flux, individual experience, and moments of rupture. Students should ask the following of each work: What kinds of things would people notice in that culture? What would it mean to understand x phenomenon from this person's point of view? In other words, how is subjectivity constructed for a person in x position in y culture?

Unit One: Media Analysis/Social Analysis

U.S. television constantly demonstrates how the commercial mass media create fearful others. Media-sustained xenophobia is one of the main factors inhibiting intercultural understanding. Many people do not know about or, even more important, *want* to know about ways of life and experiences beyond their own or to expand their imagination beyond commonly accepted goals, fears, and fantasies. To counter such unproductive habits of media reception, a teacher in any discipline can regularly tape and discuss brief examples from television (across all genres, from advertising to miniseries to the nightly news) that illustrate mainstream media's racism and narrow cultural perspective.

Certain media and politics issues are crucial to raise at the beginning of the course. First of all, a general audience will always have a cultural background shaped by concepts from the dominant culture. Each viewer brings in a set of assumptions. Class discussion can investigate how racial stereotypes function socially. First, list the countries of the world and ask what mental images come to mind about that country. Soon you will come to the point where just one or two stereotypical images represent *x* country or region. Sometimes these stereotypes are accompanied by religious stereotypes, often in reference to Islam or Catholicism, but even more in reference to religious practices, such as Haiti being represented by a mental image of voodoo. Such reduced modes of representation demonstrate the mechanisms of racism. The simplicity and paucity of "peripheral" images about "peripheral" peoples leave us with a comfortable feeling: "I already know about the issues, lives, and values of those people, and the received ideas or images I have on that subject just need to take up this tiny space in my mind."

Second, for each work seen the students should learn how to challenge or historically bracket their own reception of the work. They should ask how film form or their own cinematic or political expectations might have limited what they understood when they saw a work. In a sense, every media or literary work implicitly establishes how we are supposed to receive it and what it is "about." Clarity and persuasiveness in a film/video work are qualities we often attribute to it when it relies on intellectual structures, verbal and cinematic vocabulary, and pacing with which we are already familiar. Yet even with a conventionally constructed work, a viewer may still reject its levels of complexity, contradictions, and analyses, especially if it goes against the viewer's presuppositions.

To test this kind of rejection, analyze or give a personal response to the frequent appearance of the word *imperialism* in the films and tapes. Commonly, U.S. viewers will reveal a politically induced "blind spot" in dismissing Latin speakers' use of the word. It often induces ennui or is rejected as political rhetoric. Yet for both ordinary people and for intellectuals in South America, the word *imperialism* summarizes and explains many interacting structures, some of which go back centuries, which shape their daily lives and tie them in an oppressive way to U.S. history and the current U.S. political agenda.

Less overtly political but also important to consider are the ways that narrative fictions create closure and tension, and how they use character typage and predictable hooks (lovers, children, heroes, villains, victims) to sustain identification. In fact, the same dramatic closure, typage, and linear cause-effect discourse shape most documentaries. We should analyze how the generalizations and abstractions made in a film depend on the maker's previous political and aesthetic assumptions (rarely explicitly stated). Ask what has gotten flattened out to make this kind of work. In terms of subject matter, what does it mean for a film/tape to use positive images or to reveal negative or contradictory aspects of oppressed peoples' lives? (See articles by Linda Artel and Susan Wengraf and by Diane Waldman, in Steven, ed.)

In this unit, the films and videotapes not only deal with Latin American issues but explicitly raise issues about media form. The reading ranges from oral history and ethnography to works that criticize the very kinds of documents studied in the course. *A Man, When He Is a Man* is a documentary by Chilean filmmaker in exile Valeria Sarmiento that offers an overview of machismo in Latin America. It works on two levels; one level lets men reveal their own sexism, the other satirizes romantic conventions in Latin-American popular culture, including love ballads and fictional film. *From Here, From This Side*, a collage video by Gloria Ribe that was banned from Mexican television, offers a witty collection of found media images that interrogate Hollywood's version of Latin America and show how Mexicans view the power of the United States. These pieces deal with two aspects of women's political thinking in contemporary Latin America—the analysis of machismo and the analysis of imperialism. Both works challenge traditional documentary form. In formal contrast is a more traditionally structured documentary; *The Global Assembly Line*, by U.S. director Lorraine Gray, shows the effect of multinational corporations' closing plants in the United States and establishing runaway shops in underdeveloped countries to exploit a labor force often composed of poverty-stricken women.

Several works deal explicitly with U.S. media representations of Latin America. Some of these come from the cable-access television series "Paper Tiger Television," which analyzes the mass media from a left-feminist perspective. Two shows that take up the recurrent issues of sexism and imperialism are *Adios Machismo: Jean Franco Reads Mexican Novelas*, which analyzes photo-novels, a popular genre with a broad female readership in Latin America, and *Everyday It Gets Harder to Be a Good Housewife: Michele Mattelart Reads the Chilean Press "Avant-Coup,"* which analyzes how CIA-financed Chilean newspapers recruited middle-class housewives into publicly opposing the Allende government before its violent overthrow.

Two experimental videos, one humorous and one serious, deal with the distorted ways that Latin America is represented in our media and by our government to maintain United States political power in the region. *Out of the Mouths of Babes* by Sherry Millner and Ernie Larsen uses the directors' two-year-old daughter's language-learning to let us grasp the follies and abusiveness of United States policy in Central America. *A Simple Case for Torture, or, How to Sleep at Night* by Martha Rosler is a scholarly essay-video that juxtaposes United States news reports, opinion pieces, scholarly texts, and Central Americans' testimonials to provoke thought about how United States politicians and media create and exploit the concept of terrorism.

Readings

Andreas, Carol. *When Women Rebel: the Rise of Popular Feminism in Peru.* Westport, Conn.: Lawrence Hill, 1985.

——. "Women at War." *Nacla Report on the Americas* 24 (December-January 1990-91). Special Issue, "Fatal Attraction: Peru's Shining Path."

Artel, Linda, and Susan Wengraf. "Positive Images." In Steven, ed.

Burton, Julianne, ed. *Cinema and Social Change in Latin America: Conversations with Filmmakers.* Austin: University of Texas Press, 1986.

——. *The Social Documentary in Latin America.* Pittsburgh, Pa.: University of Pittsburgh Press, 1990.

Clifford, James, and George Marcus, eds. *Writing Culture: The Poetics and Politics of Ethnography.* Berkeley: University of California Press, 1986.

Collier, John, and Malcolm Collier. *Visual Anthropology: Photography as a Research Method.* Albuquerque: University of New Mexico Press, 1986.

Desnöes, Edmundo. "The Photographic Image of Underdevelopment." *Jump Cut,* no. 33 (February 1988): 69–81.

Flores, Angel, and Kate Flores, eds. *The Defiant Muse: Hispanic Feminist Poems from the Middle Ages to the Present.* New York: Feminist Press, CUNY, 1986. Succinct introduction, biographies of poets, and lively selections. Appropriate for undergraduates as they become familiar with at least one bilingual written text.

Fusco, Coco. "Fantasies of Oppositionality." *Screen* 29 (Autumn 1988): 80–93.

Hahner, June E., ed. *Women in Latin American History: Their Lives and Views.* Los Angeles: UCLA Latin American Center, 1976. Women from different countries and social strata tell their own stories across history from colonial times to the present. Succinct introductions to each section.

Julien, Isaac, and Kobena Mercer. "De Centre and De Margin." *Screen* 29 (Autumn 1988).

Mohanty, Chandra. "Under Western Eyes." *Feminist Review* (Autumn 1988).

Nash, June, and Helen I. Safa. *Women and Change in Latin America: New Directions in Sexual Class.* Westport, Conn.: Bergin and Garvey, 1986.

Rich, Adrienne. "Compulsory Heterosexuality and Lesbian Existence." *Signs: Journal of Women in Culture and Society* 5 (Summer 1980): 631–60.

Spivak, Gayatri Chakravorty. *In Other Worlds: Essays in Cultural Politics.* London and New York: Methuen, 1987.

Steven, Peter, ed. *Jump Cut: Hollywood, Politics, and Counter Cinema.* Toronto: Between the Lines, 1985.

Trinh T. Minh-ha. *Woman, Native, Other: Writing Postcoloniality and Feminism.* Bloomington: Indiana University Press, 1989.

Waldman, Diane. "There's More to a Positive Image than Meets the Eye." In Steven, ed.

Waugh, Thomas. *Show Us Life! Toward a History and Aesthetics of the Committed Documentary.* Metuchen, N.J.: Scarecrow, 1984.

Media

Adios Machismo: Jean Franco Reads Mexican Novelas (U.S., 1986). Video, 28 min., Paper Tiger.

Everyday It Gets Harder to Be a Good Housewife: Michele Mattelart Reads the Chilean Press "Avant-Coup" (U.S., 1988). Video, 28 min., Paper Tiger.

From Here, From This Side (Mexico, 1988). Gloria Ribe, video, 24 min., Women Make Movies.

The Global Assembly Line (U.S., 1986). Lorraine Gray, film/video, 60 min., New Day.

A Man, When He Is a Man (France-Costa Rica, 1982). Valeria Sarmiento, film/video, 66 min., Women Make Movies.

Out of the Mouths of Babes (U.S., 1987). Sherry Millner and Ernie Larsen, video, 24 min., Women Make Movies.

A Simple Case for Torture, or How to Sleep at Night (U.S., 1983). Martha Rosler, video, 62 min., Video Data Bank.

Unit Two: Rural Women

Looking at the specific details of Latin-American rural people's lives challenges college students to imagine forms of labor and social organization they may not have conceptualized before. The films and videotapes listed here incorporate different styles and genres, allowing for the discussion of the following key topics: semiotics and aesthetic issues—especially realism, anthropology, intercultural communication, national and regional specificity, and global economic structures that contribute to rural poverty all over the world. The readings use social analysis, testimonials and oral history, and case studies of the kinds of women's organizing that occurs in many poor countries with large, oppressed rural populations. Other units could be constructed around different topics that would achieve the same goal—to expand the parameters of our social and cultural understanding. In fact, the same kinds of issues raised by this unit would be important to deal with in any unit that deals with oppressed people's self-expression in film/video as well as their (and our) relation to dominant cultural forms.

Some of the films/tapes are documentaries that are similar to oral histories. These are sometimes accompanied by a published autobiography of the woman in the work or an article on the work. An exemplary film in this genre is *Carmen Carrascal*, which gives a feminist view of the life of a rural craftswoman on Colombia's Atlantic coast. It was made by a collective of women filmmakers from the capital, Bogotá. In this documentary, Carmen discusses family life, her mule, basket weaving, and domestic madness in a way that brings out feminist themes. I have written on this film in an essay that also contains a study of *A Man When He Is a Man* and the work of the Taller de Video Popular and women videomakers in the

Sandinista labor unions in Nicaragua. The essay discusses different ways of producing documentaries and differing relations to the people filmed/taped.

Other such documentaries include *Land for Rose*, directed by Teté Moraes, who headed a group of videomakers who worked with farmers for a number of years as the farmers struggled to gain homesteading land in Brazil. The tape is reminiscent of *Harlan County, U.S.A.* in the close relation between the makers and the people depicted. *Elvia: A Fight for Land and Liberty* offers a portrait of a Honduran organizer of peasants' unions. Videotaped by U.S.-based Latino filmmakers Laura Rodriquez and Rick Tejada Flores, Elvia Alvarado speaks articulately about the collective struggle of the poor in Latin America to gain justice, especially to gain decent working conditions and land. Her oral history is available, and there she discusses other issues about life in Honduras, the U.S. military presence there, her role in organizing farmers, land takeovers, arrest and torture, and the progressive role of the Catholic church, marriage and the family, and machismo.

Two other famous oral histories told by peasant women are accompanied by either a filmed portrait of the woman or of women like her. Discussion should explicitly address issues raised by the ways of representing these women, the stylistic means used in the films and videotapes, the relations between media makers and subjects, and the structures, contradictions, and psychology presented in all these documentaries. Such issues are not raised by the media makers or the films or tapes. Domitila Barrios de Chungara's famous oral history *Let Me Speak!* testifies to women's endurance under and resistance to the most savage oppression. Her lament for the lives of Bolivian tin miners is well accompanied by the videotape *Hell to Pay* by Alexandra Anderson and Ann Cottringer, which provides an emotionally moving analysis of the international debt situation through Bolivian mining women's eyes. The oral history *I, Rigoberta Menchu,* offers a similarly graphic testimonial about the savage effort to exterminate indigenous villages and culture in Guatemala. There is a finely shot feature-length documentary film by Pamela Yates and Tom Sigel, *When the Mountains Tremble*, about repression in Guatemala that focuses on the life of one woman. Here, Rigoberta Menchu herself functions in the film as an emblematic narrator who symbolizes national resistance. Since this film is shot with all the style and craft of a feature fiction and it was not advertised as a documentary, the facts of its production and distribution, as well as its style, add to the richness of the theoretical discussion about oral history's relation to a realist documentary film style.

Other documentaries, made in a more traditional expository style, deal with the global economy of agriculture. They can be viewed for information and also for the way they present information. In particular, the issue of "structures" can be raised. What structures must we understand to understand the lives of rural woman in South America? What are the limitations of such concepts, of their presentation in film and video? Without such concepts, what would be lacking in our understanding? How many ways can media present explanatory social concepts?

Consuming Hunger demonstrates how U.S. media manipulate images of starvation in Ethiopia while they neglect to cover homelessness in the United States. Although this series of three tapes is about Africa and not South America, it analyzes what the consequences are of the media's tendency to create an image of the poor as a pathetic victim, always safely other. Furthermore, feminists from Asia, South America, and Africa often address the issue of hunger as one of the principle factors shaping women's lives on an international scale. They see that hunger and malnutrition are directly caused by international capitalism and multinational corporations' sacking their arable lands, natural resources, and ecosystems. Politically conscious women in poor areas of the world all discuss the effects of malnutrition on their people's health, especially children's, as part of their self-conscious identity as *woman*. When we understand hunger as an international feminist issue, we can begin to see how for most women in the world, women's concerns mesh inextricably with issues of race, class, and international politics.

Starving for Sugar analyzes how sugarcane workers from the Philippines to the Caribbean have become pawns in world economy and politics. *The Business of Hunger* depicts how cash crops are exported from underdeveloped countries where people are starving. And bridging the gap between oral history and structural analysis is Equadorian filmmaker Monica Vasquez's *Time of Women*, which documents life in an Andean village, where the women have taken over the field work because the men have migrated to the United States to look for work.

Some of the most interesting films and tapes present or incorporate rural women's own dramatic performances about their situation. In *Sweet Sugar Rage*, Sistren, a women's theater troupe, acts out the problems that a sugarcane worker, Iris, has with the male-dominated agricultural unions and with management. Discussions after the performance help us formulate solutions. *Mecata: A New Song* was made in collaboration with a peasant theater collective that contributed to rural organizing in Nicaragua. It shows performances on farms plus the discussion of issues that followed. *Miss Universe in Peru* focuses on a bourgeois event that is *critiqued* by women agricultural organizers. The film juxtaposes the 1982 Miss Universe Pageant, held in Lima, against the reality of most Peruvian women's lives, especially in terms of the negative influence of multinational corporations. These films and tapes, taken together, raise issues about self-presentation and the dramatization of one's own issues, along with a depiction of some of the audiences for those dramatizations.

Two documentaries by North American Anglo women explicitly take up issues of documentary strategies and kinds of meanings conveyed. *Before We Knew Nothing* was made by a U.S. anthropologist, Diane Kitchen, living with the Ashaninka Indians of Eastern Peru. Kitchen's film interrogates the conventions of anthropological filmmaking and her relation to these people. I made *El Crucero* in collaboration with Nicaraguan women videomakers as an experimental documentary that, in four narrative segments, each in a different documentary style, depicts life on one Nicaraguan farm. Each movement also incorporates different sound/image relations, so as to provoke a consideration of how viewers translate media information about other countries and how documentaries convey social relations in general. I was also able to publish a complete translation of the interviews gathered on that farm.

Feature fictions made by Latin-American directors allow the class to raise problematic issues that come up in relation to most commercially successful, progressive fiction films. *Sugar Cane Alley* has many comic moments and emphasizes the strength of family bonds as it follows a Martiniquan peasant grandmother who leaves her rural house to help her grandson attend school in the capital. By concentrating on the story of that boy, director Euzhan Palcy uses a conventionally acceptable theme about the talented young male intellectual who can escape and then reflect nostalgically on his roots. *Iracema* depicts in semidocumentary style what happens to an Amazon riverboat adolescent who becomes a prostitute in Belén and is abandoned in the jungle backwaters by a truck driver. The film's naturalist narrative repeats the commercially successful formula of the doomed poor. *Gaijin* deals with the suffering and loss of social identity Japanese workers faced as they migrated to work as indentured labor on Brazilian haciendas. The film exists in the United States only in a poor-quality print, but is excellent for showing the multicultural complexities of ethnic issues in Brazil. It too has a naturalist framework about the progressive disenfranchisement of the poor (see Nochlin).

Readings

Alvarado, Elvia. *Don't Be Afraid, Gringo: A Honduran Woman Speaks from the Heart*. Translated and edited by Medea Benjamin. San Francisco: Institute for Food and Development Policy, 1987.

Chungara, Domitila Barrios de. *Let Me Speak!* Translated by Victoria Ortiz. New York: Monthly Review, 1978.

Lesage, Julia. "Life and Work in El Crucero." *Radical America*, 19, no. 5 (1985).

——. "Women Make Media: Three Modes of Production." In *The Social Documentary in Latin America*. In Burton, ed.

Menchu, Rigoberta. *I, Rigoberta Menchu: An Indian Woman in Guatemala.* Edited by Elisabeth Burgos. Translated by Ann Wright. London: Verso, 1984.

Nochlin, Linda. *Realism.* Baltimore, Md.: Penguin, 1972.

Media

Before We Knew Nothing (U.S., 1988). Diane Kitchen, film, 62 min., Women Make Movies.

Business of Hunger, The (U.S., 1984). Video, 28 min., Maryknoll.

Carmen Carrascal (Colombia, 1984). Cine Mujer, film/video, 30 min., Women Make Movies.

Consuming Hunger: Famine and the Media (U.S., 1988). Three stand-alone, inexpensive 28 min. tapes: "Getting the Story," "Shaping the Image," and "Selling the Feeling." Maryknoll.

El Crucero (U.S., 1988). Julia Lesage, video, 59 min. Facets and Foreign Images.

Elvia: A Fight for Land and Liberty (U.S., 1988). Laura Rodriquez and Rick Tejada Flores, video, 28 min., Laura Rodriguez.

Gaijin (Brazil, 1979). Tizuka Yamasaki, film, 105 min., New Yorker.

Hell to Pay (England, 1988). Alexandra Anderson and Ann Cottringer, 52 min., Women Make Movies.

Iracema (Brazil, 1979). Jorge Brodansky, 90 min., Cinema Guild.

Land for Rose (Terra Para Rosa) (Brazil, 1987). Teté Moraes, video, 90 min.

Mecate: A New Song (Nicaragua, 1984). Felix Zurita de Higes, film, 40 min., First Run/Icarus.

Miss Universe in Peru (Peru, 1984). Grupo Chaski, film/video, 42 min., Women Make Movies.

Starving for Sugar (U.S., 1988). Video, 58 min., Maryknoll.

Sugar Cane Alley (Martinique, 1983). Euzhan Palcy, film, 103 min., New Yorker.

Sweet Sugar Rage (Jamaica, 1985). Sistren with Honor Ford-Smith and Harclyde Walcott, film/video, 45 min., Third World Newsreel.

Time of Women (Ecuador, 1988). Monica Vasquez, film/video, 20 min., Women Make Movies.

When the Mountains Tremble (U.S., 1983). Pamela Yates and Tom Sigel, 83 min., film: New Yorker, video: Skylight Pictures.

Sexual Representation in Film and Video

Chris Straayer

This course analyzes systems of sexual representation in popular cinema, pornography, erotic art film, and independent film and video. It examines the functions of imagery and narrative in relation to voyeurism, exhibitionism, aggression, transgression, knowledge, displacement, the politics of sexuality, and ideologies of gender. The purpose of the investigation is not to endorse a particular position on sexuality or sexual representation, but to unravel a complex web of attitudes and cultural practices that overtly and covertly influence the viewer-text interaction, such as the privatization and regulation of sexual activity, the putting into discourse of sex, and the privileged verisimilitude of sexual imagery.

As an interface between private and public spheres, the exhibition of explicit sexual media precipitates disputes about individual freedoms and societal controls, imagination and actuality, seeing and doing. This suggests a conceptual motif for the course: boundary negotiations. Various representational systems can be studied in relation to particular boundaries that protect and maintain certain valued, yet vulnerable, entities. For example, horror films often imply that sexuality pierces the human-animal boundary, hence the generic fascination with transformation and the displacement of sexuality onto violence. Camp films use sexuality to upset societal standards and illustrate the arbitrariness of status quo definitions. Independent films and videos of alternative sexualities exclaim the denied and present the invisible.

Since extensive work has been done on issues of gender and sexual representation within feminist theory, this is a vital ingredient to the course's critical substance. An emphasis on genital sexuality, rather than sex roles, however, initiates additional considerations of importance to students of visual communication. Therefore, the course is designed with a primary focus on explicit imagery. Obviously, students should be of adult age and informed that the course includes X-rated material. Students who feel such content is inappropriate for academic study should be advised not to enroll. The professor should exercise discretion, particularly regarding what he/she shows in units three through five.

Several strategies are employed to mitigate – rather than avoid – the engagement with images of nudity and genital sexuality. Mainstream cinema genres, such as the musical, horror, and romance, are compared and contrasted to the genre of pornography. Independent, personal depictions of sexuality are studied next to more formulaic commercial products. Borderline genres such as soft porn make evident the fluidity of sexual signifiers. The use of excerpts rather than complete works, especially in the hard-core section, can foreground a scholarly stance when students might otherwise feel overwhelmed. Attitudes toward sexuality, generally articulated in the authoritative discourses of religion, law, medicine, psychology, and sexology, are presented as multiple, unfixed, and sociohistorically constructed. Readings from conflicting viewpoints and of greater and lesser difficulty are included, and primary sources are supported by surrounding secondary materials. In my selection of media artists, particularly for units two, four, and five, I have tried to support racial/ethnic and sexual diversity. All media works are noted as film, video, or film/video (film also released on video). A valuable mail order source for feature films on video (for students' home viewing) is Facets Multimedia, listed in the distributors' pages.

Unit One: The Horror of Sex

This unit investigates the generic management of sexuality by horror films. The film *Cat People* works well with readings by Davis, Evans, and Giles. Davis's description of a Jehovanist worldview, which believes that sexual activity impinges on human identity, identifies a fear that is literalized in many horror films. The particular relevance of human-animal transformations to the frightening physical changes and sexual awakenings of adolescence, for example, menstruation and masturbation, is elaborated by Laura Mulvey's psychoanalytic-based article, used here and throughout the course to discuss woman's construction as fetishized image and as victim of narrative sadism for male visual/sexual pleasure. Giles (whose article assumes a familiarity with Mulvey's) demands a sophisticated reading of film language (which then also can be employed to identify the horror discourse in *Broken Mirrors*).

Both *Videodrome* and *Broken Mirrors* investigate the intersection of violence and sexuality but with radically opposed results. While *Broken Mirrors* employs a feminist perspective to firmly establish sadism within male sexuality and the realm of the real, *Videodrome* produces an anarchy of discourses on video, pornography, sexuality, violence, and power that assigns sadism to contemporary socioeconomic conditions, depicts masochism as a non-gender-specific impulse, and ultimately eradicates the distinction between reality and fantasy. Campbell argues that Cronenberg's frequent depiction of human reproduction turned destructive challenges the animate-inanimate boundary. Bataille attacks the life-death boundary in his arguments about the simultaneous contradictory human desires toward discontinuity/personal identity and continuity/merging and about erotic violence as the attempt to come as close as possible to merging with another without losing one's self in death. *Broken Mirrors* presents the underside of Freud's famous observations on the psychology of male love and sexuality and its requisite good-bad dichotomization of women.

Screenings

Broken Mirrors (Netherlands, 1985). Marleen Gorris, film, 110 min., First Run/Icarus.

Cat People (U.S., 1982). Paul Schrader, film/video, 118 min., Swank.

Videodrome (Canada, 1983). David Cronenberg, film/video, 89 min., Swank.

Readings

Bataille, Georges. Introduction to *Erotism: Death and Sensuality*, 11–25. Paris: Les Editions de Minuit, 1957; San Francisco: City Lights Books, 1986.

Campbell, Mary B. "Biological Alchemy and the Films of David Cronenberg." In *Planks of Reason: Essays on the Horror Film*, edited by Barry Keith Grant, 307–20. Metuchen, N.J.: Scarecrow Press, 1984.

Davis, Murray S. "Part Two: Smut Structure." In *SMUT: Erotic Reality/Obscene Ideology*, 87–164. Chicago: University of Chicago Press, 1983.

Evans, Walter. "Monster Movies: A Sexual Theory." In *Planks of Reason*, 53–64.

Freud, Sigmund. "The Most Prevalent Form of Degradation in Erotic Life (1912)." In *Sexuality and the Psychology of Love*, 58–70. New York: Collier Books, Macmillan, 1963.

Giles, Dennis. "Conditions of Pleasure in Horror Cinema." In *Planks of Reason*, 38–52.

Mulvey, Laura. "Visual Pleasure and Narrative Cinema." In *Narrative, Apparatus, Ideology: A Film Theory Reader*, edited by Philip Rosen, 198–209. New York: Columbia University Press, 1986.

Unit Two: Soft Edges/Competing Discourse

The texts explored in this unit are more difficult to define and delineate than are the horror films of unit one and the hard-core of unit three. *Rate It X*, which should be taught as a media essay rather than an "objective" documentary, concerns sexist representations in soft porn and advertisements as well as their systematic support by sex role socialization. Williams reviews the history of pornography, the Meese Commission Report, the Women Against Pornography position, as well as alternative feminist views in "Speaking Sex." *Caught Looking* includes numerous feminist propornography and anticensorship essays, "100 years of porn" in explicit photographs, and a useful bibliography. Moye provides a crucial male perspective on the masturbatory use of soft porn, its reassuring address to the male viewer, as well as the acknowledgment of male sexual anxieties and limitations in the sex-aid advertisements of such magazines. Dyer considers contrary codes of looking, not looking, and posing in male pinups. Kuhn analyzes the female image in soft-core photography, including a particular convention of the "caught unawares" pose (eyes closed, body open) that facilitates prolonged scrutiny of the female sex.

WR: Mysteries of the Organism is a mixed-mode film that takes advantage of the license of "art" narrative to present Wilhelm Reich's educational/psychological/political mobilization of the healthy and powerful human orgasm. Altman deconstructs various sexologies, exposing their presumptions, prejudices, and prescriptions. Stoller returns us to the erotics of violence in his (Freudian-based) assertion that sexual excitement is generated by hostility. The film's ambiguous position invites reflection on common assumptions about sexual repression – as socially desirable or dangerous – and violent pornography – as cathartic fantasy or incitement to imitative action.

Screening a sex education film with explicit imagery, such as many of those distributed by Multi-Focus, will make evident a contrast between educational and pornographic discourses. For example, the contrast between the representation of female masturbation in the sex-education film *Margo* and that in most porn films foregrounds the constructed status of both images. In the pornographic films of unit three, female masturbation becomes a seductive, exhibitionist activity posed and photographed in a manner that discloses an altered function to accommodate the spectator.

Bright Eyes, discussed in Gever's article, analyzes contemporary representations of persons with AIDS in relation to the history of imaging illness and sexuality. The experimental film *Urinal*, also an essay, analyzes the policing of sexuality – police raids on and public exposure of homosexual and heterosexual men who engage in bathroom sex. Providing historical and political contexts, the film opposes the enforcement of "proper" sexual norms via unethical tactics that intrude on personal practices and alternative preferences. Foucault's writings on the putting of sex into discourse, the proliferation of discourses, and confession productively inform discussions of alternative sexualities and activist media production.

Screenings

Bright Eyes (U.K., 1986). Stuart Marshall, video, 85 min., Frameline and Video Data Bank.

Margo (U.S., 1972). Laird Sutton, National Sex Forum, film/video, 11 min., Multi-Focus.

Rate It X (U.S., 1986). Lucy Winer and Paula de Koeningsberg, video, 94 min., Interama.

Urinal (Canada, 1988). John Greyson, film, 100 min., Frameline.

WR: Mysteries of the Organism (Yugoslavia, 1971). Dusan Makavejev, film, 84 min., Almi.

Readings

Altman, Meryl. "Everything They Always Wanted You to Know: The Ideology of Popular Sex Literature." In *Pleasure and Danger: Exploring Female Sexuality*, edited by Carole S. Vance, 115–30. Boston: Routledge and Kegan Paul, 1984.

Dyer, Richard. "Don't Look Now." *Screen* 23, nos. 3–4 (1982): 61–72.

Ellis, Kate, et al., eds. *Caught Looking: Feminism, Power, and Censorship*. Seattle, Wash.: The Real Comet Press, 1988.

Foucault, Michel. "We 'Other' Victorians," "The Incitement to Discourse," and "Scientia Sexualis." In *The History of Sexuality, Volume I: An Introduction*, translated by Robert Hurley, 3–73. Paris: Editions Gallimard, 1976; New York: Vintage Books, 1980.

Gever, Martha. "Pictures of Sickness: Stuart Marshall's *Bright Eyes*." In *AIDS: Cultural Analysis Cultural Activism*, edited by Douglas Crimp, 109–26. Cambridge, Mass.: MIT Press, 1988.

Kuhn, Annette. "Lawless Seeing." In *Power of the Image: Essays on Representation and Sexuality*, 19–47. London: Routledge and Kegan Paul, 1985.

Moye, Andy. "Pornography." In *The Sexuality of Men*, edited by Andy Metcalf and Martin Humphries, 44–69. London: Pluto Press, 1985.

Stoller, Robert J., M.D. "Sexual Excitement." In *Sexual Excitement: Dynamics of Erotic Life*, 3–35. Washington, D.C.: American Psychiatric Press, 1986.

Williams, Linda. "Speaking Sex" and "Prehistory." In *Hard Core: Power, Pleasure and the Frenzy of the Visible*, 1–57. Berkeley: University of California Press, 1989.

Unit Three: Hard Core – Explicit Motions

This unit examines the history and generic properties of hard-core film. *History of the Blue Movie* (used with Williams, "The Stag Film") demonstrates the development of narrative and specular conventions in stag films, their informative displays, self-reflexive endorsement of voyeuristic pleasure, and frequent sense of humor regarding the cultural mythologies and personal paranoias surrounding sexuality. In other chapters, Williams (drawing on Foucault, Marx, Freud, and Irigaray) extends the discussion of pornography beyond considerations of moral limits and freedom of expression. Although Williams discusses numerous films in addition to those listed below, I suggest screening *The Opening of Misty Beethoven* in its entirety to demonstrate the genre's "musical" structure and supplementing it with clips from the remaining three films listed, which all star Marilyn Chambers, to demonstrate other particular points made by Williams.

Ellis describes the industry of pornography in Great Britain and investigates the genre's obsessive display of vaginal imagery, which is unexplained by Mulvey's scheme. Willemen's response to Ellis's article includes his concept of "the fourth look," which catches the viewer looking and reinforces the genre's mode of direct address and substitution of looking for physical contact.

Screenings

Behind the Green Door (U.S., 1972). Mitchell Brothers, video, 72 min., Mitchell Brothers.

History of the Blue Movie (U.S., 1972). Alex de Renzy, anthology released by Thunderbird, video, 120 min., Caballero/VMC.

Insatiable (U.S., 1980). Godfrey Daniels, video, 76 min., Caballero/VMC.

The Opening of Misty Beethoven (U.S., 1975). L. Sultana, Radley Metzger (a.k.a. Henri Paris), video, 85 min., VCA.

Resurrection of Eve (U.S., 1973). Jon Fontana and Artie Mitchell, video, 82 min., Mitchell Brothers.

Readings

Ellis, John. "Photography/Pornography/Art/Pornography." *Screen* 21, no. 1 (1980): 81–108.

Willemen, Paul. "Letter to John." *Screen* 21, no. 2 (1980): 53–65.

Williams, Linda. "The Stag Film," "Fetishism and Hard Core: Marx, Freud and the Money Shot," "Generic Pleasures," "Hard-Core Utopia," and "Power, Pleasure, Perversion." In *Hard Core: Power, Pleasure and the Frenzy of the Visible*, 58–228. Berkeley: University of California Press, 1989.

Unit Four: Phallus Interruptus

This unit provides alternative representations of male sexualities that critique, circumvent, or contrast the dominant patriarchal system. *In the*

Realm of the Senses, an erotic art film, and *Men Again*, an independent experimental film, contest the conventional representation of the all-powerful phallus. *Men Again* reedits contemporary video porn to foreground an incessantly demanding female presence on the audio track, which is placed against visuals of the male face in close-up. Lehman's article discusses the unconventional representation of male sexuality in *In the Realm of the Senses*, for example, its depiction of the unerect penis. Dyer ("Male Sexuality in the Media") contrasts the fragile penis to its hard and powerful phallic symbolization. Drawing on the psychoanalytic literary work of Gilles Deleuze, Studlar develops a model of masochistic aesthetics opposed to Mulvey's Freudian-Lacanian position.

The remaining films and videos listed depict gay male sexuality. Dyer ("Shades of Genet") discusses the classic film *Un Chant D'Amour* in relation to historical context and subsequent readings. *Taxi Zum Klo*, *Scorpio Rising*, and *Loads* are also classic gay films that deal, respectively, with partnership and promiscuity (including bathroom sex), macho gay motorcycle culture (with a fascist aesthetic), and a gay desire for straight men. *Hermes Bird*, in which a poetic text is read in a voice-over while the camera shows a slow-motion close-up of a penis becoming erect, not only fragments and objectifies the male body but glorifies and praises this "independent" alter-self. By contrast, *Blow Job* keeps the camera above the waist capturing the recipient's ecstatic facial reactions as his head sways between darkness and light, between control and abandonment. Richard Fung's article complements the tape *Chinese Characters*, in which the artist video-keys himself into a porn video; together they instigate an analysis of the intersection of race and sex in gay pornography. *Tongues Untied* explores issues of racism, identity, and sexuality in contemporary gay male culture. *Safer Sex Shorts*, which are explicit, purposely sexy, educational porn from the Gay Men's Health Crisis Center, propose new strategies for the educational genre.

Waugh compares and contrasts gay and straight porn, concluding his article with a discussion of *Loads*. Rubin's article (which draws from Foucault) is essential to this unit's confrontation of subjective, arbitrary, discriminatory sexual "standards" and "norms." *Pink Flamingos* promotes a discussion of camp as a subversive strategy. Sontag, Babuscio, and Newton discuss the aesthetics, politics, and transgressiveness of the camp sensibility. Davis's description of the naturalist (that sexuality is healthy and beneficial) and gnostic (that erotic reality can and should destroy the established order of a corrupt everyday reality) worldviews on sexuality can now be applied to pornography and camp and contrasted to the Jehovanist view in the horror film.

Screenings

Blow Job (U.S., 1963). Andy Warhol, film, 35 min., MOMA.

Chinese Characters (Canada, 1986). Richard Fung, video, 21 min., V-Tape.

Hermes Bird (U.S., 1979). James Broughton, film/video, 11 min., Multi-Focus and Canyon Cinema.

In the Realm of the Senses (Japan-France, 1975). Nagisa Oshima, film, 106 min., Almi.

Loads (U.S., 1980). Curt McDowell, film, 22 min., Canyon Cinema.

Men Again (U.S., 1986–89). Chuck Kleinhans, video, 18 min., Kleinhans.

Pink Flamingos (U.S., 1971). John Waters, film/video, 95 min., New Line Cinema and Films, Inc.

Safer Sex Shorts (U.S., 1989). Gay Men's Health Crisis (GMHC), video, 25 min., GMHC.

Scorpio Rising (U.S., 1963). Kenneth Anger, film/video, 29 min., Canyon Cinema.

Taxi Zum Klo (West Germany, 1980). Frank Ripploh, film/video, 92 min., Cinevista (35mm and video sales) and Facets Multimedia.

Tongues Untied (U.S., 1989). Marlon Riggs, video, 55 min., Frameline.

Un Chant D'Amour (France, 1950). Jean Genet, film, 20 min., West Glen Films.

Readings

Babuscio, Jack. "Camp and the gay sensibility." In *Gays and Film*, edited by Richard Dyer, 40–57. London: British Film Institute, 1977.

Davis, Murray S. "The War of the World Views." In *SMUT: Erotic Reality/Obscene Ideology*, 165–246. Chicago: University of Chicago Press, 1983.

Dyer, Richard. "Male Sexuality in the Media." In *The Sexuality of Men*, edited by Andy Metcalf and Martin Humphries, 28–43. London: Pluto Press, 1985.

——. "Shades of Genet." In *Now You See It: Studies on Lesbian and Gay Film*, 47–101. New York: Routledge, 1990.

Fung, Richard. "Looking for My Penis: The Eroticized Asian in Gay Video Porn." In *How Do I Look? Queer Film and Video*, edited by Bad Object-Choices, 145–60. Seattle, Wash.: Bay Press, 1991.

Lehman, Peter. "*In the Realm of the Senses*: Desire, Power, and the Representation of the Male Body." *Genders* 1, no. 1 (1988): 91–110.

Newton, Esther. "Role Models." In *Mother Camp: Female Impersonators in America*, 97–111. Chicago: University of Chicago Press, 1972.

Rubin, Gayle. "Thinking Sex: Notes for a Radical Theory of the Politics of Sexuality." In *Pleasure and Danger: Exploring Female Sexuality*, edited by Carole S. Vance, 267–319. Boston: Routledge and Kegan Paul, 1984.

Sontag, Susan. "Notes on 'Camp.'" In *Against Interpretation*, 275–92. New York: Delta, 1961.

Studlar, Gaylyn. "Visual Pleasure and the Masochistic Aesthetic." *Journal of Film and Video* 37, no. 2 (1985): 5–26.

Waugh, Tom. "Men's Pornography: Gay vs. Straight." *Jump Cut* 30 (1985): 30–35.

Unit Five: Female Sexual Pleasure–Can We See It?

This unit asks if and what an erotic media expression of female sexuality can be and looks at several women-authored texts. *Nea* is an erotic art film (see Kuhn for an analysis of the legal and economic factors relating to the marketing of this film) whose young female protagonist actively pursues sexual knowledge, trespasses filmic space (in contrast to pornography's conventional use of woman *as* space to be entered and investigated, described by Giles), and manipulates both the male characters and the plot events. *Sensual Escape* (discussed by Williams in "Sequels and Revisions") is a commercial porn video by Candida Royalle, herself a porn star, who is attempting to erotically represent and satisfy a feminine sensibility in porn for couples. In a different vein, *Annie* (Sprinkle) mixes comedy, exhibitionism, sex education, and feminist art strategies in postpornography performance. In *See Dick Run*–"a penis envy cooperative production"–a man's crotch is the focus of a persistent female/camera gaze. *Asparagus*, a gorgeously nasty animation film, symbolizes the penis while undermining the phallus.

The remaining films and videos concern lesbian sexuality. *Women I Love* promotes an alternate, lesbian sexual aesthetic and sensibility. Dyer provides an extended discussion of Hammer's work in relation to cultural feminism. Snitow's article is useful in discussing how romance shares or displaces female sexuality in *Sensual Escape* and *Women I Love*. *Virgin Machine* chronicles a woman's departure from the realm of romantic love when she visits a San Francisco scenario of lesbian strippers and sex toys. With explicit sexual alternatives, dykey domestics, and tactile visual aesthetics, *Kathy*, *Looking for LaBelle*, and *She Don't Fade* lend dimension to the representation of lesbian sexuality.

Screenings

Annie (U.S.-West Germany, 1989). Monika Treut, film, 10 min., Blue Horse Films.

Asparagus (U.S., 1978). Suzan Pitt, film, 19 min., Picture Start.

Kathy (U.S., 1988). Cecilia Dougherty, video, 12 min., Frameline.

Looking for LaBelle (U.S., 1991). Jocelyn Taylor, video, 5 min., Taylor.

Nea (*Nea-A Young Emmanuelle*) (France, 1976). Nelly Kaplan, film/video, 101 min., Facets Multimedia.

See Dick Run (U.S., 1987). Ann Alter, film, 14 min., Asymmetry Productions and Picture Start.

Sensual Escape: I. Fortune Smiles; II. The Tunnel (U.S., 1988). Candida Royalle, Per Sjostedt, and Gloria Leonard, video, 66 min., Femme Distribution.

She Don't Fade (U.S., 1991). Cheryl Dunye, video, 23 min., Video Data Bank.

Virgin Machine (West Germany, 1988). Monika Treut, film, 86 min., First Run/ Icarus.

Women I Love (U.S., 1976). Barbara Hammer, film, 27 min., Canyon Cinema and Women Make Movies.

Readings

Dyer, Richard. "Lesbian Woman: Lesbian Cultural Feminist Film." In *Now You See It: Studies on Lesbian and Gay Film*, 174–210. New York: Routledge, 1990.

Giles, Dennis. "Pornographic Space: The Other Place." In *Film: Historical-Theoretical Speculations, The 1977 Film Studies Annual: Part Two*, edited by Ben Lawton and Janet Staiger, 52–66. Pleasantville, N.Y.: Redgrave Publishing Company, 1977.

Kuhn, Annette. "The Body in the Machine." In *Women's Pictures: Feminism and the Cinema*, 10–12. Boston: Routledge and Kegan Paul, 1982.

Snitow, Ann Barr. "Mass Market Romance: Pornography for Women Is Different." In *Powers of Desire: The Politics of Sexuality*, edited by Ann Snitow, Christine Stansell, and Sharon Thompson, 245–63. New York: Monthly Review Press, 1983.

Williams, Linda. "Sequels and Re-Visions: A Desire of One's Own" and "Conclusion." In *Hard Core: Power, Pleasure and the Frenzy of the Visible*, 229–80. Berkeley: University of California Press, 1989.

Partial List of Distributors and Resources

Note: As we go to press, this list is accurate. However, since changes do unexpectedly occur, please check to verify your orders.

Almi Pictures, 1900 Broadway, New York, NY 10023, 212/769-6400.

Alturas Films, 2752-A Folsom Street, San Francisco, CA 94110.

Appleshop, 306 Madison Street, Whitesburg, KY 41858, 606/633-0108.

Asian Cinevision, 32 East Broadway, New York, NY 10002, 212/925-8685.

Asymmetry Productions, P.O. Box 5657, Athens, OH 45701, 614/592-3456.

Atlantic Video, 17750 Preston Road, Dallas, TX 75252, 214/248-3500.

Black Film Center/Archive, Indiana University, Bloomington, IN 47405, 812/335-2684 or 3874.

Black Filmmakers Foundation, Tribeca Film Center, 375 Greenwich Street, New York, NY 10013, 212/941-3944.

Blue Horse Films, Inc., 225 Lafayette Street, #914, New York, NY 10012, 212/431-0940.

Budget Films, 4590 Santa Monica Boulevard, Los Angeles, CA 90029, 213/660-0187 or 660-0080.

Caballero/VMC (video sales), 7920 Alabama Avenue, Canoga Park, CA 91304-4991.

California Newsreel (Resolution, Inc.), 149 Ninth Street, #420, San Francisco, CA 94103, 415/621–6196.

Cambridge Documentary Films, P.O. Box 385, Cambridge, MA 02139, 615/354–3677.

Canyon Cinema, 2325 Third Street, Suite 338, San Francisco, CA 94107, 415/626–2255.

Center for Cuban Studies, 124 West Twenty-third Street, New York, NY 10011, 212/242–0559.

Cine Festival, 1300 Guadalupe Street, San Antonio, TX 78207–5519, 512/271–3151.

The Cinema Guild, 1697 Broadway, Suite 802, New York, NY 10019, 212/246–5522, 800/723–5522.

Cinevista, Inc., 560 West Forty-third, Suite 8J, New York, NY 10036, 212/947–4373.

CrossCurrent Media/NAATA, 346 Ninth Street, Second Floor, San Francisco, CA 94103, 415/552–9550.

Direct Cinema, P.O. Box 10003, Santa Monica, CA 90410, 310/396–4774, 800–525–0000.

EmGee Films, 6924 Canby Avenue, Suite 102, Reseda, CA 91335, 818/881–8110 or 981–5506.

Facets Multimedia (tape rentals and sales), 1517 West Fullerton Avenue, Chicago IL 60614, 312/281–9075, 800/331–6197.

Femme Distribution, Inc. (tape sales), 588 Broadway, Suite 1110, New York, NY 10012, 212/226–9330.

Filmakers Library, Inc., 124 East Fortieth Street, New York, NY 10016, 212/808–4980.

Films, Inc., 5547 North Ravenswood Avenue, Chicago, IL 60640–1199, 800/323–4222, ext. 380.

First Run/Icarus, 153 Waverly Place, 6th Floor, New York, NY 10014, 212/727–1711, 800/876–1710.

Foreign Images, Gretchen Elsner-Sommer, 1213 Maple Avenue, Evanston, IL 60202, 708/475–1269.

Frameline, 347 Delores Street, #205, San Francisco, CA 94110, 415/861–5245.

Full Frame Film and Video Distribution (formerly DEC Films), 394 Euclid Avenue, Toronto, ONT M6G 2S9, 416/925–9338.

Gay Men's Health Crisis (GMHC), Department of Education and Videotape Distribution, 129 West Twentieth Street, New York, NY 10011, 212/807–7517.

IDERA Films, 2524 Cypress Street, Vancouver, BC V6J 3N2, 604/738–8815.

Interama, 301 West Fifty-third Street, Apartment 19E, New York, NY 10019, 212/977–4830.

Kino International, 333 West Thirty-ninth Street, #503, New York, NY 10018, 212/629–6880.

Kit Parker Films, 1245 Tenth Street, Monterey, CA 93940, 408/649-5573, 800/538-5838.

Kleinhans, Chuck, Radio-Televison-Film Department, Northwestern University, 1905 North Sheridan Road, Evanston, IL 60208, 708/491-7315.

Lesage (Julia) Video, 3480 Mill Street, Eugene OR 97405, 503/344-8129.

Maryknoll World Video and Film Library, Media Relations, Maryknoll, NY 10545, 800/227-8523.

Media Alternatives Project, Avery Teacher Center, NYU, 70 Washington Square South, Second Floor, New York, NY 10012.

Media Network, 39 West Fourteenth Street, Suite 402, New York, NY 10011, 212/929-2663.

Mitchell Brothers, 895 O'Farrell Street, San Francisco, CA 94109, 415/441-1930.

Moraes, Teté, Vemver Comunicacao, Rua Joa Borges 83, Gavea 22, 415 Rio de Janeiro, Brasil, 55-21-266-7245.

Museum of the American Indian, Film and Video Center, 3753 Broadway at 155th Street, New York, NY 10032, 212/283-2420.

Museum of Modern Art (MOMA) Circulating Film Library, 11 West Fifty-third Street, New York, NY 10019, 212/708-9530.

Multi-Focus Media Inc., 1525 Franklin Street, San Francisco, CA 94109, 415/673-5100.

Mypheduh Films, Inc., 48 Q Street NE, Washington, DC 20002, 202/529-0220.

National Black Programming Consortium, 1266 East Broad Street, Columbus, OH 43205, 614/252-0921.

National Latino Community Center, 4401 Sunset Boulevard, Los Angeles, CA 90027, 213/669-5083.

Native American Public Broadcasting Consortium, P.O. Box 8311, 1800 North Thirty-third Street, Lincoln, NE 68501-1311, 402/472-1785.

New Day Films, 121 West Twenty-seventh Street, Room 902, New York, NY 10001, 212/645-8210.

New Line Cinema, 575 Eighth Avenue, Sixteenth Floor, New York, NY 10018, 212/239-8880.

New Yorker Films, 16 West Sixty-first Street, New York, NY 10023, 212/247-6110.

October Films, 630 Fifth Avenue, Thirtieth Floor, New York, NY 10111, 800/628-6237.

Paper Tiger Television Collective, 339 Lafayette Street, New York, NY 10012, 212/420-9045.

Pennsylvania State University, Audiovisual Services, University Park, PA 16802, 814/865-6314.

Picture Start (video), 1727 West Catalpa Avenue, Chicago, IL 60640, 312-769-2489.

Sankofa Film and Video Collective–distributed by Third World Newsreel.

Short Form Releasing (television), 221 East Cullerton, Sixth Floor, Chicago, IL 60616, 312/769-2489 (same as Picture Start).

Skylight Pictures, 330 West Forty-second Street, New York, NY 10036, 212/947-5333.

Swank, P.O. Box 231, St. Louis, MO 63166, 314/534-6300, 800/876-5577.

Taylor, Jocelyn, 127 Saint Felix Street, Brooklyn, NY 11217, 718/875-9010.

Third World Newsreel, 335 West Thirty-eighth Street, Fifth Floor, New York, NY 10018, 212/947-9277.

VCA Mail Order (tape sales), 9650 DeSota, Chatsworth, CA 91311-6089, 800/458-4336; in CA, 718-0404.

Video Data Bank, School of the Art Institute of Chicago, 280 South Columbus Drive, Chicago, IL 60603, 312/443-3793.

V-Tape, 183 Bathurst Street, First Floor, Toronto, Ontario M5T 2R7, 416/538-1899.

West Glen Films, 1430 Broadway, New York, NY 10018, 212/921-0966.

William Greaves Productions, Inc., 230 West Fifty-fifth Street, Sixteenth Floor, New York, NY 10019, 212/265-6250, 800/874-8314.

Women Make Movies, 225 Lafayette Street, Suite 206, New York, NY 10012, 212/925-0606.

XChange TV, P.O. Box 586, New York, NY 10009, 212/260-6565.

Zipporah Films, One Richdale Avenue, Unit #4, Cambridge, MA 02140, 617/576-3603.

Contributors

Poonam Arora teaches film at the University of Michigan-Dearborn. She is working on a book on the representation of woman in Indian cinema.

Julianne Burton is the editor of *Cinema and Social Change in Latin America: Conversations with Filmmakers* (1986) and *The Social Documentary in Latin America* (1990). A professor of Latin-American literature at the University of California, Santa Cruz, she is currently compiling a collection on Latin-American women in the visual media.

Jackie Byars, associate professor of radio-television-film in the department of communication at Wayne State University, writes on feminist film theory and on the representation of difference in popular film and television texts. She is the author of *All That Hollywood Allows: Re-reading Gender in 1950s Melodrama*.

Diane Carson is a professor of mass communications at St. Louis Community College at Meramec and teaches courses in film studies and production. She has been a Fulbright Teaching Fellow in England and was awarded two National Endowment for the Humanities seminars. She has coedited an anthology on multiculturalism and pedagogy and publishes weekly film reviews in the *Riverfront Times* of St. Louis.

Lisa Cartwright is assistant professor of English at the University of

Rochester, where she teaches in the visual and cultural studies as well as film studies programs.

Teresa de Lauretis is professor of the history of consciousness at the University of California, Santa Cruz. The author of *Alice Doesn't* and numerous essays on feminist theory, film, semiotics, and literature, she recently edited the "Queer Theory" issue of *differences*. Her most recent book in English is *Technologies of Gender*. She is currently working on *The Practice of Love*, a book about sexual structuring, fantasy, and lesbian subjectivity.

Linda Dittmar is a professor of English at the University of Massachusetts-Boston, where she teaches film, literature, and women's studies courses. Her published work includes *From Hanoi to Hollywood: The Vietnam War in American Film* (coedited) and numerous essays concerning literature, film, and pedagogy, often from a multicultural perspective. She is a member of *The Radical Teacher* editorial group.

Nina Fonoroff continues to make experimental films and teaches film and video production at Hampshire College in Amherst, Massachusetts.

Jane Gaines is associate professor of literature and English at Duke University, where she heads the program in film and video. She coedited *Fabrications: Costume and the Female Body* (1990) and recently completed *Contested Culture: The Image, the Voice, and the Law* (1991).

Gloria J. Gibson-Hudson is an assistant professor in the department of Afro-American studies and assistant director of the Black Film Center/Archive at Indiana University. She has conducted in-depth research and lectured extensively on the images of black women in film. She has published in *Wide Angle, New York Folklore*, and the *Western Journal of Black Studies* and has contributed chapters on film to two books. Gibson-Hudson received her Ph.D. from Indiana University-Bloomington in folklore and ethnomusicology with an emphasis on the use of music in film. For 1992–93 she was awarded a National Research Council fellowship to study films by women in the African diaspora.

Christine Gledhill is senior lecturer in media and cultural studies at Staffordshire University, England. She has written extensively on feminist film criticism and edited two collections of essays: *Home is Where the Heart Is: Studies in Melodrama and the Woman's Film* and *Stardom: Industry of Desire*.

Elizabeth Hadley Freydberg is assistant professor of African-American studies and adjunct professor in the department of theater at Northeastern University in Boston. She has also taught as a Fulbright lecturer at Kenyatta University and the Goethe Institute in Nairobi, Kenya. Her publications include articles on black theater, film, and feminism, and she is currently working on a biography of Ethel Waters for Greenwood Press. In February 1992 Hadley Freydberg delivered a paper featuring Bessie Coleman at the Université de la Sorbonne Nouvelle Centre de recherches Afro-Americaines et des Nouvelles Littératures en Anglais in Paris.

bell hooks is a professor of women's studies and English at Oberlin College. A Feminist theorist and cultural critic, she is the author of six books, most recently, *Yearning: Race, Gender and Cultural Politics* (1991) and *Black Looks: Race and Representation* (1992).

Beverle Ann Houston (1935–88) was director of the critical studies program at the USC School of Cinema-Television between 1982 and 1988, the coeditor of *Quarterly Review of Film Studies* from 1983 to 1988, and a contributing editor to *Women and Film* between 1973 and 1976. She coauthored (with Marsha Kinder) *Close-up: A Critical Perspective on Film* (1972) and *Self and Cinema* (1980). At the time of her death, she was working on a book about Dorothy Arzner.

Amy Lawrence is the author of *Echo and Narcissus: Women's Voices in Classical Hollywood Cinema.* Her work has appeared in *Wide Angle, Film Quarterly,* and *Quarterly Review of Film and Video.* She teaches at Dartmouth College.

Julia Lesage is a videomaker and a teacher of film criticism at the University of Oregon. She is cofounder and coeditor of *Jump Cut: A Review of Contemporary Media.* She has written extensively on women in film and on Latin-American cinema.

Ana M. López is associate professor of communication at Tulane University. She is the author of *The New Latin American Cinema* (forthcoming, University of Illinois Press) and the coeditor, with John King and Manuel Alvarado, of *Mediating Two Worlds* (forthcoming, British Film Institute).

Gina Marchetti teaches in the departments of radio, television, and film and comparative literature at the University of Maryland, College Park. Her work has appeared in *Jump Cut, Asian Cinema, Genders, Post Script, Journal of Film and Video,* and other publications. Her book, *Romance and the "Yellow Peril": Race, Sex, and Discursive Strategies in Hollywood Fiction,* is forthcoming from the University of California Press.

Judith Mayne is professor of French and woman's studies at the Ohio State University. She is the author of several books, including *The*

Woman at the Keyhole (1990), *Cinema and Spectatorship* (1993), and *Dorothy Arzner* (forthcoming).

Patrice Petro is associate professor of English, comparative literature, and film studies at the University of Wisconsin-Milwaukee. Her book, *Joyless Streets*, was published in 1989.

Lis Rhodes is a painter, film- and videomaker, and writer. At present she lives and works in London, where she teaches at the Slade School of Fine Art-London University.

B. Ruby Rich has worked in film for twenty years as a critic, journalist, curator, and bureaucrat. She is a regular contributor to the *Village Voice*, *Mirabella*, *Sight and Sound*, and numerous other publications of scholarly and popular interest. She is currently a visiting professor in film studies at the University of California at Berkeley and is engaged in preparing a volume of collected essays.

Judith E. Smith teaches history and American studies at Boston College. She has written about the construction of family, ethnicity, and community among Italian and Jewish immigrants in *Family Connections: Italian and Jewish Immigrant Lives in Providence, Rhode Island, 1900–1940* (1985). This essay is part of a new study of representations of class, ethnicity, and gender in a set of plays, films, and television plays that foreground family dilemmas in the period 1945–60.

Valerie Smith is associate professor of English at UCLA. She is the author of *Self-Discovery and Authority in Afro-American Narrative* and has written numerous essays on race, gender, and narrative. She is completing a book on black feminism and contemporary culture.

Felicity Sparrow is a freelance writer, film historian, and programmer. She founded Circles (a feminist film distribution company) in 1979 with the aim of bringing back into circulation the films of early women directors and showing these alongside the work of contemporary women filmmakers. She lives and works in London and is currently an independent film producer.

Janet Staiger is associate professor of critical and cultural studies in the department of radio-television-film at the University of Texas. Her most recent book is *Interpreting Films: Studies in the Historical Reception of American Cinema* (1992). She is currently working on *Bad Women: The Regulation of Female Sexuality in Early American Cinema, 1907–1915*.

Chris Straayer is an assistant professor in the department of cinema studies at New York University. Her research addresses independent film and video art, gay and lesbian studies, and sexual representation.

Mary Frances Stubbs is the executive assistant to the vice president for institutional advancement at Howard University, where she also occasionally teaches film courses in the department of radio, TV, and film. Pursuing her interest in films, dramatic literature, women's literature, African-American literature, and screen adaptations, Dr. Stubbs completed her dissertation on "Lorraine Hansberry and Lillian Hellman: A Comparison of Social and Political Issues in Their Plays and Screen Adaptations" (Indiana University). Dr. Stubbs has a love for both teaching and academic administration and has held full-time positions in each.

Janet Walker resides in Los Angeles and teaches film studies at the University of California and the University of Southern California. She is the author of *Couching Resistance: Women, Film, and Psychoanalytic Psychiatry* (1993).

Andrea Weiss is an award-winning filmmaker with a Ph.D. in American history from Rutgers University. She won an Emmy Award for Best Research on *Before Stonewall: The Making of a Gay and Lesbian Community* and coauthored a companion book to the film. Her subsequent films include *International Sweethearts of Rhythm* and *Tiny and Ruby: Hell Divin' Women,* and she has recently begun production on her first narrative feature. Her essay in this volume is a shortened version of a chapter from her book, *Vampires and Violets: Lesbians in the Cinema* (1992). A New Yorker, Andrea Weiss lives in London.

Janice R. Welsch teaches courses in film, women's studies, and multicultural studies at Western Illinois University, where she is a member of the department of English and journalism and is the multicultural curriculum associate in faculty development. Her interests include film theory and criticism, women's studies, and multicultural studies, with particular interests in feminist theory and feminist independent filmmaking as these intersect with multicultural perspectives. She recently coedited *Multicultural Education: Strategies for Implementation in Colleges and Universities.*

Mimi White teaches in the department of radio/TV/film at Northwestern University. She is the author of *Tele-advising: Therapeutic Discourse in American Television* (1992), and the coauthor, with James Schwoch and Susan Reilly, of *Media Knowledge: Readings in Popular Culture, Pedagogy, and Critical Citizenship* (1992).

Linda Williams teaches film and women's studies at the University of California-Irvine. She is a coeditor of *Re-vision: Essays in Feminist Film Theory* and author of *Hard Core: Power, Pleasure and the "Frenzy of the Visible."*

Esther C. M. Yau is assistant professor of film at Occidental College. Born in Hong Kong, she has published articles and chapters on Mainland Chinese and Hong Kong cinemas. Yau completed her doctoral degree in the department of film and television at UCLA and her dissertation is on filmic discourses on women in Chinese cinema (1949–65). She coedited *Cinema and Social Change in Mainland China, Taiwan and Hong Kong*, forthcoming.

Index

Permissions